Further prai~

THE LAST CO⌐~~

"[A] hugely entertaining biography. . . . [E]xtraordinary. . . . That Ribowsky, an outstanding biographer with books on Al Davis, Satchel Paige and Howard Cosell to his credit, doesn't idolize Landry across the book's 640 pages makes his judgment all the keener."

—Allen Barra, *Dallas Morning News*

"Fascinating. . . . [R]eaders looking for a recap of one of football's greatest innovators and coaches will be enthralled." —*Booklist*

"A meaty biography of one of the NFL's legendary coaches. . . . [Ribowsky] provides as complete a picture of 'God's Coach' as we're likely to get. A must-read for fans of 'America's Team' and, given Landry's impact on the game, for Cowboy haters too."

—*Kirkus Reviews*

"Author Mark Ribowsky specializes in sports stories and often sees what others have missed. In this case, his subject is Tom Landry, the legendary Dallas Cowboys coach who has been dead for nearly a decade and a half. With added perspective (not to mention dozens of exclusive interviews), Ribowsky offers us our best opportunity yet to see this quiet, complex man as he really was . . . [and] how Landry's coaching method forever transformed the game of football."

—Barnes & Noble

"I have read every biography written about Tom Landry. And now, I am reading the last one I will ever need to read. Mark Ribowsky has captured the life and times of Tom Landry, the struggles and triumphs, the joys and sorrows, the victories and defeats like no other. *The Last Cowboy: A Life of Tom Landry* is the last and best word on the life of a Texas legend and American icon."

—SilverandBlueBlood.com

"A magisterial, meticulously researched masterpiece that reads less like a sports biography and more like a Shakespearean tragedy. Put it on your short list of best ten sports books of this year or any for that matter. It's about as good as sports writing gets. . . . Ribowsky brings every phase of Landry's 28-year reign not just to life but to a level of clarity and brilliance that few sports writers, or writers of any stripe, could match. . . . *The Last Cowboy* belongs on the shelf of every sports fan. It is an absolute winner." —Michael Levin, *New York Journal of Books*

"Based on a tremendous amount of original research and unprecedented interviews with many of Landry's teammates, players, coaches, and family members, *The Last Cowboy* tells the riveting story of a distinctly American icon." —Joe Tufaro, *Fansided*

"[T]he most thorough Landry biography that football fans are likely to come across. . . . Ribowsky shares the history of a man, a team and a sport—and some may even weep before finishing all 600 pages." —William Kerns, *Lubbock Avalanche-Journal*

"An eloquent, honest tribute to a football genius." —*Publishers Weekly*, starred review

THE LAST COWBOY

THE
LAST
COWBOY

A Life of Tom Landry

————

MARK
RIBOWSKY

LIVERIGHT PUBLISHING CORPORATION
A DIVISION OF W. W. NORTON & COMPANY
NEW YORK LONDON

For information about permission to reproduce selections from this book,
write to Permissions, Liveright Publishing Corporation,
a division of W. W. Norton & Company, Inc.,
500 Fifth Avenue, New York, NY 10110

For information about special discounts for bulk purchases, please contact
W. W. Norton Special Sales at specialsales@wwnorton.com or 800-233-4830

Manufacturing by Courier Westford
Book design by Lovedog Studio
Production manager: Devon Zahn

Library of Congress Cataloging-in-Publication Data

Ribowsky, Mark.
The last cowboy : a life of Tom Landry / Mark Ribowsky.
pages cm
Includes bibliographical references and index.
ISBN 978-0-87140-333-9 (hardcover)
1. Landry, Tom. 2. Football coaches—United States—Biography.
3. Dallas Cowboys (Football team)—History. I. Title.
GV939.L28R53 2014
796.332'6407642812—dc23
2013034731

ISBN 978-0-87140-854-9 pbk.

Liveright Publishing Corporation
500 Fifth Avenue, New York, N.Y. 10110
www.wwnorton.com

W. W. Norton & Company Ltd.
Castle House, 75/76 Wells Street, London W1T 3QT

1 2 3 4 5 6 7 8 9 0

CONTENTS

Part II
IF YOU'RE GONNA PLAY IN TEXAS

Part III
THE DEVIL LIVES IN DALLAS

INTRODUCTION

AS THE NAME GROWS FAINTER each year, for some it still carries its weight in profundity, bearing the same rock-ribbed sensibilities always reflected by his great stone face. In 2011, for example, *Forbes* ran a story urging businesses to hang tough in the midst of a killing recession. The title was "ACCORDING TO TOM LANDRY, A WINNER NEVER STOPS TRYING," apparently even in his repose, considering the tense used. Ghostly as he is now, his precepts were, the magazine noted approvingly, "appropriate for the retailing industry."[1] If Landry was not glib, when he did speak, his words perfectly adhered to the pretensions of the American sports/corporate/industrial complex—an example: "The secret to winning is constant, consistent management."[2] Not for nothing did Landry earn an obituary in the *Wall Street Journal*, under the headline "The Organization Man."[3]

Nevertheless, it was on a broader cultural level that he rose. As *the* coach during the NFL's most storied era, he became such a pop culture legend that in a *Simpsons* episode, Homer buys Landry's old fedora to rid himself of his loser image. Then there is the pivotal character named Landry in the best-selling novel, movie, and TV series *Friday Night Lights*, about the delirium of high school football in a small town much like the one Landry grew up in. And the commercial for Campbell's Chunky soup that takes place on the corner of the mythical Landry Road and Halas Drive.

By way of personal prologue, I met Tom Landry for the first and only time when he was right in the thick of his era, in early October of 1978. Though I'm quite sure he rather quickly forgot me, just another in an unending swarm of media flies he would have loved to swat away but needed to tolerate as part of the job, for me it was—and is—a sort of time stamp, etched in aspic, marking a brief encounter with football royalty. You don't meet a Tom Landry and forget the moment. This was four years after the hoity-toity *New Yorker* had placed him in the lineal descendant of mythical American coaches like Walter Camp, Amos Alonzo Stagg, Fielding Yost, George "Papa Bear" Halas, and Paul Brown, as the latest archetype of "a distinctly American institution."[4]

That very year Landry's Dallas Cowboys were tagged with the cocky marketing brand that has stuck ever since—"America's Team"—and they were the reigning NFL champion for the second time in his coaching career in Dallas, which lasted uninterrupted from 1960 to 1988. And while he would never win another Super Bowl, he had overcome the stigma he had endured as the Cowboys' architect and head coach, for the team's habitual failure to win the big one until 1971. He hadn't changed a bit over the years, still striking that inert pose on the sideline, expressionless, even diffident in service to the Lord.

Landry was long deified in Dallas, though to many he was simply sanctimonious, hollow, or, in the immortal put-down of one of his Super Bowl heroes, Duane Thomas, defined as "plastic, not a man at all."[5] While Landry was able to fulsomely express his feelings about his God, he could do little of that about his players, which not by accident kept them constantly hungry and in search of a good word from their coach. For these reasons, I was somewhat agnostic about him. But as a football buff, I admired him both for having brought a lamina of intellectualism to the game and for proving that games could be won as much by cogitation as brute force, by information that a computer and not a toothless lineman spit out.

On a personal level, Landry was just so confoundingly Delphian. Rather than any human trait, his computerized renditions of football gospel became the metaphor by which most knew him. Even when he would succumb to humanness—pump a fist in the air, whoop and holler upon sweet victory—it was so out of character it seemed staged, like someone learning to dance following numbered footprints. Besides, let's face it, as a liberal New York Jew, I had natural suspicions about this southern, Christian, Republican conservative evergreen who seemingly tolerated selective pagans in his midst if they won games for him. When I first wrote a book about a high and mighty football figure, it was a more familiar genotype. Indeed, the pugnacious, Jewish New York street kid with psychotic impulses, Oakland Raiders' owner Al Davis, was something Landry never could have been; Davis just wasn't courtly or Christian enough. Nobody ever called Tom Landry a maverick.

It didn't help Landry when one of his own players, Peter Gent, wrote the greatest sports novel ever, *North Dallas Forty*, which was published in 1973, coincidentally as Landry was basking in the afterglow of his first Super Bowl victory. Gent, who had had his problems with Landry during the author's days as a slick, rebellious wide receiver, took out his frustration on Landry for never becoming the star Gent should have been. In the brilliant roman à clef and later movie, the Cowboys, in the guise of the North Dallas Bulls, comprised a chain gang of degenerates, racists, angry put-upon blacks, and Jesus freaks numbing their constant pain with amyl nitrate, cortisol, Dexamyls, booze, weed, pork rinds, and degenerate sex, while trying desperately to meet the expectations set by their bloodless, uncompromising coach.

There would be other works by ex-players who, while they were Cowboys, had indulged themselves with, shall we say, *compulsions* such as child molestation (Lance Rentzel, Rafael Septien) and cocaine addiction (Bob Hayes, Thomas "Hollywood" Henderson, Harvey Martin, and Larry Bethea, among others). Henderson served time for smoking coke with two teenage girls, one in a wheelchair, before threatening both with a gun and sexually assaulting them. Another was convicted of arson, bank robbery, and armed robbery and killed himself at age thirty by a gunshot to the head.[6] Soon there was a whole genre of Landry/Cowboys literature about the "booze-guzzling, pill-popping, groupie-groping" Cowboys teams going back to the 1960s that "led the league in hell-raising."[7]

By the late 1980s, the FBI had interviewed several Cowboys in connection with a drug investigation, and eight of them testified at the trial of Dallas drug dealers. Speculation ran so wild about who was using drugs that not even Cowboys beau-ideal Tony Dorsett was spared from ugly rumors. Some referred to the Cowboys as "South America's Team," others to the "Cocaine Cowboys."[8] Landry's real legacy is that these modes of behavior became template on the Cowboys, expanding beyond his tenure, with the '90s breed of Cowboys, two-time champs no less, called "menaces on and off the field," "hoodlums, nutcases and out-and-out psychopaths."[9] As Gent might have said, "Hey, we were first!"

HOWEVER, THROUGHOUT his entire reign there was rarely a discouraging word in the media about Landry himself. He seemed to exist in an ether above the messiness, by his own design. Neither did the team as a corporate entity suffer any damage. America's Team was a combine that turned profits hand over fist—Cowboys jerseys and other tchotchkes have sold better than any other team's, increasing the value of the franchise to the third highest of any sporting enterprise on the globe to date. This gave Landry all the elevation and leeway he needed to be regarded as a football potentate, which he more than deserved.

The team's trademark—a five-point star—not only made for some hearty mockery in enemy locker rooms across the league but also created such enmity that a mere glimpse of it on the Cowboys' helmets was enough motivation to want to kick their tails. Think back a few years ago when Terrell Owens, then of the San Francisco 49ers, caught a touchdown pass in Dallas, scampered to midfield, and wiggled a celebratory jig on the big star painted there. Classless or not, that was something every opponent had wanted to do for four decades.

The Cowboys players, of course, knew how disconnected Landry's antiseptic image was from reality, and some would rebel against Landry as a matter of personal pride. But as a matter of public propriety, they swore blind loyalty to him. Some would swear they had a man-love for him much the way the Green Bay Packers did for the brusque but demonstrative Vince Lombardi. Of course, there was, and still is, a long line of football people who wax eloquent and emotional about Landry's own legend. But whether anyone ever really "got" Landry or his system, they did as they were told, and tasted the nectar of victory for it.

Landry had tremendous leverage and impunity, insulating him from ever having to answer for things going on in his own locker room that might well get other, lesser, mere mortal coaches fired. All Landry needed to do was plead ignorance about modern-day plagues like drugs, say that he just wasn't "prepared" for such things, and later apologize for making such a statement. When Landry said something, it was good enough to just nod in agreement and then move on. The Coach had spoken. Amen, brother.

TOM LANDRY was, of course, the polar opposite of his great rival and conquistador of the 1960s, Vince Lombardi, who was more like a blaring, impromptu trumpet solo to Landry's tight, metronomical backbeat. One of the ironies of that era was that the hard-drinking, curse-spitting Lombardi became "St. Vince," while the the mild-mannered, teetotaling church vicar was vilified as a loser. That is what winning the big one can do. But then Landry was never the "saint" type. It just didn't fit. Furthermore, he wouldn't have stood for it. From his perspective, no football coach ever qualified for that honor, least of all himself.

For Landry it meant nothing that all his players didn't love him the way the Packers loved Lombardi; what mattered was that they obeyed him at the risk of some undefined "or else." Pete Gent, who died late in 2011, once said, "His normal method of discipline is to treat you like a number. He seems to be concentrating on talking to you mainly to keep you from vanishing. He *is* a plastic man. And yet, there is this paradox—in Landry's presence you do not feel the cool platitudes of plastic and computers, you feel something more visceral. You feel *fear*."[10]

But it was more than that. Landry had a strange hold on his players that went beyond fear. The most notable example of this was the late "Dandy Don" Meredith, his first quarterback. The raw-boned but hypersensitive and troubled man, whose epic failures foretold those of current Cowboys cause célèbre Tony Romo, seemed to be always trapped in the coach's doghouse for periodically flubbing or not knowing the plays Landry sent in. Ultimately, Meredith quit at age thirty, with his body ravaged by unspeakable punishment but before he lost his sanity, and was praised at last by Landry as "the most courageous player" he had ever coached.[11] Meredith too could never quite bring himself to insult Landry in public; the closest he came was to gently chide him as "the Black Monk, a creature who could swallow himself without changing form."[12]

Similarly, few people ever really *hated* Landry or, Lord knows, denied him absolute respect. Not Meredith. Not Gent. Not Duane Thomas, who was the only Cowboy to ever demand a trade to get away from him, insisting, "I had all the freedom of a Negro slave."[13] Still, Thomas, years later, insisted that his enmity for Landry and the Cowboys had been "buried. They no longer exist."[14] Another player who had once savaged him, Hollywood Henderson, said, "You sort of didn't like him. You were afraid of him. You resented him. But when the dust settled, you wanted to be like him. When you had a family, took care of a company, managed people, you idolized him."[15] Even back in 1978, while hardly a cuddly teddy bear, Landry had at least become cuddly *for him*. Some Cowboys told me that they had tossed him fully clothed into a swimming pool at a team party, and he had even smiled a little as he dripped dry and sighed, "I've lost my authority."[16]

The Cowboys responded to him as they always did back then. The season when I was sent to Dallas to learn what was wrong with them, they wound up winning eight of the last ten games and marched back to the Super Bowl, the first team to do so five times. There they met the Pittsburgh Steelers in what was probably the most fabled Super Bowl of all. Between the teams there were no less than fourteen future Hall of Famers, five of them Cowboys, and Landry's players just missed repeating. Down 35–17, the Cowboys rallied for two late touchdowns before running out of time and grudgingly losing, 35–31.

Heartbreaking defeat was nothing new to Landry. It mocked him, tore him up inside, but from such pain he found new stimuli to win, though his great regret was that he couldn't dominate the league on a consistent basis. The first time he took the Cowboys to the Super Bowl, in January 1972, they lost by a field goal. Dallas won the Super Bowl the next year, but in the 1980s Landry would take the team to three straight conference title games, losing each time. In the yin and yang of his career, the Lord put him through hell. It was what made the man so compelling—not the winning as much as the pain.

THE MORE one examines Landry at close range, the more cracks show up in the one-dimensional image. In fact, one reason why the actor G. D. Spradlin was so superb playing the Landry character, under the pseudonym B. A. Strother, in the movie *North Dallas Forty* was that his stone-faced, frozen contemptuousness melts when he's called on to be human. When a fumbled snap costs him a championship, Strother—Landry—appears fragile, vulnerable, disbelieving, as if God himself betrayed him. This was exactly Landry's reaction after losing the first big game he was in, the 1966 NFL championship game, when his young bucks met Lombardi's Silurian warhorses and came up two yards short before Meredith threw a game-killing interception. Strother also seems helpless and torn when he accedes to management's decision to cut his aging, once-great wide receiver, played by Nick Nolte, for conduct *too* unbecoming, or too public.

In both instances, these nuances were not in the original text, but they were knowing because as knotty as he was, Landry was a man of nuance. It was not unusual for him to solicit ideas from players and carry on spirited debates during film room sessions, not to mention putting up with a lot of crap from them, witness Henderson and Martin. In *North Dallas Forty*, Gent inferred that the team spied on players to dig up dirt to be used as leverage against them, though only Hollywood Henderson was ever let go directly for conduct unbecoming.

Gent also believed that Landry was more lenient with white players than black ones, and it might have seemed plausible given his background. He was born and raised in a town where he encountered almost no black people, served in a segregated Army during World War II, and played at the University of Texas when the school had written rules prohibiting black athletes from playing on its teams. On Landry's Cowboys teams in the 1960s, reflecting the still-extant Jim Crow South—and the still particularly virulent strain in Dallas—black

players had to live in segregated housing in South Dallas during training camp, a long drive to the practice facility in North Dallas (thus
the reason why Pete Gent so named the team in his book, for the acrid
irony). They also were made to take "personality" tests to determine
if they could withstand the pressure of playing in the South. Yet one
is urged to keep in mind the times in which that happened. Even Tom
Landry couldn't do a thing about institutional racism on his home turf.

As the archetypical "southern man" that Neil Young sung about—
those with the good book in hand but perhaps not eager to broaden
its parables to the world around them—Landry was simply assumed
to be less than enlightened about race. Because many black Cowboys
wound up retiring early, and believed they were pushed out by the
organization, the assumption among many players was that "a black
player toward the end of his career didn't have a chance in Dallas."[17]
The irony, as voiced once by Hollywood Henderson, was that "you
get a lot of respect for being a Cowboy from everybody except the
Cowboys."[18] While no one ever went on record openly calling Landry
bigoted, Henderson came close: "I know that Landry is not a racist,
but he acted like one."[19] In the early 1980s, some journalists actually
tried to sell the case that the Cowboys team had purged itself of
black players because they had been trouble for Landry.

But it was a matter of common law for Landry that such reprobates—and they came in all colors and sizes—were not of Cowboys
stock. His problem was that he made exceptions to that rule when
the team was winning. He also went to the wall for selected problem children. Neither should it be overlooked that Landry drafted a
wealth of black players, many from small all-black colleges, as well
as the second-ever Mexican-born player in the NFL.

Rather than anything Landry did, it was the Dallas media that
honed a racist angle when they spread rumors in the 1980s about
black Cowboys doing drugs while giving a pass to the white Cowboys who were doing the same thing. The issue of Landry and race
is not cut-and-dried. In certain ways he seemed heroic, in others less
so. Landry personally detested racism. But the broader perspective is
that if Landry felt it was easier to be around white players, or played
favorites, he still pretty much treated *everybody* as chattel, explaining that "it's important to have a division between the team and

yourself or you give them an out—they won't have to pay the same price. When players looked at me, they knew I was gonna be pretty harsh on them."[20] Even Roger Staubach, he noted, had never been in Landry's office until the day Staubach retired. All anyone needed to confirm that Landry was color blind was to ask the perpetually beleaguered Don Meredith.

But perhaps Landry *did* change the tides, in the only way he could have in the South—by introducing a whole new equation of a team formed and sustained without regard to skin color. The Cotton Bowl was where the future could be seen, in the faces of multiethnic fans. Landry was mindful of this dynamic. And while some black Cowboys of the 1960s and early '70s thought that by condoning racism he was unwittingly fostering an atmosphere poisoned by it, others believed he was finding a way to alter centuries of history. Maybe they both were right.

LANDRY INDEED wore well. Most if not all past grievances melted away. Duane Thomas begged to return a few years later. Landry complied, though Thomas was burnt out by then. Landry forgave, if not forgot. "We get along very well," he said about their relationship in 1987.[21] All his players, it seemed, didn't only want his respect—they *needed* it.

Yes, there were hypocrisies to the Cowboys, as Pete Gent informed us. But there was a reason why children born around Dallas in the 1960s and '70s were often named after Landry. Another born in 1989, the Pittsburgh Steelers' Landry Jones, grew up to quarterback the Oklahoma Sooners for four years, sounding very much like his namesake with such pabulum as "Whether I'm a pastor or whether I'm a chaplain—whatever it's going to be, whatever ministry God calls me to—I'm going to do it."[22] But the original Landry liked to live fast and loose, at least on the highway; he drove his cars at breakneck speeds but was never given a ticket when pulled over.

Looking back, someone had to blend eras, races, and cultures into a winning template for there to be institutional change in America. That someone was Tom Landry. Quite simply, he caught the flavor of the times when strong, silent, wise leadership seemed the antidote to the chaos and cynicism all around—a lot of which began on November 22, 1963, a bright but baleful day in Dallas.

It seems fated now that both Landry and Lombardi started their head coaching careers in parallel lockstep—though with completely opposite coaching styles and philosophies—just as a new young president came to office promising America a "New Frontier." Landry, though, had to take a backseat to Lombardi for a while. But, in expanding his purview to the offensive side of the ball as creatively as he had with his defenses for the Giants—when he had invented a new formation called the "4–3" and a new position called the "middle linebacker"—Landry developed Rubik's Cube–style offensive sets that were dizzying to see and nearly impossible to figure out, with players shifting about prior to the snap.

The panoply of formations today, on offense and defense, right down to the terminology—for example, the play fake, the trap block, the stunt method of pass rushing—owe much to Landry's prototypical 4–3 "Flex Defense," the hub from which modern defensive formations are the spokes, and his hocus-pocus offenses. Nevertheless, Landry had to be patient before he could flourish. Even when he had built his team to specifications, they suffered two heartbreaking last-minute defeats to the Packers in the 1966 and 1967 NFL championship games, which were all the more bitter given that his men failed to make the big play in both. Indeed, the interception Meredith threw in the first and Bart Starr's riding Jerry Kramer's famous block into the end zone in the second are memories capable of making Dallas cry.

The latter game became so fabled that it is known by its own emblem—the "Ice Bowl," played as it was in meat locker conditions on the "frozen tundra" of Lambeau Field. For Landry, coming up short was anguishing and enraging. Still, the anger was directed only at himself, for letting the game come down to one play he couldn't control because of the frozen field—and because Fate had given Lombardi, not him, the last crack to certify *his* legend.

LANDRY WAS the tortoise to Lombardi's hare. Lombardi's teams had been built without regard for tomorrow; Landry's were to withstand turnover, to regenerate themselves to the point where he could fill a hole here and there, plug in a role player, and keep the team on its trajectory without pause. He would lose more playoff games, some painfully, but when he reached the Super Bowl in the 1971 and 1977 seasons, the opponent never had a chance.

Those games came during the height of the Landry era, one that drove the league to a higher grade of professionalism and profitability—and elevated *Dallas* too, from an under-regarded city where President Kennedy was murdered to the cradle of rich men's fantasies. The city paralleled the franchise as it first made itself a regional attraction, then a national one. Would there even have been a hit TV show about a decadent Dallas oilman named J. R. if not for the gusher that was the Dallas Cowboys? This franchise became so big that, in the current parlance, it was too big to fail. For Landry, sometimes it seemed as if his gig would never end, and that he could be moved out of his job only if he was dragged out of his office. It turns out, it pretty much went down that way.

LANDRY'S VALUES were perfectly old-fashioned and perfectly ingenuous. He married his college sweetheart. He helped found the Fellowship of Christian Athletes. He spoke often at Billy Graham Crusade rallies. But he was an ecumenical man who saw life as a constant struggle. He knew that piousness was neither a panacea nor a shield. He had much pain in his life, the sort that trivializes something like football. He would achieve a lot, but it was never perfect, the concept Landry always aspired to, at whatever cost, but could only grasp for fleetingly.

Nor was his preaching for sale to the highest bidder. Landry could fairly be called a Christian conservative and once testified before Congress campaigning against pornography. He quietly donated money to Republicans he preferred, like Richard Nixon and the Bushes of Texas. But while he could have been a kingmaker in his state, he saw no reason to publicly campaign for his favored candidates—as opposed to, say, Lou Holtz, who had his Notre Dame players appear with him in a commercial endorsing George H. W. Bush's election. Landry did do something similar, inviting President Gerald Ford to visit the Cowboys' camp during the 1976 campaign, with no overt endorsement or fanfare. Landry appeared several times on Pat Robertson's television show *The 700 Club*, but he never took the bait to bash Robertson's roster of imagined liberal enemies, preferring to instead relate how he found his faith and worked with Christian charities. Football, not flame-throwing, was his game. Neither was he comfortable with his consecration as a demigod. He more than most could cite chapter and verse to rail against worshipping graven idols. And because of him, football wasn't only king in Dallas, it *was* omnipotent. It *was* God. And Landry was the provident.

One Cowboys beat writer once wondered why it was that "I can talk to George Bush like we're about to go bass fishing together, but when I call Tom Landry on the phone or trap him on a golf course . . . I get the feeling I won't be this nervous when I talk to God himself someday."[23] Landry wouldn't have known why either. He also never would have stood for being dubbed "God's Coach." Still, his achievements are mighty, with nothing mightier than twenty-nine straight seasons as a head coach of one team, 250 regular-season wins (third to Don Shula's 328 and Halas's 318), a record twenty postseason victories, and five conference titles. The Cowboys under Landry won fewer Super Bowls than the Steelers' four and the San Francisco 49ers' three, though no one took his team to more Super Bowl games than Landry did: five.

Landry never had to work at convincing people that he was a genius. Still, knowing he was more than a coach but rather an institution, Landry protected the Cowboys' investors well, even as he was a calming figure in a country desperately seeking some sense of order and retrenchment. The team transcended its boorish, decadent, openly racist habitat and conscripted all of America as its supplemental fan base. Ultimately, the Cowboys became much bigger than Dallas, only because Tom Landry seemed like such a perfect leader when others utterly failed in that role. Down Dallas way, before there could have been an America's Team out of Texas, it was enough that, as one of the early newspapermen covering the team once wrote, the evolving franchise was a "family affair" striking deep in the heart of "boy[s] who grew up believing in God, country, and the Dallas Cowboys."[24]

It is ironic that a man who could preach in depth about the golden calf had made the Dallas Cowboys the very gilded idols he warned against. They were golden Cowboys, to be sure, and there was nothing he could do but be swept along by his creation. Those high times ended when he was done. For the legion of those who admired the manic-depressive drama of the seminal then glittering Cowboys teams, the thrill went on, even with a more glittery franchise and the grudging acceptance that all things must pass.

IN SHORT, Landry was neither a prop nor a prophet. He didn't have all the answers, but he made the most of the ones he knew, looking for any edge he could get. No coach was more of a perfectionist, an engineer (something he had a degree in), a psychologist. He could read the way the wind was blowing in the country and in his sport, though he kept the essential nature of his personal and football philosophy intact, and in his own hands. It was no wonder he loved Roger Staubach, the quarterback who won him his two Super Bowls, an equally clean-nosed technician, and ex-military man. Landry gave up his much-debated two-quarterback system for the ex–Naval Academy star, and in return Staubach created the apotheosis of the Landry system. The coach, unlike as with Meredith, was never conflicted about Staubach, whom he called "a one in a lifetime" find.[25]

The snickering irony is that some of the "straight and narrow" Cowboys, in their private moments, practiced habits that made the sybaritic New York Jets quarterback Joe Namath seem like the choirboy. It was the team's public image that kept Landry, his bosses, and the league elders happy. It also kept Landry safe in his job longer than even Paul Brown was in his. Brown, the man after whom Landry had modeled much of his coaching persona, strategies, and methods, lasted three fewer years as coach of the Cleveland team named for him. Both were fired by meddlesome owners whom they had long predated, but while the Browns were still a top team when Brown was sacked, only a steep fall from grace could have done in Landry since he did not have a losing season from 1966 to 1985 and missed the playoffs only twice. Worse, by 1985, the billionaire owner who once shared the same youthful buoyancy as the man he made his coach, went bankrupt and lost the team, taking with him Landry's lifeline.

✦ ✦ ✦ ✦

LANDRY'S MÉTIER was his ability to find answers by thinking one step ahead of everyone and renewing himself every few years. When he began running plays into the huddle not with a halfback or tight end but by alternating his two quarterbacks, football experts of the day derided it as gimmickry. But Landry had figured out back in 1960 that the game was too complicated to leave to non-geniuses. Landry was not prone to admit he was ever wrong about any plays he called, which was why some players named him "Pope Landry I"— behind his back, of course. He tended to put blame on the players for his errors in play-calling, a funny way to support his men. But Landry's quarterbacks were permitted to change the play if what they saw at the line presaged a better option. Meredith did it liberally, sometimes to Landry's consternation.

Today, plays are decided by a committee, by offensive and defensive coordinators and other coaches sitting upstairs in the press box. The poor quarterback is just part of a chain of command, the part that does as he's told. Head coaches, meanwhile, have devolved into ciphers or circus clowns, more figurehead than godhead. Consider the Cowboys' current head coach, former backup quarterback and assistant Jason Garrett, a perfectly nice fellow and more than adequate coach who most fans, even in Dallas, might not be able to pick out of a lineup. There are no more imperial coaches, or at least imperial-looking coaches. Landry was the last of the breed.

Football itself seems now to be less about coaching methods and players than about overwrought marketing and glitzy stadiums—the glitziest one, of course, being in Dallas. Like the league in which the team is still the main attraction, the Cowboys organization is an avaricious corporate monster with limited capacity for original thinking and an endless capacity for overkill. It takes bows for having a billion-dollar stadium and a multimedia scoreboard bigger than the state of Rhode Island. It invented the pole-dancing cheerleader idiom, something Landry detested but had no power to veto.

The cheerleaders, working off and advancing the marketing strategies of the team, became a franchise in itself, a conveyor belt of movies, calendars, posters, and nighttime fantasies of pubescent boys. They still prance around half-naked and gloriously white-booted, though they share the field with equally nubile squads from other teams. But they do their act as part of a $1.6 billion corporate bottom line, inferior to only the Manchester United soccer club, the Los Angeles Dodgers, and the "evil empire" of the New York Yankees. The value of the NFL is in no small part due to the Cowboys' growth, the league having been appraised at $33.3 billion, up from $11.6 billion just a decade ago. As the old joke goes, we know what the league is—we're just haggling over the price.

Again, Landry was himself a willing corporate tool. One of the few TV commercials he did was for American Express, in real cowboy garb, no less. When he ruled, players *and* coaches were far more likely to be idolized unconditionally. For his part, Landry was a model for manly comportment. In Dallas, noted a sportswriter of the era, "Some kids . . . felt their dads were not up to a certain amount of, well, respect, if they didn't wear a fedora to work."[26] Indeed, Landry's hat won him twelfth place on a list compiled by *Texas Monthly* in 2009 of the thirty people "who changed the look of our state—and the world"; the magazine noted of his headgear that "the revered head coach of the Dallas Cowboys tops a short list of men, including Humphrey Bogart and Indiana Jones, who managed to make that totem of midcentury conformity a symbol of their own individualism." The other sartorial influences in the survey included the likes of Davy Crockett, Stanley Marcus, Grace Jones, Willie Nelson, Farrah Fawcett, Eva Longoria, and Beyoncé, but it was the Landry image that, the article went on, "served a larger purpose. With Dallas tagged as a 'city of hate' after the Kennedy assassination, he became its public face: dignified, professional, and successful. He emerged as the ultimate model for our aspirations; the clothes confirmed the status we wanted to achieve."[27]

LANDRY HAD immense pride but not excess hubris. The Cowboys team was not run by Landry alone but by a holy trinity, including the egocentric general manager Tex Schramm and the nerdy but omniscient scouting and player personnel director Gil Brandt.

Landry, always gracious, wrote in his memoirs that Schramm, who hired him, "had always been the man in charge."[28] Yet the two other Cowboys mandarins were smart enough to know Landry's on-field authority was inviolate and that it was his face and voice, not theirs, which defined the team that won the most games in the 1970s. Not by chance, the Cowboys made a slew of appearances on the then-new phenomenon *Monday Night Football* and were its most heralded and eagerly awaited team. By chance, the broadcast booth included a Cowboy all its own, Don Meredith, whose manufactured "cowboy" persona won him an Emmy.

Landry was not the perfect human. He could be cruel and was prone to holding grudges. He tried to adapt to the times, but he never really could. In the aftermath of Landry's being fired by new owner Jerry Jones in 1989, the revilement of Jones for kicking St. Thomas Aquinas of Dallas to the curb was soon replaced by the rising of America's Team version 2.0. Those Cowboys won as many Super Bowls as Landry's teams had won—in consecutive years, 1992 and 1993, another in 1995—under expatriated college coaches Jimmy Johnson and Barry Switzer. Neither of Landry's successors, however, could stand Jones, and they made their stays in Dallas temporary. In the retrospective glare of so much chaos and instability over the last two decades, many in Cowboys Nation began to yearn for the creature comfort that was Tom Landry. For all their manufactured glitter, the Cowboys haven't won a playoff game in fifteen years, a fate so severe it might seem like karmic payback for trying to degrade the Landry legacy.

Landry in turn moved far from the arc of the team he had dominated. Neither he nor his wife ever attended a Cowboys home game other than for special tributes to him and to other men he had coached to stardom. With no football in his life after half a century, he was a remarkably energetic man, committing to regular speaking appearances, including some in prisons, about his unconditional faith in God, even after illness had taken away his younger daughter and even as he was dying of leukemia, which would still him on February 13, 2000.

He was far more significant than he could have imagined growing up, when life was smaller and less complicated. Yet he was quiet enough in life to be dimmed in death. The name endures, but the reasons why become diffused with time. The following pages shift the focus back onto him, and for many they reintroduce a man who during his lifetime never needed an introduction, for many reasons, not the least being that Tom Landry was something that no other man can claim. He was the first Cowboy and all too sadly, the last.

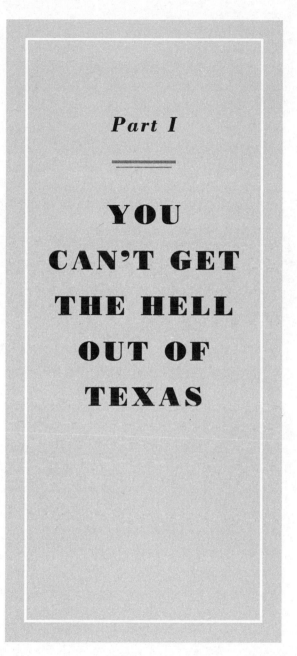

Part I

YOU CAN'T GET THE HELL OUT OF TEXAS

"IT'S A TEXAS THING"

On a hot, dewy afternoon in Austin, Texas,
late December 2011.

O N THE DAY ALICIA LANDRY turned eighty, she was still
as fetching as a Bluebonnet Belle, the high honor for which she
was a finalist at the University of Texas back in 1949. That was a
most memorable year, it also being when she and the Longhorns' fullback and co-captain, a stony-faced fellow with wavy black hair, got
hitched. She and the fellow, whom she still calls Tommy, would stay
married for fifty-one years, until he died. She is wafer thin but not at
all fragile, blonde hair shimmering as if the sun shines directly on her
wherever she goes, eyes sharp and piercing when she looks straight
at you, which she does, intently, as she speaks of him. Encountering
her for the first time, you realize why Sam Huff, the world's first star
middle linebacker and the embodiment of Landry's preternatural
theories about playing suffocating defense, would recall long after,
still with great envy, "He has the most beautiful woman in the world.
. . . She has to be the best draft pick Tom ever made."[1]

As she proves, being the widow of Tom Landry carries a certain
gossamer, of charm and éclat. She was always his alter ego, the better half who had no compunction saying what he was bound by duty
and courtliness not to say. That she reveled in that role may explain

why she hasn't been invited to many Dallas Cowboys functions, it being the apparent inclination of Jerry Jones to keep the memory of Tom Landry as incidental as possible to the current team's operations. Writing Landry out of the team's purview, impossible as that is, requires going to tacky levels, something Jerry Jones is quite adept at. For example, after Landry was forced out as the Cowboys' head coach in 1989, he was seen at Texas Stadium only three times over the next decade, not as a fan but to receive belated tributes. His last visit was in 1999. Alicia Landry has generally avoided the new venue, AT&T Stadium, née Cowboys Stadium. Ask her why her presence has been so scarce, and she tells you something that strains credulity, or would, if it did not involve a man whose name makes her facial muscles tense.

"Well," she says, as if delivering a punch line, "Jerry Jones never asked me. Well, one time. When they blew up Texas Stadium they had a big lunch over there and invited me to come and speak, and I did a little speech. But I didn't go out for the blow-up. And then at the new stadium, I've never been to a game, but Roger Staubach has a box out there and they had some musical group that performed in the stadium, and Roger had a party and asked me to come to have dinner and watch this group. So I've been in the new stadium one time, but never for a game."

The obvious questions burgeon: Is there a reason for her exile? Bitterness? Antipathy for Jones?

"A lack of interest."

That, she adds, applied to the old coach, who after his dismissal was expected not to be present any longer in the stadium he made possible. Men cut from the stock that Tom Landry was do not beg; rather, he considered himself no longer tied in any way to the team.

As she remembers, "The time they inducted Bob Hayes into the Ring of Honor, he went to that, and of course when they put Tommy in there he went. But other than that, he really didn't have any dog in the hunt. A football game is good if you care who wins. He didn't. It wasn't his job anymore." A pause. "That's why I watch Giants games. I want 'em to win so I get involved in watching their games, as did Tommy. We loved the Maras the way we loved the Murchisons. After that, well . . . it wasn't the same."

These are remarkable words coming from a woman who was the first lady of Dallas, the queen of the rodeo. They stab at the air with such ironic punch that for a visitor the room fills with a fragrant acridness, not to mention incredulity. Can it be that one consequence of Jerry Jones's reign was that Tom Landry, son of the South, came away cheering the invaders from New York when they played the Cowboys? Is it merely chance or a hidden hand from the beyond that explains why, coming into the current season, Jerry Jones had not tasted victory in four games against the Giants in his very own stadium? Remember: the old man always did know how to settle a score.

"So you don't like the Cowboys?" the visitor wonders.

"Well, there *are* no Cowboys," she avers, as if such a thing is obvious. "It's not the name of the team, it's the players in the game, and I don't know anyone playin' today."

"But what about the first few years after he left the team? He knew the players. But both of you didn't ever go back there."

"Well, we didn't have any seats. That would be one reason why. They took away our box."

Now incredulity crashes its way into seeming impossibility. The visitor is truly shaken.

"Wait a minute. I can't believe what I just heard. They took away your box?"

"Yes . . . we weren't payin' for it. [In addition to the box] our son Tom Jr. for years had bought six 50-yard-line tickets, and when Tommy retired Tom thought he'd still have those seats—and they took away those too."

"So they took away the box of the only coach the Cowboys had for their first twenty-nine years?"

"It was a very nice box too, right next to the press box." Pause. "I guess they really needed it."

"Oh, right. Because they needed space in an eighty-thousand-seat stadium."

"Whatever the reason, we didn't have seats."

"What if Jerry Jones gave you back that box?"

"I don't even know if I'd want to go. It's not important to me."

"Do you know Jerry well?"

"I don't know him at all. I really don't. I know what he looks like.

I've seen him a few times and we say hello to each other in a friendly way. But I don't know him."

"I think I understand now why the new place wasn't going to be named Tom Landry Stadium."

"Eh, Tommy wouldn't have cared. I don't think he would have even wanted that because the bond wasn't there anymore. I certainly don't care about it. And it isn't what it isn't. It's not the same Dallas Cowboys. I didn't really want the new stadium to be named after Tommy anyway. They call it 'Jerry's World,' which is more about what it is than anything Tom Landry was."

"So the Cowboys aren't your family anymore."

"The Giants are still like family. I still have dinner with Ann Mara [Wellington Mara's widow] when she comes in. We did that just last week." She waits, then, "The Giants never stopped being our family."[2]

THE COWBOYS as we knew them, to be sure, don't live here anymore. The best that Jones could do to preserve the rasher of memories was to erect a monument to Tom Landry on the sidewalk outside the originally chartered Cowboys Stadium, which was certainly more palatable than axing Landry for a second time when the time was right to elicit a nice, fat corporate sponsorship for the joint—that time being last July, when it was renamed AT&T Stadium, pocketing Jones $19 million more filthy lucre every year. It was an afterthought, a mandatory concession to the Landry legend, but at least it was done.

If Alicia Landry ever cared enough to be bitter, she's learned to live with it now. She spends most of her time in the splendid home where she and her husband lived for most of his kingly days, on tony Rock Cliff Place, a cul-de-sac in a leafy vest pocket down the road from West Northwest Highway in Dallas. Austin is still her "country" getaway, on the rolling fairways of a golf course called the Hills of Lakeway. Not that this is a surprise, but her houses are immaculate and impeccably groomed, both having been built to specification by a prissy and tidy man who turned the anomalous environs of Dallas into a modern-day Carthage through cleanliness, godliness, and King Football. Yet unlike much of "Big D," there is not a decadent, oilman chic scent inside the front doors. Call her on the phone, and she, not a butler or maid, will answer it. Splendor and luxury were never the Landry way, and his wife never tried to play chatelaine. Living large would have required snootiness and callousness, and neither of them could have even faked those qualities. Though Tom Landry was the quartermaster of Texas's burgeoning identity, his sense of self was always contained, reminding those in his charge to be humble, to walk like a man, to be cool.

It sure was a hell of a ride, one that prompts his widow to remark that being Tom Landry's wife was fun, not that the outside world could ever believe the stern-looking old coach knew what the concept of amusement was. "He had a great sense of humor, very wry and understated but right on the mark. But he never made fun of anyone. If anything, he made fun of himself. He was just such a sweet man, such a good man. He was an exceptional person. I've never known anyone like him. He didn't look down on people. He just went and lived his life and didn't have revenge in his heart. The only fault he had was workin' so hard—and maybe drivin' too fast, because he was always running behind with all he had on his mind. [Laugh] I know he forgot about me a couple times. He'd get in the car, drive half an hour and then go 'uh-oh.'"

Several hundred items of memorabilia, pictures, trophies, plaques, and sundry other bric-a-brac are placed strategically throughout the home, each one with a story to tell. Alicia Landry can walk past any of them and be transported to a place or time that stands still. As does the lingering image of him as the magic Christian in the fedora who suffered through a big-game defeat only to come through the mortal coil of trial of faith even more of a true believer.

To the world at large, Landry was no less than Job in a fedora. He too had been ordered from the heavens to *Brace yourself like a man. I will question you, and you shall answer me*. That was the least Landry could do. Keeping the faith was easy. He even, metaphorically, put his hand over his mouth, a very Job-like thing to do, saying little that one could grab onto. And if Landry wouldn't be rewarded by being able to live 140 years as Job did, the two late afternoons in New Orleans when he was carried off the field a winner were immortal enough. After the first championship, at the welcome-home banquet for the team, Landry sat on the dais drinking Dr. Pepper and listening to a band play his favorite hymn, "How Great Thou Art." His old Giants middle linebacker Sam Huff, who was there, had never seen a celebration for a football team take on the nature of a revival tent show. "Tom," Huff told him, "this is carrying things too far."[3]

Yet winning football games wasn't really biblical, not even for Tom Landry, who never liked to encourage the brokers of false prophesy by equating the result of any mere football game with something temporal. A real Christian would know better. Rather, he was manufactured and driven from within, from the roots of his soul, the same roots that nourished him deep in the heart of Texas. His habitat under that big sky was the petri dish from which all the grand theories of football sprung nearly fully formed, ingenious techniques and strategies that were simple only to him, because they were knitted from the restless ambition and rock-ribbed, orderly thoughts that captured him in childhood. There was a genuine simplicity that cloaked his intellectual and competitive components, and this was a property that kept his head level, never letting his focus stray. His life, says his widow, "was about all the people in his life who loved him, who believed in him. But it was more. He loved Texas as much as he did any person. Texas shaped his life. Texas *was* his life."

BEING A TEXAN can be a mite confusing. One of Landry's signature players from the early years was a raw-boned, tobacco-chewin', bull-ridin', calf-ropin', Wild Turkey–chuggin' Texan named Walt Garrison. He was born in Lewisville on a street with feed store, a mule barn, and the Lewisville Hotel, which he used to say was like a tight pair of Wranglers—no ballroom. Garrison wrote a book titled *Once a Cowboy*. As he will tell you, Landry taught him how to be that sort of Cowboy, one that lived "on the *inside*, where it really matters, what it should feel like, bein' it without showin' it," he wrote.[4] That sort of Cowboy used to exist, when its head coach interwove the Texas soil and soul into each of his players.

To its native sons and daughters, Texas is more than a state. John Steinbeck—not a Texan himself but a Californian who in the Salinas Valley had hunkered down with many a Deep South migrant during the Great Depression—wrote, "I have said that Texas is a state of mind, but I think it is more than that. It is a mystique closely approximating a religion. And this is true to the extent that people either passionately love Texas or passionately hate it and, as in other religions, few people dare to inspect it for fear of losing their bearings in mystery or paradox. . . . For all its enormous range of space, climate, and physical appearance, and for all the internal squabbles, contentions, and strivings, Texas has a tight cohesiveness perhaps stronger than any other section of America. Rich, poor, Panhandle, Gulf, city, country, Texas is the obsession, the proper study and the passionate possession of all Texans."[5]

State of mind. Obsession. Passionate. These are sensibilities that get into the blood, the corpuscles. The "bigness" thing misses the point. Doug Sahm, the late, great Tex-Mex singer of the 1960s, once sang a song called "At the Crossroads" in which he insisted you just couldn't live in Texas if you didn't have soul. He didn't mean the kind of soul one would normally think of when defined in musical terms, the kind that emanates from the pain of desperation and depredation, the kind that seeps out of the Deep South from the Louisiana Delta. He meant the soul defined by pride in the soil under one's boots—and in the roots under that soil, tracing back to days when Texas was a republic, accountable to itself, driving its own hard bargain to agree to accept the status of U.S. statehood.

When Rick Perry, the governor of Texas broached the idea of secession from the union, to the derision of those outside his state, within the borders it was a manifestation of Texas soul. But then again, it was Sam Houston who noted the regular presence in his state of "a class of noisy, second-rate men who are always in favor of rash and extreme measures," adding that "Texas was absolutely overrun by such men."[6] This might help explain Rick Perry and Jerry Jones. But not Tom Landry, who once applied a Twainish trope of his own to a reality that is so hard to define. "Football is to Texas," he said, with the Landry pith and borrowing some imagery from the Catholics, "what religion is to a priest."[7] It certainly was for him. He preached on the altar of the holy pigskin, which was seeded in him as a boy in the Rio Grande Valley. Landry and Texas. Neither could be separated from the other; one informed and inflamed the other.

"People don't understand it," says the woman who survived him, "but if you've been in Texas you know what it means to be a Texan. When we had our three children, Tommy laid down the law. They all had to be born in Texas. He was playing in New York at the time and, well, they couldn't be born in *New York*. We had nothing against New York. We loved New York. I still love it. But our children had to have the same blood at birth that we did. It was non-negotiable. They had to be born and grow up here."

Then, she concludes with a shrug and the only explanation that really matters.

"It's a Texas thing."

IT'S NOT impertinent but rather a simple fact to say that not everything about Texas has always been easy to digest, and no real native with a soul would have ever denied it. Texas was always analogous with bigness and crudeness, and for too long the matter of racial equality was reduced to a minor consideration, not least of all on the Cowboys. But on that historic January afternoon in 1972, when Landry won his first Super Bowl, he was carried off on a convoy of wide Cowboys shoulders belonging to Bob Hayes, Rayfield Wright, and Mel Renfro. One was a receiver, one an offensive lineman, and one a defensive back. All three were black men who gritted their teeth about the tense racial climate that grew under Landry.

When that game was played, though, as on any game day, the Cowboys weren't cleaved by race or class—they were just Cowboys, winning one for their patriarch, a very white man whose roots were one and the same as that lone silver star on the Cowboys helmet. That was the bonding between them. It came from the Texas soul that had built a pipe dream into an American dream, and an everlasting fable that men of the Landry cloth could celebrate all their lives.

Chapter 1

MISSIONARY MAN

IN TEXAS IT'S NOT EASY to forget the name Tom Landry. It's on a gym in East Dallas; the fitness center at Baylor University in Waco; the welcome center at Dallas Baptist University; the sports medicine and research center in Dallas; and various playground fences and infrastructure of all sorts. You can take a free ride on the Tom Landry Highway, a section of Interstate 30 between Dallas and Fort Worth where the signs sport an image of a fedora. If the drivers only knew how fast the old man himself used to cruise down the same strip of pavement, they'd floor the gas pedal in his honor.

Iconic photographs of him hang on many restaurant walls across the state, just as you might see the likeness of John F. Kennedy on the walls in Boston or Jesus Christ above the fireplace in living rooms in the Bible Belt. On one wall at Mia's Tex-Mex eatery in Dallas, which was frequented by Landry, is proudly emblazoned one photograph he autographed the day before Jerry Jones canned him. And though Landry's Seafood in the west end of Dallas was not named for him, it objected not a whit when it was filled to capacity for years by people who assumed it *was*.

About the only place where the name Landry seemingly *can't* be found is, again, the one place where it *should* be: on the outer wall of the twenty-first century's billion-dollar attempt to re-create the Roman Colosseum in Arlington, Texas. Indeed, more than a few people begged Jerry Jones to call it Tom Landry Stadium when the place was still unnamed months before its opening in 2010. Still, the most Jones—in his apparent obsession with downgrading Landry in the public consciousness—would bend on the matter was to have a nine-foot-two-inch statue of him erected atop the cowboy star sunk into the sidewalk outside. There, his feet are spread; his bronze arms are folded, with a metallic piece of paper clenched tightly in his right hand; and the iconic hat sits on his laminated head.

In this eternal pose, he is not much less animate than the flesh and blood man was. And if the statue is the only trace of Tom Landry in the sprawling complex of steel and concrete that owes its existence to his legacy, that legacy can be traced far more animately by heading about four hundred miles to the south, deep in the heart, or more accurately the underbelly, of Texas.

THE PLACE is called Mission, within the borders of which there *is* a Tom Landry Stadium, so named when it was erected on the sprawling campus of Mission High School in 1984. Mission, tucked into the southeastern tip of the state, within spitting distance of the Rio Grande River, has grown from a population of around thirty thousand people back then to nearly eighty thousand, and the Landry wraith still walks among them. In fact, the name hangs so pregnantly in the earth, sky, and concrete of Mission that the town may as well be called Landryville.

As its most famous native son, Tom Landry long ago turned the place into something of a shrine and an attraction—no less than "The Tourist Mecca of South Texas," as the Greater Mission Chamber of Commerce officially designated it some years ago. Oxymoron or not, the title is still used in the town's literature and on its website, along with its original motto, dating back to 1921: "Home of the Grapefruit." There are, to be sure, a lot of grapefruit and other fruit-bearing palm trees in Mission, and the air hangs heavy with their tangy sweet aroma. There is also a Texas Citrus Festival held every year, with a parade up the main drag, Conway

Avenue, which runs a straight line from the slinky Mexican border up through the McAllen-Edinburg-Mission sector of the Rio Grande Valley. Less kind to the nose is another of the town's attractions: Las Palmas Race Park.

For whatever reason, Mission either bred or harbored other famous people besides Landry. One was Lloyd Bentsen, the long-serving senator, who was born there in 1921, three years before Landry. When he ran for vice president in 1988, he uttered the most famous put-down in political history, reminding Dan Quayle that "you're no Jack Kennedy." Implausibly, William Jennings Bryan, who ran for the presidency three times and was secretary of state under Woodrow Wilson, and later faced off against Clarence Darrow during the Scopes Monkey trial, at which he adamantly denied the theory of evolution, spent a few years in Mission. More implausibly, the great Beat Generation poet and *Naked Lunch* author William S. Burroughs found refuge there for a short time so he could be close to Mexico, where he would go and buy morphine. He even mentioned the town in his confessional novel *Junky*.

Still, for all its other seductions and motley roster of past residents and occupants, it was really Tom Landry who put Mission on the map, hard as it still is to locate in an atlas.

Mission is not a very big place, around twenty-four square miles. "When you go back there, the feeling you get is that time stood still," says his now sixty-three-year-old son, Tom Landry Jr., who would be in tow when his father returned every July Fourth for the annual family picnics.[1] Although almost all of the Landry relatives have since died or left town, once you find Mission, you find Tom Landry all around you. This has been the case since long before his passing, in part because when he was alive Landry never forgot about his hometown. Over at Mission High, the librarian, Cindee Pelfrey, a longtime resident, refers to him with solemnity. "When my husband and I came to sleepy little Mission, it was so quaint and friendly—much like when Coach Landry grew up here," she says. "The first year we were here, there was a football banquet, and Coach Landry would always send one of his Cowboy players to speak. That year he sent Mike Ditka, and he passed his Super Bowl ring around the table where we sat. That thing was *big*. I could stick my fingertips into the diameter of it and had room to spare. Coach Landry came back here once in a while too. I never met him. But I felt pride to live in his hometown."[2]

There was once talk of naming the high school after Landry, but while that was shelved the town council did name the obligatory boulevard for him—Tom Landry Street, formerly Tenth Street, which stretches nearly the entire length of the city limits, between North Bryan Road and North Holland Avenue. The street was chosen because when he was a child and teenager, Landry lived in a wood-frame house only feet from it, on Doherty Avenue. The boulevard is now divided into Tom Landry East and Tom Landry West Streets. At the junction of Landry Street and Conway, you might feel that Landry—actually about a dozen Landrys—is watching you. Images of him were painted on a nearly block-long wall of a furniture-rental store by artist Manuel Hinojosa, who in 1995 was commissioned by the city to depict Landry in various stages of his life and career.

When the mural was dedicated, Landry and his wife, Alicia, came to Mission. So did Don Meredith. There the two old antagonists jointly sank their footprints into a cement plot the way movie stars do in Hollywood, to be preserved for eternity. The mural quickly became the centerpiece of a town already in thrall to Tom Landry. In fact, one suspects that by the time Mission celebrates Landry's hundredth birthday, just about *everything* there will bear his name, his image, or his echo.

AS DEEP as the name and legacy runs in Mission, Landry's roots reach all the way to France, from where his forebears came a century and a half ago to settle in the Canadian wilderness. One of those hardy settlers was named Stanislas Landrie, a lumberjack and farmer born in St. Leon, Manitoba. When he was nineteen, he migrated to the fertile farmland of Wisconsin, whereupon he became a citizen of the United States and fought with Company B of the Wisconsin Union Army regiment during the Civil War. He then moved to Bourbonnais, Illinois, where one of his six children was born: Alfred Landry, the original surname having been adapted to a more Anglicized spelling. It would also be the place where Alfred would meet his wife, Lillian, whose lineage was part French, part Scottish and Irish.

Alfred also had six children, two of whom died in childbirth. One who survived was named Harold Ray, born in 1898, but because he was a sickly child, having contracted muscular rheumatism, Alfred decided to move his clan to a warmer clime. They went all the way to southern Texas, where he landed a job with the McColl Land and Development Company in a town named for the mission chapel on Conway Avenue. Built in 1899 as a way station for Oblate priests traveling on horseback between Brownsville and Roma, the old La Lomita chapel, with its white stucco walls, still stands today, though with a good deal of neglect and corrosion and summertime heat.

A half century before, Mission had been nearly entirely inhabited by Mexicans whose ancestors lived there when Texas was part of Antonio López de Santa Anna's Mexican Republic. They may have even fought the resurrectionist rebel Texans at the Alamo. The fertile farmland and grapefruit crop had swelled the population to around five thousand, split about equally between Hispanics and Caucasians. In 1912, Alfred bought his farm just outside of town but became tantalized by the emerging urban attractions of the city proper. He sold the farm, bought a ranch house on Doherty, and worked as a bricklayer. Harold, whom everyone called Ray, meanwhile, became his pride and joy.

A marvelous athlete, Ray attracted the attention of a schoolgirl named Ruth Della Coffman, whom her future son Tom would describe as "a beautiful young woman with long auburn tresses and striking blue eyes."[3] Her parents had also migrated to Texas as farmers, bouncing from Virginia to Tennessee to Oklahoma, before moving to fragrant Mission. They were something of an odd couple. Ray was a card, a big, outgoing, friendly fellow with high cheekbones who looked as dashing as a Navy ensign in the clean white uniform he wore as a volunteer fireman. He also played football at Mission High School and on a soccer team that won a league championship in 1916. Ruth, on the other hand, was quiet as a mouse, prim and proper, deliberative and calculating.

Somehow it made for the right fit, but Ray was a year ahead of her at Mission High, and when he graduated in 1918, it seemed their romance was at an end. He enrolled at Texas A&M in College Station, a hundred miles away, though doing so carried the likely chance he would have to serve in World War I, as A&M was a quasi-military academy and every student was required to take courses in infantry training, trench warfare, and machine gun fire. When Ray arrived there in September, the entire senior class was fighting in the war— half of those who graduated from the school went into the service, a higher percentage than from any other school in America—and the juniors were scheduled to go in early fall, sophomores in the winter, and freshmen in the spring.

Ray prepared for the worst, and was relieved when the war ended two months later; he was even given an honorable discharge though he had never officially served. But he wound up living almost as on a battlefield when the soldiers streamed back to school, and over-crowding became so severe that many students like him slept in tents. That winter an influenza epidemic broke out, resulting in several stu-dents' deaths. Each time one died, a bugler would mournfully play "Taps" to a silent campus.[4]

Ray could take only so much of this, and that spring, after Ruth graduated, he returned home to her and they decided to go far away, in this case to California, where there was a postwar jobs boom. Ray went to a training school to become a mechanic, and in 1920 they married. Then, homesick, they went back to Mission, moving into a small A-frame ranch house at 1012 Doherty. The old wooden dwell-ing is gone now, torn down many years ago when the block was con-verted into a condominium complex. One block north on Doherty, however, still stands the First United Methodist Church, now an impressive contemporary adobe structure with an open breezeway off the palm tree–lined sidewalk. Back then, when it was a cramped brick building with no air-conditioning and leaky plumbing, the Landry family, dressed in their finest, with Bibles in hand, would come through the door punctually every Sunday morning to duti-fully pray. Ray would then teach Sunday school classes, something he did unwaveringly for three decades.

His weekdays were spent not in a suit but in grease-covered over-alls. He was the owner and operator of the Mission Paint and Body Shop, run from a garage just across an alleyway from the house, and a structure that also still stands. In 1921, Ray and Ruth began a fam-ily, first with the birth of a son, Robert, and then the following year a daughter named after Ruth, who was commonly called Ruthie. On Thursday, September 11, 1924—the same year that Marlon Brando, Jimmy Carter, George H. W. Bush, Chet Atkins, and Carroll O'Connor were born—came their second son, Thomas Wade Landry, who had a full head of hair and no hesitation expressing his emotions, at the top of his lungs, in his crib. Plainly, *that* Tom Landry would not be recognizable when the world at large discovered him.

THROUGHOUT HIS life Landry would pay homage to Mission, speaking wistfully of it as though it provided a refuge from the complications of living, an isle of serenity far removed from the pressures of a job that brought him precious little peace or tranquility. He would wax affectionate about how people there all seemed to know each other, and as a result "kids had a hard time getting into serious mischief," he said in his memoirs. If there was a downside to that, in the lack of privacy, he could easily turn it into a benefit: "I learned a sense of accountability early in life, accepting the fact that people were always watching—even when I wished they weren't."[5]

In this Andy Hardy–like allegory of small-town, front-porch America where nothing much happened except blessed normalcy, Landry could offer only a few examples of hard knocks, which were no more than the requisite pitfalls of youth. There was the time he bounded from the front porch when he saw his father and Uncle Arthur coming down Doherty in the latter's Model T. Failing to look both ways, Tom was struck by another car coming from the opposite direction. As he recalled, after he was taken to a hospital, his father, sister, and Aunt Viola stretched his leg taut to snap it into place before the doctor set it in a cast. Without benefit of anesthesia, Tom began to shriek in pain, making Ray Landry—who as a moonlighting fireman wouldn't so much as blink at the worst carnage or burned bodies—so queasy that he fled the room before he fainted. There was also the time when Tom fell off his bicycle, behind first, into a cluster of cactus, suffering what he called a "prickly predicament" and "horrible embarrassment" when his mother and her friends "pulled the needles out of my backside. . . . I felt like a public spectacle."[6]

The good times were gauzy memories of family outings, of padding shoeless through the dirt streets, of fishing with his father and Uncle Arthur, of learning how to shoot deer with a hunting rifle. Ray, who somehow found time to not only fight fires but also serve as fire chief for forty-seven years, allowed his sons—a third one, Jack, came along in 1931—to ride in the fire engines and the chief's shiny red Chevrolet and to slide down the poles. Sometimes, when an alarm sounded and the trucks roared out of the station, Tom would follow along on his bike for as long as he could. The boys so hated to leave the premises that Ray set up cots upstairs for them to sleep on, just like the firemen. Ray never failed to amaze his son, the way he seemed to know everyone in town. For example, when Lloyd Millard Bentsen Sr. arrived in Mission in the early 1910s, one of the first people he met was Ray, who introduced him to the woman who would become his wife, the mother of the senator-to-be. Ray was like that—a born matchmaker.

As much as Tom adored his old man, he realized early in life that because of his own shy predispositions, combined with the lisp that made him clam up even more, he would never be the kind of man Ray was. In fact, Ray was a hard act to follow, having left his own distinct marks on Mission. Today, for example, on the eastern side of Landry Street, hard by the Mission Fire Department at the junction of Francisco Avenue, there is a leafy park where firemen, on their down time, bask in the sun and on Sundays slap burgers and hot dogs on grills as their children gambol in the playground. The shingle on the fence around the park reads "Ray Landry Fireman's Park."

In 1973, the town's mayor proclaimed "Ray Landry Day" in Mission, a ceremony attended by his by-then inordinately famous son, who on that day played second fiddle to his old man. Indeed, in 1977, a year before Ray died, a local newspaper, the *Upper Valley Progress*, carried a full-page profile of him, in his spiffy fire uniform and cap, under the headline "RAY LANDRY FOUGHT MISSION FIRES FOR 57 YEARS." Nowhere in the piece was there as much as a mention of the most famous football coach in America.[7]

Perhaps because Ray was so immensely popular, his son Tom found his mother's internalized, intense qualities more akin to his own. While Ray was, as his son would note many years later, "a true public servant," his southern belle of a wife was "much more of a private person. I think I inherited my studious, perfectionistic [*sic*], and quiet nature from her."[8] That Ruth would be described in this context as the "strong, silent type" by neighbors was an odd flip of the usual male-female conventions, and one wonders if Ray perhaps bridled that his children's most rigorous guiding hand was their mother's. In a 1930s American culture, this was rare by any measure. And, as was also true of her son Tom when he matured, she would use her outward delicateness as a useful mask, hiding an inner grit and pith that would viscerally grab a hold onto the people who mattered most to her.

Although Ruth generally did recede into Ray's dominating public shadow, as was expected of the women of her era—her only foray outside the home being her role as publicity chairman of the Mission High PTA—he would often give way to her, since she had more common sense and was able to see the consequences of decisions made too lightly or for the wrong reasons. Her good-sense, conservative, steel magnolia, God-fearing ways tempered not only her husband's more restless ways but also the gushy romantic he had been in his youth.

Their middle son, who most directly mirrored Ruth Landry's prissiness about such things, would one day confess that "neither of my parents were ever overtly affectionate, with each other or with their children." It was an unusual revelation for him, given his habitual reticence to delve into personal matters that might dim the shiny veneer of a perfect family life. Indeed, it sounded like he could have said much more on the subject; instead, he left it at that, while feeling the need to clarify in the very next sentence, "I never doubted their love."[9] If Ruth Landry was not one to swath her husband or children with hugs and kisses and expressions of love, she did, with her eye for detail and demanding perfectionism, succeed at keeping them rooted to the values that made Tom Landry both a dreamer and a prude who wasted no time on anything frivolous. As he grew into his mid teens, he thus became consumed with a single-minded goal, defined by a funny-looking ball that liked to take unpredictable bounces.

THE LIVING was anything but easy in Mission, and it was especially difficult when the Great Depression hit. In the mid-1930s, women's dress shoes cost two dollars a pair; a can of corn at the local grocery, eleven cents; and a pound of steak, a quarter. Ray brought home the money, but Ruth was the one who looked after it, promptly depositing it into one of those new federally insured bank accounts. The Landrys were nowhere near rich; all four children slept in the attic, right above where Ray and Ruth slept—in the only bedroom. Few beside the very limited social set of Mission owned a car, but Ray, using his mechanic skills, could fix up an old heap better than anyone, and he rode around on some fine wheels, such as a 1937 Pontiac Deluxe Eight convertible, which drew long stares as he passed by.

Landry once recalled that his mother was able to feed the family of six on a dollar and a half a day and still had leftovers for the homeless transients on the street who became accustomed to showing up at the back door. Every once in a while Ray and Ruth would gather the kids into the drop-top and head over to the Palace Theater in McAllen, to take in a Humphrey Bogart or Jimmy Cagney movie. By taking odd jobs, the Landry boys did their part to keep food on the table. Tom's first, when he was eight, was selling newspapers on the corner of Conway and Tenth; another was carrying bags around a golf course as a caddy for twenty-five-cent tips.

All three of his sons shared Ray's love of sports. Unwilling to give up playing football in his twenties, Ray joined a semipro team called the Mission Eagles, whose game against the McAllen Bulldogs in November 1928 was written up in a local paper under the headline "EAGLES MAKE POOCHES OUT OF BULLDOGS," oddly, since the game ended in a 6–6 tie. The article included the information that Ray had "(broken) through the opposing line at random."[10] Like him, his sons were blessed with strong, lithe bodies. Robert was perhaps the best athlete in the brood. His exploits as an end (the term "wide receiver" was still decades off) at Mission High, predating his kid brother's career there by three years, led people to wonder if he would be the first athlete from the town to step up in rank as a college star. Robert was also personable, engaging, and a little reckless. Before he was old enough to get a driver's license, he sneaked into cars parked at Ray's body shop and took them out joyriding, sometimes with Tom in the passenger seat. He also once eased into the driver's seat of Ray's red fire chief's car and accidentally crashed it through the garage door. If

Robert was more a chip off the old block, encroaching rebel turf in small steps, his kid brother toed the straight and narrow path.

Tom was a deferential teen, and even the burning hot South Texas sun did not darken the pigment of his pasty face. His gray-green eyes, usually squinting in the glare of the light, were wide open and steely when he was engaged in sports. His lantern jaw was taut, his lips thin and pursed, readily agreeable to form a shy smile. If he was restrained in emotion like his mother, he could at a moment's notice channel Ray, trying to assimilate into adolescent goofiness, if with some awkwardness. At his core he was a good and dependable friend to his buddies, not needing to be asked a second time to go out to the fishing hole to kill a lazy afternoon. Tom's appearance was often deceiving; he lacked the physical skills of his older brother but made a compact with himself to do whatever was necessary to compete with Robert and the other older kids. He attacked his interest in sports fervently, sometimes maniacally.

As he waded deeper into his teens, his choice of reading matter turned from comic books to football manuals he ordered through the mail. He steeped himself in the proper techniques of men engaged in hand-to-hand combat in an era when helmets were paper thin and had no face masks, and only rudimentary pads were worn. Already he was seeing the game as a nexus of interlocking puzzle pieces and could diagram plays as a jumble of X's and O's, and do it with the coherence of a coach. Where most saw football as the simple game it is at its core, blocking and tackling to move or get to the guy with the ball, its cognitive, chess-style inner game of geometric prevision and deception on a fixed grid was catnip for a young man with a competitive streak and a keen mind.

When Tom got serious about football, it was a given that he would play quarterback, a natural inclination after steeling his arm throwing to his brother on the sandlots. There was also the excitement of perfecting the still relatively recent invention called the forward pass. This play had been proscribed in the college and nascent pro game until 1906, when it was allowed in order to "bring about a game in which speed and real skill shall supersede so far as possible mere brute strength and force of weight."[11] For Landry, passing seemed to be the flavor of the day, but even the elephantine single-wing, ground-and-pound scheme had subtleties that he could find clues and answers to. Landry came of age on the cusp of the football revolution, which was sparked by the split-T offense that would come into vogue in the early 1940s and would be mastered later in the decade by University of Oklahoma head coach Jim Tatum. And yet in the late 1930s, all across America, these theories were being tried on less glorified venues, one being a weedy plot of grass and dirt called Burnett Field. When Landry began to play on that turf in 1938, his knowledge of the game was far beyond that of the other guys.

At around five foot eight, and weighing 112 pounds, he resembled a coat rack. Neither was he overly fast, but he had shiftiness to him, excellent technique and foot movement, and toughness. He would do anything, even take the punishment of playing center at times, just to be in on a play. If he was told to play defensive back, he had a nose for the ball, where and to whom it would be going, and never held back an inch in sticking his head into the opponent's chest, hard. Never would he complain about hurting, or ask to come out.

Clearly, he got every last ounce out of what he had physically and out of personal drive that came only from inside himself. Ray had been too busy to throw a football with Tom, and there were no organized leagues in Mission. Thus, his son said years later, he had developed "something that today's youngsters aren't able to experience," learning to "cry and to fight [and] overcome all situations according to your own abilities and initiative . . . without some (adult) supervisors always looking over your shoulder. It was an opportunity to develop independence and initiative. It also meant the season never had to end."[12]

As the launch pad for his football life, Mission High is the most significant Landry landmark in the town. As with everything else, it is not far from the old Landry place on Doherty, only a few blocks to the north, at Fourteenth Street, which is today Mission *Junior* High. Burnett Field is still out back, and looking across that scarred, patchy turf, you can envision Landry as an ectomorphic galloping ghost, hair flying in the wind.

Bob Martin, the burly, affable junior varsity football coach at Mission High, who lived in a garage apartment two doors from the Landrys, took to Tom on the first day of practice. When he asked for a volunteer to play center to, as he put it, "initiate every play for our team," the only one who raised his hand was the 112-pound Landry boy. The least logical candidate for the position, he nonetheless anchored the offense his required two years on the jayvee squad. Martin was duly impressed. The following year, 1940, when Martin was moved up to coach the varsity team, he would reward the kid for his selfless drudgery. Assembling the group for the first time, Martin made Tom, who had grown to six feet though was still knotty at 145 pounds, the starting quarterback, or tailback, the positions being interchangeable in the single-wing formation that featured little passing; the long snap normally would go right to the guy who was to run straight into the line, including the quarterback, but Landry's accurate arm would allow the option for him to straighten up and throw downfield.

Martin needed a player who could both learn and lead. His choice was grateful for his trust, and years later Landry would drench Martin in huzzahs as a man whose word "became my law, his approval my inspiration," and through whom "football became my life."[13] Remarkably, Martin allowed the precocious kid to call the plays. He also put him in the defensive backfield, at safety, where Landry reacted viscerally to being victimized by a pass, developing what he called "an acute hatred for receivers. If a guy caught a ball against me, I'd try to hit him so hard he wished he hadn't. And nothing made me madder than to have someone catch a touchdown pass on me."[14]

That season, the Mission Eagles caught fire, with their tall, skinny quarterback soon being dubbed "Terrific Tommy" in the local paper. With each Friday came a greater sense of excitement as the Eagles won six of ten games and went undefeated against teams in their district, making them district champs, though they lost a heartbreaker in the bi-district semifinal regional title game, 7–6, to a school from Alice. In his first gig as a field general, Landry wisely called his own number enough to score 46 points and secure for himself a berth on the All-South Texas schoolboy team. Suddenly he was much more popular around the school, though his natural aversion to strutting his stuff made him a rather understated marquis quarterback. Indeed, when the senior yearbook would come out, he would not be the one voted best athlete; instead, to his dismay, he was "Cutest

Boy," a theme echoed by a school directory that referred to him as "Handsome Tommy."[15]

Not that such twittery would be a problem for him once his thick hair began to recede and he became more craggy than cute. But the expectations of Handsome Tommy for the 1941 season were sky-high, most of all from Bob Martin. That winter and spring, Martin, keeping Landry close by, coaxed him to play guard on the Mission High basketball team, which Martin also coached, all the way to the 1940 Rio League championship. Biding more time in the summer, Landry hooked up with a semipro baseball team, the 30–30 Rifles, most of whose players were in their twenties. When the new semester and football season came around in the fall of 1941, Martin was stoked. On his chalkboard was written a bold team mantra—"Eleven brothers are hard to beat"—and he handed out mimeographed sheets with sternly worded new rules, among them that players were prohibited from drinking Coca-Cola and letting their girlfriends wear their letterman sweaters, per the hoary puppy love tradition. A woolen badge of honor, those sweaters were theirs alone. He had also mailed each player a self-penned poem, part of which read, "You are the fellow who makes up your mind / Whether you'll lead or linger behind."[16]

For one of the players, the most impressionable one, old-fashioned rules and motivational gristle like this would not be forgotten, they would become nothing less than a cellular component of the art of coaching football. Neither would he ever waver in paying his debt to Bob Martin, for whom a box seat at the Cowboys' home games would be held years later, until the day he died.

SLEEPY MISSION hardly seemed microcosmic of the fabric of American culture back then, but there was a sense of incipient change in 1941. One vintage picture of Landry's team is a freeze-frame not just of his seminal achievements but of slow-motion sociological progress. Among the twenty-three players are swarthy faces of young men named Guerra, Garcia, Gonzalez, Pinon, Cavazos, Montez, and Linares. There is a similarly brown-skinned, slightly older man at the end of the front row: Bob Martin, whose mother was a Mexi-

can immigrant. This ratio fairly mirrored the Mexican population of
Mission, which was roughly one-third. Their presence in such a picture reflected a truism that after many decades of benign neglect or
outright hostility toward Mexicans either native-born or otherwise,
bigotry alone could not prevent rightful, earned participation in the
social fabric.

Landry grew quite close to these men, as he would all his team-
mates. Many of them would be at the ceremony when Tom Landry
Stadium was dedicated. All assumed that the great coach would have
surely forgotten them, but he knew each by name. One, Arnaldo
Vera, had several years before seen Landry at the airport in nearby
Brownsville. Vera, who was nicknamed "LaGrulla" at Mission High,
for the border town he came from, approached Landry and said,
"Tommy, I bet you don't remember me."

"Of course, I do, LaGrulla," came the reply.[17]

Landry clearly harbored not an ounce of disdain for "the brown
ones," the vernacular white Texans have historically reserved for
those of Mexican descent. The same term could have been used to
describe the players on the 30–30 Rifles, the baseball team Landry
had joined, who were mainly Hispanic. Much later, distancing himself from the racial lines of his youth—which were starkly drawn,
with whites on one side of the railroad tracks, the Hispanics on the
other—he would state the obvious in his memoirs, that "prejudice
ran deep in South Texas," and that while the football team was
integrated, "an obvious division remained with each group sticking
pretty much to itself."[18]

Mission High may not have bent the social norms as far as it did if
not for men of principle—Ray Landry, for one. Ray's 1918 graduating class at the school had not one Hispanic. A classmate's yearbook
from that year was signed by eight seniors with good solid "American" names like Robertson, Scoggins, Klopperich, Fosmire, and
Landry. Back then Hispanics were left to attend ramshackle segregated schools in their own neighborhoods, where they lived with no
electricity or indoor plumbing. Little by little, a few of their children
trickled into the white schools, aided by a general thawing among
locals. Ray Landry, a man whose word carried great weight, had
hired a number of Mexicans to work in his body shop, and he took a

stand in favor of admitting Hispanics to the high school in the mid-
1930s. Admirable as that was, however, neither Ray nor his Mission
cohorts had any great moral epiphanies about the larger problem of
race in America, in part because there were so few African Americans around to give a human face to the cause. So scarce were they
that Landry in his autobiography specifically recalled that "once in
a while I'd sit with the old black gentleman who shined shoes at the
barber shop and listen to a radio broadcast of a New York Yankees'
game."[19]

Those radios in Mission carried not much in the way of Delta
blues or rhythm and blues, but plenty of hillbilly blues stolen from
those idioms. Black culture was what whites made it to be, which
could be seen and heard at shows at the Lions Club. At one such performance, perhaps the most respected man in Mission slathered on
black face paint and sang "Sambo"-like minstrel tunes. These events
were covered in the pages of the *Mission Times*, which on one occasion wrote of three men in blackface:

> US LIONS IS SHO' FUNNY MINSTRELMENS.
> Yassuh, Mose and Rastus just had to relax here at the rehearsals
> for March 31–April 1 Lions Club Minstrel to enjoy that last joke.
> There'll be much more hilarious dialogue in the show, they say, an
> excellent musical entertainment as well as a number of specialty
> acts. Behind the blackout, "Mose" is Ray Landry. "Rastus" is F.W.
> Dooley.[20]

IF BOB MARTIN'S Knute Rockne–like dictums seemed ill directed
toward a bunch of high school kids, Martin guessed right. To them,
the regimentation had them breathing the same fire. From the season
opener, a 12–0 blanking of Edinburg, with Landry tossing touchdown passes of 19 and 25 yards, each game quickly became a no-
contest. The team's upward thrust was codified by heavy-breathing
coverage from the *Mission Times* and the *Monitor* in McAllen, often
with posed or in-action shots of Landry, the number 89 across his
chest, rumbling with or chucking the ball. Even in those faded pages,
the headlines still pop out with escalating brio:

"POWERHOUSE OF RIO GRANDE FOOTBALL"

"MISSION RATED TOP TEN TEAM FOR VALLEY GRIDS"

"HOME TEAM SCALPS REDSKINS IN 13–7 GAME
LAST NIGHT"

"WHAT LANDRY CAN'T DO CAN'T BE DONE"

The Eagles were so dominant that the 13–7 victory over their arch-rivals from Donna actually was the low point of the season—it was the only game they didn't win by a shutout. Landry took himself to task for that, seeing that he had interfered with the receiver he was covering in the end zone. Instead of placing the ball on the 1-yard line though, the referees incorrectly ruled a touchdown, and the Eagles had a blemish on their record. By then they had won the five previous games, 12–0, 25–0, 27–0, 40–0, and 47–0, and they would win the four thereafter, 46–0, 9–0, 19–0, and 33–0, with Landry doing little wrong. In fact, his outsized status had become a thorny issue, with some on the team quietly complaining that he was garnering so much publicity that they were all but ignored. Years later, the center who snapped the ball to him, Jimmy Mehis, spoke of him as many of the Eagles had in private moments, saying that "Tommy was a good football player, but there were a few others on the team better than he was. You know, a lot of people get lucky. The ball bounces up and some people catch it and run, and others drop it. Tommy caught the ball and made the most of it."[21]

For a time this subject even spilled over into the newspaper. When a *Mission Times* sportswriter got wind of it, he wrote a column agreeing that "not enough has been said for the other boys," though he concluded that "we'll hold out for the belief that Tommy has deserved everything said about him," and believed that "[his] head hasn't swelled a bit despite the adulation."[22]

Landry himself was never comfortable with the spotlight. Never in all his years would he recall his exploits as anything special. More important to him was winning the respect of his team on the field. In a late-season game he was racked up by a tackler. Ray, seeing his son with his helmet off on the sideline as the game wore on, noticed that his cheek had swollen up to the size of a ripe Mission grapefruit, and he bounded from the stands to right behind the bench. Reluctant to act like a mother hen, he politely inquired of Bob Martin, "Can I help?" Martin normally would have told him to go back to his seat, but he could tell that his quarterback needed some first aid. "Yes," he called back. "You can put some ice on the boy's face. It looks pretty bad."[23]

Ray took a close look and knew his son had fractured his cheekbone. He missed the rest of the game but despite pleas from his parents he refused to sit out the next one. Instead he donned a makeshift protective mask designed by Martin, and ran for two touchdowns before sitting out the rest of that game. It was perhaps his finest moment, and one his teammates could not have regarded as anything but doughty.

With their second-straight division crown, the Eagles went into the bi-district title game against Aransas Pass, on whose field the game would be played. By now Eagles fever gripped Mission. At a banquet at the Lions Club, the team was feted, and Landry named the Most Valuable Player. For his work, Martin was given the keys to a new Chevrolet. There were pep rallies, parades were held on Conway Avenue all week, and on Friday morning, stores closed early so that employees could, as hundreds did, board a special train at the Missouri Pacific station bound for Aransas Pass. They were not disappointed; under the lights Landry ran for three touchdowns, one of 76 yards, and the Eagles won, 19–0.

MISSION PARTIED hearty through that night and the next. But when the citizens awakened on the morning of Sunday, December 7, 1941, the radio crackled with the news that the Pacific naval fleet was in flames at Pearl Harbor. Ships were sinking, thousands of sailors were presumed dead. The Landrys, dazed, went to First United Methodist and prayed for the souls of the victims and for God to bless America. The following day, President Franklin D. Roosevelt went before Congress and declared war on "the Japanese Empire." Yet for much of the country, war was not a hard and distinct reality.

Americans had lived under the cover of peaceful isolation for two decades, far removed from the unspeakable crimes and blitzkrieg invasions carried out by deranged despots in Europe since 1938. While in Washington plans were being hurriedly made to assemble a fighting force, down in sleepy Mission, Texas, few men made tracks in the wake of Pearl Harbor for the closest Army induction center. By contrast, thousands were swept up in the Mission High Eagles' drive to win a title.

The following Friday, with the embers still burning in Pearl Harbor, the Regional 10 Championship game would be held at Burnett Field, a very big deal since the winner would be the champs of the entire area south of San Antonio. This was the highest the Mission boys could go, there being no state championship game, and Burnett was crammed with three thousand crazed souls, some of whom paid a premium price of a dollar and a half to reserve seats. For the Mission residents, the cost was well worth it, for they were fortunate to bear witness to Tom Landry's apogee as a schoolboy player: he ran for two scores, one of 65 yards, and passed for another in a 33–0 blowout.

That exclamation point to a season that reads now like a story-book fable would send him on his way to bigger and better things, but with an abiding conviction that the autumn of 1941 was an apologue of life's last fleeting moment of innocence. For Landry, the routine abominations of life would intrude soon enough, further preserving the memories he had of his magic season. In his memoirs, coming as close to elegy as this terse, inhibited man could, he would write, "That autumn of glory, shared with my boyhood friends, remains perhaps my most meaningful season in 50 years of football."[24]

Landry, who scored 130 points that season, averaging two touchdowns a game, surely set the bar high for succeeding generations of Mission High gridiron stars, such as another quarterback, Koy Detmer, who played through 1990 when his father, Sonny Detmer, was the coach. Detmer, whose brother Ty won the Heisman Trophy at Brigham Young, passed for more yards than Landry had ever dreamed of, and later played some in the NFL. But in Mission, as in most of Texas, you don't get your name on a stadium or street sign unless you change the tides of history. Only one did.

Chapter 2

A GRIM REAPER

A S THE GRADUATING CLASS at Mission High assembled in their caps and gowns in the spring of 1942, America was at war, the uneasy winds of uncertainty causing much worry about whose sons might vault right into combat in North Africa. One son of Mission, Robert Landry, had passed up going to college when he graduated three years before, and was working for Ray in the garage when the news of Pearl Harbor broke. Soon after, Ray became Mission's coordinator of civil defense, beginning a dogged four years of making sure that if the Germans somehow found their way to the borders, the town would be prepared. Toward that end, he not only put together an informal home guard of older men and high school boys who would keep their hunting rifles at the ready, but he also taught first aid classes, just in case.

Robert Landry, meanwhile, joined the belated rush to the induction center, as did nearly all of the young men in Tom's senior class. Taking a different route than almost all the others, Robert chose to enter the newly formed U.S. Army Air Forces, which, in mid-1941, was upgraded from the Army Air Corps. The USAAF offered an accelerated path to officer status, although to attain it one had to undergo rigorous academic and physical tests, then pass intensive flight training. Robert seemed to thrive on the challenge. He won his wings by piloting a small, single-engine BT-19, whereupon he was commissioned as a first lieutenant with the Eighth Air Force's 451st Bomber Squadron based in northern England. There, he began flying the pride of the force, the B-17 four-engine heavy bomber known as the "Flying Fortress," hundreds of which would drop one and a half million metric tons of bombs on Germany during the war, far more than any other aircraft would.[1]

The fleet was based at Thorpe Abbotts Field in the central English coastal county of Norfolk. From there the planes would take off into the perilous skies over England and out over the North Atlantic, where they would then head straight into the teeth of Hermann Goering's Luftwaffe on the way to bombing known German installations in occupied northern Europe. These were terribly dangerous errands. Allied planes were being shot down. Airmen who made it back to their bases often would die later of serious wounds, their planes perforated by bullet holes and rendered useless. The B-17 was considered almost impregnable, such was its long range and ability to withstand damage. But all of that was of small comfort to the family who, despite letters from Robert detailing these missions with the usual Landry breviloquence and understatement, worried themselves sick, rightly. As proud of him as they were for being the first military officer the Landry family had ever seen, all they could do was pray at First United Methodist Church that he was safe, and that if the Lord did bless and keep him he would be home for Christmas.

DURING THIS interim, his younger brother did not join him in uniform, not just yet. Tom's exploits on the gridiron at Mission High naturally attracted attention from the big Texas colleges, but so did the fact that his grades qualified him as a member of the National Honor Society and made him senior class valedictorian. His address was typically lacking in hyperbole and was reflective of the momentous crossroads of history his generation now found itself in. He was no longer the barefooted kid dangling a fishing pole in the lake, but rather a smart, centered adult, a summer shy of his eighteenth year, perched on the edge of a life about to transcend Mission. While it was only logical that Robert would enlist, providing him a way to prove himself as a man, Ray and Ruth Landry were petrified at the thought of their two eldest sons being in harm's way and so encouraged Tom to at least wait a while before doing the same, under cover of a student deferment.

The recruiters beat a path to Mission that spring, the most intent from the Southwest Conference powers SMU and Rice. They took a road not much traveled given that only a handful of Mission graduates had played football in college. But the jut-jawed wing-T quarterback, who now stood at six feet one and weighed a sinewy 175 pounds, was worth the trip on those dusty back roads. Landry too was on the move, accepting invitations from recruiters to visit their campuses. Having never ventured beyond the borders of the Rio Grande Valley, he and a buddy uneasily made the long drive on a Saturday to Houston, to check out Rice.

While he was there, he was feted by the football coaches and given tickets to the team's game that day. He later recalled that when he sat in the stands of the massive stadium, his first thought was that the entire population of Mission couldn't even fill the end zone section. He also seriously doubted that he could play on the level of what he was watching, which was prime Southeast Conference fodder, or survive some of the hits that made him wince. It seemed that the big-time schools lost interest in him after those initial meetings, because no one had made him a scholarship offer. Early in the summer, however, another invitation came, this time from Mississippi State. The coach sent Landry a couple of bus tickets to Starkville, a day-long, eight-hundred-mile journey through the bowels of the Gulf Coast. He invited Jimmy Mehis to come along, and the two of them took in the muddy landscape of an America they had read about only in their Mark Twain books. The pair was picked up at the Starkville bus depot by school officials in a 1941 limited edition Buick with a rumble seat. The trip, however, was fruitless. Although a scholarship offer was on the table, Landry became homesick quickly and made up his mind that wherever he would go to school, it would be in Texas.

As it happened, a good old boy in Mission had been using that angle on him for months. This was Vernon F. Neuhaus, who the folks in town knew colloquially as "Doc." He had grown up in Mission, then made it big in the oil industry in Houston before coming back and buying a bank on Conway. Though he split his time between Mission and Houston, where his family still lived, he also sank money into housing and office projects in the Rio Grande Valley, and today there is a park named for him in McAllen. Doc Neuhaus may have reeked of big bucks, but in his rumpled clothing and cowboy boots he looked more like a cattle rustler than an oilman. He had also gone to the University of Texas, and one day that winter he sent word to the Landry kid to come over to the bank and sit for a spell. As Landry recalled, he was baffled when he walked in and Neuhaus "wanted to talk about my plans after graduation," wondering "just what a rich, successful oilman wanted from the likes of me."[2]

What he wanted became clear by the UT pennants and other Longhorns flotsam strewn around his office. Neuhaus was now a major donor to the school and as such had a good deal of pull with the admissions people, as well as a box seat on the 50-yard line for Longhorns games. It floored the young man when Neuhaus told him, "You're just the kind of football player the Longhorns need." Landry would get this kind of soothing syrup from many people and take none of it seriously. He figured that wherever he went he would probably become lost in the shuffle, carrying water for far better players from high schools around the state almost as renowned as the campus in Austin. Actually, the Longhorns had declined as a football power in the mid-1930s but were enjoying a renascence under the exquisitely named coach and athletic director Dana X. Bible, also known as "D. X." The team made the cover of *Life* magazine that autumn as the preseason favorite for the national title, though with an 8–1–1 record, it would have to settle for No. 4 in the rankings. Given all this, Neuhaus's flattery had little effect on his would-be Mission protégé. Surely, if Tom Landry did get into UT, he remembered thinking, he would just be a kid "from a podunk school they had never heard of."

It must have shocked Neuhaus that the raw-boned young man didn't leap at the proposition. Landry was duly grateful for the attention but said he wanted to keep his options open. Neuhaus responded by saying he "sure hoped" Landry would consider going to Texas. "I assured him I would," wrote Landry in his memoirs, "that's the way we left it for the time being."[3] Such a diffident reaction no doubt made Neuhaus pant for him even more. Now, he simply had to get him, one way or another. Over the ensuing months, Neuhaus regularly touted Landry to D. X. Bible, who hadn't heard about the kid's wondrous senior season but had in fact recruited a Mission High player the year before, halfback and kicker Jack Field, who was now a key to the offense.

Bible finally decided to send one of his assistant coaches, an inimitable Longhorns notable named H. C. "Bully" Gilstrap, a three-time letterman at the school in the 1920s who would also go on to coach the basketball squad. A big round-faced, jug-eared fellow with a wry smile, he arrived in Mission in the late winter, armed with an expense account and a rap to lay on the senior who was playing hard to get. After meeting Landry in Neuhaus's office, Gilstrap took him to a restaurant down the block, the Manhattan Cafe. While Landry sank his teeth into a steak, Bully delivered the main course. Playing all the angles, he said that virtually every important person he could name in Mission—the church leaders, the oil crowd, the lawyers, the politicians—had gone to the university, and that Austin was close enough for him to visit his family. What's more, not only Jack Field but two other Mission High expatriates were on the squad, one being the brother of Lloyd Bentsen, the future senator, who also was there, at the UT Law School.

Landry still was cagey, telling Gilstrap he wasn't ready to decide where he would go—he did not want to make such a profound decision, as he mused later, "on a full stomach." With much more to digest than a rib-eye, later that day he sat down with his parents and Bob Martin and went over all the pros and cons. Neuhaus had, not incidentally, leaned on them as well, wearing down any hesitation about Tom being quickly shunted off to the bench. All agreed that the best move was to take the road that led to Austin.

AFTER GRADUATION, Landry didn't have the luxury of knocking around Mission in a convertible, taking bows and basking in past and future glory. Instead, at Ray's urging, Neuhaus gave Tom a job, not one lounging at a desk in a nice office but out in the oil fields down near Rio Grande City. Worse, he was put on the graveyard shift, from midnight to eight in the morning. The job, in the vernacular, was called "roughnecking," for reasons made evident by the work he had to do, such as threading drill bits, connecting steel tubing, and mixing and pouring cement. One would never know that corners had been cut for Landry, who with no experience should have logically been employed as a roustabout, performing the lowliest and dirtiest tasks. But it was backbreaking work nonetheless, leaving him caked in sweat and mud, and barely able to stumble into a welcome bed.

The pay was good, four dollars an hour—his earnings would last for his entire freshman year in Austin—though he must have wondered what he had done to deserve such work. Landry had no time that summer for any sort of victory lap in Mission. The first few weeks he had to drive two hours each way through a wasteland of mesquite and cactus. Then he was shifted to another rig even farther away, this time with work hours that had him baking in the blistering South Texas sun, and necessitating that he stay in a fleabag motel, having no one to talk to. Of those days he would say, "I lived a very lonely life."[4]

As the end of summer neared, he was looking forward to the usually dreaded but in this case comparative duck soup of late August football rituals, like training with the blocking and tackling sled and running two-a-day drills in full pads. There would also be one last game as a schoolboy, a state high school all-star game in Abilene. However, while working on a rig one day, he slipped on some mud-caked steps and flew ten feet to the bottom of the stairs. Landing atop a stack of metal pipes, he yelped in pain when a spigot from a steam pipe embedded in his shin, causing a hairline fracture of his bone. It could have been worse—much worse, possibly even ending his football career had the bone been fully broken. Happily, it did end his roughnecking career. Days later, he was still limping but went off to the capital city of Texas, relieved to have survived the worst summer of his life but petrified that he would wash out in Austin, just another faceless kid humbled by the daunting hauteur of the Southwest Conference.

LANDRY, WHO turned eighteen two weeks after his freshman year began and had still not seen a genuine urban center, viewed Austin as "a teeming metropolis." In truth, it was anything but. At the time, the population of the city named for the legendary Stephen Austin, the leader of the American colonization of independent Texas, was a modest eighty-eight thousand. It had also been mired in such dire economic straits over the past decade that it was given more federal aid during the Depression than any other city in the state, allowing for a minor boom fueled by construction of dams along the Colorado River, which borders it. Even so, the sum and substance of Austin comprised, as Landry noted, "little more than the state government and the university."[5]

Indeed, as the latter grew, so did the city. But if by 1942 it was considered one of the earliest "public ivy" schools, it still had a lower profile than its Southwest Conference rival: Ray Landry's far more prestigious military-themed alma mater, Texas A&M over in College Station, with its five-thousand-acre campus and student body of nearly twenty thousand, twice that of UT. Then, and now, the gulf between those two schools and their respective environs is a cultural divide, with A&M regimented, ultra-conservative, and snooty, and UT more libertarian. In matters of race though, both schools were equally pledged to Jim Crow, segregating their admissions policies and sports teams. Those pernicious customs would need two more decades of simmering outrage to burn out, if not completely. To be sure, there was a strong Ku Klux Klan contingent in Austin, and regular marches by them downtown on Congress Avenue. But so too was there a small but active nucleus of African Americans who, as early as 1906, organized a boycott of the city's segregated streetcars. By 1927, they had also founded the Community Welfare Association and the Carver Branch of the Austin Public Library, which contained one of the first collections of African American literature and art in Texas. If all this wasn't a seismic shift of attitudes, next to the wasteland of Mission it was something like culture shock, a small dose for sure, but a significant one.[6]

Landry's own maturation would be gradual. As cosmopolitan as Austin seemed to him, the fact was that he was merely going from one cloistered environment to another, with the dusty streets of Mission replaced by a campus with few roads to anything with cultural value. Not that the university wasn't a sight to behold for a self-described kid from Podunk. There was the stately Main Building, which was bathed in orange floodlights after a victory over the Texas A&M Aggies, a site that for all its pristine, nearly pastoral architectural radiance would a quarter century later be the scene of one of the most horrific crimes in American history. There, Charles Whitman, the failed UT student, would use the high wall and the light towers to shoot to death sixteen people and wound thirty-two others before cops gunned him down, ending what would be called the "Tower Massacre."[7] Such sacrilege would not have been conceivable in 1942, when the tower beckoned new students like Tom Landry into what was not a campus as much as a state of mind, one that was captured by football every autumn.

The trappings of those Saturday afternoons were already a tradition, from the orange and white uniforms and the marching band playing "The Eyes of Texas," to the appearance of Bevo the pet longhorn and the Torchlight Parade and Rally, which in 1941 was expanded from once a year, on the eve of the Oklahoma game, to each week, when a giant Lone Star flag would be draped over the tower. (The hook-'em-horns hand signal didn't come around until the mid-1950s.) It seemed almost incidental that UT technically had not won a national championship yet, and that the mythical designation had been born only a few years back, in 1936, when the Associated Press compiled a vote of sportswriters from across the country. Indeed, long before that, the rise of King Football in all of Texas had grabbed hold of the campus, inducing mass hysteria and overflowing the twenty-seven-thousand-seat War Memorial Stadium on game days.[8]

Such emotion stoked the outrage of 1941, when D. X. Bible's squad made it to No. 1 in the AP poll for the first time. That November, after blanking Southern Methodist 34–0, the Longhorns tied Baylor and lost to Texas Christian University. Next, they faced the No. 2–ranked Texas A&M, whom they had beaten 7–0 the season before on a miraculous catch, knocking the Aggies from their No. 1 ranking and a Rose Bowl date. The Longhorns hadn't won at College Station in eighteen years, but this time they wiped the Aggies out, 23–0. Yet while the Longhorns finished 8–1–1, they were snubbed by the Rose Bowl, passed over for Duke University, and their subsequent 71–7 blowout of Oregon State only hours before the bombing of Pearl Harbor counted for little. In the end, they wound up at No. 4, behind the University of Minnesota, Duke, and Notre Dame.

D. X. Bible was obsessed with taking the program to the top. Most of the players on the superb 1941 team were returning, and Bible had moved up the best of what was a strong freshman team the year before. Indeed, the jayvee team was a critical part of the Longhorns puzzle, with Bible having his pick of top-flight high school players in the state. Thus, when Landry put on his cleats for the preseason drills, still limping from his oil rig injury, he was already, as he had feared from the start, relegated to sitting behind players he had faced on the field from the AA schools during his senior year, three of whom were halfbacks ahead of him on the depth chart. Being the third-string back on a second-string team created nagging doubts in his own mind that he was Southwest Conference stuff.

The only time he would spend with the high-profile varsity players was as human fodder during joint team scrimmages. It would have to do for now, and despite his seeding deep on the bench, it was something of a relief that whatever he did on the frosh team, good or bad, would be done in relative obscurity. However, life on campus for a tenderfoot Longhorn, no matter what press clippings he had, was a gauntlet. Hazing was a merciless tradition at big-time football schools, and the kid from the sticks was easy prey. The football teams, varsity and junior varsity, were boarded at a dormitory called Hill Hall, which was more like Hell Hall for the freshmen who roomed on the first floor.

Their lives were made miserable when, at all hours, they would be called to the upper floors and ordered to perform menial tasks like shining shoes, going to the campus store for a Coke, or singing their high school fight song—that is, if they were lucky, since at other times they would be told to bend over, expose their behinds, and, as Landry remembered with a shudder, "take a hard, painful lick from a wooden paddle wielded by a big senior lineman." At those times, he could take comfort in the fact that the varsity guys usually saved their flagellation for the freshmen who had the biggest egos or talked the toughest. But not even Landry escaped the paddle.

Although the recruiters from UT would mandatorily sell prospective players on the wonders of the school's academic curricula, D. X. Bible, reflecting the reality of college athletics even then, would tell his men with a wink and a nod that their main objective was to protect their eligibility, not the strain of too much study. Landry, insecure as he was about washing out as a jock, had no intention of squandering his scholarship on proverbial basket-weaving classes; instead, he logged a full schedule of engineering courses, with an eye on returning to the oil industry not as a roughneck but as an engineer in charge of those big rigs. There was nothing easy about these classes; the required work was so consuming that during the season he had scant time for football. After all, he was eighteen now and had to consider life as a bramble of hard choices, none of which seemed to include playing sports.

Then, with the 1942 season in full bloom and Landry moving up on the jayvee depth chart, a bitter wind came blowing in from across the Atlantic. It knocked him down harder than any linebacker ever would, ending those calculations and his cloistered existence and tearing out a piece of his heart forever.

ON AN early November day that year, with Thanksgiving a few weeks away, a special-delivery letter reached Ray Landry down in Mission. As soon as he took it from the messenger and saw "War Department: The Adjutant General's Office" on the masthead—a heading that during war normally meant one thing, the worst news of all—Ray's legs weakened and he had to struggle for breath. Swallowing hard, he read the letter, desperately hoping it was a mere formality. But the first sentence of most such missives was merciless, and this one told him that his son, First Lieutenant Robert Landry, was missing in action, his plane unaccounted for after going down in the murky, freezing waters of the Greenland Sea near Iceland. No body had been recovered, and Lieutenant Landry was presumed dead.

Ray, holding the letter tightly in his hands as if wanting to strangle it, steeled himself and walked into the laundry room, where Ruth was doing the wash. Without saying a word, he put the paper in her hands. While she read the same words, her face became flushed, but she was stoic as always, refusing to break down or betray emotion.

Given that there was no confirmation of Robert's death, she said he might have survived. He was a good boy, a good Christian. God would save his mortal soul. She grabbed Ray's hand and told him he should go to the body shop and be optimistic. As usual, Ray did what his wife said. Most of all, as a family friend and neighbor named Ruth Langston once recalled, "they didn't put their grief on others, going around talking about it so many would have. They handled it themselves."[9]

Ruth called her middle son in Austin that day to give him the news. She trusted it would turn out to have a happy ending and urged him to keep the faith. But that was an instruction he couldn't obey for long. As soon as he heard about Robert, a hole was carved into the pit of his gut. He could not focus on his work or football, and sometimes sat in his room alone, nearly catatonic. Years later he would describe that "sickening emptiness" as weeks passed with no word about his brother, whose only shot at surviving was if he had been miraculously pulled from the ocean within hours of going down. Even if he had been alive when he hit the water, by Thanksgiving that possibility was nil.

Tom returned home for the holidays to find his family's optimism about Robert abating. By then his indomitable mother could put up only a brave but cracking front. As Ruth Langston said, "Ruth wasn't in shock, but she was in grief beyond words. . . . You could see on her face how much she was suffering."[10] After they ate their Thanksgiving meal in near silence, the family went over to First United Methodist Church to pray as one and to light candles for Robert, a ritual Tom would recall with great sadness, saying, "Naturally my parents weren't ready to concede Robert's death. We all hoped and prayed that by some miracle he would be found alive," but his gut told him otherwise. He went back to school dreading the inevitable, which came just before Christmas when another messenger delivered a Western Union telegram, again from the War Department, to the Landrys' door.

This time the words were even more blunt, heartbreaking, and final. Signed by Adjutant General of the Army James Alexander Ulio, it began with the boilerplate language read by too many parents: "It is my sad duty to inform you of the death of your son."

There were no details revealed, but several days later another let-ter from the department arrived with the explanation that Robert's B-17 had exploded near the coast of Iceland. Even worse, his remains were never found, nor were his dog tags or any other personal effects. "Please accept my sincere sympathy for your great loss," such cruel missives always read, hardly enough to alleviate the pain of losing a young man who died so horrifically in service to his country. When the family buried an empty casket in a symbolic funeral service in Mission in early January, the Army had sent duplicate tags, which Ray and Ruth placed inside the casket before it was lowered into the ground.

They were all stolid as ever that grim day, but the family had been blown apart, never again to be whole or even close as the years unwound. Robert's kid brother, bitten by the cruelty of life for the first time, would never be quite the same; the cavity would remain until his death. Nothing that he would write in his rather wooden autobiography bore any more emotional heft than a brief passage about the tragedy: "*Robert dead? It couldn't be. . . .* The big brother I had looked up to all my life was gone forever from the face of the earth—without my ever having told him how much he meant to me." And yet, as with the rest of the family, his manner of dealing with inestimable pain and loss was to push emotions of that sort deeper into the insular part of him that could filter out intensely personal pain. As he would go on, "I tried to shut it out."[11]

AND SO he did, and well. Rarely, if ever, did he speak about his brother's death, heroic as it was. It was as if summoning up the mem-ory of his brother would tear off the scab that allowed him to go forward. If Tom had been conditioned to be furtive in his emotions as a child, now he determined by choice to benumb them; demon-strativeness would become restrained, quiescence ingrained, and the far ends of the behavioral spectrum chopped off. In the world erected for himself, things like giddiness and out-of-control anger were asso-ciated with manifestations of weakness.

After the period of bereavement was over, Tom threw himself even further into his studies and football. He also determined that he owed it to Robert to quit hiding behind the walls of academia, to stand up and be a man and follow his steps into war—and, not incidentally, do something to avenge his death by knocking down a few Nazi planes himself. Back in November, after word came about Robert's plane, Tom had quickly traced his brother's initial steps by enlisting in the reserves of the same Army Air Force, spending weekends taking basic flight training.

Knowing he would soon be called up, he dutifully finished out a season of sporadic jayvee games in a creeping pall as war casualties began to mount and the almost giddy early war fervor turned to an expectation that there would be many awful days ahead. Indeed, as if the fun had drained away, even the heralded varsity team lost its edge. After winning their first two games by scores of 40–0 and 64–0, the Longhorns lost at Northwestern, 3–0, and muddled through the rest of the season, falling to A&M, 12–6, on Thanksgiving and finishing with a record of 9–2, good enough to come in only eleventh in the rankings.

By the end of his sophomore football season, still stuck on the jayvee squad, Landry was looking beyond Austin to uncertain horizons, which he would be able to see from above, in a cockpit of a Flying Fortress of his own. In February 1944, the call-up came and he found himself hopscotching the country, from Wichita Falls to San Antonio, to receive escalating levels of training, then to Eastern Oklahoma State College for actual flight lessons. The first time he went up, in a single-engine two-seat plane, with an instructor beside him, the engine failed. Landry, his heart pounding wildly, sat frozen as the instructor was unable to restart the engine and was forced to land the plane in a cow pasture. After that hairy experience, Landry considered himself lucky to be alive and realized that the life of a flier in wartime was one in which any number of things could go wrong, even before the plane left the ground.

He accepted the fatalism of it all, steeling himself even further to avoid letting emotions get in the way of the job to be done. There was a war to be won, and he was ready to inject himself into it. He continued what seemed like endless training, before winning his wings and going up alone in a twin-engine craft. At only nineteen, he was too young to be given command of a bomber, but he still became one of the Air Force's youngest copilots of a B-17, mastering the controls at his last training stop in Sioux City, Iowa. By the time he finally shipped out, in the autumn of 1944—crossing the "pond" on no less a transport vessel than the *Queen Mary*, which featured a nightly song-and-dance show put on by the diminutive Mickey Rooney—he was a wizened man of twenty, itching to fly over Europe and see a line of bomb explosions snaking across the landscape beneath him.

At the time, the war in Europe was rapidly nearing its climax. The Allies had successfully invaded the Continent, thrown the Nazis back in chaos, and fanned out through France, Belgium, and Holland. Nevertheless, they would still have to survive the brutal winter and the last-gasp Battle of the Bulge counteroffensive by the Nazis at Bastogne before victory could be tasted. Landry's unit of the Eighth Air Force, the 493rd Squadron, based in Ipswich near London, had carved itself a bold and dashing identity up to now, earning the nickname "The Grim Reapers." The desultory nature of the same air war that had claimed Robert Landry had smoothly coalesced around a relentless strategy of the British Royal Air Force bombing German targets by night and the USAAF doing so by day.

For a virtuous and reflective man like Tom Landry, whose early life was centered around the church, the notion that there was some mutual ground between worshipping the Holy Ghost while purposely taking scores of lives, cleanly and anonymously, without ever seeing the faces or hearing the screams of the victims, was not an easy one to resolve. Years later, the always histrionic Thomas "Hollywood" Henderson swore, for what it was worth, that Landry shouldered immense regret for raining death from the skies, such that he had "lived in a pit of remorse, shame and guilt" for "killing a lot of innocent people." Henderson believed this, he explained, because of a reaction he sensed in Landry at the coach's retirement announcement in April 1989. There an Air Force general pinned a ceremonial medal on the old coach's lapel, prompting what the ex-Cowboys linebacker insisted was "the most embarrassed I've ever seen a man. I thought Tom was going to crawl under the carpet. This man was lauding Tom for his bombing!" He posited that the conundrum for Landry was "How can you be a Christian and bomb?"[12]

One suspects that Henderson, as was his habit, exaggerated any such guilt on Landry's part, no matter how hard he tried to read his mind and body language. In truth, nowhere in Landry's matter-of-fact writings about his war experience did he articulate a shred of moral quandary, and through the years he even seemed to relish the picaresque élan shared by almost all men who put their lives on the line in combat. In future years, terse as he was about it, he tripped with a certain swagger when others, among them his players, would speak admiringly of his bomber pilot phase, which would usefully serve as a built-in rejoinder to his prissy, prudish demeanor some observers may have seen as less than manly.

Alicia Landry's response to Henderson's claim that her husband was embarrassed to wear that medal is the only one necessary: "He was fighting for his country. That's the last thing Tommy would have ever been ashamed of."[13]

Indeed, if Landry were to go by the letter of canonical law, the opposite might seem true. The pages of the Old Testament teem with counter-commandments to "thou shall not kill" such as "cursed [is] he who holds back his sword from the blood" (Jeremiah 48:10)—willful murder being the proscription for adulterers, fornicators, false idolatry, fortune-tellers, homosexuals, witches, naysayers to priests, those who cursed one's parents, women who were not virgins on their honeymoon night, followers of other religions, blasphemers, infidels, brats, the curious, people working on the Sabbath, and the firstborn of Egypt. Pertinent to the carpet-bombing of Dresden, mass murder in the name of justice was no sin if it was the Lord's command to "kill men and women, children and infants, oxen and sheep, camels and asses" (Samuel 15:2–3). To Tom Landry and his copilots, word from the USAAF high command was close enough.

And so, as one of hundreds of daunting young fliers of the 493rd, it was business as usual when the flight and bombing plans came in from central command. The chaplains blessed the pilots before each run, prayed for their souls and implored God to make sure the Allies killed more people than the enemy did, and sent them on their frightful way. It was much the same procedure that was at least symbolically followed before a team left the locker room for the football field, and thus as American a ritual as there was.

Ultimately, Tom was luckier than his brother. Most of the once impregnable Luftwaffe had been wiped out when he began guiding his Flying Fortress into German airspace, though the Nazi ground guns could still knock down an uncomfortable number of planes. He made his first bombing run on November 21, 1944, as copilot on a crew of four in a convoy of two thousand planes. Their mission: to raze the synthetic oil refineries in Merseburg, a heavily industrial city in southern Germany that would be targeted by twenty-three such attacks. Steely as Lieutenant Landry was, no amount of combat simulations during training could prepare him for the terror that even the most hardened of men couldn't push away while flying through a pitch-black night illuminated only by the light of artillery guns firing rounds into the sky. Landry would write in his memoirs of "the helpless, sinking fear I felt as we followed our squadron leader into that heart of the . . . angry black cloud of exploding flak filling the sky."[14]

He would embark on thirty missions over Europe, each fraught with the same danger, yet with each one the young flier became more battle tough and blithe about the risky business of war. Eventually, the controlled chaos of those flights became routine, from the "combat breakfast" at Ipswich—bacon and eggs and plenty of steaming black coffee—to the usual miscalculations of the generals that put the flight crews in even graver danger once they got in the air, to the improvised flight patterns back home, the problematic fuel situations, and the makeshift landings. Landry knew of only one fellow pilot who had been rescued after bailing out—all the others in his crew perished when their chutes failed to open—and the pilot was so psychologically broken that he never flew another mission. But at least he had made it back. At Ipswich, as at all Air Force bases, there was a mordant ritual. Each day a quartermaster would come into the barracks and collect the personal belongings of each flier who did not make it back, the indentation in the bed a ghostly memory of the man who had slept there.

Landry himself was literally seconds away from having to bail out into the darkness. It happened when his B-17 was on a long mission over the Netherlands. On board was a flight crew of eleven men, including lead pilot Kenneth H. Sainz and copilot Thomas W. Landry. There was a navigator, two bombardiers, a flight engineer, a radio operator, a waist gunner, two ball turret gunners, and a tail gunner. All went fine until the engines began to give out. The only way the crew could keep the engines running was by cutting fuel. Then, without warning, all four engines stopped. Sainz, who was almost as green as Landry and only twenty-two, didn't panic. As the plane began to nose dive, losing altitude by the second, they went through a checklist of possible fixes, somehow trying to get the engines up and running. When nothing happened, Sainz gave the order to his crew: "We're going to have to bail!"

Terrified but calmly preparing to jump, Landry unbuckled from his seat, checked his chute, and was about to make his way toward the rear of the plane, from where he would jump out the bomb doors. He gave a last look at the control panel and, with nothing to lose, slid the knob that controlled the fuel mixture all the way up, hoping the engines would respond. He was damn near knocked off his feet when the engines not only came alive but sent the plane roaring forward. "We got power!" he yelled above the din. Doing an about-face, he and Sainz scrambled back into their seats and lifted the nose, reversing the nose dive. Steadying its flight, they headed for Ipswich, though because they couldn't elevate the plane more than a few hundred feet above the ground, they had to, as Landry would recall, "zigzag to avoid the gunfire from the Germans in Amsterdam."

It wasn't the last time Landry cheated almost certain death. Weeks later, he and Sainz made a bombing run over Czechoslovakia, but their plane ran low on fuel on the way home over western France. The country had been liberated by then, and they could have landed at any airfield below, yet in the pitch darkness they couldn't find one; all they could see were the faint outlines of dense forestry. Sainz could have ditched the bomber in the English Channel and bailed out, to probable death in the water, but seeing a small clearing, he made a decision on the spot. "We're going in!" he cried out, and the crew, unable to steer or brake, put the big armor-plated B-17 down on its belly, with no landing gear, sliding uncontrollably through the field, digging a furrow all the way toward a thicket of trees.

Astonishingly, the plane somehow squeezed through two trees, which sheared off both wings, slowing its speed enough for it to hit another tree, hard but not fatally, and come to a stop. In the dark cockpit, the crew had prepared for the worst, hunching turtle-like in their seats, quietly praying. Jerked about from side to side, they took some painful bumps, and the plane felt as if it would crack open like an egg. When it stopped, propped against a tree, the men inside, shaken as they were, called out to each other to make sure everyone was okay. Each answered that they were. But they had precious little time before the remaining fuel might ignite and cause a fiery explosion that would cremate them all. Ripping off their seat belts they leaped through the cracked windshield onto the rock-strewn terrain below, calling out in the dark, "Let's get the hell outta here!" as they tore away as fast as they could, though the plane had too little fuel to blow.

Landry recalled the harrowing episode as blithely as a man could, noting that "every member of our crew walked out of that crash without a scratch," and that they "hiked out to the nearest road, hitched a ride from some Allied soldiers to the nearby base, and flew back to Ipswich." It was so matter-of-fact that, rather than getting some downtime and maybe a furlough for a while, they "were assigned another B-17" and days later were right back up in the sky, helping to close out the war.[15]

IF EVER a man was charmed, it seemed to be the hawk-faced kid from Texas. For all his traumatic ordeals, he sustained less physical scarring than he would have after any given football game. For Tom Landry, however, there was nothing particularly meaningful, or even particularly heroic, about his brief but extraordinarily intense wartime career. Decades later he would only say that "looking back now, I marvel at all that happened to me," that the experience had turned him "from a scared college freshman" to "a grizzled war veteran of twenty-one" who "knew what it meant to look my own fear in the face and go on to do my duty." Writing far more dispassionately than the circumstances warranted, he considered the real lesson to be that "war had tested me," and as a result he had "a confidence in myself I had never known before."[16]

During his eight-month hitch abroad, he had written letters home to his mother and father, yet believed it unnecessary to provide many details of his missions. Ray and Ruth would learn about them only in dribs, when their son came back home after V-E Day and spent the rest of the year in Mission decompressing before resuming his studies at UT. Embarrassed to brag about himself, he would grudgingly speak about the movie-worthy missions. He was, after all, just a copilot, he said.

There were no medals for what he had contributed to the survival of his crew, something that he considered not heroic but rather the simple requirements of men in war. He was more comfortable bragging about the cool-headed decisions of Ken Sainz. An honorable discharge—and survival—were good enough rewards for him. He had done his patriotic duty as best he could, been toughened and sharpened on a strop, but it was in the past now. Moreover, he would now have to fuse back into the life he had interrupted, but even a brilliant war record wouldn't be able to replace three years of inactivity on the football field. Suddenly, all those newspaper clippings about his exploits at Mission High were far in the past, and his own future seemed as foggy as the skies above Europe during one of those nightmarish bombing runs. At twenty-one, a time when most men had an idea about what they wanted to do and who they were, Tom Landry was back on square one.

Chapter 3

BIG MAN ON CAMPUS

LIKE MILLIONS OF SERVICEMEN reassimilating to the churn of an America relieved of blackouts, rationing, and the burying of men dying far too young, Tom Landry in January of 1946 warily picked up where he had left off. And, like them, he had grown beyond his years. Now twenty-one, he had filled out to a robust six foot one and a sinewy 185 pounds, with all traces of the gawky pubescent gone. He still had a hint of a baby face, but his eyes clearly had seen more than most his age, and his receding hairline, hastened by wearing vise-like pilot helmets, underscored how he had aged in the last two years.

Not that Landry had any assumptions that he would be anyone's idea of a star when he got back to Austin, where, as in most of America, things had not changed nearly as much as the men who had fought in war. Even after making the world safe for democracy, the country was no closer to being a democratic society within its own borders, with African American soldiers coming back to de facto segregation. Indeed, all across the South, there were inviolate Jim Crow laws, cross-burnings, and well-attended lynchings. Progress in civil rights would come haltingly. Not until 1948 would President Harry Truman issue an executive order integrating the military. And passage of the Civil Rights Act and Voting Rights Act would be three decades away. On the campus of the University of Texas, few felt the need to take up the cudgels for allowing blacks into the school and certainly not on the football team.

To the elders of the school, the issue was framed in spurious "separate but equal" legal rationales, which would be in effect until 1954. In 1950, a black man, Herman Marion Sweatt, sued UT after being denied admission to its law school. He lost, but with Thurgood Marshall as his lawyer, he appealed to the United States Supreme Court and won, the high court ordering the integration of the university's law and graduate schools—resulting in a major victory for the cause and paving the way for *Brown v. Board of Education.* Given where Austin is today, with the school completely integrated and the county courthouse named for Herman Marion Sweatt, one can barely imagine the breadth of racism at UT in the 1940s and how far things have come.[1]

Back then, the world in Texas was monochromatic, and racism quotidian. As far as Tom Landry was concerned, he had more pressing matters on his mind, like trying to figure out his future beyond school. He looked forward to seeing what he could do when the football team reconvened for the 1946 season, but was less convinced than ever that his future had to do with sports. He selected business administration as a major, while continuing to work toward a graduate degree in engineering, still envisioning himself as the boss of one of those big oil rigs.

Clearly, he was not quite the ascetic he had been before shipping out, and would find time now to blow off steam as would any young man hard bitten by combat. He had pledged with the Delta Kappa Epsilon fraternity, and if it wasn't exactly a prototype of Delta Tau Chi in the movie *Animal House,* there were certain expectations of frat boys, though such rituals embarrassed him. He also was still heavily invested in football, especially when it became evident that he had lost none of his football skills or instincts, though he had some rust to shake off. Having injured his leg at the spring drills, he was still a bit gimpy when the team convened in the fall. D. X. Bible, however, seeing how much effort Landry put into his drills and practices, had taken a real liking to him. Bible gave Landry a roster spot, though he was used sparingly, mainly as a backup fullback. In time, his name would pop up in the sports pages not only in Austin but also in the *Dallas Morning News*, the state's largest newspaper, which devoted a ton of column inches to Southwest Conference happenings.

The Longhorns were always in the thick of these notices. Bible had taken the team to the conference championship in 1942, 1943, and 1945—1944 being a downer, with nearly all the projected starters in the military—winning the Cotton Bowl twice and tying once. In 1945 Bible found a headline quarterback, cocksure Bobby Layne, a hard-livin', hard-lovin' Texas country boy with wavy blond hair who was a human scoring machine, cranking out points with his passing arm, running legs, and kicking foot. In the 40–27 Cotton Bowl win over Missouri in 1946, he alone scored every single point. Layne was anything but smooth; with his lumpy gut and wobbly passes, he was almost laughable. Still, he was a tenacious, frightening competitor, making something out of nothing on sheer will. However, the Longhorns never finished higher than No. 10 in the rankings those years, even after earning a 10–1 record in 1945.

Much as in 1941, the Longhorns were preseason favorites in 1946, led by the pass-catch connection of Layne and Hubert "Hub" Bechtol. Layne was only twenty at the time and a junior, while older war veterans like Landry were technically sophomores. Layne, though, made everyone else seem as if they were a virgin child. Arguably the first real football rebel, not even his marriage to a Texas cheerleader in 1946 could crimp his boozing and carousing. With a streak of argumentative, not always coherent anger, his behavior was tolerated because he could stumble onto the playing field and throw a touchdown without focusing his eyes, or for that matter pitch radar-like strikes for the Longhorns baseball team in the spring, never losing a game.

Landry had witnessed that legendary Cotton Bowl tilt from the stands, a few weeks after his discharge from the Army. He was taken up to Dallas by an old UT classmate who spilled the secret that Layne had spent the entire evening before game day in the city's Touchdown Club, putting away shot after shot of straight whiskey. Landry was duly impressed that Bobby could perform under the influence like that, but he was also viscerally disgusted. In his memoirs, Landry dispensed with Layne as diplomatically as he could. Of the two seasons they spent as teammates, he wrote, "Since I wasn't the first per-son Bobby thought of when he needed a drinking partner or party company, the stories I know of his wild side are all hearsay." Yet he couldn't help but note that Layne had "never trained. Not in high school, college, or after he became a star pro quarterback. And I've often wondered how much greater he might have been if he had"—a somewhat gratuitous slap given that Layne won two NFL champion-ships and was elected to the Hall of Fame. In the end, Landry was content to call Layne "a natural-born leader."[2]

The Longhorns won their first three games of the 1946 season by a combined score of 172–6. And Tom Landry earned some nascent exposure for himself, though not always glowing. The season's fourth game, on October 13, a clash with No. 1–ranked Oklahoma, led by a swivel-hipped halfback named Darrell Royal, was such a titanic event in the state that it was played in Dallas's cavernous Cot-ton Bowl and covered on page one of the *Dallas Morning News*. At least fifty thousand people jammed into the 45,507-seat stadium, and another five thousand were turned away. Incongruently for the times and the teams, footballs filled the crisp autumn air—there were fifty-two passes in all, and *thirteen* interceptions, and in this infectious air show, Bible even allowed the green Landry to throw the ball on a fullback option, the result being, as the game story read, that an Okie defensive back "intercepted a wild pass by Tom Landry to set up [a scoring] drive."

The Longhorns did hold on to win that bombast, 20–13, and Landry began to see even more playing time. In the November 7 edi-tion of the *Morning News* he was labeled "a promising triple-threat sophomore," having first caught Bible's eye for his punting skills. Landry's ability to throw a pass, it was noted, might be "used as additional insurance by the Longhorns." Bible also used him as a defensive back. Nonetheless, Landry spent the season mainly absorb-ing, making mental notes.

As with every good coach, Bible was feared by his men. But having seen the landscape of the game change because of the war, he didn't try to oversee this team the way he had with more tenderfoot casts. Rather, he became closer personally with the older guys, like Landry, who would recognize this as a new order of coaching. Later Landry would note that Bible "became more low-key after the war," realizing that "the Knute Rockne–type talks" of the past would ring hollow with battle-hardened veterans. To Landry, it seemed eminently praiseworthy that the coach was also "efficient" and a "fine orator."[3]

Clearly, whatever Bible was, it worked—although never quite well enough in Austin. In 1946, the Longhorns' chance to be the nation's top team went up in flames on November 16, when the underdog Texas Christian Horned Frogs harassed and snuffed Layne, holding him to 28 yards of passing by utilizing some creative defensive sets, including varying the number of linemen and linebackers. Bible was caught off guard, and the Longhorns lost, 14–0, killing any chances for a Cotton Bowl bid. The team ended with an 8–2 record and a ranking of No. 15, a bitter disappointment that sent Bible into retirement after thirty-three years of distinguished coaching.

To Bible, his second-string fullback/defensive back was a star in the making. Put in at quarterback during one game, Landry ran 30 yards on a bootleg formation. As opposed to Layne, the beak-faced war hero from Mission won the kind of praise coaches loved to dish out. According to Bible he was "modest and quiet" and "had a lot of influence without being loud or blustery," and a man who knew how to "pay the premiums [to] get the dividends."[4] Bible's successor in 1947, forty-six-year-old Longhorns assistant Blair Cherry, agreed. Cherry opened up the offense, switching from a run-dominated attack to one that encouraged passing. Layne would get to show off his whipsaw arm as the starting quarterback, but Cherry wanted to motivate him by leaving the door open to someone else getting the job, perhaps the war veteran whom he described as "as smart as they come."

When the '47 season began, Landry had been promoted to backup quarterback, in addition to his usual other chores, prompting the September 19 issue of the *Morning News* to call him "a corking defensive back and great kicker." At the time, sports editor George White saw some difficulty in the team's adaptation to the split-T offense, opining that "the Longhorns are jumpy and lack timing that will come only with practice. They'll probably draw a lot of early season penalties for being in motion and off side. Cherry thinks they'll be slow starting but he hopes to have all the kinks ironed out before the conference fireworks go off in mid-October. He believes he'll have a mighty ball club in November. If that comes through, look out!"

The opener though was a breeze, a 33–0 trampling of Texas Tech, followed by a long trip to Oregon that resulted in a 38–13 romp. However, Landry broke a finger in the latter game while making a tackle, and although he taped it up and went out to play in the next game, against the University of North Carolina, it led Cherry to tinker with the lineup. The finger was on Landry's throwing hand so Cherry moved him to fullback and made him a starter. Not prepared to defend a 190-pound fullback, the Tar Heels were a step slow, allowing Landry to run for 91 yards and score a touchdown on twelve carries in the Longhorns' 34–0 laugher. Unranked up to then, they shot all the way to No. 3 in the country.

Tom Landry's biorhythm was clearly rising high. And, as if on cue, just days after the Carolina game, there was another reward, one that would pay dividends for a lifetime.

BEING A high-profile upperclassman surely had its benefits. Landry had to be pleasantly surprised by how much easier it suddenly was to draw the attention of comely coeds. Still no Romeo, he was nevertheless soon squiring some of the more top-grade girls to frat parties. As if by devising a different sort of strategy on a chalkboard, he even found ways to circumvent the monitors who sat in the lobby at Hill Hall, keeping the rooms off limits to the fair sex. What's more, the best-looking one of all practically fell into his lap. This of course was Alicia Wiggs, the petite, drop-dead gorgeous nineteen-year-old freshman who would enter his life for a very long run.

She was raised in Highland Park near Dallas. Her father, Herbert, was a well-heeled owner of the Continental Fidelity Life Insurance Company, often traveling to Houston, where the head office was located. After graduating from Highland Park High School, Alicia planned to go to Baylor College, but Herbert insisted she attend Texas. In another six-degree-of-separation coincidence, none other than Doc Neuhaus would again influence Tom Landry's life, albeit indirectly. Doc also lived part-time in Houston and he knew Herbert, and when her father wanted Alicia to know other girls in Austin, Doc introduced her to his niece Gloria Neuhaus, one of the small number of female students at UT. Gloria, a member of the only sorority on campus, Delta Delta Delta, sponsored Alicia as a pledge, and they became roommates at Whitman Hall when she arrived in the autumn of 1947.

As it happened, Gloria was dating an offensive end on the football team, Lew Holder, another Army vet whose best friend was Tom Landry. That week, following the North Carolina game, Cherry gave his team a well-deserved day off. Gloria and Lew were going to spend it by going on a picnic in Bull Creek, a bucolic lakefront park in Austin, and Gloria dropped a hint to Lew that it would be nice if her roomie could come along. Coyly, she asked him if he could get his buddy to be her date. At the time, Landry looked anything but an Adonis. As hard as he played, games always left him battered and bruised. Now, he had a black eye and a bandage on his forehead. Yet to Alicia Wiggs he was a beautiful wreck.

"I always thought he was the most handsome guy on campus," she recalled, her head still turned by him over sixty years later. "He had really nice eyes—even the black one. He just had a warmth to him, which is why it seemed so wrong to me when people would say he was so cold and unfeeling. He could not have been more gracious and caring, a very kind and nice man. And so of course I was immediately smitten. But then so were a lot of the girls. Tommy was probably the biggest VIP on campus. He was a returning veteran, he'd be the captain of the football team the next year. People looked up to him, admired him. That's why he was such a big man on campus. I'd go and visit people in the dorms, and they'd have Tommy's picture that they'd cut from a magazine or newspaper on their desk or their wall. He was like our John Wayne. He was six years older than me and I must have seemed like a little schoolgirl."

To her great excitement, he agreed to the date, and they hit it off. During the picnic they went hiking alone, and time passed effortlessly. "We just talked, about everything, football, life, school. I never expected anything like that. I told Gloria, 'Why would Tom Landry want to be with a nobody like me?' But I think he found in me somebody he could talk to. I don't know if he really had that before. He was never a real people person, but he could open up a bit with me."

Indeed, he was convinced on the spot that he had found his better half. Though younger, Alicia was just as old world and squeamish as he was about the new boundaries of social norms that were being practiced by the likes of Bobby Layne, who, in another coincidence, had been a senior at Highland Park High when she was a freshman. There he threw passes to another future football Hall of Famer, halfback Doak Walker, who went on to glory at SMU before hooking up with Layne again in the 1950s on the NFL champion team the Detroit Lions. Bobby was a rakehell even in high school, an irresistible "bad boy" for many of the girls. But Miss Wiggs swooned more for the handsome and humble Walker. The new man in her life reminded her of Doak. Tommy Landry was, she knew, "my type."[5]

THREE DAYS after the North Carolina game, Landry could open the *Dallas Morning News* and see his image nearly eating up an entire page of the sports section. It was a striking photo of him in a punting pose, leg stretching high into the air, arms spread like a giant condor's wings, head cocked below thick but thinning black wavy hair, eyes squinting into the sky. Below it a caption headlined "PROFITABLE PROMOTION," which was followed by an article reviewing Blair Cherry's shifting of Landry to fullback. Fluffing Landry as "a 190-pounder from Mission who digs in and drives hard and low from the first step," the writer ventured that he was "sure to figure prominently" in the upcoming "traditional battle" against No. 15 Oklahoma in the Cotton Bowl.[6]

And he did. Texas took care of the Sooners, 34–14, outpassing them by a glaring 129 yards to 7 (the Okies throwing all of three passes), then rolled over Rice, 12–0. Still sitting at No. 3, the Longhorns faced a make-or-break game against Doak Walker's No. 8 SMU Mustangs on November 1. Again played in the Cotton Bowl, it was a duel between the two All-America hometown buddies from Highland Park, and a beaut, as George White wrote, a "nerve-tingler."[7]

Right from the start, there was drama. On the opening kickoff the Mustangs executed a nifty double-reverse, taking the ball 81 yards to set up a touchdown, then scoring on the even-then-age-old fakery of the Statue of Liberty play. The Longhorns tied it on a 2-yard run by Landry, for whom the glory was fleeting. In fact, he would become the goat. In the second quarter, playing on offense and defense, he was beaten by Walker, who, he recalled, "broke by me and ran all the way to the two," a 54-yard play setting up the go-ahead score.[8] The game became a tense defensive battle until the fourth quarter, when Layne threw a 14-yard touchdown pass. While the Longhorns missed the extra-point kick, they still got the ball back and, racing the clock, drove down to the Mustangs 32-yard line, where, with under a minute left, they faced a fourth-and-one.

By the writ of common football law, such a situation mandated a safe run to get the first down, whereupon the Longhorns could try to get into winning field-goal range. Layne called the safest run he could think of, by Landry. What happened next, though, would for years be a subject of contention in Austin, because at the snap Landry slipped and fell to the turf. As he recalled that horrifying moment many years later, "I can still see the look of shock and dismay on Bobby Layne's face when he pivoted to make his handoff and saw me on my knees in the mud." With no one to hand the ball to, Layne was collared and dropped for a loss, effectively ending the contest.

Landry, dissecting the ill-fated play, insisted he had set up "on the wettest spot on the field and my feet went right out from under me."[9] But *was* there any mud to slip on that day? In his story, White wrote that the game was played "under threatening skies. There wasn't enough rainfall, however, to quench a hummingbird's thirst."[10] Some would wonder if Landry had lost his bearings because of the pressure, or simply because of poor technique, which if true would have been embarrassing given Landry's reputation as a technique guy. Even so, Landry had certainly earned enough respect not to be openly questioned about a mistake, one that crushed him, with good cause. "That slip of mine," as he would call it, cost the Longhorns what would have been an undefeated season and a reasonable shot at that elusive No. 1 ranking. Falling to No. 8, they still won their remaining four games—capped off by an impressive 27–7 conquest of No. 6 Alabama in the Sugar Bowl in New Orleans. A 10–1 season got them no higher than No. 5, and a second-place finish in the Southwest Conference (SWC), behind SMU.

Layne and tackle Dick Harris made the All-America team, and with end Max Bumgardner the All-SWC first team. Landry made the All-SWC second team, having run for 340 yards on sixty-five carries, a tidy 5.2 yards a carry, and for three touchdowns. He also completed the one pass he threw, for 28 yards; had a punting average of 41.1 yards; and intercepted a pass, with a 14-yard return. Yet one dad-burned play caused him shame to no end.

"That was really the first time I saw him have to handle defeat, and one he took personally," says Alicia Wiggs Landry, who suddenly was able to watch these very high-profile events from a preferred seat. "I just felt so bad for him. He was such a perfectionist and then to slip like that. . . . Oh, he could put those things out of his mind. He could always handle defeat, but he just couldn't ever *accept* it. He didn't show it but it ate at him inside. And the worst part of it was that he thought he let down his team, which he really didn't because he was such a great competitor and everyone knew it.

"When Bobby Layne threw a bad pass, he forgot about it right away. [Laugh] Or else he could make the pain go away in other ways. Tommy would constantly go over it in his mind, what went wrong, so it wouldn't happen again. In his mind, he wouldn't *allow* it to happen again. He was just like that. He hated imperfection. It was like the work of the devil."

Fortunately he now had someone waiting for him who could ease the pain when the football Mephisto taunted him with defeat. And Lord knows he would need that. A lot.

LANDRY HAD his quirks. His new girlfriend noticed that when they went to frat parties, he would head for the table with the liquor bottles and begin to mix and stir alcoholic concoctions with great skill, but he would rarely if ever imbibe himself. It was as if he saw making cocktails as another technique to master, while keeping a distance from the taste and lure of the devil's brew. It's possible he acquired this skill during the war, while killing time at the officers' club between bombing runs; if so, he must have been a popular man there. For those who knew him, it was one more mysterious clue about a man with instincts he was loath to talk about. When it came to certain peccadilloes, the custom with Landry would be, Don't ask, don't tell. Neither would he open up about the death of his brother, something Alicia would not learn about for months. Landry was a strange bird in many ways. Everything unpleasant or unkind in his life seemed to be jammed inside him, deep inside, needing to drip out; not even love liberated some of what he had hidden away. Alicia would just shrug, knowing there was a lot more to uncover about him but giving it time. Maybe a lot of time. Until then, for Alicia the rule was, Don't ask and don't expect him to tell.

After the Longhorns' victory in the 1947 Sugar Bowl, Landry's teammates partied into the night in the French Quarter, led by the incorrigible Layne, who, sloshed to the gills, and waving a broom in the air like a drum major would a baton, directed some teammates on a bar-hopping march. Layne was once asked if Landry was one of the revelers in his train. "I don't know," he said. "I think Tommy might have been with us."[11] But not even the lure of Basin Street could draw Landry into its web that night. Exhausted from the game, in which he played a total of fifty-eight minutes, he had gone straight to his hotel room and slept through the celebrations.

This low profile didn't bother Alicia. Indeed, both of them realized they had found their respective life partners. They liked the feeling that eyes were trained on them when they would stroll across the campus hand in hand. Around school the dashing football star and the blonde bombshell were the beau ideal, a perfectly matched set. The same thought occurred to her parents after they drove from Houston to Austin during the early weeks of the budding romance. "As soon as they'd spent a few minutes with Tommy, mom fell in love with him herself," she says with only slight exaggeration. "Dad told me that she said on the way home, 'If Alicia doesn't marry Tommy I'm gonna adopt him.' When they had seen us together, she sighed and told dad, 'Herb, We've lost our little girl.'

"Yet we never talked about being in a long-term relationship. Everyone else did. We never spoke about marriage. I was only nineteen, and we didn't want to rush it. We just kept on seeing each other because it felt so right. We'd borrow someone's car and go to the movies, then go to a restaurant somewhere. It was just real easy, no pressure. Tommy was a lot of fun. I remember once we got something to eat, and they put anchovies on it. Tommy looked like he would gag. He said, 'I'm not eating meat with hair on it.'"

She laughs hysterically, as she did way back then in response to the cornball line, in thrall to a Tommy Landry few others could recognize. This was a man with a warmth and a sense of humor, albeit buried under layers of quiescent reserve, even repression. Marriage was a thought in the back of their minds, but the timing was wrong. As well, for all his popularity, he was close to broke, his scholarship money spoken for in room and board. There were other considerations too, one being that the coaches frowned on their players being married, believing it would distract from the grave tasks at hand on the gridiron. There were, of course, exceptions. Both D. X. Bible and the equally stern Blair Cherry had to accept not only that Bobby Layne had a wife but also that she wasn't enough for Layne's libido. Yet for a man like Tom Landry, a coach's rules, as Bob Martin had taught him, were there to be obeyed, at least until he had some money in his pocket.

Thus there would be a proper courtship, one that offered Alicia Wiggs a chance to learn more about him, who and what he was. As she found out, all the clues led back to Mission.

ALICIA'S TURN to meet Tom's parents came during the Thanksgiving break in 1947, when after the Turkey Day win over Texas A&M they rode the train southward, to where the grapefruit trees swayed in the wind. She was duly impressed.

"Mission was wonderful. The home of the fruits and the nuts," she says with a good-natured giggle. "And Tommy was proud of it. One of the first days we were there we went driving around. We passed all these beautiful orchards, and he stopped, got out of the car, went and picked a piece of fruit—that looked to me like an orange—off a tree and brought it to me. He peeled it and I took a bite. I said, 'This is wonderful. It doesn't even taste like an orange.' And he looked at me all serious, like I had said something terrible. 'It's not an orange, it's a tangerine.' In Mission, you have to know the difference."

Clues about who Landry was were all over the town. The close-knit but not overtly warm and hug-giving family would become his exemplar of interrelationships on a football team. He would be tight with teammates but never "love" them the way some athletes like to swear they do. Later, the teams coached by Landry would trill melodic huzzahs about their own "family," but the word "fear" was far more common in their public comments about him than the word "love," unlike the equal measure of the two words in the Green Bay Packers' teary-eyed encomiums about Vince Lombardi. Landry's players became attached to each other in a common bond and would have shed blood for one another. But love was never part of the equation.

Tom Landry, to be blunt about it, was not a particularly lovable man in the eyes of anyone except Alicia Wiggs and her mother. And this is how he wanted it. He craved love from Alicia but only acceptance from everyone else, as if the emotion of love had limits, that if applied to too many people it would become diluted and lose its special meaning. If that was the case, then he certainly wanted no part of love as a precondition for playing or coaching football, not if it would dilute the essential separation of authority between player and coach, and the focus on always becoming sharper of mind and technique.

Alicia could see the provenance of all this at Thanksgiving dinner at the Landry home on Doherty. The atmosphere was dominated by the affable but prim and proper Ruth Landry, a mother hen who made sure the silverware was laid out with perfect geometric order and the courses of the meal kept to a tight schedule. While Ray Landry's face lit up when he greeted them, and gave his boy a gentle bear hug, Ruth smiled but would not betray any physical warmth. It became immediately clear to Alicia from what tree her boyfriend had fallen.

"Tommy obviously got his personality from his mother," she confirms. "His dad was very outgoing, but Ruth was very quiet. She pretty much controlled everything and set the mood. Tommy's brother and sister were there and so was his grandfather Fred. It was all very homey and comfortable, but at the table she was in charge. It definitely wasn't the kind of Thanksgiving where people laugh and tell jokes and get loud. It was more . . . ordered."

At one point, Alicia noticed a framed portrait of a young man in an Army uniform on the dining room wall. She became curious. "Who's that?" she asked.

"That was when I first learned about his brother," she says. "Tommy had never mentioned him. The family talked about what had happened to his brother, and they were all very proud of him, but they were very stoic about it. There were no tears or anything.

"They were a family of very strong moral character, and it meant a lot to me that they approved of me because everything they said was from the heart. I could tell where Tommy got his strength from. Ray practically owned Mission. There wasn't a soul in the town who didn't love him. I think Tommy knew he would never be as popular in his hometown as his father, and I think that kept his head level. Even when Tommy became world famous, he still looked up to his dad."

Going to Mission, then, was an eye-opening experience for Alicia, telling her more about her beau than he could have ever done himself. "I could feel how important the town was to him. Mission *was* Tommy. Coming from the big city, it was so much different than what I had known as a child. Everyone knew Tommy. Everyone knew each other. You grow up with that feeling of an extended family."

LANDRY'S POPULARITY on campus would grow exponentially after Bobby Layne moved on to the pros, leaving the soft-spoken, chivalrous war veteran as co-captain and something of an antidote to the chaotic culture clash of the previous several years—the anti-Layne, as it were. He was the kind of man who could lead not only the football squad but also liturgy at the campus chapel. Moreover, as a senior he was also president of the school chapter of the T-Association, the fraternity of letterman athletes, which carries lifetime membership, and was inducted into—prophetically—the Texas Cowboys, the student organization begun in 1922. It seemed he was involved in almost every facet of university life.

Which is why being his steady had benefits for Alicia too, such as her nomination as a Bluebonnet Belle—UT's version of campus queen—and her entry into the 1948 Miss American Coed Pageant. She lost the latter contest, but by then she knew she had her big prize: Co-captain Tom Landry, who as the 1948 football season neared was thought to be Blair Cherry's favorite to play quarterback after Layne graduated. In the end, Cherry went with Layne's backup, Paul Camp-bell, and according to some of his teammates Landry felt betrayed by the decision, not that he would have ever publicly aired this gripe. The Longhorns again were expected to capture that maddeningly elusive No. 1 ranking, and no waves needed to be made. A preseason headline in the September 14 *Dallas Morning News* blared, "TEXAS GOES ALL OUT IN QUEST OF CROWN," over a snappy shot of the Long-horns backfield—Landry, ball tucked into the crook of his arm, gal-loping toward the camera.

The season began strong, with a 33–0 wipeout of Louisiana State, Campbell's slick ball-handling having "hypnotized" the Tigers, according to George White. Indeed the way Campbell, as White described it, "chunked pitchouts to backfield mates while drawing the defense in with fakes through the middle"[12] seemed more suited to the now-discarded stodgy single wing–style offense than the vari-ous passing options of the T. Backup quarterback Billy Allen threw more than Campbell did. Landry, running eleven times, picked up 53 yards and a touchdown.

For all the hype of Campbell, then, he would not be able to master the intricacies of the T offense, a fact driven home like a punch to the face in the second game, against No. 2–ranked North Carolina in Chapel Hill. A huge test, the Longhorns walked into a buzzsaw against a Tar Heels team craving revenge for the previous season's 34–7 drubbing. Worse, during the week, Landry had awoken with searing pain in his mouth, from several impacted wisdom teeth that needed to be removed by oral surgery. He was woozy after the pro-cedure and came down with a fever that night, rendering him useless in practice. Neither could he eat, resulting in a loss of ten pounds. He was still out of it on Saturday after the long, bumpy train ride to Chapel Hill, though he insisted on playing, a decision Cherry would regret acceding to. Outplayed right from the kickoff, the Longhorns were down 21–7 after the first quarter. As Cherry said, "The first quarter knocked us off balance. They were ready for us and we couldn't do anything right."

Landry in particular. In fact he helped cost his team another big game. As George White reported, after the Longhorns took posses-sion following the Tar Heels' first touchdown, "Tom Landry, fullback who was playing despite a mild illness, fumbled on his own five. North Carolina recovered and drove to a score. That was the blow that broke Texas' back."[13] The question being asked now— "What in the world happened to Texas?"—could have been applied to Landry, whose senior year was a fading problem. He was kept out of the next game, a 47–0 home laugher against the University of New Mexico. Then the Longhorns met No. 16 Oklahoma, another of the fevered rivalry games, in the newly renovated and expanded Cotton Bowl, with a Texas-record seventy thousand fans on hand. The Longhorns never found any cohesion against the Sooners, going down 20–14. Landry returned to the field the next week when the team began its Southwest Conference schedule. He ran eight times for 41 yards in the 14–6 home win against Arkansas. Then, the following Saturday, he ran eight times for 32 yards in the 20–7 road win against Rice. But the Longhorns were unranked and going nowhere. Against No. 11 SMU, they racked up a hundred yards more than the Mustangs did, yet were still carved up by Doak Walker, who scored on runs of 67 yards and 1 yard and also threw an 18-yard touchdown pass to halfback Kyle Rote in the Mustangs' 21–6 victory. Landry, who carried the ball only four times for 19 yards, got another dose of public humiliation when, the next day, a big photo appeared in the *Morning News*. It was of Walker's long run, leaving a headlong Landry, who was still playing two-way football, about to bite the turf after nipping in vain at Walker's heels in an attempted "desperation tackle."

The Longhorns would stumble again, doing no better than a 14–14 tie with Texas A&M in the final scheduled game, leaving them with their worst record, 6–3–1, since 1939, save for wartime 1944. But while Landry judged the season "a very disappointing football year,"[14] he was deemed a valuable commodity by scouts for both professional leagues, the establishment National Football League and the four-year-old insurgent All-America Football Conference. Back in 1946, in fact, Landry had already been drafted by the NFL's New York Giants, as it was the year he would have graduated if not for the war. Those were called "future" draft picks, a sort of "reservation" of talent in absentia, but the Giants' option ran out. Now, following the Texas A&M game, the AAFC's New York Yankees chose him in a secret draft meant to keep the NFL in the dark about which college players the AAFC teams would target.

Landry later would claim he had given scant thought to playing in the pros. Although both leagues had conducted a feverish bidding war for Bobby Layne, with the Baltimore Colts offering him a then-insane $77,000, which he turned down to sign with George "Papa Bear" Halas and the Chicago Bears, Landry's football purview seemingly began and ended with the college game. Believing his football career would be over after he left Austin, his plan was to parlay his business degree with graduate courses in engineering at Rice, on the premise that he would marry Alicia either before or right after graduation in the spring of 1949. After the wedding, they would live in Houston, where her parents resided and where, presumably, Doc Neuhaus would ease the man he had recruited as a Longhorn into the oil industry.

The Longhorns received an invitation to play in the Orange Bowl in Miami on New Year's Day against No. 8–ranked Georgia. The players and coaches were under no delusions why: they were chosen to be a pushover. Finally motivated, as they had not been all season, the Longhorns, in making short work of the Bulldogs, showed what might have been. The Texans piled up 324 yards on the ground in fifty-eight carries. Landry, healthy at last, played every down of the game, on both sides of the line. He carried the ball a game-high fifteen times, gaining 107 yards. He scored one touchdown on a 15-yard run in the first quarter, ran another play for 20 yards, defended perfectly, and punted flawlessly four times, for a 40.2-yard average.

It was no ordinary effort—in his memoirs he called the game "the best personal performance in my Longhorns' career,"[15] and with it the pros now took even greater notice of him. The AAFC's Yankees, not wanting to wait, had sent one of its assistant coaches, Jack White, to the game with instructions to sign Landry. In a ritual common in that era of intense competition between the two pro football leagues—one that would be repeated in the future—White was waiting on the field for the gun to sound on the Longhorns' 41–28 victory, whereupon he headed straight for Landry, contract in his pocket. When he reached him, White introduced himself, pulled out the contract, and handed it to him.

Landry took it, stuck it in the waistband of his football pants, and kept walking toward the locker room as White, trying to keep up with him, went over the terms that came attached to the contract: a $6,000 salary and a $500 bonus. He told White he would get back to him that night, before the Longhorns went back to Austin. As was Doc Neuhaus before him, White was taken aback that his prey hadn't fallen to his knees and thanked him for his aggrandizement. This Landry kid, he must have thought, was one tough nut to crack. He didn't know the half of it.

THE GIANTS' offer, which was less than half that of the Yankees', did make Landry think. A salary of $6,000 with $500 bonus was, as he would later note, "big money in those days."[16] But it was small change for the owner of the Yankees, Dan Topping, who also happened to own, along with casino baron Del Webb, the diamond-headed baseball franchise also called the Yankees. Living off the profit from his perennial pennant winners, Topping could easily afford to give $6,500 to a man he knew the rival NFL Giants were also eager to land. There was, as well, a built-in inducement for any player who signed with the AAFC Yankees: the thrill of playing their home games in Yankee Stadium, a place that Tom Landry, since childhood, had imagined was as beatific, and as far away in the worldly ether, as the Taj Mahal.

And so Landry kept his vow to Jack White, calling him back a few hours later to say he had signed the contract. His mission accomplished, White rushed over to the hotel, shook Landry's hand, and caught the long train back to New York. Word spread quickly, and only three days after the Orange Bowl, the *Dallas Morning News* carried an AP wire report headlined, "YANKS SIGN TOM LANDRY."

This surely was news to Alicia Wiggs, who was kept in the dark about there being a major change in plans for him and, by extension, for her. "I knew nothing about it, or about pro football," she says, though one of his underlying reasons for joining the mercenary world of pro football was that the bonus he would be getting days after signing the contract was all he needed to be able to join another breed, that of married men. That decision, too, was typically well thought out and geometric. Sure, love had a lot do with it, but nothing in Tom Landry's life was governed by emotions like love or hate. It simply had to add up.

As 1948 took its leave, things were indeed adding up, so well that there was no need for discussion with those who would be affected by his new course. It took only a few days more before Alicia Wiggs would not be asked, as much as allowed, to join him on that journey.

Chapter 4

A TEXAS YANKEE

TOM LANDRY MADE HIS long-awaited proposal to Alicia Wiggs in a typical Landry manner. He circled around it, laid the groundwork, then moved in, just as he would have done as a defensive back going for the kill on a downfield receiver. The game plan arose when, on their strolls to the movie theater in downtown Austin, she would never fail to stop at the window of a jewelry store and sigh longingly for a gold lapel-pin watch shaped in the image of an elfin man in a pointy hat. To him, it seemed as if the sighing got louder each time. Taking the hint, he bought the item as a Christmas present that year. This was before the $500 bonus came around, and as he would recall, "It wasn't cheap." But it had the intended effect; she was, he said, "overwhelmed by my thoughtfulness . . . and she knew I had to love her to be so sensitive to her feelings."

Of course, a word like "sensitive," if applied to the stout-hearted men of that generation, was like a slur on one's manhood and marked him among his peers as a wimp. Never willing to accept such a horrible allegation, he added in his aw-shucks fashion, "How sensitive does a guy have to be after six or eight stops at a jewelry store window? But if that 'little man' helped make me a big man in Alicia's eyes, it was worth every penny,"[1] even if it still didn't qualify her to be consulted on some big decisions he would make in his life.

However, it did ensure that she would be around for every step.

That was evident when a week after the Orange Bowl victory, he took her to dinner and out of nowhere changed the subject. "If you'll find us an apartment," she recalls him saying without emotion, "we'll move into it at midterm."

She laughs at the memory. "Isn't that romantic? Well, for him it was. It certainly showed confidence. But I didn't get what he was saying. Tommy had a roommate at the time, Tom Hamilton, a big basketball star in school, and I thought he meant Tom when he said 'we.' I said, 'You mean for you and Tom?' And he said, 'No—for us. We'll get married at midterm.' I was like *huh?* I mean, that was two weeks away. My first reaction was, 'Come on. Be serious.'"[2]

Upon review years later, Landry would insist he was being anything but cool and detached that night. It was that the usual Landry control was being consumed by nerves. Even after hours of rehearsing what he wanted to say, he just couldn't get the words out. Still, in any mental state, Tom Landry was nothing if not calculating and persuasive. Nobody, bar none, would ever see him sweat, in the figurative sense. And so even though she thought he was nuts, a day later, without needing to officially accept his unorthodox proposal, she was out looking for a love nest. When that was done, they set a wedding date: Friday, January 28, 1949.

The ceremony would take place in Houston, to accommodate Alicia's parents, at St. John the Divine Church, presided over by the Reverend Thomas Summers. Ray and Ruth, along with Ruthie and Jack, were there, ecstatic that the son and brother who survived the horror of war was the very beau ideal of the American Dream, the envy of men his age. Landry, a trifle uncomfortable and stiff in his tux and white carnation, came down the aisle flanked by his best man, Lew Holder, and ushers Dick Harris and Bobby Coy Lee, all teammates. The maid of honor was Alicia's sister Linda.

It was the classic postwar upper-class American wedding—thanks to the bank account of the father of the bride—straight out of a dime-store romance novel. Two days later, in the Sunday society pages of the *Dallas Morning News*, a photo of the stunning bride, identified as "Mrs. Thomas Wade Landry," ran next to an item headlined "ALICIA WIGGS, T.W. LANDRY ARE MARRIED." It reported that the bride wore a "street-length dress of white lace over pale blush satin,

designed with an off-shoulder neckline [and] a white lace hat . . .
trimmed with illusion and fresh flowers to match her bridal bouquet
of gardenias and white lilacs."

After a brief honeymoon in Mexico City, the newlyweds returned
to Austin, intending to live in an apartment on campus they had put
a hundred-dollar downpayment on. But when the tenant living there
refused to leave, Tom and his new wife were forced to live separately,
in their old dorms, until another apartment could be found. Following his graduation in the spring, they drove in his newly bought blue
Ford to Houston to live in a rented two-bedroom flat on Calumet
Street. There, with precious few weeks together before he would go
to New York for his first pro camp, he used his time well. Soon, she
was pregnant.

Alicia could have gone to New York with him, found a prenatal
doctor, and given birth there, but he wouldn't hear of it. There were
good, rational reasons for that, such as having to find a new doctor
and being in strange and perhaps stressful circumstances. None of
the reasons, however, were as convincing as the less rational one they
both agreed mattered most. Tom Landry may have been leaving the
soil he held dear, if only for months at a time, but the fruit of his
loins was going to be born on it, by God. Making a joke of it years
later, Landry would say, "That way if any of [my children] wanted
to run for governor when they grew up, they could claim to be born-
'n'-bred in Texas, not, God forbid, born-'n'-bred in New York City."[3]
But it wasn't a joke; it was rule one with the Landrys, and nothing
was more rational to them.

BY SIGNING with the young league, one with wobbly legs and
revolving-door teams living under the thumb of the older NFL,
Landry had no idea what he was getting into. As Alicia recalls, "We
didn't really think there was much of a future in football. Tommy
saw it as more like a lark, a chance to keep playing and make some
money when he was young, and put some away for when he'd start a
real career. My dad gave him a job selling insurance in the off-season
for a few years. You have to remember that pro football then was
nothing like it is now. We never even saw a pro game on television;

they weren't being broadcast yet, definitely not in Texas. There might be a few lines about a game in the papers. I was just glad Tommy could do what he loved doing and make some money from it. Anything that would help us build a nest egg was welcome. But nobody who played pro ball then believed it was anything like a permanent job."

Landry had little sentience about the NFL, knowing not much more about the pro game than that Paul Brown was the author of many of the mail-order football manuals he liked to read. Still, he became sold on the insurgent élan of the AAFC, which was founded in 1946 by the Barnum-like Chicago sportswriter Arch Ward, who had similarly created the baseball All-Star Game in 1934. Setting itself apart from the stodgier NFL, the maverick league presented a new set of cultural realities for Landry. For one, this would be the first time he would share locker room quarters and field space with black players, who were, for the most part, still being kept out of the older league. That the football Yankees were an integrated team was a considerable irony since Dan Topping, a smug man of impeccable sartorial tastes and straight and narrow conventionalism, had no objection to carrying on the de facto segregation of the high and mighty baseball Yankees until 1955.

The AAFC owners could boast both pulling moral rank on the NFL and drawing black fans at a time when the older league seemed stuck in racial resistance. On the other end of the divide, many of the AAFC's spotlight players were black, such as the Cleveland Browns' bruising fullback Marion Motley, the indomitable lineman Bill Willis, and long-limbed fullback Joe Perry. The football Yankees freely suited up black players, led by the fireplug-like, blazing-fast, five-foot-four (on a good day), 170-pound halfback Buddy Young.

The Yankees were actually one of the few financially successful franchises in a league that was really a showcase for Paul Brown's Cleveland Browns, arguably the best team in all of football. They had won all three AAFC crowns barely breaking a sweat, usually on the laser-like passing of Otto Graham, whom Coach Brown had converted from a single-wing runner to a pure dropback quarterback. In doing so, and by having Graham protected by a semicircular, moving pocket, Brown had birthed the modern passing era. He was so intent on having things his way that he was the first coach to call all his team's plays from the sidelines, sending them in with a "messenger," usually guards being rotated in.

Brown also had a knack for scouting remarkably good players, a carryover from his days coaching the Ohio State Buckeyes. There, he won a national championship in 1941, before, as a lieutenant in the Navy during the war, he coached the Great Lakes Naval Station boot-camp team in some big-time competition against top college teams. He then accepted a kingly offer from Cleveland businessman Arthur McBride to become part owner, vice president, general manager, and head coach of the original AAFC team there, which was eventually named after Paul Brown in a vote by fans, though at first it was called the Brown Bombers.

Brown was given a $20,000 salary and 15 percent of the team's profits, and he earned every dime. He ran the team as an absolute autocrat, instituted not only by micro-detailed football theory but also by method. He used IQ and personality tests to determine the best fit for each position, different ones requiring specific mental capabilities, and filmed both games and practice sessions. Football people at first thought these methods were twaddle, but in time they emulated them. Brown may not have been as urbane and elegant as his college counterpart, Bud Wilkinson, whose Oklahoma Sooners reflected their coach's anal-obsessive eye for detail and precision, but beside Brown most coaches looked like refugees. Landry, who became transfixed by Brown, took note of these seemingly unrelated factors, such as attitude, body language, haberdashery, and other tonsorial matters, almost as much as Brown's playbook.

BECAUSE THE main objective of the AAFC was to force a merger with the NFL, the Yankees' rivals weren't really the Browns but the crosstown Giants. A team that had won three NFL titles since forming in 1925, but none since 1938, the Giants had seen the rise of many Hall of Fame players during the long reign of its head coach Steve Owen, as well as an unfortunate habit of losing playoff games. They were run by an old-world Irish family, the Maras, the patriarch, Tim Mara, running the team as a kitchen-table operation with his sons Jack and Wellington. Both were quickly given ownership interests in the club in 1930, when Jack, twenty-two and right out of Fordham Law School, was made vice president. Eight years later, after Wellington had gone the same route, he was made an assistant to Jack, then secretary, and then vice president. When Tim retired in 1941, Jack became president, but it was the affable Wellington who carried the most weight, forming close relationships with the players while Jack would keep to his office, taking his kid brother's advice on who to sign, for how much, and for how long. Even at practices and training camps, Wellington's squinty-eyed smile was a fixture.

The Maras did share one thing in common: they were all tight with a buck, as they needed to be, what with the team's operating costs always draining the revenue generated by erratic attendance at the cavernous Polo Grounds. The Yankees, who went 8–4 in 1948, had actually outdrawn the Giants at the gate, aided by the allure of Yankee Stadium. In truth, both leagues were pretty much ragtag, though the NFL had found a semblance of hard-won stability since its founding in 1920, as the American Professional Football Association, at a Hupmobile dealership in Canton, Ohio, with Jim Thorpe as its commissioner. Renamed the National Football League in 1924, in the two decades since its birth all but two of its founding franchises were defunct, the survivors being the Chicago Bears, née Decatur Staleys, and the Chicago Cardinals. While the franchise shifts and revolving-door teams were dizzying by the late 1930s, the lineup was set for a while, split into eastern and western divisions. Its headquarters was now in Chicago, its membership national in scope and making inroads in the big markets on the popularity of the college game; an early game had even been televised, albeit to a very limited number of sets, in 1939.[4]

By a decade later, the league was a viable entity, anchored on each coast by a glamour franchise, the New York Giants and the Los Angeles Rams, and centered in its backbone by two Midwest franchises, Papa Bear Halas's Bears and Earl Louis "Curly" Lambeau's Green Bay Packers, ferocious rivals and polar opposites. The crusty Halas loved to pound out yardage, while Lambeau was smitten by the pass and turned loose quarterback Sid Luckman to heave long spirals to Don Hutson. Halas and Lambeau would fight to a draw, each winning six championships, before Lambeau left the scene and Halas stopped winning. Attesting to the league's staying power, both teams were by the late 1940s "old guard," the new wave embodied by the "Hollywood" team in LA, with pinup-boy quarterback Bob Waterfield and superb ends Tom Fears and Elroy "Crazylegs" Hirsch.

Fatefully, Tom Landry was injected into the pro game in the cusp of its awakening as a cultural staple, its balletic and violent character a measure of the times, or at least getting there. While pro football was a good match for the postwar working class–driven lunchpail ethic—the explosiveness of the pass, the overall technological/militaristic metaphors, and the rags-to-riches fantasies of a nation in the middle of an industrial boom—baseball's unhurried pace had a long-entrenched clamp on the national imagination. Linguistically, getting to (and hopefully beyond) first base was all the allegory a man really needed. In fact, the 1950s would be baseball's apotheosis, when life would indeed seem to be reborn every spring. Forever young and putatively clean nosed and indestructible heroes like Mickey Mantle were the virtual saints of American manhood in full bloom.

Football, especially the pro game, had to make do as an off-season placeholder for the next baseball season. But it was getting closer every day to its own time, and its renaissance.

LANDRY ARRIVED at his first pro training camp at Cheshire Academy in Cheshire, Connecticut, with his future as uncertain as his league's. The AAFC had been whittled down to seven teams, three in the Eastern Conference (Yankees, Baltimore Colts, Buffalo Bills) and four in the Western (Browns, Chicago Hornets, Los Angeles Dons, San Francisco 49ers), none of which, save for the indomitable Browns, was guaranteed to make it beyond the season. It was of some comfort to Landry that the Yankees were like a Confederate outpost in the heart of the North. Though they were related more to football than any kind of sociocultural statement, the team's player acquisitions in 1949 decidedly centered on the Southwest Conference.

Besides Landry, the SWC stars who came to the Bronx included the Longhorns' halfback Pete Layden, Texas Christian University's end Bruce Alford, Baylor's halfback Jack Russell, and Texas A&M's tackle Martin Ruby. Some of the veterans were also southern boys. Two were ex–Ole Miss players who had been named to the All-America team, two-way end Barney Poole and offensive tackle Frank "Bruiser" Kinard. And then there was the ex-Okie Orban "Spec" Sanders, one of the last great all-around players who twice led the league in rushing. Another, halfback Noble Doss from UT, had been named All-America in 1946, the year Landry returned from the service.

If Landry was up for a cultural change, he sure got it. In addition to seeing African Americans who weren't porters or janitors, his Yankees captain was a Jew, Arnie Weinmeister, a superb defensive tackle who would go into the Pro Football Hall of Fame despite playing only six years, the briefest career of anyone with that honor. As few blacks as Landry had ever known, he had met even fewer Jews. But if by nature he would keep a distance on certain levels, never really growing personally close to any of these men—several of whom in turn took his aloofness as arrogance—the main thing they learned about their new teammate was that he acted that way toward everyone, white or black, Protestant, Catholic, or Jew.

The truth was that he did not feel that he fit in on a team of odds and ends, thus he kept a distance. He would even tell Alicia during their nightly phone call that he wasn't sure he wouldn't be cut. The Yankees' coach, Norman "Red" Strader, a former All-America fullback and coach at St. Mary's College of California, as well as a lieutenant commander in the Navy during the war, not only ran a back-breaking camp but also allowed the players, especially the veterans, to impose their own pecking-order rules on the rookies, who were treated shabbily. "Football was their job and rookies presented a threat to their livelihood,"[5] Landry would recall of having to endure the same sort of demeaning orders as a pro that he had as a college freshman. There was no paddle this time, but there were days of lugging around the ice bucket and being made to croon "The Eyes of Texas Are Upon You" in the cafeteria.

WHEN THE team got to New York in early September, Landry found plenty of time to let his eye wander about the canyons of the big town. Along with the single players and those whose wives had also stayed home, he was put up in a midtown Manhattan hotel, the Henry Hudson. Suddenly he was living large. He was given free passes to Yankees baseball games and watched his first big-league game from the stands, the home team beating the Boston Red Sox in the season's final game to win the American League pennant. Many years later he would write of that day, of being there as "all of New York went berserk. What an introduction to the fantasy of professional sports in America. And I was now a part of that fantasy!"[6]

He also got to see Friday night fights at Madison Square Garden, was given discount tickets to Broadway shows, and had his tab picked up at "in" eateries like Toots Shor's. One can imagine the wonder of it all for the kid from Mission to wade through bustling rush-hour crowds on the streets, the pace of the city and the glare of its lights creating an energy field around him.

"He loved it," says Alicia. "He couldn't get enough of the city. He'd take long walks without knowing where he was going. I think one time he wound up in Brooklyn somehow, but he found his way back. He got to memorize the subways. He must have been something of a rube at the beginning, because he would talk to strangers, which of course they tell you not to do. But then he was a big man, he looked like an athlete, nobody would ever mess with him."

She goes on, "I think he fed off the excitement, all the hustle and bustle. He never really changed who he was. He wasn't an extroverted person. But he definitely became more outgoing and confident being in that atmosphere." The Texas hick had become a Texas Yankee.

BY THE time the season began, Landry seemed to recede a bit. Strader gave the starting quarterback job to another rookie, twenty-two-year-old Don Panciera, a fourth-round draft choice out of the University of San Francisco who had turned down the NFL's Philadelphia Eagles. Neither could Landry get much time running the ball, not with his competition being Buddy Young, who could run 100 yards in 9.4 seconds, the fastest time in football, and fullback Bob Kennedy, who had jumped to the new league from the Pittsburgh Steelers. Also ahead of Landry on the depth chart were Lou Kusserow, who had been named to the All-America team while a Columbia and also played linebacker; rookie Sherman Howard; and second-year man Lowell Tew. Landry would have to settle for table scraps on offense, though the punting job was his from the start and he was sure to see much time at defensive back.

The season opener, in Buffalo, got the Yankees off on the right foot. Trailing 14–0 after seven minutes, they scored on an interception return, then tied the game in the fourth quarter on a 76-yard drive kept alive when Landry, out of the backfield, snared a 35-yard pass from Panciera and Tew capped the drive with a 2-yard touchdown run. Getting the ball late in the game, they drove downfield, and with just over a minute left, Harvey Johnson clinched the win, 17–14, with a 21-yard field goal.

Though they then had the misfortune to play the Browns in Cleveland, the Yankees still came away with a swagger despite the inevitable loss, actually outplaying the Browns in the bowels of massive Municipal Stadium. The Browns didn't have Marion Motley, who was out with a knee injury, and the Yankees put heavy pressure on Graham, who completed only four of ten passes for a mere 36 yards. But as the great teams do, the Browns capitalized on two huge turnovers, scoring on an 84-yard interception and a 27-yard fumble to win, 14–3. Stoked by the effort, the Yankees won their next five games, a span that saw Landry be given more time on offense running the ball, something that was noticed by the *New York Times* sports section. Though he wasn't yet a starter, sportswriter Roscoe McGowan noted in the October 22 issue that "Tom Landry, the 6-foot, 200-pounder, will replace [Buddy] Young quite often. Landry has shown a lot of ball-carrying ability and in addition is a fine, long distance punter."

Nine days after that blurb ran, on Halloween, Thomas Wade Landry Jr. was born in Houston. The day before, when Alicia had gone into labor, Landry had to keep his mind on the next game, against the Baltimore Colts. After the match, a 21–14 victory in Yankee Stadium, he hurried back to the Henry Hudson, biting his nails while waiting for a call from Houston. Finally, the next morning it came. As soon as he heard Alicia's voice he blurted, "What did we get?"

"A boy," she said.

As he would recall about that moment, it was all he could do to mumble incoherently. But for a manly Texan, that his firstborn was a son could not have been more satisfying. Still, though he would pull no rank in deciding what to name the boy, which he said was Alicia's call, it seemed preternatural that a boy with his pedigree, who checked in at a hefty nine pounds, should also carry his name. Given the wonder of it all, it was almost cruel to the new daddy that he would have to go through weeks before he'd be able to see and hold the first fruit of his loins.

The rest of that day he found himself welling up with emotion, not that he showed it to anyone around him. Thinking more personal thoughts than he could table, he finally sat down and wrote a letter on hotel stationery, addressed to "My Darling Wife." Expansive and mushy by Landry standards, it ran to three long paragraphs, which while it included some typical Landry corn—being such a big boy, he wrote, "we might have to make a tackle out of him instead of a quarterback"—but closed with some uncharacteristic, not easily dispensed syrup:

> *Have I told you how much I love you? I would like to tell you a million times more than I do. I guess today I miss you more than ever. To think that today we two have become three is really something. I could almost get sentimental, but you would never believe it. . . Let's make the next month fly by. I love you lots. Tommy, Sr.*[7]

SITTING WITH a record of 8–3 and staying close to the Browns in the Eastern Conference, the Yankees would go into a tailspin, losing three of the last four games, one of which was the biggest learning experience in Landry's tender pro career. That was the second tilt against the Browns, in Yankee Stadium on November 20 before 50,711 screaming fans. Injuries in the defensive backfield led Red Strader to start the raw Texan, immediately making him a marked man for Paul Brown and Otto Graham and for the Browns' superb receivers Dante Lavelli and Mac Speedie. As Landry reminisced later with a shudder, "They threw at me all day. Mac Speedie turned me inside out and hung me out to dry. He set the official AAFC record for receiving that day—well over 200 yards." While Speedie didn't catch a touchdown pass, Graham completed nineteen of thirty-four passes for a jaw-dropping 382 yards. At *halftime* the score was 31–0, which is how the game ended. Landry's epilogue to that game was that it was "the most embarrassing athletic performance of my life."[8]

But what he learned was the foremost lesson of the game: that beyond the X's and O's, a good football team, and definitely a *great* one, gets to that level by ruthlessly exploiting other teams' vulnerabilities, never letting their heel off their opponents' throat. Paul Brown was not a man to take pity on his opponents; he wanted to snuff the Yankees' offense, and he did. If Brown quickly forgot the game, the poor bedraggled defensive back he had victimized would not. Paul Brown may have been his intellectual beacon, but Tom Landry would neither forget nor forgive Brown for hanging him out to dry like that.

The close of the regular season was another hard knock, the Yankees being pasted by the 49ers, 35–14. That left the Yankees with a record of 8–4, three games behind the Browns, one game behind the 49ers, but good enough to grab a playoff spot. For Landry the season was a mixed blessing. While the sting of the second Browns' humiliation stuck in his craw, he had much to be proud of. He ran twenty-nine times for 91 yards, had a 44-yard interception return, and punted fifty-one times for a 44.1-yard average. But all their good work only got the Yankees a return trip to San Francisco for the December 4 playoff game against the tough 49ers.

After the last game of the season, Landry flew to Houston, landing in the wee hours of Monday morning, and spent most of the next week getting to know Tom Jr. For a time it seemed the playoff game might not even take place. The 49ers players, opening a scab that had been festering in the league, were threatening to go on strike unless they were paid $500 for the game. Amazingly, metaphoric of the times and the sport, the AAFC teams weren't paid extra money for playoff games. Perhaps more amazingly, no one but the 49ers took a stand. The players eventually buckled, and the game was played before a frenetic crowd of 41,393. The gate proceeds went right into the pockets of the owners, lumber magnates Tony and Victor Morabito.

The 49ers were clearly the better team, but the Yankees hung tough in a contest the *New York Times* game story headlined as a "WEST COAST THRILLER." After tying it at 7–7 on a 26-yard touchdown catch by Buddy Young, the Yankees fell behind, 17–7, in the third quarter.

At that point they eschewed a feeble ground game—Landry, starting at left halfback, carried three times for minus 3 yards—to fill the air with footballs, but completed only seven of twenty-five passes, with three interceptions. Meanwhile, the great 49ers quarterback Frankie Albert completed eight of seventeen passes and ran for 51 yards. Still, Landry had a vital role. As the *Times* reported on December 5, "It was a great defensive battle that saw the kick put back in the game of football as Quarterback Frankie Albert of the 49ers and Tom Landry of the Yankees engaged in one of the most spectacular punting duels ever seen in the West." Indeed, Landry punted ten times, sending one into the ionosphere for 75 yards. But the 17–7 score stood, ending the Yankees' season.

As it happened, he was right at home for the last game on the AAFC schedule that year, which actually became the last AAFC game, period. Held at Rice Stadium in Houston on December 17, it was an exhibition called the Shamrock Charity Bowl, pitting a league All-Star team against the league champs, Paul Brown's machine-like Cleveland Browns. The Browns won again, 12–7, with Landry getting in only as a punter. However, six days earlier the warring leagues had agreed to a merger rendering the AAFC a relic. Before the 1950 season would begin, three of its teams, the peerless Browns, the Colts, and the 49ers, would directly fuse into the NFL. Three other teams would merge with existing NFL teams in their respective regions, the Yankees being divided among the two New York NFL clubs, the Giants and Bulldogs; the LA Dons integrating into the Rams; and the Bills, into the Browns. The players on the remaining AAFC team, the Chicago Rockets, would be put in a general dispersal draft.

And so did the AAFC go into that good night, the legacy of the pigskin New York Yankees negligible but for the one man on its roster who would achieve football immortality. On January 18, 1950, the dispersal draft was held to populate NFL rosters with the best and the brightest from the AAFC, but if peace was at hand in pro football in New York, the draft was anything but a show of comity. Weeks before, the imperious NFL commissioner, Bert Bell, had decreed that the entrenched Giants, by seniority, would be permitted to nab the first six players from the Yankees. The Bulldogs, an abjectly bad team that had moved from Boston the year before and had won but one of twelve games, would get from the rest. The Giants chose Arnie Weinmeister, defensive backs Harmon Rowe and Otto Schnellbacher, guard John Mastrangelo, end Dan Garza—and Tom Landry.

The new Giant happily spent the rest of the winter and the spring easing into fatherhood. He headed north again, to the Giants' summer camp at Saranac Lake in upstate New York, but though his son was just a toddler, Landry didn't want to be separated from the family, and after camp would break in late August, Alicia and Tom Jr. would follow him up on a train. The three of them would live in a series of hotels around the city, at first in Long Beach in a waterlogged boardinghouse called the Commander.

In camp, Landry developed a quick and easy teacher-student relationship with the Giants' coach, Steve Owen, whose knowledge of the game far eclipsed that of Landry's previous coaches, college or pro. Owen took an instant liking to the Texan, as indicated by a blaring headline in the sports section of the August 5 edition of the *New York Times*: "TOM LANDRY IMPRESSES: GIANT QUARTERBACK'S WORK IN TRAINING PLEASES COACH OWEN," which also gave the impression that Landry was going to be the wheel of the offense. In addition, Owen wanted to use him as fullback, defensive back, and punter, saying, "I figure he'll be one of our most valuable players."

Landry was a mite surprised by his apparent status, but more so at the professionalism that set the Giants apart from the defunct Yankees. The Giants also were loaded with talent. Weinmeister and Schnellbacher would be named to the All-Pro team, as would quarterback Charlie Conerly, a craggy-faced Mississippian who had been an All-America player at Ole Miss and fought with the Marines in Guam. Fullback Eddie Price was on his way to two All-Pro seasons the next two years. The biggest nova though was a quick, instinctive, remarkably adhesive defensive back, Emlen Tunnell, who in 1948 had broken the Giants' longtime color barrier. Tunnell, born in Pennsylvania coal-mining country, had served in a segregated unit of the Coast Guard during the war, then starred as a quarterback, halfback, and defensive back for the University of Iowa, before the Mara clan signed him, thereby finally integrating the Giants. He would be chosen to play in the Pro Bowl every season from 1950 to 1957 and would become the first black player elected to the Pro Football Hall of Fame.

Landry, meanwhile, was quietly becoming an important, if less heralded, piece of a new Owen powerhouse. As comfortable as he was on the field, he felt he had landed in an atmosphere of kinship that for the first time brought football to an adult level. The Maras had demanded of the Giants a business-like method of operation from the front office down through the coaches and the roster. The veterans didn't bother with adolescent hazings, and Owen's reliance on expertise filtered into his players' attitudes. They practiced with a crisp, precise sense of order and moved from team skull sessions with enthusiasm, eager to learn new plays that Owen and his assistant coaches would scrawl across the chalkboard. Fifty and grizzled, Owen was a traveler on pro football's rocky journey to respectability. An Oklahoma cattle rancher, oil rig boss, and sometime pro wrestler, he played two-way tackle for Phillips University, before migrating to the pros with the Cleveland Bulldogs in 1925. Soon after, he became a member of the original Cowboys—in Kansas City, where an early NFL team used that name—before being sold to the nascent Giants in 1926 for $500. He would recall later in his distinctive drawl, "I had seen a lot of fat hogs go for more than they paid me."[9]

Owen became the team captain a year later, when the Giants won the championship, and by 1930 he had begun a long run as head coach, and part-time player for a time, never having signed a contract for the job; instead, back when real men were good for their word, he and Tim Mara simply had a handshake agreement. A constant contender, his Giants won titles in 1934 and 1938, the former in the instantly famous "Sneakers Game," when Owen, trailing the Bears 13–3 at the half, had his players nix their cleats for sneakers that had been scrounged up from the nearby Manhattan College locker room, to navigate the icy field in the Polo Grounds, whereupon they tallied 27 unanswered points to prevail 30–13.

Owen, a squat man whom the players called with affection "Stout Steve," had an easygoing demeanor and, after decades of barking to players and referees, sounded like he was gargling gravel. He seemed not to be the deepest thinker in the world, but he was right up there with the best strategists in the game. A practitioner of the standard 6–2–3 defensive set, with six hulking linemen up front, two fairly immobile linebackers, and three defensive backs, he would at times experiment to deal with halfbacks roaming out of the backfield to catch passes—borrowing the new-look "Eagle" defensive formation of the late 1940s, a 5–2–4 set in which the four deep defensive backs covered the halfbacks downfield, from the Philadelphia Eagles' coach, Earle "Greasy" Neale.

For men like Neale, such ostensibly minor numerological designations actually meant big changes because of the new responsibilities they required in each tier of the defense. Owen for his part knew he had to think up something the Paul Browns and Greasy Neales hadn't. He didn't exactly know what it was, but with the plethora of defensive backs he had, he had more leeway than most coaches to defend the pass. For Emlen Tunnell, chemistry was all important. "I guess I got sold on defense," he said in 1957, "when I teamed up with Tom Landry, Harmon Rowe and Otto Schnellbacher in 1950. That was the best tackling backfield I ever saw. Everyone knew what the other fellow was going to do and that's what made it such fun. . . . The thing you have to learn is what pass pattern each receiver prefers, because every man has a favorite. You have to learn what fakes and feints he uses. And you have to learn whether he's quick or whether he's fast. Don't look so surprised. There's a difference."[10]

That area of expertise was the holy grail of defense for Landry, who felt it was well within his purview to explain the difference to his teammates as part of the common good. Landry himself was not quite a star, but on an intellectual level he grasped more of the pass-coverage game than most veteran players. He too sensed a common cause and esprit in the defensive backfield, and team-wide. In his first Giants camp, he had some down-home familiarity, rooming with fellow Texan Randy Clay, a halfback who had played on the same Longhorns team in the late 1940s, and backup quarterback Travis Tidwell from Auburn University. But Landry spent the bulk of his work time with Tunnell. As Alicia Landry says, "It was like they were coaching that part of the defense themselves." Touching on the undertones of such a relationship, she adds, "Their races could not have mattered less; Tommy never saw anyone in any category other than his position on the field. He just admired great athletes and never saw anything else that would affect that."

Not that there was a perfect symmetry to these relationships, and off the field there was little if any real simpatico to them. Tunnell made that point in later years when he said Landry was "a born student of the game," but added that he "was kind of weird." When Tunnell, Schnellbacher, and Rowe would go out for a beer after a game, "Tom would disappear. He was always with his family. You never knew what was going through his mind. He never said nothing."[11] Still, Landry would never have dressed up in blackface for a minstrel show and think nothing of it, as his father had. When Tom Landry came north each summer, to be sure, there was around him more of a sensitivity to matters of race. Because the NFL, at the time, played no farther south than Washington, southern men like Landry had to live in a social context very different from what they experienced back home. Agreeing with it wasn't mandatory. Accepting it was.

What Landry surely knew now was that his world *was* of a different hue. He was sharing locker room space with Jews, blacks, and men who came from the coal mines and inner-city streets, all of whom had been baptized or bar-mitzvahed. And all of them were top-level football players, as good or even better than the palefaced Texas alumnus. This must have required some adjustment in his perspectives. But at Saranac Lake in the summer of 1950, all he really thought about was his place on his new team. As camp broke, Steve Owen had reappraised him. Owen was no longer talking about Landry as a quarterback but eagerly plugging him in as the first-string punter and starting defensive back. His education would continue, its prime objective being simple enough: defending against those hated pass receivers, ready to lay some hurtin' on them. At this point on the long road out of Texas, that wasn't a half-bad goal.

Chapter 5

"OKAY, TOM,
YOU EXPLAIN IT"

FOR ALL THE STRIDES the professional football game had
made, at the start of a new decade it was still the poor relation
in American sports. The haughty college coaches particularly held it
in contempt, with Army's crotchety Earl "Red" Blaik ridiculing the
pros as "show business" and insisting that "a fiery team like Tennessee would cripple a pro club." To George Halas, them was fightin'
words. Blaik, he fired back, was "stupid." Greasy Neale pointed out
that he had taught the pro T offense to the Army team in 1942, at
Blaik's request.[1] Still, pro football was a curio to many, a sometimes
intriguing way to go through baseball withdrawal, but not entirely
big league.

Unlike the regimented, almost mannerly college game, a pro game
could be sixty minutes of carnage. Some players on the field acted
as if they were escapees from a psycho ward, and the lack of rules
only let them do so with impunity. Years later Landry liked to recall
a shiver-inducing linebacker for the Colts and 49ers, Hardy "The
Hatchet" Brown. A Texan who, as a child, had witnessed the murder
of his father, Brown made his name in the era before face masks. In
fact, he helped usher in that era by leaving offensive players' faces
looking like bloody pulp. Landry remembered when The Hatchet,
who was actually a fantastic player and one of only two men to play
in the AAFC, the NFL, and the future American Football League,

"hit a runner's jaw with such force that the man's eyeball popped out and dangled on his cheek by a tendon."[2]

The elders of the sport had only themselves to blame for much of its ill repute, thanks to their own clownish behavior, such as when the Browns' owner demanded, in vain, that the Chicago Cardinals pay the medical bills of a Browns player injured in a game between the two teams.[3] Indeed, nobody thought to keep skilled doctors on the payroll for such injuries. Typical was the Giants' team "physician," a foppish fellow they called "Doc" Sweeney who got the job because he was Steve Owen's brother-in-law. One time when Landry came stumbling out of a game with his lip spouting blood, the brother-in-law began to stitch it up, but then he realized he had forgotten to run thread through the needle. He laughed his head off while Landry sat in pain helplessly on the training table with the empty needle embedded in his lip.

The game, like the country, was going through growing pains in an uncertain time. The decade ahead would involve a tug of war between tradition and rebellion. Each year would bring the culture closer to new and bolder idioms in all manner of arts and leisure, science, and politics. Already, the novel invention called television, which would be a prime carrier of these new norms, was a booming cultural staple, having proliferated from forty-four thousand sets (thirty thousand of them in the New York City area alone) to six *million* sets in 1950. Four infant networks confined to the Northeast in 1947 stretched from coast to coast by 1950. While the CBS network had developed a color broadcasting process, NBC beat it to the punch, going on the air in color in 1953.[4] The instant gratification served up at home was so threatening to the movie studios that they waged a public relations crusade against television, fearing it would kill the film industry.

Though they could hardly know it at the time, the children of postwar America—to be labeled forever as the "baby boomers"—would mature in a direction quite different from their forebears. The boomers would grasp their very own cultural devices and heroes in sports, movies, and music, all under the cover of the placid but stern, grandfatherly guise of Harry Truman and then Dwight David Eisenhower. Technology and the population were growing exponentially, creating a thriving middle class and a whole new buffet of cultural appetizers, such as a T-shirted Marlon Brando, James Dean in a Porsche Spider, TV sitcoms, the Kinsey Reports and *Playboy* magazine (both ripping the veil off human sexuality), and visually compelling sporting forms like pro wrestling and roller derby. Sports, in fact, from the start commanded a huge chunk of the television schedule, with baseball establishing a foothold in big-city markets through deals with local stations and soon a national game of the week.

Pro football didn't have the popularity to do much business on television just yet, but Red Blaik was right in calling it show business. Sports heroes were no longer of the white-glove variety described on the radio for many years by sportscasters like Graham McNamee who sounded as if they were English lit professors. Athletes were now being portrayed in the papers and on local radio as people who sweat and who failed, and their flaws made them more human even if their private habits were submerged by friendly reporters. Athletes were still larger than life but with a hint of vulnerability. They hurt, they bled, they got up and got back into the competition. What better game incorporated those elements and tropes than football? There was every reason for those in the pro football inner circle to believe that if they stuck it out, their game would bloom.

THE GIANTS' 1950 season began on the road on September 17 against the Pittsburgh Steelers. Such out-of-town openings for the New York football teams were usual, because their baseball overlords needed to keep their playing field at the Polo Grounds manicured for the pennant race and prospective World Series games. The Giants wouldn't even see home turf until their fourth game, on October 15. Still, they passed the initial test when, down 7–2 in the fourth quarter, Landry made the game-changing play, scooping up a fumbled ball and running 37 yards for a touchdown, the turning point in the 18–7 win.

The Browns were next on the schedule, the first time the Giants (but not Landry, who still had scars from the carving he had taken the previous year) would meet the perennial champs of the AAFC. Owen was so obsessed by the date that on the eve of his own team's opening game he took a detour to Philadelphia to watch the most eagerly awaited football game in memory at the time, the Browns' initial NFL game, a Saturday night affair against Greasy Neale's defending champion Eagles. Many old liners hoped Neale would teach Paul Brown and uphold the honor of the entrenched circuit. Brown approached the game as if it were Armageddon, devising ways to deconstruct the famed "Eagle Defense." On that night his receivers, Mac Speedie and Dante Lavelli, set wider than usual, beat the overmatched Eagles defensive backs from the get-go, while tanklike Marion Motley ran the ball unchallenged. The Browns dismantled the Eagles, 35–10.

Owen surely shuddered, but he had to rig something that would at least slow down that thresher of an offense. Because the Giants had the next Sunday off, Owen had two weeks to work out a few things. And for that he leaned on the smartest player he had. As Landry would recall years later, Owen "just drew the thing up on the board and handed me the chalk and left it to me to explain it. I remember it to the day. It's where my coaching started. I was 25 years old. They called it the Umbrella Defense because it had the effect of an umbrella opening. It worked very well. Emlen [Tunnell] played next to me. We sort of worked things out on our own, on the field."[5]

When the Giants took the field in Municipal Stadium, by which time the Browns had also destroyed the Baltimore Colts, 31–0, the Umbrella was revealed. The defense came out in a 6–1–4 formation, but the new wrinkle was that the two ends would peel—or, as the terminology had it, "flex"—back when the halfbacks came out of the backfield on pass routes, making it functionally a 4–1–6 formation, or sometimes a 5–2–4 when Owen would insert a second linebacker in passing situations. By all this the Giants would be able to cover every potential receiver with somebody, even if just long enough to disrupt the receivers' patterns. Whether it would work or not would be up to the two flexing ends, six-foot-two, 215-pound Ray Poole and six-foot-two, 205-pound rookie Jim Duncan. To Paul Brown it must have looked like he could steal candy by merely throwing short to Motley out of the backfield, but Owen had the inside linemen "stay home" and always keep Motley in their sights.

What also would make or break the defense was how far the

umbrella opened. That was where Tunnell and Landry came in, having to make the right educated guess about which receiver Otto Graham would go to, since at a certain point the receivers would outrun the linemen and it would come down to man-on-man coverage. To the amazement of everyone, not least of all Paul Brown and the 37,647 fans in the spacious concrete mausoleum by Lake Erie, the Giants' defense seemed to indeed stymie all the Browns' usual weaponry. Neither did the Giants' offense do much, but when fullback Eddie Price scored on a 1-yard touchdown run midway through the first quarter and the Browns sputtered, things began to happen that no one had ever seen. As Landry recalled of the game, "Graham didn't complete a pass on our defense in the first half. We intercepted three. We had both Speedie and Lavelli double-covered." When Graham finally started clicking, rolling out and throwing underneath the deep coverage, the Giants adapted by blitzing the ends and rolling up the cornerbacks.[6]

It still wasn't easy. Graham, trailing 6–0 in the fourth quarter, moved his team to the Giants' 9-yard line, but Landry batted away a pass for Lavelli. Then on second down, Graham collided with Motley on a handoff, squirting the ball out for linebacker Dick Woodard to pounce on. The Browns' quarterback had one last shot with four minutes left, getting to the 11-yard line. But on fourth down, his end zone pass was deflected by a leaping Schnellbacher. In his breathless game story in the *New York Times*, Lou Effrat foamed, "For the first time since they were assembled in 1946 by canny Paul Brown, the mighty Cleveland Browns today suffered the humiliation of a shutout. . . blanked, 6–0, by Steve Owen's Giants in one of the all-time great upsets." Effrat noted that "an aggregate of 3,660 minutes" had passed "and yet the Browns, until today, never had known the misery of a whitewash. But then, it is to be doubted whether the Browns ever had been pitted against so great a defense as Owen's charges confronted them with."[7]

While the game didn't immediately alter the axis of pro football, historians of the sport would retroactively tag those sixty minutes as the dawn of the modern era of defense. In his incomparable 1984 updated bible of the sport, *The New Thinking Man's Guide to Pro Football*, Paul Zimmerman, who covered pro football for almost half a century, beginning in the 1960s for the *New York Post* then *Sports Illustrated*, wrote that "the birth date of the 4–3 defense was officially September 24, 1950."[8] In his zeal, Zimmerman got the date wrong—because of the bye week, it was actually October 1. And, in truth, in real time, one would never have known the import of this game. Effrat, writing for the self-described "newspaper of record," was a lonely town crier. Indeed the Giants had the bad timing of playing a game in Cleveland the same afternoon that the National League pennant was being decided at Ebbets Field in Brooklyn, when the "Whiz Kid" Philadelphia Phillies beat the Dodgers on a dramatic home run by Dick Sisler in the top of the tenth inning. Most of the town's other sports sections put out the next day were awash with stories and columns about baseball-related matters.

On that October 2, the *Post* gave not a word to the football Giants. The *Daily News*, which sold two million copies a day, the largest circulation of any newspaper in America, found space for a whittled-down, two-hundred-word facsimile of the AP report on the game under the headline "GIANTS CHECK GRAHAM, UPSET CLEVELAND, 6–0." More generous was the *New York World-Telegram*, which sent reporter Bill Lauder Jr. to Cleveland. In his write-up, he waxed that "the master of the defense—Steve Owen—beat the master of the offense—Paul Brown. . . . There wasn't anything wrong with the Browns. It was just that the Giants were better. In fact, they were great."

THE GIANTS had been so focused on the Browns that, with the second match only two weeks ahead, they fell prey, 17–6, in the home opener to the Steelers. Then the Browns marched in. With the baseball season over, there was indeed a crackle in the air. The Polo Grounds was filled with 41,734 people. Bowing to the reality of widespread sports betting—a prime lever in the growth of pro football—some papers reported the Browns as 14-point favorites. But again Owen had gone to the drawing board. His new wrinkle now was in the secondary, where he really opened his umbrella by implementing Em Tunnell at the top of a "triangle" alignment. From his perch Tunnell could see the field from sideline to sideline and be able to zero in on the receiver with his blazing speed.

This likely was the first sighting of what would be called a "free safety," though Tunnell was nominally the left halfback, the term at the time for a cornerback, with Landry the right halfback, and Rowe and Schnellbacher the left and right safety, respectively. More important than the terminology was that in a man-to-man coverage league, a rover safety was a new idea, one that would make the zone defense standard. However, when the Giants looked up at the scoreboard at half time, they were again behind, 13–3. Still, their defensive schemes held Graham in check, resulting in three interceptions and eight sacks, and Landry recovered a key fourth-quarter fumble to help turn the game. A crushing 200-yard Giants ground game put two scores on the board late, for a 17–13 win, marking another milestone: the first time Paul Brown's team had ever lost twice to the same team in any season.

This time, the conquest merited space in all the papers, even those far away. In Dallas, the *Morning News*, picking up an AP wire story about the game, prominently noted Landry's recovered fumble. Paul Brown, the stench of defeat prompting him to overreact, said his team was "over the hill."[9] If he meant to challenge his players, it worked. The Browns rolled on to win their last six games of the season, finishing with a record of 10–2 and in first place in the east. In New York, meanwhile, Owen was playing the same motivation game; after the Giants lost a game to the lowly Chicago Cardinals, he told the press his team "stunk." When he took some heat for it, he deadpanned a mock apology: "It has been brought to my attention that the past tense of stink is 'stank,' not 'stunk.'"[10] In the end the Giants too finished 10–2, setting up a rubber match with the Browns in a semifinal playoff game. Now they would need to defeat Paul Brown a *third* time.

In retrospect the Giants never had much of a chance in that December 17 game, which, unlike the old AAFC playoffs, guaranteed an extra payday for the players. Amounting to one-twelfth of their salary, such compensation was made possible by the partnership the league had for several years with the ABC network, which broadcast a game of the week and the playoffs, with Red Grange doing the color commentary. Owen's team came in banged up and was a 7-point underdog. Landry, his shoulder throbbing, was one of the walking wounded. He implored Doc Sweeney to numb the pain, but Sweeney thought it might open him up to greater injury, and refused. As Wellington Mara recalled years later, "Tom just kept pleading with him to no avail. So Tom played anyway. He wasn't about to miss that game."[11]

When the dance began on a numbing seventeen-degree day on an icy field in the half-filled Municipal Stadium, the crowd numbers held down by the bitter cold, it was clear that Paul Brown still hadn't figured out the Umbrella Defense. Neither was he prepared for Owen's latest strategy, which had the defensive line unbalanced to one side and the backfield to the other. Though the conditions created a defensive battle, with gains made in inches not yards, in an echo of 1934 *both* teams, unable to get traction on the ice-caked turf in cleats, wore sneakers and gloves. The Browns, mainly on bootleg runs by Graham, got close enough to kick a first-quarter field goal, and the 3–0 lead held into the fourth quarter until the Giants finally began to move. They got to the Browns 4-yard line, and Conerly threw a touchdown pass—but the play was wiped out by an offside penalty, and the Giants settled for a game-tying field goal. With the sun setting and the first sudden-death overtime in league history looming, Graham now took command. He guided his men down the field, thrice running the ball himself, gaining 45 yards, and with fifty-eight seconds left, Lou "The Toe" Groza kicked a 28-yard field goal. The Giants kept fighting, but a late Browns safety ended the warlike affair, 8–3.

Landry, stoked by pain and adrenaline, was particularly ornery during that game. "He was hollering and yelling and screaming when the offense was on the field," Mara said. "When a Cleveland tackler hit one of our players who appeared to be out of bounds and Tom interpreted this as a 'cheap shot,' he rushed over and was all over the guy and ready to fight before they separated them."[12]

The Giants walked off convinced they were the better team, a sentiment reflected in the papers the next day, such as Gene Ward's plaint in the *Daily News* that "the Giants deserved a better fate."[13] The Browns would go on to beat the Rams in the championship game, but smart as Paul Brown was, he knew he had escaped. He also couldn't help but read the tea leaves in the hard rise of the Giants.

Tom Landry, too, was rising. To a thinking man's player like him, the game could be maddening, all the crazy marks on a chalkboard not overriding the simple fact that there were only eleven men on the field for each team, and that somewhere down the line at least one of them would be left out of position, usually at the worst possible time. In his world, perfection simply did not exist; it was a mocking, elusive goal. Which was why there would need to be constant tinkering. These philosophical, logistical, and numerological conundrums would keep him tossing and turning in his bed at night. Yet he had made considerable progress in 1950, with two interceptions and two fumble recoveries in addition to his always reliable punting. Best of all, he was locked in on a stable team with owners who loved him like a son. Indeed, never would he feel he belonged on a team as much as he did now, long before running one from the sideline was anything close to a reality for him.

WHEN LANDRY went home for the winter and spring, it was not to hibernate in leisure but to continue working toward what still seemed a better long-term bet than anything football might offer him. He resumed his studies at Houston University for a postgraduate engineering degree, while also putting in time selling insurance for his father-in-law, a job he detested for its static drudgery. Needing the money to keep coming in from football, he kept himself in shape with a daily regimen of calisthenics, pushups, and runs around the high school track, but it was a measure of the obscurity of the pro game back home that this occupation seemed to be a mystery to his neighbors.

Laughing about it now, Alicia Landry recalls that "nobody knew what Tommy was doing. They didn't have pro football on television in Texas at the time. Nobody knew any of the teams. When we would get back after the season, people who knew us would ask, 'Where have you been?'" Indeed there were times when Landry himself wondered if this sport of paupers, not kings, was a waste of his time. At those moments of reflection, he would tell Alicia that there was "something missing" within his routines of football and fatherhood. Worse, he would say he was a bad father, and that he didn't really know how to be a dad because of his preoccupation with the game. "As a father, he felt a little lost," she recalls. With him holed up in their basement studying football films, she would sit there and watch too, knowing not the slightest what she was seeing or what he was looking for in that grainy celluloid. "I just didn't want him to be alone," she says.[14]

Often she would plead with him to relax, and she would drag him out of the house, having her parents babysit so the young couple could return to their old college routine of going to the movies and eating out several times a week, but it was as if he could never sit back and take a deep breath before football beckoned. That was why she would take Tom Jr. and go north with her husband, even though it meant uprooting the child. "He needed us," she says. "As much as Tommy loved the big city, he was still really a small-town boy and he would get homesick. His family was everything, it was his anchor." And so wherever the head of the family went, they all went. Tom Jr. would barely remember it years later, but he was enrolled in a fairly upscale preschool in Manhattan. The newspapers ran pictures of him being toted around through various streets and parks, his hand being held by his father. It was an odd life for a two-year-old, but one that his old man justified as a kind of extended-family expedition. "For two transplants fresh from the open spaces of Texas, the opportunity to live part of the year in the world's biggest city really did feel like an adventure," he would later write.[15]

The adventure for Tom Sr. was pro football, playing for the big-city team the NFL office, most of all Commissioner Bert Bell, wanted badly to be the league's prime attraction. Bell, a nervous, chain-smoking social climber, was the original owner of the Eagles and later co-owner with Art Rooney of the Steelers before being named commissioner in 1946. He had big visions, or phantasms. When the owners objected to putting a team in Los Angeles because of the distance teams would have to travel getting there, Bell overruled them. But he believed a winning team in New York was key to business success, and he was as happy as the Giants players were when they began getting red-carpet treatment around town.

Suddenly enjoying the sort of sweet life he had tasted with the defunct football Yankees, the two self-described hayseeds from Texas found themselves part of the trancelike bustle of the big town. Regularly they and other Giants husbands and wives would leave the kids with a babysitter and ride the D subway downtown for a play and dinner at the hot eateries, like Toots Shor's midtown restaurant. The perks continued to grow in 1951 when the Giants were almost as good as the year before, going 9–2–1. By now Steve Owen had become so dependent on Landry that before one of the games with the Browns, and with Conerly hurting, he penciled his defensive back and punter in as a potential quarterback, a move headlined in the *New York Times* as "GIANTS PUT LANDRY IN ATTACKER ROLE."[16] He didn't play quarterback in that game, but his play in the defensive backfield helped keep the team on track. Their only two losses that season did them in, though, with both coming at the hands of the not-so-over-the-hill Browns, whose season record was 11–1. Because the league had pared the postseason to a single game between the American (formerly Eastern) and National (formerly Western) Division winners, that meant the Giants were out of luck while the 8–4 Rams made to the title game, losing to the Browns, 24–7.

The Giants, striving to take the last elusive step up in 1952, won their first three games. In the third one, against the Browns in Cleveland, Landry put the game out of reach with a late interception that he ran back 30 yards for a touchdown, the final score being 17–9. The defense once more snuffed Graham, who completed only fourteen of thirty-five passes, and kept the Browns to a mere 21 yards of rushing on twenty-three attempts. But only three times in the last nine games did the Giants score more than 17 points, though they did end the season in style, beating the Browns again, 37–34, to finish with a 7–5 record. Clearly, even with high-profile halfback Frank Gifford, who had been an All-America player at the University of Southern California before being drafted in the first round, and another halfback from the previous year's first round, SMU's Kyle Rote, the lack of firepower hurt. For Landry, literally so. In a game in Pittsburgh, both Conerly and his backup were injured, both on frightening hits by the Steelers' malevolent defensive end Ernie Stautner, a ten-time NFL Pro Bowler. Owen now had no choice but to throw Landry in as quarterback.

As he would recall, still singed by the memory, "I'd never taken a snap as a pro and didn't know any Giants' offensive plays . . . so in the huddle I'd kneel down in the dirt and scratch out the pass routes." He was able to joke about how proud he was that he led the team to a touchdown—one that made the final score 63–7, which he noted was "the worst shellacking in Giants' history." Just to prove that it was no fluke, he played quarterback again the next week, and the Giants lost again, to the Redskins, "allowing me to retire with a perfect 0–2 record . . . as a professional quarterback."[17] Amusing as this story would be as banquet speech fodder, at the time it was no joke. Indeed, Landry left out that Stautner had broken his nose, even with the rudimentary single-bar face mask Landry wore.

Stautner, for his part, would only relish the moment, more so years later, such as when he recalled that he was "foaming at the mouth" when he "broke through, doubled up my fist, and smashed him in the face, right through his face mask. The blow broke his nose, bloodied him up, knocked him over. I just casually started walking back to the defensive side when Tom jumped up and pounded me on the back. I kept going. I know I'd done a bad thing, but I hated the Giants."[18] Rather than hating Stautner, however, Landry would appreciate such amoral bloodlust on the field. When it came time for him to hire men to teach the art of being rough, tough, and dirty, he would place a call to Mr. Stautner.

THE GIANTS' ebbing was not something Paul Brown experienced with his team, Brown's knack for instant regeneration was remarkable. Though the Browns had a mundane record of 8–4 in 1952, they made it into the title game against the insurgent Detroit Lions, who had become an instant contender after having traded for Bobby Layne the year before. Now both a pro-level quarterback and drunkard, the swashbuckling, hiccuping Layne heaved nineteen touchdowns and threw for 1,999 yards during the season as the Lions tallied a record of 9–3 before polishing off the Browns, 17–7, to earn the team's first crown since 1935. Layne, who still holds the Lions records for career passing yardage, would lug the team back to the championship game the next two years, only to lose to a reanimated Browns team each time. The Detroit-Cleveland logjam would not be broken until 1956, by which time all the pieces would be firmly in place for a renaissance in New York.

During the interim Landry's progress had continued apace. Over the 1951 and '52 seasons he intercepted a pass in seven straight games, which is still a team record, and his machine-like punting was a given. So ubiquitous was he that he led the team in the number of minutes played the former year, and the second-most number of minutes the latter. His role was expanding, as was his family. Alicia was again pregnant, and as the 1952 season neared, they prayed that she would deliver before he would have to go north. She missed by a few days. He was in camp when their daughter, named Kitty, was born. With a summer pro football camp being as close to jail-like conditions as a free man could experience, he again cursed that he could not be on his turf for the arrival of another scion from good hardy Texas stock. Fortunately the Giants had a late September game in Dallas, against the Texans, a team that textile mogul Giles Miller had formed from the remains of Ted Collins's revivified New York Yankees, as a short-lived attempt to establish a pro football team in Texas, and Landry would sneak a side trip to Houston.

This was a portentous stage in Landry's life. Nearing thirty, he was now the father of two, owned a home, and held a postgraduate degree. It was often only an afterthought that he also happened to be a fixture on a team rounding into the centerpiece franchise of a sport about to take off. The next year, the Giants would make important changes that would focus his thoughts more on the game. After a dreadful 3–9 season in 1953—rock bottom being a 62–14 mugging by the Browns—Steve Owen was finally given the gate, ending his long run of twenty-four seasons and 151 wins, still the most by any coach in the team's history. Replacing him was Jim Lee Howell, a six-foot-six former Marine and part-time Arkansas pig farmer who had been Owen's ends coach. The move was unexpected since it was assumed that Mara's sons would elevate the cocksure Brooklyn-born line coach Allie Sherman, who instead was let go. Howell's knowledge of the game was shallow, and he mainly bellowed a lot at players. His big-lug persona, however, was perfect for what Wellington Mara had in mind, which was for Howell to serve as a beard for a much more important "get"—a man whom Mara had known for years and who was sure to overstep Howell, yet one who was too risky to make head coach.

Accordingly, Vincent Thomas Lombardi was introduced that off-season as the Giants' new assistant coach in charge of the half-backs, a properly low-level job for the forty-one-year-old son of Italian immigrants who had never coached at any level in the pros. Indeed, perhaps only Mara would have offered him a job, Mara having kept tabs on Lombardi ever since they had been classmates at Fordham University in the mid-1930s, when Mara was editor of the school paper. The Fordham Rams of that decade were known for their "Seven Blocks of Granite," the mastodon offensive and defensive lines that transported the team to national prominence. Lombardi, the right guard, never received much press, his name buried in articles highlighting All-America players Alex Wojciechowicz and Ed Franco, and he got by, not on raw talent, but by wringing every drop from his anatomy and his will despite standing just five feet eight and weighing 180 pounds.

After graduation from college, during the depths of the Depression, Lombardi took a job as an assistant coach at St. Cecilia High School in Englewood, New Jersey, where he also taught Latin, chemistry, and physics for a $1,000 salary.[19] Whip-smart and more than a little arrogant, with a big, gap-toothed smile and a wide vocabulary of four-letter words, he moved up to head coach, making the schoolboy team arguably the best in the country by winning every game it played for four straight years. In 1947 he returned to his alma mater as an assistant coach, but the timing was bad. Fordham football had lost its sheen to such a degree that the school would within a decade end the program. That led Lombardi to take a more secure job as a line coach for Red Blaik at Army.

Lombardi was a man of oversized appetites, impulses, and contradictions. He drank martinis and smoked cigarettes one after the other, not even stopping when he would express his tenacious faith in God, something he wore on his sleeve as a onetime divinity student who nearly became a Jesuit priest. As egotistical and manic as he was, he could also grow equally depressive, wrestling deep in his soul with a mass of insecurities. No one could have told him he wasn't head coaching material, though his experience was confined to East Coast football. When Mara asked him about coming to the Giants in 1954, Lombardi assumed he meant as the new head coach. Lombardi listened, but when Jim Lee Howell was named, Lombardi petulantly told Mara he was going to remain at Army, something that Red Blaik thought was preposterous given that the pro job would pay more and better advance Lombardi's career.

Blaik, who was close with Mara, persuaded Lombardi to change his mind and accept the role of Howell's assistant coach in charge of the running backs. The undercurrent of that episode was that Mara would have liked to hire him as top dog, but the ill winds of bigotry could make such decisions prohibitive, given that Lombardi was a Catholic. At this time, any non-Protestant, as with any non-Caucasian, was deemed a risk. Bigotry was still so entrenched within the NFL that even Catholic owners like the Maras and the Rooneys held back hiring their own kind, based on the same sophistries that had kept blacks on the sidelines for so long. Not since 1921, predating the color barrier, when Fritz Pollard coached the seminal NFL team the Akron Pros, had there been a black coach at any level in the NFL.

Mara would offer Lombardi only a two-year deal, enough to demonstrate that a man who had been baptized and believed in the infallibility of the Pope could command the attention and allegiance of Protestants. Even after signing, Lombardi didn't feel sanguine about it and again hedged. Mara assuaged him by promising him the head coaching job after Howell left. It was a promise he would not keep. But at least he had the assistant coach he wanted. The other assistant coach he wanted would be an easier get.

IN TRUTH, Mara was far more sold on Tom Landry than on Vince Lombardi. Landry, bearing none of Lombardi's excess baggage, was a company man who could ascend the corporate ladder. As an immediate objective, Mara wanted Landry to play a critical role to resurrect the team's bread-and-butter defense, which had flagged in 1953 because of the heavy pressure the limpid offense put it under. Mara and Howell, beginning to acquire some good raw material, traded to get from the Rams linebacker Harland "Swede" Svare and drafted defensive back Dick Nolan, a swarthy native New Yorker who had starred at the University of Maryland. Nolan was cut in the Landry mold, not overly fleet but smart and an insatiable student of the game.

The same could be said of two new defensive backs, safety Herb Rich, who came in another trade with the Rams, and an eighth-round draftee from Ole Miss, corner Jimmy Patton, an aggressive ball hawk. These players were sorely needed for a defense unit getting long in the tooth, and Mara turned to Landry to hold it together until more reinforcements arrived. He would continue at cornerback but with a larger purview, as a player-coach in charge of the defensive backs. His importance was such that he was to be the only defensive coach, whereas Lombardi was one of three offensive assistants.

In the small football universe, the promotion was news: the *New York Times* gave it a full story on January 14, 1954, headlined "LANDRY GIANTS' PLAYER-COACH." This expansion of Landry's role might have made for a delicate situation, given the egos of the other players. But Landry was conceded to be the smartest football tactician on the team, if in not the league, and had been an informal coach all along. Owen had frequently begun a tutorial about the Umbrella Defense only to stop after a few sentences, hand the chalk to Landry, and tell him, "Okay, Tom, you explain it."[20] Landry had been calling signals in the defensive backfield for years, based on his intuition and instinct.

For Landry, being given a title meant little outside of the few more dollars it would put in his pocket. But he agreed to the change, which in effect made him both labor and management at the same time, at a raise, up to $11,000 a year, a real bargain for the Giants. Coyly, Mara also promised him a bonus at the end of the year if, he said, "we have a good year."[21] Landry, thus entrenched, conducted his coaching business as an absolutist, certain of his theories and unwilling to bend them no matter what. Where Lombardi would listen to suggestions by his players, Landry would shut them out. And while Lombardi courted the archetype of a hard-ass, the players rarely saw him as that. Dick Nolan called him "a pretend tough guy."[22] Frank Gifford would describe Lombardi as "a real guy, a warm, funny guy."

Nobody could have ever called Tom Landry a warm, funny guy. But he, too, was a study in contrasts. Unlike Lombardi, Landry had no real desire to be loved the way soldiers did their commander in battle. Rather more Eisenhower than Patton, he wanted to be officious and distant. On the field and at the blackboard, Gifford said, "he was kind of cold." Removed from that role, he warmed up. Gifford fondly remembered he and Landry taking their young children out in their strollers and talking not about football but their lives. Those times, he said, Landry "was a different person."[23] In fact, he too was playing a role, a distillation of Paul Brown's stoicism and his own standoffish reticence to connect with people on a personal level. All he ever cared about, through most of his Giants tenure, was giving instructions in winning football, and that escalated into an obsession, as if he were running away from something on the outside to be able to throw himself so totally into his job.

Landry was the best exemplar of his theories. His number 49 always seemed to be in, on, or near a tackle downfield. And while he rarely came off as angry, there was no doubting that he often was, and you couldn't miss it when he was. Cornerbacks *could* be rough and tumble then. They could take chances creeping up toward the line to defend the run because passers were nowhere near as accurate as they are today. Allowed to make contact with a receiver all the way down the field then, as opposed to today's game, which limits such contact to within 5 yards from the line of scrimmage, corners could mug, hold, or kidney-punch receivers. As Paul Zimmerman noted, "Once upon a time cornerbacks like Herb Adderley and Night Train Lane would go half a season without getting beaten deep." He quoted Tom Brookshier, the Eagles' corner who later became a broadcaster, "We played more like outside linebackers in today's 3–4 defense. We'd come up on the run a lot faster than they do now." Even so, Brookshier added, "If you got beat long back then, the crowd would come out of the stands looking for you."[24]

Landry would hit receivers so hard, and with such disregard for his own health, that he would actually scare them. Glenn Davis, who followed his storied "Mr. Outside" days running the ball for Red Blaik at Army, with two years playing for the Rams before a knee injury ended his career, had a run-in with Landry in 1951. The first pass he caught, he said, Landry "smeared me. It hurt, and we both knew it." Moments later Davis beat Landry for a touchdown, after which, 5 yards behind the end zone, an enraged Landry "tackled me anyway." Davis, in a fashion common now but not then, got up and slammed the ball where Landry was still on the ground. "Here," he yelled, "if you want it so damn bad." Landry viewed that sort of behavior as out of bounds, never mind his feral tackle. As Davis recalled, "He chased me all the way to our bench."[25]

To Nolan, Landry stood out not for his professorial qualities but as "a tough egg" who would "knock your brains out." Once, Landry hit the Colts' tight end Jim Mutscheller so hard that Nolan said "he drove him through the air until Mutscheller turned upside down. His head was straight down, and his feet were straight up in the air."[26] Seeing moments like that, other Giants defenders would unload on opponents with everything they had. And yet Landry, as with the Davis incident, rode such a moral high horse that he either didn't or wouldn't admit applying a cheap shot on anyone else, while never allowing anyone else the benefit of the doubt—not even Paul Brown. In one of the Giants' many tussles with the Browns, Landry, who never washed away the bitter taste of the dressing-down Otto Graham gave him in their first meeting, caught Otto in the open field on a scramble. A salivating Landry launched into him, helmet to rib, plowing him to the ground.

"Cheap shot! That's a cheap shot!" Brown, a few feet away on the sideline, screamed to both Landry and the officials.

Taking great umbrage, Landry, with amazing self-assurance, and a ton of gall, disputed the point. "You know better than that, Paul," he addressed the old master,[27] whose privileged rank and status would normally preclude anyone talking back to him, much less with actual *condescension.*

The lesson of this fleeting vignette was that Landry didn't much care who liked him or not, a trait that suited him well as a coach. And if he cut Paul Brown no slack, he surely wouldn't with his own teammates now under his charge. He refused to let anyone slide or ignore his skull sessions, and was a stickler not only for technique but also for punctuality at blackboard meetings. Once the Landry template was established, being five minutes early for a meeting meant one was ten minutes late and subject to a fine of ten dollars. Each player had to be able to explain the complexities of reading the stances and initial moves of receivers as a tip-off to where they were headed. Landry went over the same instructions again and again, to the point of stupefaction, until he was satisfied his men could repeat them by rote, and then work them on technique on the field to make sure they knew what it all meant.

Even with, or maybe because of, the added responsibility, 1954 turned out to be his best season on the field. That year he intercepted eight passes, the same number as Tunnell; recovered two fumbles; and averaged 42.5 yards on sixty-one punts, without a single block. The Pro-Football-Reference website, which uses complex methodology to assess an "approximate value" for any given player per season, rates Landry as the most effective Giant in 1954, his approximate value of 22 being second best in the league to Browns defensive end Len Ford and tied for the sixth best in NFL history. By more conventional standards, he was named to the All-Pro first team, albeit as a punter. As a unit the Giants' defense had a league-high thirty-three interceptions and yielded only 15.3 points a game. Not by coincidence the team rebounded to a record of 7–5, finishing out of the playoffs but with reestablished credibility. Mara wanted to extend the same player-coach arrangement into the 1955 season. Landry was agreeable, but he found out what a Wellington Mara promise was worth went he went to the owner after the '54 season to ask for his bonus. Mara refused. As Landry wrote in his memoirs, "It seemed I'd misunderstood; Wellington had meant that if the Giants' *organization* had a good enough year, he would consider giving me a bonus. And while the box office take had admittedly improved over 1953, he told me the Giants couldn't afford to pay me any more than my contract called for. I walked out of his office disappointed and a little irritated."[28]

As it happened, Lombardi had felt the same slap when Mara refused to pay *him* the same promised bonus. While Landry simply shrugged and made mental notes about the kind of man Mara was, Lombardi characteristically turned on his heel. Prepared to walk out on his contract, he contacted his old school, applied for the head coach job there, and was hired, but only weeks later Fordham finally dissolved the football program. Lombardi next asked for his old job at Army back. Red Blaik, again believing that Lombardi would be better off with the pro team, tipped Mara off about it. Mara then again intimated to Lombardi that when Howell stepped down, he would be in line to get the job.[29]

And so, like Landry, Lombardi returned for another season, though with the same suspicion the players already had that to Mara they were little more than chattel. Neither Landry nor Lombardi could trust their boss, and both would keep in mind Mara's disrespectful treatment. For Mara, the consequences would be profound.

Chapter 6

"SAM'S MY MAN"

THE 1955 GIANTS WERE again strong, and for once balanced, with Lombardi's brutally effective running attack eating up enough clock time for the defense to catch its breath. Landry for his part was still peripatetic and a thorn in receivers' anatomies. Otto Graham again collided with him in one of the games against the Giants that season, sustaining a hit that left the Browns' quarterback so woozy he had to leave the game. As a result, Graham, broadening Paul Browns' "cheap shot" lament about Landry, said that the Giants as a whole played "dirty football" and were out to "get" quarterbacks. Landry's response, as usual, was succinct and unapologetic. "A lot of us tackled him," he said. "I don't know how he was hit on the head. But nobody was out to 'get' him—we were just there to stop him."[1]

Dirty or not, the Giants couldn't climb out of the hole they put themselves in, losing the first three games and going 6–5–1 for the season. Mara by then had reached the conclusion that Landry's coaching expertise had eclipsed his value as a player, and made him an offer to become a full-fledged assistant coach in charge of the entire defense, a "coordinator" in parlance not then common but applicable to both Landry and Lombardi by 1956. That meant Landry would need to retire as an active player, lest his attention be divided, and for Landry the timing was right for such a transition.

He was now in his thirties and had in fact been thinking of retiring and finally getting a real job and career back home. Hard and reckless as he played, and still as tough as nails, he had also grown susceptible to nagging injuries. His knees ached all the time and sometimes it was all he could do to get himself out of bed. He wouldn't say a word about it, but time had clearly taken its toll. Never a gazelle, his career thirty-two interceptions being a tribute more to his brain than his feet, he was a step slower, which was a killer for a cornerback in a league being built for speed. Plainly, he was a dinosaur in the back field. And so, having been convinced that the players he had tutored were committed to him, when the new offer came Landry quickly accepted. The February 9, 1956, issue of the *New York Times* reported, "LANDRY QUITS AS PLAYER; BUT HE WILL STAY WITH GIANT ELEVEN AS DEFENSIVE COACH."

While his promotion entailed a bump in salary by another $2,000, Landry was no more convinced that his future was with football. Still, when he traveled north for another summer camp, now freed of the torture of sweltering in full pads under the August sun, he was officially in charge of the defense. Mara had hired no other assistant coach to back him up. This was indicative of several things. First, Mara believed Landry to be such a savant that any assistant would be extraneous. Just as significant was that with the Giants, even with Landry, defense was regarded as the stepchild. The guys who scored the big points were still the stars. Offense was thought to be what the fans paid to see.

On the Giants rosters, two-thirds of the players were offensive ones, as were almost all the top draft choices from year to year. Offensive meetings always were held in the bigger rooms, while the defense generally met in cramped quarters. When game lineups were printed in the paper, it was always the offensive squads. Defensive players, shown little respect, often thought of themselves as living in a penal colony, and Landry, exploiting that shared peevish comradeship, turned it into collective pride and snarling disrespect for pampered offenses, including their own team's. In doing so, the second-class, chain-gang image common to league defenses began to change. Now, it was the *defense* that would be where the Giants' biggest brain—Landry—was.

Wellington Mara would once say, "It was as though Landry lectured to the upper 40 percent of the class and Lombardi lectured to the lower 10 percent,"[2] or more bluntly, "the lower portion of the mentality." Landry, he also said, "knew there were only three or four people in the room who knew exactly what he was saying."[3] While these easy inductions surely sold the offense short, it's true that under Landry, the smartest Giants were of the defensive persuasion. It's true, too, that Landry didn't bother trying to get through to the rest, because he would want them traded or cut anyway.

Given his influence over Howell, he could do just that. When *that* reality became clear, players who had regarded him as a joke, a school marm whose clinical calculus seemed a waste of time in a game where animal brutality ruled, would trip over themselves getting down the hallway to his lectures. Most were still confused after the sessions, but Landry would say, "Just study it, over and over, go over it every day at breakfast, lunch and dinner, and it'll start to make sense." Simplifying his teachings is a risky business, but mainly his defensive scheme broke down to creating individual zones within the traditional man-to-man defense, with each man not only being responsible for a specific offensive player but also, seemingly with contradiction, holding his ground so as not to leave an area of defense open. This way, if a receiver entered an area, he would be defended or shunted out of it and into another, to be picked up by that area's sentry—not unlike the grid of the national missile defense system. The only defensive player allowed relative freedom was the middle linebacker, who had to tear through holes in the line and wrap up the fullback when, per the system, the probability of him getting the ball was high.

Contrary to much regurgitation of lore overly generous to him, Landry did not really invent the 4–3 formation or the middle linebacker position that made it the featured attraction. Greasy Neale's various permutations of his Eagle Defense included a 4–3 scheme, which by nature means there was a middle linebacker involved. Historians generally credit George Halas as the first to utilize a regular middle linebacker, Bill George, in the mid-1950s. George, at six foot two and 230 pounds, had been playing middle guard in a five-man front when in a 1954 game against the Eagles, the quarterback kept on popping short passes just over his head into the vacant middle. George got so sick of it that he told his coaches, "Hell, I could break up those passes if I didn't have to hit that offensive center first."[4] Freed to do just that, George intercepted a pass right after that and soon became a holy terror and a future Hall of Famer. In the Bears defensive system his position was called "Mike," the shorthand many teams would use for their own middle linebacker, though not Landry, who was operating in his own ether.

On the Giants the middle linebacker position, held by Ray Beck, went by the code name "Meg," the strong-side linebacker (the one on the side of the tight end) was "Sarah," and the weak-side line-backer, "Wanda." Beck, a former Georgia Tech All-America guard, had played on the offensive line until Landry thought that, at six foot two and 224 pounds, he had the size and speed to be thrown into football's new role. Landry's vision of the position was far beyond what George was doing, and beyond the ken of the sportswriters whose limited knowledge of the game rendered them incapable of any nuance.

Neither did Landry invent the art of studied intuition, to fore-see the probabilities, or "tendencies" as he called them, of a team's response to specific down and distance situations. Still, the hours he put into culling them by watching game films was radical. The Landry way was not to try and fight through blocks but to play the angles and use inertia and momentum to direct those blockers away from the middle linebacker—the key to the 4–3 set. Landry likened it to the work of an industrial engineer; attackers were ushered, or fooled to go, to one side when the play went to the other, leaving ball-carriers out in the cold and Giants tacklers cleaner shots, a brilliant application of Newton's law of motion.

Naturally, a knowing guess, or rather an educated prevision— there were no guesses allowed—was where it all started. Rather than purely reacting to the developing play, the defensive unit, having memorized the tendencies Landry had compiled, would already have an idea what the play would be and be able to react faster. In addi-tion, on a microcellular level, the players learned to decipher before-hand the little tipoffs—"keys" as they were called—to the play that the halfbacks, fullbacks, and receivers unconsciously gave away when they took their stance: which foot was forward, how they leaned or didn't, in essence how their body language betrayed them.

Landry swore that if a fullback lined up a certain way, he *had* to be getting the ball and couldn't possibly run a pass route, and vice versa. Unlike Lombardi, who was prone to get so frustrated when his charges were slow to pick up a key point that he would pound a balled-up fist on a luckless board, Landry never raised a hand or an octave in his voice. He would stare, hard, at someone who didn't get it until the man would wilt. Landry could seem bloodless, even vampirish, and certainly mulish. There was no use in questioning anything he adumbrated. Dick Nolan once had the temerity to try. "He said a certain thing would happen and I said, 'But what if the guy does this instead of that?'" Landry firmly told him, "He won't." "Let's say he does," Nolan persisted. "He won't," Landry repeated. The two of them went on like this until Nolan gave up. Sometimes Landry would be proved wrong on game day. But, Nolan said, "if he wasn't right, he wouldn't admit it."[5] The Giants' defense once tacked a sign up on the locker room wall that read, "THERE ARE NO WHAT IFS," underscoring but also perhaps gently mocking their coach, something they needed to do for their own sanity.

Landry's schemes succeeded because other teams didn't know how to exploit them optimally or how to equally read the defense's moves. Not that the system worked every time. Paul Brown, who was always thinking a step ahead of Landry, beat the Giants five out of six games from 1953 to 1955, the lone non-win being a 35–35 tie. But things go wrong all the time in football, things that no coach can control. Landry one day would be able to write chapter and verse about that.

As it stood on the eve of the 1956 season, Landry had his system and some people he swore by. More and more they came via the trade route. A fourth-round pick brought from the Rams defensive back Ed Hughes, who was much like Dick Nolan, and both were nearly analogs of Landry. Neither was fast or nimble, but with a radar-like intuition for where the play would go, they would mesh well on the field. Off the field, Hughes would marry Nolan's sister. Landry could also boast having defensive tackle Roosevelt "Rosie" Grier, a third-round pick the year before from Penn State who, at six-five and 300 pounds, made it impossible for any one man to block or even much deter him. All were pivotal; none was a game changer.

In 1956, however, Landry would need to look no farther than what the tide, and Mara, brought in to find the crux of his defense and prove that everything he preached was indeed football gospel.

THE 1956 season was a milepost for many reasons. That year marked the modern marriage of the NFL and television. The broadcasting arc had progressed since the tentative early sightings of pro games on local stations. The DuMont Television Network had televised a Sunday game of the week until 1955, when the network went broke. Bert Bell then sold rights to broadcast the league's title game for $100,000 to NBC, which paid $1 million to continue doing so for five years. Cannily, Bell also peddled his regular-season games starting in 1956 to CBS, though many franchises had their own local television deals. Teams were hiring regular announcers for local broadcasts, which were limited only to road games, broadcasts of the home contests being blacked out so as not to eat into the gate receipts. The Giants' TV "voice" on those games, for example, was Chris Schenkel, a personable, low-key voice that helped carve for the New York team and the league an identity of top-notch professionalism.

Bell and his minions in the league office had to be giddy that his vision was coming to fruition, with a team in New York ready to roll aces. So strong had the Giants returned to prominence in 1955 that the Maras concluded that being quartered in the increasingly corroded Polo Grounds would hold them back. They longed to put their team on a grander stage, the grandest of all, the pale-blue Parthenon across the Harlem River, its frieze-frame facade as famous a landmark as there was in sports. There was a winter vacancy sign on it ever since 1951, when Ted Collins's Yanks had folded. At the same time, the baseball Giants' flinty owner Horace Stoneham planned no upgrading of the Polo Grounds, and with cause—he was secretly preparing to join the Dodgers' owner Walter O'Malley in mutual wanderlust. By the end of the 1957 season, both National League baseball teams would jilt their loyal fans and make the long jump to greener vistas, the Dodgers to Los Angeles and the Giants to San Francisco.

Wellington Mara popped his buttons in glee when Dan Topping and Del Webb agreed to allow him use of Yankee Stadium. Within those cavernous walls there would be a pigskin powerhouse to go along with the baseball dynasty. And it was a perfect venue for Tom Landry and Vince Lombardi to pad their resumes.

THE EFFECTIVENESS of Landry's Socratic, oddly incongruous football methods was so striking that within the Giants there arose a teeming sense of rivalry. Landry's defensive players wanted to prove themselves ready for the next task by trampling the Giants' offense, something that would increasingly become a matter of intense pride and provoke a definite spike in motivation for men on both sides. As it happened, Landry had a real fight on his hands there, with the con-comitant rise of Lombardi. Like Landry, Lombardi was big on repeti-tion ad nauseam, but he concentrated on getting his men to master one single play above all others: the power sweep, a throwback to stone-age football, featured a convoy of pulling guards and backs, blasting defensive people out of the way for the ball-carrier.

Back then, when he was actually somewhat reserved around fully grown men, Lombardi had not known what to do with a professional team offense. He tried his Fordham/Army split-T offense, which was built around the option play, meaning the quarterback would do as much running as passing. When Charlie Conerly was told of the plan, the gimpy-kneed old Marine damn near revolted. Lombardi then went with the more traditional set, though he wasn't sure if he wanted Conerly or the younger Don Heinrich to play. The latter was better at throwing long passes and as such more popular with the fans than the aging Conerly, who had sometimes been booed off the field the previous seasons. Lombardi thus touched off one of foot-ball's seminal quarterback controversies, with Giants crowds taking sides and alternately chanting for the one who wasn't playing. It was an uncomfortable dynamic but one that wrung the most out of each, something Landry tucked into the back of his mind.

Lombardi's squad wasn't quite storied yet, and like Landry he had

more refining to do. Both, however, were getting closer, and more confident. As wildly opposite as these two de facto co-head coaches were—
as Wellington Mara famously noted, "You could hear Vince laughing
or shouting from five blocks away. You couldn't hear Landry from the
next chair"[6]—they were on the same fast track, already engaged in a
personal race to the top, which was where the Giants were headed as a
team. The Giants' defense began the 1956 season with two critical new
defensive linemen who arrived in trades: tackle Dick Modzelewski and
end Andy Robustelli, who, typically on Landry's squad, had little in
common except their ability to understand his theories. Modzelewski
was a former All-America player and an Outland Trophy winner at
the University of Maryland. With a reputation for clashing with his
coaches, he had to explain why he'd been on three teams in as many
years and, before the 1956 season, traded twice within three days.
Robustelli, meanwhile, had come much further as an unlikely stand-
out, having been a Navy veteran and son of immigrants. Barely noticed
at tiny Arnold College in his native Connecticut, he was drafted as a
twenty-six-year-old rookie in the nineteenth round by the Rams, only
to bloom and make the All-Pro team in 1953 and 1955, though at age
thirty-one few thought he had much football left in him.

The Giants had also drafted in the third round a chirpy, cherubic-
faced kid from coal-mining country who was a two-way tackle and
sometime guard during an All-America career at West Virginia University. Robert Lee Huff, who answered to the name of Sam, had
been a co-captain at the East-West Game and the Senior Bowl, then
starred in the College All-Star Game. He was expected to play on
the offensive line but had no idea what he stepped into at the Giants'
summer camp at Saint Michael's College, a sprawling Catholic
school in a place called Winooski Park in Colchester, Vermont, just
outside Burlington. Founded by Edmundite priests in 1904, this was
a typical venue for Mara to hold his team's camp, on the theory that
if everyone experienced the collective suffering of being at a Catholic school, even an empty one in the summer, they would learn real
discipline. The place was suitably spartan, with no air-conditioning
in the dorms, sputtering water in the showers, and a brocade of bad
sewage wherever one went. The result made being out in the broiling
sun seem a relief.

For Mara and Lombardi, the priests' daily invocation on the field and Sunday Mass at the Chapel of Saint Michael the Archangel seemed like old times. But Landry, rugged individualist that he was, felt entombed in a Catholic necropolis. Two weeks in, he was having second thoughts about staying in a job that required such stifling asceticism and sacrificed quality time with his family. He poured out another emotional letter to Alicia, writing, "Don't think you're the only one who is lonesome. Don't ever think these football players can take your place. I miss you so much. We've stood it before, so I guess we can this time. But let's hope this is it. Maybe I'll get a break next year and have a job that will support us."[7]

If Saint Michael's made Landry think about getting a real job, it made Sam Huff think about simply getting out. From the start, Huff's first pro camp was torture, Sam having stepped from college stardom into the firing line of Jim Lee Howell's mouth. While Giants fans might also remember Huff from the color commentary he provided during radio broadcasts of the team's games for years after his career, today he is president of the Middleburg Broadcasting Network in his native West Virginia. Casting his memories back to that month in purgatory, he makes Winooski Park into his own rendition of Gorky Park.

"I hated Winooski so bad I still can't remember it. I blocked it out of my mind. I had come straight from the College All-Star Game in Chicago, me and Don Chandler [the Florida Gators' punter-kicker drafted in the fifth round], so we hadn't been home for two weeks and were homesick to begin with. And right from the start Jim Lee Howell would yell at me, and he didn't even know my name! He'd call you by your number. He'd say, 'Number 70! You can run faster than that, goddammit!' And I was the fastest guy on the line! We'd run 40-yard sprints and I'm first, and he's yelling at me! Lombardi would yell at you but he knew who you were. [Laughs] Lombardi was the master. You felt great because Lombardi yelled at you. There's the difference."

At the time, Huff rarely heard or saw the defensive coach. "I didn't know who Tom Landry was, or Lombardi, but I still didn't know Landry even after camp because I never talked to him that whole month. He ran the defense and never said anything to anybody else.

It wasn't until later that I found out he didn't talk to anybody, period, on the field. He'd just stare at you. And when you made a mistake, he'd look at you and shake his head no, like, 'Aren't you ashamed of yourself? I taught you better than that.'"[8]

There was talk that, at six feet one and 250 pounds, he was too short for the guard position and too light to play on the defensive line. But not only had working in the mines back home made him strong as a country hoss, he also was extraordinarily fast on his feet. Huff, who had a wife and child back home, had driven a somewhat hard bargain, at least for Wellington Mara, when he demanded a contract with a $7,000 salary, $2,000 more than the normal rookie income. Splitting the difference, Mara gave him $6,000. And yet he now felt like a whipping boy.

In truth, he might have taken Howell's verbal abuse as a compliment, given that the coach's favorite target, for years, was Frank Gifford, the marquee halfback who even in the early 1950s had begun to appear in commercials and in small roles in films. Evidently believing that Gifford needed motivation to keep his ego in check and his mind on football, the coach regularly belittled him as "Mr. Hollywood" and taunted, "Do you want to be a football player or a movie actor?" Gifford had to fight back tears, and later he would say, "I never had a comfortable moment around Jim Lee Howell."[9]

Under these circumstances, it was impressive indeed that Gifford during Howell's tenure would make the All-Pro team five times and in 1956 win the Most Valuable Player award, a fact that seemed to impress Howell not in the least. Always convinced that there was some dog in Gifford, the next year Howell would publicly, and dimly, call Gifford "the worst player in the league."[10] Huff himself would note that Howell's treatment of his star player was "absolutely embarrassing." Being in Howell's firing line so got to Huff that after a few days at camp he decided he had enough. He wasn't alone among the rookies. "Jim Lee yelled at Don Chandler, too—a punter! Who yells at a punter? Don and I were rooming together and one day we just said, 'Fuck it, let's just get the hell outta here.' So we took our playbooks and went into Lombardi's office to turn them in." When they did, Lombardi was dumbfounded.

"What the hell are you doing?" he roared.

"We quit," Huff said.

"Like hell you are!"

Lombardi, who knew better than to try to physically stand in their way, sputtered on as the pair left the building and, hauling valises with their clothes, got into a cab they had called for and headed for the Burlington airport. Recalls Huff with a hearty cackle, "That's how young and naive we were. We didn't know what flights there'd be or anything. That's when we found out there were no planes that could get us out of Vermont that day. We just looked at each other and said, 'What the hell do we do now?'"

Lombardi answered the question for them. He had gotten into his car and followed them. He lumbered into the terminal, saw the two expatriates, and thundered, "Get the hell back to camp!"

"That was the only thing we could do," Huff says. "But he also agreed to speak to Howell and get him to go easier on us. So, back we went. I'll tell you what, though. If there'd been a plane out of there, I can't tell you what would have happened. All I know is it didn't happen. Maybe Fate didn't let it happen."

LOMBARDI MOVED Huff into the right guard position to lead the power sweep that gave Frank Gifford a reason to keep playing for Howell and not turn into a full-time Mr. Hollywood. The rookie was in that role when the season began, as usual, on the road until the Giants' landlords were done with Yankee Stadium. The opener required a long trip to San Francisco, where the Giants ran up a 17–0 first-quarter lead and won, 38–21. They then played the Chicago Cardinals and lost, 35–27, in a game that featured a 66-yard interception return by the immortal Dick "Night Train" Lane. Particularly worrisome to Landry was that the normally anemic Cardinals offense racked up 223 yards on the ground a week before the Giants had to go into Cleveland.

The game against the Browns, on October 14, however, became the turning point of the season, storied for two reasons. One was the electronic espionage the Giants used to pilfer Paul Brown's plays. The Cleveland coach had been sending plays onto the field via a wireless radio signal from a sideline microphone to the helmet of his new quarterback, George Ratterman. The league had approved the new technology, which the Lions and Cardinals were also using. Two days after the Giants' 21–9 victory over the Browns, General Manager Ray Walsh rashly, and perhaps foolishly, crowed about the eavesdropping. Walsh said the Giants had used a makeshift system in which scrub defensive end Bob Topp, armed with a radio receiver on the bench, heard the signal and relayed the information to Gene Filipski, who had been acquired from the Browns and knew Brown's play terminology. Filipski, in turn, tipped off Landry. "It was one of the nicest days we've ever spent in Cleveland," boasted Walsh.[11]

However, Brown denied the Giants had one-upped him at his own game, saying that Walsh's revelation was "not true" and that he, Brown, had used the radio only for two plays before putting the microphone away because of the crowd noise. And while a smug Walsh said the Giants would continue to use "this phase of communication only when necessary," Commissioner Bell, concluding that the controversy was foolish, quickly outlawed any further use of it. The ban stood for three decades, until such transmissions from coach to quarterback became more secure. The story grew so mythic that Frank Gifford, in retelling it years later, insisted that the Giants had that day blanketed Jimmy Brown, who in reality wouldn't be playing for the Browns until the next year. Yet it all but obscured a more important turning point: the changing of the guard, literally, at middle linebacker. That happened when Ray Beck went down with an injury, sending Landry scrambling for a replacement during the following week.

Rather than try to use one of the existing linebackers, he followed through on an idea he had been toying with since he'd seen the rookie guard from West Virginia in camp: switching Huff to the defensive side of the ball, as had happened with Beck. "Tom was the first guy to seek linebackers with speed and mobility, and guards have to be able to move and still wipe people out," Huff says. "He'd already come to me. He said to me, 'Sam, have you ever thought about playing linebacker?'"

"Hey, you're the coach. If you really want me to try it, I will."

Lombardi, stocked with many good offensive linemen, had no objection, so Huff took a few tentative steps at the new position during practice. When he did, he can say without disputation all these years later, "Well, I'll tell you what, it was like I was born to play it. I'd played some middle guard in college but this was a new world for me. I'd always played down in a three-point stance and now I was up, with my hands on my knees and I could see everything. I was just like a fullback looking over the whole field. Before that I'd never seen over the center's head! That week, after Ray got hurt, Tom gave me his playbook. That was the first time I ever had a playbook and it was the size of a phone book. It's like, where do you start?"

Ready or not, Huff found himself couched between the two other linebacker positions, played by Cliff Livingston, Swede Svare, and at times Bill Svoboda, and he made Landry proud with the speed at which he carried his 250 pounds. He was sometimes a blur and made tackles as if in a frenzy. Though maybe only Tom Landry knew it, having Huff on his side of the ball was when the middle linebacker position was born in earnest. To the world at large, it would take a while longer. The *New York Times* wouldn't give Huff his first notice until the next week's premiere at Yankee Stadium before 48,108 fans, the biggest home crowd the Giants had ever had. After the 38–10 laugher against the Eagles, Lou Effrat noted only that Huff was one of the "operatives" who aided in the win. At the time Huff didn't know whether he would be shuffled back to the offense when Beck became healthy, and he was warily trying to slog through the thicket of Landry's playbook. "I don't understand all this, Ray," he said to Beck in midweek.

"Well, by God you better, 'cause you're takin' my job."

Indeed, Landry confirmed this to Beck, telling him, "Ray, Sam's my man."

Against the Eagles at the stadium—"the dirty Eagles," as Huff says Landry always called them—Beck had been moved back to guard. The middle linebacker position indeed belonged to Huff, who had no idea how important he would be.

LANDRY'S DEFENSIVE schemes placed an impossibly large responsibility on his middle linebacker. At the time they probably would not have worked with anyone other than Huff. In a 1960 book called *The Pros*, by Robert Riger and Tex Maule, Landry dissected the 4–3 formation using an array of precise diagrams and giving the lay public a sense of what it must have been like in a Giants defensive skull session. According to Landry's tracing of the evolution from Greasy Neale's Eagle Defense to his 4–3 schemes, stage one required the middle guard to drop back, forcing the defensive tackles to tighten and take more of an inside route on their rushes to protect him. In the next phase, the ends lined up inside the two outside linebackers to protect *them*. Thus, as Landry wrote, "The linebackers are the key," with vast responsibilities to make the hit. And since the objective of the other ten defenders was to contain and shunt the player with the ball toward the middle, the middle linebacker's play would make or break the system.[12]

Huff found himself picking up minutiae he never knew existed. Today, those teachings are still fresh in his mind. "The 4–3 was either an inside or outside," he says, according to down, distance, and tendencies. If an inside run was anticipated, "the two tackles, Grier and Modzelewski, would shut off the middle, take the inside holes off guard. The ends, Robustelli and [Jim] Katcavage, would come in from the outside, and when the quarterback handed off to the running back, he was my man—I came up the middle. If it was an outside, Rosie and Mo came through outside the guards and I'd follow the ball carrier outside. It was all done to free me up."

Before each play Landry would signal to Huff what he wanted. "Both hands on his hips meant an inside. Folded arms was an outside. You might think Paul Brown would be able to see that and make the connection, but that wasn't so easy. Paul was 50 yards away, and he'd still have to send in his play—he couldn't wait until the last second. And the quarterbacks didn't really change a play at the line then. Besides, you still had Grier up there, and you had to block him. And we were constantly changing coverages, which was unheard of. We switched up depending on the team and the situation. If they played a split backfield, we called Red, or an outside 4–3. A tight backfield was Blue, an inside 4–3. Andy [Robustelli] would call the switches on the line.

"Yeah, it got very complicated, but the more we played together it was very simple. If you played it right, everything would be automatic, the shifts, the coverages. This was when defense came of age.

We were the only ones to play it right. Because no one else had Tom Landry."

LANDRY'S TROOPS may have cringed at the volume of his playbooks—Don Smith, the team's PR man then, told a joke that after one of the defensive players lost a page from the playbook, "we found it at a Chinese laundry. Someone had exchanged it for a dozen shirts." Nevertheless, what was in the playbooks would become instinctual and executed with boldness. Herb Rich, a safety who had come from the Rams, said the coaches there "loved to embarrass you if you took a chance." Landry, on the other hand, "taught you not to be afraid to take chances. Tom would say, 'Anticipate! Get there ahead of him. Go on the snap of the ball.'"[13] However, the players constantly had to toe a razor-thin line between regimentation and individuality. Even making a fabulous play at times wasn't a good enough excuse for deviating too much from the system.

Says Huff, "You couldn't win an argument with him. If he thought you went outside the box, you'd get the look, the stare. You could tell him, 'But, Tom, I made the play.' It didn't matter. He'd say, 'You gotta play my defense. Don't make me look bad, Sam.'" Only in Landry's world could a man saving a game with a crucial tackle make Landry believe he looked bad as a coach. These types of responses seemed to come from an odd warp, independent from the moment at hand, even the game at hand, from a need to be right. Similarly, while Landry would be free, if typically clipped, with his praise for these men, he rarely if ever congratulated any of them in real time. Consequently, they never knew if they had done what he expected of them, which was likely his objective, to keep them always giving more and more. The sting of his terse critiques was something they all felt at some time or another.

At those moments, Huff adds, "the only thing he'd say was 'You know better than that,' and you'd slink away with your tail between your legs." Even so, Landry was so protective of his men that when blame was due, he would never lay it on anyone, by name, either in team meetings or when he spoke with the reporters. "Tom never second-guesses you," Jimmy Patton once said. "The only time he uses I is when he says, 'I take the blame.'"[14] To a man, they came to see him as a unique sort of leader, strange in many ways, but whose words were the mystic key to the kingdom. Gifford could never figure him out. "Tom's a nerd. He's so shy, so square," he once said. "Why does anyone think he's intimidating?"[15] Yet the same nerd made mountains move. "In defensive strategy," Gifford said, "Tom went far beyond Paul Brown. And in my estimation, defense is what wins football games. The offense gets the hosannas and the genuflections and all that crap. But the defense wins it—and Tom Landry was the absolute master of the science of defense."[16] While it may have sounded like he was master of the obvious when he would say things such as, "I don't believe a defense can be sound unless every man knows what he's doing in every situation," Landry *literally* meant *every* situation.

As had Landry, his flock played not only cerebral but also trash-mouth football. During one game Rams halfback Dan Towler bulldozed into the end zone, smacking his head into the stanchion of the goal post, which back then was sunk into the ground just across the goal line. It knocked him cold, and as smelling salts brought him to, Dick Nolan, perhaps the Giants' closest analog of Tom Landry, began taunting him. "You come through there again, you sonofabitch, and I'll really hit you!"[17] Neither did Landry show *his* players mercy. Nolan remembered when *he* went down after being smeared on a tackle that separated his shoulder. He was writhing on the ground in searing pain, only to look up and see Landry, who had come over from the sideline. "You had bad technique on that play," was the first thing Landry said.[18]

As heartless as he could seem, for the Giants there was some comfort in moments like that. If he was even one degree warmer, he just wouldn't have been Tom Landry.

Chapter 7

"AS DIFFERENT AS DAYLIGHT AND DARK"

SPORTS, LIKE THE REAL WORLD beyond the turnstiles, were ready to be molded, or remolded, into a whole new and not altogether serene paradigm in 1956. Events were happening too fast for easy inductions and comprehensions. That year, on the international front, Egypt nationalized the Suez Canal, precipitating an attack by Israel in tandem with bombings by Britain and France. The first attack was open aggression in the name of Israeli security, but in the end it failed. Soon enough, a United Nations resolution would impel the Israelis to withdraw, and as a consequence of the hostilities, the Arab axis began to limit oil imports to the West. In Cuba, Fidel Castro came down from the mountains to foster a revolution in what was a colony and playpen for American capitalists and mobsters, who bankrolled the bloodthirsty regime of Fulgencio Batista. The Cold War was getting no warmer as the Russians invaded Hungary in defense of the bogus Warsaw Pact. In South Asia, Pakistan became an Islamic republic.

At home, contrary to the hopes of an aging generation, the joyful subversion that was rock 'n' roll had refused to die, but the much larger cultural imperative, civil rights, was still being fought to the death. In many ways, however, life remained simple. Gasoline stood at twenty-two cents a gallon, and the average cost of a home was

$2,280. The absurd moral homilies of *Father Knows Best* were the collective, if never achieved, illusions of every American family. The clatter and confusion of this soundtrack lay safely beyond the borders of sports, but the figurative blood spilled in the razing of the color barrier in baseball and football was not lost on hoary team owners.

When the Giants had an exhibition game in Dallas against the Baltimore Colts, the black players—Em Tunnell, Rosie Grier, Roosevelt Brown, and Mel Triplett—had to be booked into a "colored" hotel, as was the case pretty much everywhere throughout the Jim Crow South. Brown, making light of it, wondered aloud where the "Mau-Maus of Kenya" were going to be put up.[1] The next day there was a scheduled publicity luncheon at the hotel where the bulk of the team stayed, and the Giants' bus came by to pick up the black players, who refused to get on, the hypocrisy of the event too bitter a pill for them to swallow. Impatiently, Wellington Mara came off the bus to confront them. "You guys never said anything about this before," he said. Grier, speaking for his brethren, responded, "We shouldn't *have* to say anything about this." According to Grier, Mara had an instant epiphany. "Wellington said, 'I promise you we'll never again have to separate our team.' So we got on the bus, and we never stayed in separate hotels again."[2]

Because Tom Landry despised the racism, he was at once in conflict with many fellow Texans' embrace of their "states' rights" of the time. And while he took no public stand on the matter, his commitment to civil rights ran deeper in his own Texas soul. "A black football player is your brother, that's how we all saw it," says Sam Huff. "Tom felt about it exactly as I did. He was quiet, but when something like that happened he'd shake his head and you'd know he was pissed off—hell, that was his state, he was embarrassed by that.

"Here you had a Tom Landry, a guy from Texas, and he's coaching Rosie Grier and Em Tunnell, two of the greatest ballplayers ever to play. And on short-yardage situations, Tom brought in Rosie Brown, and we'd have two black tackles in front of me. That's Tom Landry. That's how he handled the problem, that's how Lombardi handled it. A great coach can make attitudes change."[3]

✦ ✦ ✦ ✦

SOME OF the most thorny cultural issues were now being discussed freely by a new sports cognoscenti. For the first time in the post-war era, sports journalism began to ascend from the jockstrap sensibilities of *The Sporting News* to a more classical, broader literary context reminiscent of the Grantland Rice age, albeit with a harder, edgier beat. On August 6, 1954, a new glossy, full-color magazine hit the stands, its intent to grab the eye and mind with prose and photography equally penetrating and artistically flavored. Bankrolled by *Time* magazine patriarch Henry Luce, the new weekly, *Sports Illustrated*, had the gift of timing, both taking advantage of and heralding the new paradigm of seamless sports seasons and either real or contrived drama and lyricism to any given sporting event. It also gave bylines to writers not often associated with the grinding treadmill of sports, such as John Steinbeck, William Faulkner, A. J. Liebling, and Budd Schulberg. Although *SI*, as it would become abbreviated, would not turn a profit for a decade, it grew in reputation and influence along with the events and people its splendid scribes and shutterbugs tended to—just in time for the pro football evolution.

Thus, things were deceptively peaceful through the meridians of sports now that franchises were reaping the rewards of the postwar, baby-boom gain in disposable income and recreation time. By mid-season 1956, pro football was a different animal, refined in its brutality, with a pretty face—Frank Gifford—carrying the ball and a cool new order, replacing the scabs and warts of Hatchet Brown and the drab gray visage of Paul Brown.

For Landry and Lombardi, ensconsed in the most famous stadium in the world, the autumn of '56 was their own proving ground. While still not known to the general public, these two upwardly mobile tyros had established their respective hegemony so ferociously that the rivalry between their two squads had by now escalated to tribal level. With the stakes high, the two coordinators would petition Howell to give their respective squads more field time during practices. Landry was also the kicking coach and lobbied Howell for more time doing that too, which Lombardi believed was a waste of time, an opinion he would soon change. As Howell would recall of his top adjutants, "They were fussing all the time."[4]

In Landry's bromidic autobiography, one can distinguish a touch of sarcasm when he wrote about playing second fiddle to "Lombardi's flashy, innovative, and star-studded offense" in "a city accustomed to excitement and glamor of bright lights and big stars."[5] Huff was, as ever, more direct. "Oh, we hated those guys' guts. We ran over so many offenses and the offense ran over so many defenses that the toughest competition for each squad was when we faced each other in practice. That was the real game! We didn't like each other one bit. We wouldn't allow them to make a first down. We'd get Lombardi all steamed up." On the practice turf, no profanity or slur was off-limits to the warring sides. Howell's imprecation of Gifford as Mr. Hollywood was freely requisitioned by the defense, which delighted in the fact that Gifford hated it.

On Sundays, Landry and Lombardi would separately lead their units onto the field, and the antagonism between the squads would continue. Lombardi would bark at the defense during games, "Get the goddamn ball once in a while!" Huff would call to the offense after they went three and out, "Would you assholes go out and hold them for a while this time!" When Gifford wrote one of his several books about the Giants' good old days, he interviewed Huff, who couldn't resist reminding him, "Jesus Christ, did I hate you." Of the personal slurs Gifford heard from his own team, Gifford says it "wasn't a joke . . . and it stung."[6] But winning was the salve.

LANDRY'S RELATIONSHIP with Lombardi, the subject of endless fascination over the years, was more complicated than anyone knew back then. In fact, Landry was ambivalent about his opposite in many ways. The offense-defense rivalry by extension meant there was a degree of tension between the two of them. Landry took immense pride that the defense always seemed to be better than the offense. When Lombardi evened the scales, Landry refused to yield any ground. The rivalry, then, was real and obvious. As Landry put it with typical terseness, "Though Vinnie and I became great friends, we each had our own agenda."[7]

Landry regarded Lombardi's foul-mouthed volatility and juvenile aspects of his personality as the sort of thing a coach should avoid. While not going as far as to call Lombardi a classic manic-depressive, he apparently believed it. Landry, says Sam Huff, used to have his own pet name for Lombardi back then: "Mr. High-Low." In his memoirs, Landry said that Lombardi was "loud, aggressive, gregarious," with a "New York Italian personality," and that "any time the offensive team had a poor game, you could count on Vince being in a foul mood for the next two or three days." He continued, "If you risked talking to him during that time, he might snap at you or just respond with an angry grunt," hastening to add, "But you learned never to take it personally. That was just Vince."[8]

Off the field, they could discuss football as shop talk, bouncing ideas off each other, in one or the other's office or living room. Their wives, whom both men knew were their better halves, and who could get them to give in on any argument, became friends. Landry recalled that Lombardi's "emotionally volatile personality" gave him an "expressive, warm and caring nature. When you got to know Vinnie you couldn't help but love the man," and that "his old-world-gentleman style thoroughly charmed Alicia."[9]

Landry could not help but admire Lombardi. He was smart, sharp, and a better actor than Landry could have pretended to be, and at that stage of their lives Lombardi was more unapologetic about citing religion as his salvation. Both shared the same impatience with a lack of perfection, and the notion that it was unachievable. Both were voracious game-film watchers, and it was Lombardi who proposed that the Giants do what he did at Army: take Polaroid pictures of the defense during games so the quarterback could see for himself how he was being defended. Landry thought it was a splendid idea for the defense as well, embellishing in real time what his men had seen on the game film. For several years, none other than Wellington Mara, acting as the conduit in the rudimentary system, dropped the pictures from the press box inside a sock to an aide on the field.[10]

In truth, if Landry had some of Lombardi's molten emotion, and Lombardi some of Landry's self-control, each would have been the perfect coach. Their respect for each other drew them closer, to the extent that Sam Huff says now that they were indeed "close friends" and that the two of them roomed together in camp and on the road. Knowing how interconnected they were as rising stars in football, and because the rivalry turned up the heat for both, they accommodated each other, even if it made them uncomfortable. Some thought they never really pulled it off. Given the rawhide competition between the the two coaches, Gifford said, "I don't know if it ever turned into a friendship."[11]

To be sure, Landry was turned off by Lombardi's two-day silent broods, and Lombardi was disdainful of Landry's prissiness and distance when it came to the usual bonding rituals of men who share locker rooms. One example of the latter was the daily off-the-record confab dubbed the Five-Thirty Club, which was meant to court and condition local sportswriters. It was a nightly event in Howell's office between the coaches and general manager, and sometimes Wellington Mara and even Doc Sweeny, along with the writers. They all talked football, drank martinis, played cards, and shared some dirty jokes. Landry, who could mix a mean martini and at times would knock back one at a restaurant, was not part of these festivities, such rites of manhood being too unnatural and pointless for him to pull off. While certainly not unpopular among the team's brass, neither was he one of the boys, and many wondered if he was too prickly, self-righteous, and standoffish for his own good.

Landry also had a disconnect with Lombardi about something they never openly discussed, a subject they both felt was best left unspoken—the always sensitive and intensely personal matter of religion. This was apparent when Landry's jaw would clench tighter as Lombardi would go off on some booze-fueled profane rant. Again, Landry was no prude, having said prayers during the war with men of all religions who couldn't have acted like choirboys on a bet. Still, that Lombardi was hot-blooded and Italian was not a sufficient excuse to blaspheme the Lord in nearly every sentence.

Nor, from where Landry sat, was it possible to ignore that the Lombardis' marriage was strained, with Vince often neglecting the woman in his life.[12] In fact, Lombardi's son, Vincent Thomas Lombardi Jr., who in 1956 was nine, later would endure the same neglect as he faced the pressure of being the scion of a living legend. "My father," he said, "wasn't always pleased with who he [was]. The time he spent in conversation with his God was an attempt to rec-oncile [being] a good person and what he knew he had to be to be successful."[13]

To Landry, given his vague sense of unease about missing some core value in his own life, Lombardi was a cautionary example. Landry too believed religion could ease his imperfect soul, but he had no impetus, or time, to explore it, though he surely would not have sought the cover of religion to gauze over those imperfections. As for Lombardi's inner rage, Vince himself may have had the best reason for why he behaved as erratically as he did, describing the football environment he lived within as a breeder of "madmen."[14] Yet it was precisely Lombardi's flaws that ironically benefited him more than Landry's uptight, ethereal propriety. Lombardi was far more a "player's coach," the proverbial mensch, than Landry could have ever been, which propelled Vince more urgently and ensured that if he won on his own, he would be seen and judged in deeply human terms. In the end both sensed that they needed to stay con-nected as best they could, lest they give in to the natural human temptation of wanting to succeed at the other's expense. They would work hard at not betraying any such impulse, and given how fast they were moving up the ladder, that may have been the hardest thing they ever did.

JIM LEE HOWELL, however, made it easier for them. His bombast may have been a way of justifying his presence, and compensating for there being little room for him to get in the way of Landry and Lombardi, and that he shouldn't even try. Because the results were so handsome, his laissez-faire approach became a model of leader-ship in a new era. As the *New York Times* noted upon reflection three years into Howell's term, "Like a good general, Howell [has] kept tabs on the whole affair, but left a good share of the work to his subordinates."[15] Red Smith, the sagacious *Herald Tribune* columnist, wrote of him as an "administrator and coordinator, and that appar-ently is the way to do the job today." The *New York Telegram*'s Joe King agreed that Howell had developed a "logical evolution" in the pros "to a peak of specialized skill."[16]

The "good general" tropes suited Howell just fine, given that his role as a cipher became something of a running joke for Giants players and observers. Mara was right about him. He required no great huzzahs for himself, nor did he need to be asked to praise his assistants by name. Landry, he would say, was "a perfectionist like Paul Brown," "a warm person but not with his players . . . he expects them to go out there and do their jobs," and "he's smarter than anyone."[17] Howell also codified Lombardi and Landry as equal partners by famously saying they were "as different as daylight and dark," and lauded them as a brain trust that made life delightfully easy for a head coach. Conversely, Howell never took a deep bow. "I would like to say I developed them," he once said, "[but] they had it when they came in . . . they were great coaches and fine people."[18]

Among the Giants, their bellowing figurehead made for much jocularity. Oft quoted in Giants literature was what Kyle Rote said in later years: that in the old days "I looked into Lombardi's room and he was working away on the offensive game plan. A few doors down, I looked into Landry's room and he was putting the finishing touches on the defensive game plan. At the end of the hall, I looked into Howell's room. Jim Lee was sitting back in a chair with his feet up on the table, reading the newspaper."[19] Howell himself made this sort of twittery in bounds, with the self-effacing one-liner that Gifford later attributed to him, and which became Howell's epitaph: "All I do is pump up the balls and blow the whistle."[20] Landry himself once noted that Howell had actually cribbed the line from his mentor Steve Owen, who had said, "A coach's job is to blow up the footballs and keep order, and that doesn't take much help."[21]

A more common assumption among historians is that Howell must have been a wise man indeed to oversee such a successful operation and play off the respective strengths and ambitions of Landry and Lombardi. It helped, to be sure, that he racked up a 53–27–4 record. And that was no accident. Howell counterbalanced his top deputies by lightening and taking the edge off their nitpicking perfectionism. Fearing that the players would be overworked and overtrained, Howell pulled rank when it came to practices, keeping them all but perfunctory, and these too became fodder for levity. In 1958 Effrat ran in the *Times* a half-jested example of a typical Giants practice:

Monday—Off.
Tuesday—Loosen Up. Easy does it.
Wednesday—Work hard.
Thursday—Work harder.
Friday—Start to taper off. Drill 1 hour 15 minutes.
Saturday—Complete tapering off. Drill 30 minutes.
Sunday—Hope for the best.[22]

Yet the team almost always came into games fresh and primed. And for his reputation, Howell had much to thank Landry. Unlike Lombardi, who said little of him, his defensive coach would describe Howell with much warmth, a rarity for Landry. Howell, he wrote in his autobiography, was "a long-legged, soft-spoken, teddy bear of a man," "a fine football man [with] great public relations skills," and "a gentleman who never had an ego problem." Landry also noted that Howell's way of "allow[ing] his coaches to learn what it took to become a head coach" was "something I struggled with and didn't do as well when I became a head coach." Rote's enduring image of Howell, Landry said, was "a misleading exaggeration."[23] Alicia Landry today speaks fondly of Howell, saying, "He was very smart. He let them do what they felt like doing because he saw how much they knew."[24]

Sam Huff, not a man to mince words, says this of his old head coach: "The thing about Jim Lee Howell pumping up the footballs, it was basically true. His pregame talk was to read the itinerary. He'd tell us what time the game would be over and, 'Don't be late on the bus 'cause we gotta catch the plane so get in there and shower.' But I will say this: Jim Lee Howell was smart because he let the two best coaches in the league coach and he got out of the way. I'll give him that." Indeed, Huff can look back and see Landry growing more and more in stature every year, if not always to appreciate what sort of influence he had. "Tom would never have thought of himself as a genius," Huff says. "He didn't see those times as anything special. Tom wasn't the type who would ever get sentimental about things—not like me, I'm a sentimental slob. I cry at anything. I cry thinking about how special those times were."

He goes on, "Tom should have relished it. We were making history, making the *league*. We didn't realize then how special it would be the rest of our lives, and I don't know if Tom ever did. I don't think he could ever see that he was doing more than coaching a defense. That's a little sad to me."

Landry would come to realize this too. "I didn't fully appreciate," he admitted, "the unique opportunity Vince and I had with the New York Giants until years later."[25]

IN 1956 the Giants finished 8–3–1 to win the Eastern Division (the league had gone back to Eastern and Western Divisions in 1953) in a year when the Otto Graham–less Browns fell to earth—albeit temporarily—and finished 5–7. It was the first time in their six seasons in the NFL that the Browns weren't a fixture in the championship game. That would be fought out between the Giants and Papa Bear Halas's "Monsters of the Midway," the Chicago Bears, who ironically enjoyed a renaissance after Halas gave up the coaching reins that year to sixty-one-year-old Paddy Driscoll, who had coached the original NFL Chicago Cardinals back in the 1920s (Halas would be back in 1958). Driscoll brought the Bears in at 9–2–1, not on the strength of their famous defense but on the tireless legs of fullback Rick Casares, who ran for a league-best 1,126 yards.

The title game, played on December 30, 1956, at Yankee Stadium, is today a bookmark in history, as the first real showcase of middle linebackers, Sam Huff and Bill George. At the time, the field seemed to be tilted toward the latter, who was only twenty-seven and at his peak, a unanimous All-Pro selection. Huff, on the other hand, was learning the ropes of Landry's more complex system. The black-and-blue aspect of what was expected—coincidentally, those were respectively the main colors of the Bears and Giants—became the theme of the reportage around the game, which, *New York Times* columnist Arthur Daley wrote, "will not be a demonstration of gentlemanly politeness."[26] In truth, the Giants were a far better balanced team. That season, they scored 99 fewer points but also allowed 49 fewer. As a unit, the defense had seventeen interceptions, split among *eight* players, led by Tunnell's six and Huff's three. Gifford rushed for 819 yards, caught fifty-one passes for 603 more yards, and scored nine touchdowns, one behind Alex Webster's total, and would win the league's MVP award. Charlie Conerly, coming off the bench to relieve a shaky Don Heinrich in every game, threw ten touchdowns and won back the fans.

The Giants, whose last game was on a Saturday, were able to send a scouting party to Chicago for the Bears' finale the following day, with Landry, assistant coach Ken Kavanaugh, Kyle Rote, and chief scout Jack Lavelle bringing back critical observations, such as that the Bears' top defensive back, J. C. Caroline, would come in at half-back.[27] The game was played amid frayed nerves because of a number of unexplained bomb scares around New York City, a pipe bomb having been found during the week in a phone booth at Grand Central Station and another one that would be found in a phone booth in the grandstand at Yankee Stadium. The game was also played in bad weather, twenty degrees with knife-stropped winds of thirty miles an hour, making for a day that *Sports Illustrated*'s top pro football writer, Tex Maule, described as "a gelid December afternoon."[28] The crowd for the event would be 56,836, some five thousand short of capacity in the gaping park.

The overconfident Giants seemed almost blasé about the clash. They dedicated only *one* day during the week to a full-blown practice, while the Bears had five, including one on Christmas Day. In the minutes before the game, Jim Lee Howell, whose wife had given birth the day before, was handing out cigars to his stooges in the press and seemed unconcerned about the field conditions. Outside, the turf had frozen over and was "as hard and slick as a slab of marble," as Landry would say.[29] When the players came out to warm up, they could not get traction with their cleats, slipping as if on ice skates. Fortunately, Wellington Mara had kept his eye on the weather reports during the week and had a strong sense of déjà vu.

As an eighteen-year-old, Mara had watched his father's Giants play the Sneakers Game over at the Polo Grounds. Now, repeating history, Mara had ordered dozens of pairs of rubber-soled Keds from Andy Robustelli, who owned a sporting goods store as a side business. This time the Giants came out wearing them and proceeded to skate by the unsure-footed Bears, who also had brought sneakers but didn't wear them until it was too late, when they were already out of the game, down 20–0 early in the second quarter. The Giants played with what sportswriter Jimmy Cannon called "a wild gladness."[30] They were at their peak on both sides of the ball. The two Bears quarterbacks, George Blanda and Ed Brown, completed twenty of forty-seven passes, with two interceptions. Casares ran fourteen times for 43 yards, Huff dogging him at every turn. Gifford, meanwhile, caught four passes out of the backfield for 131 yards, one for 67 yards; Alex Webster rumbled for two scores; and Landry's defense was impenetrable.

The final score, 47–7, excused the hyperbole it generated in the press. Gene Ward's *Daily News* game story read, "The Monsters of the Midway' were ground into the icy terrain of Yankee Stadium, their spirits spattered and their bodies battered by the Giants, who played as though they had wings on their sneakers." Before the game Bert Bell had threatened to levy fines for rough stuff; he needn't have worried. The Bears behaved like lambs brought to slaughter, a real disappointment to the more rabid onlookers. Effrat lamented that "the one-sided contest was not an unduly rough one. There wasn't a real fight all day."[31]

While almost fifty-seven thousand people might have seemed like a large crowd, the number actually underscored that as a big-time sport, pro football wasn't quite there in the Big Apple, at least not like it was in, say, Cleveland. As Gifford recalls pointedly, "For all New York's newfound love for the Giants, pro football still couldn't fill Yankee Stadium for a championship game. An NFL championship game not sold out!" Neither was the game the main story in some of the sports pages the next day. The *Post*, for one, placed it on the lower half of its sports page one, headlined "IT TOOK GIANTS ONLY 5 MINUTES TO WIN TITLE." The big story reflected a different sign of the times: Mississippi State's refusal to play in a basketball tournament in Kentucky against a New York team that included black players.[32] As well, Maule's *Sports Illustrated* take on the NFL game ran a mere six hundred words.

Despite the not-quite full house, the game was profitable. The gross receipt amounted to $517,385, including $205,000 from NBC to televise the game nationally. The winning players' share came to $3,779.19, a new league record, as was the losers' cut of $2,485.16.

But for Tom Landry, who could not have known that he and his middle linebacker were about to become billboard headliners, there was no great feeling of portentousness about the championship. That night, the rest of the team engaged in the rites of victory. Gifford was brought out on stage by Ed Sullivan and glad-handed. Nearly the entire team gathered at Toots Shor's, where they were given the entire back of the joint for boozing, carousing, and toasting. Instead, Landry began to pack up for the trip home to Texas with the family.

Tom Landry Jr., who was only seven at the time, remembers that moment of beatification as if it were yesterday: "I was standing with my mom in the Stadium Club after the game, waiting for dad to come in, and when he did everyone in there stood up and cheered him, because it was really his defense that had won the championship. Oh, he was pleased, you could tell that. But to him, you know, that was just his job. Even then he was a very controlled man."[33] Alicia Landry adds that while her husband never let his facade crack at such memorable milestones, she could sense relief more than personal vindication. "Those were the times when the weight of the world was off his shoulders—at least until the next game."

Landry himself would later say that championship games never really seemed climactic. Because football preparation was year-round, he did not see the sport as composed of distinct seasons but rather as a continual cycle, with no beginning and no end. Sometimes championship games would be a letdown, even in victory. In his memoirs he would recall the malaise he found himself in 1956 as everyone else around him was giddy with exhilaration. "Despite the thrill" of victory, he wrote, "the accomplishment left me feeling strangely unsettled and unsatisfied."[34]

VICTORY DID bring some comforting spoils. "We all became toasts of the town," Alicia Landry says of the fawning that accrued to the Giants in the wake of their title, such as the tables that would be held in reserve at popular establishments. They became regulars at the chichi watering holes like Mike Manuche's, P.J. Clarke's, and Jack Dempsey's, and down at Toots Shor's there was even a bonus for the normally overshadowed defense. "Toots loved the defensive guys," Sam Huff says. "Toots knew the game, and he'd put us up front, at the best tables. We got our drinks before Frank did! He'd put the offensive guys way in the back, next to the toilets." Not that Gifford was suffering; everywhere else he was being bathed in adulation and offered moneymaking opportunities, such as in commercials for Lucky Strike cigarettes and Arrow shirts. Kyle Rote, another handsome and articulate hunk, was soon doing sports reports on local television in the off-season. All of these perks were not merely for vanity's sake but necessary given Wellington Mara's habitual penury, which Huff says never turned into magnanimity.

"In 1956, I was the defensive rookie of the year and we won the championship. I was making $6,000, and when Wellington gave me my next year's contract he gave me a $50 raise. Fifty dollars! I was barely making enough to pay my rent. I said, 'You're giving me *$50!*?' and he thought I was thrilled. He said, 'Sam, I think you're worth it.' I told him, 'Mr. Mara, I need more than that, 500.' And I got it, too. *That* shocked me." If not on the players, Mara did spend some good coin on the operation. The Giants organization was unarguably in the big league now. It had two team doctors and three dentists as well as a handsome office suite on Fifth Avenue. The *New York Times* lionized Tim Mara whose "vision and patience are paying off now,"[35] his original $2,500 investment having been parlayed into a profitable concern. And Landry's defensive line had turned into a star chamber.

Robustelli and Grier were named to the All-Pro first team in 1956, as was Tunnell. (Huff lost out to Bill George.) But adulation is a fickle thing, wholly dependent on success, as the Giants learned in 1957. That year, as defending champs, they faltered. They lost the opener to the Browns in a 6–3 defensive war, before shifting into high gear and winning seven of their next eight games. Finishing badly, the Giants dropped the final three, to the 49ers, Steelers, and the eventual champion Browns, and ended the season with a 7–5 record.

The Giants' stumble, however, was through no fault of Landry's defense, which yielded only 17.6 points a game; Lombardi's offense stalled slightly but enough to account for the key defeats. The defensive unit had another year under their belts and ascended in the public eye, unlike their unsung coach. Dick Nolan, for example, didn't make the All-Pro team but earned a profile in the *New York Times* by Gay Talese, who had just begun his career as a sportswriter before moving upward to the pages of *Esquire* and then writing best-selling books. In hailing Nolan as a "defensive expert," Talese gave the quiet Texan who tutored him his first real shoutout in the press: "Other players before him [Nolan] have had to assume equally unromantic roles, to wit: Tom Landry. He played defensive halfback on the Giants for six years and never received a piece of fan mail. 'In six years, nobody ever asked for Landry's picture,' said a Giants' publicity agent. 'Now Landry is one of Howell's assistant coaches, and he is even more obscure.'"[36]

AFTER THE move to the Bronx, the Landrys took up residence for a time at the Concourse Plaza Hotel, mere steps from Yankee Stadium and in the shadow of the massive Bronx County Courthouse, which loomed behind the rightfield bleachers. An opulent place when it opened in 1923, the twelve-story hotel had begun to lose its luster, as had the neighborhood, made up of predominantly immigrant Jews and their first- and second-generation American offspring. By the end of the decade, the Concourse Plaza would be abandoned by the large number of Yankees and Giants players who lived there with their families in-season, and soon after would become a welfare hotel. For the Landrys of Texas, it was something like their old dorms in Austin. There, in close quarters with other Giants itinerants and their families, the wives washed their husbands' uniforms after each game, something they had to do themselves because Mara wouldn't pay anyone to do the team's laundry.

"A very family kind of atmosphere," is how Alicia Landry remembers the Concourse Plaza. "We must have walked up that hill a thousand times. The stores there all knew us. There was a grocery store we loved that you could just call and tell them what vegetables you wanted, and they'd send someone to the hotel with them." It was all very homey. Before most of the players had a car, much less a driver at their disposal, Frank Gifford, married then to his first wife, Maxine, would pick up their children and other players' children at a school a few blocks away and walk them back up the hill like a scout troop.

An occasional cosmopolitan breeze blew through those musty

corridors. Gifford remembers a few famous folks, such as David Niven and Gordon MacRae, staying at the Concourse in its fading glory. Jaws hung open when Ernest Hemingway once came through the door. A VIP of sorts in her own right was Charlie Conerly's wife, Perian, a blonde and strikingly beautiful southern belle who had become a gadabout socialite in the big city. In the early 1950s she began to write a society column for her small hometown newspaper in Mississippi. By the mid-1950s, the column was being syndicated in major newspapers. In *her* Plaza Hotel, the staff meticulously packed her expensive silverware each late December until she returned the next fall.[37]

Perian Conerly was a kind of Pied Piper for other Giants wives not so well versed in socialite tastes, such as they were in the Bronx. As Alicia Landry recalls, that included tromping over to the courthouse and sitting en masse in a courtroom to watch murder trials. Their favorite day of the week wasn't necessarily Sunday, when they would be planted as a group at the games in seats with no cover against rain and snow, but Wednesday, which was matinee day on Broadway. With the kids in school, they would follow Perian into the subway and go to the latest hot show, where, unable to afford good seats, they would each pay a dollar and a half for a standing-room ticket.

Much as Tom and Alicia enjoyed the city vibe, the concrete jungle began to lose some appeal. The old splendor of the Concourse Plaza was hard to appreciate when the room had no kitchen, dinner was cooked on a hot plate, and the dishes were washed in the bathtub. For Tom, little of this mattered so long as he had an extra room to set up his projector. That room would inevitably be dubbed "Landry's Lab" by players who were roped into coming by each night for supplemental, after-hours film-watching sessions— a ritual Sam Huff always dreaded but profited from. "I learned more football in Tom's apartment than I'd learned all through high school and college," he says.

However, for Alicia the collegiality of living in the Bronx dimmed fast, especially when there was literally no place for their kids to play. "There was a park down the street, but one day a policeman came over and said, 'Tell those kids to quit playing in the park because they're killing the grass.' Imagine that." When they would return for the 1957 season, it was not to the Concourse Plaza. Instead, they were back downtown at the Excelsior Hotel, where Tom Jr. and Kitty's playground was suitably Texas-sized—Central Park itself. Even so, she says, "Tommy and I were starting to get itchy about wanting to stay home all year. We never said anything, and for Tommy it would have been a ticklish situation because he was so important to the team, but I think Giants management probably could sense that something was gonna give soon, and that keeping Tom might be a problem."

Their upward mobility in New York was mirrored back home. When he returned after the 1957 season, the brood was on the move again. Alicia's father, his business done in Houston, returned to Dallas, and the Landrys followed, buying a home in the Lake Highlands section of northeast Dallas. Amazingly, even as an elite coaching assistant in the NFL, Landry was still buttressing his income by selling insurance for Herb Wiggs. Fortunately, this time, he and Alicia had timed their family planning right. On March 4, 1958, she gave birth to another daughter, Lisa. With residual guilt about not seeing his first two children born or able to spend time with them until months after, he now hovered around and doted on Lisa. Still, he would recall, "I wanted to make up for missing Tom Jr.'s and Kitty's birth. But I knew I couldn't. And the reminder of how my football career had disrupted our family life increased my determination to build another career that would better provide for my family and allow us to live in Texas all year round."[38]

The Giants' owners didn't know it in New York, but Landry had already made up his mind to leave the team. In fact, had they known, Wellington Mara might have had to make a decision he was loath to make, one that would induce Landry to stay. Instead, Mara, feeling no great urgency to disturb the status quo, kept Jim Lee Howell securely in place. One reason was that Mara didn't want to have to choose between Landry and Lombardi as the one he should elevate to head coach. Mara simply trusted that both would be around as long as he needed them to be. He never dreamed either would go anywhere.

When Landry came north for the 1958 season, he steered clear of the now-dimming seductions of Manhattan. He rented a small house in Stamford, Connecticut, not far from Andy Robustell's home, with whom he would carpool down the New York State Thruway or take the train, which stopped at Yankee Stadium. Sometimes they would be joined by another neighbor in those parts, a headache-inducing, self-promoting man named Howard Cosell, a rising radio and some-time TV sportscaster who liked to play favorites, according to which athletes and coaches aggrandized him. Many in the sporting crowd detested him. Landry tolerated him as a kind of sociological study of the species called the "New York Jew." As with his black, Jewish, and Catholic peers, Landry would study men like this, learn what made them tick, then bid them farewell without ever really forming a personal attachment. He also might have appreciated that a new era in sports culture was almost upon him, an era that would neatly accommodate, elevate, and even venerate people who made a ruckus around themselves.

That was something Landry would never do himself. No matter where he called home, there was a studied consistency in his lifestyle, entirely centered on his family and football, if not always in that order. "One thing about Tommy," says his widow, "he always had breakfast and dinner at home. No matter what he had to do, he'd make time. He wanted to maintain a normal family life." If it seemed like he was overdoing it on that count, it was probably because he was actually more isolated from the family than ever. What's more, he knew it. Which was why he was now prepared to make a change in his life, in a couple of important ways, a change he hoped would resolve that nagging "unsatisfactory" feeling.

Chapter 8

"LORD, I NEED YOUR HELP TODAY"

TIME AND TIDE WAITED FOR no man in 1958. When pro football found itself pulled into the modern era of American culture, Tom Landry was burrowing deeper into the profession he had doubted could ever take him to a higher level of self-reward. This was good timing, as his life was now a fuller spectrum than it had ever been. The birth of Lisa Landry that March was only the beginning of a chain of events and revelations that would escort him through the rest of his life. As it was for him, 1958 arose as a crucial crossroads for the NFL and for its great urban hope, the Giants. After the downer of 1957, another also-ran season would likely have been cause for some housecleaning on the team and for the reputations of Landry and Lombardi to have taken a hit. The way the season began, Landry recalled, "I wished I had stayed in Texas."[1] The Giants, still mired in the mud of the previous season, lost five of six summer exhibition games. The first hurdle of the regular season was the Browns, who seemed primed for another dynasty.

The biggest reason was Jimmy Brown, who, as a 220-pound guided missile, made offenses shudder. Brown, who never looked like he was hurrying until he got the ball, had an uncanny ability to shift gears on pure instinct. He could become either a sprinter in the open field or a human battering ram pulverizing tacklers with a stiff-arm or a helmet into the chest. No amount of strategy could slow, much less stop him. "When Jimmy Brown came to the Browns," says Huff, "he lined up right behind the quarterback. There was no trickery to it. You knew what he was going to do. We called that formation 'Brown,' for him, and when we did call it, we just hoped and prayed. I never played against anyone who made me feel that way—scared to death."[2]

The two of them would become enmeshed in a serial drama, a romanticized battle royal in which victory and defeat would be traced directly, if simplistically, to which one got the best of the other. No matter that sixty men or so played the game—all eyes were on two numbers: 32 and 70. Brown had won those tangos twice in 1957, and portentously for Huff, in 1958 most football pundits had just about given up on the Giants' ability to revive themselves. Huff and Landry took that personally, and it became a major theme in a wider lens. Before the two teams met for their first game, on November 2 in Cleveland, Arthur Daley noted that "the burly blond from the West Virginia hills undoubtedly will dog Brown every inch of the way."[3]

And he did. That day in Municipal Stadium, Brown ran for 113 yards, but on only thirteen carries because Lombardi's offense controlled the ball, getting off sixty-eight plays to the Browns' thirty-six. Mel Triplett, running for 116 yards, outgained Brown, and the Giants rang up 337 yards while giving up 201. Still it took until Conerly's third touchdown pass, and second one to Alex Webster, late in the game before they put it away, 21–17. At that point the Giants' record was 4–2, the Browns' 5–1. By the time they met again, at Yankee Stadium in the season's climactic game, the Eastern Division was riding on the outcome. The Giants had kept pace, winning six out of their next seven games, including a tremendous victory, 24–21, over the league's newest rising power, the Baltimore Colts, thanks to a late field goal by veteran kicker Pat Summerall. By then, there was a discernible rush of excitement to Giants games at Yankee Stadium, with crowds rhythmically chanting, "Dee-fense! Dee-fense!" and sometimes, "Huff! Huff! Huff!"—a phenomenon that Landry traced as the genesis of public consciousness about what really won games. Huff indeed was reaping the rewards, being named to the All-Pro first team in 1958 and 1959.

Entering the final Sunday, the Browns were 9–2 and the Giants

8–3, but having won their earlier match, the Giants, with a win, could sneak past the Browns—even though if they did, the Giants would have to play the Browns again the very next Sunday to determine the division champ. A snowstorm dropped six inches on the field, but it deterred neither the fans, 63,192 of whom showed up, nor the redoubtable Jimmy Brown. On the first series, Brown took the ball, broke a tackle by Huff, and rambled 65 yards for a touchdown, his record-tying eighteenth of the season. Brown ran for 148 yards in all, but his team would not again get into the end zone. In the fourth quarter, with ten minutes left, the Giants tied the game at 10–10 on a nifty option pass from Gifford to Bob Schnelker. Five minutes later, they moved into field-goal range, but in the mounting snow, Summerall missed from the 25-yard line. At two minutes the Giants got one last shot, taking the ball at the Browns' 43. After three incomplete passes, it was fourth and ten. Most everyone believed that Coach Howell had to go for it, seeing that a 49-yard field goal in these conditions was folly. Lombardi assumed so, and grew apoplectic when Howell sent in the kicker. Lombardi briefly argued, then walked contemptuously away, arms folded, when the decision was made.

Summerall had endlessly worked out the delicate synchronization of the snap and kick process with Charlie Conerly, the ball holder. But Summerall had been injured in the last game and hadn't kicked at all during the week, nor did he handle the kickoffs that day. When he got to the huddle, Conerly blinked. "What the hell are you doing out here?" he said to Summerall, who nonetheless proceeded to calmly drive the kick of his life, the ball floating as if forever through the flakes and darkening sky before finally nestling between the goal posts. "It was the most remarkable field goal I ever witnessed," Landry would recall. Lombardi sheepishly ran out to glad-hand Summerall. "You son of a bitch," he twitted, "you know you can't kick a ball that far."[4] Landry, in character, never did glad-hand the kicker, who had come to know that was par for the course. "I knew," he said, "not to take it personally. That was Tom."

Part *deux* of the dance—same teams, same site, same big crowd— a week later needed no such drama. It was a resounding triumph for Landry, his defense throttling Brown as never had been done before nor ever would be done thereafter. With Huff stuck to him like lacquer, Brown gained 8 yards on seven carries. Meanwhile the Giants ran wild, rushing for 211 yards, so controlling the ball that not only Gifford and Webster ate up 157 yards but Triplett and spare halfback Phil King also outrushed Brown. The old warhorse Conerly rubbed it in, dashing for a 10-yard touchdown.

Knowing the Browns had to go to the pass, Landry's men had fun with quarterback Milt Plum, sacking him six times and intercepting him three times, once by the ubiquitous Huff. The 10 points the Giants put up in the first half were all they needed. They shut out the Browns as they had in 1950, exactly 101 games ago—the last time Paul Brown had suffered such a humiliation.

This was the Landry defense *in excelsis*—as the Browns' kicker Lou Groza said, "Only one man could have done that to us. Tom Landry."[5] After the game, Robustelli quieted the locker room and to great huzzahs presented the ceremonial game ball to the defensive coach, something that was, Landry would say, "one of my proudest moments ever in sports"[6]—albeit something he never did in kind with any of them. For Tom Landry, being able to single out anyone for praise, or to get even a little emotional over such football mimes like awarding a game ball, wasn't in his DNA.

BEATING THE Browns on consecutive Sundays may have seemed worth a trophy, but the third straight Sunday would bring an even stiffer test—as Howell scribbled on his chalkboard that week, "Next the Colts!" By now, no team was scarier, the Colts having been purposely built from scratch since a Baltimore shirt-company owner, Carroll Rosenbloom, paid $200,000 for the charred remains of pro football's first team in Dallas. Under head coach Wilbur "Weeb" Ewbank, a dwarfish, chubby-cheeked gnome and Paul Brown protégé, the Colts became a machine that cruised to the Western Division title, riding the mortar arm of former Steelers reject Johnny Unitas.

The spindly legged Unitas, behind an offensive line anchored by massive tackle Jim Parker, was able to thread passes mainly to the bookish Raymond Berry, whose astigmatism didn't keep him from grabbing the ball while running precise patterns. When defenses geared for the pass, 218-pound fullback Alan "The Horse" Ameche rumbled for big yards. The Colts' defense was just as daunting. Ewbank had appropriated Landry's 4–3 scheme, with second-year pro Don Shinnick the man in the middle. The Colts' defensive front, led by the magnificent end Gino Marchetti, beer-bellied Bronx native Art Donovan, and ill-fated Gene "Big Daddy" Lipscomb, looked like a Sumo wrestling team. Stacked against this cast, the Giants seemed almost Lilliputian. Before the game Lombardi remarked, "If anyone had told me two months ago that we'd be here today in the playoff I'd have asked him to give me a whiff of the opium pipe he was smoking." It was Landry's defense that got them there; as Daley wrote, "Tom Landry, a defensive genius, molded his platoon into a superlative unit."[7]

This time the weather was balmy, in the fifties, and three days after Christmas the stands were packed with 64,185 rabid fans. But inside the Giants' locker room things were hotter. The team held a vote on apportioning shares of the playoff money, and Frank Gifford talked most of the team into approving a full share for backup quarterback Jack Kemp, though he had spent the season on the taxi squad. Sam Huff, who always had a grudge about not making enough money, objected, leading to what Gifford called a "fight," the extent of which he has never specified and one that Huff says never happened.[8] Something, however, stoked Huff because he made two huge plays in the first half, forcing Unitas to fumble on the Colts' initial drive, then blocking a field goal attempt on their second drive. The Giants also intercepted a Unitas pass. But they too were slipshod. Heinrich threw an early interception, bringing old man Conerly off the bench. After the Giants took a 3–0 lead, Gifford imploded, fumbling twice in consecutive series, leading to a 14–3 Colts' lead.

The Colts owned the stat sheet on this day, with their offense gaining 452 yards to the Giants' 266. Unitas strafed Landry's secondary for 349 yards, twelve of his passes going to Berry for 178 yards. In an odd vibe, the Colts at times seemed to be playing at home, as they had brought their cheerleaders, marching band, and hordes of fans dressed in Colts regalia, including kooky antler-eared hats. Yet the Giants didn't crumble under pressure. Landry's boys stopped the Colts on the 1-yard line early in the third quarter, and Conerly took his team 99 yards down the field, aided by an electrifying 86-yard play in which Kyle Rote reeled in a pass deep downfield and fumbled, only for Webster to scoop the ball up and run to the 1. Mel Triplett took it over the goal line to make the score 14–10. The Giants then took the lead when Conerly threw a 15-yard strike to Gifford.

As the clock ticked down to another championship, Landry's charges were superlative. Late in the fourth quarter, when the Colts moved to the Giants' 27-yard line, Robustelli and then Modzelewski sacked Unitas, taking the Colts out of field-goal range. The Giants needed only a first down to run out the clock. Lombardi called a sweep by Gifford right toward Marchetti, who as he clutched at Gifford felt a heavy load. It was Big Daddy Lipscomb crashing down on him, shattering Marchetti's ankle. As Gino was carted off the field, referee Ron Gibbs made a gravely imprecise spot of the ball, placing it inches short of a first down, prompting howls from Gifford. (Gifford claimed years later that just before Gibbs died, he admitted that "maybe Frank was right.")[9] Now, with the ball on their own 40-yard line and around two minutes left in the game, Howell made a decision that would be second-guessed interminably. He refused to gamble and had the Giants punt the ball, to deafening boos from the fans. Unitas started with the ball on his own 14.

Landry's defense needed to come up big, just one more time. But Unitas, in a masterful use of the clock later defined as a "two-minute drill," methodically chewed up yardage. He found Berry three times in the open, and got the team close enough for the Colts to kick the tying field goal with seven seconds left. Watching the kick sail through the uprights, Huff cursed the fates but wasn't entirely crushed. Believing the game, and season, were over, ending in a tie, he said to Gibbs, "I'm going home happy, we're both getting winning shares."

"Not yet," the ref replied.

"Holy Christ," Huff, eyes imploring otherwise, told him, "you mean we keep playing?!"

Impossible as it seems now, most players had not the slightest idea that there was a sudden-death overtime, there being no such provision for regular-season games that ended in a tie. At midfield, Gibbs explained the rule to the captains, and the game began anew after the Giants won the coin toss. As twilight was falling, and with it a cold, gloomy, surreal backdrop in the now-lit park, an exhausted Huff wondered how he would be able to go back out on the field. "We'd shut 'em down, but when you play an overtime . . . it's like you gear yourself to play sixty minutes. You give everything you've got. You're tired, you're miserable. You had to stop those guys all over again, the greatest quarterback that ever played. How do you stop Unitas? You'd have to shoot him."

The Giants took the ball on their own 20 in overtime, moved it to the 29, and on fourth down, Howell—this time much more logically—again played it safe and punted. The 69-yard cannon shot by Don Chandler backed the Colts up to their 20-yard line, from where Unitas once more piloted his team downfield. They moved so breezily that a field goal wasn't ever a consideration. Lacking the usual Landry discipline, the Giants' incredibly hard-working defense was out of gas. Finally it was third and goal from the one. As Huff remembers, "We were all up on the line. I was down in a three-point goal-line stance, on the inside shoulder of Rosie, but I guessed wrong. Ameche came off tackle outside of Rosie, and he was a hell of a running back. Jim Parker opened the hole for him and that was it."

After all these years, Huff's memory is still a bit clouded about that moment, which he would rather forget. Rosie Grier, injured in the second half, was actually gone by then. And while Parker did take out his man, the biggest block was made by Jim Mutscheller, who took out *three* Giants, knocking Cliff Livingston sideways into Katcavage and Modzelewski. Lenny Moore, not known for his blocking, took care of Em Tunnell, who was also up on the line but not anywhere near Ameche when he barreled, untouched, into the end zone at the 8:15 mark. For a split-second, all was silent. Then a crowd of Colts fans rushed over and surrounded Ameche in glee. The Giants, still not sure it was all over, slowly began to wander off the field, in a daze.

In the papers the next day, the drama was framed by an instantly famous AP photo of Ameche, head bowed, coming right to the camera through that massive hole, the image of which took up nearly the entire back page of the *Daily News*. Much of the post mortem centered on Howell's decision to punt on fourth down when the

Giants were leading by 3. Unlike the fans, though, Arthur Daley, as most in the press, cut slack to the coach who was so good to them, and wrote that it would have been "sheer idiocy" and "madness" for Howell to have tried for a first down; Red Smith agreed that the call "seemed wise." Daley, reaching for something metrical, summed up the afternoon by positing that if the game "wasn't the most exciting football game ever played, it will do until an even more implausible cliff-hanger is performed. This was one for the books, an unforgettable episode crammed to the gunwales with dramatics and heroics. . . . This was a football game. Wow!"[10]

However, because it had been so riveting and seesaw, the plot thickening in so novelistic a manner, the black-and-white images so boldly cut into the fabric of a culture falling under the spell of bodies in motion, both balletic and brutal, this game begged for a more definitive statement. And it was Tex Maule who provided one. In his review of the game in the January 5, 1959, issue of *Sports Illustrated*, the headline "THE BEST FOOTBALL GAME EVER PLAYED" stretched across a double-truck display, the story given not a few paragraphs but five full pages of text and dramatic photographs, the last its own freeze-frame of Ameche on the ground in the end zone. Maule's lead read, "Never has there been a game like this," and the last sentence belonged to Ray Berry, who said, "It was the greatest thing that ever happened." Soon, that would indeed be the coda forevermore for those three hours of revelatory midwinter madness in the Bronx.

But was it the greatest game ever played? The question would be asked increasingly in future years as that facile conclusion began to be scrutinized in light of the sloppiness of play and the urgency to brand the contest, and the sport, with a metaphoric exclamation point. Huff brushes the question off, though for reasons of his own bias. "It was the only championship game to end in a tie," he insists. "Does that make it the greatest? Didn't make it the greatest to me. It ended in a goddamn tie!" Landry, who had to be crushed that his lieges had been so gritty but couldn't make the big stop, and who typically betrayed no emotion after the game, on his part made no particular effort to be elegiac about the proceedings. In his memoirs he dryly recounted the basic details with no embellishment other than that the contest was a "legendary milestone in the history of the sport," one that "by thrilling millions of television viewers marked the time and place when America discovered professional football."[11]

All those who had participated in the game knew well that on an artistic level it was far inferior to others before it, and a good deal many after it. But Landry was right that the game certainly was a belated "Where have you been all my life?" prophecy for television viewers who might have only been semi-sentient about the sport before. Pro football was now hopelessly addicted to TV, and vice versa. The audience that day grew to 45 million, even with the broadcast blacked out in New York, as viewers took to calling others saying, "You gotta see this!" Though, with grotesque mistiming, the video signal had gone out briefly late in the game, only to be recovered in time for the last run, to the massive relief of the network and Bert Bell.

When NBC had paid $1 million for a five-year exclusive on the championship game, it seemed risky to some media wags. Now it seemed like a bargain, given the increased rates for commercial time the network would be able to charge. It also was of inestimable value to the main protagonists, mostly Unitas, whose eighteen-year career was rife with achievement, including three MVP awards and ten Pro Bowl appearances. But so would it be for all eleven future Hall of Famers who roamed the field that day: five Giants—Gifford, Huff, Brown, Robustelli, and Tunnell; and six Colts—Unitas, Berry, Moore, Parker, Marchetti, and Donovan (Ewbank, too, who won arguably the *second*-most fabled game ever, as well, with another team in New York a decade later). And it would open the door for two other men who were seen fleetingly on sideline shots. One would walk through that door within weeks, the other within sixteen months.

LOMBARDI KEPT it to himself, but he knew that he was a lame-duck assistant coach for most of the 1958 season. Either he was going to be the Giants' head coach in 1959 or he would leave. He was hardly sentimental about staying with his old school chum Wellington in gratitude for giving him a job when no one else would. Only days after the game against the Colts, the Green Bay Packers requested permission to broach Lombardi about becoming their new head coach after a miserable 1–10–1 season. Lombardi had a year left on his contract, but the Maras knew they were in a bind. Jim Lee Howell, coming off a great year, was secure, but Lombardi's value was high in football circles. While the Maras might have gotten How-ell to take one for the team and accept a cushy front-office job, they hedged. At first trying to pull a shuffle on Packers owner Dominic Olejniczak, they slyly suggested that the Packers could instead have another of their brilliant coaches—the one named Landry.[12] This certainly signaled that the Maras held Vince in higher regard, some-thing that did not get by Landry. Worse, Olejniczak, declining the gracious offer, said he wanted to talk to Lombardi first.

That's when the the Maras knew they had lost him, but they had one more card to play. As a condition for letting Vince go, the Giants wanted the Packers to agree to let the Giants petition Lombardi about coming back to New York if they wanted a new coach. Their thinking was obvious—that for Vince there would be no upside in Green Bay, which had the league's smallest market and the worst win-ters, as well as a team thought to be beyond repair. What's more, Lombardi himself was a bit hedgy. With Red Blaik retiring at Army, the job Lombardi really lusted after was open, and he began discus-sions with the brass there, only to be shot down with the same excuse they had once assured him didn't exist: that Army hired only their own kind, former cadets. Seething, Lombardi believed it was really because his "last name ended in a vowel,"[13] and, sulking all the way, agreed to terms with the Packers.

Lombardi was indeed ambivalent about going from the Big Apple to a place so quaint that the stockholders of the team were the citi-zenry of the town. The Packers had made sure to feed his ego and need for control by making him a virtual czar, his word immediate law. Yet for the first couple of years, he went back and forth about whether he would stay, confiding to friends back in New York that the Giants' top job might be very attractive to him. On February 16, 1959, two weeks to the day after Lombardi signed his new contract in Green Bay, Tim Mara, the Giants' patriarch, died at age seventy-one, meaning that the team had lost both its father figure and its favorite son. The Giants had a good deal left with which to go on, but the truth was that no matter how good the defensive coach was, or what his ambitions and intentions were, a pale, soft-spoken Methodist from Texas could never have replaced an emotional Catholic from New York as a son, and quite likely as a head coach.

LANDRY'S OWN expatriation from the Giants had been portended as far back as 1951, when there was a pitiful attempt to bring pro football to Texas for the first time. The failure was so big that the impoverished Dallas Texans didn't even make it through the season. With five games left, the league relocated the team to *Hershey, Pennsylvania*, amid the Amish, who had no idea what football was, and had them play out the schedule on the road. After that 1–11 season, Carroll Rosenbloom annexed the franchise, which, as the Colts, would rule a half decade later. Down in Red River country, meanwhile, a family of oil barons and real estate venture capitalists would make it their business to feed a geographic nationalism and create a *big* success of it. Most set on the idea was Clint Murchison Jr. (in the Lone Star dialectic, it was pronounced "Murkison"), who was only in his early thirties but had the boundless ambition and deep pockets of his daddy, the quintessential oil man tintype Clint Murchison Sr.

The latter was a millionaire many times over and unafraid to use his money to crush people he didn't cotton to. Those people turned out to be mainly Democrats, all of whom he took to be Communists. Thus Murchison Sr. became a natural ally to the FBI director J. Edgar Hoover and was able to bankroll smear campaigns. In return, Hoover and his companion Clyde Tolson invested heavily in Murchison's oil business.[14] The elder Murchison set up his sons, Clinton Williams Murchison Jr. and John Dabney Murchison, in real estate, and by 1956 they were thriving, having branched out into publishing and construction, and on the periphery of sports. Whereas Clint Sr. was a self-made good ol' boy, Clint Jr. rode the gravy train through academia, with an impressive detour as a fighter pilot in World War II. Eschewing a commission when the war ended, he and his brother returned stateside, John to Yale, Clint to MIT to earn his master's degree in math, where he got straight A's.

Many called Clint Jr. a genius. Preferring to hang with fellow intellectuals, he would take his private Lear jet to New York and Boston for white-glove affairs at the Yale, Harvard, and Dartmouth clubs. He loved meeting up with other MIT alumni over dinner, to discuss scientific theories and the latest peer-reviewed papers. But whenever the topic would turn to social matters, he would clam up, as if afraid of his own shadow—an image not recognizable behind closed doors, where he was anything but a milquetoast. Though he had married early, Clint Jr. carried out a string of affairs, many of his conquests having been pimped by his best friend, Bedford Wynne, the son of Clint Sr.'s business partner Toddie Lee Wynne. The latter's other son, Toddie Jr., also became interlocked with Clint Jr., keeping his secrets and forming an inner circle that shared his profits.[15]

In Texas a man is supposed to have the cold, steely nerves and reckless daring of a riverboat gambler, and the younger Clint had that gene for sure. In 1956, he won a mention in *Sports Illustrated*, not for any sporting reason but because of his ruthless eviction of a surfing club in Hawaii so he could build a hotel and condos on the grounds.[16] Yet as cold and cutthroat as he was in business, to Clint Sr. he seemed too antisocial, too brainy, and too impetuous. The old man often had to finish some deal or other that his boy had begun, only to tire of it or forget about it. Such behavior, which once led to Clint Jr. losing $500,000 on a bad real estate deal, had convinced the head of the clan that his namesake was a ten-gallon risk—"unbalanced" and "erratic"[17] were his words for him—and when the latter began sniffing around for a pro football team to own, big Clint would have nothing to do with it. The idea seemed that dumb.

Clint Jr. accepted the challenge as a way to prove something to the old man. Frail as the son appeared, he had actually played football at MIT. Looking to the pros for the first time in 1952, when he was only twenty-nine, Murchison seriously contemplated putting in a bid for the moribund Dallas Texans franchise. But when he asked Bert Bell for twenty-four hours to put together a proposal, Bell committed to a bid from Rosenbloom. Not giving up, Murchison subsequently tried in vain to buy a minority interest in the Washington Redskins. Then in 1954, when the San Francisco 49ers were up for sale, he entered the fray, wanting to move the team to Dallas. But that failed too. Next Murchison saw an opening in 1958 to buy the Redskins outright from George Preston Marshall, again with the idea of moving the team to Dallas. The deal would be for $600,000, and it would permit Marshall to continue running the club for five years, but just before the papers were inked, Marshall demanded the duration be increased to ten years. "Tell him to go to hell," Murchison told people close to Marshall. "The deal's off."[18]

After coming so close, Murchison would eventually hit paydirt with a more direct route: looking toward his own backyard, vowing that he would put a homegrown team deep in the heart of Texas, thereby tapping a gigantic, still untapped market. And even though Clint Murchison Jr. knew little of Tom Landry, nor Landry of him, time and tide were about to conjoin them.

BY 1959, Tom Jr. and Kitty were no longer tots, and going to school in different cities was confusing. "We felt like we were perpetually in a revolving door," the son recalls. "Constancy was a big thing in dad's life, and yet my sister and I would go from playing in wide open spaces to playing on the roof of a hotel."[19] While Landry had committed to the game by becoming a coach, he had seen little trickle down in the way of benefits from the Maras, who were making money hand over fist. Neither did Howell seem to be going anywhere fast. As Landry had sensed, America had discovered pro football, and he had established an unmistakable imprint on it. Yet he was fast coming to the conclusion that his shelf life as a coach would expire, and he would then need to find another line of work. It wasn't just the Giants in which he saw no future; it was pro football itself that had little upside. "I was planning on leaving football altogether," he would say years later. "I'd done everything I'd ever wanted to do in football. And because there was no 'next level' I wanted to achieve, I found myself with no clear direction in life, no purpose. . . . I felt I'd reached a major crossroads in my life, but I didn't have a clue as to which way I should go."[20]

WHAT WOULD point the way for him came a few weeks after he had returned to Dallas following the Colts game, when he stumbled on an answer to what it was that put him in the malaise he couldn't shake. As Frank Gifford said, Landry was "cool and calculating," and "always appeared to be looking beyond the game itself, searching for an unknown key. He had to know why things happened."[21] Nothing that Landry had rationalized about his overall life, however, could balance the crudities and contradictions—and hypocrisies— of his profession with the sense of order and morality he demanded for himself, and it was even more disconnecting that his faith had become a mere habit. Indeed, he thought little of it when, as winter gave way to spring, a friend named Frank Phillips asked if he wanted to come to a prayer breakfast at the Melrose Hotel in downtown Dallas.

"I wasn't at all interested," Landry recalled. But still he went, eating bacon and eggs with forty or so businessmen before the workday began, and then listening to a few of them read from and interpret the Bible. The first discussion, he remembered, centered on the Sermon on the Mount, from the Book of Matthew. At the time, for all of the rituals of his church-going, he had rarely read the Bible. When he had, he admitted, it had been "confusing and irrelevant." For some reason, that morning "the meaning of Jesus' words . . . seemed to jump right off the page at me," perhaps the most trenchant being the passage about the rains, floods, and winds that "beat upon the house; and it fell not: for it was founded on a rock."[22] In the years to come, he would metaphorize that rock often, as if it were his Gibraltar, from where he summoned his inner strength and convictions. He began now to pore over his King James Bible for similar inspiration and meaning, and in it he believed he had found the ligature Gifford meant, the one that seemed inherent in the patterns of thought between football and human existence. According to Landry, he would use "the same sort of scientific, analytical approach that enabled me to break down and understand an opponent's offenses" to find "the basic keys of the Christian gospel."

In truth, such revelation didn't make Landry feel taller, but instead *smaller*; all his clean living, he said, wasn't worth a damn in this new purview, because his Bible was telling him that he "was as much a sinner as anyone in the world," and demanded unconditional, ongoing revelation. That was a universal commitment for a Christian— in Lombardi's Catholic faith they called it "world without end,

amen"—and Landry knew he was in for the long term, if he committed. As he would say, that was a very big *if*.

Indeed, he wasn't quite sure about diving in the way he would need
to, not in the beginning. He never did etch a start date to when he
"gave myself to Christ," the phrase that would tumble from his lips
for the rest of his life. There was no "sudden 'born-again' experience," he wrote, no apocalyptic changeover, no lightning bolt sent at
him under a full moon at the stroke of midnight. Neither would he
say that what he called "my new Christian experience" made a discernible difference, or that it "instantly transformed me into a much
better person." All he could commit to was going back to the Melrose each Wednesday morning, to look for more salvation, to keep
on reading his Bible, and to pray his heart out, until "I was willing
to commit my entire life to God." He was still not certain where his
life was going, in and out of football. For now, it was good enough
that football was no longer his main, and at times sole priority, and
that when he went back to work he had "a sense of confidence and
peace about the future—whatever it would be." It even surprised him
that he felt so sanguine, saying a decade later that "all my intellectual
questions no longer seemed important, and I had a curiously joyous
feeling inside."[23]

Alicia Landry, who had always been the more punctilious about
religion, watched him dig his way into hagiology, keeping what he
was discovering to himself. "It was a very personal thing to him," she
says, "because I think he was trying to figure it all out, and he had
to do that by himself, with no one else giving him answers he had
to find for himself. I knew of course that he had not been happy. He
mentioned to me once that he'd set all these goals for himself, and
after he'd achieved them, he felt like, *then what*? He needed something more than wins and losses, something where the goals didn't
go away when you won and crush you when you lost. He needed to
know something else was out there that meant more than that. And
he found it, in Christ."

She goes on, "That seems pretty basic, but you'd be surprised. As a
Methodist, we never think like that, it was more about living your life
according to a set of values. And when Tommy was sure he understood what being born again was, he opened up about it to me, and I

followed him into it. I became born-again too. That became our way of life, and we had a better life because of it. We didn't go around screaming it, we just lived it."[24]

BY THE time he traveled north for the 1959 season, religious homiletics began to creep into his public utterances, but nothing that was beyond the normal presence of religion in a sports locker room. "He didn't preach that jazz," says Huff, a man not to mince words. "We had a prayer service because football is war without guns. Every team does that. Before you go out of the locker room, you say a prayer. Get us by, Lord. But he didn't do anything different. That's how it is in football. Except they got this goddamn quarterback doing all that preaching. You leave that bullshit in the locker room. Landry knew that."

Huff, naturally, was referring to quarterback Tim Tebow, whose Rodin-like, silent but very public prayer pose at midfield caused heated debate in 2011. It was self-promoting in a way Landry never could have been about religion. Indeed, Landry described an almost monklike insulation to his daily prayers, saying, "I begin each day now with a person-to-person effort to contact Him [and saying by example] 'Lord, I need your help today when we make squad cuts.' . . . At the end of the day I take inventory. Was my criticism of the quarterback handled right? . . . When I get out of touch with Him, I flounder. Power seems to ebb away, and that restless feeling returns."

Pious though he could be, then, and as public as *he* was about his faith, Landry once noted that among his daily assurances from the Lord was, "Did I get across to the squad my moral convictions without preaching?" What's more, he reeled from outward displays of religious showmanship. "I'm afraid," he said, "these little 'God help me score a touchdown' and 'God helps me be a winner' testimonials mislead people and belittle God. I don't believe God plays favorites like that. Neither do I believe God cares who wins a football game."[25] To some Cowboys looking to get into his good graces, it was almost an act of faith simply to have Landry know they were running with him and Jesus. Pete Gent would recall that on his first day as a Cowboy, blackboards at the Thousand Oaks training facility were covered not just with football diagrams but bus schedules to the town's churches. Gent, a sinner by nature, felt compelled to accede to Landry's clear wish that the players ride those buses. He even rode to one with Landry and his son. "That Sunday," he wrote, "I became a full-blown Methodist. I never went back, but in retrospect I think that by landing that first Sunday punch I gained a little extra time in the NFL. It was worth it. One Sunday as a Methodist." Pause. "I should have gone twice."[26]

To be sure, Landry's faith was not always easy to take. What's more, if he felt curiously joyful, he didn't tend to show it much. Huff, as did other Giants, wondered if he was using religion as a crutch, to convince *himself* he *could* feel the joy deep in his heart, when in fact he didn't. It wasn't that Landry was insincere; rather, it was as if he was somehow overcompensating. Huff knew Landry well enough to tell him to his face when he was getting too evangelical, such as years later when Huff gently rebuked him for "carrying things too far" after Landry's first Super Bowl triumph. Yet Landry would just let flak about his public testimonials of faith bounce off him the way Nazi antiaircraft fire had around his B-17. He knew his way home.

Still, Landry wanted to be more than merely admired. He wanted to be *accepted* as Lombardi was, as a man of real flesh and blood and pain, and on some level Landry rued that he never was seen with any shading, only in black and white, or rather cold gray. Alas, nothing he could glean from his Bible would explain why Lombardi was feared and loved at once, while Landry could only be *respected*. Huff says, "Tom talked a lot about, well, as a coach I can't let anyone see me get emotional, I have to think two plays ahead, I need to be in control. And all of that was true. But at the same time I think all that was a cover, too. I loved Tom. I'll even go further. Tom Landry was the most wonderful person I ever met in my life. Tears come to my eyes when I think of Tom. He was a genuinely kind and caring man, a gentleman. But I don't think Tom could reveal much of himself. When he found God, he didn't have to; he could talk to God and leave it at that.

"You know, we all have pain we try to extinguish. I've never said this publicly before, but for the grace of God I would have killed my older brother. He was bigger than me and he would beat the shit out of me. So one day I got a gun, put it in his ribs, and pulled the trigger. I didn't kill him only because the gun misfired. That was God saving *my* life. So God bless Tom for his faith. I admired that, because he didn't just say he believed. He lived it."

Pat Summerall recalls a Landry so intensely private that when he visited injured Giants players in the hospital—contrary to his normal bloodless reaction to them lying in pain on the field—"he made sure those things weren't publicized. Landry's Christian beliefs were very strong, and even though he never talked about them, we knew it."[27]

Landry was the most cryptic of men, one who wanted to make the pastoral side of him take precedence. He also wanted to make sense of his world, where Christians made money in a secular profession and derived godly justification for walking in victory off a gridiron littered with other fallen Christians. But, unlike Tim Tebow, nobody ever wanted to beat Landry because of his expositions of faith. They wanted to beat him only because he would have done anything on God's green earth to beat *them*. And in the end, that and not anything he heard in his daily communions, was probably what kept him around the game, and from hearing any heavenly directives to leave it behind.

AFTER LOMBARDI had relocated to Green Bay, Wellington Mara, to his relief, still had Landry, who was putatively the next in line for Howell's job. But even if Landry wanted it, the matter became complicated with the reentrance of Allie Sherman, who had returned the previous year as a scout, then replaced Lombardi as offensive coordinator. Sherman was suddenly a hot property. Greasy Neale praised him as "the smartest football player I ever coached," Lombardi was said to want as him an assistant in Green Bay, and Art Rooney reportedly offered him the head coach job in Pittsburgh. Howell had no problem touting Landry, but he was obviously tight with Sherman, always had been, and Allie quickly found himself the subject of talk that *he* was next in line. As Sherman recalled, "Jim Lee had been telling me for several years that he might be retiring soon, and I realized I might have had a shot at the head-coaching job. And when I was offered the job as offensive coordinator, there were indications that I would probably replace Jim Lee."[28]

Sherman had another advantage. At thirty-three, he was willing to wait for his shot. Landry wasn't, not with Texas calling him back home. He also was nowhere near as ambitious as the Brooklyn-born, streetwise Sherman. The Maras felt no need to rush Howell out and give him a cushy front-office job—something that Howell would later say would have indeed made him retire from coaching. Instead, Howell pushed on, his behavior becoming most peculiar. Pat Summerall, for example, told of the big coach treading the corridors of summer camp like Marley's ghost, wearing long blue pajamas and carrying a stopwatch, evidently looking to time people in the 40-yard dash down the hallway. In meetings he would digress and rail about the dangers of homosexuality, signs of which he thought were afoot everywhere.[29]

Like Lombardi, Landry didn't begrudge the head coach his job, but he didn't intend to stay around either. Though close to quitting football, and having resolved early during the 1959 season that it would be his last in a Giants parka, he had already started looking for other possible jobs in the game. The year before, when Coach Bear Bryant left Texas A&M for his alma mater, the University of Alabama, Landry learned that Dallas oilman H. R. "Bum" Bright, a 1943 A&M grad, who was a millionaire by age thirty-one, was put in charge of recruiting a new head coach. Taking the initiative, Landry called Bright, who knew almost nothing of Landry but agreed to grant an interview. After they met in his office, Bright said, he was "singularly unimpressed," his biggest reservation being that a man with so little personality and oomph could not possibly persuade high school kids to play football in College Station instead of, say, following the Bear to Tuscaloosa.[30]

Seeing how little he mattered to the colleges, Landry knew that any future he had in football was on the pro level, but he was coming to believe that the born-again motif applied to his life in general. Indeed, with the decade about to end, it was perhaps time to leave football and become the white-collar professional he had educated himself to be. As usual, he kept this to himself, saying nothing about leaving during the season, in which he earned his most public exposure yet. That year, the Giants' defense yielded a paltry 170 points, the lowest in the league, giving Allie Sherman's offense such a head start that they rang up more points than anyone but the Colts. The

Giants finished with a 10–2 record, also the best in the league, and one game better than Baltimore, who they would again face for the championship. Getting there, Landry took on guru-like properties. In October, after a 70-yard interception return by Swede Svare helped the Giants beat the Eagles, Tex Maule wrote in *Sports Illustrated*,

> Landry has a few "pick-off" plays for his defense—plays in which a defender will purposely play a little out of position in order to lure an unsuspecting quarterback to throw into apparently unguarded territory. Svare's interception . . . came on a pass thrown into what must have seemed a very vulnerable spot. It wasn't. As [Eagle receiver Tommy] McDonald found out, there were no apparent vulnerable spots in last Sunday's Giant defense.

Maule called Landry "one of the most astute defensive coaches in football,"[31] but was one-upped by Arthur Daley in his December 23 *New York Times* column, published just before the Giants would tackle the Colts in the title game, this time in Baltimore. He quoted Jim Lee Howell rhapsodizing, "Defensive football has become a highly developed science, and the Giants have the world's leading scientist in Tom Landry. He's the best defensive coach in the business." There was a large head shot of the eagle-faced, grinning, and now quickly balding Landry alongside explications in his own words about the art and science of defense, and what had gone wrong the year before. According to Landry, his mission in pro ball had been to "study the men, the patterns, and what to expect. Then I began correlating this to the over-all design and really learned what an intricate, fascinating subject defense can be."[32]

As he spoke, he may have believed that he had accomplished his mission, and that it was about over. But if so, he was living a more charmed life than he thought. Howell's quote about him would get around and take on a life of its own. Within months, it would be truncated by some in the press as "Tom Landry is the best coach in the business." By then those words would be his virtual calling card, gaining him more ascent and responsibility than he ever would have foreseen, as well as the need to have to prove them to be true.

Part II

IF
YOU'RE
GONNA
PLAY IN
TEXAS

Chapter 9

BIG DOG

BACK IN DALLAS, Clint Murchison Jr. had laid all the necessary groundwork to join the NFL's ruling class, though he wasn't the only swell scouring the landscape to bring a team to the city. That had also become the goal of another scion of a full-flowered Texas oil baron, twenty-six-year-old Lamar Hunt, whose father, Haroldson Lafayette "H. L." Hunt Jr., had been called the richest man in the world, his wealth estimated by *Fortune* in 1957 as between $400 and $700 million. In 1958, the younger Hunt, worth around $50 million himself, offered to buy the floundering Chicago Cardinals and move them to Dallas. But in 1960 the owners of the team, the Bidwill family, got a better deal from the NFL to move the team to St. Louis and remain in charge. Hunt, who had seen how many people wanted to buy that and other NFL teams, came away with a different idea: to rustle up a bunch of them and start a whole new league, with him as owner of a Dallas franchise.

Hunt cannily lined up a rival team in Houston, to be owned by fellow oilman Bud Adams, who had also tried to buy the Cardinals. After one last gasp to get into the NFL, which ended when both Bert Bell and George Halas insisted to Hunt that the elder league was not going to expand in the near future, in August 1959 Hunt and Adams held a press conference in Adams's boardroom to announce the new six-team American Football League, which would commence games in the fall of 1960. Despite the felicitous relationship between Hunt and Bell, the latter knew that with moneybags like Hunt and Adams to contend with, the NFL would have a real fight on its hands. Hunt, for example, had secured the use of the Cotton Bowl for his home games, a huge asset. Indeed, it took all of a month for Bell to flip-flop. Having been wary of trying again in Texas, the old league suddenly *needed* a team in Dallas, pronto, lest Hunt and the new circuit have dibs on the town and the whole state, especially since they already had Houston covered.

Enter Clint Murchison Jr., who had sworn by all that was Texas that he would bring a team to Dallas. Once Bell blessed that objective, Murchison was in demand. It was Halas—acting for the league he had fostered to enormous growth—who went to Murchison to ask for assurances that he could shepherd and maintain a new team where there had been only failure. Halas was convinced Murchison could—and why not? The entire payroll of the twelve-team NFL was only $3 million,[1] which came to around one-tenth of Clint Jr.'s net worth. The new franchise would cost $600,000, far from the $100 membership fee each seminal NFL owner paid for a place in the league, but chump change for a Murchison.

To make it look like a corporate endeavor, Murchison had gotten a few of his bobos to invest some of their own millions in the team, including his brother John and the Wynne brothers, Bedford and Toddie Jr.,[2] but their amount of seed money and number of shares of stock were small. Clint Jr. held nearly all of the stock. Yet, unlike Hunt, he shunned publicity. In fact, during the team's rollout, at Murchison's behest, Bedford Wynne, a pleasant and outgoing man who had a law degree and was active in *Democratic* Party activities, of all things, acted as team spokesman while Clint set out to hire the first crucial personnel.

Actually, he had no business doing so. Despite Bell's turnaround, no money had been paid to the league yet, and most league people, including the commissioner, figured that the new team would not be able to get off the ground until 1961. There *was* no Dallas team in point of fact, and there would not be until the other owners voted on giving the Murchison group, and another group awaiting approval for a new team to play in Minneapolis, their charters, something that wouldn't happen until the annual owners' meeting in January 1960. Neither could any players be *legitimately* signed until a dispersal draft could be held to populate the new teams, and that would also happen at the winter meeting. Until then, no contracts with Murchison would be legally binding in the league's eyes.

Not that any of that mattered to Murchison, for whom being accepted as a *potential* owner, and a promise to pay the league $600,000, was as good as any stinking charter, and he was not prepared to keep his powder dry for three months, never mind a year. The NFL owners may not have sensed any urgency in getting their first southern-based team up and running, only established, but Murchison could hardly afford to let his opposite number, Lamar Hunt, lay down roots and claim the allegiance of his town. And so Murchison, on his own, did all he could to get the team going. Using his political clout, he was able to keep pace with Lamar Hunt by calling in his chits with Dallas politicians, including Mayor Robert L. "Uncle Bob" Thornton, and officials of the State Fair of Texas, which operated the enormous, 75,500-seat Cotton Bowl, located within Dallas city limits in the Fair Park section.

Hunt, of course, had gotten all these folks on his side first, and whatever he agreed to pay as a rental fee Murchison would match. Although Uncle Bob was happy to have two leagues playing in the stadium, the rivalry posed a conflict. The two teams would strain the uncertain loyalties of a city of 750,000 and quite likely divide the overall pool of fans, making it highly unlikely that either could succeed. For both teams, the key was to draw from the outer exurban areas, where another 250,000 people lived. Hunt, steaming about the "other" Dallas team—the one that didn't really exist—was at least relieved that, having gotten there first, the Texans would have first call on preferred home dates at the Cotton Bowl, putting the NFL club in the embarrassing position of needing to schedule games there on Saturday nights.

Early as it was, the private argument between the two filthy rich men would become the heart of an escalating war between the leagues, which would get a lot uglier before it was over.

HAVING GOTTEN what he wanted, Murchison next turned to the whos. The first on his list was Tex Schramm, the former general manager of the Rams. He bore a resemblance to Gene Autry, the wildly popular "Singing Cowboy" and native Texan, which seemed to validate the assumption common to those who didn't know him well that Schramm was another homespun son of the prairie who could make order out of chaos. Because of his name, which in full was Texas Earnest Schramm Jr., Schramm was often assumed to be a native Texan, and he enjoyed posing as such, even if he was actually born in San Gabriel, California. His father, Texas Sr., *was* a native Texan, but his job as a stockbroker carried him and his family to the West Coast. His son did return to attend the University of Texas, graduating in 1947 with a degree in journalism.

To be sure, Schramm had a way with words, and also with good fables, many about himself. He liked to tell tales of his football days in Austin, where there is no record of him ever playing the game.[3] But Tex told them so well, he may have believed he *did*. Like Landry, Schramm didn't need to embellish that he was a distinguished Army Air Force veteran, having served for four years and making captain. After he got out, he married and became the father of a two-year-old daughter, and went to work as sports editor of the *American States-man* in Austin, for $35 a week. Then his father, who knew people in the Rams organization, got his boy a job as their publicity man, at $100 a week.[4]

It was 1948, three years after the Rams had moved from Cleveland to Los Angeles, which had no pro football tradition. To Tex, that necessitated building—or "merchandizing," as he called it—the team's image around the fast, glamorous pulse of Hollywood. He would hand out passes to movie stars so that at least there would be some beautiful people sitting in the mostly empty seats in the continent-wide expanse of the Los Angeles Coliseum. Acting like a press agent, he planted stories in the newspapers and magazines about the hunkier players, like former UCLA and Michigan All-Americans Bob Waterfield and Tom Harmon, sometimes in beefcake layouts so as to attract women fans. Waterfield's 1943 Las Vegas marriage to sexy actress Jane Russell suddenly became news again.

Schramm didn't stay a PR man for long. The owner of the team, Daniel Reeves, thought the world of Tex and soon gave him the general manager's job, which Reeves had previously tried to handle himself, badly. Schramm once related that *someone* had to take the job from Reeves, whom he said had "a drinking problem" that rendered him useless.[5] By the late 1940s, Schramm was making bold moves to augment the high-octane Rams passing attack, mirroring the fast, glamorous LA vibe. He acquired Elroy "Crazylegs" Hirsch in the AAFC dispersal draft and switched Tom Fears from defensive back to receiver, arguably the game's first wide receiver, split out from the offensive line. He also drafted Norm Van Brocklin, who impressed few scouts while at Oregon. A year later, the Rams were in the championship game. A year after that, when Van Brocklin threw for 554 yards in a game, still a record, and Hirsch set a receiving yardage record, they won it all.

Bert Bell was overjoyed that he now had glitter franchises on each coast, and he often consulted Schramm on elevating the league's image. The other general managers began emulating his innovative scouting methods: concentrating on finding talent the scouts overlooked, such as in small colleges, and setting up a far-flung and sophisticated network of amateur scouts whom he put on retainer to the Rams. Through the mid-1950s the team remained a top draw, and Schramm was running the most heralded front office in the league. He employed publicity men, including a young Tex Maule— a Schramm kind of guy, having been a trapeze artist with the Barnum & Bailey Circus. When Maule left to become the PR director for the original, lamentable Dallas Texans, in came an LA public relations man named Alvin Ray Rozelle, better known by his nickname Pete.

Working for Schramm certainly did lead to bigger and better things for those two. Schramm too moved onward and upward. In 1957, he saw an opportunity, not coincidentally at a time when the Rams were being eaten alive by internecine feuding between Reeves and his partners. A job had opened up three thousand miles away in New York, one that offered him the chance to catch the wave of the new booming creature that was sports television: president of CBS Sports. Ironically, despite being out of football, the position would give him even more influence on the sport. Over the next three years, one of his roles was to expand the network's coverage of NFL teams by bringing into the fold the few remaining teams that were still broadcasting their games on local or other networks. One of them was the Packers, whom network people thought had too small a market to care about. But Schramm foresaw a far wider audience for them, the entire Upper Midwest, and even though they were a bad team, he once recalled, "I cut the Packers a check for $15,000. I threw in more money, thinking it would be good for the network in the long run."[6] Typically of Schramm, the insight and timing were uncanny, and only months later Vince Lombardi came to Green Bay.

Schramm became busy planning for the upcoming 1960 Winter Olympics in Squaw Valley, New York, an event he convinced CBS to pay to broadcast, contradicting most television people who believed winter sports like skiing and bobsledding were poison to red-meat American audiences. But Schramm would be right. That was the Olympics when the U.S. hockey team upset the mighty Russians for the gold medal, and when figure skater Carol Heiss captured the fancy of viewers. These prescient decisions made Schramm a very important man, but he soon itched to get back into football. With amazing providence, late in 1959 the NFL reversed itself on putting a team in Dallas. Within days he was sitting in Clint Murchison Jr.'s office giving him the big-talking routine Schramm had mastered. Bluntly, he told Murchison his team would lose $2.5 million before he made a dime, but that under anyone other than Tex Schramm it would never turn a profit.

Murchison blinked at the price tag but was convinced he had to have this man working for him, and offered him the job of president, at the top-shelf NFL salary of $36,500. But it didn't end there. Schramm was able to command a stock option package no other league executive could have imagined for himself—he was given the open-ended option to purchase 20 percent of the team's stock, at the price it was right then, meaning that no matter when he wanted to exercise the option, he would be buying shares at their 1959 prices. That could wind up being either a windfall or nothing, depending on whether the team would still be around long into the future. And just in case it would fail to get a charter in January, he was permitted to hold onto the CBS job at the same time he began working for Murchison. While this was clearly a conflict of interest, both the league and the network cut him the slack to do it.

It was late October 1959, and Schramm came to Dallas. But he attacked the job like a piranha, ignoring that he couldn't legitimately sign staffers or players. Within days he was spreading around more of Murchison's money, with his first hire being Gil Brandt, a man as inscrutable as Schramm and as brilliant. A puckish, twenty-six-year-old Milwaukee photographer by trade, Brandt had gained a reputation in the game as a rather shadowy freelance scouting guru who prowled the back alleys of the football hinterlands in search of diamonds in the rough, making information on such gems available to pro teams but at a price. Back when Schramm was running the Rams, pro scouts weren't allowed to bird-dog the workouts of the talents chosen to play in the annual late-summer College All-Star Game in Chicago against the NFL champs, but Brandt, without anyone really knowing how, was able to get a front row seat at practices.

He had files on virtually every player on every college team, and seemed to know every coach, along with their wives, children, and distant uncles. His Rolodex was thick as a Texas steak. Because Brandt got close enough to college kids to be able to persuade them which team they should sign with—which was whatever one was paying Brandt at the time—Schramm had kept him on a retainer. Now, he used him again. While the NFL had not a single player under contract in Dallas, and with the dispersal draft months away, Schramm had paid his friend Daniel Reeves $5,000 for a list of undrafted, unsigned players compiled by the Rams' scouts, a breach of protocol that fazed neither man. The problem was that no one knew where to find them—except Brandt. Schramm reached for the phone and called Milwaukee.

"Do you want to sign some players for me?" he asked the photographer.

"Give me the names," he replied.[7]

Thus did the team-that-wasn't begin to acquire its first board pieces, the players signing what Schramm called "made-up contracts," as opposed to actual, legally binding contracts. They were given documents copied verbatim from the language of the standard NFL player contract, with mastheads that read only, "Dallas Football Club," the team not having officially committed to a nickname. Informally, "Dallas Steers" was bandied around at first, but Schramm thought "Dallas Rangers" sounded better. At the time there already was a Dallas Rangers, a Texas League baseball team, but he was told they were soon to go out of business. Until they did, however, the new franchise really *had* no name, and anyone who signed with them ran the risk of being back out in the cold after the New Year. But Schramm went ahead, anyway, wading into a new war for players precipitated by the American Football League's having wasted no time scouring the land to fill its rosters, its supply of funds to do so having been bolstered by a deal Lamar Hunt had engineered in June with ABC to broadcast the new circuit's games for a modest $2,125,000 a year for five years.

That deal jolted the fattening elders of the NFL, not because of the money but because it would be shared equally in socialistic fashion by all eight teams so that no team would go bankrupt—a development that proved so successful it would force the NFL's rabid capitalists to make the same arrangement when it came time to renew its relationship with CBS. The AFL owners were brash and confident, and admittedly off their rockers to wage a fight with the NFL—they proudly called themselves "the Foolish Club"—and they readied themselves in a hurry. That fall they held a college draft, leading the NFL to move up its own draft to during the season—too soon for the not-yet-official Dallas Football Club to participate, another hurdle Schramm had to navigate. And the AFL would even come away with the biggest prize in the eyes of both leagues: LSU halfback Billy Cannon. He had signed with the Rams for $50,000, but when the Houston Oilers drafted him and Bud Adams waved $100,000 under his nose, he signed with *them* too. Adams's lawyers went to court, claiming that Cannon's Rams contract was invalid because their general manager—Pete Rozelle, Schramm's protégé—had "manipulated" Cannon into signing.[8] Adams came away with the prize.

Players, any players, were at such a premium in the signing war that even some of the free agents that Schramm and Brandt were signing had to be shielded from the AFL. Brandt became the Cowboys' chief "baby sitter," keeping them under lock and key until they were safely signed. Nor did it matter how iffy a kid's background might be; one, a lineman named Byron Bradfute, had been kicked out of Abilene Christian University for drinking beer, but he was signed nonetheless—an early indicator that if Schramm was sold on a player, he was blind to the player's behavior off the field, something that would both behoove and bedevil Landry in the years to come. All Schramm asked of his players, and all other employees, was that they put team ahead of everything else, even their own families.[9] The team *was* the family, in the same sense as a Mafia family.

The last missing element in the creation of the Dallas Cowboys was a coach who could work with Schramm while also understanding his ego and need to be patronized, and accepting his word as law in the front office, yet whose acumen was nonpareil when it came to decisions made on the field. Schramm believed he had the perfect candidate. He knew Tom Landry as both a player and a coach and, living in New York and going to the Giants' home games, saw how Landry's defenses changed the game. That Landry was a Texan didn't hurt either. But Schramm found that he had a fight on *his* hands, from *two* incipient teams in the AFL: Hunt's Texans and Bud Adams's Houston Oilers. For a few weeks Landry sat on the offers from both—Adams, offering $65,000 for five years, shot the moon.[10] There were no tampering rules then, and Landry could have accepted any offer, but he thought it prudent and respectful to his team to wait until the season ended.

That wasn't good enough for Hunt, who was working at breakneck speed and couldn't wait. He went ahead and hired Hank Stram, a highly regarded assistant coach through the 1950s, one of his jobs being at SMU. But Schramm and Adams would hold the door open for Landry.

WHILE THIS subterranean intrigue was going on, the Giants went to Memorial Stadium in Baltimore on December 27, 1959, for the championship game rematch with the Colts. And for a while it seemed that Landry would be able to go out on a high note. This time the Giants won the stats battle, 323 yards to 280, and Landry's defense sacked Unitas six times. Gifford had more yards rushing, 56, than Ameche and Moore combined. After Unitas had thrown a 60-yard touchdown pass to Moore early in the game—which Landry took blame for, having guessed wrong by calling for doubling the receivers and leaving Moore in single coverage—the Giants controlled the game but could score only three field goals, leading 9–7 going into the fourth quarter. Then the sky fell in. Unitas ran in a 4-yard touchdown and tossed a 12-yard scoring pass to Jerry Richardson; a Conerly pass was intercepted and run back for a touchdown; and just like that the game was out of reach, 28–9. It ended with a score of 31–16 and the Giants just as dazed as the year before, not knowing what had hit them.

If Landry hadn't known for sure that he was done in New York, he did now, with the bitter taste of two crushing defeats in the big game. Not able to convince himself that it would be acceptable to turn his back on the NFL, he had progressively moved toward Schramm's offer. But before he would make the decision known, he owed it to Wellington Mara to see him one more time about the Giants' coaching situation. Mara, who could not have been pleased that one of his own would be coaching a team in the same division, and trying to beat his Giants twice a season, hoped that loyalty and another semi-promise might still keep Landry in New York.

As Landry wrote in his memoirs, Mara "wanted me to know that when Jim Lee Howell took his planned retirement soon, I'd be first in line to become head coach."[11] Landry, not to mention Lombardi, had heard *that* one before. He also knew that Howell probably would step aside only if Allie Sherman was getting the job. By then, as well, the secret was out that Landry had other offers. In fact, on the day of the Colts game the *New York Times* already had him accepting one of them, with the headline reading "LANDRY REPORTED LEAVING GIANTS" and the UPI story below reporting that he "will take a coaching position with the Houston club of the new American Football League within a week."[12] That was half right. Landry *would* be taking a position, the very next day in fact, but not with the Oilers. Mara no doubt knew it. As Alicia Landry remembers it, Mara actually made a hard offer to his lame-duck defensive coach to take over the reins in 1961. If so, he couldn't have meant it, and made the offer knowing he had nothing to lose, given that as Alicia says now, "We had decided we were going to go home."[13]

In retrospect, Murchison and Schramm had only one advantage

in landing Landry—they were the NFL team. Otherwise, it was the riskiest move. Schramm could not deny that it was a "gamble" for Landry, given that "we didn't even have a franchise yet."[14] In fact, it wasn't really a job, more like a binder to hang around until such a time when it *became* a job.

Accordingly, Landry approached it with intentionally lowered expectations. He had made some tentative plans to open an insurance office, the engineering career now scrapped for something more secure, and would say later that if the coaching job lasted "only two, maybe three years, [it] could buy me the time I needed to build my business to the point I could adequately support my family. . . . So while the position didn't look very secure, I realized it could serve as a solid bridge to life beyond football."[15]

He left New York with a legacy that was only then reaching its peak. During the season, his star pupil Sam Huff was given an encomium that not even Gifford had received: Huff's granite-carved mug appeared on the cover of no less than *Time* magazine. Having discovered the growing mass appeal of pro football, the weekly chose the most apt face and personality—at least to the New York cognoscenti—to personify a long dissertation bearing the cover line "PRO FOOTBALL: BRAWN, BRAINS, AND PROFITS" and the title "A MAN'S GAME." Proclaiming "this is the year of the defense," the author of the unbylined piece wrote that Huff was "a confident, smiling fighter" with a "devout desire to send a thick shoulder into every ball carrier in the National Football League." In many ways, the article was as much a paean to Huff's mentor, who was introduced to the public at large this way:

> The mind behind the Giants' muscle is Defensive Coach Tom Landry, 35, a sharp-featured, whisper-voiced Texas hick who learned his trade in the Giants' defensive backfield under coach Steve Owen. Using the pros' basic 4–3–4 "Umbrella" formation, Landry has plotted a score of basic defensive plays, each capable of several variations tailored to the particular [team's] offense.[16]

A lot of space in the article was given to explaining, as best as a lay writer could, about tendencies, keys, and the like, marking a real watershed in the way the abstruse inner game of football was written about for a mainstream audience. A year later, the Huff persona was given an even better, more visual treatment when Walter Cronkite sang his praises on the October 30 edition of the popular early-Sunday-evening half-hour television series *The Twentieth Century*. Titled "The Violent World of Sam Huff," the episode was directed by documentary filmmaker Nicholas Webster, who treated the subject as seriously as his next film for the series, "Alert! Defense in the Missile Age," and as entertaining as his future directing stints for *Bonanza* and *Get Smart*. Miking up Huff during a game to enter what was indeed a brutal province, Webster presented in grainy, vérité-style black-and-white images the sounds of grunts, groans, and guttural prattle, to Cronkite's somber narration. The film stands as one of the best and most watched of all early sports documentaries.

Landry's Giants defense had reached such a level that it was not given another official defensive coordinator, who would have been held to unreasonable expectations. Instead, Swede Svare was promoted to player-coach, his job to maintain the 4–3 defense, which had become standard around football. But soon that defense would be almost entirely dismantled, and Huff would lose the enormous altitude he enjoyed playing for Landry. That, Huff says now, was something that he sensed the day he lost his coach, and for that he's always believed that Wellington Mara blew it.

"I know damn well he did! And I called him every damn thing under the sun. I couldn't believe Tom was gone. Think of it this way, we were the first America's Team. And then he left and made another team that. If Wellington Mara had to give up his left nut to keep him, then that's what he should have done."[17]

CLEARING OUT quickly even for him, Landry was in Dallas the morning after the Colts game to meet Schramm and give his official yes to the offer. At the time, no one in Dallas had a clue what the future of pro football would look like, and the prodigal son from Mission was hardly a household name. Around town, it was of substantial interest that a new NFL franchise bearing the city's name had been born, but no one called the team for tickets or planned a parade for the players, which would have been rather difficult to do since there was no team phone number to call or any players to see. With those and a million other details to tend to, Tom Landry, not a year into his born-again life, would have ample reason to get out of bed each day, look skyward and plead, "Lord, help me," and then wonder what he had gotten himself into.

In his adopted hometown, the citizens had seen fleeting accounts of his rise in the heart of Yankeeland. After his signature game, the 10–0 whitewash of the Browns in the 1958 playoff, the *Dallas Morning News* attached to a wire story its own headline about the game that read "BIG D'S LANDRY DESIGNED BIG DEFENSE FOR BROWNS."[18] Before the '59 season, the *Morning News* ran a story headlined "INSURANCE MAN LANDRY GOES IN SEARCH OF GIANT POLICY."[19] Months before, in the spring of that year, a young sportswriter for the paper, Sam Blair, first came upon him at a Texas alumni luncheon where the Longhorns' coach, Darrell Royal, who would win the first of his eleven SWC titles that season, was going to speak.

As Blair remembers, "This tall, trim young man with even less hair than I have now walked up and said, 'Sam, I'm Tom Landry.' And, honestly, if he hadn't introduced himself, neither I nor a lot of other people there would have known who he was. He was a national name by then, but he was sort of a stranger in his own town. He kept a low profile. He told me, 'I live here in the off-season, and if I can ever help you, just give me a call. I'm in the book.' And he was—Fleetwood 7-5914, I still remember it. I said great, and several times a year I'd call him for a quote or something. And then suddenly he was the coach of this new team in Dallas."[20]

The first inkling of that development appeared in December 1959 when there came a profusion of stories, one doctoring Jim Lee Howell's huzzah—"HOWELL SAYS LANDRY BEST"—followed by "HOUSTON PRO CLUB SHOOTS FOR MOON" (the Oilers' offer to Landry), "LANDRY DELAYING DECISION ON JOBS," and "LANDRY HEADING SOMEWHERE?"[21] Finally, after Tom met Tex, the headline on December 29, 1959, would read "RANGERS HIRE TOM LANDRY." It took only a few minutes the day before for them to come to an agreement on the details—Landry would reap a $35,000-a-year deal over five years—and Schramm was so confident that he had brought to the meeting a personal services contract, not from the Dallas Rangers but rather the Tecon Corporation. That was Clint Murchison Jr.'s main holding company, operated by his partner Robert Thompson. Pending league approval of the Dallas franchise, this was the only means of binding Landry to the nascent team.

The wonder is that Landry agreed to such a provisional arrangement. But when Alicia found the Murchisons to be, as she says, a "darling couple," he had all the recommendation he needed. The money was never an issue—Adams had ponied up nearly twice what Landry accepted. Neither did he have a problem acceding to Schramm on business matters and Brandt on players to be signed. Indeed, that's how he wanted it. As Bum Bright had discerned, Landry was no recruiter of young men, and knowing this himself, he had never given a hang about scouting players. And as far as the business end went, from where he sat that's what they invented millionaires for, not men in cleats prowling muddy sidelines. Landry *did* have his own demands of Schramm. Tex, he said, could have his hegemony upstairs and could draft whomever he and Brandt wanted, but the field was Landry's duchy; neither Tex nor anyone else could cross that invisible barrier. Of course, that was something Schramm readily admitted *he* didn't care about, and so all seemed perfectly interwoven.

Landry did seem perfect for Dallas. At the announcement, Schramm defined him according to script, as a man from Dallas, a family man, a man of God, a man who was certified as the greatest coach in the game. Landry took it all in stride, with a little smirk that the city would come to know as his happy face. The newspapers could call him coach, but as the *Morning News* pointed out the next day, if the team for some reason were denied membership when the NFL owners meet in Miami Beach, his contract "would be null and void [and] he will be paid a certain sum for the risk he is taking. He said that in such an eventuality, he will be free to take another job, including the post he has just given up with the Giants."[22]

Landry would in time admit that Jim Lee Howell's oft-quoted and more oft-misquoted panegyric made him uneasy. "It was very nice for Jim Lee to say that, but it put me on the spot," he opined. "It's not easy to live up to that sort of thing."[23] So he knew he would have to do more than establish a decent team. He would need to have the

best team. Little wonder he thought it wise to hang on to his job selling insurance. What's more, even Schramm and Murchison weren't
totally sold on him. Schramm would later say that signing Landry
was "a very big gamble" because assistant coaches usually washed
out as head coaches.[24] Murchison, who had pledged to spare no cost
in erecting the team, seemed to be hedging his bet somewhat. Rather
than sinking heavy coin into a team office headquarters and practice
field and facilities, he barely spent a dime on these things. The team
office became a large musty room on the second floor of a nonde-
script building on Yale Boulevard off North Central Expressway, the
first floor leased to an automobile club.

The practice field was—ironically—called Burnett Field, bringing back some fond memories of youth for Landry, though the field
behind Mission High School was probably in better condition than
the one used by his players when the baseball Rangers weren't playing
on it. The empty grandstand made ghostly noises, and the grounds
smelled like a cow pasture from plumbing that was always broken.
In the locker room, rats the size of armadillos had no fear of the
humans. Often the players would get to their lockers after practice
and find their shoes half-eaten. The training room was the women's
bathroom, which had pink walls, just the stimulus to elevate a man's
testosterone levels. "We didn't call it a locker room," says Mike Connelly, an offensive lineman on that first roster. "It was an outhouse we
shared with the rats."[25]

Still, the fact that the not-yet team was carrying on business as
usual, as if it already had a charter, and with an attitude to boot,
caught the other general managers around the NFL by surprise.
Schramm believed that if he could sign as many free agents as the
budget allowed, the league would let the new team begin to play
in 1960. He once proudly recalled that when Paul Brown tried to
recruit a player and the kid told him he already had a contract with
the Dallas Rangers, Brown recoiled. "What the hell are you talking
about?" he said. "They're not even in the league!"[26] Yet, at least one
owner—the *biggest* owner—was quite willing to help the new team,
even at his own expense. The circumstances involved SMU's lanky,
fun-loving quarterback Joe Don Meredith. Known by his middle and
last name as a two-time All-American who even then was a lightning

rod, Meredith was adored in victory, damned in defeat, but always a picture of James Dean cool with his crewcut and swaggering gait.

From the start, Murchison had his eye on Meredith as the quarterback he wanted to lead his team, picturing in his head all the Mustangs fans that would follow Meredith into the Cotton Bowl. While Lamar Hunt had the same idea, drafting Meredith as a "territorial pick" for his Texans, the new league didn't appeal to Meredith. Still, without a draft pick, all Schramm could do was sign him to the same personal services contract with Tecon—the first player officially signed by the nascent team. The contract was for five years, the same length as Landry's, not that it would mean anything if the team wasn't approved, in which case Meredith could still be taken by any other NFL team in the upcoming draft. But the shock was what Murchison agreed to pay him—$150,000 over the life of the contract, a then-astonishing sum for a rookie and only marginally less than the greatest coach in football was to get.

Halas took care of the rest. Fearing the repercussions if the AFL Texans got a head start in Dallas, Papa Bear conspired with Murchison on a plan by which the Bears would use one of their draft picks, a third-round one, on Meredith, as if upholding the imprimatur of the league and in effect taking him off the market. Assuming all went well in Miami Beach, Murchison would repay Papa Bear for his help with draft picks. Halas even went as far as to tell the other owners not to draft any player signed by Dallas. Schramm then went out and signed another high-level stud, New Mexico halfback Don Perkins. "They gave me a little money up front," Perkins recalled, "and I got to keep it whether I made the team or not. I said, 'Why not?' "[27] However, Carroll Rosenbloom wasn't playing the stooge for Schramm, and his Colts drafted Perkins. Though Dallas would eventually be ordered to compensate the Colts with a ninth-round draft pick in 1961, it was a cheap price to pay for a player of Perkins's caliber.

Trying to head off Lamar Hunt, Schramm also went after Billy Cannon. Cannon hadn't yet signed with the Rams, but Pete Rozelle, Schramms's old ward and replacement as general manager there, put his foot down. If Schramm signed Cannon, Rozelle warned, "you might not have a franchise,"[28] inferring that Rozelle would get the NFL to come down hard on the franchise-in-waiting. Schramm prudently backed off—though Rozelle's threat backfired when Cannon eventually spurned the NFL, giving the old league a black eye right off the bat in its war with the novices. Schramm and Landry would have to make a go of it with very few players of real talent. But Schramm had done enough, had too many assets in place, for the league to possibly take it all away in Miami. Or so he thought. One owner who Murchison had crossed, though, was lying in wait, looking for revenge.

IN AN AIR of paranoia about impending war with the new league, the NFL owners convened at the Kenilworth Hotel in Miami Beach on January 20, 1960. Murchison, Wynne, Schramm, and Landry all attended, looking to mix, mingle, and establish goodwill with owners they had made sure to send nice Christmas gifts to, especially their benefactor, Papa Bear Halas, whose almost unitary power was exercised in his role as head of the league's rules committee. That seemed to make approval for the Cowboys—an aye vote by at least ten of the twelve teams—a slam dunk. But the meeting would not be as serene as they thought. For one thing, Bert Bell had died suddenly on October 29 while he was watching an Eagles-Steelers game at Franklin Field. It was a genuinely sad and tragic turn of events, one that some believed might derail the whole league, such had been Bell's czarlike standing. By example, one of his last acts had been to recognize the existence of the first NFL players union, the National Football League Players Association (NFLPA), which had enormous consequences for the future of the sport.

The Dallas Rangers weren't the only new NFL franchise awaiting its official charter in Miami. Actually, *four* ownership groups came in with high hopes, the others representing Minneapolis, St. Louis, and Miami. The Minnesota franchise, the Vikings, had been an original AFL team, but owner Max Winter acceded to an NFL entreaty to join the elder league, with the understanding that it could not begin to play until 1961. The matter of expansion was put off though while the owners set about choosing a new commissioner, which became a nightmare. For nearly seven days of screaming, hair-pulling hissy fits behind closed doors, they were unable to agree on whether to go with the pro tem commissioner Austin Gunsel or the 49ers' attorney Marshall Leahy. They then began to seek a compromise candidate; the one put forward by Wellington Mara and Paul Brown, Pete Rozelle, won the vote. The new, boyish NFL commissioner owed much to Schramm and favored approval of the new Dallas franchise, but he learned quickly that the owners more often than not would muck up a good thing.

As it happened, one of the most powerful and choleric of owners, the flinty George Preston Marshall, was balky about the Rangers. Marshall clearly held a grudge against Murchison going back to the aborted sale of the Redskins years before, when the millionaire had told him to go to hell. The two men had grown into bitter enemies, though Murchison hoped it wouldn't jaundice Marshall's vote in Miami Beach. Fat chance. For months Marshall had been tipping his hand, vowing not to let a new team in Dallas encroach on what Marshall insisted were his territorial rights anywhere below the Mason-Dixon Line, especially since he had put together an array of southern stations on the Redskins' radio broadcast network. Marshall liked to bill his club as "the team of Dixie"—something that perhaps explains why through the years he signed so few black players to his team.

Marshall, seemingly sitting pretty, needed one more vote to keep Murchison out, and he found one, right in Halas's backyard, in the owners of the soon-to-be-relocated Chicago Cardinals, Violet Bidwill and her new husband, Walter Wolfner. For two more days, *that* debate raged, taking the goodwill out of the visitors from Dallas; as Tex Maule noted in *Sports Illustrated*, the group "had grown progressively gloomy," and had "nearly given up all hope of being admitted to the league in 1960."[29] Schramm was said to have lost five pounds from worrying and pacing the carpet in his room, but Murchison was not a man easily denied. He had already begun to challenge Marshall's territorial claims by leaning on his friends in Congress to rule that the Redskins' radio network was a monopoly, and a Senate antitrust subcommittee chaired by the crime-busting Estes Kefauver declared exactly that—one month before the Miami meetings. The timing made Marshall rightly suspicious, and even more intransigent about denying Murchison.

Rumors flew about what extent Murchison had influenced the

politicians, and his apparent relationship with Bobby Baker, Lyndon Johnson's infamous Senate aide who would be convicted in 1967 of larceny, fraud, and tax evasion. Baker claimed, in a 1978 *Playboy* interview, that Murchison had delivered to him $25,000, which Baker promptly delivered to Kefauver.[30] In any case, when Marshall arrived in Miami Beach, he didn't care about his radio network as much as Murchison had thought. Instead, Marshall's biggest gripe had to do with the fact that Murchison had something he wanted. It wasn't a player or a coach or front office executive. As it happened, the fate of the NFL, all professional football, and maybe the free world rode on a novelty song. How this happened was another testament to Clint Murchison Jr.'s endless reach, sentience of the smallest of details, and love of double-dealing. The song in question, which was never played outside Washington, DC—where it's still played on game days—was called "Hail to the Redskins," a college-style fight song written in 1937 by Marshall's then-wife Corinne Griffith and the Redskins' bandleader Barnee Briskin, whose 110-piece marching band played it with gusto on the field during games.

The song became a bone of contention in the late 1950s when Marshall fired Briskin after some sort of dispute and he and Corinne divorced. Briskin asked her to sell her portion of the copyright to him, and she did, sticking it to her ex-husband, who now could not have the song played without permission. Marshall audaciously kept on using the song anyway, and Briskin played dirty. He went to Murchison, whom he knew, and sold him rights to the song for $2,500. It was a wonderful piece of leverage for Murchison to have, and a month before the NFL meetings he rubbed Marshall's nose in it by ringing him up in DC with feigned outrage. "Does the Redskins band intend to play the Redskin fight song?" Murchison demanded to know.

"They sure will," said Marshall.

"The hell they will," Murchison growled, enjoying himself immensely. "Nobody plays *my* fight song without *my* permission."[31]

Marshall came to Miami Beach obsessed with getting back that darn song. Knowing how desperate Murchison was to be admitted to the NFL, Marshall himself provided the solution: if Murchison would sell "Hail to the Redskins" to him for the same $2,500, all would be forgiven and Dallas would get its team. The logjam broken, a vote was taken and it came up 11–0 in favor of Dallas, with an abstention by the Wolfners. With the proverbial whimper, Dallas had itself an NFL team, for a song. Marshall had also intended to fight to make Murchison's team wait a year before it could play, but he gave in on that fight too. The Cowboys were permitted to sign three players from each NFL team, choosing from among eleven players left unprotected from each thirty-six-man roster in an expansion draft to be held in February. The existing teams would split $550,000 of the $600,000 Murchison paid the league. The new club would go into the Western Conference but would be a "swing" team for 1960, playing each of the other twelve teams.

Schramm could now make tickets available, merchandise team gear, officially put the name and logo of the NFL on contracts, and be able to take Landry and Meredith off the Tecon payroll and transfer their contracts to those that bore the full legal force of the Dallas Rangers of the National Football League. However, if there was peace inside the corridors of the NFL, the league was in for the fight of its life. The AFL meant business, and in December it hired as its first commissioner a man whom Jimmy Stewart could have played in a Frank Capra movie.

Joe Foss had tuned up for the job by being a Marine fighter pilot who was awarded the Congressional Medal of Honor, and then a two-term governor of South Dakota. He had come aboard for three years and was useful in manifold ways, as a legitimate American hero and a political operative with friends in Congress whom the league would need. And he was still a fighter. Only minutes after the NFL approved of a new team in Dallas, Foss put on his Marine face and declared, "This is an act of war." That same day, the AFL owners had their own meetings—in Dallas—and elected Lamar Hunt president of their league. The two men then announced a $10 million antitrust lawsuit against the NFL for violating *their* territorial rights, as specious as that seemed. Rozelle hissed back, saying the AFL had moved into "our territory in New York and Los Angeles and San Francisco. Why shouldn't we be allowed to move into Dallas?" Hunt's retort was to compare the AFL to "a little dog going into the backyard of a big dog," while the NFL was "going into the little backyard and asking the little bitty dog if there's room for him."[32]

It almost seemed as if the main front in the war between the leagues was the battle for Dallas, a city few in football had cared much about. In an opening salvo, Foss began to work the cloakrooms of Congress with the hope of denying the entrenched league its exemption from antitrust laws. Indeed, Rozelle would find himself in front of a congressional committee pleading for its members not to do that, the wearying effect of which would be obvious within a few years.

In the meantime, all that the second team to sink its flag into the soil of Dallas could do was make big promises. "We will have the big-league team," said Murchison with plausible logic, "because we will be playing the establishment big-league teams."[33] But nothing about the Dallas team would be establishment, or big league, at least not for a while.

Chapter 10

"IS THERE A TEAM IN DALLAS?"

THE INAUGURAL SEASON OF pro football in Dallas would proceed in the same time frame as the presidential campaign that transformed American politics. In the gracefully metaphorical words of the young candidate who would be chosen in a squeaker of an election, a "torch has been passed to a new generation of Americans, born in this century, tempered by war, disciplined by a hard and bitter peace." Seeking new ways of dealing with changing tides, John F. Kennedy summoned entry into what he called a "new frontier." That new generation would need to hold that torch through a cultural tinderbox, the air cracking with both an excitement and a dread. Down in Dallas, the firstborn of a new NFL generation seemed to fall right into this ethos, by dint of their already bold strokes and youthful head coach.

Thomas Wade Landry had almost nothing in common with John Fitzgerald Kennedy except relative youth in their respective professions—Kennedy was forty-three when he became president, Landry thirty-five when he took the Dallas job. But both the son of New England and the son of Texas benefited from the national hunger for new leaders, though they would need to steel themselves and keep that torch from dropping in spectacular failure. Just as Kennedy was surrounded by the "best and the brightest" of counsel—who for all their erudition would make some grievous mistakes—so too was Landry given co-counsel that would help drive his agenda.

To be sure, the yoking of Landry, Tex Schramm, and Gil Brandt made for providential and organic fit. They would agree by consensus on players, but there would be no overlap of their individual spheres. Because Brandt, content with his scouting obsession, had no desire to pick up on football strategy or business, he posed no threat to either Schramm or Landry, all three of whom would carve out their own turf and protect it. Neither did Murchison, who knew a thing or two about delegation of authority, feel a need to exercise his ego by posing as George Halas or the Maras and meddling in his Big Three's affairs.

Landry's first order of business was the hiring of assistant coaches. His choices, from a very shallow talent pool, were Babe Dimancheff, the Steelers' running backs coach, who would have the same responsibility in Dallas; Tom Dahms as coach of the defensive line, the same job he had held at the University of Virginia; and for the offensive line, Brad Ecklund, an assistant at Oregon who had played center for the Yankees team Landry broke in with and for the original Dallas Texans. No offensive or defensive coordinator need apply—Landry would be both, as well as one-third of the troika trying to form a usable cast from the expansion draft held in Los Angeles in March. While there, Landry gave a rousing—for him—five-minute speech making the case that the league should do all it can to bolster the team in its war with Hunt's Texans, by freeing up more than eleven players from each of the NFL teams' rosters. He had taken the job, he said, to fight for the honor of his league against the AFL Philistines, and had assumed that the NFL would make some decent players available to give the new teams a break. The league, he said, "doesn't want any weak clubs. . . . That hurts everybody."[1]

Looking back years later, he said, "I felt like I was begging." But he could have saved his breath. This time even Papa Bear Halas felt he had done all he could for the new franchises. Landry came away with a hash of pros old and young. The best of the lot were halfback L. G. Dupre (from the Colts), defensive back Tom Franckhauser (Rams), linebacker Jerry Tubbs (49ers), and Jim Doran (Lions), a great athlete who was past his prime. Landry couldn't wring much from his old team, but when the Giants made Don Heinrich available, he jumped on him, mainly because the now-thirty, former fair-haired boy who could never move Charlie Conerly out, might help mold Don Meredith into a real quarterback instead of a strutting party boy with an aversion to the intellectual side of the game.

"We chose players for their offensive ability first," Landry said, "because we needed an exciting team. We were competing with the Dallas Texans. Playing against established NFL clubs, we knew we wouldn't win many games, but we wanted to give the customers a show, at least. We didn't have time or material to build a strong defensive club."[2] Still, he knew it would be potluck. His team had the quickest start-up of any sports franchise in history, and perhaps of any major corporation in history, one that was still without a conclusive name until March 19, 1960, when it became the Dallas Cowboys.

This alteration was almost incidental. The team had been informed that the Dallas Rangers baseball team was staying in business, sending Tex Schramm back to deep thought about a name. "Cowboys," he believed, was a perfect match of team and habitat, coating a simple childlike image with the gravy of regional pride. It rolled off the tongue easily and appealed to men, women, and children. Saying it like a native would—*DAY-LASS CAH-BAWUHS*—sounded so good, so *Texas*, it made you want to say it again and again for the hell of it. Not everybody agreed. Bedford Wynne, for one, hated it, once recalling, "At first blush, you thought, 'That's ridiculous. It's corny.'"[3] It was also in use by several college teams, such as Oklahoma State. Wynne pitched for something more modern and snazzy—"Jets"—something any Texas oilman had plenty of. But Murchison agreed with Schramm.

On such small linguistic nuance does Fate—and dynasties—sometimes hinge. Had there been no preexisting Dallas Rangers, a football tree would have grown in Dallas, to be sure, but would it have been the Rangers or Hunt's Texans? Would the Dallas Rangers ever *sound* cool or marketable enough to become a billion-dollar operation and ordained as the team whose hometown was *America*? Naturally, not a soul would have foreseen anything like that happening. At the time, a name was just a name. But if Tom Landry was keeping his expectations low, he already had a leg up, because in this case a name would be much more than just a name.

DALLAS IN 1960 was 104 years old, and like its two pro football teams, it was nowhere near fully grown. It had evolved as a bastard child, its fertile farmland and framing nexus of rivers valuable enough to be claimed by both the French and the Spanish, before it became a protectorate of Mexico in advance of the Texas Revolution. When American settlers began to populate the Red River Valley, a Tennessee lawyer and land developer named John Neely Bryan built a settlement there and named it after a friend of his, Joe Dallas. In 1845 it was annexed by the United States government, and a year later the name extended to the surrounding county. Then in 1856 the city of Dallas was incorporated. It was mainly prairie then, landlocked but accessible by the rivers that allowed it to become a commercial center and grow into what it is today: 358 square miles teeming with two million people, comprising one-fifth of the vast Dallas–Fort Worth metroplex, the fourth-largest metropolitan area in the country.

Oil of course became the sine qua non of Dallas, though not one drop of oil has ever been pumped from the ground it's built on. Rather, it was where men who owned the oil rigs around the state came to count their profits. But before there was oil, there were cowboys. Cattle was the first commodity that drew entrepreneurs here, then came cotton, a profitable enough trade for the state to both align with the Confederacy and adopt slavery as a societal norm, and for families to lose forty-five thousand fathers, sons, and brothers defending that norm.

Reconstruction forced Texas to find more technological pursuits, which centered primarily but not solely on oil. Money soon began flowing through Dallas from petroleum, banking, and transportation industries, paving the way for future investment gold mines such as telecommunications, energy, health care, and medical research. Today, Dallas has followed the trend of every big American city, its white residents moving out to the suburbs, leaving once-segregated streets to be populated primarily by Hispanics and African Americans. Multiculturalism, as a result, is one of its proudest traits. It even votes *Democratic* in elections. *This* Dallas is not the Dallas that warily greeted the Cowboys. *That* Dallas could still summon up images of cowboys, cattle drives, and chaps right out of the pages of Benjamin Capps and Elmer Kelton, the Dallas author who inspired Frank Loesser to write a show tune called "Big D." But what no one wrote or composed about *that* Dallas was that its streets were marked for specific feet, some for whites, some for blacks, with common ground rare.

In Big D, as in Texas writ large, blacks had a rich, proud history of hard-earned respect as sharecroppers during the Depression. Yet in its biggest cities, no ground or respect was given. Not all white residents accepted this pro forma segregation. In the 1950s a growing number of businessmen led drives to pass ordinances such as those barring back-of-the-bus transportation and separate drinking fountains. But progress was painfully slow, deadly so for those who died hanging from trees—to its everlasting shame, from 1882 to 1968, there were 493 documented lynchings in Texas, third in number behind Mississippi and Georgia.[4] The sunset of segregation was tangible in 1960, but so too was the stench of bigotry and death.

Unlike some of the city's other businessmen, Tex Schramm needed to confront the segregation issue head-on, not only because Landry wanted the team to stay together on the nights before home games but also because visiting teams would need lodging. Schramm was aware of incidents such as the one Landry's Giants had run into, which was repeated when other teams had come to town for exhibition games, and he would not stand for it as the general manager and moral barometer of the new franchise. But he had a high hurdle to clear—not one hotel in Dallas permitted blacks to stay in its rooms. Schramm had to go around them, appealing to businessmen in the city with some influence, a number of whom had been working with local civil rights figures to keep Dallas from becoming a racial tinderbox as were other big cities in the South. Schramm lobbied them hard to get a hotel to bend and one did, the Ramada Inn out at Love Field—on the condition that the other hotels wouldn't retaliate by spreading the word around and causing whites to avoid the Ramada. Less than courageous as this was, it had to suffice. Then, in 1962,

Schramm once recalled, the team "moved down to the Sheraton downtown, and that broke the hotel barrier."

That, too, was a small victory, since as he added, "Dallas still had a restaurant problem," among others.[5] Indeed, the black players could not find a place to eat or even stand on the street, much less a place to live during the season, in much of Dallas—at least not the "good" part of town. The dividing line was the Trinity River, snaking along the western border of the city on its near parallel route with the Red River, which ran the entire length of East Texas, from Gainesville to Houston. West and south of the Trinity was where blacks were expected to confine themselves, generally in the Oak Cliff section. North Dallas was there for them to frequent temporarily, by bus, to work in the white folks' homes, before heading back south.

It was something that Texans like Meredith—and Landry—were accustomed to all their lives, as it was for black men like Frank Clarke, born Franklin Delano Clarke in a small Wisconsin town just as segregated as Dallas. Although he was an All-State player and won a scholarship to the University of Wisconsin, it was promptly rescinded when word got out that he was dating a white girl. After he transferred to Colorado, his coach told him he would never start in place of white players, and when the team played in the Orange Bowl, he and the other black players, he said, "were afforded an escort who took us to the black side of town."[6] Yet when Clarke got to Dallas, it seemed to be racism of a deeper, meaner streak. There, he saw for the first time the epochal symbol of segregation: the fountains marked "white" and "colored." As he once recalled, "I had never seen this. It kind of takes your breath away. You go, 'Holy smokes. How far away are we from lynchings?' Though we didn't have any cause to be threatened, I could not divorce myself from the fact that we were in Texas."[7]

To some of the white players from less restricted parts of the country, the matter-of-fact nature of racism in Dallas stung them as much as it did the black players. Dallas was more than recalcitrant; it was emphatically, rabidly unyielding, and as such a haven for right-wing extremists of every bent. Not only blacks but Catholics, Jews, Hispanics, liberals, pacifists, social workers, Fifth Amendment scholars, and anyone else not in the majority had cause to feel like they were viewed with fear and loathing. Big D was run by big money, by ultra-right-wing billionaires who broke out in night sweats that they might lose their porcine fortunes, and perhaps their daughters, to blacks and their Freedom Rider friends, whom they freely labeled "nigger lovers." The Ku Klux Klan and the John Birch Society operated in plain sight in Dallas, and the *Morning News* casually labeled President Kennedy as a "Socialist" for his civil rights agenda, which included his brother Robert using his power as attorney general to allow black students to get through the doors at Alabama universities in Birmingham and Montgomery.

Tellingly, while the governor of Texas, John Connally, was in no way segregationist, few gifted blacks felt compelled to make a similar push at the doors in Austin, Houston, and Dallas. The Lone Star State just seemed immune to integration. Indeed, Connally was worried by the baleful winds that blew in Dallas, as was his close ally Lyndon Baines Johnson. Clint Murchison Sr., who had written fat checks to the Richard Nixon campaign in 1960 and was still vexed that Johnson had helped carry the state for Kennedy, was prepared to write fatter checks to defeat him in 1964. The winds were blowing harder, and uglier, by the day.

To some, Dallas was the "Hate Capital," and there was nothing that the NFL and its team in this crucible could do to ameliorate that in any direct way. That was what was insidious about it—that segregation just seemed so *normal*. In fact, Mike Connelly says he didn't even realize there were such things happening in Dallas at first. "I was naive. I'm from LA. I'd been in the Marines with black guys. I didn't think a damn thing about racism. We'd fool around in the locker room, black guys would rag on my 'honky ass,' I'd rag their 'black asses.' It's what you do in a locker room. Then around my second year I'd become friends with Don Perkins, who I loved. I said, 'Let's go eat somewhere,' and he said, 'I can't, they won't serve me.' That's when I realized why he had to drive an extra twenty minutes from Oak Cliff every day to practice. I was stunned this was happening."[8]

In fact, men of goodwill like Connelly *were* naive, and on the Cowboys there were a number of unreconstructed racists, at least according to the feelings of certain black players.[9] If Landry knew who they were, none were lectured about it. There were no incidents on the team, no demonstrations of racially inimical conduct. Besides, if there was any mitigating factor to the pathetic spectacle of black men who represented the city not being able to live in its better quarters, it was that even the whitest of Cowboys weren't exactly welcomed around town. "Hell," says Connelly, "we were *all* outcasts. Nobody wanted to see us play, and they weren't crazy about serving us outside the stadium, either."

Dallas may have been booming, but it had no soul, just oil profits and hatred flowing through its veins and the smell of desperation wafting down the streets. It was where modern-day speculators came as gamblers did to Las Vegas, to get lucky at the table by making an investment in something, anything, a bond, a stock, real estate. If you just gave it time, it would come up blackjack. And when you did win, you could go on sprees at Neiman Marcus and pretend you were like the Murchisons and the Hunts and the Adamses.

The acerbic former Dallas sportswriter Skip Bayless once described the town as a "stainless steel melting pot" and its nouveau arriviste in the 1960s this way: "Everybody was looking for the latest watering trough. Everybody seemed to be swapping wives. If your neighbor had two cars, you had to have three—a Mercedes, a Rolls, and a Jag. 'The deal' was everything. The most admired people were the ones who knew how to make the most money. Unfortunately, people thought the men with the most money had infinite wisdom, too."[10] Within this society grasping for meaning—never mind that many of those monied men wound up blowing all of their treasure, including monied men of the Dallas Cowboys—a fedora would become worshipped as a symbol of status and the top of the leisure class. A TV show in the 1970s bearing the city's name was no more than a veiled rendering of the Murchison clan's twisted family values. Yet very little in the city of Dallas in 1960 seemed particularly meaningful or endearing or on the cusp of something more than just big. And that included its NFL football coach.

THE NEWLY minted Dallas Cowboys faced enormous problems finding serviceable players. The pickings had been so slim that even by late spring the team still hadn't filled the thirty-six-man roster. Looking around, Murchison would have another good laugh at George Preston Marshall's expense, when he acquired something else Marshall wanted: Eddie LeBaron, the Redskins' lilliputian but bravehearted quarterback for the past decade who had had an All-America career at the College of the Pacific. Standing just five foot seven and weighing 168 pounds, "the Little General," as he was called, had a huge heart. He had been a Marine lieutenant in the Korean War before he joined the weak Redskins team, throwing for a lot of yards and making the Pro Bowl four times. Tired of losing and earning peon's wages, LeBaron, who had earned a law degree during his off-seasons, said he would retire after the 1959 season and Marshall left him unprotected.

When Schramm swooped in, LeBaron was intrigued, not least of all because the Cowboys would set him up in the law office of Wynne and Wynne—as in the Wynne family that owned a piece of the team. But, according to LeBaron, the main reason was "my chief desire, deep down . . . to play for Tom Landry." Figuring that at worst he would benefit from the usual stellar Landry defense, "I wanted to play on a team which could stop someone."[11] But the signing was costly. Marshall cried foul that because LeBaron hadn't officially retired, the Redskins were owed compensation. That was an argument Murchison couldn't find a song to barter his way out of. When the league agreed with Marshall, the Cowboys had to forfeit their first-round pick in the 1961 draft, leaving them with no first-or third-round choice (the latter was bartered to Halas for shielding Meredith) and crippling any chance for them to land a blue-chip player when they would finally participate in the draft.

The entire spring and summer became an ongoing cattle call. And when the team found suitable facilities for their summer training camp no closer than Forest Grove, Oregon, near Portland, on the grounds of Pacific University, a mob of players, either cut from other teams or just living a dream, followed the Cowboys all the way there, turning Landry into more of a traffic cop than a coach. When Schramm had looked around for a camp site, the Portland Chamber of Commerce assured him that in this fold of the bucolic Pacific Northwest the cool breezes held the temperatures below eighty degrees in the summer. But when everyone got there, the thermometer flirted with a hundred degrees almost every day, though these were the sort of days the team would have to get used to in Dallas.

Forest Grove also brought the first wave of sportswriters who would be covering the Cowboys, a contingent that would fit neatly into a midsize sedan. The first to make it up there was Sam Blair, who with veteran scribe Charles Burton would be covering the two new pro teams for the *Dallas Morning News*. "There was nobody who knew much about pro football," says Blair, "but Charles was an easy call because he'd been with the paper since the mid-1930s. I was the most qualified among everybody else for two reasons. I had the home telephone numbers for Raymond Berry and Tom Landry, which was now unpublished, so that chance meeting in 1958 set me up for a job I'd have for thirty years. But back then we were all pretty much in the dark and in a very small club. There'd be maybe two or three writers at the games for the first several years."[12]

This undersized claque also included Bud Shrake and Dan Jenkins of the *Dallas Times Herald* and Gary Cartwright of the *Fort Worth Star-Telegram*. A year later, another writer from the latter paper, Frank Luksa, would get the assignment, as he remembered, "for one reason—they asked people in the newsroom if they would cover the Cowboys, and I was the only one who put his hand up. And I wasn't gaga about it, either."[13] They, like almost all young sportswriters in North Texas, were heavily influenced by an editor and columnist named Blackie Sherrod, a kind of Damon Runyon chased with Bull Snort who flitted through the doors of all three papers in his day, pollinating by example a slick, homey, and hard-boiled style of writing. Back then the *Times Herald*, the only afternoon paper among the three, had the highest circulation, around 170,000, its liberal editorial slant playing to the bourgeois in contrast with the *Morning News*' conservative, white-glove pretensions. The *Morning News* hit the stands first, delivering the score of Cowboys' games, albeit to what would be a rather indifferent public.

To be sure, no one in the management arc of Dallas journalism had any idea what import, if any, there would be in breaking Cowboys news. That would need to be a lesson learned when, and if, someone succeeded in making the team a real attraction. For now, that was the job of Tom Landry, in whom lay the future of more people than he could have ever imagined at the time.

Blair, sharp of eye and pen and nearing eighty, can attest to that. He would, in 1969, originate the cottage industry that became Dallas Cowboys literature, with a now-buried treasure of a book called *Dallas Cowboys, Pro or Con?* Recalling those weeks in Forest Grove, he wrote of them as "a weird adventure. There really were some capable players there but there were also some fugitives from *Whose Zoo?*"[14]

And there were a lot of them. No fewer than 189 men came through steamy Forest Grove, almost all to be sent packing within days, not surprising since the first chore Landry had for anyone in his camp, then and thereafter, was to put them through the hell of a mile run in the midday sun—an exercise that Burton wrote of under the headline "COWBOYS GREETED BY LANDRY'S MILE."[15] This phrase—"the Landry Mile"—would cause grown men to wince and even weep in every Cowboys camp for the next twenty-nine years. When word of this got back to *Sports Illustrated*, it ran a semi-serious item that read:

> If track men can run the mile in four minutes, how fast should football players be able to run it? Five minutes? Six minutes? An hour and a half? Dallas Cowboys' Coach Tom Landry decided to find out. He measured off a mile course on the turf at the Cowboys' training camp in Forest Grove, Ore. and told the boys to get out there and break the six-minute barrier.
>
> None did. The best time was 6:19 by Greg Altenhofen, rookie end from Oregon. Slowest time was a 9:06 by Bob Griffin, Arkansas center. The University of New Mexico's Don Perkins, who has run the hundred in 10 seconds flat, collapsed after five of the six laps, walked the rest of the way. Landry intends to keep the boys at it, and if football fields are ever lengthened to 5,280 feet, the Cowboys will be a team to be reckoned with.[16]

For a good many in Forest Grove, it was their Last Mile. For those who survived, there were two-a-day practices in full pads and long film and blackboard sessions in airless dorm rooms. Indeed, the vibe between Landry and his first batch of Cowboys was strained. Perkins almost quit in camp because he had come in overweight, not expecting a Parris Island regimen. Indeed the only thing that cooled the air was Landry's glacial way with other humans, which was another cause for discontent. Some would believe in retrospect that Landry was sinking his own ship by turning off so many players. A defensive back on that first Cowboys team, Tom Franckhauser, said, "I felt if Tom had been more personable with his players in those early days he might have gotten more out of them. A lot of us didn't particularly like his standoffish attitude."[17]

The portrait of Landry sent back from Oregon by the sportswriters was of a stern, joyless martinet who said little beyond boilerplate clichés and resisted any open show of emotion. In New York, it didn't matter that he wasn't one for empty bravado, that he spoke in clichés and had no use for butt-slapping, glad-handing rituals with players. But now that he was a head coach and an instant celebrity in his hometown, such quirks seemed pathologically unfit for the inborn swagger of Dallas. Landry, trying to explain why his diffidence was part of the coaching psyche he had learned from Paul Brown, would say things like, "The players don't want to see me rushing around and screaming. They want to believe I know what I'm doing." [18] Paul Brown, however, was a man with too many championship rings to count. Who was Tom Landry? For the time being, that was an open-ended question. But Landry couldn't be bothered with personality issues. There were also too many questions to answer about a team that was filled with football chaff.

After fleeing Forest Grove in midsummer, the team spent two more weeks out of town, at the St. John's Military Academy in Delafield, Wisconsin. At that point, the triumvirate was still searching for players. One of the last was acquired minutes after a preseason game, in Pendleton, California, against the Rams. After the game, rookie Rams guard Mike Connelly was told he was traded to the Cowboys. Connelly's response was, "Is there a team in Dallas?" Connelly, who had gone to Utah State after a two-year stint in the Marines, was totally in the dark when he got to Big D. "That game was on a Friday night and they told me to be in Dallas on *Saturday morning*. They were having practice the morning after a game played two thousand miles away. You had to learn to change your whole thinking, throw out the way you'd done things before. And I was a rookie. Some of those other guys had been with the same team for five, ten years, their whole world was turned upside down. You gotta blame someone, and who better than the coach you don't know? So there was a lot of bitching about Tom." Sizing Landry up, Connelly says, "I liked Tom. Most of the guys hadn't been in the military. I'd been in the Marine Corps. I'd seen a lot of aloofness. Tom got that as a military guy. I thought he was nice and polite. He didn't say a whole lot. It was, 'This is the way we were gonna do it,' and that was it. And he grew on us. We weren't gonna win many games, but we still couldn't wait to get out there because we were learning stuff about football we never knew before."

One of the older guys, offensive lineman Bob Fry, had also come to the Cowboys from the Rams, where he had played for seven years. A former All-American at the University of Kentucky under Bear Bryant, Fry was smart and skilled, and would neatly transition into coaching after his playing days. Fry began to notice some similarities between Landry and the Bear. "Bryant was more of a personally overwhelming guy, but Tom was too in his own way because his fingerprints were just all over everything, every detail. Some guys didn't like Tom because he was tough on them. I couldn't care less about that. We had to get better players, but I went out there thinking we'd win every game because of him. We never lost because we were unprepared, I'll tell you that."[19]

ASIDE FROM Meredith, LeBaron, and Perkins, Landry had little to work with, which was why Schramm, in his old PR mode, busied himself in the run-up to the season getting reporters to run human interest stories about the players Dallas would soon see. Meredith was a natural, a local rakehell with enough personality to make up for the lack in Landry. Dallas got to know that "Dandy Don" had an encyclopedic knowledge of country tunes. Without warning or reason he would break into a crude rendition of his favorite, Kitty Wells's 1952 twangy hit "It Wasn't God Who Made Honky Tonk Angels," which became something of a theme song for him. At the same time, LeBaron, Meredith's polar opposite who would hold the quarterback position while helping to groom him, was portrayed as a kind of Renaissance Man, because he had that law degree and a practice in Midland, Texas, and as a David among Goliaths. It was a natural story line that the most fan-captivating pieces played the same position, but for Landry it would become a headache he didn't need.

"He wanted to get Meredith some time because he had the ability, he was the hometown boy with a big following at SMU," says Connelly. "But he was just such a clown all the time, and that's what caused trouble. Tom bent over backwards, he was so patient with Dandy, but he hated that he had to wait for him to get serious. Because he would come in and wouldn't know the audibles. He'd look at us in the huddle and sing his songs. He wouldn't know what the hell was going on out there. He'd call an audible, but he'd call the wrong one. It really got to where you didn't even want him around."

Meredith was far more complex than he seemed. His self-erected Li'l Abner schtick was a facade for massive insecurity dating back to childhood, when he was stricken with polio and kept in his crib for seven months. When he recovered, he was left with skinny legs and hammertoes. He was also susceptible to injury, but similar to Tom Landry at that age, he wanted to prove to himself that he was as good an athlete as his older brother, Bill Jack. Meredith had a lot of courage, which he would need, but he never answered the riddle of who he was, a riddle he once believed he could sort out in divinity school. He had his life story boiled down to a few humorous lines, liberally dispensing southern-fried nuggets such as that he was first and foremost "Jeff and Hazel's baby boy from Mount Vernon, Texas"—a phrase he would cash in on a decade later when he became an overnight media icon.

For whatever reason, Meredith had no desire to learn the nuances of being a quarterback, much to the consternation of Landry, LeBaron, and Don Heinrich. Denne Freeman, who covered the Cowboys for the Associated Press, coined a useful metaphor for Meredith: "Don had that gunslinger mentality and wanted to throw the bomb. Tom wanted him to read defenses."[20] To Landry, Meredith was the gridiron equivalent of the Texas rubric "all hat, no cattle"—all helmet, no brains. He would constantly need to prove otherwise.

✦ ✦ ✦ ✦

LANDRY WAS dealt a killer blow when in August he lost his best runner and best defensive back, both suffering injuries while practicing for the College All-Star Game. Perkins broke his ankle, and former Arkansas All-American Jim Mooty, whom Schramm had filched from the AFL New York Titans, tore his thigh muscle. Landry knew it would be impossible to throw all kinds of esoterica at players with limited time to understand them. Instead, he installed four basic formations, placed the emphasis on fundamental blocking and tackling technique, and used a stripped-down playbook, with a few variations of each play according to on-the-go reads and the tendencies of the opposition. But mainly he left it up to LeBaron to get him points.

Landry could praise the Lord that he had Eddie. He could also rejoice that, if little else, he had a gem at middle linebacker. That was Jerry Tubbs, a former member of Bud Wilkinson's undefeated, twice-national-champion Oklahoma teams of the mid-1950s. Born in Throckmorton, Texas, Tubbs was one of the most-storied college players of his day, having been a two-way All-America center/linebacker and won the Walter Camp Award for player of the year. He was drafted in the first round by the Cardinals and then traded to the 49ers, but San Francisco misused him as outside linebacker, negating his blend of brute power and lithe quickness, which had become notable when he had run the ball in college. Tubbs was also an Academic All-American. When he was undecided about quitting the game, 49ers coach Red Hickey left him unprotected and Landry had to have him.

On the eve of the season the Cowboys were a team of spare parts about to be sent into battle, not with anything resembling a pep talk from their coach, but with reams of words unsaid and implied. In that frame of history, obeying Landry had a simple, intrinsic imperative: to keep from getting on Landry's bad side. As Connelly confirms, "Getting chewed out by Tom was scary. If he yelled and screamed, you could live with that. But Tom was like Peter Lorre in a scary movie. He wouldn't raise his voice. He'd say, 'On that play when they got Eddie, you weren't watching out for the inside move by the tackle. You know better than that, we've gone over it again and again.' It was all nice and calm but you'd be shaking, scared to death of making the same mistake." The reward for making a good play was a silent pat on the back, which from Tom Landry meant you would live to see another morning. If you did, Landry wanted you to be gnarly. When told that someone in Forest Grove had called the Cowboys "the nicest boys we've ever seen in a pro club," Landry replied, with a thin grin, "I don't know whether that's good or bad."[21]

THE FIRST game the Cowboys played was a preseason match against the 49ers up the Pacific coastline in Seattle's Husky Stadium. They lost 16–10, but Landry said, "I am very encouraged, and so are the players. We think we can beat somebody now."[22] Red Hickey added, "The Dallas club is no patsy. I'm sure they won't finish in last place in the National League." Those were common sentiments as the Cowboys made their way through the tune-up games, losing to the Cardinals 20–7 before getting the key to the Cotton Bowl for the long-touted exhibition game against the two-time defending champion Colts, who beat them 14–10.

But the most important number for the Cowboys that night, not to mention the NFL, was the number of people who came to see Johnny Unitas toss a few passes: "in excess of 40,000 fans" is what Charles Burton wrote the next day. It was an estimate given to the press by Tex Schramm but, which Burton noted, included a horde of children, five of whom were allowed in free with each purchase of a $2.75 end zone ticket, a policy that would continue into the season in the face of something less than a stampede to see Cowboys games. Things progressed as well as could be expected. The games, superfluous as they were, stayed close, and football people were saying very nice things about the Cowboys. Weeb Ewbank's take was, "They've got some good ballplayers. They've got more than I had my first year in Baltimore," and "They've got a fine team. They already have that Landry touch. They have real good balance between offense and defense. They looked like a team that's played together a lot longer than six weeks." As an event that proved the Cowboys were big league in every respect, Burton wrote, it was "a smiling success."[23]

Just not for Landry, for whom the closest thing to a smile came the following week when he looked across the field and saw Jim Lee Howell on the opposite sideline. Although the game was a mere tune-up for the Giants, played in Louisville before a small crowd, Landry prepared with a grimness even for him, and the Cowboys made him a winning coach for the first time, taking the game 14–3. Afterward, Frank Gifford dropped into the Cowboys' locker room to greet Landry, telling some of the players, "I bet that you win more games than you lose. I wouldn't say that if it were anyone except Tom Landry coaching. He's going to surprise you."[24] The next week, after they lost to the Packers in the preseason finale, Vince Lombardi, who himself had to weather a rough baptism in Green Bay, with a record of 1–10 in 1958 before bettering it to 7–5 in '59, said he told Landry, "We made you too strong," meaning that the league had given the new team perhaps too many breaks. In its preseason pro football preview, *Sports Illustrated* boldly predicted, "The Cowboy pass defense will not be the NFL's worst," and that "with their air attack, their good short-gaining ground game and their good defense, it will be a great surprise if the Cowboys finish last."[25]

THE FIRST Cowboys game that counted was played on the night of Saturday, September 24, 1960, against the Pittsburgh Steelers, a team with title aspirations. Yet Landry predicted, "We'll fool 'em, and you can take that any way you want to."[26] The game had a built-in appeal beyond the obvious, as a homecoming for both Landry and his former Longhorns teammate and hero of Highland Park Bobby Layne, who had outstayed his welcome, and bar tab, in Detroit. After joining his old Lions coach Buddy Parker, he was now pitchin' and elbow-bendin' in the Steel City. Another feature attraction at the game was the TV cowboy couple Roy Rogers and Dale Evans. They flew in during the week to appear on a show on Dallas's channel 8 called *Cowboys' Home-Coming* and perform before the kickoff. The game being a high-priority item in the Fifth Avenue offices of the NFL, Pete Rozelle flew to Dallas to be in attendance. At game time, the night was a comfortable seventy-two degrees, but rain began to fall, cutting into what was almost entirely a walk-up crowd, advance tickets having sold poorly. Just in case, Schramm had papered the Cotton Bowl with free passes, including for children.

Yet despite all that and reams of free publicity in the papers, the stadium was no more than a third filled, mostly with curiosity seekers and stragglers uncertain of what to do on a Saturday night. Not everyone was in a festive mood. Roy and Dale were supposed to sit in the back of a convertible—not on horses—and take one lap around the field while waving to the crowd, but in one of the end zones they had to duck for cover from a hail of ice cubes thrown at them. At eight o'clock, the ragtag home team—Parker had called them "a bunch of strangers"[27]—came out decked in their garish royal blue and white uniforms with oversized white stars on each shoulder, white helmets with a blue star over each ear, and blue socks with two horizontal white stripes. Subtle they weren't. They stood stiffly in a single line at attention during the national anthem and before a procession of marching bands, then went out, and early in the game scored on a thrilling 75-yard pass from Eddie LeBaron to Jim Doran.

LeBaron threw another touchdown to 49ers castoff Fred Dugan. After a short run by erstwhile Packer Don McIlhenny, the Cowboys went in at the half leading 21–7. The Steelers tied it in the third quarter, but LeBaron threw another bomb to Doran, covering 54 yards, to retake the lead. Little Eddie was a terror, piling up 345 yards, but Layne, even in deterioration, was in hog heaven against the Cowboys' odds and ends. Stumbling onto the field again, he threw a 49-yard touchdown pass, then another for 65 yards. The Steelers escaped, 35–28. Landry and his team left the field contented that they had thrown a scare into a fairly good NFL team. The offense was miles ahead of the defense, which must have been the unkindest cut for the old defensive master. But, for now, Landry was after excitement, and he had produced a lot of it. Burton called it a "thrilling but losing battle." As for the coach, one headline noted, for only the first time, that "LANDRY IS HAPPY (ALMOST)." His diagnosis was, "Our players tried hard, but they were up against a good football team."[28]

Positive spin aside, the game did have its pleasant surprises that Landry might be able to extend long term. A lightly regarded receiver, Frank Clarke, who had caught a total of ten passes in three years with the Browns, made the team because Landry sized him up as a

Ray Berry type, such were his soft hands and intricate moves. In the opener he grabbed two long heaves for 75 yards, the kind of yardage-to-catch ratio that would become common for him. And LeBaron was perfectly willing to throw the living heck out of the ball to keep the fans excited, no matter how few showed up. Schramm said the opening-day crowd had reached "around 30,000" and left it at that, never giving a specific total.

However, the fact that the Cowboys had to cede the traditional Sunday afternoon sinecure to the Texans on opening weekend dulled whatever buzz the team had made. Sixteen hours later, Lamar Hunt's team took the same field in their bright-red jerseys and helmets, not with a lone star on them but with the shape of Texas in white and Dallas marked by a gold star. The attendance in the same rainy weather was estimated to be 42,000, if Hunt's PR people could be believed—though Hunt too had practically stood on street corners during the week handing out freebies. Unlike the Cowboys' game, there was scant excitement, but the home team won, shutting out the LA Chargers, 17–0.

Few around Dallas thought it mattered which home team won that weekend, but the Texans played off the NFL connection well enough. The AFL had certainly given *them* every advantage, even establishing the league office in Dallas, in the same Mercantile National Bank Building where the Texans had their offices. Unlike the NFL with the Cowboys, the other AFL teams stood aside and let Hank Stram sign native college heroes such as North Texas halfback Abner Haynes and TCU linebacker Sherrill Headrick. Stram's quarterback was the veteran Cotton Davidson, who had starred at Baylor. Stram also beat Paul Brown to the signing of Stanford receiver Chris Burford. Haynes would lead the AFL in rushing that year. LSU halfback Johnny Robinson, who like Billy Cannon had signed with the NFL, voided his contract with the Lions to sign with Hunt. Once with the Texans, he switched to strong safety, where he would set the standard for that position. Playing much of the season with a broken neck, Headrick developed a cult following and won the affectionate nickname "Psycho" for his inhuman pain threshold. The Texans' defense gave up the fewest points in the league.

Realizing that it might indeed be easier to peacefully coexist with the Texans than to knock them out, Tex Schramm, pumping out wishful thinking, said, "That inferiority complex about Dallas as a major league city ought to be finished. The people have proved they're great football fans. It's quite possible both pro teams will draw big crowds this year."[29] The Cowboys' second game, also at home, brought in the Eagles, who were en route to winning the championship that year, driven by the now-graybeard quarterback Norm Van Brocklin and his trio of receivers, Tommy McDonald, Pete Retzlaff, and Bobby Walston. They also had Chuck Bednarik, one mean Slovakian middle linebacker who that season would splatter Frank Gifford, putting him out of the game for two years with a concussion. The game was a madcap affair, with *nine* interceptions, four thrown by the Eagles, five by LeBaron. Through three quarters, amazingly, Philly led only by a hair, 13–12, and the Cowboys were flying after LeBaron hit Clarke with a thrilling 75-yard touchdown pass. The Eagles took leads again in the fourth quarter, only to see Dallas come right back each time before time ran out with the Eagles holding on, 27–25.

Few seemed to notice the inert-looking figure on the sideline sending out signals—Landry had not yet taken to wearing a fedora and tailored suits, and in his drab baseball-type jackets or rain slickers he appeared more like an equipment manager. But Landry's wide-open offense kept things exciting. In the first road game, against the Redskins, the Cowboys were down 19–14 in the last quarter and lost 26–14. The first blowout came the next week when the Browns traveled to the Cotton Bowl and waltzed to a 48–7 win before a crowd of 28,500, but then in St. Louis the Cowboys *led* in the fourth quarter, only to lose on a late field goal, 12–10. With the Cowboys sitting at 0–5, not even Johnny Unitas's first regular-season visit to Dallas could rouse the town; only around 25,500 saw him heave five touchdown passes in the Colts' 45–7 victory. The next week, the Rams brought in only 16,000 to see another rout, 38–13.

By then, the team was burned out. The Cowboys' tour of the league produced no wins and few additional close encounters, and soon the novelty wore off in a city of archetypical Texas bravado and hubris, especially about football. They went to Green Bay, where they were subjected to a 41–7 pasting, and their last game at home,

a 26–14 loss to the 49ers, barely drew 10,000 fans. To Landry, that
proved what good taste the town had. As he would wryly remember,
"Perhaps the most encouraging thing about that first season was how
few hometown fans came out to see us lose." Once, he said, he trotted onto the field with the team, looked around, and thought, "We'd
shown up on the wrong date." On one of those rainy days in Dallas, when the few in attendance moved to shelter, the Cotton Bowl
seemed like "a completely deserted stadium."[30]

Still, he did have a shining moment, back where he had first made
his name, when after a 17–7 loss to the Bears, the Cowboys traveled
to Yankee Stadium for a game on December 4 that Landry had been
waiting for all season. "Oh yeah, that was a *big* game for us up in
New York," Mike Connelly says. "Tom didn't say it, but we could tell
that was his whole season right there."

There was a kind of nostalgic glow about the game, even in New
York, where Howell's team was out of the race and Jim Lee was perfectly willing to update his oft-misquoted quote about his old assistant, whom he now said "is the greatest coach in football. I've always
said that, and I mean it."[31] In the *New York Times*, Arthur Daley
made like Zane Grey:

> Tom Landry, an old range rider from Texas will come a-moseyin'
> out of the mesquite today, plumb tuckered out from the way them
> varmints treated him on the prairie before leaving him for the buz-
> zards. His lips are dry, his throat parched. He's thirstin' for victory
> for him and his bedraggled Dallas Cowboys.[32]

While the old range rider had never mounted a horse in his life,
he was surely thirsty for his first victory. During the bus ride from
Newark Airport to the team's midtown hotel on the day before the
game, Alicia, who accompanied her husband on every road game,
was excitedly talking to him about what show they could see and
which of their old haunts they would go to for dinner. As Cowboys
linebacker Gene Babb recalled years later, "Tom had his hat on, and
he was looking straight ahead, and I don't know that he heard a word
of what Alicia was saying." It was, Babb said, as if "he was already
at the ballgame on Sunday."[33] Landry snapped out of his catatonia

upon hearing a loud welcoming roar when his name was announced. As the game progressed, the Cowboys caught fire, storming back from a 21–7 deficit to tie it at 24–24. The crowd of 55,033 was clearly rooting for the visiting team to get that elusive win. For Landry, it was a chance to show up the 4–3 defense he had made into a league backbone. The Cowboys rang up 328 yards, one more than the Giants' total. "We had Sam's number all day," says Connelly. "Other teams just couldn't figure out the 4–3, but they didn't have the guy who invented it."

Trailing 31–24, LeBaron again took his offense down the field, hitting Billy Howton with a touchdown pass from 11 yards out to salvage a very exhilarating tie. Sam Huff, smiling, says that was the Giants' gift to Landry. "It was like, 'Hey, Tom, thanks for all you did for us, Here, have one on us.'"[34] Landry would recall that after the final gun, "we all stood there stunned for a while, not believing." His enduring reaction was that "it was great, just great," which for him was getting lathered with glee.[35] But back home, few celebrated. Landry remembered landing that night at Love Field, where "an overwhelming mob of two fans crowded around the gate to welcome us home. One of them held up a sign that read, 'Well done, Cowboys.'"[36] Their final game was in Detroit, in the snow against the Lions, where they fell 23–14. While it was a hard-fought contest, what happened outside the lines was more significant.

Dandy Don Meredith, figuring he wouldn't see any action in the game, decided to get some the night before, as he went about "introducing myself to the Motor City." The next day, he could barely focus his eyes when Landry suddenly told him he was going to start the game. In a funk, he put on his uniform and was about to walk out onto the field when a teammate told him, "Maybe it would be a good idea to put your pants on before we go out." Properly pantsed, Meredith got outside when Landry, turning on a dime, told him he *wasn't* going to start after all. During the game LeBaron took another frightful beating, turning Landry livid that the officials never flagged the Lions for any roughing penalties. By the fourth quarter, Landry, again looking to Meredith, told him to warm up. Tired of being kept on a string, he refused and sat on the bench smoking cigarettes the rest of the game. Landry never said a word about it, but Meredith knew there would be repercussions. That snowy afternoon in Motor City, he would say with classic Meredith sarcasm, was when he realized that "Tom and I were going to really have a lot of fun together."[37]

Landry's final take on his winless maiden season was to josh in his memoirs that the team had "peaked a little too early," at Yankee Stadium, dutifully noting that after all the hubbub of his hiring, he had compiled "the worst record in the NFL in the last eighteen years." Twelve weeks after the first Cowboys campaign began, contrary to *Sports Illustrated*'s forecast they placed last in almost every category. They scored an average of 15 points while giving up 31. LeBaron threw for twelve touchdowns and 1,736 yards, but he also had twenty-five interceptions. No rusher gained more than 362 yards. The kicker made only six of thirteen field goals. Landry though was typically Landry. "At least," he said, "we had made progress."[38] But even he was hard-pressed to say where.

Chapter 11

A VIRTUE
OUT OF WEAKNESS

IF THE FIRST SEASON WAS a character-building embarrassment, the Cowboys still held a crucial winning card against the Texans in the war between the leagues: the pipeline of visiting NFL stars who streamed into town. Thus, the two Dallas clubs remained stalemated in friendly warfare—Clint Murchison Jr. even attended Lamar Hunt's Christmas party clad in a red Texans blazer (in return, Hunt would pop out of a cake at a surprise birthday party for Murchison)—with attendance for both teams' games dropping off steadily during the season, notwithstanding all the freebies and promotions. Hunt's team certainly had the more creative of the latter, including Friend of a Barber's Day—if you showed up in a white smock you got in free. The idea behind the promotion was that loquacious barbers would drum up interest in the Texans by yapping about them to their captive customers in the chair. Attendance at the Cowboys' games averaged an embellished 21,000; the Texans', an equally fanciful 24,500. And the Cowboys caught a break when the far better-stocked Texans finished the year with a mediocre 8–6 record, second in their division to the Chargers, who lost the AFL's first championship game to the Buffalo Bills—a game played not at either team's homefield but in the Cotton Bowl, which had been chosen for a Texans' coronation, to around 18,000 people.

The AFL was playing a strong propaganda game too. After the

season a story appeared in the *Houston Chronicle* speculating that because of their failure to draw crowds, the Cowboys were already considering leaving Dallas for Minneapolis, no matter the incipient Vikings. Tex Schramm, knowing a plant when he saw one, responded with humor, saying that if attendance would determine such an exodus, the Texans "would move to Anchorage, Alaska, and the Oakland Raiders will move to Opelousas, Louisiana."[1] If Landry was looking forward to the next season, he would have to find a way to collect a few solid players despite having lost a first- and third-round pick. The draft was in Philadelphia in late December, and when he and Schramm arrived, the latter had a plan in his mind, one that he hoped would reel in not just a serviceable player but the mother lode: Bob Lilly, TCU's All-America defensive tackle.

Nabbing such a phenomenal talent seemed impossible, but Schramm went to work doing what he did best: finding a way to get his man by hook or by crook. As it happened, most NFL teams had given up on Lilly, since Lamar Hunt's Texans had chosen Lilly in the AFL draft six months earlier and offered him the sort of meed that Hunt trusted would scare off any NFL team from wasting a pick on him. And he was almost right; everyone did stay away from Lilly—except Schramm, who was thrilled when Lilly told him he would sign with the Cowboys if they could get his draft rights because he wanted to play in the NFL. This explained why Lilly had held off signing with the Texans. Even so, the rest of the NFL assumed he would, and he was still on the board after twelve picks.

That was when a salivating Schramm paid a little visit to Paul Brown. His Browns were next in line, and Brown was perhaps the only other league bigwig who was prepared to pick Lilly. As the clock ticked down, Schramm made Brown offers to squirrel away his pick. Brown dawdled, asking for more, but in the end he couldn't resist Schramm's bedrock offer, which included the Cowboys' first pick in the 1962 draft and veteran tackle Paul Dickson. Lilly, who was in San Francisco for the East-West Shrine Game, couldn't wait to get to Dallas, and when he did, he signed for a salary of $16,000, not Lamar Hunt type of money but more than enough for him. He showed up at the Cowboys' summer camp at St. Olaf College in Northfield, Minnesota, with the air of a star, "shuffle[ing] around the St. Olaf College campus in faded blue jeans and a plain white T-shirt, his blond hair waving like a field of unknown hay atop his 6-4, 250-pound frame," as a starry-eyed Sam Blair wrote in the *Morning News*.[2]

Landry hadn't seen a player quite like Lilly, who had size but little muscle mass or natural speed yet always seemed to be in on a tackle. The coach started him at right end, anticipating him being able to seal off wide runs such as the Packers' sweep play. However, Lilly didn't know what he had signed onto. He would be behind the learning curve all season and would have been the first to attest that playing for Tom Landry was no country picnic.

Neither were the Cowboys going anywhere just yet. If not for Lilly, the team's first draft was a washout. Hunt got the last laugh on another local boy made good, Texas Tech linebacker E. J. Holub, who chose to sign with the Texans even though Schramm had used his second pick to draft him. Besides Lilly, of the twenty college players the Cowboys drafted, only two made it onto the roster, as benchwarmers. The only other break they got was when they took a flier on Oregon State halfback Amos Marsh, who had gone undrafted. Landry desperately needed speed in the backfield, and not only would Marsh stick with the club but that season would be their second-best rusher and one of the top kick and punt return men in the league. Even so, it was obvious to Landry that, once again, progress would be a relative term, measured not in yards but inches.

IT HAD hardly escaped Landry's eye, as preoccupied as he was with merely competing, what Lombardi had managed to accomplish in Green Bay. Landry was ever gracious in his comments about his old confrere, but Lombardi's stratospheric one-year rebound into the NFL elite set the bar high for Landry. Thus, it would become a matter of utmost pride and an obsession for Landry to clutch his way closer to the level of Lombardi's team. To some of his old Giants cohorts, Landry and Lombardi had intertwined themselves as they branched out on their own. Frank Gifford once said that the two men "exchanged each other's playbooks. Lombardi used Landry's defense all the time."[3]

That was true, if a bit overblown since Landry's 4–3 defense was now standard issue in the NFL. What's more, Landry never thought he could use the power sweep the way Lombardi did, because the Cowboys did not have the big, rangy offensive linemen and battering-ram backs to make it work. That wasn't Landry's style anyway. Cerebral as he was, his offense wasn't based on raw power but baffling deception. As he once explained, "The Green Bay system of offense—we call it the basic system—was that you were going to run the power end regardless of what the other team put against you. Run that play over and over. It was all execution. So Lombardi had to develop the players to an emotional pitch, keep them doing their best all the time against a defense that knew what was coming. . . . Our system is different. We run a multiple offense and must take advantage of situations as they present themselves. Everything we do from every formation doesn't work against every defense, so we have to concentrate, we have to think."[4]

Obviously, Landry could not ignite the kind of visceral emotion Lombardi could, nor ever become a saint in quite the same personal way, although he too would have on his team grown men willing to take a bullet for him. Given his dispassionate ways, he could only go to his strengths, which was to out-teach, outguess, and outfool everyone else. He was practically bursting with new, daring concepts—especially since he had been handed the keys to the offense for the first time—but knew he had to keep things relatively simple for players who had been around the block but never been taught anything beyond the rudimentary. The whiz-bang stuff he had in mind would have to wait. As Bob Fry recalls, "All the multi-formations with everybody moving and shifting around came later. It was tough enough for us to just get everybody to make a simple block."[5]

Little by little, Landry began to implement elements that would make it harder for defenses to figure out what was coming. Even so, there was a growing kinetic, thinking-man's quality to his formations, such as when the running backs would shift, then shift again before the snap, or when a back or even a receiver would arise from his stance and slowly jog behind the quarterback all the way to the other side of the field. In an additional formation, an extra receiver would come out of the huddle and line up between the line and another receiver—in the proverbial "slot." Sometimes three receivers would line up on the same side. Or Lebaron or Meredith would take the snap in the "shotgun" passing formation founded by Red Hickey in San Francisco, with the quarterback standing seven yards behind the center, providing an extra second or so before the defensive linemen closed in. And with the runners having a wider angle out of that formation, Landry would draw up plays with inside draws and shuffle passes to the backs.

It was all being designed and given trial-and-error auditions so as to provoke maximum confusion. Motion, blurring of the defense's vision, the quarterback calling out an audible at the line . . . everything was thrown into the mix. Even the linemen got in on the deception. They would fully rise up as one before setting back down again, the object being to block the view the linebackers had of the running backs, even if only for a critical split-second—a tactic Landry called "the Hitch." The key to any great leap forward for the Cowboys was the quarterback. Landry yearned for the time he would feel good enough about Don Meredith to put him in and not regret it. Meredith had to be kept around because of the absurd money Murchison was paying him—though the $35,000 a year he was making may have seemed less to Dandy Don than everyone else, since, as Mike Connelly says, "on top of that, he married millions."[6]

Still, all the money in Dallas couldn't buy him any love with the coach who made him his pet project. Landry spent more time with Meredith than any other player, another sore spot for some of the veterans. One, defensive end Larry Stephens, recalled, "Tom never said much to the rest of us." Part of it was that Meredith was an accomplished brown-noser. As Stephens put it, "Don always seemed to have some idea of what Landry felt about the team,"[7] even if he was just pushing a load of jive on the coach. Dandy Don was one of the very few players who ever got across on Tom Landry, though it would be pushing it to say that Landry ever really warmed to Meredith or anyone he ever coached. More accurately, he and Don shared an ongoing psychodrama, trying to find common ground that wasn't there—not even when Meredith would amble onto the field, usually to get buried, then dust himself off and somehow make lemons out of lemonade. Even then, he earned little from Landry but that frozen stare. Among the players, there was a belief that Landry was cruel and humiliated Meredith, making him an example of how rough Landry could be on slackers.

Bob Lilly, a slavish admirer of Landry, pointed out that "Coach was already aware of the fact that Meredith would be the starting quarterback and the future of the Cowboys, but he was afraid of destroying his confidence by rushing into the position too quickly. Being a Dallas Cowboys quarterback in those days was not considered a glamorous position. It required a strong survival instinct."[8] Meredith, though, was hardly the only player who vexed Landry. In summer camp that year, he dropped a bomb on veteran linebacker Wayne Hansen, who when he showed up twelve days late was fined $1,200, a full month of his salary.[9] But Hansen was a marginal player, and 1961 would be his final season. Meredith, on the other hand, had a world of promise, and pain, ahead. As impatient for success as Landry was, in Meredith there was a necessity to show forbearance, a quality Landry would need to repeat with far more thorny players down the road. Balancing his natural decisive instincts against a selective double standard for his most talented players, in fact, would be the most delicate and maddening thing he would ever do.

The common assumption with Meredith was that Landry would sooner or later stick him in a game and let the dice roll, though Meredith's rookie year was a megaton bomb; he completed only twenty-nine of sixty-eight passes in 1960, with two touchdowns and five interceptions. For many around town, it didn't matter. Reflecting this attitude, a headline in the *Morning News* midway through the season pleaded "MORE MEREDITH, PLEASE."[10] Landry would try to appease them, though he did press Eddie LeBaron back into service for 1961, something he felt badly about, knowing how much punishment the little man would take. "The worst thing I ever did for Eddie was talking him into playing for us," Landry would say. "I guarantee you those guys took a great beating. I hate to say those early teams were awful, because it would be a discredit to so many of those great guys, but we were weak. We just didn't have the personnel."[11]

IN THE off-season run-up to 1961, Landry had no false hopes. Again with a wry wit, he lamented, "I guess we'll have to send Don

Perkins a football and tell him to run all summer."[12] The Cowboys were essentially the same team when the season got under way against the Steelers before an estimated crowd of 23,000 at the Cotton Bowl. The game would be an exhausting ordeal. Meredith hit Clarke with a 44-yard touchdown pass in the first quarter, but Bobby Layne brought his team back to lead 14–10. After Meredith botched a drive with an illegal pass in the third quarter, Landry went to LeBaron. He sent in a trick play in which Amos Marsh took a handoff and pitched it back to Eddie—familiarly known as the "flea-flicker"—who threw a 45-yard touchdown pass to Billy Howton.

Landry then returned to Meredith, but he threw two seemingly game-killing interceptions, the second one taken back for a touchdown and a 24–17 Steelers lead with four minutes left. Exasperated, Landry again sent out LeBaron, who by passing brought his offense 75 yards down the field and found Dick Bielski for a 17-yard strike with a minute left. But Layne, eschewing a tie, tried pulling out a late win, only to have a pass intercepted by Jerry Tubbs. Landry stuck with LeBaron, who cranked up a 40-yard pass to Howton, setting up kicker Allen Green's winning field goal, leaving the crowd, as Sam Blair wrote in his game story, "howling" as it "staggered from the stadium, still not believing what it had seen." He added, cheekily, that "the Cowboys rode from nowhere to a first-place tie in the Eastern Division."[13]

The headline the next day, spread across a full page of the *Morning News*, preserved the first-ever Dallas Cowboys victory: "COW-BOYS WIN, 27–24, IN FINAL SECONDS."[14] For Landry it was a great relief, and in his restrained euphoria he came away, typically, sensing a strategic advantage in how he had alternated his two quarterbacks, never mind that he had done it out of desperation. "Meredith played well," he said, "and he learned a lot. It just takes experience to get the necessary poise. In time, he'll be able to do like LeBaron did in the last few minutes."[15] Landry wouldn't say who would start the next game, against the newly expansion Minnesota Vikings. It would be the beginning of a coy cat-and-mouse game that would become standard procedure over the next two years.

The Vikings had incredibly won their first-ever game right out of the box, beating the Bears no less. Still, the Cotton Bowl matchup of two fledgling teams drew only around 20,500 people, who intimately witnessed another gem. The Cowboys led 14–7 in the fourth quarter and iced it late when cornerback Don Bishop pried the ball loose from a Vikings receiver, and Meredith, who started and passed for 163 yards, found Marsh for a 20-yard touchdown pass and the win, 21–7. After the Cowboys took an expected beating in Cleveland, they went to Minnesota and decimated the Vikings, 28–0, Meredith throwing for two touchdowns, LeBaron one. That ran their record to 3–1, and they were breathing rarefied air, still in first place. Landry also had a new wrinkle: to alternate his quarterbacks, not sporadically, but on *every play*. Blair in his game story applied a term for the method, noting,

> Landry has used the shuttle system before but never received nearly as much publicity with it as San Francisco's Red Hickey did a week ago when he rotated three quarterbacks in the 49ers' 49–0 rout of Detroit. This time, however, the Cowboys won with it and that does make quite a difference.[16]

The implication was that either Landry or Hickey had cadged the idea from the other, though it was clear that as far as the press corps was concerned, Hickey was old news and this was Landry's baby. Landry explained the genesis of it as merely a response to a pressing need. He had that week put a number of new plays in the game plan, and needed a conduit to send them into the huddle. "We didn't have two of anything but quarterbacks," he would say, "so we had to alternate LeBaron and Meredith. If we had had an extra guard or end, I probably would have used the same system as Paul Brown. But all we could spare was an extra quarterback." With the shuttle, he would have, he said, "a lot more information available to me when I call a play. I have what the quarterback coming off the field has to tell me about the situation on the field, and he is in the best position of any player to tell what the defensive reaction is."[17]

Landry could, and often did, discourse on the efficacy of the shuttle, winning headlines from the friendly press such as "LANDRY SPARKLES AS SIGNAL CALLER."[18] But the players were left dizzy seeing

the quarterback change every down. A few of them believed it was a
sign of weakness instead of a wise course. Connelly, for one, says he
thought the shuttle was "nuts." And a rude awakening came quickly.
For the next game, the 3–1 Giants made their first trip to the Cotton
Bowl, a marquee attraction that drew the biggest crowd there yet, an
estimated 42,500 people. They got an early thrill when Meredith hit
J. W. Lockett for a short touchdown pass and a 7–0 lead, but thereafter it was all Giants. Intercepting each quarterback twice, one interception being returned 101 yards for a touchdown, the Giants with
Y. A. Tittle—the ancient and beautifully bald quarterback who had
been traded to the Giants after a decade with the 49ers—put the win
away with two touchdowns, 31–10. The next week, the Eagles came
in and attendance dipped back to around 25,000 as the Cowboys
were dispatched 43–7.

Then came another return to Yankee Stadium. This time the
place was packed with over 60,000 fans looking for the Cowboys'
blood, not to praise the head coach moseying on in from the prairie. Landry's boys were a two-touchdown underdog and would not
have Meredith for the game, an injury to his throwing elbow keeping
him out. LeBaron threw two early touchdowns for a 14–0 lead, but
the Giants clawed back, going ahead 16–14 in the fourth quarter.
As he had in the opener, however, LeBaron moved his team up the
field, close enough for Green to win another nail-biter with a 32-yard
field goal. That one, too, felt like winning the championship. Defensive back Dick Moegle recalled that Landry was actually "jumping
around, yelling in the dressing room."[19]

Crashing back to earth, the Cowboys were not to win again
that season; they were blown out of every game, losing by scores
like 31–17, 37–7, 35–13, 38–17, and 31–13. The best they could do
was a 28–28 tie against the lowly Redskins, who four weeks later
beat them 34–24 in the finale and once again avoided a winless
season. During the free fall, Landry pulled the plug on the shuttle
and counted on LeBaron to somehow stanch the bleeding. Meredith, hung over from the nights before, mostly sat and smoked
cigarettes—perhaps he was grateful LeBaron and not he was being
buried out there. After each fresh loss, Landry would repair to the
coaches' room, dress quickly, and head for the bus. He would be

stewing in frustration, having seen all discipline and smarts on the field drain away before his eyes. Bob Lilly, for example, was invisible the whole season, slowed by a bad knee. Told by Landry he had to play, regardless, he had the knee shot with Novocaine. His failure to jam up the running lanes made it impossible for Jerry Tubbs to perform functionally at middle linebacker in the 4–3. Fed up, Tubbs would shout at him through his mask, "Lilly, close the trap. You're going to get me killed."[20]

Neither did Landry have any sympathy for his, or anyone's, pain. In this respect, he was no different from any other coach. Football rosters carried thirty-six players at the time, a full ten bodies fewer than today, which put extreme demands on everyone to get himself on the field and stay there. It was almost like being at the front during a war: only a stretcher, and proof that you needed one, could get you out. Landry had some standard pablum for that too. "The mark of a pro," he would facilely tell hobbling players, "is if you can play hurt. If you can't play hurt, you can't play in the NFL."[21] Lilly had reason to wonder whether, despite all the Cowboys' self-congratulations about signing him, Landry would get rid of him if he gave in to the pain.

Landry could find some small solace that he had won four games and that he'd made more incremental progress. The Cowboys were ranked sixth in passing, Clarke led the league with 22.4 yards a catch, and Perkins rushed for 815 yards. Amos Marsh was always a step from taking one a long way. But the team scored just 16.9 points a game and gave up 27.1. If there was anything to be happy about, it was that the Texans, in going 6–8, slipped behind the Cowboys in attendance—even Hunt knew it was useless to pad his crowd figures much, leaving the estimate for his last two Cotton Bowl dates that season at 8,000 and 12,500. In truth, even those numbers were inflated, and it was reported that neither team cleared 10,000 paid admissions for the *entire season*.[22] The year before, when Hunt claimed that the public was demanding a postseason "dream game" between the Cowboys and the Texans, the peerless Blackie Sherrod retorted in his column, "Dear hearts, the way the 'public' turned out for both the Texan and Cowboy games this year, it could ill afford to demand anything, even mustard for the hot dogs."[23]

✦ ✦ ✦ ✦

IN 1962, the third year of Landry's five-year plan, the Dallas Cowboys still lacked their own first-round pick in the draft, that having been bartered for Bob Lilly. When it was the Cowboys' turn to choose, they made jaws drop by taking with their eighteenth pick TCU quarterback Sonny Gibbs. It was incomprehensible for many reasons. One, Gibbs was likely the most bizarre-looking quarterback ever, standing at six foot seven and weighing 230 pounds, with a mortar of an arm and the speed of a snail. Two, he was a such a poor student he had another year of college eligibility left, meaning the Cowboys had to take him as a "future." Three, with so many holes in the team to fill, and their next pick not until the *sixth* round, why in the world would they use the only high pick they had on another quarterback, with the high-salaried Meredith presumably on the verge of stardom?

Tex Schramm seemed pleased that he had "shook everybody," and insisted Gibbs was "a good long-range choice."[24] The real shock was that Landry, tantalized by the kid's arm, went along with it. A convincing explanation was that Landry wanted to send a message to Meredith to buckle down or else. Still, one can scarcely believe that Landry would have signed off on Gibbs had he not been persuaded by Schramm, who may have taken Gil Brandt's word for it that Gibbs was a gem. Flightiness may have made for some good ink for Tex, but Landry needed some level-headed, sober judgment from his GM.

Schramm's quirky drafting did, however, net him a find with the eighty-second pick: George Andrie, who played defensive end at Marquette—but not for the past year, when he played not at all because the school had dropped its football program. At six foot six and 250 pounds, and fast enough to have played *receiver* at times, he was the sort of athletic freak Landry coveted, and he had to have him. Three other draftees would make the squad: guard Donnie Davis from Southern University, defensive tackle Guy Reese, and running back Amos Bullocks, the last taken in the twentieth round. Schramm and Landry also talked Pettis Norman, a tight end from the small black college Johnson C. Smith University, away from the Texans, who had taken him in the AFL draft. Other talented rookies were signed as free agents, including Mike Gaechter, a world-class sprinter at Oregon—he had run the third leg on the world-record-setting 4 × 440-yard relay team that year—who hadn't played football until his senior year.

By the time the final roster was set, no less than thirteen rookies, and arguably the best athlete of them all—Cornell Green—had made it. A muscular and lithe six-three, 205-pound All-America guard on the Utah State basketball team, Green had been drafted by the NBA's Chicago Zephyrs and thought he would play pro basketball. His brother was an outfielder in baseball who in 1959 became the first black man ever to play for the Boston Red Sox. Cornell had never played football, but Brandt projected him as a tight end and signed him as a free agent for $1,000, which Green considered found money. "I never planned on playing for the Cowboys," he recalled, "I figured I'd go there for a week and they'd cut me.[25]

Camp that year was at Northern Michigan University, in Marquette, and by the time it began, Landry had added three new assistant coaches. He let go Babe Dimancheff and brought in his old defensive backfield mate, thirty-year-old Dick Nolan, who had been traded to the Cowboys by Allie Sherman in his ongoing purge of Landry's defense. In Dallas, Nolan was initially made a player–backfield coach, and paid a quick dividend in the rise of Cornell Green. Green knew so little about football that when he got to summer camp he wore his pads backwards for the first three weeks before someone told him how to wear them right. He didn't cut it as a tight end, but Nolan moved him to cornerback, where he excelled. Nolan, who would become a full-time assistant coach after a midseason injury, could boil down the 4–3 defense in simple, coherent ways, which itself was a stride forward in the overall molding of the team. Green took to him and decided to chuck basketball. For their original $1,000 investment in him, the Cowboys would reap monumental benefits.

Landry also lured Jim Myers into the pros after two decades in the college game. Myers would coach the offense, which would move Brad Ecklund to work the defensive line with Tom Dahms. Landry then tapped Ermal Allen, once a four-sport letterman at the University of Kentucky and a two-way quarterback/defensive back for

Paul Brown in the AAFC days. Allen had been a sponge for Brown's highbrow methods, and Landry wanted him not as a coach but as a "special assistant," a right-hand man who could help analyze films and chart other teams' tendencies. However, all these aides said little that Landry didn't program them to. As Mike Connelly says, "There was no question who ran the show."

BY THIS time Landry's offense had certainly grown more ambitious. Each set was identified in a similar fashion to the color-scheme terminology he had originated with the Giants—the I (two running backs stacked behind the quarterback), the Brown (both backs set to the weak side, the one without the tight end), the Red (backs split with the fullback to the strong side), and the Blue (both backs set to the strong side). But with all the permutations based on the tendencies of the defense in each down-and-distance situation, there were some *sixty* variations of each set. Sometimes they went on a quick count, sometimes after one shift, sometimes after a shift where a flanker or a running back went in motion, sometimes after a second shift. Of course, no one was more qualified to defang a 4–3 defense than the man who had invented it.

"Having spent so much time myself on the 4–3," he recalled in the early 1970s, "I realized that the basis of its effectiveness was recognition—recognizing what possible plays your opponents' offensive formation was setting up and then making your defense adjustments. My thinking went like this: If this is the case, let's keep the other team from recognizing *our* offensive intentions. We'll show them one formation, and while they're adjusting their defense we'll shift into a different formation and run our play before they can ever start to readjust."[26]

This was nowhere near as easy as he made it sound, because in his system every player had to make individual reads and adjustments. If one didn't pick up on something, the whole house of cards would come tumbling down. Connelly, who was switched from guard to center, found out that he was the steward of the offensive line. "You had gaps or you had players in the gaps, then you had the tendencies of each team's defense in each formation. You had all these ways to line up and you had to know what you'd do in like a split-second, how to block, and who. With most teams it was, 'You take that guy, I'll take this guy.' But Tom put in all these odd-man lines and shifting to one side or the other. If there was a linebacker in the gap, the guard and I would double-team him. Even while you were making the block, you were reading, because if he's moving a certain way you knew the linebacker would go the other way and a free lineman would have to take him. Tom's thing was that every defense had a weakness that could be exploited. We were light years ahead of other teams, but with our teams in the early years, the big teams could still come in and manhandle us."

Allie Sherman, who had indeed succeeded Jim Lee Howell in 1961 and was irritated that his reign in New York was being judged against the abstract of what might have been had Landry or Lombardi stayed, made the same point, almost damning Landry with faint praise in 1962. "Tom is a bright coach," he said. "Tom can key his guys to our offense. But if his guys fall down on him and don't hit, he can't win, can he?"[27] Neither could Landry win unless his quarterback would make the offense work. Thus, all of Dallas waited for him to hand the ball exclusively to Meredith. Instead, in 1962, he again went with the crude shuttle rotation he had tried the year before, with LeBaron and Meredith alternating play by play. It was the only way he felt comfortable with Meredith, whom he had no choice but to play. It would be folly to keep a $30,000 quarterback incarcerated on the bench for a third year. But he seemed to ignore that this system would be even more demeaning to Meredith. Landry's overarching objective was to mold a complete set of players carved in his system, when the flotsam of the early 1960s teams would come out in the wash. The biggest question was whether he himself would be able to last that long.

THERE WERE a few real positives coming into the 1962 season. One subtle change for the better was when George Andrie won the job at right defensive end. He was one of *three* rookies who started on the defensive line, along with tackles John Meyers and Guy Reese, while Bob Lilly at right tackle was only in his second year. The papers would dub them the "Maverick Line" for their tender years. "They might be the youngest defensive line in history," Landry marveled. "I don't remember three rookies ever starting in the front four."[28] Andrie seemed to make the line whole, easing the burden on Lilly a bit, and became the first Cowboy to be named to the NFL All-Rookie team. Still, there seemed not much hope for a major breakthrough.

The Cowboys lost five straight games in the preseason, then opened at home against the doormat Redskins before a crowd said to be 15,730 but in truth was maybe a third of that. And while the offense accrued a 483–286 edge in the number of yards gained, and Frank Clarke caught ten passes for a remarkable 240 yards and three touchdowns, it was never easy. Landry went again with his quarter-back shuttle, and Meredith threw two touchdown passes, but he also threw two picks. The team could salvage only a 35–35 tie. Still, Bud Shrake, now with the *Dallas Morning News*, came away impressed, writing in a column headlined "COWBOYS ARE GROWING UP," his proof being that they had "punished people in a way that makes the Cowboy future considerably more interesting."[29]

The next week, the Steelers came in and took an early 21–7 lead. The Cowboys fought back but could not catch up, going down 30–28. It was a game that featured both Bobby Layne's then-record-breaking 188th and 189th career touchdown pass and, in a considerably rarer sight, Tom Landry damn near melting down. That happened late in the game when, with the Steelers up 21–14, LeBaron dropped back into his end zone and sailed one long and far. Frank Clarke ran under the ball, caught it, and ran all the way to the other end zone, sending the intimate Cotton Bowl crowd into a frenzy—but only until the referee dropped a flag and awarded the Steelers a safety. No one really knew why the play was wiped out, and the crowd became, as the *Morning News* reported, "an angry mob," leading the referee to use a sideline telephone to call the press box and tell the public address announcer that a Cowboys lineman had held in the end zone, which by rule was a safety. "Now will you please explain this to 'em and let us play the game," he pleaded.[30]

The explanation did little to calm the crowd or Landry, who was enraged that he had lost 9 points on one play and bolted onto the field, pointing a finger at the ref and screaming, "You better be right!" about the rule. Both Landry and Buddy Parker said they never knew a rule existed that awarded points on a penalty—hard as it is to believe now that any NFL coach wouldn't know that. (Actually, the touchdown wouldn't have stood anyway, as Clarke had caught the pass after coming in from out of bounds.) Landry would recall not only that "I was so mad" but that, even worse, his minister was in the stands watching his tantrum.[31]

Admirably, the Cowboys then came up big with two huge upsets on the road, a 27–17 victory over the Rams behind LeBaron (a bad ankle kept Meredith out) and a win over the Steelers, 42–27. Those games wrapped around a manhandling of the Eagles, 41–19, at home, with Marsh returning a kickoff 101 yards. Meredith and LeBaron had been splendid to that point, benefiting from a conservative game plan dominated by a strong ground attack. In the Pittsburgh game, when the Steelers bunched up for the run, LeBaron riddled their secondary with five touchdown passes, three to Frank Clarke. That was the context when Tex Maule wrote a piece about the Cowboys in the November 5 issue of *Sports Illustrated* with the title "A SHUTTLE SHAKES UP THE PROS," a logical assumption with the team record at 3–3–1. But as with the year before, the second half of the schedule went sour. After they beat the 'Skins to go 4–3–1, they came home for their biggest game of the season, against the Giants, an event that brought 45,668 fans to the Cotton Bowl—for once, Schramm had no reason to exaggerate. Landry, playing a hunch, went with Meredith the whole way, to his regret, as Dandy Don cracked along with everyone else. The Cowboys fell behind, 27–0, and lost, 41–10, with Tittle completing three touchdown passes.

Landry stuck with Meredith the following week, and this time *he* threw three touchdown passes against the Bears, though the Cowboys blew a 33–24 lead and lost on a late field goal, 34–33. After a loss in Philadelphia, they returned to the shuttle and had a watershed win against the Browns before being smeared by St. Louis then New York in the finale, to finish 5–8–1, a tease of what could have been. Indeed, in 1969, Tex Schramm would bend history by recalling the season as a landmark of sorts, crowing that "there we were in 1962 leading the league in offense. And with *nothing*!"[32]

Actually, the quarterback shuttle produced twenty touchdowns and twenty-one interceptions, and the offense finished ninth out of fourteen teams. But for all the shaking up Landry had done, the result left a familiar sour taste, and the usual ambivalence about whether football was his long-term life plan. "I had never forgotten," he would say, "what Alicia and I had realized when I took the job: I was bound to get fired sooner or later. I'd already made it to the three-year mark. . . . Any more time was gravy."[33]

WHILE LANDRY would recall that he'd had to "ignore the critics who called me indecisive" about choosing a permanent quarterback, any such critics were drowned out by the sound of silence in Dallas on this matter, and of the Cowboys in general.[34] The same could be said of Hank Stram and his Texans, who that same year had accomplished what no professional team in Texas ever had: winning a championship. Turning Lamar Hunt's money into success on the field, the Texans rampaged through the league behind a formula that made Landry drool: Len Dawson's wily quarterbacking, Curtis McClinton's powerful legs, an enormous defensive line, and quick, smart linebackers. Yet even with all that upside, Dallas mostly yawned.

Beneath the inflated attendance figures, official records showed that the Texans had again drawn a mere 10,000 paid admissions, even less than the Cowboys, who had attracted all of 10,050 paying customers. For both teams, it would have taken 30,000 paid admissions *per game* just to break even. Hunt and Murchison vowed to soldier on, and *Sports Illustrated* called their mutual hemorrhaging of family fortunes a "millionaire's standoff," noting however that "now the nerves and the checkbooks are beginning to fray," and that "it seems unlikely that money alone will determine the winner." Indeed, the Cowboys, whom writer Joe David Brown said were "going about their business almost sedately," were surmised to be better positioned than the "razzle-dazzle" Texans, by dint of being "an adequate National Football League team and the reputation of that league behind them." The article went on:

Currently, the most popular suggestion is that the teams play each other, and the winner leave town. Some civic leaders have

expressed dismay because they claim the battle is dividing the loyalties of a city that has always been united. The Lions Club and the
Jaycees, for example, publicly are supporting the Texans, while the
more powerful Salesmanship Club has sided with the Cowboys.
A note of class consciousness has also crept into the struggle: it
is claimed that the more socially prominent people support the
Cowboys because the Murchisons and Wynnes are more "social"
than the Hunts.[35]

Coyly, Clint Murchison Jr. ventured that the smart thing to do
would be to move to another city, ruminating that "if you stayed and
threw away money, you would be a fool in everyone's eyes," then adding the punchline: "That's why I think Lamar should start looking for
another city." In fact, Hunt, having eyed Atlanta and Miami, already
had, and had in his pocket a sweetheart offer from Kansas City, the
mayor of which promised to triple the team's season ticket sales and
to expand the hoary Municipal Stadium, where the baseball Athletics played. That Murchison was able to lose money easier than
Hunt was underscored when it was pointed out to Lamar's father,
H. L. Hunt, that staying in Dallas would cost his son a million dollars a year. At that rate, the elder Hunt sniffed, "it will take him 150
years to go broke." But wags correctly noted that at a million a year,
Clint Murchison Jr. "wouldn't go broke for three hundred years."[36] If
anyone had any doubt about that, the *Sports Illustrated* piece noted
that "whenever he has the chance he hops one of the 17 planes in the
Murchison air fleet and flies off to Spanish Cay, the three-mile-long
sand and coral island he owns in the Bahamas," and his biggest kick
in life wasn't his football team but jumping out of those planes, as he
said, "with a beer in my hand."[37]

In the end, the battle of the fops was broken in the spring of 1963
when the AFL's $10 million antitrust lawsuit against the NFL went
to court. By then, Hunt had gotten the suit to include the demand
that the Cowboys be ordered out of Dallas, the Texans having gotten there first. When the judge dismissed the case, it was the death
knell for Hunt. Turning on a dime, he took up the Kansas City offer
and moved his team at breakneck speed to that city. He renamed the
team the Kansas City Chiefs. Finally, after a three-year trench war,

the city was the Cowboys' alone. But what exactly did the Cowboys win? Even the judge in the antitrust case had made mention of the fact that "interest and attendance at both the NFL and AFL games in Dallas has been disappointing, and that the city might not be as good a location for a professional football team as was generally believed."[38] Or, as Frank Luksa twitted, "They flipped a coin—and the winner got to leave."[39]

This was probably the best option for Hank Stram. He never could have hoped to compete with Landry the way the press sucked up to him. In January 1963, when it got out that a letter to Stram had been mistakenly sent to Landry's office, Gary Cartwright burnished it into a psalm of Landry worship in the *Morning News*:

> The long shadow of The Image—Tom Landry—burns [Stram's] cheeks daily. He is the helpless misfortune of anyone who rides in after the public has inhaled an opinion: there will never be another Gene Tunney, another Sarah Bernhardt, another Orville Wright, another Felix the Cat. There will never, for that matter, be another Tom Landry, just as there never was. . . . The Image [is] a dogma as unshakable as motherhood and the Easter Bunny.[40]

AS THE head coach who would be staying in the Big D, at least for another two years, Landry was slowly but surely evolving into a New Frontier monogram, stolid and smart, if hardly glamorous in the JFK mold. The writers were indeed smitten with him, not least of all Tex Maule, whose paean to the shuttle system carried the subhead "How Landry Made a Virtue out of Weakness." Landry surely could think out of the box and run a teetering ship tightly, establishing an air of high professionalism even in defeat. The details were getting more complicated, yet more often than not there was an informal name for the way the Cowboys blocked, or didn't—the "lookout" block became a team specialty, which happened when a player missed a block and turned and yelled to the quarterback, "Look out!"

For Landry, whether or not a play went well or nowhere would evoke the same reaction. The Cowboys, he would explain, had a *system*. Not the man but the *system* was supreme, the metaphysical talisman that would provide all the answers, given patience and better personnel. That, and the power, glory, and graces of God in heaven, to whom you could only assume Landry had a direct line. It would take him a while, longer than Lombardi had taken, to turn his team into a winner, but the symmetry between them was no less tangible than it was in New York. Vince had shown him that there really was something to hold on to when the fit was right. The Packers had run their sweep all the way to the championship game in 1960 and held a fourth-quarter lead before the Eagles pulled out the win, 17–13.

Crushed by the defeat, Lombardi vowed never again to lose a title game, but he almost walked away from the job right there. The day before, he'd had a secret meeting with Wellington Mara, who told him Jim Lee Howell was finally moving to the front office as player personnel director. Mara had promised Sherman the job, but Mara first made a stab at Lombardi, who was admittedly homesick and never had the same familial bond with the Packers' board of directors that he did with the Maras. After some soul searching, however, Lombardi stayed put. Mara couldn't possibly match the perks Vince had in Green Bay, where he was also general manager and paid a bonus for each winning game, as well as awarded stock in the team. That stock went through the roof when the Pack went all the way in 1961 and '62, destroying Sherman's Giants both times. But more than that, Lombardi knew that having come through his blue-collar, ethnic baptism in Green Bay, that was where he belonged.

Just as Landry's congealing environment was right for him, in the bosom of evangelical Christians, oilmen, dreamers, schemers, and cultural lines split between pickup trucks and Coupes de Ville. He'd still have to turn up the team's performance a notch, many notches. Yet one could almost sense that he and Lombardi had a showdown looming down the road.

LANDRY HAD staked out some solid ground on his own. "I think what fans liked about him is what we liked about him, that he said what he meant and had that consistency and confidence about what he was doing," says Sam Blair.[41] And how could they not, given how the press stroked Landry? His stoicism was always a major theme, and Landry never was at a loss for words explaining why his sideline demeanor was so stiff. Calling the world he isolated himself in "a total concentration of focus," he insisted that when a big play was made, he didn't react because he hadn't even been watching it, preoccupied as he was with the *next* play, and the one after that. Another rationale was that his players would lose focus if they saw that he did. Landry didn't need to be reminded that he was a one-dimensional figure during games. He admitted years later that his demeanor "wasn't such a positive trait off the field."[42]

The plain truth was that Landry didn't react with standard human emotion because he never learned how; it was simply how the man was constructed. Or, trenchantly, how Ruth Landry was constructed. If he was distant and seemingly uncaring, any understanding of his roots would explain why. As Blair recalls, "I met his dad once, very quickly, and you knew right away Tom took after his mother. Ray had moral fiber just like Tom's, but Ruth had that stoicism, that do-right, no-nonsense way of living. What made Tom unique was that he was so dang intense. There was something inside him that burned." Mike Connelly agrees: "What few people knew was how torn up he could be on the inside." As a result, Landry would never be able to relax as long as he had a game to coach. And at least one old ally had no doubt his old protégé would get it right.

"You wait a while," said Jim Lee Howell. "Tom will build a winner down there in Dallas."[43]

Chapter 12

"IT WASN'T DALLAS. IT WAS DANTE'S INFERNO"

THE 1963 SEASON, WHEN THE Cowboys had Dallas all to themselves, would also be the season that Don Meredith had the quarterback job all to himself. Landry had dropped this news on Sam Blair during the off-season in a way typical for the almost neighborly relationship between the coach and the small circle of sportswriters on the Cowboys beat. "I was in the office and I needed to get a Cowboys story so I rang up Tom at home, and he said, 'Don Meredith will be our number-one quarterback, and will be from now on.' Tom never steered me wrong, so I went with it. To Tom, it was just shooting the breeze with me, but that was a real scoop."[1]

Landry of course had hoped he could keep Dandy Don on his toes and at least a little more serious-minded with the looming figure of Sonny Gibbs on the sideline, itching to get in. However, Gibbs became a disaster. Lackadaisical from the start, he showed nothing in summer camp, prompting the call to go out to Eddie LeBaron once more to hold off on his law career and prepare his thirty-three-year-old body for more punishment in relief of Meredith. Gibbs would stay stuck to the bench all season, never to play in a game, and was then let go, to stand as the Cowboys' worst draft pick of all time.

Otherwise, the 1963 draft brought in one major stud. Finally owning a first-round pick they didn't need to barter or connive for, at number six the Cowboys chose Alabama's All-American linebacker

Lee Roy Jordan. The big defensive gun on Bear Bryant's 1962 national championship team and the '63 edition that went 10–1, Jordan was coming off his last college game, when he made an incredible thirty-one tackles against Oklahoma in the Orange Bowl. Still, many scouts had wavered about Jordan because of his smallish size, six foot two and *maybe* 200 pounds. Bryant told Landry he couldn't go wrong with the kid, that he breathed fire and with his speed made tackles from sideline to sideline. Jordan did just that in camp—Landry called him the best rookie he ever coached—and even though early in the season he punctured a kidney and missed the last seven games, Landry had a hunch his middle linebacker of the future was in his hip pocket.

The usual mob of draftees and free-agent stragglers came through camp, which was now held on the campus of California Lutheran College, founded only five years before in the sleepy, smoggy ranchlands east of LA. Landry was so taken with the "pleasant valley Sunday" atmosphere that he would make it the team's permanent camp site, which suited Mike Connelly just fine. Landry still had his men punish their bodies with the Landry Mile, but as Connelly says, "It wasn't far from LA, and on our off-days I'd lead a bunch of guys over where we could get a drink. We'd sit in the sidewalk cafes taking in the sun, and it was like a paradise. I could've kissed Tom for bringing us out there."[2]

When the team reluctantly traveled back to Dallas in late August, only Jerry Tubbs and cornerback Don Bishop were left on defense from the original Cowboy roster. The offense was at least stable, Landry having junked the shuttle, which Gary Cartwright had written "belongs with the anachronisms, the double-breasted suits and 'We've Got a Boy in the Navy' stickers and nostalgic waste of the past,"[3] though the death of the shuttle was greatly exaggerated. For now, at least, Meredith had the job. Things looked so propitious for the team that the nation's most obsequious Landry courtier, Tex Maule—to whom Landry seemed to be "a tall, soft-spoken young man who, given a bit more hair, would be handsome enough to play the lead in a TV western serial"—ventured in the preseason issue of *Sports Illustrated* that "the youngest club in the Eastern Division may very well be the best [and] should win the Eastern Division championship of the National Football League . . . proof that one of pro football's soundest and most intelligently operated franchises is on or ahead of schedule in its quest for a league championship."[4]

Liberated at last, or so he thought, Meredith imploded out of the gate. He led the Cowboys to four straight losses and six in the first seven games, including 41–24 and 37–21 thumpings by the Browns and Giants, respectively. Meredith, who still had problems assimilating Landry's plays, became walking pulp early and threw eighteen interceptions, but usually he kept his team in the game with his seventeen touchdown passes. In a 31–24 defeat to the 49ers in early November, which the Cowboys somehow lost despite a 532 to 394 edge in yardage, Meredith completed thirty of forty-eight passes for 460 yards (fourth most in league history) and three touchdowns. As a result, Cartwright penned a profile in the *Morning News* revealing Meredith's struggle to keep focused after his wife divorced him for the second time and took their young daughter with her.

"No other athlete in Dallas," he wrote, "has been handled with such verbosity, passion, intelligence, ignorance, curiosity, analyzation, objectiveness, and irony. Few could take it." Dandy Don, he said, "is a sensitive person [with] complexities, problems, and agonies. He says, 'I've got a song on my lips but my wretched heart is breaking,' and he pops his fingers into a pistol, shoots you in the navel and skips away like a leprechaun. Part of this is natural. Part is affected. Most is exaggerated. Landry, a basically somber man, didn't understand this, at first."

Landry, for his part, dishing praise on his beleaguered quarterback, said he had "a more serious attitude. He was trying to do the things we wanted. . . . His recognition [and] willingness to set up strong in the pocket are the two big things in his success recently."[5] Another time, after Meredith had smartly reacted to his receivers being double covered, Landry enthused, "I'll bet half his completions were to secondary receivers. That's the knack of a great passer. . . . That's what Y.A. Tittle has going for him."[6] Still, few, if any, believed the future would be without discord between those two. Least of all Meredith.

That season Don Perkins again went to the Pro Bowl. The tight end platoon, with Lee Folkins and Pettis Norman, gave the passing game a new dimension, with Folkins making the Pro Bowl as one of the league's leaders in receptions at that position. But the Cowboys finished ninth in offense, and the hoped-for bump in defense never materialized, ranking tenth and giving up 27 points a game. Their record was 4–10.

HOWEVER, ALL such matters were rendered immediately trivial when on a brilliantly sunny Friday morning in late November, shots were spat from a rusty World War II, bolt-action Mannlicher-Carcano rifle only three miles from the Cowboys' workout grounds. On November 22, 1963—the second day of infamy in Tom Landry's lifetime—the team was on the practice field going through their paces before leaving to play the Browns on Sunday. As Pettis Norman recalls with a shiver still, "The crazy thing, scary thing, was that that morning Frank Clarke and I were on the practice field and we were talking about Kennedy coming to town, which was a really big deal. And Frank said, 'What if some nut took a shot at the president?'"[7] The two bright, young African Americans were sharing a dark laugh about the Dallas they had come to know, a highly charged, unashamedly racist place rife with all manner of far-right-wing lunatics. In fact, once there, Kennedy would enter a hornet's nest.

Although the trip was intended to mend the fences within a Texas Democratic Party riven by Kennedy's advocacy of civil rights, some advisers had warned him to avoid the "Hate Capital," that deranged nuts would be lurking in the shadows. Days before, mock "Wanted" posters, with pictures of JFK above the words "Wanted for Treason," began being tacked to lampposts. The first word that Clarke's joking prevision had come true was from a distraught Cowboys official who had heard it on the radio and told Landry, whose blood seemed to drain from his face. Jerry Tubbs, sensing something was wrong, asked Landry what happened. "Oh," he said the coach told him, "some nut just shot Kennedy," whereupon Tubbs recalled, "We went on about our business."[8] This telling makes it seem as if Landry, perhaps blinded by his own political bent, was remarkably callous about the tragedy. But others remember that he was ashen when he halted practice, sent everyone home, and watched the unfolding tragedy on

TV almost in a stupor. In his autobiography, Landry called the day "an emotional low point for the Cowboys, the city of Dallas and the nation."[9]

To be sure, down in the heart of Texas a couple of the players were not overly distressed that John Kennedy had been murdered. Pettis Norman remembers, "We had some racists on the team, you know, rednecks. I knew of one or two. I don't remember anyone cheering when Kennedy was shot, and we had people of all colors and backgrounds who were shocked, and stayed that way for the rest of the season. But not everyone was in mourning." Later in the day Landry told the press, "I don't think we could play a game today, no matter what. Everyone just went solemn like a big drain plug had been pulled out. Then I just kind of got sick. I don't know how this will affect the team. I just don't know."[10]

As events unfolded in a surreal, apocalyptic fog, Cartwright noted, "For the Cowboys, as to all Americans, it became a very small and ugly world Friday afternoon." The AFL quickly canceled its Sunday games. Rozelle, however, decided that the NFL show must go on, though with no TV coverage, his stated reason—that the slain president had been a football fan and "sportsman"—being an obvious dodge protecting owners who didn't want to lose gate receipts. It was the worst decision, he would admit later, he had ever made. Even as Tex Schramm was saying, "It sounds petty to even talk about football at a time like this,"[11] the Cowboys packed up and headed for Cleveland, unprepared for what they would face but aware that extra cops would be deployed at the stadium and players' introductions dispensed with.

The most surreal part of the weekend was the ludicrous farce of a football game played on a bleak day in a cavernous stadium between two teams with no heart for it. The match drew just over 55,000 people, 30,000 short of capacity, all of whom didn't know how much they should cheer. The only visceral reaction came when the Cowboys appeared and boos poured down on them, not the usual kind given a visiting team but the type for a public enemy. That was the first sign that the team from Dallas was indeed going to be scarred with stigmata. As Meredith aptly put it, "It was like going to the lions with the Christians."[12] By game time, it had gotten worse. Minutes before, the nation had witnessed the horror of a murder on live TV, when Jack Ruby shot Lee Harvey Oswald in the garage of the police station. As Bud Shrake described the atmosphere in the Cowboys' locker room, "The players talked about it quietly and Tom Landry walked around the room with his head down, as if his thoughts were elsewhere. . . . 'This seems useless,' one player said. 'Who cares?'" Schramm said, "I'm still not sure we're doing the right thing by playing this game."

Pettis Norman couldn't wake from the nightmare. "I said to myself, 'What the hell's happening back home? People are being killed all over the place.' It wasn't Dallas. It was Dante's Inferno." Not that it really mattered, but the game, played in a daze by both teams, ended in a 27–17 Browns win that Shrake called a "silly and frivolous" exercise.[13] Dallas had brought much of that enmity on itself, and as a result had much rehabilitation to do. Few could have imagined that the football team they largely ignored would be a crucial part of that reclamation.

THAT TEAM had no choice but to push ahead, though it seemed unclear where they were headed. Tom Landry was the least sure of the road he was on. For all the respect he had won for himself, his team's mediocrity was an issue since his contract would be expiring at the end of the 1964 season, and as that clock ticked down, Landry once more believed he might be in the last mile of his coaching "sidelight." Four seasons had blown by, and that whole time he had never been secure enough in the job to give up selling insurance during the off-season. Mike Connelly, who was working his way toward becoming a stockbroker, earned a license to sell mutual funds in the early 1960s. One off-season he nearly had to rub his eyes when he ran into his coach at the same office.

"Tom was there trying to do the same thing I was. He was selling funds, I think it was for Mutual Benefit Life. I mean, we all had jobs. Meredith was in real estate for a construction company. But you just didn't expect Tom Landry to be sitting behind a desk pushing a pencil. But he was good at that too. He helped me get some clients, which was very generous of him since we were competitors in that field."

Landry had cause to remain circumspect about the Cowboys. The team's record under him was 13 wins, 38 losses, and 3 ties. In his memoirs he lamented the "growing public criticism I'd received at the end of the '63 season," that fueled "continuing speculation about my future."[14] Actually, given the ennui about the Cowboys, there was no great outcry, as Sam Blair says, "no big bonfire lit, no mobs carrying torches and pitchforks calling for his head. They really didn't care one way or another." Landry's invincibility in the press, however, was springing leaks. Shrake, in a *Dallas Morning News* column, wrote of "an army of fans and gossipers within the trade, who thought Landry was nearing the exit here," though Shrake benevolently noted that "it is all but impossible for anyone who has not been closely connected with the Cowboys . . . to realize the problems Landry, Schramm, and the rest of the organization have felt."[15]

Before the 1963 season, Landry had been offered a contract extension but turned it down, figuring he hadn't earned it and unsure that he wanted to go on in the game. For Murchison, being rebuffed by anyone was cause to make sure it never happened again. After the season he wasted no time making another pass at Landry, with an offer no coach could possibly refuse. It would be for *ten* more years and bump Landry's annual salary up to around $50,000, more than Lombardi's, and would include the same stock-option sweetheart package Schramm had obtained, reserving for Landry the right to purchase a 20 percent share of the franchise whenever he chose—at its 1959 prices. The extension would kick in after the 1964 season, but signing it now would allow Murchison to say it was an eleven-year contract, making it sound even more generous. Landry indeed couldn't refuse, and for the first time he knew he was in, all the way, as a career coach. Said Murchison: "We've been trying to get Tom to sign this contract for a couple of years. He didn't know whether he liked us. I guess we finally wore him down."

Reporters were summoned to Murchison's office for the announcement, with the owner gloating that "the Cowboys have made history again." He went on, "This will round out Tom's years with us at an even fifteen. This is in line with my philosophy that once you get a good man, you keep him." Shrake noted that Landry "grinned and blushed a bit" before saying, "I am grateful for the expression of confidence Mr. Murchison has shown in me."[16] In his clipped accent the name came out as "*Murtchison*," Landry still not inured to saying it as "Murkison." That prompted one of the press wags in the room to joke, "That's it. Clint thinks in another eleven years Tom might learn how to pronounce his name." Landry, gushing about the deal, was more expansive in later years: "Ten years! I couldn't believe it. And neither could anyone else. No coach in any professional major-league sport had ever received an eleven-year commitment. And all I had done to deserve it was to compile a terribly unimpressive record."

As Landry construed it, Murchison made the move in order to "shut people up" who had criticized him. Landry also would have no hesitation attributing the deal to a higher authority than even Clint Murchison Jr. It was, he said, "a clear indication of God's will for my life. And I never again doubted that coaching was to be my life's calling."[17] After listening for so long, the Lord had indeed spoken. With dollar signs, stock options, and ten more years' worth of either joy or suffering. Nearing his fortieth birthday, Landry would be standing on the same sideline until he was at least fifty-two. Whether or not he would claim bigger and better prizes as the future played out, he'd be a Dallas Cowboy for what seemed like forever.

THE 1964 season began with arguably the second-biggest piece of the Cowboys' puzzle in place, next to Bob Lilly. In the draft, Landry and Schramm, again gambling, used the first pick they had, at number seventeen, to nab Mel Renfro, University of Oregon's quicksilver All-American halfback/return man who for all his talent seemed like damaged goods. The previous year, he injured his hand so severely that a nerve was severed in his wrist—though how this happened was at first covered up. Renfro, it was said, had become so distraught over the Kennedy assassination that he slammed his hand against his bathroom mirror, which shattered and sliced his wrist. However, it later came out that he had actually had a domestic incident with his wife, who cut him with a knife. The injury scared off other teams but opened the door for Landry and Schramm. The coach pronounced Renfro "the finest college athlete in the country" and "worth the gamble."[18] In fact, Landry was hot for speed, that attribute being by far his top drafting criterion. Renfro, who had also played defensive back and was part of Oregon's 1962 relay team with Mike Gaechter that set the world record of 40 seconds in the 440 event, was slotted in at free safety, opposite Gaechter as strong safety. For the next fourteen years, Renfro would be in that defensive backfield.

Landry also used a future pick to hold in reserve arguably the world's fastest human, Bob Hayes, a five-eleven, 190-pound blue streak who at Florida A&M would concurrently hold world records in the 60-, 100-, and 220-yard dashes, and the 200 meters. His time of 9.1 seconds in the 100 would stand for eleven years. Hayes also played halfback on the A&M football team but was gearing up for the 1964 Olympics in Tokyo, and he had another football season of eligibility left before the Cowboys would be able to sign him. But Landry was already dreaming of Hayes flying downfield and catching long passes. While he waited, he added a short-term spike in the passing attack by trading for two fading but still dangerous long-ball targets, the elastic-limbed Tommy McDonald and Buddy Dial, who had been out in the cold in Pittsburgh since Bobby Layne retired after the 1962 season.

Landry, firming up his coaching staff, also brought in for the first time someone with some heft and not just a football functionary. All the original assistants were sacked, and Red Hickey, who had quit the 49ers after losing his first three games in 1963, would coach the receivers. Ermal Allen came down from the computer banks in the office to coach the offensive backfield. Jim Myers and Dick Nolan stayed on as the offensive line and the defensive backfield coach, respectively. The biggest move, though, was to keep Bob Lilly at right defensive tackle, the position Landry had switched him to during the '63 season. Lilly turned into a wrecking ball on the inside, and the only thing he needed to really blossom was a fellow tackle who could tie up blocking linemen and free Lilly to rush the quarterback. To effect this, Schramm traded for the Colts' ingot-like Jim Colvin.

Lilly's development had allowed Landry to take his 4–3 defense to its apogee. As Lilly recalls, each lineman still had to "control one gap apiece, except for the middle linebacker who had to control two gaps, on either side of the center,"[19] perpetuating the counterintuitive method of driving blockers out of the way through momentum, into other defenders' zones so that those targeted for blocks could slide away, get to the ball-carrier, and make the hit. Landry, as was his wont, had a catchy, pseudo-militaristic name for the system— the Flex, a term applied informally in New York for his defensive schemes as an adjunct to the Umbrella. This made perfect sense; the point was to render the 4–3 even more flexible. Asked to master its nuances that summer, Lee Roy Jordan could get no further than the outside edges. "All I really knew then was that the Flex was a way to play both an inside and outside 4–3 at the same time, so that we wouldn't be caught guessing wrong. People were saying Tom put it in to stop the Packers' sweep, and it was set up to stop the running game because Tom believed that was always the key to a game. But it was a passing defense too. It was balanced, more coordinated, we could play more combination coverage because that extra time let the linebackers and defensive backs play in loose zones, cover more ground."[20]

As this suggests, Landry indeed rigged his defense to snuff the gaps of the Packer sweep. Seeing the Cowboys' evolution, Sam Huff noted this from afar. "The strong-side tackle," he says, meaning Lilly, "had to hit and control. Some called it playing the piano. Your weak-side tackle was flexed [and] it took care of Lombardi's counters and Run to Daylight. With the Flex there is no daylight." To the peerless football historian Paul Zimmerman, the Flex was "a triumph of the cerebral,"[21] which was turf all but conceded to Landry. But it was also a triumph of Gil Brandt's well-financed venture scouting. If anything made the Cowboys, it was the soldering of all those zones of responsibility by Lilly and Renfro. Jordan, who would soon fill the last critical zone, at middle linebacker, can't think of a more important Cowboy than Renfro, being that "the defensive backs were the last line of coverage."

Landry, the old defensive back savant, gave them enormous responsibilities, expecting them to make sure there was never an open receiver, ever. When it became clear that Renfro seemed to have radar built into his brain, he rose as the Cowboys' version of Emlen Tunnell, freelancing all over the field but never blindly or without a designed coverage. "I was responsible for any pass that comes down the middle," he once said. "This allows the cornerbacks and even the linebackers to play their outside zones a little tougher."[22] As it happened, the refinement of the defense came at the same time that the Cowboys would come onto the field *looking* different, their uniforms updated to mid-1960s' mod. Before, the team had been cut in the square cloth of Tom Landry. When they traveled, they had to dress in conservative coats and ties, unwittingly reflecting a New Frontier/Rat Pack vision of cool, but when they showed up for games in their uniforms with those stripes and shoulder patches out of the 1920s, they were nobody's idea of cool or class. Schramm had believed those uniforms would "make the Cowboys easier to recognize in cities where we play only once each season." Now, though, with too few wins in them, it was time to drag the team into the space-age sensibility of men blasting off in dashing silver bubble suits.

The jerseys Schramm ordered were minimalist but eye-catching: solid white or blue with just a dash of two thin stripes on the sleeve. There were no stars on the shoulders. For the pants, he gave meticulous instructions to the Rawlings company, which supplied all the NFL teams' uniforms, that he wanted a material that was different from the norm, something that would make them shimmer. And the company gave him just that, with a color called "metallic blue," which would seem to change from silver to a light blue according to how the sun hit the pants.[23] Schramm thought about ordering new helmets too, replacing the lone star on them with a silhouetted boot and spur. He felt that people around the country didn't associate the star with Texas. But as the fates would appreciate, the star stayed, big and bold and blue set against metallic silver/blue and a center divider of blue and white bars. "The image," Zimmerman once wrote, "was perfect—nobility, wealth, purity."[24]

The new color scheme would become the most eye-pleasing "look" in sports. Two decades later, even that would be the stuff of myth. In 1983, after his Redskins won the Super Bowl, the balmy fullback John Riggins, stirring up trouble as usual, said that the only difference between the Cowboys and most teams was that they had better-looking uniforms. By then, the Cowboys had long sparked the modernization of football style and glitz. However, when Schramm unveiled the new uniforms and helmets in January 1964, and said, "No first-rate team wears second-rate uniforms," Landry didn't hide his dissent. "I always thought our uniforms looked pretty good," the coach told him. "I've never seen a good-looking uniform win a game."[25] To Landry a uniform was no more than work clothes, but he had to suck up being overruled by Schramm on trivial matters like these, and every time he did, Tex strutted a little more.

Tex had other sartorial strategies in mind. During their first four seasons the Cowboys had dutifully followed informal NFL protocol and worn their blue-shirted home uniforms at the Cotton Bowl. Beginning with the 1964 season, they would wear their spiffy new duds almost exclusively with the white jerseys, at home and away. Apparently this was something of a trend, wearing white at home, in that the Colts, Browns, Cardinals, and Redskins all did that in 1963. Schramm, an old TV guy, could foresee the game as an extension of *Walt Disney's Wonderful World of Color.* The fans, he pointed out, "can see seven visiting teams in different colored uniforms here instead of all of them showing up in white. And when the day comes that everyone has a color television set, maybe we'll get away from white altogether."[26]

Give the man his due; he knew his atmospherics. NBC was already broadcasting the AFL games in color, and CBS would follow by the late 1960s. Even in black and white, the Cowboys' shades of silver and white would resonate in a dashing, debonair, new-age way. Schramm was also partial to putting the surnames of his players across the back of their uniforms, which the AFL had done from the start, but the NFL office would sooner have had its teams wear Bermuda shorts than copy the league it was fighting. On the eve of the 1964 season, Gary Cartwright wrote with some relief that the Cowboys' new look was "a refreshing contrast to the little stars and junk which adorned the suits they have worn since inception," but he couldn't help but note that, "unfortunately, the new finery will be filled with the same old football players."[27]

THE LONG and loose-limbed Don Meredith looked particularly dashing in silver and white when he came in for the 1964 season safely ensconced as the starting quarterback. But the season couldn't even get off the ground before Meredith nearly went down for the count. In the annual exhibition game against the Packers in the Cotton Bowl, the scabrous middle linebacker Ray Nitschke blasted him on a rollout, tearing cartilage in Dandy Don's left knee. With Eddie LeBaron having retired, there was no capable quarterback on the roster. Schramm traded for Bart Starr's young backup in Green Bay, John Roach, but Meredith, knowing how much Landry was counting on him, played on, prompting team trainer Clint Houy to say that Meredith "had more guts than brains."[28] Bum knee and all, he was under center in the opener against the Cardinals, for which 36,605 fans came out. And they were rather rude to Meredith, who, with a touchdown and two interceptions, was given little sympathy playing on one good leg, en route to a 16–6 loss.

The next week the Cowboys beat the inept Redskins, 24–18, but Meredith threw two more picks and Roach had to come in and mop up for him. This scenario, when the offense let down the defense, would unfortunately be replayed numerous times over the year. Landry's Flex made a demonstrable impact, elevating the Cowboys to No. 4 in defense among the fourteen teams. Those efforts had been bolstered by a key move. Rookie Dave Edwards had been playing weakside linebacker, requiring him to cover, with great difficulty, swift receivers. Jerry Tubbs thought it would suit the mulish Edwards if he covered the tight end. Landry agreed and flipped Edwards to the strong side, moving Chuck Howley to the weak side. It worked smoothly, especially when Jordan inevitably replaced the aging Tubbs in midseason in the middle slot.

Still, it was another painful campaign for Landry and Dandy. In the third game, in Pittsburgh, Meredith staked his team to a 10–9 halftime lead but was sacked seven times and taken out after a late hit by defensive back Clendon Thomas. Roach wasn't much more effective, completing two of eight passes with two interceptions—the killer on a fourth and goal at the Steelers' 1-yard line late in the game. The Steelers hung on to win 23–17, and on the plane ride home Meredith suffered a collapsed lung and was rushed to the hospital. Roach had to start the next week in a critical match in Cleveland against the Browns, who would interrupt the Packers' dynasty to win the NFL title that year for Blanton Collier, the unenviable replacement for Paul Brown after the Browns' peevish owner Art Modell fired the living legend the year before. Roach had a touchdown pass to Pettis Norman, but the Browns beat up the Cowboys, 27–6.

Next was a home game with the Giants—a team Landry might have had trouble recognizing, as Allie Sherman had almost fully dismantled the old defense, sending Rosie Grier to the Rams in 1963 and Sam Huff to the Redskins and Dick Modzelewski to the Browns the following year. Dandy Don returned that week, throwing three more interceptions but leading the Cowboys back to a 13–13 tie (they cost themselves a win with two missed field goals late in the game). Meredith came away with a slightly separated shoulder and a split lip, but he was back in the next game, a rematch with the Browns. He threw for 228 yards and after a 1-yard Don Perkins run, the Cowboys led late in the third quarter. Meredith then seemed to ice the win when he hit McDonald with a 37-yard scoring pass, but the play was wiped out after the refs ruled that he had made the throw after crossing the line of scrimmage. When he overthrew Frank Clarke on the next play, the Browns' Bernie Parrish intercepted the ball and took it back 54 yards for the 20–16 win. While the Cowboys lost the game, it was a morale builder for Meredith. After that week, he went on a tear, beating the Cardinals, Bears, and Giants in succession, throwing three touchdown passes in the latter contest. The Cowboys, as a result, were back in contention with a record of 4–4–1, and a crowd of three hundred met them at Love Field after the Bears game.

But then came, inevitably, the annual collapse, as the team went on to lose four in a row, including the unkindest cut for Landry, a 45–21 defeat at home to Lombardi's Packers, with Bart Starr pitching three touchdown passes. Meredith had to miss that game, and by then he was quite nearly the walking dead—almost immobile, he had gone an ugly six for twenty-four against the 'Skins the week before. Steve Perkins of the *Morning News* coined a new category pertaining to Dandy Don: "yardage lost attempting to live."[29] Meredith returned for the last two games, closing out the season with a 17–14 win over the Steelers, which gave the Cowboys a 5–8–1 record, yet another bitter disappointment for Landry.

As usual, there were pluses. Clarke made the All-Pro first team, with sixty-five catches, 973 yards, and a league-high fourteen touchdowns. McDonald caught forty-six for 612 yards, though he was traded to the Rams after the season. Lilly made the All-Pro first team for the first of six straight seasons and seven of the next nine. Renfro was runner-up to Washington halfback Charley Taylor as NFL Rookie of the Year, led the Cowboys with seven interceptions, led the league in punt and kickoff return yardage (his 1,435 combined return yardage was a rookie record), and made the Pro Bowl. Conversely, Buddy Dial, who Landry had touted as the best receiver he would ever have, was oft-injured and reeled in only eleven passes. Dial and Landry clashed regularly, the old former All-Pro never getting used to the coach losing interest in him.

Perhaps the high note was hit before the last game, when Schramm signed Bob Hayes to what-was-a-monstrous rookie contract, $100,000 a year for five years. Weeks before, "Bullet Bob" had set the Olympics on fire, winning one gold medal in the 100 meters and another running the anchor leg of the 4 × 100-meter relay, both in world record time. Clearly, he was the biggest star in sports, and Murchison had to have him. For Landry, it was a gift he sorely needed.

HAYES WAS sure to put fannies in the seats at the Cotton Bowl, where crowds were increasing slowly. While they weren't yet at the point where Murchison could think in terms of a profit, he could afford to wait a little longer now that the NFL had cast its fate with a little welcome socialism. If the very idea of Marx and Engels knocking at the door would have normally made the Murchisons and the other oligarchs in the ownership class apoplectic, in the charmed business of sports ownership it was perfectly sensible, especially when crowds refused to buy the product. That happened after the U.S. Congress passed what was called "the most important piece of legislation in the history of sports,"[30] giving all fourteen teams in the NFL equal shares of the revenue generated from the league's television contract. Now, small-market teams like the Packers need not beg for a few extra bucks while the big-market teams prospered, earning a fortune from high ratings and elevated commercial prices.

By the mid-1960s, the pro football boom was in full swing, and it was a trend that Tex Schramm had helped create by playing on his influence with the TV crowd. The bond he forged between the sport and the medium hardened in 1964 when CBS renewed its NFL package for $28.2 million for two years, treble the previous fee, and led NBC to invest $35 million in the AFL the next year. The pro game, once the step-child of the colleges, was now rolling in dough. And the Dallas Cowboys needed every penny of their cut to survive. Moreover, the NFL as a whole needed a war chest, seeing how strong the junior league had gotten despite a very uneven, sometimes amateurish product. Indeed, there were whispers that the only way the NFL could stay solvent was to merge with the AFL and bring it under the NFL banner, thereby removing the AFL teams as competitors for the top talent. As it was, in 1965 the insurgent league had beaten the NFL to the biggest college star: gimpy-kneed Alabama quarterback Joe Namath, who easily tossed aside the advances of the St. Louis Cardinals to grab a then-breathtaking $400,000 offer from Sonny Werblin's New York Jets. "Broadway Joe" brought his cannon arm and outlaw's scent to the biggest TV market as the new avatar of the impudent league. Sensing NFL blood, some AFL owners dared to believe they could put the NFL out of business. That was when the NFL turned to its still-wobbly franchise in Dallas, putting its fate in the hands of the wily, round-faced general manager.

It was in fact Tex Schramm who would eventually save the league's bacon and carve the future structure of the sport. That in itself was just one indicator that the Dallas Cowboys team was already something greater than the sum of its parts. It wasn't a winner yet, and some of its crowds could fit neatly into the Yankee Stadium bleachers. But by the mid-1960s, with Tex Maule carrying hod for the coach and Schramm guiding the league's strategy, the little bitty dog was now starting to growl. Little things pointing to something larger were happening. In Dallas, one could look beneath the surface and see ways in which the Cowboys were influencing the city, the culture within it, and that far beyond.

RACE, OF COURSE, was the most important cultural sticking point, the canary in the coal mine. Landry never directly called attention to it, but because he built his teams giving prime roles to the few black players he had, the Cowboys reaped a base of fan support among the city's African Americans. While they were relegated mainly to end zone seats—the Cotton Bowl's equivalent to the back of the bus—the presence of black fans didn't please all white fans and may have even kept them from coming out in full force. As more black players would come to the Cowboys, the lamentable racial landscape of Dallas became a festering problem for the team. In 1960 there were five blacks on what had been expanded to a forty-five-man roster. In 1961 there were eight; in 1962, ten with the additions of Pettis Norman and receiver Donnie Davis; in 1962, ten; and in 1963, ten. All of them had to take the long drive from Oak Cliff to North Dallas, but no one seemed to have the stomach for civil rights demonstrations in Dallas, which still awaited its first burst of social activism.

As with the first generation of Cowboys players, younger men who had grown up in a more tolerant America were dumbstruck that the city surrounding them was in a state called denial. Pete Gent, who made detailed notes for future use, was most offended by the casually festering racism in Dallas, seemingly exempt from the Civil Rights Act that was made into law his rookie year. "I was shocked," Gent, who died in 2011, once said, "that in 1964 America, Dallas could have an NFL franchise and the black players could not live near the practice field in North Dallas—which was one of the reasons I titled the book *North Dallas Forty*. I kept asking why the white players put up with their black teammates being forced to live in segregated south Dallas, a long drive to the practice field."[31]

There was no answer other than that was just how it was in Dallas. Landry, knowing there was nothing he could do, went about his business hoping that Jim Crow could be ignored. It was of some comfort, at least, that racism in the NFL was by now losing its staying power. Coaches were color blind when it came to fielding the best players available. And yet nearly two decades after college football had integrated, in the Deep South all-white teams were still the norm. Bear Bryant had wanted to integrate the Kentucky team but was rebuffed by the university. He had the same intention at Texas A&M, where he was told, "We'll be the last football team in the Southwest Conference to integrate." Bryant replied, "Well, then that's where we're going to finish in football."[32] Because Bryant's team won anyway, especially at his next stop, at Alabama, where his team won three national titles in the first half of the 1960s without a single black player, the race issue remained moot.

As ever, the best Landry could do was let social change take its course, not to lead it. For some black Cowboys, that didn't seem quite good enough. Mel Renfro admits that he never took to Landry and Schramm during his Hall of Fame career in Dallas, partly because the racial double standards never seemed to bother them much, something not helped by Landry's coldness on a human level. Picking his words carefully, Renfro says, "My first five years I didn't like him very much. He had a plan that would make us better players and people, but some of us never bought into it at the time. When you're young and maybe a little angry, you form certain attitudes."

Renfro, a soft-spoken man with a rumbling intensity, goes on: "Tom was aware of racism. When we played an exhibition game in 1965 in Birmingham, Alabama, Tom warned the black players that there were some places that we perhaps shouldn't go. It was like he was saying: don't make waves, don't cause problems. To me, that was capitulation. I was insulted by it. My feeling was: Why even go to Birmingham? Did it mean anything to them that black people were being lynched there? Some black players thought Tom was a racist. I don't believe he was. Tom Landry was a very fine man. But I couldn't really defend him then because I was sensitive to the issue of segregation."[33]

Renfro went further in the late 1990s when he said of Landry, "Here's a guy who was supposed to be a Christian, and yet he's condoning segregation."[34] He pulls back now, clarifying, "I've had a chance to think back, and I realize now that Tom didn't make those decisions like where to play. Tex Schramm made those decisions," leaving it at that. However, Pettis Norman, perhaps the most politically active of those Cowboys, cuts the same slack for Schramm. "When I came to the Cowboys," says Norman, "we were being assigned rooms in camp and on the road by race. And in '65, '66, I said, 'Tex, it's time for us to stop this.' I suggested we assign rooms by last names, and he did."

As for Landry, he says, "The fact is, Tom would *not* play in cities where our players had to eat separately. In New Orleans, he refused to let us stay at the segregated hotels. He'd find places where we could eat and stay together. Tom Landry did not condone segregation. Tom knew all about my participation in sit-down demonstrations when I was in college in Charlotte, North Carolina. He could have said, 'Why get a troublemaker?' These were the kind of things some of the black players overlooked. There was a lot of anger, and people needed scapegoats, on both sides." Schramm's quiet unraveling of Deep South modes of racism had a subtle but dramatic impact, allowing Landry some cover. "Tom could say, 'Tex is handling the situation,'" says Frank Luksa, "and that would mean Tex would *have* to make things happen. Tom was putting the heat on Tex because if anything good was gonna happen, it would be from above, trickling down, not trickling up."[35]

Landry's Cowboys were, like any other team of the day, well stocked with southern boys conditioned to demean men of color. The core of them—Bob Lilly, George Andrie, Ralph Neely, Chuck Howley, Dave Edwards, Harold Hays, and Lee Roy Jordan—seemed to underline their redneck reputations by keeping hunting rifles in their lockers for after-hours duck and rabbit shooting. The briny Jordan was despised the most by some black players and by the team's sole white liberal, Gent. "Oh, I hated him," he said of Jordan in the late 1990s. "He was a racist, sorry bastard. I have absolutely no respect for him as a man."[36] Jordan indeed may have had an indelicate way of dealing personally with other players, but no one, not even Gent, considered him less than the ultimate warrior on the field. Renfro describes his relationship with Jordan as "gold." Jordan nonetheless had to live with the bigot rap. He says now, "Some guys thought I was a racist because I'm from Alabama, but most of 'em learned real quick that the only thing I disliked was a player that wouldn't play hard."

For Landry, whatever racial schisms there were never boiled over during his long tenure, it being the Cowboys law that such distractions had no place on the field, where every man shared a communal bond. And neither did the city ever boil over. Racism was gradually—very gradually—disappearing in the town, and when it was almost completely gone, at least in the de facto sense, many like Alicia Landry would never be able to figure out why it took so long. "It was the way it was in Texas, and you knew it wasn't good, but you didn't know what to do about it," she says. Indeed, a long time before the NFL had the moral and economic force to wield some muscle—such as pushing Arizona to adopt Martin Luther King Day as a state holiday or else the NFL would refuse to allow the Super Bowl to be played there—the league and even the U.S. Department of Justice had no recourse but to take a cautious approach.

Alicia could look around decades later and say, "I don't think there's any prejudice in Dallas now and hasn't been for years. Nothing."[37] She may be a bit naive about that, but the point is well taken in the broader context—that Tom Landry didn't change just a team or a sport but a city, and perhaps the way Texas thought, because of the racial composition of his football team. Of course, he had to be careful about it, not lurching too far from the cultural median. But could he have taken a stronger stand? In 1964, Jim Brown wrote a sort-of Black Power manifesto, a book titled *Off My Chest* in which he famously said, "I say the hell with integration—just don't segregate me." This was in the aftermath of heavyweight champ Cassius Clay's shocking refashioning of himself as Muhammad Ali and declaring his fealty to the Nation of Islam. Brown followed soon after, claiming speciously that 99 percent of African Americans embraced the Black Muslim philosophy of racial self-separation.[38]

To most white Americans, this movement, with its optics of bow-tied men in suits that bulged with the outline of firearms, was nothing but ominous, portending violence and in some cases spouting virulent anti-Semitic doggerel. Following the Kennedy assassination, the most highly visible and voluble Black Muslim leader, Malcolm X, declared that it was "a case of chickens coming home to roost."[39] Not long after, in March 1964, Malcolm broke with the Nation; a year later, he was gunned down while speaking in a Harlem ballroom. All hell was breaking loose in the racial subculture, far from Tom Landry's ken but with every chance that some of his own black players might fall in step with Jimmy Brown's postulations. All Landry could say when asked for an opinion of Brown's book, which was excerpted in *Look* magazine, was to blandly demur, "I don't think it'll make a difference." It was wishful thinking, of course. As Gary Cartwright wrote wisely, and bravely, of the brouhaha,

> Some of Brown's contentions I know are correct. There is in professional sports a maxim that the Negro athlete "is not quite as

bright as his white colleagues." There is the general feeling that sports should win some kind of Nobel Prize for its compassion in hiring Negroes in the first place. And every coach in pro football makes a conscious effort to carefully prune his squad so that no more than one-fifth to one-fourth of its athletes are Negro. The Cowboys have 10, few of whom they could do without.[40]

If Landry was doing some racial "pruning," that was part of the problem. But it's an issue that can never be settled one way or the other. Landry's place in the stubborn but atrophying landscape of segregation in his town will forever be ambiguous, just like so much else about him.

Chapter 13

"WE'RE READY TO CONTEND"

THE 1965 SEASON BROUGHT a new contract for Don Meredith, with a modest bump in salary that took him to around $27,000 a year for the next three years. He and his coach had become so interlocked that they were something like a comedy team, with Tom Landry playing a slow-burning, patronizing, and often cruel Abbott to Dandy Don's incorrigibly adolescent Costello. Their comic timing was certainly perfect and served as a cushion of reassuring stability while faces and eras changed around them. Landry, standing in the front of the meeting room, would be sprinkling what he called "appropriate Bible verses" into his football instruction, while in the back suppressed laughter caused shoulders to heave over something Meredith said under his breath.[1] Meredith, in retrospect, was the first test case of Landry's patience and tolerance for someone he didn't understand, and whom he feared would cleave the iron-fisted discipline Landry wanted.

Indeed, Landry bridled constantly that Meredith was not only undercutting but also openly mocking him. Meredith's usual plea about any playful pokes at Landry—"Aw, don't take me seriously"— merely underscored that according to Landry Law, *everything* was to be taken seriously. During one practice, Cornell Green intercepted a Meredith pass and was chased around by Dandy Don brandishing his helmet like he would crown Green with it. Everyone in the field cracked up except the guy with the whistle. "Gentlemen," Landry intoned, "nothing funny ever happens on a football field—if we can help it."[2]

But in Landry's system of disciplining players, Meredith rarely was slapped with a fine, more evidence of the bizarre double standard that at some times made Meredith into a whipping boy and at other times a privileged character. It may well have been that Landry knew he needed a square peg like Meredith, that having too many automatons wasn't the best way to build a team—and that if there was to be one exception for human frivolity, Dandy Don was it. Meredith held a good deal of metaphoric power. In the long lens, by challenging Landry like no one else did, at least until years later, he delineated how much playful resistance was acceptable, and allowed everyone else to live vicariously through him.

That was no doubt a good idea in cultivating a healthy team dynamic, though Dandy Don was clearly pushing it when he would all but ignore the plays Landry sent in, something that became more frequent and more obvious. Landry could only burn slowly when, as Pettis Norman recalls, Meredith would be too busy telling a joke or singing in the huddle to hear the messenger deliver the play. "Or he'd forget what the play was that was called and just shrug and say, 'Okay, just run the last play again.'" While Meredith made it seem as if it was a simple snafu, Norman sensed he was doing this intentionally, as a show of independence, or because he really thought he had a better play for the situation. "Don would laugh about it, and you got the feeling he was laughing not because he screwed up but because he was getting away with it, showing Tom who was boss."[3]

Says Mel Renfro, "My third year Tom moved me to wide receiver in certain spots, and in the huddle Don was the funniest guy in the world. When the play came in, he'd say, 'Uh-uh, I'm not gonna run that play,' and he'd call his own. Tom was never happy with it, but he had it both ways. If Don threw a bad pass, Tom could blame him for it. If he threw a touchdown, Tom would be able to make it seem that it was his call and not acknowledge that Dandy had changed the play. He never could give credit to Don in a situation like that."

No other player had Landry by the short hairs like this, but Landry indeed did not allow Meredith his conceits easily. More merciless in his treatment of Meredith than anyone, he pointedly criticized Don even if he had played a good game, and constantly chirped at him, "Keep your head in the game." Meredith had company in one respect: no Cowboy received direct praise from their coach. Renfro recalls, "You'd sit in those film sessions on Monday and you'd be on pins and needles. If you made ten great plays and one bad play, he wouldn't say anything about the good ones, just the bad one. He called out every little mistake."[4] Meredith, the highest-paid player at the most critical position, naturally was the most picked on, especially because, as Frank Luksa said, "Tom just never thought Don took it seriously enough."[5] Even an old cowhide-tough cuss like Lee Roy Jordan wished Landry had eased up a bit on Meredith. "I was very close to Don, and Tom didn't know how sensitive Don was. He really hurt Don's feelings. After a while, it was like he dreaded going out there."

Jordan goes on, "Tom didn't know how to handle players who had problems outside of football, married life, divorces, and so forth. He didn't know how to relate to that, and Don always had a lot of personal shit goin' on. So everything kinda mounted year after year."[6]

IN HIS mid-twenties, Meredith was aging fast and being worn down. He was not nearly the carefree Dandy Don he used to be. As handsome, hunky, and funny as he was, and as tolerated by the coach, he still was plagued by insecurity that Landry only exacerbated. It couldn't have gotten by Meredith that Landry, when he coached the South squad in the 1965 Senior Bowl, said nicer things about his quarterback that day—Joe Namath—than he ever had said about his own team general in Dallas. Mike Connelly observes, "Even in good times, Tom never really showed any warmth to Don. That wasn't Tom's way, and you learned to live with it. But we'd grown up with Don, seen him go through hell, and we'd come around to love the guy, for all his faults. We wanted Don to be our Johnny Unitas. But he never really got serious until Tom lit a fire under his ass by bringing in some real quarterbacks."[7]

That surely was the plan in 1965 when the Cowboys pulled in not one but *two* of the most heralded quarterbacks in the land, both of whom would be elected to the College Football Hall of Fame. First, as a future pick, came University of Tulsa's Jerry Rhome, a Dallas native who had grown up in the black Oak Cliff section, where his mother taught elementary school. Rhome, a sawed-off little guy reminiscent of Eddie LeBaron who paid little heed to the safety of his anatomy, played recklessly while passing and running his way to nearly every school quarterback record.

He became eligible for the draft in 1964, when he still had his senior year to play. And what a senior year it was. In the Heisman Trophy vote Rhome came in second to John Huarte, Notre Dame's matinee idol quarterback who was drafted and signed by the New York Jets only to become an afterthought when Namath arrived in New York. If Rhome wasn't enough, the Cowboys used their top pick in the 1965 draft on Craig Morton, a big man who moved like a snail but had a strong, accurate arm. Born in Flint, Michigan, he thrived at the University of California, Berkeley, being voted the outstanding player on the Pacific coast. Because he took to another Michigan native, Pete Gent, that pair became known among the grizzled veterans as the team's "flower children." Murchison paid each of them more than Meredith would get, even with his new deal. Indeed, that the club was unwilling to give Meredith a contract longer than three years was an implied threat itself. Moreover, there were actually *three* high-profile quarterbacks Meredith had to worry about—another being the Navy All-American Roger Staubach.

A courtly, highly intelligent young man, Staubach was born in Cincinnati and attended Catholic school there before he went to Annapolis as a third-class midshipman and won the Heisman Trophy and Maxwell Award in 1963. That same year, he led the academy to a 9–1 record and a No. 2 ranking in the country, losing only to No. 1 Notre Dame in the Cotton Bowl, despite the star quarterback's completing a Navy and Cotton Bowl record twenty-one passes. Staubach, at a lean, wiry six foot three and 190 pounds, possessed a more accurate than powerful arm and thickly muscled legs that made him a dangerous runner. Most of all, he was an eager student who had a way of willing his teams to victory. A man with sharply creased manners and military-style, yes-sir, no-sir obedience, he was obviously all that Meredith was not. Almost too contrived to be true, Staubach had married his high school sweetheart and likely never strayed—a latter-day analog of Landry.

Still, Staubach was not in great demand. Not only because his arm was not the strongest, but because, even though he had completed his college career, he had taken a course of study outside Annapolis and therefore had a year of eligibility left. This meant he couldn't be signed until 1966. Also as a commissioned naval officer, he had four years of active duty to serve. In addition, Schramm and Brandt had to contend with the AFL Chiefs, who had approached Staubach. When the Cowboys finally picked him, Staubach admitted that he did not particularly like Dallas, his Navy teams having lost to SMU and Texas in the Cotton Bowl. It didn't help that the idealistic man who had entered the academy because he had idolized Navy hero John F. Kennedy was traumatized by the assassination, and the late president's sister-in-law Ethel Kennedy had told him he had failed in "representing the country" by losing to Texas, as she said with a sneer, "down there."[8]

However, the Cowboys' trump card was a man named Danny Peterson, an assistant at Annapolis and a longtime crony of Gil Brandt. Peterson, given the task of reeling Staubach in, made the case that the NFL existed in the tradition of a military academy. That made the sale—as well as the fact that the Cowboys would pay Staubach $100,000 over ten years, a $10,000 bonus, and $500 a month while he was in the service, provided he would give up his Navy commission and come to play by 1970. These were extraordinary concessions to make for a man who might never play again. Brandt also apparently tried to curry favor with the Navy, to keep Staubach from shipping out to Vietnam. (Pete Gent insisted that Brandt had done just that for him, saying that after being drafted into the Army, "I ended up failing my physical four or five times. Gil knew the right people.")[9] But Staubach had volunteered for a tour of duty in Vietnam, as a Supply Corps officer in the port of Chu Lai in the Quang Nam province, where would serve until 1967. When he was done there he would still have stateside duty to fulfill.

Inescapably, the mass importation of quarterbacks had to burn Dandy Don's neck. Worse, he was scheduled for off-season knee surgery. Although Landry was committed to Meredith, he was intrigued with the tall, dark Morton, whose slow feet were offset by a strong and accurate arm. In these and other ways, including his rebellious streak, Morton was similar to Meredith and thus posed the same potential headaches for Landry. Rhome, on the other hand, was like Staubach, a strong runner, offering Landry the luxury of a mobile and fast quarterback for the first time. Given the unique talents of each, wags immediately began wondering if Landry would unearth a *three*-quarterback shuttle system, with one for every situation—if they didn't collide with each other getting on and off the field.

Meredith, with his new contract as comfort, played the good soldier. "I'm happy I got what I wanted and I hope they got what they want," he told the press, referring to the Cowboys. Still, he couldn't help deviating from the company line in the Dandy way, saying with a glint that Schramm "told me that no player on the Cowboy team was in a more secure position than me. But I checked our roster and counted nine or ten players with quarterbacking experience. Then I knew what he meant: The position is secure, but I'm not."[10] All Landry could do was assure him. "We'll get you more protection next year," he had told Meredith at his locker after the final game of the '64 season as he shook his quarterback's left hand, the right one having been mangled in the game. After a pause, Meredith watched Landry walk away. "Promise?" he called after him.

THE NEW pair of quarterbacks, along with Bob Hayes, were the big stories out of Thousand Oaks when the 1965 season began. Just as significant in the long term, however, was the arrival of defensive end Jethro Pugh, an eleventh-round pick from an obscure black school in North Carolina, Elizabeth City State College. Perhaps the best eleventh-round draft pick ever made, Pugh was a six-foot-six, 260-pound mother lode with quick feet and powerful hands. With him, the defense that had surprised everyone the year before now earned from Bob St. John a designation that would soon become oft-heard—the Cowboys, he wrote, first using the phrase on August 18, had a "doomsday defense."

Two massive yet nimble offensive linemen were plugged in as well. One, center Dave Manders, had been chosen by the Cowboys as an undrafted free agent in 1962, quit during camp and hitchhiked eighty miles to his home in Michigan, worked as a plumber, and played in the United Football League for $50 a game, before calling Brandt and asking to rejoin the Cowboys. The other, tackle Ralph Neely, a two-time All-American at Oklahoma, had been drafted by the NFL Colts and the AFL Oilers. He signed with the Oilers, but when the Colts traded him to Dallas, he went there, at the cost of the Cowboys' having to send two draft choices to Houston. Manders displaced Mike Connelly, who was moved to left guard, and began a career that lasted thirteen seasons; Pugh wouldn't be through for fourteen years, Neely ten.

All the holes that needed attention had seemingly been filled. But then, on August 11, three days before the Cowboys' first preseason game, in the Coliseum against the Rams, race riots broke out in the simmering Watts section of Los Angeles after white cops stopped a black motorist and used harsh force to subdue him. For the next five days Watts burned, set afire by its own residents, and before the fires were put out, thirty-four people had been killed, over a thousand injured, and more than three thousand arrested, nearly all black. Again, reality had intruded on the mundane business of football, forcing cancellation of the game, which was moved to the following Tuesday, after the embers had cooled. Though the field was ringed by National Guardsmen, unnerving both teams in the Rams' 9–0 victory, the Cowboys had to ponder how close their own city might be to such a paroxysm. One thing they could take comfort in, at least, was that all signs pointed to 1965 being, at long last, their breakout year.

The initial sign was that the Cowboys beat the Packers for the first time, 21–12, in their annual exhibition game in the Cotton Bowl that summer. This time, they played before a *real* crowd, 67,954, the largest for a pro football game in Dallas history, all of whom left the building breathless after having seen Meredith hit Buddy Dial with a 46-yard touchdown pass and Chuck Howley intercept Bart Starr to set up the go-ahead score. Landry was heartily enjoying his quarterback smorgasbord, liberally using all three in preseason, doing little for Meredith's confidence and prompting Dandy Don to fatalistically say, "My Daddy always told me, there's a place for you, Don, and you'll find it—someday, somewhere."[11] Not until days before the opener did Landry take Meredith out of the fryer and put him back in the fire, as starting quarterback.

The first game was against the Giants in the Cotton Bowl, before 59,366 paid customers, a regular-season record, and the Cowboys' defense was as stifling as the moist, ninety-seven-degree afternoon. Landry's defense didn't allow Allie Sherman's team a first down until the third quarter, held them to 139 yards, and sacked their new quarterback, the journeyman Earl Morrall, five times and intercepted him twice. Although Meredith was himself sacked six times, strong running by Don Perkins and Perry Lee Dunn made it easy, and Dandy Don delighted the crowd by hitting Hayes with a 45-yard spiral to close out the 31–2 win. Hayes, who caught two balls for 81 yards, was feted at a Cowboys' luncheon days later and was named Cowboy of the Week by a local dairy, which presented him with a month's supply of milk. "Coach, if I'm late for practice," he ribbed Landry, "you'll know I'm home tryin' to drink up all this milk, 'cause I don't have any kids."[12]

The Cowboys were surely giddy drinking in their victory. The next Sunday they wasted the Redskins, 27–7, at home before 61,577 fans, the offense rushing for 160 yards, though Meredith heard some boos while completing only six of twenty-one passes—a harbinger of what was to come. The Cowboys went into their annual nose-dive earlier than usual, losing their next five. Against the Cardinals, Meredith went nine for twenty-five and missed a wide open Hayes in the end zone, leading to a bitter 20–13 defeat that prompted Landry to stick the knife into Dandy Don. On the plane home, he told a reporter, "I'm going to have to make a decision about Meredith. We can't go on without a passing game." The decision was to bench him, with the insistence that "we're making the change in fairness to him, as well as the team."

The team, however, was close to open rebellion about it. Most players, not least of all Dandy Don, believed Landry had done him an injustice. Years later, Buddy Dial said about it, "Don had a *long* memory. . . . Dandy, he didn't forget." At the time, though, Dial said Meredith "didn't want to hurt anybody, or get even, all he wanted to do was win, and that's a class act . . . he just kept it to himself."[13]

Against the Eagles, Landry dusted off the shuttle, injecting poor Rhome and Morton into a system they couldn't possibly have fully grasped. They threw for a combined 250 yards and three touchdowns, but Morton also coughed up the ball, which a lumbering Eagles lineman picked up and carried 62 yards for a touchdown. Still, the quarterbacks played well enough. It was the collapse of the Cowboys' running game and the defense that did them in, the Eagles winning 35–24. With the powerful Browns up next, in Cleveland, Landry couldn't make up his mind about the quarterbacks even during the game. Before a packed house of 80,451, the largest for a Cowboys game thus far in their history, he went mostly with Dandy Don, who responded with two touchdown passes. Still, he was yanked at times for both Morton and Rhome, who together completed one of eight passes, keeping the Cowboys stalled. As Browns defensive end Bill Glass remarked after the game, "I really wasn't worried about the Dallas offense except when Meredith was running it."[14] The result was a hard-fought 23–17 victory by the Browns.

The next week brought an enormously important barometer game, against Lombardi's Packers in Milwaukee's County Stadium, their second home. Landry again put Meredith on the bench and started Morton, causing more bafflement and anger. That day, on a pleasantly balmy forty-degree afternoon, the Cowboys' defense cleaned Bart Starr's clock, holding him to four completions in nineteen passes for a paltry 42 yards and sacking him five times—net, the Packers had minus 10 yards of passing. What's more, the Pack could gain only 73 yards on twenty-nine rushes. "I can't remember," said Starr, "when our offense has had a tougher time." But it went for naught. Landry's game plan called for Morton to shock the Pack by throwing long, but Hayes missed the game with a pulled leg muscle. Morton had success only when handing off to Perkins, who ran wild with 133 yards, and because *he* was sacked *nine* times, the Cowboys' own net passing yardage was minus 1. It was the sort of game in which only the strongest survive, as if on iron will—the sort Lombardi feasted on, and he came away with a 13–3 decision.

With four straight losses, and the quarterback situation "definitely chaotic,"[15] as Clarke later put it, the reeling Cowboys pulled into Pittsburgh on Halloween. Meredith was back and began well, but then he came apart, finishing just twelve of thirty-four passes for 187 yards and throwing two interceptions. Meredith did find Gent for a touchdown, but in the fourth quarter the Cowboys bumbled to a 22–13 defeat. Afterward, Landry was in such a snit that he could not repress his emotions. So that the snooping press wouldn't hear him, he locked the door to the locker room and addressed his men. Biting his words hard, he told them, "This was the first time I have felt truly ashamed of the team's performance." He went on, in a voice so hushed the players had to strain to hear him, "Maybe the fault is in the system, with the approach we are . . ."[16]

At that point his voice choked, his shoulders heaved, and he started quietly sobbing, real tears running down his red cheeks. No one said a word. All that could be heard were nervous coughs and Landry's high-pitched bawling, a stitch in time that for many players would be the most indelible memory they would ever have of their Cowboyhood. Pettis Norman is still startled by it. "I didn't know what to make of it. Landry had never shown a bit of emotion before. It was like, is he having a breakdown? He said, 'I let you down. I apologize. I did a poor job, I didn't prepare you correctly.' And we knew that. Because he made a lot of changes at the last minute. He over-thought it, which is what Tom did sometimes. I always appreciated Landry for doing that. It proved he was human."

Actually, according to Sam Blair, Landry was even more on the edge when he did his mea culpa. "I didn't even write this, but when he locked the door and cried, he told them, 'I don't know if I'll be with you next year. I just can't do it anymore.'"[17] If Landry was close to falling on his sword, that was something he kept to himself. When he related the moment in his autobiography, it was with some shame, writing, "I don't know who was more embarrassed, me or the players."[18] Tom Landry Jr., however, believes it was more the real Landry than anyone would have realized. "That was Dad being himself. The players saw his compassion and how much he cared for them. And that was really the beginning of the rise of the Cowboys."[19]

As it happened, Meredith was the only player who broke the silence. He rose and took the blame himself. And as soon as his eyes dried, Landry seemed to be the first to agree. He couldn't resist telling the press, "We'll seriously consider going with Rhome and Morton the rest of the season." A *Dallas Morning News* story in midweek was headlined "COWBOYS TO SWITCH HORSES AGAIN." But as Landry later explained, the decision on whether to virtually end Meredith's career as a Cowboy caused him convulsions. "That Monday and Tuesday were two of the worst days of my coaching career. Everyone—public and press alike—had turned on Meredith. With good reason . . . I tossed and turned for two miserable nights. I prayed for wisdom to make the right choice." Finally, he met with Dandy Don, who he said was "somber, ready for the blow he knew had to be coming." Instead, Landry shocked him. "Don, I believe in you," he said. "You're my starting quarterback the rest of the year." Meredith, he recalled, "began to cry. Then we both cried."[20]

These tearjerker scenes were unknown to the fans, and if they were cathartic for both men, in Dallas the news that Landry was sticking with Meredith only meant that Dandy Don would be subject to even more vociferous booing at the next game, which was at home against the 49ers. Meredith, says Luksa, "was vilified more than any other athlete in this town ever. He was booed on sight in pregame, when he was in the game, and when he came out of the game." The flinty coach, meanwhile, as if immunized by his long-term contract, escaped even mild censure in the papers, the closest to it being a Gary Cartwright column after the loss to the Steelers that printed some fan letters, one lamenting that "Landry has thrown away too many games."[21] Meredith was squarely the one on the hot seat against the 49ers, and the game turned into a classic Dandy Don roller-coaster ride. After he found Hayes for a 24-yard touchdown pass to go ahead, he fell behind in the fourth quarter, then hit Hayes again for 34 yards to go ahead 36–31. The Cowboys won 39–31, and Meredith jogged off the field to fickle hurrahs. Not that they had a lasting effect. After eleven games, the Cowboys' record stood at 4–7.

One of their worst defeats may have been even more maddening than the comedy of errors in Pittsburgh. That was the rematch with the Browns, and 76,251 fans—more than had ever turned out for any football game, college or pro, in Dallas—watched on the edge of their splintered seats as a swashbuckling Meredith, playing with a broken rib, closed the gap to a touchdown with four minutes left. Then, with the ball deep in the Browns' territory, he threw two interceptions, the last one from the 1-yard line, clinching the Browns' 24–17 win. Meredith was showered with boos, but more humiliating was the next day's *Morning News*, in which Gary Cartwright penned arguably the most memorable and cruel snark ever applied to an athlete in Dallas.

Parodying the stilted prose of Grantland Rice, he wrote, "Outlined against a grey November sky, the Four Horsemen rode again Sunday. You know them: Pestilence, death, famine, and Meredith."[22] Meredith was said to be devastated by the crack, and it so angered the team that Cartwright was dubbed "Poison Pen Cartwright." Pete Gent years later insisted that Cartwright "doesn't know how many times he came close to a savage beating" had not a forgiving Meredith intervened on the scribe's behalf.[23] As rock bottom as the loss to the Browns was, the Cowboys won the last three, with an efficient Meredith relying heavily on the redoubtable Hayes, whose blinding speed was impossible to defend downfield. He would reel in forty-six passes over the season, averaging a stunning 21.8 yards a catch, and score twelve touchdowns, all in addition to returning punts and kicks.

For their strong finish, the Cowboys and their 7–7 record, second-best in the anemic Eastern Division, earned them the dubious reward of playing in the Playoff Bowl. Officially the Bert Bell Benefit Bowl, this was a consolation game between the two divisional runners-up played from 1960 to 1969 at the Orange Bowl a week after the title game. The players got an extra payday, but they ridiculed it as the "Loser's Bowl," or as Vince Lombardi, who was in it twice, called it, "the shit bowl . . . a hinky-dink football game held in a hinky-dink town played by hinky-dink players. That's what second place is— hinky dink."[24] Landry also thought little of it, and even though his wrung-out team was ravaged by the Colts, 35–3, being there was at least a marker of progress.

There were other markers too. Hayes, voted onto the All-Rookie team with Neely, also made the Pro Bowl along with Renfro, Lilly, Howley, Andrie, and Cornell Green. Meredith, with twenty-two touchdowns and thirteen interceptions, led the league with three game-winning drives. The defense ranked third, and the offense climbed to seventh. No one had to wonder who would be running that offense in the 1966 season. Indeed, Meredith might have allowed himself the private fancy that the worst was over and that the fans and the coach might even have his back.

AT FORTY-ONE, with only traces of hair and the onetime dashing young football savant, Tom Landry had become a different, more human man. He had come to rethink his prudish distance from the common pursuits of pro athletes who shared the same space for six months every year. For one thing, he was surprisingly agnostic when it came to the subject of booze, of which there was a steady stream around the Cowboys. Tex Schramm was a conspicuous drinker, and alcohol was part of the tools he used to conduct business. When Landry told him about the Giants' Five-Thirty Club, Schramm found the idea appealing, not least of all because Tex had a glass in his hand most of the time anyway. As Bob St. John wrote, with Schramm's approval in the latter's 1988 biography, Tex "enjoys his drinking. . . . He does not do things halfway."[25] He was partial to J&B Scotch and appreciated, said one Dallas writer, "loyal Schrammites to share it with."[26]

Landry himself was less uptight about drinking than he had been in New York. Feeling comfortable with his power, he was not self-conscious now about having a drink at wet press sessions, at which it would have been all but impossible for anyone to stay dry. Landry's glass was kept filled, and he found it comforting to drain it. One sip could pack a Texas wallop.[27] Even for a born-again Christian there were times as a coach when he would take any relief he could get. As for his players, Landry relaxed his instinctive restrictions. "He treated us like men," says Mike Connelly. "On the plane coming home after a game, everyone had a beer. Tom arranged that. He knew after a loss we'd all be up all night blaming ourselves, so the beer would be waiting for us, win or lose." Up in first class, notes Sam Blair, Landry, Schramm, and Murchison would be swilling a higher grade of booze, Landry generally a scotch and water before burying his nose not in a playbook but a Louis L'Amour western novel.

For the Cowboys proletariat during those early years, liquid courage and relief were mandatory. For many of the moguls in Murchison's jet-set crowd, the arrival of the Cowboys was a good excuse to party hardy, to break open bottles of tequila, rum, Jack Daniel's, and Johnnie Walker. The score of the game? *What* game? Each time the Cowboys were at home, the diamond-decked, Rolex-wristed revelers would be numb long before kickoff. Sometimes they came straight from a stay on Clint's private Bahamian island—a refuge never offered to any of the players who bled for him. Murchison, wrote *Sports Illustrated*, "is having the time of his life [heading] the richest and most ardent fan club in the history of football."[28]

Murchison's Cowboy Club, the VIP section of the club level, had a distinct *Animal House* quality, and this was an element of the Cowboys' mystique-to-be: that the head coach was a lonely counterweight to all the rich man's hijinks going on upstairs, which struck some as a playhouse for philanderers. One observer called the Club "the wildest place in the history of the world . . . everyone seemed to have a girlfriend there [and] it was like a big game keeping the wives from finding out. It's almost inconceivable how much we drank and how unfaithful everyone was." The happily married, outwardly shy, and clean-living Murchison was perhaps the biggest of the leches. After Murchison made a deal with Dallas-based Braniff airlines to ferry about his team, stewardesses in the airline's Pucci line of couture were habitués in the room. Stories were told of the original Cowboys cheerleaders, the Cowbelles, who were pert high school girls in modest hoop skirts, being given "tryouts" in there.[29]

What was going on upstairs was always something Landry avoided at all costs, putting helpful space between the blue-nosed coach and the idle rich vulgarians and fornicators who bankrolled the team. And they seemed afraid to offend him, encroach, or step on his toes in any way. For Murchison, his $600,000 investment was the most satisfying, if not nearly the most profitable, return he ever had, and he wanted nothing to disturb the formula that earned him props in *Sports Illustrated* as "A BIG MAN EVEN IN BIG D." Murchison, wrote one scribe, had a "happy gift for mixing business and pleasure while doing his level best to make a profit out of both."[30]

In the less than luxurious Cotton Bowl grandstand, beer would have been welcome had Dallas not had blue laws barring alcohol sales on Sundays—making the Friday and Saturday night games particularly helpful. Nowhere in fact was the disconnect between the Cowboys' elite and the fan base the team needed to win over more obvious than the Cotton Bowl, a place once described as "a Depression-era project [where] the bathrooms were little more than outhouses . . . and the stadium's general-admission seats were separated from the reserved seats by strands of chicken wire. It was a blue-collar stadium, where blue-collar fans watched a blue-collar team."[31]

Back then, when Cowboys fans and players were blue collar, the games weren't nearly as much a reason to party as they were to get drunk. More and more, Meredith, with ample reason, was seen in hotel restaurants on the road with a glass of scotch in his hand. Once Pete Gent arrived, the two of them hit it off, fusing a new cultural alliance as they would repair to Gent's apartment and get raging drunk and, increasingly, high on the 1960s' mandatory turn-on, marijuana.[32] For Dandy Don it was a happy trade-off for giving up cigarettes and one that would endure long beyond his football days. (His good pal Willie Nelson once vouched, "I can't say personally that Don got high for every Monday Night game he did, except for the 40 or 50 times we did before he headed to the booth.")[33] They were hardly alone. Guard John Wilbur, a free-spirited Stanford product from San Diego, once said, "I won't say everyone smoked pot, because under Texas law it's still fifty years in jail for smoking pot. But I will say it was a prevailing thing at the time. Every college student smoked it, and all of us had been to college, so what did you expect?"[34]

If Landry was in the dark about such pastimes among his players, he wore a metaphorical blindfold. For the Cowboys, getting loaded on booze and pot became part of their routine. Just getting through one of Landry's four-hour film sessions on Monday morning required, as one writer called it, "a two-drink minimum."[35] A protocol had formed over time: no drinking was allowed within Landry's purview, but what anyone chose to ingest at home or on the way in was their own business. According to Gent, ultra-potent vodka gimlets were the team's drink of choice: "You didn't have to drink a lot . . . to feel it. I immediately became a drunk, going from not drinking to drinking every day." Dave Edwards, he insisted, had a champagne fountain next to his bed. Whenever a player had a party, the scene would become, Gent said, "insane."[36]

If there was booze on one's breath, Landry could pretend not to notice. As long as everyone did their work and played their behinds off, they were given their private conceits and habits. In time that would come to include recreational drugs, which were tougher to detect and easier for Landry to leave alone. There were potential risks in this laissez-faire approach, but for now these were just grown men doing things that grown men do. Thus the beer that flowed on the charter flights signaled that the overarching impresa of the Dallas Cowboys in their march to respectability wasn't the big star flayed across their helmets. It was, for varying reasons, a crystal glass or a Styrofoam cup filled to the brim with country comfort.

LANDRY BY 1966 was seeking more sophisticated modes that might give his team that last push over the hump. He hired what was likely sports' first team shrink, Dr. Ray Fletcher, an industrial psychologist whose job was to prepare employees to mentally mold themselves to the objectives of their companies. As Bob Lilly recalled, Fletcher was supposed to "give everyone a sense of direction and, believe me, it worked."[37] Tex Schramm also brought in a shrink, SMU psychologist Dr. Robert Stoltz, to help iron out *his* domain. His role was to develop a common language that the hundreds of college coaches and scouts whom Gil Brandt sent questionnaires to each year could use to rate players on a 1 to 9 scale, rather than trying to understand the varying colloquialisms and dialects that came back on those forms.

This was trickier than it sounds; as Schramm said, "It took us years to come up with the dimensions that define a player. . . . Then there was another problem. How did we assay the qualities of the scouts who were feeding the information into the computer."[38] The computer, of course, would become the virtual trademark of the Cowboys organization, which began using banks of them as early as 1962, compiling the down and distance tendencies that Ermal Allen put into notebooks for Landry, who called the computers "just another weapon that we had to do the job that had to be done," and Schramm's zeal for them "a bit crazy."[39] Getting an edge, any edge, justified the investment in hardware that seemed applicable only to the mass storage and minute analysis of information in commercial industry, high-technology medical research, and census-keeping.

Landry, the holder of a master's degree in engineering, had good company in his appreciation for information technology. Murchison had his MIT math pedigree and fancied himself something of a human computer. For him, bringing in the best computers was as gratifying as bringing in the best players, and as it happened, in 1964 there was a hi-tech breakthrough. A second-generation computer, the IBM 1401—with transistors replacing the old bulky vacuum tubes, reducing the size and cost of each machine—captured a third of the world market, with more than ten thousand units sold. The Cowboys organization was among the buyers. Schramm hired an IBM technology guru, Salam Quereishi, to create a quantum table of values on college athletes, in which criteria for each, such as character, quickness, body control, competitiveness, mental alertness, strength, and explosion, could be analyzed on a tiny three-by-five card. Game performance each week was analyzed in the same way.

To be sure, Landry came into team meetings armed with a sheaf of computer-proved failures that needed to be fixed. In *North Dallas Forty* there is a scene in which the coach scolds his team, "We played far below our potential. Our punting team gave them 4.5 yards per kick, more than our reasonable goal and 9.9 yards more than outstanding." If Landry never actually was as robotically didactic, Gent said that on the Cowboys "they literally rated you on a three-point system. On any play you got no points for doing your job, you got a minus one if you didn't do your job, you got a plus one if you did more than your job. And they would read your scores out in front of everybody else. . . . Tom thought that everyone should know who was letting them down." However, Gent wondered if the grading might have been influenced by nonobjective factors, in that "I began to notice that the guys whose scores didn't seem to jibe with the way they were playing were the guys Tom didn't like."[40]

Don Meredith, as it happened, was the most likely to fail such actuarial analysis, since his game was based less on regimentation than improvisation. Still, Landry made no exceptions, and some would assume he took extra delight in reading back Dandy Don's anemic scores, a form of payback for his openly flaunting plays that the coach sent in. But if Meredith felt that way, he could find at least some relief that every other Cowboy experienced the exact same heat at one time or another.

Back in the mid-1960s, no other team had these issues, IBM having had no rush of orders from around the leagues. Still, people were watching what was going on in Dallas and seeing what the future would look like. Indeed, the chance to tap into Schramm's brain was enticing, though when he proposed in 1961 sharing scouting information in an informal "combine," most other general managers were wary of giving him the keys to their files. Thus, the first combine, formed in 1963, included the Lions, Eagles, and Steelers, leaving Schramm to join with the only two teams that would partner with him, the Rams and 49ers. The expansion New Orleans Saints joined in 1967.

Such foresight by his coaches and front office finally led Murchison to provide them big-league facilities—even if they were the ones Lamar Hunt left behind on the North Central Expressway, which came with nicely manicured and rat-free practice grounds built on an old parking lot. For Murchison, who didn't bother to take an office for himself in the complex, the biggest kick in the world was to come down from the high-balling haut monde and rough it with the team. He would frequent the locker room at games and practices not with a shot glass in his hand but as a silent observer, the players not knowing who he was. "There'd always be this guy standing at the door wearing old clothes," Connelly recalls. "We thought he was a guy who picked up the bags and put them on the bus. Sometime around the second year someone was asking if anyone ever met Clint Murchison Jr. And Meredith said, 'Well hell, that's him right over there by the door.' I expected a guy like him to be wearing silk suits and smoking fat cigars, not look like a truck driver." For Murchison, it was a way to separate himself from the craziness up in the Cowboy Club, where any resemblance to a working-stiff ethos was gaucherie.

LANDRY HAD bought a spacious new ranch home on a quiet lane at the end of Midway Road in the tony Bluffview neighborhood of North Dallas, so named for its sweeping, cliffside views of the duck-laden Bachman Creek tributary of the Trinity River. The Highland Park Methodist Church was down the road, which was convenient; if Landry needed to have faith in the team, he needed more to have faith in himself. Religion, he once said, helped to "take some of the pressure off" the job.[41] For him, religion may not have been a prop but a crutch. Landry's catechisms could indeed be odd. Bob Lilly remembered that when he first witnessed Landry etch his holy trinity on the blackboard—God, family, football—"Every guy, and I mean *every guy*, in that room turned around and looked at each other in amazement. We all thought the same thing: *Coach has his priorities backward*. In [our] minds the order should have been football, family, and God."[42]

If Landry's children had religion stamped on them, Tom Jr. points out that "Dad never pushed me. Just like he never put any pressure on me to play football. I played because I enjoyed it. I wasn't overly big, but I was a pretty good defensive back. I could have gone to Texas like he did, but I went to Duke because I wanted to study law there. Unfortunately, I spent more time in the hospital than on the field and I gave up football, and that was fine with Dad. I got my law degree and he was extremely proud of that. He may have even been relieved."

AROUND THE game, one could almost feel that the Cowboys were getting ever closer to the magic ring of the Packers. Indeed, both Landry and Schramm believed they were following the same pathway, albeit in polar opposite ways. Lombardi was stone age; Landry was new age, his weapon of choice being not the bellow of a voice but the hum of a computer. Once ho-hum in Dallas, the Cowboys now were selling tickets for real, stoked by the greater attention paid to them in the newspapers—which in a growing symbiotic alliance had discovered that the interest they had helped to stoke in the team was selling more papers. By 1967, the press corps had accordingly grown exponentially, with as many as twenty scribes on the Cowboys beat.

Naturally, the press had a perfect peg in the stormy Landry-Meredith relationship. Now, because of the elevated expectations,

Meredith was living in a funk, his confidence brittle. Every down, he seemed to bring a new crisis or a threat to his health. Once, when he was tackled hard by Sam Huff, his sore ribs burst open and he found himself covered with blood. "Now you've done it, Sam," he drawled. "You've killed me."[43] Early on, Landry, perhaps a little too cutely, would cite the danger to Meredith's anatomy in defending his indecision about Dandy Don, saying it was partly to protect him from being seriously damaged, as well as from the "psychological abuse" he would take from impatient fans. Of Meredith, he would write in his memoirs, "A lot of people over the years have assumed . . . that I never really liked or respected him because of his fun-loving, flippant attitude. But that's just not true. I liked Don from the start and he very quickly earned my respect as a football player,"

But he couldn't in good faith leave it at that, adding, "He aggravated me at times, all right" and "I'm afraid I didn't understand Don as well at the time as I wish I had . . . at times our differences did create tensions between us." The feel-good coda was that "Don and I were a lot more alike than either of us realized at the time. He cared just as much about football and winning as I did. We just showed it in different ways."[44] Meredith, never hearing anything like that from the coach in real time, bought none of this. Though he never publicly uttered a word of criticism about Landry, then or after, he vowed that when he got into a game, he would play no matter what injury he sustained, a vow he would make good on, with mixed results. In truth, neither man understood the other, and both seemed not eager to try to bridge the enormous personal gap between them. Gary Cartwright, in baroque terms, wrote of Meredith as "a 13th-century troubadour persecuted for his good intentions" who saw Landry as "the Black Monk, a creature who could swallow himself without changing form," and that "if Landry understood the depth of Meredith's paranoia, he never let on."[45]

Landry had no reason to understand Meredith, only to constantly hope he would grow up. And with the Cowboys rising, they were attached at the hip, restlessly, fitfully. Landry could not deny that Meredith had talent and Texas-sized courage. If Landry was God's chosen coach, by extension Dandy Don had to be God's chosen quarterback. Not Craig Morton and not Jerry Rhome, both of whom would seem like loiterers as Landry, reluctantly, kept blessing the head of Don Meredith. However he felt about Landry, Meredith was being eaten inside out, not only by the painful stewardship of the team and the ever-more frequent booing but also by his personal travails. In 1966 his wife left him and took their daughter to live in California, and he would begin to see a psychiatrist and turn up his inhalation of alcohol and weed with Pete Gent.[46] Sometimes, it seemed the field was the last place in the world he wanted to be. But the field was where he would be, for some of the most convulsive moments in football history.

Chapter 14

"THE BASER INSTINCTS OF MEN"

AFTER HAVING ITS NOSE RUBBED in the dirt by the AFL for five years, the empire struck back in 1966. It happened when Hungarian-born Pete Gogolak, the first side-winding, soccer-style kicker in pro football, played out his contract with the Buffalo Bills and refused to resign with the team. Claiming to be a "free agent," a term not used before in sports, Gogolak, in 1966, signed with the New York Giants, breaking the gentleman's agreement between the leagues not to sign each other's players. In response, the AFL elevated to commissioner the dead-end kid from Brooklyn, Al Davis, who advocated no less than unconditional surrender from the NFL. He gave his league the green light to sign two marquee quarterbacks, the Rams' Roman Gabriel and the 49ers' John Brodie. Davis didn't know, however, that he was just a PR prop. Although the contrasting personalities of Davis and Pete Rozelle were the public images of the leagues, the real action would take place behind the scenes, among the same pair who had waged the war for Dallas, Tex Schramm and Lamar Hunt, who were still friendly enemies. After Schramm got approval from Rozelle to, as he said, "let me try on my own," he called Hunt, who was about to travel from Kansas City to an AFL owners' meeting in Houston, and asked him to stop over at Love Field.

That was where they held a private "summit" in the VIP lounge and drew up a master plan that would be finalized on June 8, 1966.[1]

In the rapprochement, Davis was aghast that the elder league had won concessions such as territorial indemnities to be paid by the AFL's Jets and Raiders to the Giants and 49ers and Gabriel and Brodie being returned to their old teams. There would be a common draft of all AFL and NFL teams, who wouldn't face each other during the regular season until 1970, when the two leagues would be realigned into an expanded twenty-eight-team league split into two conferences. This gave the AFL and NFL four more years of autonomic home rule, but a championship game between the leagues would be played after the 1966 season. The game would be televised the first two years concurrently by CBS and NBC, though for most pro football fans the big fish fry would still be the NFL title game, at least until the AFL could prove it belonged on the same field. Hunt proposed calling the climactic game a "Super Bowl," which the owners rejected as too facetious. The fans, however, took to it, and by the third go-around, the owners adopted it as the official name. Davis, humiliated by his own league, fled back to Oakland, as part-owner of the Raiders, with a seething hatred for most owners and especially for Rozelle, who was anointed commissioner of the soon-unified NFL, the job Davis yearned for.

AS FOR the Dallas Cowboys, Landry reckoned the timing was ideal for his team to be the vanguard of the new order. His Flex Defense was his signature, and to make it breathe harder, he needed someone to fire up his players. That was when Landry reached back into his past to the day Ernie Stautner left him half-dead in the dirt in Pittsburgh. Stautner had retired as the game's meanest defensive lineman in 1964 and a sure future Hall of Famer. He was working as an assistant coach for the Redskins when Landry made him an offer to coach the Cowboys' defensive line. "When Tom handed me a playbook [I saw] all the keys listed for the tackle," Stautner said. "When I was playing tackle no one ever gave me keys."[2] He took a crash course in the Landry way and learned well. He would be with the Cowboys until the end of Landry's tenure, his craggy just jaw and scowl a threat to every lineman to get meaner and tougher.

Landry also had a pair of new fire-breathers on the other side of the ball, running backs Dan Reeves and Walt Garrison. Both were the antithesis of the Landry-Schramm architectural blueprint of strong and fleet über-athletes. Indeed, they seemed more like the kind of guy Landry had in 1960, milk horses rather than the thoroughbreds he had now. Reeves, who shared the same name as Schramm's old boss with the Rams, was a quarterback at the University of South Carolina and had caught no one's attention as the school went 8–21–4 during his time there. Signed with the Cowboys as a free agent in 1965, he was tried at safety and halfback and made the team on grit alone. He played little during that season, but he had a nose for the goal line, scoring three touchdowns. Garrison, a halfback drafted in the fifth round out of Oklahoma State in 1966, made the cut because he not only could block—he *liked* to stick his often bloody nose into blitzing linebackers—but also was a natural homeboy, a native of Denton, Texas, and an actual cowboy who performed on the rodeo circuit in the off-season.[3]

Few knew, and Garrison sagely didn't let on, that he was no rube, having been named to the Big 8 Conference All-Academic Team. The honest-to-goodness cowboy had scant speed, but like Reeves he had a knack for a big play. Though neither Reeves nor Garrison—who roomed together—would start a single game in 1966, they still had an impact, mainly on kick returns but also when Landry would sneak them into the backfield and have them go out for passes. Reeves could throw the option pass, as well. Landry in this way kept the Cowboys at least symbolically an everyman's team. Now, with computers all around and shrinks almost literally acting as assistant coaches, he was what he once thought he might be, an industrial engineer, with an appropriate motivational rap. He would post signs on the locker room wall with an affirmation, not in *football talk* but in Landry-speak, part academic, part Martian, sometimes biblical, all meant to elevate the players' brain power and inure them to higher physical and metaphysical demands. A typical one from the early 1970s could have made sense only to him:

WILLPOWER
Intellect tires, the will never.
The brain needs sleep, the will never.

The whole body is nothing but objectified will.

The whole nervous system constitutes the antennae of the will.

Every action of the body is nothing but the act of the will objectified . . .—TL[4]

BY THE mid-1960s, the fever that gripped Landry whenever he played the Giants had waned, mainly because Allie Sherman managed to take a near-dynasty and systematically pawn off almost every single player from the Howell-Landry-Lombardi era. So as soon as Lombardi began to own the league, Landry's obsession shifted to the team from the Upper Midwest, from where his ancestors migrated. Bob Lilly recalls coming in one day and seeing a quote tacked up on the bulletin board that read, "The quality of a man's life is in direct proportion to his commitment to excellence." Lilly asked who had said it. He was told Vince Lombardi.[5] Landry would also, implicitly, use Lombardi as a foil, by positioning his team as the anti-Packers, and of course himself as the anti-Lombardi.

Pete Gent noted that at the beginning of each training camp "Landry would come and speak, and the first thing he would explain was the history and development of his offense and of modern football, and he would cite the Packers as the perfect example of what we did. He'd talk about the simplicity and execution and talent of the Packers. He'd say, 'The Packers are this, and we are the opposite end, but we are willing to give up a few more mistakes . . . to beat them on the big play."[6] Says Mike Connelly: "That was Tom's way of getting us to hate the Packers. He wasn't the type to say, 'Let's rip out their fucking throats,' so he would make it seem like our way was the only way to beat them. You keep hearing it and you'd start believing it."[7]

Landry then was constructing his team with the express purpose of checkmating the Packers. While he couldn't try to copy the Lombardi offense, Landry did borrow some of Lombardi's blocking schemes. His main thrust on defense was to stop the stampeding power sweeps of Paul Hornung and Jim Taylor. In Landry's playbook, Lombardi's Gothic, foreboding image hung over every page, leading Landry to counter it with his pseudo-militaristic terminology. The Cowboys shivered each summer when the next edition of the playbook was given to them, a daunting read to be sure, and once, Pete Gent, seeing a rookie try to get through it, told him, "Don't bother. Everybody gets killed in the end."[8] Having written the novel, Landry now had to channel it into a championship. Until then as Cowboys guard John Wilbur once said, Vince Lombardi was the "monkey on Tom Landry's back."[9]

LANDRY AND Lombardi had remained steady if not overly close friends. At their annual August dinner at the Landry home, they would relax and banter about any number of things while sitting on the back porch, drinks in hand. "I used to quietly come out to the porch and sit there listening," says Tom Landry Jr. "I wanted to be a fly on the wall when they revealed the secret of life, but all they talked about were mundane things. It was like neither wanted to let the other know what football ideas they had. They were competitors now, and they began to act more and more like it. Those get-togethers stopped around 1966."[10]

If Landry had been fixated on drawing the distinctions between his team and the Packers, now that the Cowboys had risen to a level where they threatened the Packers' preeminence, suddenly *Lombardi* was getting a tad paranoid about them. "Even in preseason he didn't want Dallas to beat us," recalled the wondrous Packers defensive end Willie Davis.[11] Because Landry felt the same, when he finally beat Lombardi for the first time, in that preseason game in 1965, the win was like sweet nectar. A year later, the Cowboys would show off what would be called "the most explosive team in football history."[12] No one would have debated that Landry had the best pure athletes in the league, guys whose physique and speed made Lombardi's aging warriors seem sclerotic. Indeed, many believed a new order was at hand. Preseason polls of sportswriters in 1966 by UPI and AP picked Dallas to win the Eastern Division while the Pack trailed behind the Colts in the Western Division. Tex Maule, naturally, again picked the 'Boys, though Landry, playing it cool, maintained that "Cleveland is very definitely the team to beat."[13] But, as always, his eye was really on Lombardi, and vice versa.

The Cowboys wired the Eastern Division, winning their first

four games by scores of 52–7, 28–17, 47–14, and 56–7, and Gary Cartwright was dipping his pen not in poison but in sucrose. Where Meredith was "pestilence" only a year ago, the scribe's story after the October 3 blowout of Atlanta was headlined "MEREDITH HITTING POTENTIAL AS TOP QB." Cartwright, noting that Meredith had signed a deal to record country music records, wrote, "Dandy Don is zooming in on a different type record, the kind that wins championships," and "It is difficult to fully appreciate Meredith's amazing contribution."[14] After he completed nineteen of twenty-six passes for 394 yards against the Eagles, Philadelphia coach Joe Kuharich said, "Man, Meredith was on the money. [He] now has the protection and man you can tell the difference. Don's now the quarterback they've been saying he could be. Landry just stuck with him through it all [and] it's paying off." He added, "Dallas just doesn't appear to have a weak spot. You look for that. It wasn't there."[15] Sam Blair's take on Meredith was, "He never was so Dandy."[16]

All was copacetic between coach and quarterback. "DON LIKES LANDRY WAY" read the headline in the October 22 *Morning News*, and Meredith was talking big. "What Tom [has] said is true. When the Cowboys start winning, we're going to win more consistently than any team who ever won in this league. More than Cleveland, more than the Giants, more than Green Bay. And the reason is Tom. . . . You get tired of a guy being right so often. You almost wish he could be wrong some time. . . . I used to fight believing Tom. I really rebelled against it. It was immature and I was stupid. . . . When every man on this team learns and accepts this about Tom, Dallas will be the world champion." He added, "It's literally true that I'm a different man. . . . I've never enjoyed life as much as I'm enjoying it now."[17] It was still early in the season, with plenty of time for it all to crumble again, but this time that didn't happen.

With one game left in the season, the Cowboys' record was 9–3–1. Meredith had again taken a steady pounding, leading a Cowboys player to say, "Dandy can't even bend over to tie his shoes without getting a splitting headache." Fortunately he could sit out the last game, against the Giants in New York, since the Browns were beaten earlier the day before, giving the Cowboys the division crown. When they beat the Giants 17–7 that day, the fans sang sardonic choruses of "Good-bye Allie, we hate to see you go," which might have made Landry wonder if such serenades might have been aimed at him had he been given that Giants job.

WHEN THE Cowboys returned home as the first expansion team in any sport to be in a title game, Murchison was walking on air. After the plane landed at Love Field, he took the microphone and gleefully announced, "Welcome to Dallas, home of the Kansas City Chiefs."[18] The *Morning News*' front page that day crowed, "CHAMP (YEAH!) COWBOYS," inches from the headline for the lead story: "FRESH TROOPS LANDED BY U.S. IN S. VIETNAM." At the airport there were 5,000 "hysterical" fans waving signs saying "Cowboys Uber Alles" and "Landry for President," and hard as it was to believe, chanting "We want Meredith!" With cause. He would be voted league MVP, just one of many milestones. Dave Manders was the first Cowboys offensive lineman to go to the Pro Bowl and Lilly, Howley, and Hayes were first-team All-Stars. The cream was Landry being voted Coach of the Year for the first time. It seemed such a coronation that almost overlooked was one little detail: the Cowboys would now need to dispose of Lombardi's defending champs, in the NFL Championship Game on New Year's Day in the Cotton Bowl.

Age aside, the Packers proved they were nowhere near extinction, going 12–2 on the strength of the best defense in the league, allowing just 11.3 points a game. Their offense was still potent too, coming in fourth. Landry's team mirrored them in reverse, his unstoppable offense leading the NFL with an amazing 31.8 points a game and his defense ranked fourth, yielding 17.1 points. Seven Packers made the All-Pro first team: Starr, tackle Forrest Gregg, guard Jerry Kramer, defensive end Willie Davis, middle linebacker Ray Nitschke, cornerback Herb Adderley, and safety Willie Wood. While the Cowboys tried to tamp down their smugness and swagger about having eclipsed the Packers, it could not be overlooked that they had never played a game of this scale. Cardinals quarterback Charley Johnson ventured, "I just don't think that Don Meredith, Bob Hayes, Dan Reeves and the guys the Cowboys offense depends on are ready for that type of pressure."[19] Lombardi gave a terse analysis—"We've got the defense to stay with them"[20]—and wrote on the blackboard a pregame ode that went:

> I have seen the wicked in great power
> And spreading himself like a Green Bay tree
> Yet he passed away and lo, he was not;
> Yea, I sought him, but he could not be found.[21]

Lombardi also had a simpler homily: "The hay is in the barn. The team is ready."[22] The Vegas boys agreed, making the Pack a 7-point favorite. Landry, playing down expectations, said, "The Packers should be favored, they've got the record. But our boys feel pretty confident."[23] Meredith came in loose as ever, appearing in the locker room with his face apparently covered in stitches. He said he had tripped and fallen through a plate-glass window and would be unable to play. "You could've heard a pin drop," Dan Reeves recalled. "Then coach Landry walked in and he peeled it off," Meredith having had a makeup artist put on a mask of scars. "We all wanted to choke him to death for scaring us like that. But we all just cracked up."[24]

Dallas was fogged in right up until game time, but eventually the day brightened and the turf was fast, the temperature a comfy forty degrees. With the game blacked out on television in Dallas, every one of the 40,000 available seats was sold within five hours and 75,504 fans crammed into the Cotton Bowl. The homeboys then trotted out of the tunnel—and promptly fell on their faces. Before Meredith could get his hands on the ball, the masterful and opportunistic Bart Starr found Elijah Pitts with a 17-yard scoring pass before, on the ensuing kickoff, Mel Renfro's fumble was returned for a touchdown. That, Landry would understate, made it "an uphill battle." By the end of the first quarter, though, the Cowboys had tied the game. But the Packers were always steely and machine-like, especially Starr, who confused the Flex by sending his backs crisscrossing out of the backfield for short passes. Meredith was almost as good, throwing for 238 yards, though Lombardi had his defense blanket Hayes, who caught only one pass for 1 yard.

The Cowboys stayed close, but when Starr connected with the ageless Max McGee for a 28-yard touchdown pass with five minutes left, making it 34–20, the game looked over. Even so, Lilly blocked the extra point and gave Meredith some wiggle room, and he promptly hit Frank Clarke with a stunning 68-yard scoring pass, which Clarke would call "the biggest thrill of my life."[25] Raging now, the defense sacked Starr, batted down a pass, and dumped Jim Taylor for a big loss, forcing a punt. The Cowboys got the ball back at the Packer 47 with 2:19 left. With the crowd deafening, Dandy Don hit Clarke with a 21-yard pass. Clarke then beat safety Tom Brown into the end zone and Meredith cranked one for him, but Brown held Clarke. The interference penalty put the ball on the 2, first and goal, with 28 seconds left and a tie game and overtime hanging in the balance.

Reeves ran the ball to the 1-yard line. But now came a perfect storm of blunders. First, left tackle Jim Boeke rose out of his stance a split-second before the snap, incurring a penalty that took the ball back to the 6. Meredith next tried a dump-off pass to Reeves, who hadn't told the quarterback that his eye had been scratched on the previous play; his vision blurred, Reeves flubbed it, bringing up third and goal. Another pass play was called, for Norman in the end zone. As he now recalls, "I was open but Don threw short and I dove out of the end zone and caught it on the 2. I got up to run but my knee was still on the ground, and they tackled me anyway."[26] Meredith would confess later to Frank Luksa that he hadn't enough faith in Landry's call and short-armed the throw, fearing an interception if he put the ball in the end zone.[27]

So now it came down to one play, with 17 seconds left and the clock running. Landry sent in the play—"Fire 93, G pull"—a Meredith rollout with the option to pass or run it in himself, depending on whether the linebackers came up or dropped back. However, Clarke, who had been lining up at tight end, was replaced by the bigger Pettis Norman in a goal-line offense. Clarke was supposed to stay in, replacing Bob Hayes for more blocking power. Instead, Clarke ran toward the sideline, leaving Hayes out there, baffled. Landry, evidently caught up in the high drama, didn't notice the snafu and didn't call a time-out, nor did Meredith. The wily Packers *did* notice. Loading up their rush to blow by Hayes, they poured in. As Hayes recalled, outside linebacker Dave Robinson "just grabbed me and tossed me aside like a sack of feathers."[28] The 240-pound Robinson then barreled into Meredith just as he rolled out, clutching him by the shoulder pad as Dandy Don, trying to fight him off, flung a wobbly pass into the end zone. The Packers' Tom Brown nestled the ball for the game-saving interception—a crucifying pick that would haunt Dandy Don to his dying breath.

Robinson many years later would admit to Sam Blair that he had been offside on the play, but the officials missed it.[29] Not that it mattered. For Landry, there was only agony, his priceless reaction—turning away in disgust, wincing, his eyes shut, jaw clenched—forever preserved on film. The jaw remained jutted when, at the sound of the gun, he dragged himself out to midfield and shook Lombardi's hand in congratulation. Landry, who may have believed it was his time, must have felt about half past dead walking forlornly off the field. Later Vince aggrandized his old confrere and rival profusely, as did Starr, who said of the Cowboys, "That is a great team."[30] Although Landry could not have known just how much so, had his team won, the victory would have altered history in many ways. Decades later, *Sports Illustrated* recalled the game with the rhetorical question "Ever wonder what NFL life would be like with the 'Landry Trophy' instead of the Lombardi Trophy?"[31] In retrospect, the stakes for Landry were indeed that high, and the failure that scarifying.

Meredith, who would again have to overcome revilement in Dallas because of the interception, graciously took the fall, if not entirely. "It was my mistake for not noticing Hayes and sending him off," he said. "It was Hayes' mistake for not getting out of there on his own. It was Tom's mistake for not sending Clarke in for him."[32] He predicted that the Cowboys would be back in the title game next year, but the recriminations would endure all summer. The satisfaction of crashing into the NFL elite couldn't gauze the sting and the feeling among the Cowboys that "somebody had died" in the wake of the game. Landry kept his sights high and never would yield in his refusal to admit he had erred. His autobiography recounted the game briefly and without emotion, with the cop-out observation that "none of us had noticed that Hayes was still in the game," and the soothing coda that "we were the youngest team ever to play an NFL title game. Everyone knew Dallas would be back."[33]

Landry still had his comforting phalanx of media pipers. Tex

Maule in his *Sports Illustrated* game story never mentioned the Hayes mess-up, and cast Landry in defeat as "an unruffled man" who displayed his "normal icy calm."[34] Landry thus could subtly shift blame elsewhere, such as onto poor Boeke, who would lose his job after one more season. Landry also cut Buddy Dial before the next season, ending his long career, after Dial confronted him after the game about the play calling. In time, Landry would belatedly be criticized for it. Pete Gent, who was injured and didn't play in the game, eviscerated him for an air of "chaos" on the sideline when calm was needed, and that it was not uncommon for Landry to become so overwrought that he called the wrong plays. Some would even turn psychologist and construe that traumatic moment as proof that Landry must have had a subconscious compulsion to see Meredith fail, based on the perception that, as one latter-day revisionist insisted, Landry "truly did not like Don Meredith, not as a player and not as a person."[35]

That assumption does not quite jibe with how Landry had stuck with Meredith, praised his courage, even cried with him. Yet that tortuous afternoon was in retrospect the most indelible sign that something irretrievable had been lost between them, and that the uneasy trust that had been earned on both sides had taken a hit. What neither could have known was that much worse was yet to come.

THERE WAS much to feel good about in the wake of the defeat, mainly in Landry's own determination that "we had it," meaning momentum that would lead to an overtime victory had that pass been on target. The *Dallas Morning News* headline "AMAZING COWBOY RALLIES THWARTED BY GREEN BAY" was in itself a feel-good spin on the game, from which the Cowboys took home a loser's share of $6,527. While Lombardi would extend his legacy on a relaxing day under the LA sun the next week, feasting on Lamar Hunt's Chiefs in the first Super Bowl by coasting to a 35–10 win, there already was keen anticipation about the Cowboys displacing them in 1967. What's more, Landry had no intention of conceding any of his play-calling authority or methods. "I have," he said, "no apologies to make."[36]

He still kept running the team like a country store, albeit one with computers on all the shelves. Landry would never conduct any team business until he'd had a sit-down breakfast with Alicia and the kids, and he still allowed her to watch game film with him. Tom Jr. recalls that "all the coaches would come over during the off-season. It was like a movie about a team in a small town, like a *Hoosiers*, everyone liked to keep it a family thing." In this prism, if Landry's behavior toward Meredith could seem to some like intentional malice, to Landry it was more like a tough-loving dad.

For the players, Landry's quirks and distance were constant irritations, but as the team rose they found themselves working harder for him, including their level of physical punishment. Some, like Meredith, felt little gratitude for their labor and for their willingness to put their bodies through the wringer for Landry. Buddy Dial, like Meredith, had played through terrible injuries, believing the Cowboys' coaches expected him to play regardless. When Landry axed Dial, he left football with an addiction to pain-killing drugs that would become nearly debilitating. Twenty years later he would need extensive treatment to kick the habit—an epilogue not uncommon among football players of his era. If Landry knew anything like that was going on in the locker room, he didn't think it was a problem. Just as plausibly, he didn't know, nor did he have an inkling that his demands for perfection provided a major stimulus for his men taking such risks.

Pain-killing measures were not exclusive to the Cowboys, and all teams around the league explored whatever methods were available to get people on the field and as wired for combat as possible. Tales have been told of locker room tables featuring bowls of different-colored pep pills for players to come by and scoop up as if they were Good & Plenty. But there may well have been an urgency to do so under Landry that few teams experienced—including in some ways the Packers, who could soothe pain with victories and championships. "As the years went by," Connelly says, "there was a *lot* of pressure on us to win. I don't think anybody felt their job was safe." Accordingly, perhaps without him even knowing it, Landry was breeding a culture of excellence that led his men to partake of the drug buffet too casually for anyone's good. This psychology might explain why the Cowboys were a team of extremes, and why cultural lines were drawn more starkly for them than for other teams. Playing in a city where racism and hate tainted them all, and for a stifling coach who barely permitted breathing unless it was in the playbook, seemed to bring on a kind of Newton's law, where living in one nation under Landry and God sparked an equal and opposite reaction, led by the openly rebellious core of "flower children."

In John Wilbur's estimation, besides the fact that "just about everyone was smoking pot" on the team, this was the least of the recreational drug behaviors developing under Landry's uncritical gaze. The big rush for certain Cowboys, Wilbur maintained, was amyl nitrate, a very dangerous stimulant inhaled through the nose that was then available over the counter in drugstores. He recalled that "we'd go to the beer bars, the cowboy bars, and those amyl nitrates would get you high for thirty seconds. . . . It was the redneck way of getting high." But there were also other cheap rushes such as mescaline and speed, the latter of which he said was all over the locker room. "The team used to dispense it . . . there were these little white boxes in everybody's locker." Yet another, Dexamyl, was touted by some veterans as a performance enhancer, which had immediate appeal for players held to high standards, though "they were pretty good about not letting the new guys do it. It was just for the old guys. I was kind of into the beer and speed. . . . And amyl nitrate."[37] Gent would say the abuse of that drug was so rampant that "I was surprised nobody died from using [it]."[38]

IF LANDRY'S expectations and his own reputation made many of his men believe they had to walk the extra mile for him—even when they could barely stand up—not even Gent claimed that the coach mandated any of this. At best, he was too naive to know about the extent of it, and at worst, he let it happen with a willing blind spot. The Cowboys of the era still blanch at the memory of those long cold needles penetrating flesh and bone. The most harrowing scenes in *North Dallas Forty* dealt with this, but they were no more disturbing than the scenes in the Cowboys' locker room, which Gent said was stocked with "rows of syringes."[39] As Norman recalls, "Both of my knees had to be drained all the time, but I never took pain medication because I was afraid of what it would do to my health. I played eleven years with two bad knees and constant pain, but I wouldn't let anyone come near me with one of those needles, except once when I took a shot of cortisone and I hated it. It's a vicious cycle. You don't want to do it but you have to. Then all of a sudden you wake up and you can't walk normally the rest of your life."

In Norman's opinion, such implicit compliance was dictated from upstairs, not from the coaches. "One of our doctors told me that Tex protected him from malpractice. That tells you all you need to know." Landry for his part seemed eager to ignore the issue altogether, as he would in his memoirs, and was smart enough not to give anyone an ultimatum to play with an injury. Neither did Gent directly slam Landry for it, though the win-at-all-costs philosophy spoke for the coach. "They seldom tell you to take the shot or clean out your locker," Gent said. "They leave you to make the decision, and if you don't do it, they will remember, and so will your teammates. But worst of all, so will you—what if the team loses and you might have made the difference?"[40] Ralph Neely disagreed, saying, "I cannot remember an instance where a player was made to feel he had to do this where he was put in the position of feeling he might lose his job."[41]

In retrospect, the weirdest part might have been that players pumped full of pain-killers were seen by management as good soldiers, while those who smoked some weed were moral degenerates— a common refracted reality of the times. Indeed, Landry made an antidrug sermon part of his Sunday morning liturgies, devotionals that implicitly were to be taken more seriously than team meetings. But Walt Garrison, whose drug of choice was a tall bottle of Wild Turkey, never could quite take them seriously. "Some of the speakers Tom brought in were really good. Some were ex-football players who had gone into the ministry and, man, they could sell that Bible. . . . I'm not exactly sure what it was [they said]. Nobody ever listened."[42]

It seems hard to fathom that Landry didn't see the disconnect. Perhaps he believed he could smooth over the contradictions—and the necessary pain-killing methods—with a good dose of Christian temperance. Suspecting that such casuistry was part of the Landry facade, Buddy Dial sarcastically called him "the Reverend T.L."[43] Frank Luksa believed that Landry actually didn't know all that was going on, because "he didn't *want* to. It was easier that way to deny what was going on." In the end Landry, taking the safe route on these matters, gained an extra benefit from the cold distance he kept from the players, allowing him to overlook what he didn't need to see. But the problems festering in his locker room would find deeper mud down the road when success would be the most destructive drug of all.

THE VIBE in Thousand Oaks at summer camp in 1967 contained a strange brew of old and new currents. The Cowboys' first winning season had taken the team so far that it accumulated almost mythical properties in Dallas and the exigency for a grander scope. Clint Murchison Jr. relocated the Cowboys' offices again, now to the Expressway Tower, an opulent fifteen-story glass structure at 6116 North Central Expressway that Murchison built on property he had bought expressly for the purpose. He put the organization on the eleventh floor, its picture windows offering sweeping vistas of the city. He also rented out a ground-floor space to the Playboy Club, which catered to the same upscale, male-dominated crowd that Murchison hosted in the Cowboy Club at the Cotton Bowl during home games.[44] Not for a minute did Murchison consider that his coach might be embarrassed to have as neighbors cleavage-displaying young women wearing bunny ears and cottontails. The Cowboys were the hippest party in town, and the juxtaposition fit. Neither did he mind if players repaired to the Playboy Club after a hard few hours at the practice facility, which was under a big bubble behind the building. Landry already had the squares' allegiance; could it hurt if they were balanced by Hugh Hefner's ideal of 1960s American manhood?

Tex Schramm, for one, saw no downside to that equation. Working from the same idea, he junked the Cowbelles that off-season and created a new cheerleading squad, one that would remind no one of high school girls in hoop skirts and sweaters. Instead, the Cowgirls were professional go-go dancers hired to shake their pompoms while wearing hot pants and tight vests, showing off ample racks and bare midriffs. When Landry learned of it, he nearly had cardiac arrest. Years later in his memoirs, he was still exercised, saying that while the Cowgirls "transformed sideline entertainment," and that it was an example of Schramm's lust to foster "a high profile image of style, flair, and maximum visibility," it also "sexually exploited the young women by pandering to the baser instincts of men."[45] Alicia Landry says he had another worry. "Tommy wanted the Cowboys to be role models. He wanted the little boys in Dallas to emulate the players, not think about . . . other things. I guess he didn't think football and sex mixed."[46]

He took his case to Schramm, who brushed him off. While Landry never would change his mind, he also realized Schramm was right—football and sex *did* mix. Still, to appease traditional morals Schramm would send the Cowgirls to perform at charity functions and USO tours all around the world. When the notion arose that there was a rivalry between the Playboy Bunnies and the cheerleaders, he produced a virtuous member of the latter to attest that "we're not stewardesses, hookers or Playboy Bunnies."[47] Virtuous T and A became a key to marketing success. No Cowboys vestment ever returned a higher yield or caused greater proprietary zeal than the cheerleaders. When the porn movie *Debbie Does Dallas* was being made a few years later, word came that the lead character was a Cowboys cheerleader, dressed in the official garb with the Cowboys' emblem. Aghast, Schramm sued, successfully, to prevent such infringement. But Schramm got what he needed from the movie, not only in its wink-and-nod PR value but also for a moral justification of the Cowgirls, most of all for Landry. Schramm once amusingly told of arguing with the coach about the image of the cheerleaders, Landry's objection being "all the flesh they were showing."

"Tom," Schramm said, "just go to the beach and look around."

"Well, they're not wholesome."

As Schramm recalled, he happened to have a copy of the skin flick in his office. "I put the tape on the machine. It was a scene in the shower, with all these guys and girls going at it, an orgy in the shower. He [Tom] stood there looking at it in disbelief," though apparently he didn't turn the machine off. Finally, Tex turned to him and said, "Tom, *this* is not wholesome." Concluded Schramm: "He nodded and left and never said anything about it again."[48] Landry may not have been mollified. For years, as if compensating in his soul for all that pulchritude on the sideline, he lectured about the evils of pornography, and in 1980 testified for prosecutors in the obscenity trial of a local bookseller who had adult fare in the back of his store. According to a *Dallas Times Herald* account,

> Landry, who appeared as an expert witness on community standards . . . had made an earlier trip to the courthouse . . . to view an untitled 12-minute "peep show" that portrayed sexual intercourse and oral sex. Landry testified that he addresses 8,000 to 9,000 people each year . . . and said he nearly always spoke on the problem of obscenity and pornography.
>
> "I speak on the philosophy of humanism which is creeping into our society . . . ," Landry explained.[49]

To a true believer such as Landry, a seemingly *good* thing like "creeping" humanism (perhaps he meant *hedonism*) can be construed as something like pestilence and plague. But he was a realist too, enough to understood Schramm's point: if anyone was to benefit from selling sex in the name of the Cowboys, it would be the men doing Dallas.

MURCHISON, WHO once hedged his bets on the team, now was the biggest man doing Dallas. In that role he was ready to build what he really wanted: a properly respectable and decadent home field. The corroding Cotton Bowl with its blackening neighborhood was deemed dangerous by the white population and no longer feasible. At first he brought to the city a proposal for a civic bond issue to finance a new stadium in a more affluent section of Dallas. Mayor Erik Jonsson, however, refused, sending Murchison to look beyond the city. He liked what he saw in Irving, across the northwestern border, and began negotiations with civic and business leaders that continued into the 1967 season. Finally, in December, Murchison and Schramm announced the plan for a stadium in Irving designed by architect A. Warren Morey. It included a retractable roof and luxury "sky box" suites that could net Murchison millions each season. Construction would cost $35 million, which was actually cheap for the era, considering that the similarly designed Houston Astrodome had cost the same when it was built in 1965.[50] The Cowboys were hopeful they could move in when the merger with the AFL was to begin, in 1970, but the problems with the newly charted Texas Stadium were only just beginning.

Moving up into an elite group of teams inevitably meant that the competition would want to tap into the Cowboys' business model by luring away front office executives. Schramm was locked in, but Bedford Wynne, whose role as secretary treasurer was far less critical, was open to jumping ship for a meatier job, and when Houston millionaire John Mecom Jr. paid $8.5 million to put a new team, the Saints, in New Orleans in 1967, Wynne did just that. Craving the next best thing to a Schramm, or so he thought, Mecom lured Wynne away to be his general manager, getting an added bonus when Wynne brought along Larry Karl, who had been promoted from the PR department to become Schramm's assistant general manager. Leaving Dallas, though, became a slip then a fall. Wynne and Karl couldn't bear Mecom's penny-pinching nor the blustery obstructionism of Saints coach Tom Fears and quit during the Saints' very first training camp.

Booming growth certainly had rewards. Yet, for all that the Cowboys organization had prospered, and offered its members a security blanket, the shattering loss to the Packers revived the usual insecurities and uncertainties in Dallas. The 1967 draft, the first common draft of the NFL and AFL, netted only one intriguing player. A Gil Brandt special, Rayfield Wright was a typical Cowboys man-mountain, but he was easily ignored by pro scouts who rarely bothered to visit small all-black Deep South schools such as his, Fort Valley State College in Georgia. At six-seven and 235 pounds, Wright had gone there as a basketball player, and his speed—he ran the 40-yard dash in 4.7 seconds—agility, and vertical leap were such that when he turned to football, he was put on the offensive and defensive lines, at tight end and safety, and he also punted. Landry had no idea where to play him, and for two years he would experiment with Wright at tight end and on both lines, but even with Ray as a scrub, Landry knew he had to hold onto him.

Landry's main problem entering the 1967 season, as evidenced by the way the Packers had blanketed Bob Hayes, was easing the burden on Hayes by adding another big, fast receiver. This need was so grave that Schramm traded for one, Lance Rentzel, who on the surface was the last type of player Landry would ever want. The son of an Oklahoma City millionaire, Rentzel had played with Ralph Neely on the Sooners before Bud Wilkinson soured on him and was about to drop him from the team. He then gave Rentzel a rather odd initiation ritual. With the Sooners set to play their archrival Texas Longhorns in the Cotton Bowl, Wilkinson told him that if he were able to get to Dallas by himself for the game, he could play. Rentzel borrowed a car to drive there, then, when it broke down, he hitched to the Cotton Bowl, arriving three hours before the game. Wilkinson indeed let him play, and Rentzel went on to have an All–Big 8 career as a receiver, rusher, and punter.

A handsome square-jawed guy with wavy blond hair and a rebel streak, and probably too intellectual for his own good, Rentzel first clashed with crusty Norm Van Brocklin, the Vikings' original coach, after the team drafted him in 1965, and he was barely used for two seasons. He also had an unresolved dark side, which arose in September 1966 when he was arrested for exposing himself to two young girls in a Minneapolis playground. The Vikings kept him out of jail by sending him to psychiatrists. He was put on probation while he continued playing, and Rentzel would later admit, "I just couldn't get myself to understand that I was sick in some way . . . part of a deep, mysterious neurosis." The incident was kept quiet, going unreported in the papers, but around the league it was an open secret, though nothing that seemed overly serious. Van Brocklin even joked about it, hanging him with the nickname "Flasher," and Rentzel passed it off as a "momentary aberration." However, all sides thought it best if Rentzel left town.[51]

Enter the Cowboys. When Schramm ran the deal to acquire Rentzel by Landry, the coach quickly signed off on it, partly on the recommendation of Craig Morton, who was tight with Rentzel and had been sharing an apartment with him in Dallas. When Rentzel finished a hitch in the National Guard in San Antonio and came to Thousand Oaks, he wowed Landry with his speed, hands, and mercurial moves, which made Pete Gent and thirty-three-year-old Frank

Clarke expendable. Shifted to backup tight end, Gent knew it was the beginning of the end for him as a Cowboy, while Clarke would play only one more season. Rentzel meanwhile fell right in with Gent's Cowboys claque of boozing, toking flower children, secure in the knowledge that Landry was sold on him and was giving him a major role at flanker.

Though his teammates knew of the flashing matter, and a few of the rednecks, mainly Lee Roy Jordan, called him a "fag"[52]—a mark of their ignorance about the nature of Rentzel's problem—most said nothing about it and befriended a man who not coincidentally seemed poised on the edge of stardom. As for the flower child who was going to pitch him spirals, and had suffered the ecstasy and excruciation of stardom, Don Meredith had gone through much soul searching of his own that off-season. Getting as far from Dallas and his painful divorce as he could, he spent seventeen days visiting military bases in Vietnam, after which on a stopover in Tokyo he met a woman he soon married. He came home with a new wife and a sense of inner tranquility. When he dropped in on Gent, the two smoked dope and Meredith said he was prepared to do whatever Landry wanted him to do, that life wasn't worth the tension that always developed between him and the coach.

"The moment Don said that," Gent remembered, "I said, 'Uh-uh. If you do that, you're dead. Because he's going to see that as a weakness'" Indeed, Gent maintained, Landry would lay the blame on Meredith for every failure by the team.[53] But Dandy Don was sick and tired of being sick and tired. The fans were ready to pour more abuse on him. He seriously didn't know how much more he could take, mentally and physically, without winning. And so he toed the line. "We hoed the crops, now it's time for the harvest," was his latest homespun creed as the season approached.[54]

Landry too had his mind on the last hurdle everyone would need to clear to get to the land he promised them. He spoke a lot to the press about the psychological demands of the game, which he said dwarfed playbooks and computers. He was speaking in the collective sense, but after what had happened on the goal line against the Packers, and the lingering trauma of it, he may have wondered if he could come away with his own sanity after another loss like that.

Chapter 15

LESS THAN
ZERO

DON MEREDITH'S NEWFOUND peace and tranquility ended quickly, and with tormenting déjà vu, when his ribs were fractured during a preseason game in San Francisco. In a contest that featured an ornery Walt Garrison cold-cocking a 49ers linebacker, precipitating a bench-emptying brawl that included fans jumping into the fray, Meredith, whose new wife was expecting the birth of their son, hung tough, as usual, but eventually gave way to Craig Morton, who finished out the exhibition schedule. Dandy Don, his ribs tightly wrapped if not fully healed, was back when the Cowboys opened the regular season on September 17 with a stern test. They had to travel to Cleveland to play the Browns, who were ornery too, having been victimized two years in a row, first by the Packers in the NFL Championship Game, then beaten out by the Cowboys in the Eastern Division.

The Browns would be glad that they were shunted into a new division in 1967, when the league expanded to sixteen teams. What's more, even minus Jimmy Brown, who had quit the game two years before for an acting career, they were a better offensive team. With the shifty Leroy Kelly providing a seamless transition, making the All-Pro team for three straight years, they trailed only the Cowboys in yardage in 1966 while retaining a strong defense. The Browns' coach, Blanton Collier, couldn't wait to get Landry's team in his building for the opener, which drew the usual rabid capacity crowd of over 80,000 on a balmy, sixty-eight-degree day. It was a daunting task for Landry, the Cowboys never having won in Municipal Stadium. But Collier's quarterback, Frank Ryan, had a sprained ankle, and the Cowboys' defense intercepted him three times, sacked him four times, and held the Browns' runners to 11 yards.

Meredith completed fourteen of twenty-five passes for 205 yards, finding Hayes and Reeves for touchdowns. Reeves also rumbled for 114 yards. There had been talk that the Cowboys were a one-year fluke and would fall back to earth in 1967, but after the convincing 21–14 victory, Meredith pronounced, "If you don't beat the good teams, you don't deserve to be champions. And we are."[1] He then proceeded to shred the Giants in the first home game, 38–24, with four more touchdown passes. But his life was no closer to being dandy. Landry stewed when Meredith passed up a sure running touchdown and threw to Rentzel, who was ruled out of bounds when he caught the ball. Afterward, Landry, citing the play, said, "That's why I don't have any hair."[2]

Next came the Rams at the Cotton Bowl, meaning a date with LA's manic coach George Allen, an obsessive-compulsive Richard Nixon look-alike who habitually licked his thumbs and schemed up ways to unnerve his opposition. That week, Allen had sent two adjutants to Dallas who sat in a car and spied on the Cowboys' practices. When Schramm saw them, he filed a protest with Pete Rozelle, but Allen laughed it off and said the Cowboys had had someone spying on *his* practices. Landry was more intimidated by Allen's defense, which was driven by the "Fearsome Foursome" line of Deacon Jones, Merlin Olsen, Lamar Lundy, and, this year, Roger Brown, replacing the retired Giants expatriate Rosie Grier. The Cowboys' own Doomsday line was almost as fearsome, but during the game Meredith's receivers seemed to be running their routes on eggshells and dropped a number of passes. One pass caromed to Rams defensive back Ed Meador, who took the ball in for a touchdown to break open a close game, making the score 21–6 in the third quarter. The Rams, en route to a division title, won, 35–13.

The Cowboys got by the Redskins, 17–14, the next Sunday, but Meredith was knocked silly by blitzing linebackers and one time emerged from the huddle stumbling around like a drunk before the snap. Landry, though, left him in the entire game, saying later, flippantly, that he didn't notice Meredith's condition because "I'm so used to seeing him that way, I can't tell the difference any more." Meredith was flip too, saying it was just "another day at the office."[3] However, he developed pneumonia during the week and was so ill his wife called an ambulance to their home. He was put in an oxygen tent for the next week, with Landry later recalling, "Very few people realize how serious Meredith's condition was. An average man, even an above-average man, wouldn't have made it back on his feet for months, much less back to playing football. Courage is what did it. It was February before he ever felt good."[4]

Landry gave the ball to Morton, who had a rough day against the expansion Saints, completing just eleven of twenty-nine passes for 128 yards and throwing two interceptions as the Cowboys just slid by, 14–10. He rebounded to beat the Steelers, hitting twelve of sixteen for 256 yards and three touchdowns, two to Hayes and a late 5-yard toss to Norman, to pull out a 24–21 win, but then he threw three interceptions in a 21–14 road loss to the Eagles. Soon after, Meredith was back—looking sticklike after losing twenty pounds—for two walkovers against the two expansion doormats, the Atlanta Falcons and the Saints. But he had lost his early-season edge. Against the Redskins, Landry found himself reprising the old shuttle, alternating Meredith and Morton, which did nothing to prevent an ugly 27–20 loss at home. Even though Rentzel caught a team-record thirteen passes for 223 yards, he also dropped a key pass.

The Cowboys' record now stood at 7–3. They were cruising in their anemic division but fortunate to have faced the expansion teams three times. They closed out the season doing no better than splitting four games, beating the mediocre Cardinals and Eagles, losing to the unbeaten Colts and 49ers. In the matchup against Johnny Unitas, Meredith was awful, completing ten of twenty-seven passes for 106 yards and throwing four interceptions, while Johnny U went twenty-two of thirty-nine for 275 yards. He was, however, picked off three times, twice by Mel Renfro, and the Cowboys led 17–10 in the third quarter. The Colts came back with a 13–0 fourth quarter to

American Gothic: The Landry family, its roots firmly planted in Mission, Texas, in 1928. Beaming patriarch Harold Ray Landry and his prim wife Ruth could be proud of their clean-cut, God-fearing brood: elder son Robert, daughter Ruthie, and baby boy Tom, in front, whose carefree smile would become rarer as the years rolled on. *(From the collection of Mission Historical Museum)*

Ray Landry, third from the right in the first row, was the first in the family to win notice for his athletic prowess, such as when he was co-captain of this schoolboy soccer team in 1916. He was also a star on the Mission High School football team, paving the way for his sons to follow in his cleat marks. *(From the collection of Mission Historical Museum)*

Rather than in sports, Ray Landry left his mark as one of Mission's most celebrated citizens. In his spare time, he served as chief of the Mission Fire Department nearly up until his dying day. Here, he stands, second from the right, in front of the firehouse with his fellow firefighters and their pride and joy, the spanking red fire truck in which his sons were given rides and even slept in some nights. *(From the collection of Mission Historical Museum)*

For the Landry family, home was not a castle but a simple two-story A-frame house at 1012 Doherty Street. Today a garden apartment complex stands on the hallowed turf where Tom Landry came of age and once tossed footballs to his football coach, who lived two doors down. *(From the collection of Mission Historical Museum)*

The Mission Paint and Body Shop, located across an alley from the Landry home on Doherty Street, was Ray's place of business. The structure he owned for decades still stands today under its original name, seen in this recent photo with the kind of vintage pickup truck in the driveway that Ray would have tended to back in his day— proof that, in Mission, time has for the most part stood still. *(From the collection of Mission Historical Museum)*

The living may have been easy in Mission, but as a Deep South town in the heyday of Jim Crow, racism was ingrained. Even a decent man like Ray Landry had no problem performing in a local minstrel show in blackface under the name "Mose," an event covered without shame in the town's newspaper. Such casual racism was something his son would need to resist and change, in subtle rather than major ways, as a big-time coach. *(From the collection of Mission Historical Museum)*

The First United Methodist Church, seen here circa 1920, was a looming beacon, its arches and columns only steps down the block on Doherty. However, while Ray taught Sunday school here, and his children's presence was mandatory at liturgy and class, Tom's religious attachment was more a duty than a commitment until the late 1950s, when the confused young pro football player, husband, and father needed to find his way. *(From the collection of Mission Historical Museum)*

Mission High School, an impressive architectural sight in this archival photo, was where Tom Landry grew to young manhood and found his calling, honing his athletic skills and leadership qualities on the weedy turf of Burnett Field, which fanned out behind the building. *(From the collection of Mission Historical Museum)*

A baby-faced Tom Landry, seen here in the middle of the second row with a full head of dark hair, was hardly a star when he began playing on the Mission High football team. His brother Robert, seated directly in front of him, was a far bigger name. *(From the collection of Mission Historical Museum)*

By 1941, with Tom filling out and maturing into a star quarterback/defensive back, the Eagles won their regional division and finished No. 2 in the state. Landry, seen at the far right in the back row wearing number 89, seems a bit distant from his teammates, and in fact he was so good that some of them resented the attention he got. Also notable are the Hispanic faces on the squad, a rarity in Texas then. *(From the collection of Mission Historical Museum)*

Landry, a great natural athlete who blended skill and intellect, also played guard on the Mission High basketball team that won its league's title in 1940. He is immediately identifiable in this team shot, crew cut and all, second from the right in the second row, beside his coach, mentor, and neighbor, Bob Martin, who also coached the football team and marveled at Landry's abilities. The two remained close until Martin's death decades later. *(From the collection of Mission Historical Museum)*

Landry grew to manhood with pain and fanfare. After Robert perished while flying a bombing mission in World War II, Tom became a bomber pilot, as well, surviving several harrowing crash landings. He then became co-captain of the Texas Longhorns as a fullback and defensive back, leading the team to a top-ten finish in 1947. With his square jaw and wavy hair, there was no more dashing a figure on campus. *(The Dolph Briscoe Center for American History/The University of Texas at Austin)*

Presaging the heartbreak that would taunt him as a coach, Landry's collegiate career had its low points. The lowest was this play, when Landry, number 24, allowed 1948 Heisman Trophy winner and future NFL Hall of Famer Doak Walker, number 37, to catch the pass and run it 54 yards, propelling his SMU Mustangs to a victory over the Longhorns for supremacy of the Southwest Conference. *(The Dolph Briscoe Center for American History/The University of Texas at Austin)*

Besides a national reputation at Texas, Landry gained a wife, reeling in his greatest catch, Alicia Wiggs, in 1949. The handsome co-captain and gorgeous Bluebonnet Belle finalist, seen here in a stunning pose from the competition, made heads turn on the Austin campus. *(University of Texas)*

Landry, entering pro football at a time when it was part circus, brought some well-needed discipline and scholarship to a feral game. After starting with the New York Yankees of the All-America Football Conference in 1949, he moved into the NFL with the New York Giants the next year. The archetypical coach's pet, he further cemented himself into the plans of coach Steve Owens with his picture-perfect punting, in addition to his defensive backfield duties. *(AP Photo)*

Landry retired as a player after the 1955 season to become the Giants' defensive backfield coach, though he actually ran the entire defense. As "the best assistant coach in football," he made defense the focal point of a championship team in 1956 and altered the face of the game. He is pictured here with his charges in 1958, including two future Hall of Famers, middle linebacker Sam Huff, kneeling in front in the middle, and defensive back Emlen Tunnell, standing just to his right. *(AP Photo/John Lindsay)*

The men who would dominate the game for two decades had a friendly but ferocious rivalry as assistants with the Giants, seen here in 1957. Landry, on the left in the back row, was as cold as line coach Vince Lombardi, front left, was volatile. Both, however, were ambitious and went elsewhere when nominal head coach Jim Lee Howell, beside Landry, kept the job, with Lombardi going to Green Bay in 1959. *(AP Photo/NFL Photos)*

In 1960, it was Landry's turn to take the reins of a team, though few envied his task in building the expansion Dallas Cowboys from scratch. Striking a commanding pose in his Cowboys T-shirt, he would need to weather a winless first season and three more losing years before turning the team around and justifying his physically and intellectually challenging methods. *(AP Photo)*

Landry's hiring and longevity as the Cowboys' coach traced back to the faith shown in him by Clint Murchison Jr., the team's millionaire playboy owner, and the loyalty of the team's president and general manager, Tex Schramm, both of whom flank him, left and right, in this photo taken after Murchison signed Landry to a then-unheard-of eleven-year contract on February 5, 1964. Schramm, a brilliant and powerful football man, had to accept Landry's eminence, and his loyalty would be put to the test a decade later. *(AP Photo/DMN)*

The first wave of the Cowboys' success crested with quarterback Dandy Don Meredith and his favorite receiver, former Olympian sprint champ Bob Hayes, who are shown huddling privately with their coach before the NFL title game in Cleveland in 1969. The explosive combination powered the Cowboys to three title games in the '60s—all ending in crushing defeat and humiliation for Meredith and driving him into early retirement. *(AP Photo)*

After losing two epic NFL title matches against Lombardi's Packers, another title game to the Browns, and a Super Bowl to the Baltimore Colts, Landry found the winning formula in the early 1970s with courtly but ferociously competitive quarterback Roger Staubach, the ex-naval officer who earned the nickname "Captain Comeback" for his many late-game miracle rallies. But even Staubach had run-ins with the coach over his being allowed to call plays. *(© Bettmann/Corbis)*

Landry had to bend his rules of discipline and conformity to keep the scabrous Duane Thomas mollified and running wild, such as when he took this handoff from Staubach and headed for pay dirt in Landry's first Super Bowl victory on January 16, 1972, beating the Miami Dolphins 24–3. But Thomas went too far. After labeling Landry a "plastic man," he was traded the next season, though he later tried a comeback with Dallas, in vain. (© Bettmann/Corbis)

Landry, having finally broken his big-game jinx by pummeling the Dolphins in Super Bowl VI, enjoys a ride off the field at Tulane Stadium atop the shoulders of his players. Though some black Cowboys groused about Landry's handling of the combustible racial divisions on the team, all would have run through walls for him. (AP Photo)

Tom and Alicia, pictured here in the late 1960s, became the first couple of Dallas, and could still make heads turn, though he joked that only she kept her good looks. She was the great strength in his life, outgoing and personable, and the perfect buffer for him, freely saying what he held back from. *(From the collection of Mission Historical Museum)*

Landry, who became arguably the most famous Texan in the nation, greets the second-most-famous Texan, former president Lyndon B. Johnson, after the Cowboys won the 1971 NFC title. Landry, a staunch Republican, was a magnet for political heavyweights looking to bask in his glow, but he usually kept his distance, unwilling to be used as a prop and confining his testimonials to the frequent appearances he made for the Billy Graham Crusade and Fellowship of Christian Athletes. *(AP Photo)*

While his son prospered in Dallas, Ray Landry remained the most admired Landry in Mission. Here, in the early 1970s, he and Ruth are among a group of distinguished citizens greeted by Texas governor Preston Smith, in the middle. *(From the collection of Mission Historical Museum)*

Ray and Ruth were still a happy, handsome couple into their seventies, but Ray and his son were dealt a devastating blow when Ruth, whose stoicism so greatly influenced Tom, died in 1975 at age seventy-six. *(From the collection of Mission Historical Museum)*

Ray, still fire chief in Mission, was slowed down only by a stroke in the mid-1970s. He fought hard to recover but died in 1978 at age seventy-nine. Today, his memory endures as indelibly as that of his son in Mission, where this sign adorns a park beside the old firehouse he ran nearly his entire adult life. *(From the collection of Mission Historical Museum)*

Landry built another powerhouse in the mid-1970s, taking the Cowboys to the Super Bowl three times in four years, led by future Hall of Famer Tony Dorsett, who ran for over 12,000 yards in his eleven-year Cowboys career. While Dorsett quarreled with Landry over his playing time, he put that aside at functions such as this 1982 dinner in Washington, DC, when Landry received the NFL's Board of Governors Award. *(AP Photo/Ira Schwarz)*

Thomas "Hollywood" Henderson wears a full-length fur coat after the Cowboys beat the Rams in the 1978 NFC title game, and signifies that he is on his way to his third Super Bowl. Arguably the best linebacker in the game, he pushed Landry to the limit with his insubordination and cocaine habit, until he was fired late in the 1979 season after nearly brawling with an assistant coach. *(AP Photo)*

Landry's agony was as legendary as his conquests. The most agonizing may have been what provoked this grimace, when Jackie Smith dropped a touchdown pass in Super Bowl XIII in 1979, the key play of the 35–31 defeat to the Pittsburgh Steelers. That loss kept Landry from repeating as champion and marked his final appearance in the climactic game. *(AP Photo/file)*

The Cowboys' thirty-year homegrown tradition ended in 1989 when the team was sold to brash Arkansas tycoon Jerry Jones, who coldly fired Landry and hired crony Jimmy Johnson. Despite howls from the fans and the media, Jones won three titles in the 1990s, but has seemingly been cursed ever since, to the joy of long-memoried Landry loyalists, including Alicia Landry. *(Cowboys © Bettmann/Corbis)*

The morning after he was dispatched by Jones in the "Saturday Night Massacre," on February 26, 1989, Landry made his last trip to the Cowboys' training facility to clean out his office and say a final farewell to some of his players. Never an expressive man, his contemplative gaze and distant, private thoughts spoke volumes about how much his pride was hurt. *(AP Photo/RFN)*

Landry's dejection over his firing was mitigated somewhat by his induction into the Pro Football Hall of Fame a year later. Here, at the ceremonies in Canton, Ohio, on August 4, 1990, he clutches a bronzed bust depicting his famous face known to every fan of the sport. *(From the collection of Mission Historical Museum)*

Although Jerry Jones resisted for several years while seeming to downgrade the Landry era, he gave in to the inevitable and granted the coach his place in the Cowboys' Ring of Honor on November 7, 1993. Given a massive ovation by the fans, Landry seemed to go out of his way to avoid making eye contact with his successor, Jimmy Johnson, just behind him, after the halftime ceremony. *(AP Photo/ David J. Phillip)*

Tom and Alicia, seen here during his retirement years, shared a half century of memories, reminders of which line the walls of their homes in Dallas and Austin. To Alicia, he is still "Tommy," the dashing Longhorn who swept her off her feet. *(From the collection of Mission Historical Museum)*

More than a few believed that when the Cowboys built a glitzy new $1.15 billion home in Arlington, Texas, which opened in 2009, it should have been named Tom Landry Stadium. However, Tom did live to see a stadium bear his name that cost a lot less but mattered much more to him—in his hometown, where his old team, the Mission Eagles, play their home games. *(From the collection of Mission Historical Museum)*

Down Mission way, where Landry's journey to fame and legend all began, the Last Cowboy is perhaps best memorialized in this vivid mural on Conway Avenue, commissioned by the town and painted in 1995 by artist Manuel Hinojosa. Landry's life had many turns, but the great stone-carved face always remained the same, the signature of a singular man whose influence was a product of and was as large as Texas. *(From the collection of Mission Historical Museum)*

win, 23–17, on a Lenny Moore 2-yard run. Though a 9–5 record got the Cowboys into the playoffs, it felt as if they had backed in, and their first-round game would be against the Browns, who were looking for revenge.

For Meredith, who had taken to wearing a plastic mask inside his helmet to protect a broken nose sustained against the Eagles, the up-and-down season had ended, aptly, with sixteen touchdowns and sixteen interceptions and his fewest yards per game since 1962. Even so, Meredith, Perkins, Hayes, Renfro, Jordan, Howley, Neely, and Green went to the Pro Bowl, the last three named to the All-Pro first team. And Lance Rentzel did in fact bloom. He caught more passes than Hayes, fifty-eight to forty-nine, and was nearly as explosive with an average catch of 17.2 yards, only 3 less than Hayes. He also had eight touchdowns, just two less than Hayes. But the offense's ranking still fell to No. 6, and the Doomsday Defense, put under a greater burden, also dropped to No. 6.

The Browns, however, came into the Cotton Bowl for the Christmas Eve Day playoff game after the same sort of lackluster season, with the same 9–5 record. They were also hurting. Meredith, who junked the plastic mask that had been hindering his breathing, needed to do little but hand off the ball after stunning the Browns with an 86-yard lightning bolt to Hayes to put the Cowboys up 21–0 in the second quarter, his second touchdown pass. Securely ahead, the Cowboys would chew up the ground and the clock, running forty-six times for 178 yards and neutralizing the threat of Leroy Kelly, the league's best rusher that year. Meredith needed to throw only thirteen times, completing eleven for 212 yards, before Landry allowed him to bask on the bench in the fourth quarter while Morton mopped up the 52–14 romp, a game that not even Landry could find fault with. His postgame comments were a stream of superlatives, saying it was "the best team effort we've ever had," and that Meredith was "tremendous" and had turned in "the best performance of Don's professional career."[5] He even sought Meredith out at his locker with a personal greeting.

"Merry Christmas, Don," he said.

Extending his hand, Dandy Don replied, "Yeah, I think it's gonna be an okay one."[6]

✦ ✦ ✦ ✦

VINCE LOMBARDI, whose glorious old bastards showed they still had plenty of life, beat up on George Allen's Rams 28–7 in his team's first playoff round. That gave the Packers home field advantage for their next title tango—with the Cowboys, who had to make the dreaded trip to Green Bay for a New Year's Eve rematch. It was the first time they would play in Lombardi's Arctic-like lair since 1960, and to make matters worse, they had never beaten the Pack in a regular season game. Nonetheless they were a cocky bunch, even arrogant. After beating Cleveland, Jerry Tubbs said, "Now that the warmup's over, we're ready."[7]

Though they'd be underdogs again, it was of some comfort to the Cowboys that with Paul Hornung now retired and Jim Taylor traded to New Orleans, the Packers' offense had fallen to No. 9. Bart Starr had his worst season in a decade, throwing only nine touchdowns and seventeen interceptions. Their stifling defense also fell, to No. 4, though it had four Pro Bowlers. In truth, both teams had taken a step back from the year before. Still, the Cowboys' defense had allowed the fewest rushing yards in the league and had pretty much shut down the Packers' offense the year before, taking away the vaunted power sweep. But for the horrendous opening minutes, Landry's boys had outplayed them. As Norman recalls his team's attitude before the redux, "We absolutely believed we were better than those guys. We thought we'd run them off the field."[8]

But that was the rub—the field. With Lombardi in charge of the grounds at Lambeau Field, it really *was* a home field advantage.

LOMBARDI, NOT known to many, had been a victim of his own magnum success. He had been persuaded to give up smoking but was suffering from periodic dizzy spells, nearly keeling over in the locker room a few times. He confided to his priest that he was having stomach pain and was chewing antacid tablets like candy. When his doctor urged him to have a rectal exam, he flinched and growled that no one was going to "stick that goddamn thing up my ass."[9] If there was indeed a medical condition, his deterioration was aggravated by the mental strain of having to keep winning. He had also been having irritating squabbles with the team's owner and had dropped hints about retirement. In fact, even the year before, the *Dallas Morning News* had asked "LAST GO FOR LOMBARDI?"[10] There was no chance, though, that he would leave while his team was still capable of winning another championship, even if it might kill him.

In Dallas, meanwhile, talk about the midwinter weather in Green Bay dominated the run-up to the game. Because they played half their games in a moderate climate, the Cowboys, like the Rams before them, were hung with the label of a "warm weather team." Such teams almost always played wide open football geared to speed and slick moves, while teams in the polar climes generally pounded out the yardage inch by inch. It did not bode well for the Cowboys that the Packers had trounced the Rams on a thirteen-degree day. Landry, however, dismissed the notion. "I don't expect the weather to be a factor," he said, pointing more to which quarterback had the "hot hand."[11]

Lombardi was also playing down the deep-freeze effect. Contrary to the notion that he wanted a frigid surface, he had the team purchase an $80,000 electric coil system developed by General Electric that was laid under the turf. Vince was so proud of it that the day before the Cowboys game he took visiting writers onto the field and, like a science teacher, explained how it worked. By then the Cowboys had arrived, with Gary Cartwright writing upon arrival that if hell ever did freeze over, "It would be here."[12] The temperature was seventeen degrees and snow was falling when the Cowboys emerged from their plane and removed from the luggage compartment numerous sets of extra parkas, hoods, sweatshirts, socks, and thermal underwear. When they practiced at Lambeau on Saturday, though, it was in the mid-twenties and Lombardi's subterranean electric blanket was keeping the field toasty. "Everything's okay," said a pleased Landry, according to Alicia, who recalls, "That night, we all went to a party for both teams, and Vinnie got up and spoke, and he was so funny. One thing he said was that he was going to have the field heated. He wanted the game to be played on even terms, and we all believed him."[13]

The next morning, Landry answered a wake-up call at the Holiday Inn in Appleton, where the Cowboys were lodging. Through the windows the sun was shining brilliantly, a good sign—but then the operator said, "Good morning, it's 8 A.M. And the temperature is 16 below zero." Good morning, indeed. With the wind chill it felt like fifty below zero outside, a record chill in Green Bay. By game time, it had "warmed" to thirteen below, breaking the previous NFL record for the coldest temperature ever recorded for a championship game, five degrees above zero, when the Cleveland Rams met the Redskins in 1945, a circumstance that no doubt helped convince the Rams to move to LA the next year. When the Cowboys boarded the bus to the park, the wind snapped at them, turning their faces beetlike. The wind chill was around minus forty. But at least Lombardi's heating system still seemed to be working. Both he and Landry agreed that it was good enough so that the teams would wear cleats, not sneakers, during the game.

After they emerged for warmups—an impossible task on this day—two hours later the players, in their parkas and with clouds of smoke billowing from their mouths, were gasping from the frigid air rushing into their lungs like liquid mercury. Landry had brought from home only a cloth overcoat, gloves, and his felt fedora. His face was already the color of bubble gum, his extremities numb. Seeing him freezing before his eyes, the Cowboys' equipment manager Jack Eskridge went to Toddie Lee Wynne, who had come to Green Bay with several coats, one of which was fur-lined. Eskridge asked Wynne if he could borrow that one for Landry, as well as the fur-lined hunter's cap that went with it. He also took three pairs of long underwear and a hooded sweater, all of which Landry would pile on. Barely able to move, and still not much warmer, he would later say he felt like a "polar bear with arthritis."[14]

The conditions were not brutal enough to keep the team's rabid fans away. In the stands, slabs of concrete with no roof or decks to provide shelter, every seat was taken, the fans hunkering down under blankets in down coats and ski masks, thick sheets of steam rising above them as if they were in unison puffing on cigars. The Cowboys' wives and VIP guests were stuck in the stands with them, and some generous Packers fans took mercy on them and gave them extra socks. Out on the gridiron, Mike Connelly, back at center because of a Dave Manders injury, tried practice snaps wearing gloves for the first time. "You ever try to snap the ball with gloves on? You can't."[15] In the locker room Bob Lilly looked for anything that might help, including rolling Saran Wrap around his feet. Tough-guy Stautner at first forbid anyone from wearing gloves—"Men don't wear gloves in this league," he decreed.[16] But when they saw that the Packers wore them, no one obeyed Ernie.

At kickoff time, Lombardi's electric blanket had suddenly stopped working, leaving the gridiron a solid sheet of gray ice, getting icier and slicker. Footing was almost impossible. A fall on the field was like landing on a bed of nails. Lombardi seemed rather casual about it all. Noticing this, Landry knew he had been conned. "Vince," he wrote, "realized his advantage,"[17] a coy way of saying what many in Dallas said, that Lombardi had no intention of giving the Cowboys an equal playing field that day. Lee Roy Jordan believed then, and now, that "Lombardi turned the heat off to try and slow down Bob Hayes."[18]

The Packers, old hands at conditions like these, moved around so easily that Renfro insists, mistakenly, they *did* wear sneakers. The Cowboys, by contrast, looked as if they were in a Halloween parade. Trying to cover every inch of their exposed flesh, some wore ski masks under their helmets. More than a few Cowboys didn't think the game should go on. "Absolutely. It should not have been played," says Renfro.[19] Some of the visitors wondered if the conditions were not only bad but possibly life-threatening. Pete Rozelle would have been the only one to make such a call, but Rozelle, no dummy, had chosen to forgo Green Bay for Oakland that day, where the AFL Championship Game would be played after the Cowboys-Packers match.

Meredith looked at the gray slab and thought all the preparations of the preceding week were for naught. "We thought we had an advantage in our speed, our quickness, our multiple formations," he would say. "We had studied hard and knew what to do. Suddenly we couldn't do anything we had done all season. Our game plan was gone down the ice."[20] Lombardi, it seemed, may have won the game even before the opening kickoff.

THE OFFICIAL game-time temperature of minus two degrees with a wind chill of minus twenty-three was warmer than the actual temperature; during the game the chill would be measured as minus forty-six. It was so boreal that Tex Maule found reason to channel himself, writing of "the gelid confines of Lambeau Field," finding a new context for the line he had used at Yankee Stadium a dozen years before.[21] Frank Gifford, the color commentator for CBS's broadcast of the game, had the first memorable line of the day, telling viewers he had taken "a bite of my coffee."[22] On the opening kickoff, referee Norm Schachter put his whistle to his mouth then found the whistle was stuck to his lips. He had to rip it off, taking part of his lip with it. Because his and the other officials' whistles were frozen, none were used that day; instead, they had to scream things like "He's down" to end a play.

While Landry had vowed not to let the Packers get a jump on them like the last time they met, the game began in eerily similar fashion. The Cowboys, their joints icicles, were mainly bystanders and *again* were staring at a 14–0 deficit in the second quarter. Lombardi, figuring that Landry would bunch his defense trying to stop the sweep, eschewed it almost altogether and let Starr drop back and throw into the teeth of the swirling wind. Remarkably, he did so without as much as a slip, hooking up mainly with Boyd Dowler over the middle. Neither did the Cowboys discuss ways of adjusting. When they went to the sideline, everyone headed for the butane heaters behind the bench and sat there, mummified in giant parkas, teeth chattering, a situation Landry would say was "weird. You couldn't find anybody you wanted . . . or keep up any communications. It was very confusing on the sidelines."[23]

In fact the Cowboys never really adapted to what Lombardi was doing; they were more occupied with simply trying to get some traction. Linemen tried to excavate the ice by kicking at it with their heels or pounding on it with their bare fists, to little good. By the second quarter, Renfro, his fingers stiff and numb, would become the first reported to have frostbite. Meredith was fortunate to complete anything. In the first half, he was four for thirteen and didn't improve much thereafter, going ten for twenty-five overall for a mere 59 yards. Hayes, who caught only three passes for 16 yards, would be dogged for years by the NFL Films depiction of the game, in which he was shown lining up with his hands jammed into the waistband of his pants and barely moving when he wasn't the intended receiver—a sure "tell" that the Packers caught on to early, but apparently not Landry.

But just as the year before, the tide turned, if for no other reason that the Packers couldn't possibly perform at peak levels for long. Even if the conditions were to their advantage, they were only human. Linebacker Lee Roy Caffey would say later, "I have never been so numb or hurt so much from the hitting. . . . We were just as baffled by these conditions as the Cowboys were."[24] Catches they had made earlier now flicked off their frozen fingers, sure tackles were broken by the Dallas ball-carriers, and linemen were starting to get through to Starr. In the second quarter, Cowboys end Willie Townes got to Starr and caused a fumble. George Andrie scooped up the ball and ran it 7 yards for a touchdown. Moments later the Packers' Willie Wood fumbled a punt, setting up a 21-yard field goal to narrow the Packers' lead to 14–10 at the half.

The Cowboys gave Starr no breathing room in the third quarter—they would sack him eight times in all—and the offense seemed to be getting comfortable with the field. Taking the ball with six minutes left in the game, Meredith had a second and five at midfield. What happened next made Landry indeed seem like a genius, though it was actually the doing of Reeves, who had a suggestion in the huddle. "Don," he said to Meredith, "these guys force hard on the run. Let's try 'fire pitch.'"[25] That meant the option pass, which was always a possibility with Reeves on the field. During the season he had tried it seven times, completing four, two for touchdowns. The Packers' secondary had to keep it in mind, but after Reeves took a pitchout from Meredith and ran a few steps to the left, both cornerback Bob Jeter and safety Willie Wood began coming after him. When Reeves then stopped, squared up, and cocked his arm, Jeter recalled, "I said to myself, 'Oh, my Lord, what have I done?'"[26]

Reeves, seeing Rentzel alone deep down the sideline, lofted a fluttery pass through the wind. Rentzel was so open that he could turn, come back for the ball, and grab it at the 20, still 5 yards ahead of the nearest defender, who couldn't catch Rentzel as he pranced into the end zone. Back upfield, Reeves leaped into the air and into Meredith's arms. Other Cowboys raised clenched fists. Landry cracked a thin smile. The extra point made it 17–14, Dallas, the stunning nature of the score silencing the muffled fans. Lombardi, no longer smug, barked at several of his players. With just under ten minutes left, the Packers missed a field goal, and when they got the ball back on their own 32 with 4:50 to go, it was Lombardi who needed late lightning. In the CBS TV booth, the great play-by-play man Ray Scott intoned, "This possession could represent the Packers' last chance."[27]

Starr had no good choices. Running was useless, and the footing for receivers was so treacherous that he needed to keep the passes short. Landry played his defense straight-up, no blitzing, the deep backs hanging back to protect against an unlikely deep pass. In protecting the lead, Landry was willing to exchange short yardage for keeping the clock moving. And it came with a grievous price, as the Cowboys began yielding too much cheap yardage too fast. Starr began by attacking the left side of the Cowboys' line, sucker-ing Townes and Pugh with play fakes inside before throwing short to Donny Anderson and Chuck Mercein, who had played little during the season but was built low to the ground and could remain upright on the icy field. Near midfield, Starr found Dowler for 13 yards down the middle, taking it to the Dallas 42. Here, Starr tried the same half-back option pass that worked for Landry, but Townes crashed into the backfield and buried Anderson for a 9-yard loss.

Two plays later, it was third and eight, inside two minutes left. Starr, with the season on the line, threw short again to Anderson in the left flat. Howley seemed to be there, but Anderson jerked hard and How-ley lost his footing. Anderson ran for 9 yards. First down, at the Dallas 30. Starr then floated a soft pass in the left flat to Mercein. Turning in the play of the game, he stayed on his feet as he moved down the sideline, and when linebacker Dave Edwards slipped, he rumbled 19 yards to the 12, with just over a minute left. The Packers were now in sure tying field-goal range, that is, on a normal day. But in an echo of Johnny Unitas in sudden death at Yankee Stadium, Starr had only a touchdown, and victory, on his mind. Zeroing in on the end zone, he called a trap for Mercein, who ran it to the 3. Anderson then crashed over the right tackle for 2 yards, ringing up a first and goal at the one. Now, with the Packers close enough to taste victory, the Cowboys' linemen braced for the impossible task of keeping them out of the end zone. Starr sent Anderson up the middle, but he could gain only a foot. On second down he ran the same play and got nothing. The ball sat two feet away, and it was third down with sixteen seconds left.

Lombardi now made a decision that would create much second-guessing. He had one time-out left, which normally a coach would have saved in case he needed time to set up for a last-second field goal, in this case to send the game to overtime. But Lombardi took the time-out right then, banking everything on the next play. Starr trotted over to the sideline, hands in his pants, and conferred with his coach. When a man in a CBS parka with a handheld camera came close, Lombardi chased him, screaming, "This is my office. Get outta here!"[28] During the time-out, the Cowboys' linemen dug out as much of a trench as they could in the ice on the goal line, some of them having stripped off the rubber coating around the spikes on their shoes, lengthening the metal so they could kick harder into the ice. They reminded each other that if they snuffed a run, to stay on the ground and not get up, to writhe in fake pain if need be, to do anything to keep the Packers from getting another snap.

Starr finally trotted back out with the play—"31-Wedge," a variation of the quarterback sneak, a play he seldom called for an offense that almost never needed the quarterback to take the ball in from close range. As he explained after, "I knew Donny wasn't getting any footing. He almost fell down before I could get the ball to him the second time he carried. I figured I wouldn't have as far to run and I wouldn't have as much chance to fumble, so I called the wedge to Kramer's side."[29] The number "31" was the hole between center Ken Bowman and the right guard Jerry Kramer, who would plow into the left tackle, in this case Pugh, giving Starr an alley. To blunt them, the defense needed its own tidal surge to stand the blockers up, gumming up the timing and closing the alley. In the defensive huddle, it was decided that Pugh would stay high, Townes low. Landry would say that he was expecting a roll-out pass, which would give Starr a chance to throw the ball out of bounds and reserve time for a field goal. But as Starr barked out the signals, Landry had a gut feeling. "Watch the keeper now!" he barked.[30]

At the snap, with Starr grunting, "*Hut!*" Kramer fired out fast, relating later that "I got off real good with the ball. Pugh was playing on my inside shoulder and I took my best shot at him."[31] Pugh was caught by surprise, having expected Anderson to carry it up the middle, and he slipped. When Starr followed the block, Howley shot through the gap and hurled himself at Starr, but he had already fallen over the goal line. Norm Schachter stood above him, arms upraised. Mel Renfro also fell to the ground. "When Starr snuck through," he says, "I just rolled over and screamed."

Lombardi was mobbed by his players on the sideline. The fans exploded, some streaming onto the field, though with thirteen seconds left the Cowboys got the ball back, deep in their own territory. All the Cowboys could do was fling two prayers, which fell incomplete. The clock had run out on Landry again, the bell tolling a 21–17 defeat. As the fans rushed onto the ice and began dismantling the goal posts, he made the long walk off the field, a lonely wraithlike figure, hood hiding his face. Lombardi's smiling face seemed to be shining brightly in the dusk. By beating the Cowboys again in excruciatingly dramatic fashion, he had created football mythology. Indeed, Kramer's block was immediately the stuff of myth.

The Cowboys, meanwhile, stumbled into the locker room, physically spent and mentally crushed. Rentzel recalled it as a "tomb" and said, "Some guys were crying, others sat there bleeding inside."[32] Some arose from a catatonic, glaze-eyed state to smash fists into their locker, cursing the fate that had burglarized them again, telling themselves that those weren't tears in their eyes because Cowboys, after all, don't cry. But that day, they did.

A TIGHT-JAWED Landry held a brief session with the writers. Bob St. John would write the next day that Landry, "measuring his words so they don't spill over," said in his monotone voice, "This thing hurts so bad I don't know if it's worse [than the first defeat to Lombardi] or not—no, it hurts more this time," and "It's very difficult to play football in this kind of weather. I've played in 8 degrees and 4 degrees but I've never heard of anybody playing in weather like this."[33] As galvanic a figure as Lombardi was in his glory, Landry was equally isolated in his agony. The next day's *Morning News*, in which the page-one headline was "PARADISE LOST ONCE AGAIN FOR THE COW-

BOYS," published a photo of the coach as he left the field, his eyes looking at the ground, his hood and hat brim casting a shadow on his sallow face. The caption was simple and accurate: "MAN ALONE."

It was, as usual, left to Meredith to shoulder the blame, and this time he did with an almost surreal calm and grace, even poetry. At one point he was interviewed during the postgame broadcast by Frank Gifford, with whom he was friends, and discoursed thoughtfully and almost Shakespearean about glorious defeat, saying how proud he was of his teammates and that in the figurative sense they really hadn't lost, their effort being a reward of its own. CBS executives were so impressed with him that they sent word through an operative at the game to inform Meredith he would have a job as a color analyst waiting for him when he retired.

On the flight home, when cases of scotch were substituted for beer because of New Year's Eve, no one felt like toasting. Meredith, said Sam Blair, was a "melancholy figure," sitting in a trance in the rear of the plane watching some teammates play cards, glass of scotch in his hand. Blair approached him and tried to make conversation. "I'm sorry," Meredith told him, "but I just can't say anything about the game. I hope you understand." He then began to ramble, saying, "All I have to say is, there was trouble on every corner and it just didn't seem like Christmas," then spoke by heart some lines from Edgar Allan Poe. He mumbled something about coming back to the game only as a TV commentator. Halfway through the flight, Landry came looking for him. According to Blair, Meredith wore "a grave expression" as he said to Landry, "This ol' body has been good to me . . . but I have this offer from CBS and . . . . ,"[34] before Landry stopped him, saying this was no time to make a profound decision. As Landry remembered in his memoirs, "I told him he was being too hard on himself for his performance under such dreadful conditions."[35] Landry then returned to the front of the plane. Meredith, said Blair, "stood alone, his head bowed toward the wall. He was crying."[36]

After he got home, Meredith was diagnosed with pneumonia. However, he got out of bed to accept a joint invitation to appear on *The Tonight Show* with Bart Starr. Johnny Carson asked Starr whether the Packers would have had time for another play if the quarterback sneak had not been successful. Starr said he didn't know. "You wouldn't have," Meredith said, with a twinkling eye. "You sure wouldn't have."[37] CBS was right about him; he was a natural for TV. Meredith was approaching thirty, his contract was up, and he was involved in a number of business ventures on the side. What he needed to decide was if all this football madness was important or necessary anymore.

WHILE LOMBARDI luxuriated in Miami, having crushed Al Davis's Raiders by a count of 33–14 in Super Bowl II at the Orange Bowl, Landry had to deal with the demons of defeat. On the flight back to Dallas he was, said Frank Luksa, "very calm, but the defeat really, really hurt him." Landry could only envy how Lombardi had developed character in his players, and on some level he blamed himself for that, though he also wondered if he had failed his men by not toughening them to the point of ignoring adversity. The Cowboys, he believed, had done far too much complaining and not enough playing on that bitter day. Landry was no poet, yet perhaps he had the most lyrical coda for the mythic game. Said Luksa, "For as long as I knew him he made just one reference to it. He said, 'You can recognize the Cowboys. They're the ones with the broken hearts and the frozen fingers.'"[38]

The biggest of the broken hearts belonged to Landry himself. Says his son, "He was quieter than usual that winter. I got the feeling he was replaying the game over and over in his head, changing this or that. He'd watch the film of the game, alone, and he'd come out of the room shaking his head."[39] Landry had no answers for what had happened—and that was the worst thing about it. An executive at NFL Properties at the time, Steve Taylor, who later became a psychiatrist, told of Landry coming into the office a few weeks after the game, and "all of a sudden he just started talking about those two [Green Bay] losses. He wasn't really talking to me—anyone would have done—it was just something he had to say." According to Taylor, Landry said, "It's a lack of character, in the team and in myself. We just don't have what it takes. Maybe we never will. Maybe I never will." Recalled Taylor, "He talked like that for a while, and I didn't say anything. It was like a window had been opened. Then it shut. I never saw those kind of quotes from Landry again."[40]

"He was, what's the word, morose," says Landry's widow. "He was terribly disappointed. He tried not to show it, but how can you not be affected by losing like that? It broke his heart. He felt he let everyone in Dallas down." Neither would he forget. Years later, Lee Roy Jordan said, "Out of nowhere, Tom said to me, 'Why did you take a step to the left when Bart took it in?' Even all that time later he was *still* pissed off. He just couldn't let go of it."

INSTANT CLASSIC that it was, the game spawned headlines such as the one in the *Dallas Morning News*: "CHILLED IN ICEBOX BOWL: C-C-COWBOYS F-F-FROZEN OUT."[41] It became de rigueur to refer to it as the "Ice Bowl," played on "the frozen tundra of Lambeau Field." When NFL Films president Ed Sabol wrote the script of the highlight reel of the game, the one aimed for a Dallas audience—another was produced for Green Bay viewers—those two phrases were included, to be spoken in the film not, as is assumed, by the legendarily stentorian narrator John Facenda but by a lesser known announcer, Bill Woodson. Because Lombardi believed "frozen tundra" highlighted the failure of his heating system, he ordered it cut from the Packers' reel. The Cowboys, of course, were only too happy to have it in theirs.[42]

The Ice Bowl replaced the 1958 "greatest game ever played," in the perspective of a new football generation. There were exponentially more witnesses on TV in 1967, a time when pro football's ratings had surpassed those of Major League Baseball. To be sure, the Cowboys' profile had become almost as bold as the Packers', and the bar for them was raised higher, putting them under greater pressure to finally win, more than the Packers felt since they were seen as having achieved their last hurrah. There was, too, a certain arrogance to the Cowboys' losing, a belief by many in Dallas that they were entitled to win, even if they didn't. That arrogance would be part of the legacy they were forming, with consequences good and not so good.

There would, tooth by jowl, be increasing criticism of Landry for losing, though not among the general public or media. Pete Gent, who had broken an ankle and missed his second straight title game, watched the Ice Bowl from a hospital bed, blitzed on Demerol, and once more blamed the coach for bum strategy. "Landry," he said, "was not going to say, 'Boy, what a stupid thing I did to run a prevent defense, when they are running in the face of a 40-mile-an-hour gale and the wind chill is around 50 below zero,' "[43] his point being that had Landry played a little more aggressive, daring defense, Starr would have had to throw into the teeth of that ill wind. This was something few players disagreed with, and none but Gent dared say openly.

But the unkindest cut of all for Landry wasn't anything he may have done wrong strategically. It was that he would never get even with Lombardi, whose legacy as God's chosen coach was established because he had been able to beat Tom Landry twice at the wire.

THE PEACE between Dallas and Dandy Don Meredith was an uneasy, tenuous one. Just days after the game, a *Times Herald* story by Steve Perkins was headlined "MEREDITH RETIRES." Perkins had overheard Jerry Tubbs tell a teammate that both he and Meredith were going to quit before the next season, and not bothering to ask Meredith, Perkins ran with the quote, forcing Meredith to deny it. But his ambivalence was clear in a Bob St. John column that began, "Don Meredith, the Great American Enigma, is now standing at the crossroads of a pro football career, which heretofore has been bad, good, painful, frustrating and excellent," and surmised that the only thing that would bring him back was pride.[44]

Also ambivalent was Landry, who said Meredith's 1967 season "was not a good year because of his physical problems. . . . Don is at the point where he has matured at most things. Nobody ever masters them all."[45] While he stressed that a quarterback can require twelve years to fully mature, it didn't sound like he was prepared to wait nearly that long with this particular quarterback.

Part III

―――――

THE DEVIL LIVES IN DALLAS

Chapter 16

"WE NEED TO REVERSE THIS TREND"

THE COWBOYS CAME OF AGE just as America was degenerating into an apocalyptic hellfire. Having nearly heard the shots that killed a president and breathed the fumes of the nation's worst race riots, the team from Dallas seemed to have an inherent connection to a culture coming apart at the seams. The Cowboys may not have won anything yet, but their epic death-matches with Lombardi's Packers put them squarely into the progression of social transformation that was fomenting so much trouble. Clearly, the Cowboys were going one way—up—and the Packers the other. The price the Cowboys had to pay for their impudence was merely losing a couple of games. Others paid a much higher toll. The spring of 1968 was the start of the apocalypse. On April 4, Reverend Martin Luther King was shot to death at the Lorraine Motel in Memphis, where he had gone to support striking sanitation men. Then, with barely time for the country to exhale, in the early morning of June 6, Senator Robert Kennedy was murdered in the kitchen of another hotel, the Ambassador in Los Angeles, after he had claimed victory in the Democratic presidential primary.

As it happened, the day after King's assassination Tom Landry was scheduled to address businessmen on topics of faith at a Layman's Leadership Institute workshop in the Sheraton-Dallas Hotel. Jarred by the news, and more angry than sad, he stopped holding his tongue about social matters. In almost acidic terms, he combined religious tent-show fervor with a wagging finger about the disintegration of the country he once knew. "I believe that every American . . . is genuinely concerned about the direction America is going," he began. He then tore into a curdling culture in which "snipers stalk and looters run rampant," and ridiculed what he called "a furious rush to pass gun-control legislation," which he called "more of a conscience-easer than an anti-toxin."

He endorsed another Christian conservative of the era, Paul Anderson, who said of "free love" that "it destroys you physically and mentally." He denigrated the Supreme Court for ruling that "you can't pray in schools because an atheist says you can't." He channeled UCLA basketball coaching giant John Wooden's credo that "places our faith in the hands of the Savior," which was his solution to all the ills he saw around him, and particularly to the decline in competitiveness among the soft and sensitive athletes of the day. Landry's language is strikingly familiar in the light of current-day neoconservative doggerel about the evils of liberal causes, big government, makers versus takers, and gun control. "It has become fashionable," he said, "to expect the government to guarantee almost everything. No longer are our young men asking for an opportunity to prove themselves, but they only ask, 'What are the benefits?' . . . the sentiment in the U.S. today is that if you don't like rules or laws, forget them."

The first priority, he insisted, was that "we need to reverse this trend. We need to renew our competitive spirit, reestablish character, and apply discipline."[1]

Such was the Magna Carta of Thomas Wade Landry, with much simmering outrage, half-truths, sophistries, and fire and brimstone. But unlike Wooden, he made no effort to understand what King and Kennedy had represented in life. In fact, in that regard he was much closer to his nemesis Vince Lombardi, who that same year endorsed a Pride in Patriotism Day held at Lambeau Field. Taking place right before the last game he coached for the Packers, on December 7, 1967, the event was described as "a flag-waving answer to young anti-war demonstrators and draft card burners,"[2] with stirring marching-band and choral renditions of "This Is My Country" and "God Bless

America." Pete Rozelle clearly had no qualms about enlisting in this partisan crusade; at halftime Lombardi received a one-word cable from the league office reading, "Wonderful."

And yet Lombardi was far more nuanced than most people could have imagined, more than Landry to be certain. For one thing, Lombardi, as a Catholic from New York, grew up as an FDR Democrat and never shed that sensibility. He was an ardent supporter of John F. Kennedy in his race against Richard Nixon in 1960, and a long-time friend of the Kennedy clan. In 1968, his name was floated as a vice presidential running mate for Hubert Humphrey, until Lombardi pulled out, telling friends he was "too much of an idealist" to be anyone's lackey.[3] Landry had his own nuances, and hedges about being too easy a catch for right-wing politicians who craved his endorsement and never got it, but he didn't mind being on the ramparts defending an embattled establishment. Indeed, so pleased was he by the reaction from those in that corner that he repeated his speech a month later at a Fellowship of Christian Athletes coaches banquet in Atlanta.

What was missing was any sense of irony that his own kingdom was everything he decried in the outside world, or that his opprobrium about the decline in competitive thirst in the country was something he believed infected his own players—at least in the dying moments of games against the Packers. To be sure, given his team's behavior off the field, Sodom and Gomorrah could have been names on the backs of Cowboys jerseys. Landry had seen the world change, and the soothing sinecure of Texas was no longer a means of insulation from the turmoil outside. Not incidentally, it was reported the same day of his speech, the North Texas Conference of the United Methodist Church, having been urged by some of its parishioners to take a stand against the Vietnam War, released a statement that it had no immediate plans to either publicly support or condemn the war that was tearing the country apart, in itself a daring departure from blind patriotism.

It's unclear whether Landry, perhaps the most prominent North Texas Methodist, had any input into the decision, but the statement was Landry-like in its careful reluctance to come down on one side or the other, citing "the diverse positions by hundreds of Methodists in North Texas [that] reflect the lack of unanimity on Vietnam which extends across our nation."[4] Such safe neutrality, however, was becoming less feasible. The quagmire of Vietnam was being brought home daily through television, no more saliently than by America's most trusted man, Walter Cronkite, in February 1968. In the convulsive aftermath of the Tet Offensive, which razed the military's delusions of impregnability, Cronkite found rice paddies soaked in the blood of American soldiers. He then came home and plaintively averred, "It is increasingly clear to this reporter that the only rational way out then will be to negotiate, not as victors, but as an honorable people who lived up to their pledge to defend democracy, and did the best they could."[5] The coverage didn't alter the course of the war as much as it did the parameters of dissent about it. Landry's sermons would thus need to be topical, but without committing to any political cause. It was a tenuous line to walk, but in doing so Landry was able to solidify his image as a fellow in whom either side could find the lesson they craved.

The sports establishment, still a pseudo-militaristic bastion of conservatism, couldn't insulate the dissent. Openly declared critics of the war were still few, but at the top such voices included megastars such as Joe Namath, Mets pitcher Tom Seaver—and Don Meredith. As a result, such emboldening of outrage seeped into other causes. In Dallas, particularly, the slow death of Jim Crow was no longer good enough for some players. As a frustrated Don Perkins told a reporter in his hometown Albuquerque in 1967, "Do you know my wife Virginia and I would be embarrassed to have you visit our home in Dallas? We'd have to take you to a nice restaurant. Why? The Negroes on the Cowboys can find only roach-infested houses. . . . It's always been the same story. The apartment selector service refers us to an out-of-town owner and then the owners won't even talk to us."[6]

Mel Renfro was all too familiar with that con game, he and his wife having been turned down for an apartment promised to them *five* times. Not putting up with it any longer, Renfro joined with a lawyer and Dallas state senator Oscar Mauzy, who represented him pro bono in a federal Fair Housing Act lawsuit—to the consternation of Tex Schramm, who tried to talk him out of it. Recalled Renfro, "He said, 'Mel, you can't do this. You just can't do this.' Tex was afraid of the white hierarchy in Dallas, the real estate industry, [which] had been putting pressure on him." Renfro pushed ahead, and the suit became a major test case against de facto segregation. Schramm, mindful of the solid black fan base in town, later assured Renfro, "If you're going to do it, I'm with you all the way," and claimed the Cowboys hired an attorney to handle the case, which Renfro says never happened.[7]

The case, the first of its kind in Dallas, was heard before Federal Judge Sarah Hughes, a liberal state judge appointed by President Kennedy and a close friend of President Johnson—Hughes had administered the oath of office to him on *Air Force One* in the aftermath of Kennedy's assassination. Friendly to Renfro's case, she ushered it forward and in the early spring of 1968 issued a landmark ruling effectively ending segregated housing in Dallas. Though the ruling allowed African American players to finally live in North Dallas, those same doors were still not fully open for the less than famous prospective residents of Oak Cliff. It wouldn't be until the mid-1970s before compliance was anything near total. Renfro received hate mail for years. More active in the cause than ever, he once said the King and Kennedy assassinations "tore me apart. I stayed drunk for a week after the King thing, and I got real militant, had an attitude, and of course the Cowboys didn't like that." In recourse, he claimed, "They fixed me by not paying me any money,"[8] his perennial All-Pro status notwithstanding. If true, then such pettiness was for Schramm a form of Jim Crow in itself.

In truth, not much changed on a wide scope, and incantations of faith, family, and football were still largely admired at a time when an old-guard scoundrel like Nixon won the White House. Even if the football men of past generations were becoming anachronistic, and the game was moving forward without Lombardi, Brown, and Halas, Landry would be there, and bear the weight of their ghosts.

THE COWBOYS' great expectations for 1968—Landry's reservations about character aside—were shared by nearly the entire sports literati. Tex Maule was on board, yet again, in his *Sports Illustrated* preview, and so was Jimmy "The Greek" Snyder, the Las Vegas odds-maker and tout on the CBS pregame shows who was becoming a self-promoting Cassandra in the booming business of football betting. Even more than before, Landry's stable of coaching scions had made it to the wish lists of other teams. His longtime right hand, Dick Nolan, had been hired that winter as the 49ers' new head coach, a position he would hold for eight years, patrolling the sideline in a Landry-style business suit and developing Landry-style Flex Defenses.

Meredith, his latest deliberations about retiring over, was so eager to get to Thousand Oaks that he went out a week early, even in the midst of the NFL Players Association's first strike. After a lockout by the owners for the first time, the strike was settled within days when they yielded some minor symbolic concessions to the pension fund. When the players walked back into camp, Meredith was overweight from months of gorging on Tex-Mex dinners at a Dallas restaurant owned by a friend, and from living *la dolce vita* in Majorca, where he earned a few pesetas posing for swimsuit ads, as well as Palm Springs and Reno.[9] At camp he went on a severe diet and stopped smoking cigarettes, which an observer said "caused him to look a bit crazed."[10]

Darts from the press aside, Dandy Don appeared to have shrugged off the traumas of the losses to the Packers the way Landry could not, but on the surface the two men finally seemed to be on the same page. In a long *Sports Illustrated* profile by Bud Shrake that was published in September 1968, Meredith related, "Landry is a hard person to get to know. Now I love him to death, but [in the beginning] I wasn't sure if I could take him." Indeed, Meredith still had some rebel in him. Tex Schramm said in the article, "Last spring I told [Meredith] he had to join the adult world. He got mad and stormed out of my office. The next day he came back and said, 'I'm not gonna join your adult world. I'll live in my world and you live in yours.'" Shrake also told of Meredith sitting in a quarterback meeting with Morton and Rhome while Landry drew diagrams on a board. Meredith was taking drags on a cigar—his alternative to cigarettes—and when Landry turned around and asked a question, Meredith "stuck the wrong end of the cigar into his mouth. He coughed, sputtered, spat shreds of tobacco over his playbook. Morton and Rhome laughed, but Landry stared down at Meredith with as stony and humorless a face as he could manage."[11]

Landry kept his inner thoughts about Meredith to himself, but it was clear who he meant when he would say things like, "I guess we can do everything except win the big one."[12] That was the thematic cross that all the Cowboys would come to bear, but Meredith was beginning to think he would have to give Landry a championship in order for his life in Dallas to get any easier, and that he had one chance left to deliver it to him.

IN 1968, knowing his over-the-hill gang wouldn't be able to cheat the odds again, Lombardi arranged to step down as head coach of the Packers and stay on as general manager, a position few believed would demand his interest or passion. They were right. Lombardi soon felt powerless—his worst fear—and the team crumbled under his mild-mannered successor and old defensive coach Phil Bengston, who himself would be eaten alive by having to follow Lombardi's massive footsteps. For a while it seemed that Lombardi's stamp would be enough to carry the team through again. In the last preseason game, the Packers defeated the Cowboys 31–27, and they clocked the Eagles 30–13 in the season opener. But the rest of the campaign was a struggle, and they finished 6–7–1, the Cowboys exacting a small measure of revenge by beating them, 28–17, in the Cotton Bowl on October 28, before a season-high crowd of 74,604.

At season's end Lombardi, deciding to move on for the sake of his health and sanity, requested a release from his contract. The decision left hard feelings among the fans and board of directors, with whom he had more than a few arguments. If they wanted, they could have made it difficult for him and enforced the contract. Instead, they let him go, believing Lombardi when he said he was retiring from coaching for good. Only a year later, he made his return, as coach and general manager of the Washington Redskins.

Landry moved on too, into a now symbolically different football universe, taking what he could from the maddening defeats to Lombardi and aware that there would forever be a void. At the same time, he would need to establish a new focal point while bracing for other foes, and in 1968 the resurrection of an old one. He moved swiftly, and deftly, honing his offense into what he had always foreseen it could be. Frank Clarke had retired, holding the Cowboys' record for the number of touchdowns by a receiver in a season, fourteen, which would stand until 2007. Hayes and Rentzel, however, were a nearly unstoppable long-range tandem, and they would only get better after Landry hired for the '68 season, Ray Berry to coach the receivers, *and* Ray Renfro, the former Browns receiver, as coach of the "passing offense." Indeed, Landry now had expanded his assistant coach cadre from three to seven, having also hired Bobby Franklin to handle the secondary and Jerry Tubbs, now two years retired, as the full-time linebacker coach.

Excessive or not, it worked. The Cowboys tore through the league like a thresher, scoring the most points in the league and chewing up good teams as if they were Texas prime rib. Meredith, again running the league's top offense and given optimum field position by the Cowboys' second-ranked defense, had his best season. After a 59–13 opening-game slaughter of the Lions in the Cotton Bowl— when he completed sixteen of nineteen passes for 228 yards and two touchdowns—a headline on September 18 read, "A DANDY TIME IN DALLAS." And when a sore knee kept him out of a November game in Chicago, Craig Morton presided over a 34–3 blowout, sparking chants in Dallas of "We want Morton!" Dandy Don took it in stride. "Naw, it doesn't bother me," he clucked wryly, "until the guys on the bench start it." Landry too was unmoved, standing pat. As the *Dallas Morning News* put it, "MEREDITH THE MAN: COWBOY COACH MAKES IT CLEAR."[13] It sometimes seemed that Landry couldn't win, even when he did. There would always be some in the Cotton Bowl who would not be satisfied, for whatever reason, and volubly register discontent about it. Trying to be affable, Landry noted, "They used to boo us when we lost. Now they boo us when we win."[14]

Win they did. Over the season, Meredith completed 55.3 percent of his passes, had twenty-one touchdowns and twelve interceptions, earned an 88.4 passer rating, and went to the Pro Bowl for the third straight year. His sixteen-fumble fiasco of 1964 was a distant memory, Meredith having fumbled only twice in the 1968 season. The tandem of Rentzel and Hayes was amazingly balanced, finishing fourth and fifth in the league, respectively, in receiving, Rentzel with fifty-four receptions for 1,009 yards and six touchdowns, Hayes with fifty-three catches for 909 yards and ten touchdowns. Don Perkins, in his last season, was ranked sixth in rushing, with 836 yards. Garrison had five touchdowns in only forty-five carries, Reeves four in forty. The defense, meanwhile, recovering from its 1967 ennui, choked the life out of teams, holding them to 13.3 points a game and finishing second to the Colts in number of yards allowed.

Once more, the Cowboys' overconfidence ran high, to Landry's dismay, but there was little he could do to tamp it down after the Cowboys beat the Giants 28–10 to close out the season at 12–2, the next-best record in the league to the Colts' 13–1. Don Shula's team had struck gold when the thirty-four-year-old retread Earl Morrall stepped in for the injured Johnny Unitas, threw twenty-six touchdowns, and won the MVP award. This seemed to portend a championship game that would whet fans' appetites even more than the Cowboys' two clashes with the Packers. In the playoffs, the Colts did their part, winning the Western Conference by beating the Vikings 24–14. All the Cowboys had to do was get by the Browns, which was nobody's idea of a stroll in the park. While the Cowboys had taken apart the Browns in the second game of the season, 28–7, in the Cotton Bowl, their fourth straight win over them, the Browns hit their stride in midseason, winning eight in a row, including dishing the Colts their only loss, 30–20, in Baltimore.

Blanton Collier's team had the third-best offense in the league, built around Leroy Kelly, who ran for 1,239 yards and sixteen touchdowns. Unsung quarterback Bill Nelsen had connected with silky Paul Warfield fifty times, twelve for touchdowns. The Browns' defense had three Pro Bowlers: tackle Walter Johnson, corner Erich Barnes, and safety Ernie Kellerman. What's more, the playoff game would be in Cleveland. A trip to Municipal Stadium, by frozen Lake Erie, was daunting, and Landry, once bitten, was wary when Collier, as had Lombardi, promised the field would be in good condition. There were flurries the morning of the game, played on Saturday, December 21, and while there was no frozen tundra on a thirty-three-degree afternoon, the turf was a bog of mud that caked up on the players' cleats.

Like the Packers, this was weather the Browns always liked, especially a mudder of a horse like Leroy Kelly. They also had a rabid horde of 81,497 people squeezed into the drafty old park. And yet for once the Cowboys didn't have to dig out of an icy or muddy hole. Even though Meredith threw an interception that led to a Browns' field goal late in the first quarter, Chuck Howley stormed in on a blitz, jarred the ball from Nelsen's grip, and returned the fumble 44 yards for a touchdown and a 7–3 lead. The Cowboys were playing a new wrinkle—zone on the strong side, man-to-man coverage on the weak side—and had stymied Nelsen, whom they would sack three times. Kelly and Warfield were held in check. After a field goal made it 10–3 in the second quarter, a blown coverage turned the game around. Nelsen aimed one long pass downfield for Kelly, who was supposed to be covered by Howley, but the veteran linebacker was momentarily confused, letting the mercurial halfback get open for a 44-yard touchdown pass that tied the game. Meredith then moved to the Browns' 30-yard line, but Mike Clark missed a field goal as the half ended. That seemed to let some air out of the Cowboys' momentum.

In the second half, Meredith wasn't bad as much as he was cursed. On the first play, he threw a sideline pass for Hayes but hadn't seen linebacker Dale Lindsey standing between him and the ball. Meredith, following the Landry playbook to the letter, expected Lindsey to be where he should have been, but Perkins had blocked Lindsey into the area where the ball had been thrown. Lindsey, by instinct, batted the ball into the air with both hands, then plucked it and rambled 27 yards for a touchdown—the sort of fluke that always seemed to haunt Meredith, and not the last one on that day. On the next possession, third and four, Meredith tried to hit Rentzel at the Browns' 35-yard line when, inexplicably, the ball caromed off Rentzel's hands and into those of Ben Davis, who took it to Dallas's 36. Kelly then scored on a 35-yard run.

In the span of two and a half minutes, a tie had become a 24–10 hole. For Landry, this was the tipping point in a relationship with Meredith that always seemed one play from divorce. Having seen enough of the man he had stuck with through so much troubled water, when the team got the ball back, he told Meredith to have a seat. Morton came in at quarterback. In the Cowboys' lore, this is probably the most bloodless, and least glorious, frame of Tom Landry's three-decade stewardship of the team, based on what such a move might have done to the fragile psyche of a man whom Landry had taken pains to shield. As Sam Blair recalled, "Several weeks earlier, Landry had said he wouldn't pull his No. 1 quarterback when he believed there still was a chance to win a game."[15] But that was exactly what he did.

Dandy Don was the type of quarterback who could put clusters of points on the board, with lightning suddenness. And Landry himself would say that the interceptions that afternoon "weren't entirely Don's fault."[16] But Landry was a creature of the moment and a hunch bettor, at times to his regret. By the time he was yanked, Meredith had completed three of nine passes for 42 yards and had thrown three interceptions. Whether or not the last two had been his fault, the offense he was directing could muster all of 82 yards, while Nelsen was on his way to a 203-yard afternoon. Time was wasting away. Landry's motivation, he said later, was that "we needed a psychological lift" and "Morton was the only thing I had that I could use," though he did add that he had no intention of embarrassing his starter. "I never even thought whether Meredith was doing a good job. We had to get some life." What's more, he said Meredith agreed that it was the right move.[17]

Pettis Norman's take, now as then, is to simply ask, Why not? "I think at some point, if things are going bad you have to say maybe a change is needed. Something like that isn't personal. You're not thinking of any player's feeling at a time like that, you're trying to get a spark of some kind going."[18] On the other hand, Bob Hayes believed that Landry's pulling Meredith was "one of the worst things he ever did."[19] The operative word for many would be "humiliation."

Morton for his part came out flinging, and he immediately found Rentzel for a 48-yard gain that moved the ball to the Browns' 15, though the drive stalled and Clark missed a chip-shot 22-yard field goal. Minutes later Clark made a 47-yarder, trimming the deficit to 24–13, and in the fourth quarter the defense forced a fumble. From the Browns' 40-yard line, still with a hope and a prayer, Morton sailed another pass to Rentzel, but it was picked off. Nelsen then guided a drive ending in a touchdown to put the game out of reach. A superfluous touchdown pass to Garrison made the final count a still unsightly 31–20 at the gun. Tex Schramm, who had watched the game as if it were the death of a man he had known the entire decade, found Meredith on the sideline as the clock ran out, and embraced him, both men quaking in sobs. With the Browns having won a date in the NFL title match with the Colts, who would trample them, Landry again left a field in late December feeling lifeless, his head filling with the minutiae of what went wrong. Unlike the losses to Lombardi, there was no sympathetic lifting of the pall that hung over the team. And nobody asked for sympathy. Howley acknowledged that there were no excuses this time. "We can't say it was too cold. We can't say the field was frozen. We can't say we needed one minute more. We can only say we did a bad job, and it was a team effort."[20]

"COWBOYS BLOW THEIR THING" came the headline in the *Morning News* the next day, that "thing" apparently being pride. Bob St. John's lead cast them in a dark mythical shadow as the reincarnation of the "Ancient Mariner" and a "Greek Tragedy." Another headline was more direct—"COWBOYS WORST HOUR," taken from Landry's confession that "this is by far the most disappointing day I've ever had." The frustration was palpable all around. "A whole year shot in two and a half hours," moaned Schramm in the losing locker room, there being not enough vodka in the world to make the game go away. Landry had to keep repeating that he didn't yank Meredith because of how he was playing. Almost pleading for understanding, he said wearily, "It's hard to explain unless you've been there."[21] Meredith, who was there and didn't understand, again played the fall guy, blaming himself for "bad passes." But he said little before politely excusing himself and disappearing into the trainer's room. Some believed he had been through too much torture, and wondered if he would subject himself to it again.

Landry, perhaps already looking ahead to life without Dandy Don, didn't seek him out afterward, as he had in the past to assure him that next year would be different. In his mind, Meredith may have already been out the door. Literally, he was. When the Cowboys boarded the team charter back to Dallas, Meredith dropped into his seat for a few minutes, proceeded to fire up a joint, then took a drag and passed it to Pete Gent, who was so shocked that his buddy would smoke pot on a plane with Landry on it that he quickly put it out. Meredith then jumped up and said, "Let's get the fuck out of here," and the two of them grabbed their coats and bags and walked out the back exit of the plane, minutes before takeoff. Wandering around the airport, they ran into Frank Gifford, who was heading home to New York, and decided to fly there with him. As Gent later recalled, "We sat down, and Don lit up another joint, handed it to me. I puffed and handed it back to Meredith, and then he handed it over to Gifford, who looked at it and immediately put it out in his drink! I looked at Frank and just shrugged my shoulders as if to say, 'The guy's on a death trip.'"[22]

The two Cowboys, who hadn't gotten permission to jump the team flight, spent a few days at Gifford's house, where the old Giant who had once played with Landry saw how out of it Meredith was, a condition he blamed on Gent's bad influence. Gifford, whose success in the broadcast booth masked the trouble he'd had adapting to life after football, said to them, "I'd give anything in the world to trade places with you." Gent laughed hard. "Frank," he said, "you are so fucking dumb. I'd give anything in the world to trade places with you!'"[23] Still, Gifford's plaints seemed to have gotten through to Meredith. He and Gent returned to Dallas, and a contrite Meredith apologized to his coach. Landry though had already let it slide.

"I didn't have the heart to fine them," he wrote in his memoirs. "I would have liked to skip that flight myself. It was a long, grim trip back to Dallas."[24]

It seemed that all trips back to Dallas in late December were grim.

CRUEL FATE had once more denied Landry the spoils of winning the big one, and one can only wonder—yet again—how it would have altered the history books had the Cowboys made it to the Orange Bowl on January 12, 1969, when the gloriously subversive Jets tamed the Colts and leveled the pro football playing field. Instead the Cowboys were again relegated to the extraneous Playoff Bowl, where they beat their fellow also-ran Vikings 17–13 in the same Orange Bowl a week before the Super Bowl was played. For what it was worth—not much, the winning share being a mere $1,200 per player—Meredith played the first half, completed fifteen of twenty-four passes for 243 yards, threw a 51-yard touchdown pass to Hayes, and was named the game MVP. It did nothing to insulate Meredith from another storm of criticism. As St. John wrote of him after the loss to the Browns, "he will naturally—and it fits—wear much of the burden of this defeat on his shoulders."[25]

Of course, Meredith's courtiers would pin the blame for that loss on the man they believed had humiliated Dandy Don. As that mode of thought went, Landry betrayed his true feelings—he could not trust Meredith to bring him victory. Pete Gent, always the pitchman of these imprecations, would claim that Landry had inexplicably gone into the game with an offense not suited to the muddy field, and that giving Meredith the hook "cost us the game"—for the third straight season of playoff misery. Landry, who knew these games had not represented his better coaching efforts, nevertheless refused to shoulder a scintilla of blame. Gary Cartwright, perhaps nailing the way Landry's mind worked after such deathly defeats, wrote that in classic Landry-think, as the coach saw the first fluke interception, "unfortunately [Lindsey] was in the wrong place. It wasn't that Landry was wrong; Cleveland just wasn't right."[26]

Meredith, who never bothered to claim bad luck for his big-game flops, may have been looking for a push out the football door. The television offer kept growing as a viable, even preferred option. Gifford, as much as he missed the game, was making more money than he ever did playing football, with none of the battle scars. Meredith was torn about what to do. He had two more years on a contract that would be hard to walk away from. He was still a refreshingly carefree bloke at times. Walt Garrison tells the classic story of a night on the town with Dandy Don, who shot a $400 wad on beer for himself and buying rounds for the house.

"God darn, Meredith," Garrison told him, "how can you afford to blow all that dough?"

"Whadda ya mean?" Meredith said. "I just made $400."

"How do you figure that?"

"Hell, I had $800 worth of fun."[27]

The psychological drama of dealing with defeat and abuse from the fans, the media, and Landry had more than justified Meredith's visits to his psychiatrist. Sometimes Meredith acted as if he wouldn't mind if it all—not just football—came to end. On a team flight that season, the plane took off in a snowstorm, a big boom was heard, and it began to fly erratically. Beer cans were rolling down the aisle, and the stewardess, crawling on her hands and knees, was scream-ing, "We're in trouble!" While most of the players prepared for the worst, Meredith, who hadn't given up smoking for long, took a long drag and a swig of beer, turned to Walt Garrison, who was sitting next to him, and said calmly, "Well, it's been a good 'un, ain't it?" As Garrison remembered, "He couldn't have cared less if that plane went down. He didn't actually care. And everybody knew he wasn't bullshitting either."[28]

LANDRY DIDN'T have similar torn emotions, and he didn't need to since he again faced no great umbrage about the latest wrenching defeat in the press. In fact, Landry, as did all the Cowboys, caught a break by Meredith's being an effective lightning rod for fan and media storms. Beyond the locker room, few slammed the coach for yanking Meredith, and some, like St. John, even gave Landry the benefit of the doubt by rationalizing that "Landry, in theory, only gave up on Mer-edith this particular day [hoping] to shake things up."[29] Still, Landry, likely feeling a bit guilty about giving Meredith the hook, allowed years later that "he'd been deeply hurt when I pulled him in the Cleve-land game."[30] But the coach had come to the conclusion that he could no longer roll the dice with Dandy Don, and that Meredith simply was his personal King Creon, his goofiness only a fleeting respite from his other mask, the one carved in tragedy and Sophoclean mis-ery. Although St. John had written a December 24th column in the *Morning News* entitled "EPITAPHS PREMATURE IN DANDY DILEMMA," the reckoning between Landry and Meredith had come.

Meredith, after unwinding from the loss to Cleveland, spent the off-season in an odd limbo. He was apparently ready to quit. In the Bud Shrake profile of Meredith published in *Sports Illustrated* months earlier, several clues could now be seen in a starker light. Meredith had already cushioned his football afterlife. He had bought into a 2,300-acre South Texas ranch with a landing strip, had done

well in the stock market, had some oil properties, and was a partner
in a Dallas restaurant called Dandy's.[31] Still, Meredith couldn't close
the door on football and kept waiting for clues that Landry would
assuage him. But Landry, promising Meredith nothing, told the press
that "if Morton should turn in a superior performance in preseason,
then he would be the starter" and "this year Morton knows he's
ready." Morton indeed did, saying that "Don is one of my favorite
people, but I'm going to camp to win the job." Meredith, playing it
cool, said the right things, such as "I don't think it'll happen, but if
it does, then he's the better quarterback and Dallas will be a better
team;"[32] however, the notion that at his age, after nine seasons at the
helm, he would need to win the job was mortifying.

Worse, that off-season he suffered yet more personal agony when
in late June his wife Cheryl gave birth in a Dallas hospital to a
daughter named Heather, who was born with defects that had not
been detected earlier and had no apparent cause. Meredith, according to Gent, "felt tremendous guilt. He blamed his wild life and all
the sleeping around that he did."[33] His daughter had to be institu-
tionalized before her first birthday and grew up both blind and deaf.
Meredith must have asked himself endlessly what he had done to
deserve such a horribly disordered life. In his ruminations he decided
that football no longer had any place in that life. Even so, he found
it hard to cut ties with the addictive lifestyle that went with it. Two
weeks after Heather's birth, on July 4 no less, he asked Landry for
a meeting. Landry complied, cutting short his holiday activities to
meet Meredith at the Cowboys' offices. Seeing him in a despondent
state, Landry believed that his quarterback "wasn't sure he wanted
to play football anymore." Though Meredith had wanted to see for
himself if the coach would try to talk him out of retiring, Landry
instead listened to his myriad reasons for wanting to, then looked
at him with no tenable emotion or affection and offered some blunt
advice. "If that's the way you feel," he told him, barren in emotion,
"retiring is probably the right decision."[34]

Even if Meredith had a foot out the door, it wasn't what he wanted
to hear. He always had coveted Landry's respect, but even more some
simple human concord. Had he gotten it that day, he would have likely
given football another go. But while the coach may have believed he

was brooking his own self-interest out of empathy for Meredith's, it came out as typical Landry aloofness. As a result, Meredith left, his heart broken. Gary Cartwright would report years hence that "despite his success in television, some folks suggest that Meredith never recovered from all the criticism he took as the face of the Cowboys during those years. I've heard it told that he was devastated that Landry didn't try harder to talk him out of retiring in 1968."[35] Of course, it's also possible Dandy Don was hoping Landry would make the decision for him, so he could get started on the new life he'd been thinking about.

With relief that a decision had been made, either by or for him, Meredith left the game officially the next day, his farewell being announced at a press conference at the Cowboys' offices. Landry dutifully stood beside him in what he described in his memoirs as "an emotional scene,"[36] though fewer tears flowed than one-liners cracked by a relaxed and relieved Dandy Don. "I was gonna say that my reason for retiring was that I had bought this one-third interest in a New York bar," he said. "But I decided to play it straight." He stressed that quitting "had nothing to do with how I feel about being equipped to play another season," praised "an awfully lot [sic]" of Cowboys fans, and said he wanted to remember "the fond memories." Offering that he'd made up his mind a while ago, he added, "I wanted to be certain, but I was running out of time. I did not want to go to training camp with this mental attitude. . . . I have been playing football for something like twenty-four years. I have no distaste for the game for it's been very, very good to me. But now I want a different type life. I want to spend more time with my two children and my wife."[37]

Landry then said, with good cause, "I firmly believe that my decision in 1965 to stick with Don was the most important decision made in this club's history," and that Meredith was "very sincere in his feeling and under that circumstance I completely agreed with his decision." And Meredith, ever the good soldier, oozed of his now ex-coach, "I've come to love this man. I can tell you about his professional ability in just about any era you want to talk about. But he's also the finest man I have ever known. I will miss him a great deal."[38]

Few had actually hated Meredith, and no one in the press or the peanut gallery vilified him by calling him a quitter. Most simply seemed happy for him that he would no longer be in the line of fire. His checkered legacy was contextualized as part of the larger Cowboys' narrative of pain; a *Morning News* column was titled "THAT MAN CALLED DANDY: MEREDITH SYMBOL OF FANS' FRUSTRATIONS WITH COWBOYS."[39] Gifford, who revered both Meredith and Landry, tried to ease his pal into the CBS broadcast booth right away, but Meredith had other things to do first—one of which was to go on, as Gent called it, a "binge of self-destruction" that alarmed everyone around him and made them genuinely fear for his life.[40] Meredith, however, would soon surface on an even grander scale, plying his old schtick into a persona that would bloom into nothing less than a cultural tintype, just as pro football found its ultimate media niche.

But not without enduring, conflicting emotions. Gifford noticed a strange dynamic whenever Landry's name was mentioned in Meredith's presence, especially if Gifford praised the coach. No matter how Dandy-like he was at that moment, there would be either an uncomfortable silence or an emotional outburst by Meredith. In time, Gifford recalled, "We finally agreed never to discuss Tom Landry in order to maintain our friendship. Don at times would become maniacal on the subject of Tom."[41]

THOUGH IT was barely noticed, it was the end of the line in Dallas for another longtime Cowboy. By 1969, Pete Gent was a wreck, having suffered among other things a broken neck and leg, a fractured spine, a dislocated ankle, and a broken nose half a dozen times. The pain from these injuries was what had led him to the medications he used, several of which he was addicted to. But it wasn't his brittle nature that prompted Landry to move him out. Gent seemed to love tweaking the Landry sensibilities, and he even got to do so as host of a weekly in-season TV show in Dallas. What ripped it for Landry was when Gent, before the Cleveland game, propped himself up against some equipment bags, puffed on a cigar, and listened to the Beatles' *White Album* on a portable tape recorder while everyone else was deep in thought about the game. Several reporters even wrote about it in the paper.

There was a symbolic thrust to Gent's being discarded along with Meredith. It was as if Landry hoped he could snuff the "flower power" contingent on his team as a way of creating a more serious, disciplined, and surely less pungent air in the locker room. Indeed, Landry would consciously replace Gent by acquiring the anti-Gent from Philadelphia: Mike Ditka, the former five-time All-Pro Bears tight end who was a last vestige of football's brawling, cussing, blue-collar past. Gent meanwhile was put on waivers and the first bus out of town, winding up with the Giants, though he was cut before the season began.

Gent would, to great reward, obsess about Landry after he left the game, honing his memories and erecting a caricature of the man he could convey with a few well-chosen lines such as, "The only way I kept up with Landry, I read a lot of psychology—abnormal psychology."[42] Gent, nevertheless, like his buddy Meredith, went through a private hell in his withdrawal from football, finding little about himself that he liked. "When I retired I didn't want to live," he once said. For that, too, he blamed Landry. Still, Gent, in a moment of reflection, attested that he had lived in rarefied air serving under Landry, and he could never bring himself to deny Landry his props. "Over the course of a high school, college and pro career, an athlete is exposed to all sorts of coaches, [including] great ones who are geniuses breaking new ground in their game," he said. "Tom Landry was like that. . . . When you are young, you think you are going to meet men like this your whole life. You think the world is full of genius, and it isn't until you leave the game that you found out you may have met the greatest men you will ever meet."[43]

Actually, Gent's dismissal from the team was no different from that of any number of Cowboys who produced diminishing returns due to age or injury. Mike Connelly was one of those. Before the 1968 season, he told Landry he had one more year left in him. He was thirty-two and felt like 102 after nearly a decade of getting pounded on the offensive line. "The second I told Tom I'd only be around one more year, he had no use for me. I wanted to finish in Dallas. It had gotten to be a lot of fun after we started winning. But the next day he called me in and told me he traded me to Pittsburgh. He wasn't being vindictive. He took what he could get for an old beat-up lineman. I appreciated that he told me himself. Tom always did that with the guys who came of age with him. I wish he'd been a little more sentimental and kept me that last year. But if he wasn't sentimental about Dandy, he wasn't gonna be sentimental about me."[44]

MEREDITH EXITED just as Roger Staubach entered. After he had completed his stint in Vietnam, Staubach returned to the States in 1968, and while he was serving on a base in Pensacola, Florida, the old itch returned, leading him to attend on his own initiative the Cowboys' summer camp in Thousand Oaks, mainly to prove to himself and Landry that he still had a pro-grade arm. While there, he grabbed headlines, then reported back to Pensacola, to resign his commission in 1969 and begin his delayed pro career. Knowing he would have Staubach that year had made Landry's decision not to placate Meredith any longer an easier one. For the immediate future, Landry committed to Craig Morton as his starter, Morton having earned it after spending years on the bench. Expendable now was the frustrated Jerry Rhome, who asked for and was given a trade, to the Browns.

Staubach, who joked that he had gone from the Cowboys' No. 4 to No. 2 quarterback without even being there, was treated like royalty by the media and the fans. In fact, Staubach was a singularly heralded second-stringer, yet Landry kept him waiting, unwilling to gamble his hard-won spoils on an unproven quarterback, though one with the look of winner. In fact, while Staubach was no live wire off the field, and boasted of his squareness, he seemed to have a sizzle about him. In a battle of star power, Morton had no shot. He also did himself no favors with the coach by earning a reputation as the biggest party animal on the team, dimming even Dandy Don's star in that department.

Staubach would draw barbs from his teammates as a blue nose. Most of them were personally fond of Morton. However, Landry could not deny that Staubach was the kind of quarterback he dreamed of, and one who had beneath his gentlemanly exterior a go-for-the-jugular attitude and instinct. At the time, the biggest rap on the Cowboys was the absence of just this quality. The preseason issue of *Sports Illustrated* noted that "the Dallas Cowboys are the best team in football. They scout well, pick wisely, have one of the most intellectual coaches and field the finest 40 physical specimens you'll ever lay eyes on. Nonetheless, they may not win the most games." An unnamed coach was quoted as saying, "They don't beat you up when you play them, and they have the people who could do it. They aren't killers." For that, Landry was given a mild slap, for not having "forged the intense, Lombardian desire which animates pro football dynasties.[45]

Staubach lay in wait, with the promise of changing all that.

ANOTHER NEW, key face entered in 1969: Calvin Hill, Yale's big and versatile halfback, a man with thick thighs, nimble feet, and a highly functioning brain. No one doubted Hill was one of the best pure athletes in the country, but the scouts and general managers, in the group-think of the era, couldn't help but regard him as tainted by the lower-quality competition in the Ivy League—an old bugaboo indeed, with no Ivy League running back having been drafted in the first round since 1948. Rarer still, he was a black Ivy Leaguer, though he defied facile stereotyping at every turn. His selection with the Cowboys' pick at No. 24 caused snickers around the league, but Landry, Schramm, and Brandt were sold on him as another best-athlete-available choice. Hill had also been a champion long and triple jumper, had played linebacker and tight end, ran the forty-yard dash in 4.65 seconds, and scored inordinately high on the Cowboys' IQ and psychological tests given by chief scout Bucko Kilroy. Hill also almost short-circuited the computers when all his attributes were analyzed. Of the four thousand athletes who had taken the psychological test—called the Wonderlic Test—Brandt said Hill was in the top 2 percent.[46]

He was a natural by Landry standards. The son of a Baltimore construction boss, Hill was such a devout Baptist that he was attending divinity school in the off-season. Nevertheless, Hill still departed from the Landry mold in his politically liberal application of religion, one of his musings being, "I think the church needs to be more socially oriented. . . . We know it's there on Sunday, but I believe it can be a weekday thing, too." Hill was a public critic of the Vietnam War, often quoting Martin Luther King's demands for the church to lead the peace movement. A sense of excitement accrued to him, and he would get a shot at the big time far earlier than anyone expected because the Cowboys' ship was suddenly springing holes. In 1969, fullback Don Perkins became the latest of the originals to retire, and the loss of other active players during the preseason threatened the new season before it began.

Late in the preseason, Bob Hayes and Craig Morton were injured during an otherwise satisfying 25–9 victory over the champion but Joe Namath–less Jets, before a sellout crowd in the Cotton Bowl. Hayes separated his shoulder, which would cost him six weeks, and Morton dislocated the forefinger on his passing hand, keeping him out of the first few games. Willie Townes was out for the year with a leg injury. Dan Reeves had had off-season knee surgery. And Mike Ditka was damn near killed when a driver ran a stop sign and plowed into his car. Fortunately, he walked away with a broken jaw, cuts on his face and knee, and four loose teeth. A dentist told him he should sit out a month so the teeth could harden into place. Ditka wouldn't hear of it. "Pull the sonofabitches," he said. As a compromise, he had his jaw wired shut and wore a cushy rubber mouthpiece when he made his debut as a Cowboy, in game one.[47]

The casualties forced Landry's hand. Despite having no pro experience, both Hill and Staubach would be pressed into action for the opener—though Staubach too was hobbling, having a cracked bone in his lower back and a bruised kidney from a hit during practice. Going with the neophyte was especially distressing for Landry, who, when it came to quarterbacks, was always ultra-cautious. But with Meredith retiring so close to the start of the season, Jerry Rhome gone, and Reeves's iffy knee, all he had was Staubach, who had just retired from the Navy in early June and looked awful in the exhibition games. Anticipating his eventual arrival, Landry had allowed Staubach to take a Cowboys playbook back to Pensacola, and had even sent a case of footballs to him in Vietnam when he was stationed there, so he could keep his arm in shape. While he hadn't expected Staubach to leave the bench much during his rookie season, the ex-midshipman was under center for the season opener against the Cardinals in the Cotton Bowl—where he had played twice in college and lost both times.

Landry's main task with Staubach was to keep "Roger the Dodger" in the pocket and not panicking and scrambling around, which would put him at greater risk. Indeed, if *he* went down, God only knew who could take the snaps. But Staubach was not easily tamed, and he would never lose the habit to run, which drove Landry up the wall. The problem for Staubach was that his receiving corps was anemic. Although Ditka had revolutionized the tight end position by alternating bone-crunching blocks with deep pass routes over the middle, at thirty his body was battered. Landry wanted Ditka less as a tight end than as a symbol to reinforce the new, tougher attitude Landry sought. With Ditka and Ernie Stautner, the Cowboys had arguably the two men who could most easily make other men wet their pants.

Still, there was only one viable deep threat now: Rentzel. Wisely, Staubach looked for him against St. Louis and found him twice for game-busting plays, one for 75 yards, the other for 53. Staubach, who needed to throw just fifteen times, ran for a touchdown as well, in a 24–3 walkover. Little wonder Morton recovered faster than expected and was back for the second game. Staubach, fitfully, went to the bench, a place he absolutely detested, watching Morton lead the team to a 21–17 win over the Saints, with Hill rumbling for 138 yards and two touchdowns. As the tremors of summer gave way to another autopilot season, the Cowboys galloped out to a 6–0 record and finished 11–2–1, losing only to the Browns and Rams.

Hill, who would make the All-Pro first team and be voted rookie of the year in a landslide, was spectacular, his 942 rushing yards second only to Gale Sayers's 1,032. He was an even three for three with two touchdowns on option passes. Hayes returned after four games and caught forty passes; Rentzel, forty-three with two touchdowns. Morton had his best season, throwing for 2,619 yards, twenty-one touchdowns with fifteen interceptions, and a league-best 8.7 yards per pass attempt. Garrison, the plow horse, ran for 818 yards. The offense came in No. 2; the defense ranked fourth. Satisfyingly to Landry, though it hardly eased the past, he beat Lombardi's Redskins twice, 41–28 and 20–10. As a sadly ironic footnote, they closed out the schedule with the second of those wins, on December 21, 1969, the last game Vince Lombardi ever coached.

The opening playoff round would bring in the 10–3–1 Browns, who had destroyed the Cowboys, 42–10, in the regular season and could now barely hide their arrogance. After the earlier game, in November, one of Cleveland's linebackers merrily mocked Landry's team, saying, "We were standing there laughing at them. They would run at us and we would knock them down."[48] Tackle Walter Johnson predicted that the Cowboys would be so "keyed up they can't play their game." Lee Roy Jordan tried to generate some motivation by telling his teammates that the Browns were "saying we're going to choke."[49] The biggest problem the Cowboys had, however, was that they needed no reminders that choking seemed to be what they did best.

Chapter 17

THE LORD
TAKETH . . .

DAYS BEFORE THE DECEMBER 28 rematch with the Browns, Craig Morton gave his take on the Cowboys' overall attitude. Whereas in November they'd been loose, he said, now they seemed "nervous, afraid, scared."[1] Amazingly, he said this as if it were a *positive* thing.

Hopes that they would finally have a decent field under their feet were dashed when it rained in Dallas for days and right through the game. Even though on game day it was fifty-one degrees, Bob Hayes would recall that "it was an all-around shitty day—raining and cold—and the field was muddy and in terrible shape."[2] Three thousand fans who had bought tickets stayed home. And, once more, a game that mattered got away early. On the first series the Browns' punt floated short. Hayes, waiting to return it, let the wet ball hit the ground rather than risk catching and dropping it. The ball took a crazy bounce sideways, toward Rayfield Wright, a downfield blocker. He tried dodging it, but the ball ticked him as it squirted between his legs and was recovered by the Browns at the Cowboys 34-yard line Bill Nelsen then took his offense into the end zone for a 7–0 lead. Morton, meanwhile, misfired on his first six passes, his runners couldn't move the ball, and the Browns surged to a 17–0 halftime lead. As the Cowboys trudged off the field, boos, as Sam Blair wrote, "grew and swept down upon them like an avalanche. The fans weren't booing one player now. They were booing the entire team. This had never happened in the Cotton Bowl."[3]

Strategically, Landry had tried flipping Mel Renfro and cornerback Otto Brown in covering Paul Warfield, which Cornell Green later called a "stupid" move,[4] since the old pro receiver ripped the young Brown apart, catching eight balls for 99 yards. Other Cowboys later spoke of Landry's changing the game plan at the last minute, causing confusion. Whatever the case, Morton never got on track, going eight for twenty-four for 92 yards and throwing two interceptions. With Leroy Kelly again running through the mush, the Browns' lead ballooned to a remarkable 38–7 in the fourth quarter. That was when Landry pulled Morton, who had come in the year before when Landry pulled Meredith. It was another example that, with the Cowboys, things didn't change; they were just reordered. Staubach did toss a meaningless touchdown pass to Rentzel to make the final score 38–14.

Afterward Kelly piled on, saying that "Dallas is a fair-weather team,"[5] and no one in the opposite locker room felt much like denying it. Pettis Norman called the defeat a "low point,"[6] which was taking in a lot of ground, and "total devastation." Hayes sadly quipped, "It looked like we were playing on a wet field and they were playing on a dry one."[7] Morton, now in the role made famous by Meredith, stood bowed at his locker and apologized for a hellish performance. And Landry, Staubach recalled, "looked like a beaten man that day . . . the lowest I've ever seen him. He was ashen."[8] Not even the humiliations by Lombardi seemed to haunt him as much as the trio of losses to the Browns. "I don't understand it," he said, insisting, "We have a fine team, a very fine team."[9]

The press was merciless, with no slack for the coach. "Landry has taken them almost to the top . . . almost," wrote Sam Blair. "Now they've slipped. The Cowboys are nobody's darlings anymore. In the aftermath of their biggest mess yet . . . Landry is the target for more harsh words than at any time in his career."[10] Word began to go around that Landry's time had perhaps passed, though his team had won more games in the last three years than anyone except the Colts. To some around town, the Cowboys were worse than big-game losers; they were close to old news, with their coach a tarnished icon,

Blair noting that during the season fans had shown up with a banner reading, "Mickey Mouse wears a Tom Landry watch."[11]

Even with his ambivalent feelings about his old coach, Dandy Don Meredith felt for him. The night after the loss to the Browns, the quarterback-turned-stockbroker, who often was seen in the stands watching his old team play, phoned Landry and asked if he could drop by his home. It was the first time he had ever been to the house, and when he got there he hoped the roles would be reversed from a year ago, that he'd be able to talk Landry *out* of football before it could eat *him* alive. As Landry recalled it in his memoirs, Meredith counseled him, "Get out of this rotten business, hang it up, forget it, get out."[12]

Landry laughed. A man who had endless permutations when it came to drawing up plays, he had no options for himself other than continuing on and vindicating Clint Murchison's faith, and his own. Murchison in fact went on record that day in the *Morning News* with renewed confidence in his coach, saying, "No one has mentioned any unhappiness with Tom to me, and I suggest they not. . . . We've won a conference or division title the last four years [and] I'm looking forward to the seventies, the decade of the Cowboys."[13]

If the coach appreciated the succoring, he entered the new decade knowing that a record 42–12–2 over the last wasn't nearly good enough. Indeed, he would need to own the next one. For a team that couldn't win a playoff game, that seemed like a preposterous notion. As the *Morning News* said that day, of all the work to be done by the team, "Landry's job is obviously the toughest. He may be looking for the Golden Fleece." Or, as a *Peanuts* cartoon that was pinned up in the Cowboys' locker room read, for all to see, "There's No Heavier Burden Than a Great Potential."[14]

IT SURELY had to gall Tom Landry that he was once again bound for Miami to finish a season in the ho-hum Playoff Bowl. In fact, he was so disinterested that he sent his boys out with no game plan and told them to do what they wanted, whereupon the Rams wasted them 31–0, fulfilling George Allen's game plan to run up the score on the team he hated. Meanwhile, the NFL champs, the Minnesota Vikings, a team that entered the NFL a year after the Cowboys, carried the old league's battle flag into the last Super Bowl of the decade. Landry's cosmetic clone, Bud Grant's "Purple People Eaters" defense, anchored by linemen Carl Eller and Alan Page, had beaten the Browns 23–20 in the last NFL title game. And if anyone doubted that the old-guard NFL was dead, they would know for sure when the world championship was won by the man who built the AFL and lost the battle for Dallas: Lamar Hunt, whose now superbly honed and massively proportioned Kansas City Chiefs exposed the Vikings as an undersized, slow Potemkin champ, bullying them in a 23–7 victory.

Landry, however, was not only among the small circle of elite coaches but also the apotheosis of his team, which had gained innumerable fans in cities far beyond Dallas. Because it was built in his image, really smart guys like Hill and Staubach, who were polar opposites politically, were united in their excitement playing for him. Landry's continuing relevance was amazing given that the sensibilities of his old world clashed so virulently with those of a growing number of modern-day players. "I've come to the conclusion that players want to be treated alike," he once said. "They may talk about individualism, but I believe they want a single standard. . . . If a player is contributing and performing the way he ought to, he will usually conform. . . . We just can't get along with a player who doesn't conform or perform. No way."[15] This was not far removed from Vince Lombardi's canon, yet it is much harder to imagine Lombardi enduring as long and relevantly as did Landry.

In truth, Landry wasn't as remote as he seemed. There were important exceptions to the distance Landry kept between himself and the players, mainly in his relationships with Dan Reeves and now Mike Ditka. Landry would play tennis with both during breaks in Thousand Oaks, which because of the extreme competitive zeal of all three led to some long and intense matches on the court. Ditka particularly intrigued him. The brutish, boorish tight end was his alter ego, a man's man not given to niceties—one time he grew so enraged over who knows what that he tore a phone book in half—and Landry lived vicariously through him, biting his lip when Ditka would spew endless profanity. That Ditka seemed afraid of *him*, and would have shut off the cussing with one word from Landry, was a wonder. It was also true that Landry allowed Tex Schramm enough room to fantasize that he stood on the same plane as the coach. Schramm, by nature, could not have been as sanguine as he insisted about taking a back seat to Landry. Tex often looked for ways to elevate himself, even if at Landry's expense. After the most recent loss to the Browns, Schramm, sounding like Boss Hogg, said, "We plan to reevaluate the entire organization and the systems therein," before catching himself and adding with a smirk, "This is not applicable to the head coach."[16]

Schramm, smart as he was, had foreseen in the team what Landry had not. It had been Schramm's plan all along to solder the Cowboys' name to all that was big and remarkable about Texas—and, not incidentally, all that was homegrown about Tom Landry. And that was exactly what had happened. The team had bonded the scent of excessive wealth with the pungent scent of the stockyards and given the Dallas Cowboys a cachet that just kept feeding on itself. A skeptic, minority owner Bedford Wynne, had seen with his own eyes the power of the name he had hated at first. As he recalled, "We found that everywhere we went, [we were] a source of mystique. There was just an intrigue nationally with Dallas—the oil, the wealth."[17]

While nobody really quite "got" Landry, they did come to expect him to be there on the sideline, ratifying and reifying all that the Cowboys were. Had Lombardi been cursed by the heartbreak that always found Landry, it's doubtful football fans would have seen him with half the pity they did for Landry. All over the football map, in fact, there was just as much impatience for Landry to finally win the big one as there was inside the Dallas city limits.

TEXAS STADIUM wasn't ready for the transition to a new decade and football order. Rather than making its debut as Clint Murchison's intended $25 million Acropolis, it had become a Texas-style boondoggle. Murchison's big idea, a retractable roof, went through several stages of design, none of which could be made feasible without danger of the whole roof falling in. With union strikes, bad weather, and cost overruns that grew into the millions, both the architects and the construction crews were baffled about what to do.

Murchison cared not a whit that the price tag had escalated to over $30 million. He and his brother John owned over a hundred companies worth an estimated $1.25 billion. He believed nothing he did with his money could ever go wrong. Hoping to get it right, he continued pouring assets and cement into the stadium. Eventually, he had to downsize his fantasies, but the stadium still wouldn't be completed by the start of the 1971 season. The Cowboys would break in the new age of the NFL in the Cotton Bowl, a mocking relic of a bygone era that the team had already transcended with its streamlined, computer-age modalities.

Stadium woes aside, the once-ragtag Cowboys were now the model for a sport on a hard upward thrust. Even methods that originated elsewhere were taken to a higher level of sophistication by Landry. The Wonderlic IQ exams, for example, were first used by Paul Brown when he returned to the game in 1968 as the point man for a new AFL franchise, the Cincinnati Bengals. Brown would have the team in the playoffs by 1970, at which point Landry was *still* learning from him. Landry wasn't the only coach doing so. The Wonderlic, for example, was becoming standard around the league. The test, a standardized fifty-item, twelve-minute, multiple-choice questionnaire seeking logical free associations with English, math, and science concepts, was created by sociologist E. F. Wonderlic for use in schools and businesses. A typical question was one that would be perfect for Landry to have to answer:

> PAIN is the opposite of: 1. poison, 2. torment, 3. agony, 4. comfort, 5. punishment.[18]

Of course, the players, never giving it any credibility, merely acceded to answering questions that had nothing to do with football. Pete Gent once spoofed the test in one of his writings with a question that went:

> What would you rather do? A. Kill your mother. B. Jack off. C. Read a book. D. Eat live baby ducks.[19]

What Landry saw in such oblique questions, though, few other coaches would have. He also added his own touches of free association by inputting the criteria of some of the Cowboys' team shrinks. If it meant nothing to the players or outsiders, to Landry every question, every response, contributed in some way to his evaluations. There was no consistency to it; no team was more diverse in background, world culture, religion, politics, or even nationality. Yet the players all seemed to be filial, sharing that elusive, mysterious Dallas Cowboys' gene. It never would have mattered a whit to Landry that, as a team, they reeked of star power. Out in Los Angeles, Thousand Oaks had grown with them. The once sleepy suburb had exploded into an "in" place, and as such a magnet for movie people and attendant gossip. It was, Bob St. John once wrote, "a city where daily soap operas come to life, or late afternoon philosophical martinis, and where a great deal of the population is devoted to hedonistic pursuits."[20]

The Cowboys rivaled the baseball Dodgers for celebrity sightings, and summer practices drew the likes of Burt Reynolds, Kenny Rogers, and Glenn Campbell. After Lance Rentzel, who lived in LA in the off-season, began a high-profile romance with sex kitten actress Joey Heatherton, it became the major story of camp in 1968. When an otherwise-occupied Rentzel missed practices and Landry fined him $850, no one doubted it was worth every penny. The counterweight to all this was that Landry, blessedly, never went Hollywood. Other bigwigs in the organization ran around like rutting sows, turning the front office into a Grace Metalious novel where everyone seemed to be "doing" someone who was not his wife—the most active being Murchison himself, who was so friendly with Gil Brandt's wife Anne that when they divorced in 1975, Anne rebounded quickly, marrying the big boss.[21] If Landry could do nothing about such matters, it was at least comforting that within this Caligula subtext, Tex Schramm would stay married to his high school sweetheart, Martha Anne Snowden, until her death in 2002.

And Tom Landry? As Bob Hayes once reported, "Tom is truly devoted to Alicia. I can't imagine him playing around with women; in fact, I'm not even sure he played around with Alicia during the season,"[22] an assumption that she pleads the Fifth to. As far as anyone knew, Landry's sole vice was speed, on the field for his players and off it for himself, behind the wheel of his Grand Prix, his retort to those who wondered why his foot was pressed so hard against the gas pedal being simple and obvious: "I'm in a hurry."

If Landry wouldn't surrender to the seductions of fame, however, he was quite aware of his own now very famous image. At home he had filled his closet with fedoras of different shades of gray and brown to match the dozens of tailored suits he wore exclusively on the sideline, where he couldn't be merely a coach but *Landry*. Others in his train felt the same demand, not to be Landry but to be cut in the same mold. It was comical to see the assistant coaches trying to mutate somehow into Landry-bots and sycophants. Once, when Landry had a coughing fit during a chalk talk, a Three Stooges–type scene ensued, with Dan Reeves and Ernie Stautner, Hayes recalled, running to get water for him. "They both hit the door at the same time and got stuck in the doorway," recalls Mike Connelly. "It was one of the funniest sights I ever saw."[23] Even Iron Mike Ditka, trying to speak in the cerebral language of Landry's locker room aphorisms, used words he didn't know and couldn't pronounce. Seeing Ditka attempt to say "objectification" then give up and mutter, "Aw, fuck, just kick some ass," was worth staying after school for.

IN 1970, the year the NFL merger went into effect, each league was refashioned into a conference that retained its historic identity to the respective original leagues, the National Football Conference, or the NFC, and the American Football Conference, or the AFC, each with East, Central, and West Divisions. Television also perpetuated a sense of continuity; CBS would broadcast the NFC, and NBC the AFC, with the home team in each interconference game determining which network covered it, and the rotation between the two networks for the Super Bowl, which began with the 1969 game, was carried over. The price tag for these games was stratospheric, and when the networks' deals with their leagues ran out in 1969—CBS had carried its games for $18.8 million, NBC for $36 million—they re-upped at twice that amount, and would do the same every four years.

Starting that year too, ABC moved into the picture with an entirely new concept: a prime-time Monday night game broadcast each week, completing the loop between pro football and entertainment, a daring idea that cost the traditional third-rated network $8.5 million for a mere thirteen games. Each of the twenty-six teams reaped around $1.7 million from these deals, $500,000 more than the year before for the NFL teams and $800,000 more for the AFL teams.[24] The television blackout for home games continued, but only until 1973, when Congress lifted it for games sold out seventy-two hours in advance, despite Pete Rozelle's argument that only seven teams were assured of weekly sellouts even with blackouts. There was still a strong New York skew to the announcing teams at the networks, which included Pat Summerall, Frank Gifford, Kyle Rote, and Al DeRogatis—all former teammates of Tom Landry. Tex Schramm was proved correct yet again when the AFL innovation he had wanted to annex for the NFL in 1965, putting players' names on the back of their uniform shirts, became mandatory for all teams.

For Landry, it had to be of some comfort that the pro football world had in effect hit the reset button, not exactly wiping the slate clean of recent history but charting a new horizon on which every team started equal. If only it was as easy to forget all those miserable endings. Still, it seemed almost in the spirit of rebirth that the Cowboys' maiden first-round draft choice of the new era was a running back, even after Cal Hill's wondrous rookie year. Schramm again reached for the prototype of the big, fast, and shifty back, plucking Duane Thomas from the small but profoundly important West Texas State in Canyon, eighteen miles down the Panhandle from Amarillo. Though it was a mostly white school, the coach, Joe Kerbel, specifically recruited black players, one of whom was Mercury Morris, with whom Thomas was teamed in the backfield before Morris was drafted by the Miami Dolphins.

Thomas had a hard act to follow—Morris had become the NCAA's leading rusher in history, in a single season and over his career—but similar to Hill, at six foot two and 215 pounds he was built like a linebacker with room to easily grow. He could play halfback and fullback and block like a truck, having helped Morris into the open field enough to set his records. As a senior Thomas ran into the headlines himself, gaining 1,072 yards, tenth best in the nation. One scout called him "a do it all back. One of the greatest ever. A Jim Brown."[25] Brandt had made him his top-ranked running back, but the Cowboys never thought he would still be available by the time they picked, at No. 23. Or would he? The scuttlebutt among the scouts and other very serious people in the league was that Thomas, gem that he was, was perhaps too much of a risk. It wasn't that he was outwardly a problem. He had never been in trouble with his coaches, or the law, and had been pleasant and chatty with the press. Nor was he a low-IQ case, having finished his education at the University of California, Irvine, during the off-season. But one scout went on the record, anonymously, in a national sports magazine, calling Thomas "lackadaisical" and saying that he had "financial problems," namely unpaid bills.[26]

Red Hickey, who had scouted him and told Landry that Thomas would displace Hill in the backfield, had a final discussion with the coach days before the draft. He again advised Landry to take Thomas—"if you think you can handle him." Landry, who was licking his chops, ignored the negatives. "I think I'll try to handle him," he decided.[27] As if scripted, as team after team chose players and left Thomas on the board, Landry, Schramm, and Brandt knew they had lucked out. Landry, thrilled to get him, had no idea what he was in for. That applied to a very puzzled Calvin Hill too. When he learned his team had drafted Thomas in the first round, Hill was in the hospital recovering from a blister on his foot that had become so infected it required his foot be placed in a cast. Landry had recently assured Hill he was going to be the fulcrum of the entire offense in 1970. Now, he had to wonder if Landry had told Duane Thomas the exact same thing.

OTHER ADDITIONS would cause fewer ripples but become just as vital. The Cowboys' third-round pick was Clemson's quarterback-turned-receiver Charlie Waters, whom Landry took to because Waters was so eager to play he said he'd even give it a go at defensive back. Though Landry almost cut him, the defensive backfield was in a state of flux. Landry couldn't even promise longtime starters Mel Renfro, Cornell Green, and Mike Gaechter that they wouldn't be backups when the season began, and to prove his point he leaped at the chance to land Herb Adderley when the five-time Packer All-

Pro and future Hall of Famer suddenly became available just weeks before opening day. At thirty, he still had plenty in the tank.

Waters and Adderley were just two of a horde of new defensive backs to enter the fray that season. Mark Washington, drafted in the thirteenth round out of Morgan State, also caught Landry's eye, as did a very free-spirited free agent, Cliff Harris. A safety and kick returner from Arkansas's Ouachita Baptist University, Harris, it was said, would crash through a wall if he had to, leading to the nickname he would earn in Dallas, "Captain Crash." In camp he was mocked because he liked to wear lightweight placekicker's padding so as to keep his speed and agility on kick and punt returns. He was also so high strung that before practices, as with games later on, he would turn green and barf up his lunch. Landry was so impressed that Harris, signed for a bare minimum $5,000, was made the starting free safety. Waters became his backup, but the move would start a tandem that would link them the way Garrison and Reeves were. The two would become inseparable, spending long nights on the town bar-hopping, and uniting as business partners in several ventures after retiring. When Harris was called into the National Guard after six games, Waters would replace him for the balance of the season, with splendid results.

With Adderley installed at left corner, Green was moved to strong safety, displacing Gaechter. The latter had been on slippery turf with the coach ever since 1966 when, on Landry Mile day, he jogged a quarter-mile warmup, having been told he wouldn't have to do the full mile for another ten minutes. Instead, he was ordered to get right to it. Gaechter blew his top. "What's wrong with you all around here?" he raged at the coaches, Landry included. "I thought you were supposed to be a smart coaching staff." Then, alluding to Landry, he said, "A man has an IQ of a hundred and fifty and he can't even give me the right time."[28] He was too valuable to move, but after he ruptured his Achilles tendon in the 1969 Playoff Bowl, he became a memory. He sat out the entire 1970 season then was traded to the Redskins, but soon retired. Indeed, Landry seemed to be less patient and more irascible than ever. One day when several players and assistant coach Jim Myers were late for a meeting because a truck had overturned on the Central Expressway, jamming up traffic, they were fined $150 each. Myers tried explaining to Landry, "Hey, god dang, a grain truck overturned. You shouldn't fine these guys. Or me." The coach didn't as much as blink. "You gotta plan for that," was his answer, one that was absurdly funny to all but him.[29]

Landry made further refinements that summer. Willie Townes was out for the year with an injury, but he was less missed because of the presence of six-foot-five, 250-pound defensive end Pat Toomay, a sixth-round pick out of Vanderbilt who had also played linebacker and jumped center on the Vandy basketball team. Tall, quick, and smart, he was a valuable backup on the Doomsday line, perfectly handling the intricacies of the Flex. But Toomay would not be a long-term investment. Though he was a superb student of the game, and the son of a career Air Force officer, he also was suggestive of Pete Gent, a free-thinking man and vocal critic of the Vietnam War. Thus, he said, "I found that there were constraints for me being around Landry. Dallas was very image conscious. When the ownership and management turned on the TV, they wanted to see a particular kind of guy saying particular things. I would push that envelope. That got to be a frustration."[30]

Another pivotal change was on the offensive line, with Rayfield Wright given the starting right tackle spot, where he had excelled the year before when Ralph Neely broke his leg. Landry would also name him co-captain, with cause since Wright was arguably the most popu-lar Cowboy, and the man excavated holes for the running plays like no one else in the game—all while never making more than $16,000, in retrospect an absolute crime and a prime exemplar of the Landry-Schramm philosophy when it came to most players' salaries: you took what you were given and blessed the Lord for being a Cowboy.

THE 1970 season began as if the 1969 one had never ended. Once again Craig Morton, now the highest-paid Cowboy, was a casualty, slowly recovering from off-season shoulder surgery. For an ultra-ambitious Roger Staubach, this created an avenue of opportunity. He had lobbied Landry during the off-season and vowed not to see the world from the bench again, even as Landry constantly reminded him that quarterbacks needed three years' experience before they could be trusted. After one practice, Staubach snapped. "How can you judge every individual by the same yardstick?" he pressed him, anger rising. "If you do that, I don't have a chance. . . . You've got to judge every individual separately!" As Bob Lilly recalled, "Staubach went nuts [and] I think Coach Landry was a little shocked by his reaction."[31]

Still, Landry was resigned to suck up back talk from Staubach the way he hadn't with Gaechter, knowing what Staubach's potential was. Staubach, however, never did quite believe the coach was on his side enough, and never adapted to Landry's henpecking of his players when they made a big play, and even more so when a big play was made in spite of a deviation from the playbook. Even many years later, after Landry died, Mel Renfro met up with Staubach and Morton at a banquet. "They were talking about Landry, and said some of the same things I felt about Tom. Roger mentioned when he threw a pass a certain way and it wasn't the way Tom wanted it thrown even though it went for a touchdown. Tom gave him hell for it, and Roger never got over it. That surprised me, that it ran that deep. I remember the first time he told me that, it was in 1969. I laughed and said, 'Roger, now you know what it feels like to be a Cowboy.'"[32]

Staubach was so set on winning the quarterback job that Meredith, who'd had to fend off Morton in his day, offered some advice to his old backup: watch your back. What's more, Staubach seemed to have made allies in the right places. That summer, Tex Maule dissected the team with an acerbic pen in a *Sports Illustrated* piece. He argued that Staubach was the man for the job, given that Morton was, he wrote, "brilliant" at times but was "suspected of being frivolous" and "taking the game lightly," and that he'd been "scared to death" for the Browns' game. Staubach was praised as "a fiery leader" and a "more emotional leader than Morton, if not quite as accurate as Morton," and with him, "the Dallas El Foldos might even get the winning habit."[33]

The fans loved Morton, for sure: they voted him to receive the Favorite Cowboy award the previous year, the prize for which was a free vacation in Acapulco. For the players it was a tough choice. Most were tight with Morton, but Staubach was seen as preferable for his versatility. Morton had increasingly become one-dimensional as a deep-pass threat and would be sacked if receivers weren't open, while Staubach's happy feet would keep the play alive. Moreover, Staubach did not reflexively mouth Landry-style platitudes about faith and family in the locker room. And even though he did live by those standards, the Cowboys constantly tried to corrupt him. In Thousands Oaks, for example, according to Bob St. John, they would sneak willingly amorous young women into his dorm room, then listen at the door. Usually Staubach would engage them in conversation and pull out pictures of his wife and kids. When he was retired and addressed a Cowboys reunion, he told his old confreres, probably sarcastically, "Well, guys, the things I'll miss the most are the booze and broads."[34]

Staubach earned his stripes among the players, not for any pass, but rather the time in 1976 when, kept waiting for a meeting with Schramm at the team offices, he shinnied onto the ledge that wrapped around the building, eleven floors up, and crawled to a spot outside Schramm's window. Tex almost had a coronary. "I guess I got his attention," Staubach would mirthfully recall.[35] Staubach also surprised the black players, who had expected a stereotypical Christian conservative but found a man eager to befriend them, one who would engage them in discussions about the heavy issues of the day. Even if he would rarely come to their way of seeing things, he would understand their feelings. Morton would shy away from such matters: He was flaky but no knee-jerk liberal. During the summer of 1969, when the players again went on strike, Morton was one of the dozens to cross the picket line. After three days the strike collapsed and the players returned to work, with so little for their trouble that Schramm was seen gloating.[36] Morton's betrayal of the union made it reasonable to assume that he was committed more to getting in good with Landry than to the cause of player freedom. If so, it had uneven returns.

Landry did more than shake up the team that summer. He shocked people when, late in camp, he decided to bench Bob Hayes for Dennis Homan, a scrub receiver with few of Hayes's abilities who had caught sixteen passes in two seasons with the team. Landry explained to a baffled press that Hayes hadn't been working hard enough and was in less than peak shape. Even if that were true, the inglorious demotion of Dallas's first African American All-Pro superstar in favor of a white man from Alabama was immediately construed by some black players as the sort of opprobrium that only a black Cowboys star could have received. Mortally offended, and more so when the papers ran headlines such as "BULLET BENCHED FOR SHOOTING BLANKS," Hayes held his tongue at the time, but in his 1990 autobiography he let the recriminations fly. Landry, he wrote, "resented that I was outspoken, especially about black-white relationships on the Cowboys, because he saw it as a challenge to his authority."[37]

Accordingly, Hayes saw devilish motives to typical Landry conduct. For example, there were times when "he would treat me great, put his arm around me at practice, walk with me, ask how I felt, and tell me his whole game plan depended on me. But at the start of every season, he would go to the press and complain about my blocking, my concentration, my weight, what have you. I guess he did that to motivate me, but I would have felt a lot better if he had spoken to me in private."[38] He could still hear Landry's sparrow-like trill slicing through the air at practices, ordering him to "run that route until you get it right," even when he did get it right. These were familiar complaints about Landry, and some other players might have been envious that Hayes had actually felt the coach's arm around him. But within the hues of Hayes's world, "Tom needed to make an example of someone [and] I was that someone."[39] And more and more, Craig Morton became an enemy.

Hayes began to think there was more to it when Morton aimed a preponderance of his passes to Lance Rentzel. "I won't say that Craig was an out-and-out racist," he said, "but a lot of players . . . were angry because Craig wouldn't throw the ball to me and he was always looking for Lance Rentzel. And then Craig went to the coaches and told them he didn't have confidence in me and got me benched." To those around the team then, this would have been hard to swallow—by no one more so than Morton himself, whose own tenuous job security was hardly conducive to any sort of veto power on who should or should not play. Hayes became convinced of the conspiracy, however, when Staubach came out of a quarterbacks' meeting with Landry and told him, "Bob, I didn't do it. I didn't do it." As a result, Hayes would never trust Morton, whom he branded "lazy" and "a playboy with some personal problems," noting that Morton had "once got arrested for urinating on a street in Dallas."

Hayes admitted that if Morton threw more to Rentzel, one good reason why was that Hayes was almost always double-teamed. But all this meant to Hayes was that Morton lacked the "mental toughness" to risk taking a big hit while waiting for Hayes to outrun the coverage. Hayes, studiously avoiding swabbing Landry in the grease of outright racism, chose his words very carefully, leaving his harshest imprecations more generic, such as that Landry "was so used to my speed that he took it for granted."[40] But the benching contretemps nonetheless was a microcosm of a general racial curdling within the Cowboys, one that would influence the course of some very important careers. If Landry could feel that happening, he didn't attempt any effort to defuse a clearly ominous situation.

Perhaps he was simply too overwhelmed by how to field a competitive team. For all the evaluations in the off-season, the benching of Hayes was one indicator that Landry was willing to shake things up to find some alchemy that would work. As it happened, Landry's lineup that year began with neither Hayes nor Morton, meaning Landry would have to hand Staubach the ball in the opener in Philadelphia. The result was a conservative, ground-and-pound onslaught that amassed 198 yards on forty carries, 117 yards by Hill, 30 by Garrison, in a 17–7 win. Staubach threw just fifteen times, completing eleven passes for 115 yards, while the defense harassed quarterback Norm Snead all day, intercepting him three times and sacking him twice.

This set the pattern for the season, over which that devastating running attack would lead the league with 2,300 yards. For most of it, Cal Hill needn't have worried about his job. With Duane Thomas starting the campaign on the bench, Hill continued running wild, thriving in a system that, unlike Lombardi's plowing sweeps, sent runners wide and had them cut back, finding creases in the defense's pursuit patterns. "Landry was a running back's dream," Hill once explained. "He always geared the running game to a particular back's talents. He'd never attack the heart of a defense; he wanted to get you one-on-one with somebody. Shifts, rolls, influences, everything to help you, and always with a very logical reason behind it."

Other coaches, like George Allen, he said, would go right for the heart of the defense, "afraid of making a mistake." Landry, always seeking the big play, rolled the dice. If a play failed spectacularly, it didn't mean he guessed wrong, only that the next one might be the one that broke.[41]

Conversely, the running fixation dropped the team's passing yardage to sixteenth in the league, and the overall offense to tenth. Morton again would find his way to a swift recovery and be back under center in the third game, a loss in St. Louis, but his arm had lost demonstrable strength, another reason why Landry amped up his ground attack. Morton soon began to lose confidence. He tried changing his throwing motion. He went to a hypnotist and tried self-hypnosis. Hayes later enjoyed telling of the time when Morton borrowed his Firebird and left a tape in the tape deck. When Hayes played it, he heard the voice of Morton repeating over and over, "I will not throw an interception! I will not throw an interception!"[42] Whatever the subterranean baggage the Cowboys were carrying, if Landry actually believed he could benefit from sitting Hayes, he now had to deal with the fact that *Rentzel* was drawing double coverage, effectively eliminating any deep threat. Homan, who had average speed, was catching only a handful of passes.

By the sixth game, the Cowboys were 3–2, facing a date with the world champions in Kansas City. Here is where Landry decided he had held out Hayes long enough. He also had to give Thomas more playing time when Hill's back began to bother him, only two weeks after he had rushed twenty-nine times for 117 yards against Atlanta. Thomas would ravage the Chiefs' defense, streaking for 134 yards on twenty carries and running in two touchdowns. He had a 47-yard burst in the third quarter that left jaws agape. Indeed, while in full gallop, he swiveled, turned completely around to shake the last defender, and cruised in to the end zone, putting the Cowboys up 20–10. Hayes then broke it open with an electrifying 89-yard touchdown pass from Morton, who at least on that play looked for him right from the snap. The impressive 27–16 win was followed by a close win over the Eagles the next week and a close loss against the Giants. The Cowboys' record was now 5–3. And then everything fell apart, for the whole country to see in prime time.

✦ ✦ ✦ ✦

THE NADIR of the 1970 season, and perhaps the new decade, came in the rematch with the St. Louis Cardinals in the Cotton Bowl on November 16. It was no ordinary midseason football game. For one thing, the Cardinals had been the surprise of the league. Coming off a 4–9–1 season the year before, they arrived in Dallas with a 6–2 record, one game ahead of the Cowboys, and riding a strong ground attack of its own behind the sudden emergence of fullback MacArthur Lane, who would run for 977 yards and a league-high eleven touchdowns that season. For another, the game was the first to begin under the lights, on a Monday night, a new vibe that Dallas would need to get used to, as would every other place where the sport was played and observed.

This brave new world of football was the most obvious manifestation of something new and different about the appeal of the game, something Don Meredith had an integral part in. The brand of sporting and cultural expansion known as *Monday Night Football* was an idea that Pete Rozelle had sold to Roone Arledge, the canny president of ABC Sports, who hoped it might lift the perennially third-place network to a higher plane. Although Meredith had held off working on television for a year, the move made sense. His presence beside the prickly Howard Cosell formed the oddest of all TV couples, the homiletic Texas hick and the preposterously prolix New York Jew, bouncing one-liners off each other in a running gag of one-upsmanship that would all but overshadow what transpired on the field.

For "Danderoo," as Cosell dubbed Meredith, the rewards would be great but so would the toll of sudden stardom. When Frank Gifford joined them a year later, he would feel as if he were in a combat zone sitting between two men with monstrous egos and clinical insecurities, though Meredith could savor the bouquets thrown his way as the aw-shucks cowboy by deflating with surgical pinpricks the man the world loved to hate. Soon reports began to surface of Monday night barroom promotions at which people fired gunshots at television sets when Cosell came on, and while this seemed fun in a postmodern violent America, the credible death threats that also streamed in were anything but. No matter the nature and consequences, good and evil, of this new cultural staple, one could argue that the new paradigm in sports entertainment took hold on that Monday night in Dallas.

The Cowboys-Cardinals game was remarkable football theater in which Meredith was the hook. The Cowboys cooperated with this script by playing perhaps their worst game ever in the Cotton Bowl, which turned morgue-like as the Cardinals took a punt back for a touchdown in the first quarter and then ran wild, gaining 242 yards as they kept pushing the game out of reach. Morton completed only eight of twenty-six passes and threw three interceptions, and when Staubach relieved him in the fourth quarter, with the Cowboys down 31-0, he went two for eight and tossed another interception. The Cowboys turned the ball over six times; the quarterbacks were sacked four times. As the night went on, it just got colder and uglier. In the second half, a rumbling in the crowd began to grow louder until it was deafening: "We want Meredith! We want Meredith!"

Dandy Don became uncomfortable as his old team went from bad to worse, and he was clearly embarrassed by the chanting and by not knowing what to say, given his mixed emotions about retiring. As the chanting built, the director of the show made it the focal point of the telecast, cutting from crowd shots to the red-faced Meredith, and Cosell kept prodding him to make an untoward comment about Landry, in vain. The harshest thing Meredith said was, "There's no leadership out there." He replied to the chants by saying, in jest, "I'm not going down there, not on a night like this," then his tone became progressively sadder. As if it were a car wreck on the field and not a game, he confessed that he had some great stories to tell, "but I can't tell funny stories when something like this is going on." If Meredith was despondent, ABC was giddy; the next day the ratings showed that rather than lose any of the audience during the 38–0 blowout, the numbers *increased*. This was the new reality of pro football and television.

Meredith left the Cotton Bowl heartsick. And Cosell for years would continually prod him to backbite Landry during the frequent telecasts of the Cowboys' games on *Monday Night Football*. But as Dandy Don became more polished, if not nearly as carefree as his performances would suggest, he deflected the subject of Landry with breezy, innocuous one-liners, an example being to say that in a personality contest between Landry and Bud Grant, "neither would win." Once, when Cosell opined on the air that Meredith despised Landry, Dandy Don refused to take the bait, saying later, "I'd rather speak for myself on something that personal."[43] Of course, he never did. For Meredith as for most everyone else who had worn the star on his helmet, loyalty to Tom Landry—even if it seemed like a one-way street—carried a lifetime membership.

LANDRY, FOR whom such matters were inconsequential, came away from the ignoble defeat almost numb. Linebacker Steve Kiner recalled another crying scene—sort of. "There were tears running down his cheeks," he said, but "he didn't sound like he was crying. He didn't whimper . . . he said that he was real disappointed in the team and he was sorry he hadn't done a better coaching job, that he had let us down, and basically he said it didn't look like we were going to make it to the playoffs this year, that we had pissed away our opportunity."[44] Landry's memory of that locker room scene was similar. He was, he said, both condemning and contrite. "I've never been through anything like this," he recalled telling his men. "The game was embarrassing to us all. You guys didn't really want to win. Maybe it was my fault, I don't know, but it was the worst perfor-mance of a Cowboys' team I've ever seen."[45] Staubach, looking back, took only one thing away from Landry's remarks—that he "pretty much said he didn't think we could win."[46]

After Landry gave his mixed message, many of the Cowboys seemed to believe he had given up on them, and on himself. Bob Lilly was moved to get up and say, essentially, that Landry could go fuck himself. "He doesn't win games, we do!" he growled.[47] In the papers the next day there was a funereal tone. "DEATH RATTLE FOR COWBOYS?" was the headline in the *Morning News*. Moreover, Fate seemed Landry's enemy. Hill, having racked up big numbers for the season, broke a leg in the Cardinals game and suddenly was gone. Cliff Harris got his call-up from the National Guard, and he too was gone. Still, even if hanging by a thread, they were 5–4 and had time to recover. Landry at this point decided to ease up on his usual regimentation. At the Tuesday practice that week, he allowed the players to scrimmage on their own. "Just go out today and play some touch football," he told them. This was his way of letting them "loosen up," he said.[48]

"He didn't ride us so hard," says Mel Renfro. "We didn't know if he'd thrown the towel in on the season or was just letting us clear our heads of all the pressure, and for some of us that meant years and years of pressure. Basically, what he did was to let us realize for ourselves that it was all on the line. He worked on us, our pride. It was a basic instinct. He would never have said that we should hate our opponents, but that's what he had to do. It was brilliant. We were having fun and getting a focus."

Pettis Norman felt that, beginning that week, "Tom did his best coaching. The season was on the line and the team looked like it was falling apart. Tom just wasn't going to let us slip. He wanted us to change our thoughts from strategy to feeling like we were all in this thing together, to develop an emotional attachment to each other, and with Tom. We'd gotten away from that. We were putting ourselves under way too much pressure to excel, physically. But Tom knew football is a mental game, a human game. You gotta want to kick the shit out of people."[49]

For the next game, in DC against the Redskins, the Cowboys came in with a threadbare playbook. Landry let Morton call his own plays. Trailing 7–3 after a sputtering start, they detonated in the second quarter. Thomas ran in for one score, and Morton threw touchdown passes to Rentzel and Garrison. Leading 24–7 at the half, the team kept pouring it on. Thomas, who rumbled for 104 yards, put two more touchdowns on the board in the second half, one on a 35-yard burst. Morton completed twelve of fifteen passes. The defense sacked Sonny Jurgensen six times. Mark Washington ran a kickoff return for 100 yards. The 45–21 blowout made a statement, in boldface type. "That was really when the Cowboy mystique took hold," Renfro remembers. "We'd found that missing element, that no more Mr. Nice Guy thing. We may have had our arguments with each other, but when we played you, you'd have to drive a stake through our hearts to kill us. We were gonna make you pay for every mistake. And that was when teams began to fear us—and hate us, which we loved."

Having found their groove, the Cowboys indeed had a new bounce and balance, accommodating the physical and the intellectual as they ran the table on the rest of the season, winning the last five games to close out 10–4. Helpfully, the Cardinals fell back to earth, losing four of their last five games and handing the division title to the team they had run out of the Cotton Bowl. By then, Landry had gradually reinstalled his recondite playbook and strategies—something that the thorny Cowboys, who had pledged to win not for him but for themselves, believed might ruin the groove. Emphatically, it didn't. Indeed, Landry's shifts and formations now were the coups de grace for a team that could physically dominate. The last two games of the regular season were perfect exemplars. First they went to a glacial Municipal Stadium and won an epic defensive struggle against the Browns, 6–2, on two field goals, holding Leroy Kelly to 18 yards on seven carries. They then came home and buried the poor Houston Oilers 52–10 under an avalanche of 549 yards, 187 of them by Bob Hayes alone. Somehow, the same man Morton had once refused to throw to hauled in four consecutive touchdown passes from the man Hayes believed was an "out-and-out racist." That was how far the Cowboys had come.

FOR MOST of the season, Lance Rentzel had been sensational, his habitual tardiness to practice and profusion of fines abating neither Landry's reliance on him every Sunday nor the growing unease about Rentzel's dark side. Then, on November 19, coincidentally just days after the crushing loss to the Cardinals, he left practice and stopped his car in front of a house where a ten-year-old girl was playing. Calling the girl over as if to ask a question, he rolled down the window and exposed himself, in a virtual replay of the incident in Minnesota. He quickly sped off, but the girl told her father, who called the police. The girl remembered the license plate, leading cops to Rentzel's apartment, where he was arrested and subsequently released on bail. As had the Vikings, Schramm and Landry tried to keep the incident quiet, and with the support of his teammates Rentzel played in the Redskins game. The coverup fell apart when a paper in Oklahoma City, not Dallas, broke the news the day before the next game, the Thanksgiving contest in the Cotton Bowl against the Packers.

That night, Rentzel addressed the team at the hotel, sobbing that he would voluntarily take a leave of absence following the game the next day until the case was adjudicated. The players wanted him to stay on. With the scandal out in the open, however, Landry and Schramm weren't as supportive. In fact, Pete Gent would claim that the team had initially, and quietly, sought to pull some strings to get Rentzel off the hook, but because the girl was "the daughter of a Highland Park lawyer who they couldn't buy off . . . Lance was fucked." Finally, on November 30, Rentzel was charged with indecent exposure.[50] The scab was torn off, and Landry and Schramm went into damage control mode as the Dallas papers belatedly blared headlines about the story for days, treating it, as Gent put it, with the gravity of "a presidential assassination."[51] Around town, the reaction was tumultuous, with crude jokes about Rentzel and bumper stickers cropping up reading, "KEEP IT IN YOUR PANTS, LANCE."[52]

Knowing it would be a major distraction to keep him around in the interim, Landry banished Rentzel, refraining from even mentioning his name. Soon, neither did the press nor the broadcasters. Watching the ensuing Cowboys games on TV, Rentzel could hardly believe that "it was as if I had never existed, that I'd never been part of the Dallas Cowboys."[53] Landry went further, as if wanting to purge the whole squalid business from the Cowboys' history as best he could. In his memoirs, as he would other messy interludes over the years, he wrote not a word about Rentzel's problem or the circumstances of his exile. In such matters that reflected on what the public assumed to be his moral fiber and code of good conduct, cribbing from the Joe Stalin playbook was a small price to pay for ablution.

Chapter 18

"A VEHICLE FOR CORPORATE EGO"

HEADING INTO THE FIRST playoff derby of the new decade, and a new NFL calibration, the league and its heavily marketable team in Dallas—whose formula for success was psychodrama and melodrama, which translated into rising ticket sales and TV ratings—were on a roll. The Cowboys were many things to many people, outlaws and straight-arrows alike. While the franchise reflected the great wealth of its home base, its mystique was carved by not only arrogance but also heartbreak, which gave a human sheen to everyone in the uniform, as well as to the glacial coach on the sideline. Individualists lived in a sometimes tense symbiosis with a coach who preached team above ego. For any number of reasons, the team had sizzle, the cutting edge of a league on a hard path into the cultural and commercial stratosphere.

Tom Landry couldn't help but feel blessed by the material he had that had jelled into a juggernaut during the 1970 season. By its end, Craig Morton, for all his self-doubt, led the league in number of yards per pass completion and passing touchdown percentage. Duane Thomas in two-thirds of a season ran for 803 yards with a league-high 5.3 yards a carry. Hayes led the league with a 26.1-yard average catch. The ground game was so effective that it made for some deceptive stats. The Cowboys were ranked tenth in the league in offense but only because they led the league in the number of carries (522) and rushing yardage (2,300)—they never needed to pass much. The Doomsday boys did the rest, leading the league in least number of yards allowed and surrendering but one touchdown in the last four games. And if any more fuel was needed to light the fire of the new "us-versus-the-world" Cowboys mind set, it was delivered when only two of them—Mel Renfro and Chuck Howley—were deemed worthy for a Pro Bowl invitation.

The playoffs matched the Cowboys first against the Detroit Lions, the "wild card" entry, in the Cotton Bowl. On a cold, wet, thirty-five degree day, neither team could move the ball much. Morton would complete a ghastly four of eighteen passes for 48 yards; the Lions quarterback, Greg Landry, five of twelve for 48 yards. But Thomas, given the ball thirty times, broke out for 135 yards, and Garrison ran for 75. An early Clark field goal held up, and a late safety, with Andrie and Pugh swarming on Landry in the end zone, made the final score 5–0. Still the Cowboys again had to sweat it out after Greg Landry was pulled and his backup, Bill Munson, moved his team to the Dallas 29-yard line with under a minute left. Munson then tried to throw a pass to Washington, but Renfro was on him like a leotard and made the game-saving pick.

This, the NFL's first-ever playoff game not to feature a touchdown, put the Cowboys in the maiden NFC Championship Game on January 3, 1971, a ticket to the Super Bowl being theirs if they could get past—mercifully—not the Browns but the San Francisco 49ers, coached by Landry protégé Dick Nolan. Landry had to be relieved he wouldn't need to prepare yet again for another conservative, plowshare offense like the Packers' and Browns', though he assessed his players in superlatives that week, saying, "This is the best team we've had in Dallas. The defense is better than it's ever been . . . the cornerbacks are better." He pointedly omitted the quarterbacking, but only because of "Craig Morton's injuries."[1] Sizing up the 49ers in the films, he would go up against a team almost completely dependent on the pass, something that his defenses normally feasted on by messing up the timing of the quarterback-receiver designs. Even so, the 49ers' All-Pro combo of John Brodie and Gene Washington had gained more yards by air than any other team, with Brodie producing twenty-four.

The smart money had the 49ers a 3-point favorite, and their motivation was raised by the fact that this would be the last game they played at ancient Kezar Stadium before moving to Candlestick Park the next year. "'49ER FEVER' SWEEPS FRISCO INTO FRENZY," reported the *Dallas Morning News* the day before the tilt, and indeed the Cowboys would need to survive the emotional surge across the ball and in the stands. The first half was a rough go, but the defense got them through it, keeping the game to a 3–3 tie. At that point, Landry would say, "We went into the locker room feeling kinda down. . . . Everyone came in mumbling." Morton had been dreadful again—he would complete seven of twenty-two passes for 101 yards, but he and the team were saved, as they had been the week before, by Thomas, who piled up 143 yards on twenty-seven carries. Eventually the Cowboys began to wear down the 49ers on the both sides of the ball. Brodie, his running game mired, threw forty times, completing only nineteen. Early in the third quarter, on his own 14, Brodie faded back to pass. He rolled out and, harassed by defensive end Larry Cole, tried to throw the ball into the ground. Astonishingly, Lee Roy Jordan was able to dive for it and make the interception. He got up and scrambled to the 13. From there, Thomas broke loose for a touchdown and the lead.

After the 49ers got the ball back, Brodie threw a long pass toward Washington, but Renfro made another interception. Several plays later, Morton pitched a 5-yard scoring pass to Garrison, a rusty nail of a man who had insisted on playing despite back spasms, cracked ribs, and a swollen ankle. Suddenly down by two touchdowns, Brodie spent the last quarter feverishly looking for a big pass, but he could only hit one, too late, for a 26-yard touchdown that made the final score 17–10. For once everything had gone right, not wrong, and Landry could walk off the field tall and proud, and no doubt relieved that he wouldn't have to shake Nolan's hand in defeat. He could even be a bit haughty. "We had to run the ball and to contain Brodie," he said. "I believe we did both." Admitting that "I'm kinda tired now. I was just emotionally drained in the last quarter," he asked someone to get him a cold drink. Then, with a wan but toothy smile, he appropriated a moment that had been a decade in coming.

"You don't know how good this feels," he said. "They needed it, they worked for it, and they got it." He needed it more. And now he could exhale, at least until the kickoff of his first Super Bowl appearance.[2]

ALMOST IN disbelief, the *Morning News* ran the headline "COW-BOYS DO IT . . . IN THE BIG ONE" the next day, with Bob St. John vouching for a team that had found the holy grail. The previous Cowboys contenders, he wrote, "relied very much on trickery. . . . This one does not. It is physical."[3] That had been the ticket to Miami, for the season's climactic game, which as the first-ever Super Bowl of the new era would suffer the rather embarrassing irony of pitting the Cowboys against a team that was actually far older, the Colts. They had been relocated into the AFC for the sake of balance, and had convincingly beaten the Raiders in the AFC title game. But few players would pretend to be playing for the pride of the old AFL; rather they would play for their own.

Both rosters were rife with top-tier talent at every position—except, perhaps, the most important one. Not only was Morton viewed with skepticism around the media meridians, but John Unitas, back at the helm at age thirty-seven, had a mediocre season himself, his arm withered and his knees gimpy. However in this popularity contest, Morton was cooked. For example, Morton Sharnik in his Super Bowl preview in *Sports Illustrated* called the Cowboys "a team without a quarterback" and boiled the game down to the battle line between "two dissimilar players . . . the cool, quiet [Morton] and Mike Curtis, Baltimore's violent, voluble linebacker."[4]

The game, on January 17, would be an even money wager, the bettors hedging their bets on both teams. The Colts, who would be reminded of their sorry, epic defeat to the Jets two years before simply by being on the very same Orange Bowl turf, had compiled a 11–2–1 record during the season, but several key players from that earlier team were gone—as was Don Shula, who had borne the brunt of the shame and left the still-contending team after the 1969 season to coach the expansion Miami Dolphins. The man who replaced him, Shula's offensive coordinator Don McCafferty, mirrored the team, as an unexciting football chess-master not unlike Tom Landry. The craggy-faced former Paul Brown protégé was no slouch; no other first-year coach has ever gotten as far as McCafferty did in 1970. Landry surely respected McCafferty and his team, but the Cowboys came in strutting. Clint Murchison Jr., anticipating a party to end all parties after the game, sent a jaunty telegram to Landry when he arrived in Miami: "I have taught you all I can. From now on, you're on your own."[5]

The Colts were more dangerous than the Cowboys' VIPs believed. Unitas had reliable targets in Eddie Hinton and Roy Jefferson, as well as the perennial All-Pro and future Hall of Famer, right end John Mackey. The Colts' backbone was their defense, not just the beastly Curtis but twenty-three-year-old man-child defensive tackle Bubba Smith and veteran strong safety Jerry Logan. Even though the Cowboys had their own graybeards, the game loomed as a generational battle, something the Colts probably hoped they had seen enough of already.

Both teams endured the mandated two-week wait for the game, the league insisting that the climax of all the tribal excess around the event needed such a prelude and refusing to foresee the downside that teams might succumb to ennui and come out rusty. With this in mind, Landry tried to keep his players aroused, even in the literal sense. Reaching back to the injunctions of Bob Martin in high school, after the team arrived in South Florida, Landry had them stay in a different hotel than the team's headquarters at the Galt Ocean Mile Hotel in Fort Lauderdale, and prohibited any contact with their wives or girlfriends, even phone calls, until after the game. "Tom wanted us to be as angry as we could be," says Lee Roy Jordan, with a wry grin. "He wanted us isolated, angry, horny and ornery, ready to come out snorting like killer pigs."[6]

The next day, in the bright, warm late afternoon sunshine, the players had to wait out the insufferable pregame pomp. But the Cowboys, in their metallic blue road jerseys—the "bad luck" ones—seemed more at ease than the Colts. The game's first five minutes were, as Tex Maule wrote, "spectacularly dull,"[7] the first four series ending in punts. On the last one, after the Cowboys were unable to cash in on a diving, juggling interception by the ageless Chuck Howley, the Colts fumbled and Cliff Harris recovered the ball on Baltimore's 9-yard line, but the Cowboys had to settle for a field goal. After another punt, Morton found Hayes streaking downfield and hit him perfectly between Logan and Charlie Stukes for a 47-yard gain, but again they could only notch a field goal.

The two blown chances cost the Cowboys. Early in the second quarter came the play that is still talked about as Fate's unkindest cut to Landry. Unitas flung a third-down pass down the middle for Hinton, who leaped but could only tip the ball, slightly slowing its speed as it came right at Renfro, who also instinctively leaped and stuck a hand out. The ball appeared to graze his fingertips and continued on its path into the hands of an extremely surprised Mackey, who was loitering in the deep zone, and he slid past Charlie Waters and rambled for a 75-yard touchdown, with Waters jumping up and down protesting that the catch was illegal. Renfro too protested to an official, who told him, "Shut up."

Unlike today, a pass back then could not be deflected from one receiver to another unless it was touched by a defender. The replays and game films showed that Renfro did touch the ball. But the Hall of Famer maintained after the game that "somebody touched the ball. I don't think I did." Renfro himself couldn't say for sure though, citing the self-inflicted injury in college that took some of the feeling from his right hand. He still cannot say.

Renfro had stumbled into the most controversial play in Super Bowl history, elegized by John Facenda in the NFL Films highlight reel as proof that "the clouds of chance will overshadow the plans of men."[8] Landry didn't put up much of a stink, knowing that if he did, his team wouldn't be able to put it past them. As it happened, for all the hubbub, the play didn't have a happy ending even for the Colts, because their rookie kicker Jim O'Brien, who would say later he had been "awfully nervous," clanked the point-after, leaving them with a 6–6 tie. Landry's biggest problem was that Morton seemed no less edgy himself. Clad in a natty blue plaid suit and gray fedora, the coach was unusually animated as he constantly conferred with the fluttery quarterback. And after Howley and Jordan hit Unitas, causing a fumble, Morton took the team smartly down the field again, hitting Thomas with a 5-yard touchdown pass for a 13–6 lead. Andrie then blasted Unitas, breaking his rib and putting him out of the game. Earl Morrall came in, reversing the dynamic of Super Bowl III, and brought the Colts to the Dallas 2. But Howley, who was a human torpedo all day, broke up Morrall's goal-line pass on the last play of the half.

The Cowboys kept getting the breaks when the Colts' Jim Duncan fumbled the second-half kickoff, and the Cowboys had a first and goal at the 2. Now, though, the pendulum began to swing. Thomas took the hand-off and dove for the goal line, where Curtis stripped the ball from him and Duncan fell on it. Or did he? Dave Manders may well have recovered the ball, but the referee was convinced when the Colts' Gargoyle-faced defensive tackle Billy Ray Smith got in his face and screamed, "Our ball!" Weeks later, Bubba Smith would confide to a newspaperman that Manders indeed had gotten to it first.[9] Still, Dallas led 13–6 entering the fourth quarter, and seemed charmed when Howley again intercepted Morrall in the end zone, and on the next series, Cornell Green pried the ball from Hinton after a long pass and the Cowboys fell on it in the end zone for a touchback—the Colts' *seventh* turnover.

Morton, needing one good drive to salt the win away, instead blew up. He threw a short pass for Garrison, but the ball was tipped, intercepted, and carried to the 3-yard line, from where the Colts ran in the tying touchdown. Then, taking the ball on the Colts' 48 with just under two minutes left, a game-winning field goal within perhaps 15 yards, Morton was sacked back on Dallas's 27. Now, on third and 34, Landry might have been wise to kill the clock and send the game into sudden death, since with the clock running he had no time to send a play in with a shuttle back. Morton, for the only time all day, had to call his own play. He rolled to the right, pursued by two Colts, and almost blindly threw a pass 10 yards downfield for Reeves, who leaped for the high, wobbly ball only for it to go right through his hands—never did a game rest on so many skittish fingertips—and be picked off by Curtis, who ran it to the 28.

This shocking turn of events left the Cowboys dazed as the Colts ran the ball to the 25, then sent in O'Brien, a man called "Lassie" for his long, shaggy hair. Nerves and all, on the last play Lassie lifted his leg and nailed a 32-yard field goal with 5 seconds left. It all happened so suddenly. Rather than a great cheer from Colts fans in the

Orange Bowl, there was tepid murmuring as the ensuing kickoff and failed return ended the game. The Colts began bounding around in celebration. Bob Lilly disgustedly flung his helmet the length of the field, smashing it like a grapefruit. Landry, whose abstinence dictum couldn't prevent another failure, shook hands with McCafferty—the rookie coach—and trod off, again a loser, again watching his men make the last mistake.

There had been so many mistakes that Maule, who had christened the greatest game ever played in 1958, led his *Sports Illustrated* review by opining, "Perhaps the game should be called the Blunder Bowl from now on."[10] Indeed it would be. The Colts were so guilty about being a champion on such terms that Bubba Smith refused to wear his Super Bowl ring.[11] Chuck Howley, voted the MVP of the game in defeat—still the only time that has ever happened—accepted the trophy with palpable embarrassment. In Dallas, the dog-and-pony show wasn't the slightest bit amusing. "'SUPER' DAY DRIBBLES AWAY" and "DOOMSDAY AFTER ALL," read the *Morning News* headlines, with Bob St. John venturing that the Cowboys "have come a step closer" to a ring but "that step constitutes more broken hearts and bitterness than, perhaps, the club has ever experienced."[12] Clearly, the players were furious at Morton for snatching defeat from victory, and more so when on the bus ride from the stadium to the hotel, Morton acted not the least bit upset by the loss. Renfro recalled being in tears and looking over and seeing Morton "goosing his girlfriend and laughing."[13] That was when Morton lost his teammates, if not his coach.

LANDRY, WHO again escaped any great umbrage after the defeat, quickly set about reframing the narrative that there was something different about this loss, something less painful than the others. Obligatorily, he said, "We beat ourselves," and "We're disappointed, but not ashamed. . . . My gosh, three tipped passes gave them all their points." He also hastened to defend Morton, who he said made the right call on the critical play because "we were going for the win,"[14] a stretch to be sure, and insisted the game wasn't as sloppy as it was hard fought. "I haven't been around many games where the players hit harder."[15] In his memoirs, he wrote, "I saw reason for hope. . . .

I thought maybe, just maybe, we'd broken through the mental barrier."[16] So too did Cowboys fans, three thousand of whom were waiting at Love Field to cheer their fallen heroes when the team returned home that night.

Landry certainly could be proud that his men hadn't quit on him. Indeed, many shared the rationale that they didn't lose; they just didn't get the title. This of course fit with the arrogant gospel according to the Cowboys, as did the ex post facto conspiracy theory that Renfro still espouses today: "the league wanted the Colts to win," that team being eternally an old NFL franchise, no matter the realignment. "Pete Rozelle didn't like that the NFL had lost two Super Bowls in a row. We were still the party-crashers. I don't know, there was something tainted in that game." Renfro's own employers were not overly sympathetic to his plight. Much like Landry never letting Jordan forget the play he didn't make in the Ice Bowl, years later Clint Murchison Jr. passed Renfro in the hall and said, "Mel, why did you lose that game for us?"

Renfro recalls, "I freaked. I guess it was supposed to be funny, but it wasn't to me. I went through hell because of that one play, with the fans, the media. Charlie Waters should have tackled Mackey when he caught it. But I always got the blame, and it bothered me for a long time. I thought Tom should have backed me up, but he didn't. It was all unfair. That play had nothing to do with the outcome of the game, but everyone thought it did."[17]

The inability of the Cowboys to put the wreckage of the Blunder Bowl behind them produced what Pat Toomay called "cognitive dissonance" among some of the players, "a collective restlessness" that was, he said, "too great to dissipate in an off-season."[18] Coincidence or not, during the months that followed, several Cowboys got into trouble. One rebellious linebacker, Steve Kiner, head-butted an usher, at a rock concert in Tennessee and was busted for disorderly conduct and resisting arrest. Oddly, while no drugs or alcohol were found on him, he was also charged with being under the influence of both. He was let off after paying a fifty-dollar fine.[19] A year later he was arrested again for narcotics possession. This time the charges were dropped.[20] Morton was charged with indecent conduct and abrasive language" by a cop who, as Bob Hayes liked to remind people, said

Morton had urinated in the street, though Morton called the charge "bullshit,"[21] he was fined fifteen dollars.[22] The last thing on some players' minds, it seemed, was the next season and how painfully *that* might end, especially since there would be even more pressure to win, for Landry and for the swells upstairs who would at last be able to revel in a swanky new habitat for the team. But even that upped the Cowboys' profile, and the ante.

FROM THE minute Duane Thomas had arrived, a devil's bargain was brewing. Thomas could run like hell, but he portended trouble, given that he thought the worst of his new bosses and was perfectly willing to act in ways that would put their patience to the test. Thomas had been groomed in an environment completely alien to that in Dallas. He loved his West Texas State coach, Joe Kerbel, a garrulous man who treated his players like buddies. To Thomas, little that he saw on his pro team satisfied his gnawing feeling that the black players were being ripped off by management and misused by Tom Landry.

Never mind that practically *every* Cowboy was being seriously underpaid, but Thomas didn't help himself financially by choosing a Dallas agent named Norman Young, who had accepted a truly chintzy contract for Thomas. It called for a $25,000 bonus but only a $20,000 salary for the first *and second* years, and just $22,000 for the third, plus performance incentives, including $50,000 more for his Rookie of the Year season.[23] It wasn't nearly enough. In the off-season Thomas found himself billed by the IRS for $10,000 in unpaid taxes, which Young was supposed to handle for him. He began getting calls from creditors about charges that Young allegedly rang up. Thomas was startled to learn that $100,000 of his money was gone. He fired Young and, with little money left and alimony and child payments overdue, borrowed some cash from a friend. Then he broached the possibility of renegotiating his contract. Informally, Gil Brandt, who had promised Thomas when he signed with the Cowboys not to worry, "we'll take care of you," told him it might be doable. But when Thomas met with Schramm, the answer was succinct: "Sorry, son."[24]

Stung, Thomas spent the off-season in LA, stewing and getting more militant about racism. When he spoke with Brandt, he told the scouting guru he was retiring from the game to take a job with Levi Strauss. Brandt said he couldn't do that, promoting Thomas to retort, "Hey, Gil, the Civil War's over."[25] Thomas told a local TV station he was retiring from the game but then subsequently hired Jim Brown as his adviser, who urged him to play the upcoming season at the same salary, then drive a hard bargain. Thomas went along, but he became obsessed in his rage for the team, including Landry, whose aloofness he detested. "Tom never once called me in and said, 'Duane, you had a great year,'" he would recall. "That was all I ever asked. Instead, what I got from him was . . . the face, the chin, the compressed lips."[26]

In fairness, this was a familiar complaint on the team, and from Thomas it was an especially ironic one, since from the beginning he himself had been uncommunicative. As Sam Blair wrote, Thomas had a "faraway look in his eyes [as if] he must be hearing a zither somewhere."[27] More than a few Cowboys players assumed his insulation was magnified by the use of drugs of some sort, the most suspect one being LSD. Lee Roy Jordan surmised that Thomas's roommate during his rookie year, Steve Kiner, "introduced him to things that would destroy your brain cells."[28] Landry hedged on the point, claiming later, "I hadn't had any exposure to the effect of drugs on a player's personality or I might have suspected Duane of using drugs," leaving it that "his mood swings and his drastic change in behavior simply baffled me."[29]

Stories were told about Thomas, such as the time he spent at practice meticulously counting blades of grass on the field, or sitting on a curb outside the hotel early on the morning of the Super Bowl, head down, looking, as Morton said, "zonked."[30] Of the drug rumors, which would persist for years, Thomas retorted, "It's a damn lie." He said he'd been on the curb because he'd just gone for an early-morning run, which hardly made sense on a game day. He tried to turn the flak back at teammates, who he said were taking "all those damn bennies" and were so drunk they were "hung over for games . . . in the fourth quarter they're breathing heavy in the huddle and I was just getting started."[31]

Whatever stimulus provoked his behavior, he now began to isolate himself, saying nothing to anyone, but not before saying all he wanted to say. At one of the most extraordinary press conferences ever, held on July 21, 1971, in Dallas, he blistered Landry as "a plastic man, just not a man at all"; Schramm as "completely dishonest, sick, and totally demented"; and Brandt as a "liar." That however was only a preface to a more troubling premise. "The problem is I'm black," he said, so quietly he could barely be heard. "If I was white it would have been totally different. They would have done me justice." The Cowboys, he added, treated their black players "like stupid animals," and he predicted, that "a revolution is coming in pro football. Players like me are tired of being on our knees all the time. I want equality."[32] Though Thomas's opinions were shared by other Cowboys, he had clearly gone over the line by labeling Landry a heartless cipher in a web of bigotry.

As Paul Zimmerman, who co-wrote Thomas's 1988 autobiography, noted, "Players had called Brandt and Schramm names before. No big deal. But in Dallas, Landry was God." As a result, he said, "The national media came down on Thomas with a vengeance."[33]

Landry took the high road. "I really have no comment regarding what he called me," he said. "I've always gotten along fine with Duane and always thought a lot of him. I know he came up the tough way and in a tough environment and doesn't seem to accept anybody helping him." It was perhaps the first time Landry had to wade into the discussion about black men and their environmental baggage, and in that vein he went on, "As far as black players being treated badly, I know what I feel and to me there is no difference . . . no difference in my eyes. If there is a difference then it's on their side, not mine."[34] His courtiers in the press weren't so kind. Sam Blair reported the next day that "some of the players here indicated they felt Duane had gone too far when he jumped on Coach Landry." Blair called Thomas "the strange one" and editorialized, "From personal observations, it is most difficult to find any validity to Thomas' statements that he was yelled at by coaches because he was black." Bob St. John, also succoring Landry, wrote,

> You can criticize Tom Landry for many things—and he has been—
> but he isn't plastic and he is ten times the man most men will ever

be. And insinuations that Landry is racially prejudiced are absurd, ill-thought out. I'm sure Duane has been treated unfairly . . . but now he has turned around and been unfair himself . . . he has over-stated his case [and] over-killed his adversaries.[35]

Others in the media would inevitably shunt Thomas into the cli-chéd refuges that white people generally assumed existed for the ben-efit of angry black athletes; soon, Thomas was suspected of being, in the mold of Muhammad Ali, a member of the Nation of Islam. This assumption took hold when he returned to Thousand Oaks eight days after his press conference, accompanied by a mysterious, baleful-looking black man wearing a dashiki who said his name was Ali Khabir. When Thomas introduced him to Landry, Khabir refused to shake his hand. "That's fine with me!" Landry responded.[36] Jab-bing Landry more, Thomas demanded that his adjutant be given a tryout, in vain, whereupon, Cal Hill once said, "there was a rumor going around camp that Duane and the Muslims were going to kid-nap Tex. Next morning, Tex had four or five guards around him. It was wild."[37] To say nothing of highly distractive on the eve of a new season in which the expectations were enormous.

Landry and Schramm, their patience worn, had no choice but to make a move that was sure to stoke new speculation about how the Cowboys dealt with problem players who happened to be black. After putting out feelers around the league, Schramm made a trade with the New England Patriots, exchanging Thomas along with scrub receiver Honor Jackson and backup lineman Halvor Hagen for third-year halfback Carl Garrett and a first-round draft pick. How-ever, getting rid of Thomas wasn't quite so easy. His life with the Patriots lasted all of five convulsive days, during which he physically threatened reporters who came near him. On his last day, he walked off the practice field after the coach, John Mazur, an old Notre Dame guy, instructed him to take a three-point stance. Thomas, ignoring him, remained in a higher, two-point stance in order to, he said, see the field better, adding with infinite irony, "That's the way we did it in Dallas."[38]

In fact, Thomas was hardly the first player to have an epiphany about Landry after being separated from him. Years later he acknowledged, "Whatever I felt about Tom Landry, he was never a 'Because I say so!' coach. Never. If you didn't feel right in something, you told him. People don't understand that about Landry. If you're in a position that's not comfortable for you, Tom will go with you and let you do it your way until you screw up. If you're in a pattern, then based on your read of the linebacker drop, you make your own adjustment. Tom would say, 'Good adjustment.' "[39]

Mazur had no intention of saying anything to Thomas. After Thomas refused to give blood and urine samples for drug tests as required for his physical exam, the Patriots notified the league office that they were canceling the deal. Landry and Schramm were aghast, but Pete Rozelle ruled that Thomas had indeed breached his contract and the Patriots were within their rights. He determined that Jackson and Hagen would stay with New England but that Thomas was still the Cowboys' property. Garrett, who had been thrilled to run behind the Dallas front line, was crushed about having to go back to the Patriots.[40] Thomas, though, did not immediately rejoin the Cowboys, who seriously debated whether they too would declare his contract null and void. He went to LA, hired a new agent, took the same drug tests he had refused, and passed. Hoping to dicker for a new deal, he and his agent then went to Schramm, but Schramm agreed to take him back only on the same terms. Thomas, his other option being to sit out the season and return as a free agent, agreed to put on the metallic silver and blue again.

So back he trudged to Dallas, not an ounce less seething and emphatically on his own, his verbal attack on Landry following him like radioactive dust. Neither did he attempt to smooth things over. His once-again teammates tried as best they could to find nice things to say about him. Pettis Norman's analysis of him is that "Duane was out there but he wasn't a bad guy, he was an angry guy, and that led him into some bad choices."[41] Yet it seemed beyond explanation that Landry, ceding more and more ground to Thomas, allowed behavior he never had tolerated from anyone. Even Dandy Don Meredith always remembered to publicly butter up Landry, and Pete Gent's aspersions percolated for years until he could write about them.

Thomas, on the other hand, did not hesitate in directly challenging Landry, who would recall, still not knowing why it got so out of hand, that Thomas "would sit in meetings, never opening his playbook, his stocking cap pulled down over his eyes as if he wasn't paying a bit of attention; then we would walk out on the field and he'd do exactly what I had been talking about as if he had memorized everything I had said. He refused to do warmup calisthenics with the team. Instead he would walk down to the far end of the field by himself and go through the most incredibly rigorous training routine."

Thomas also willfully flaunted the coat-and-tie rule on road trips and would refuse to answer roll call. The silence became eerie, and seditious. When Landry would call him into his office for a one-to-one talk, the coach did all the talking. "Each time I paused, waiting for him to respond, he'd just sit there staring at me, not saying a word until I would finally dismiss him." Landry seemed determined to bend as far as he could lest he be judged as racially insensitive. As the situation settled into an awkward tango, Thomas, who had put in little training, was placed on the inactive list for the first four games of the 1971 season, and Landry dodged the subject of disciplinary measures he might take for Thomas's insubordination. Happily, Thomas had lost none of his skills, making it easier for Landry to exchange his pride for keeping the running back firmly in his plans. Surely, he figured, the kid would grow up. "I cared about Duane," he said. "He was obviously a troubled young man. I wanted to help him just as much as I wanted to help the team."[42]

Still, if he thought of Thomas as his personal reclamation project, Landry knew all the while that he was wrong in what he had told Red Hickey; he *couldn't* handle Duane Thomas. But if bending over backward to prove to the world otherwise allowed Thomas to channel his malevolence for the team's overlords into one big game after another, so be it, at least in the short term. It was bizarre, it was ridiculous, it was unhealthy. And only on the Cowboys could it seem anything approaching normal.

WHILE THOMAS was making Landry into a villain, others were canonizing him. In the spring of 1971, a documentary called *A Man and His Men* had premiered in SMU's McFarlin Memorial Auditorium. It had been produced by a young Christian film house in Michigan, which announced plans to circulate the movie in junior high and high schools around the country. The opening was something of a big deal in Dallas, and Landry attended with a number of Cowboys players.[43] But the ongoing Thomas episode was proof that, as Paul Zimmerman wrote of the team, the Cowboys were "a curious mixture. They were predominantly a good-ol'-boy team. . . . Whites generally hung out with whites once practice was over, blacks with blacks."[44]

This once-shrouded topic began to seep into the national discussion when the pugnacious Tex Maule dropped it into a sourish précis in *Sports Illustrated* about the team he had dubbed the "Dallas el Foldos" when summer camp began. It was titled, in full, "Big Ifs in Big D: The Cowboys, Who Haven't Won a Big Game, Are Plagued by Quarterback Doubts, Complacent Vets, Angry Blacks and No Confidence." Wrote the erstwhile Cowboys courtier, "Most of the black players on the club are less than enchanted with Dallas and the attitude of its citizenry toward blacks." Maule quoted an unnamed player as saying, "Sure, they cheer us when we're on the field, but they can't see us off it. They make you feel like an animal act." Reflecting the era's evolving, harder-edged style of sports journalism, Maule ventured, "Moreover, a few of the white players have no love for the blacks and don't bother to conceal it," though he allowed that this was "a situation that exists on other clubs as well."[45]

Maule wasn't bold enough to belatedly blame Landry for any of this, and the coach who had been so politically voluble only a few years ago as a defender of the establishment was smart enough to stay away from the topic. But the black players under his imprimatur were clearly an angrier bunch than they once were. A prime example was Pettis Norman, a man with so low a public profile that, during the 1970 Super Bowl, Jack Buck, on the CBS broadcast team for the game, kept calling him "Norman Pettis." But in the early spring of 1971, Norman made headlines when he took a lead role in a protest march of 250 civil rights and other civic leaders after the city's lone black councilman, George L. Allen, was passed over by the council as mayor pro tempore in favor of a white councilman. Pettis, a friend of Allen's, seconded his nomination and was so outraged by the vote that he stood up in the gallery and pointedly asked each councilman to "justify" his vote. Days later, he locked arms with Allen in the demonstration.

"There had never been a march like that in Dallas," Norman says. "Martin Luther King never came to Dallas. We'd gotten assurances from the council that George would be given the position, but they lied, they stabbed him in the back. It was an affront to the African American community, and we weren't going to sit back by and let this happen, so I led the march and spoke out. And after it was over a reporter came up and said, 'How's it gonna feel playing in Kansas City next year?'—meaning that because I was a Cowboy and black, I couldn't be so outspoken about issues like that. My answer was, 'If I gotta go to Kansas City to be a man, then Kansas City here I come.' My principles weren't for sale."

There was, indeed, a feeling among the black players on the team that they paid a price for such candor, and that Landry, Schramm, and Brandt preferred a certain type of player for the Cowboys. This seemed to be especially so in the case of black players. As Pat Toomay believed in the mid-1970s, "You are made to feel that dignity and self-respect are imagined qualities: you are a superb physical creation, expertly trained, but in all probability mindless. Many players have been infected with the impression that they are tolerated only because they are necessary pieces in a monumental chess game, a vehicle for corporate ego."[46]

The real or imagined price for causing contrary waves was steep for Duane Thomas, the most prominent example of someone who was *not* the type of black man the Cowboys by nature coveted. Even as he led the team to the heights, Thomas was a pariah for many in a still racially on-edge culture, not only in Dallas but around the country. Indeed, while both Pettis and Renfro played an immense role in the city's racial progress—and would make their post-career homes in Dallas, where they are successful business owners—the hate mail they received for their public crusades didn't ease for a long while.

What's more, it surely seemed that Norman had marched himself right off the team when on May 19, 1971, he was traded, not to Kansas City but to San Diego, along with defensive linemen Tony Liscio and Ron East, for thirty-year-old Lance Alworth, once the game's best wide receiver who had helped define the flamboyant élan of the AFL (and would become the first AFL player to be inducted into the Hall of Fame). Landry and Schramm became tempted when "Bambi," as Alworth became known, for his floppy ears, doe eyes, and graceful strides, had become a pariah on his own team. Having declared bankruptcy, divorced one woman and married another, Alworth, in vain, sued the Chargers for $5.6 million in money guarantees he claimed were never backed up—incredibly, even in 1971, Alworth was making a puny $55,000 a year—though he dropped the suit shortly before the trade.[47]

Sid Gillman, the Chargers' wily coach and general manager who, like Landry, had been his team's only head man, once said of Alworth, "I love this boy like I do my own son."[48] Now, with an out-of-shape, injury-prone Bambi coming off his worst season and hinting at retiring, Gillman put him on the market. Alworth was equally tempted to play for Landry. He also needed the bread. And so he agreed to a trade that coincidentally solved one of Landry's festering problems—Lance Rentzel. In April, Rentzel, who in December, as expected, had been charged with indecent exposure, received probation and naively hoped Landry would take him back. Instead, he became trade bait for the other Lance, in a three-way deal in which the Rams kicked in tight end Billy Truax and wide receiver Wendell Tucker. The move seemed perfect for both Lances, though neither would last long with his new team. In 1973, still troubled, Rentzel would be arrested again, for possession of marijuana,[49] and suspended by the league for the entire season. After copping a plea bargain to avoid jail time, he quit in 1974.

An easy induction to make at the time was that a bloodless Landry was similarly sacking Norman for un-Cowboy-like behavior. Instead, he says that Landry actually went out of his way to keep him from such a perception. "On the day I was traded, Tom didn't want me to find out from anyone but him. I was working as a vice president of a bank and he called and said, 'Can you wait until I get there?' and then drove an hour through afternoon traffic all the way across town so he could tell me about the trade. He wanted me to understand why he made it, and I did. There were circumstances that made sense. He said, 'Pettis, you know how much I respect you. I would never have let you hear about it on TV.'" At the time, such respect for black men by white men ensconced in the power structure of sports in Texas was still rare; black admittance to the big state universities, and their teams, had increased only to a trickle. Landry was still caught in a delicate social fabric and long-entrenched intolerance. He was no crusader for justice, but on the team he ruled, he would take that kind of long ride for anyone who had shed blood for the team. *That* was the kind of solidarity he had no trouble standing up for.

THE COWBOYS were still riding against the wind, but now they could almost taste their destination. "Seventy-one was a mission," says Mel Renfro of the mind set of the team. Bob Hayes, arguably the most important Cowboy after some stormy times, had played out his contract after the 1970 season and became a highly sought-after free agent. Rumors flew that he would sign with the Jets, giving them a deep threat Joe Namath would have killed for, but in the end Hayes, who'd had to take a pay cut the year before, chose to re-up with Dallas for another five years, now as the highest-paid receiver in football, at a salary of $55,000 a year sweetened with a $25,000 signing bonus and bonus clauses.[50] Even Don Meredith seemed to want back in on the Cowboys' threshold to a championship. Two years into his announcing gig, he had grown itchy for the game again. He met with Schramm and asked if the Cowboys would be interested in having him back. Tex, who went to Landry with the idea, came back with a polite but firm no, and Dandy Don, his residual doubts about quitting too soon finally extinguished, went back to the ABC Monday night booth, where dysfunctional ego-induced competition was almost as unbearable as being the Cowboys' quarterback. In fact, the Morton-Staubach competition resumed on an even higher level of anxiety. Landry, with the former needing more off-season shoulder surgery, still couldn't make the latter his starter and copped out by reviving the dreaded quarterback shuttle when the season began, alternating game by game, a decision that made the reporters acerbic—"QB QUIZ: WHO'S ON FIRST?" read a mocking headline in the *Morning News*[51]—and both contestants squirm.

"I don't have any choice but to do what he wants," said Morton, holding his tongue. Characteristically briny, Staubach offered, "I personally believe in a one-quarterback system. I believe one quarterback should assert himself and be the one you depend on."[52]

When the shuttle reemerged, so did the painful images of the Meredith-LeBaron, Meredith-Morton days. Jordan says, "Well, I was never a fan of it, but who were we to say anything? When Tom wanted our opinion, he gave it to us." Unable to hold his tongue, however, Staubach would over the entire season make pointed comments to the coach in front of the team about the infeasibility of the shuttle, which irked Landry to no end and may have kept Staubach on the bench longer than he might have been.

Instability was elsewhere, as well. The raucous Steve Kiner, who had grown tired of waiting for Chuck Howley to retire, had developed a drug habit, getting hooked on cocaine. When he demanded a trade, he was quickly accommodated. Kiner left throwing darts. "Landry and Tex," he said, had "turned a blind eye" to his drug use, a charge that would be repeated in the future. "They didn't value any of these people as human beings. They didn't say, 'This person needs a little help here. We need to show a little kindness.'"[53] This skew overlooked Landry's patience in coping with Duane Thomas.

For Landry, chaos was always part of the equation, and something to smooth out. Corny as he could sound, his trite apothegms sufficed for inspiration. His mantra entering the 1971 season was, "The hardest championship to win is the first. After that a club knows that it is capable of winning and it gains a great deal in confidence."[54] That message seemed to have gotten through when the season began. The Cowboys broke fast out of the gate, though Landry's shuttle plans were put on hold when Staubach suffered a broken blood vessel in his leg and Morton got the start in the season opener in Buffalo. The oft-criticized Morton was effective leading the team past the Bills, 49–37, in a wild fireworks show—he completed ten of fourteen passes for 221 yards, including for two touchdowns—and even with Staubach ready to go the next week in Philadelphia, Landry stuck with Morton. The Cowboys won again, 42–7.

Staubach meanwhile felt he had been misled by Landry, and moped on the sideline when Morton again started the following week against Washington. Landry believed this was necessary given that George Allen, who had come to the 'Skins that year to succeed Vince Lombardi, had whipped his team into a frenzy by trashing the Cowboys. Landry was his prime target in the NFC East, and Allen carried on with a neurotic madness. The longtime NFL executive Don Klosterman observed that Allen was "obsessed" with besting Landry. "If a light bulb was out in the hall, he'd screw in a new one and say, 'Can't beat the Cowboys that way . . . they don't have this kind of sloppiness.' He was just nuts on the subject."[55] John Wilbur, the ex-Cowboy whom Allen had brought to Washington, recalled that the manic coach built his distaste for the Dallas team into "hatred" and that he "never referred to the Dallas Cowboys any other way than the 'Goddamn Cowboys.'" Allen's first speech when he came to town was a rant: "our enemy is the Dallas Cowboys. You've got to have hate in your heart for the Cowboys. If you don't, we can't beat 'em."[56]

Allen had traded away almost all of his draft picks for aging veterans, including seven of his old Rams players. Nevertheless, the "Over the Hill Gang," as Allen called his geriatric players, had won their first two games before they traveled to Dallas to meet the team of his obsession. For Landry, subduing them was vital, and so he went with the more polished quarterback. But Morton again let him down. He was off the mark all day, going eleven for twenty-six, and this time the running game also sputtered. Down 17–9 after three quarters, Landry yanked Morton for Staubach, who completed six of nine passes and moved the Cowboys to within a point. The 'Skins, though, held on to win 20–16, an impressive task in the Cotton Bowl, and proof that the Cowboys had a dangerous new rival to deal with.

Landry was so torn about the quarterback situation that he became schizoid, soon alternating the two suitors for the job by each *half*. In the next game, a Monday night match with the Giants, Staubach started and gave the Cowboys a 13–6 lead, but when he took a hit that knocked him temporarily cold, Landry inserted Morton, who stayed in for the entire second half, winning the encounter, 20–13. Victory or not, the unsettled quarterback limbo prompted Dandy Don Meredith, up in the TV booth, to violate his oath against openly unloading on his old coach. "Landry's responsibility as a head coach is to pick a quarterback," he angrily huffed. "Now, after he has spent this long with them [if] he doesn't have any idea which one is best, then get another goddamn coach."[57]

Staubach, his senses restored, was so offended about being pulled from the game that when Landry strode by his locker afterward, the old Navy officer sprung from his chair and told the coach that what he had done was "uncalled for," adding, "You'll never understand me,"[58] as if his habit for sulking was by itself enough reason for him to be given the permanent job. Landry detested loose-lipped, emotional outbursts like that, and held his own tongue. "I admired Roger's will to play," he would write in his memoirs. "I just wished he'd be less vocal in his disagreement with me."[59] Landry would have to put up with a lot of guff from Staubach, enough to lead people to wonder—as with Duane Thomas—about Landry's selective double standards with players of their caliber. To be sure, he would back off from returning fire to both men, excusing their impudence, knowing how valuable they were. As well, Staubach's childish tantrums were almost a welcome relief from Thomas's creepy silent routine. And Staubach's static did nothing to disrupt a most satisfying evening, which also featured the return of Thomas, who darted for 60 yards on nine carries.

But with their new hippodrome in Irving at last ready, there was another leg to the Cowboys' equation, one that would turn up by a few notches the pressure to win, and to do so with the fattest bottom line. It was a certain sign of the times that the team that had put Dallas on the pro sports map—and the city on a higher plane of attention, even envy—was going to become a whole other breed of corporate animal after it stopped playing its home games there.

Chapter 19

. . . AND THE LORD
FINALLY GIVETH

THE TRANSMOGRIFICATION OF the NFL into a spiral of excess and nearly demonic commercial rapacity began on October 24, 1971, twelves miles west of Dallas. That was when Texas Stadium finally opened its gilded doors to football. While it had actually opened a month before, for a ten-day Billy Graham Crusade, on that day the Cowboys played the New England Patriots in the sixth game of the season. As was the case for much of the season, the hero was none other than the heretic of the Cowboys congregation, Duane Thomas, who notched the first touchdown of the new generation, blowing through a hole and streaking 56 yards in the first quarter of an eventual 44–21 blowout. Clint Murchison, basking in the glow of a building he had built, ushered former president Lyndon Johnson around the locker rooms before the game and helped himself to an array of tall glass potables in his luxury box during it. Pleased by the Caligula-like setting, and the easy win, the editors at the Dallas *Morning News* on September 18 ran a succinct, swooning headline: "1ST CLASS."

Upon closer inspection, Texas Stadium was an odd sort of Acropolis. Clint Murchison, stubbornly clinging to his idea for a roof that would allow for fans to be protected while having the feel of an outdoor game, accepted a half-and-half compromise: an "open dome." A visually striking and even scary rectangular peekaboo hole rose directly over the gridiron, which among a tapestry of steel girders, planks, and scattered light towers made the roof seem unfinished. Making the best of it, Murchison explained that the hole was there "so God can watch his favorite football team play," though it was taken for granted that if God wanted to watch from a luxury suite, even He would need to pay full price.

Of no lesser import, all those who had paid their way into the stadium expected their comforts to be a prime concern for Murchison. Yet once in, they immediately were disabused of that notion by the lack of air flow and acceptable air-conditioning, which only worsened during the burning autumn-afternoon games, when the Texas sun would glare against the huge scoreboard and make it impossible to read. As Pat Toomay wrote of the place, "Texas is noted for its grandiose self-image, and true to form, Texans have built the largest sauna bath in the world right in Irving, Texas. . . . The stadium rises out of the Irving bottomlands looking like a colossal Big Mac: the Irving Cheeseburger. [It is] one of those rare facilities in the nation where spectators, sitting stock-still on their hands, can expect to lose as much weight during the course of a game as the participants."[1]

The Irving Cheeseburger had 65,000 metallic blue seats packed into two tiers, with the end zone seats especially cramped. At least as important as the number of rumps in those seats would be the advertising signs splattered all over the place, including a three-sided Marlboro Man out in front of the stadium entrance with video screens in constant motion, one billboarding the three different movies showing in the stadium theaters.[2] Located twelve miles from downtown Dallas, the stadium was accessible only by the new nexus of superhighways, which carried mainly newer, upscale Cowboys devotees and not the carryover blue-collar Cotton Bowl refugees. It was the rich of Dallas after all who had built the place.

Murchison, knowing he could hit up the well-heeled to get his esplanade built without having to take a dime from Irving or any public funding, reaped $18 million of the price tag in revenue bonds, kicking in the $7 million balance himself. Many of those bond-holders also shelled out $50,000 for what was then a novel concept: a discrete private "suite" with all the amenities of a posh hotel room, *plus* tickets for their guests at each home game, at the price of $1,296 each. Mur-

chison saw cash cows, or steers, everywhere he looked. Orders for
season tickets to Texas Stadium came pouring in, and he drove a hard
bargain because he knew he could—anyone buying a season ticket
would need to pay $4,272, including a "seat bond" that could run
anywhere from $250 to $1,000 depending on location, which would
bear zero interest but annex the seat in perpetuity. Seat-owners would
forfeit them unless they committed to buying them each season for
the next *thirty-two years*.

That fetched Murchison over $30 million the first year alone. In New
York, Giants fans were famous for passing down their season tickets
from generation to generation because they wanted to. In Dallas, at
least some would because they *had* to. At the Cotton Bowl there had
always been enough tickets for walk-up game-day sales. That ended
in 1971. From then on, Dallas was a "season ticket town," the bulk of
them owned by corporations, almost none by regular fans.

Texas Stadium, by transforming the Cowboys into a wild, money-
snorting bull drunk with excess, instantly rewrote the manual for
sports ownership. In '71, Murchison's golden goose began with 176
luxury suites. Only a decade later, when these modern-day staples
would be part of every stadium in sports, there would be 381, at ten
times the price. And owners' fanatical desire to have them was the
prime reason why Al Davis would take his Raiders from Oakland in
search of luxury box profits in LA, though they wouldn't be enough
to keep him there long.

At the beginning, the vibe of Texas Stadium was rather sedate,
especially when compared with the rowdy mobs at the Cotton Bowl.
Applying a very selective standard of morality, the free-flowing champagne, tequila, and scotch up in the luxury boxes notwithstanding,
Murchison allowed no booze sold to the fans in the stands, a prohibi-
tion that would not be lifted until the 1990s. Being beyond the Dallas borders probably had something to do with it. The stadium was
in a gray and desolate area. With no place else to go, early arrivals
could only loiter in the parking lot before the gates opened. Even so,
tailgate parties were not part of the Cowboys experience, as an ordi-
nance of the City of Irving banned open flames and open containers,
and it would not be lifted until the mid-2000s when the team was
preparing for another move.

For some, the new vibe coincided with that intended by Landry's team. One longtime fan quoted by Gary Cartwright years later believed that the Cowboys "cultivated a mildly snobby character with their multiple-set offense, reliance on computers, and Landry's unemotional approach. But moving to Texas Stadium pushed their elitist reputation to a new zenith." According to Cartwright, the notion of human contact, which was almost mandated at the Cotton Bowl, was now "only optional, very optional" to the team. Thus were Texas Stadium crowds to be caricatured as swells in fur coats and three-piece suits who, said Cartwright, seemed to be "too cool" to cheer.

The biggest noises came from commercials on the giant screens and the anachronistic marching music of the Cowboys' band, not counting the lustful barnyard squeals directed at Schramm's hot-pants cheerleaders. Still, the fans kept streaming in, and almost none gave up their season tickets, which irritated the front office, knowing how much more it could sell them for. If a ticket-holder died, the Cowboys would look for a reason to take the tickets back, such as the renewal was mailed in a day or two late. This, said the fan, was "emblematic of the attitude searing pro football's soul. Teams no longer wanted fans: They wanted clients."[3]

The Cowboys players, when they saw the magnificently polished grounds they would call home, wondered if there were now rules of etiquette to follow. Bob Lilly asked if it was okay to spit on the meticulously groomed artificial carpet—which, as Schramm pointed out, was not the same as AstroTurf but a new, more grasslike invention called, naturally, "CowboyTurf." The dampened acoustics of the thick walls led Calvin Hill to say that playing here "seemed like we were in an opera house or something."[4]

The coach of the soap opera known as the Dallas Cowboys was living in higher style, having moved to a French Colonial house on Rock Cliff Place, a cul-de-sac in a more upscale part of the Bluffview section. Here, Alicia Landry, the queen of the Cowboys' realm who for years lived in uncertainty and on tight budgets, could relax the purse strings just a bit, within the broad context of the Landrys' sense of frugality and humility. Not that he didn't see some avenues of reward, with a cue by Tex Schramm. By the late 1960s, Schramm had hungrily opted to take advantage of the sweetheart deal given to him at the beginning by Clint Murchison, and bought shares of the Cowboys' ever fattening stocks, at their 1959 prices, which made Schramm a part-owner of the team and, as Sam Blair noted, "a fairly wealthy man."[5]

Landry, who had been given the same terms when Murchison extended his contract by ten years in 1964, didn't do the same; he was unable to justify a greater reward that had not been earned, at least in his value system. Decadent frills like a stadium that located his team in the middle of a new football universe may have been a proper reward for Murchison, the overlord of the team's asset sheets, but to the coach of a team that had not fulfilled its birthright, the arena was just another golden calf, a false idol, gilded and gelded, mocking his failures. Besides, he wasn't so sure that a coach had any business aligning so inextricably with ownership in the modern era. That was a sticky spider's web foreseen by Paul Brown when he let Art Modell buy him out in Cleveland so that Brown could coach without added entanglements and pressures.

Unlike Papa Bear Halas, playbook Platos like Landry and Brown were wary of smooth-tongued liars playing front office politics, every reason why Landry kept a distance from Tex Schramm. Thus, even when Landry did buy stock in the Cowboys, it would be as a short-term transaction that gained him little of the Cowboys' overall wealth. And, for him, that would be just fine.

THE INTERIOR tension about race among the Cowboys' black players was exacerbated by the move to Texas Stadium, where the sizable Hispanic and black fan base was financially frozen out of seats. Clint Murchison Jr., unapologetic about it, found rationales in institutional economic racism. "If we discriminated against them, we discriminated against them," he said, meaning minority fans, "but no more than all America discriminates against people who don't have money to buy everything they want."[6] Creditably, the complexion of the Cowboys' rosters remained more variegated than that of many teams. One of their newest additions, kicker Toni Fritsch, arrived by way of Austria, Landry having found him while on a European excursion scouting those whip-legged European soccer players. He had to go all the way to Vienna to find Fritsch. Concurrently, there were homegrown "rednecks," some of whom thought it was hilarious to show up for a team Halloween party one year dressed in white hoods and robes emblazoned "KKK."[7] And there were not only Europeans but also Mexicans, mainly in the string of kickers that began with Danny Villanueva, whom Fritsch replaced in 1971.[8] The brown-skinned Cowboys, as with the black-skinned ones, were accepted by the fans with reluctance; many of these players received hate mail, and would for years.

It was testament to Landry that in the midst of all these rip currents, he had his team running on all cylinders with remarkably few stumbles. The newly returned Duane Thomas, negotiating the CowboyTurf as if it were a glide path, ran for a long touchdown in that first game at Texas Stadium. The following week at Wrigley Field, with his 65-yard effort the Cowboys ran up 342 yards against the ever-tough Bears defense—but lost, 23–19, after committing several turnovers, three fumbles and four interceptions, three thrown by Morton, who was otherwise brilliant. That, though, was the last time the Cowboys stumbled for the rest of the season. Through it all, Thomas maintained his spooky silence and bizarre behavior, something that he would recall was directed by God so as to guide him "through the valley of death."[9] Landry, letting bygones be for now, raved that "Duane is just an amazing fellow."[10] Thomas was so good that the newspapers stopped savaging him.

Within the rank and file of the team, things weren't so copacetic. Indeed, the line Thomas had crossed by openly making Landry into an enemy backfired badly. By doing so, he had frozen himself out, with all the other Cowboys now wanting nothing to do with him personally. Thomas, not helping himself, turned off his teammates with alarming ease. In one game against the New Orleans Saints, he was hit hard and got up limping. On the sideline, Jethro Pugh put an arm around him and asked, "How's the leg?" Thomas, snarling, said, "Are you a doctor?" Incredulous, Pugh pushed him away and spat at him, "Fuck you, man."[11]

Another time, Mike Ditka patted him on the back before a game and said, "Good luck." Days later, as though Thomas had been boiling about the innocuous gesture, he told Ditka, "Hey, man, don't ever hit me on the back before a game. It breaks my concentration." As the always irascible tight end recalled, "I said, 'Hey Duane. Go fuck yourself.' That was our conversation."[12] The upshot was that players who had their own grievances with the coach were, because of Thomas, resolved to support Landry at all costs in his ongoing cold war. Once, the coach's biggest thorn, Bob Hayes, who, contract notwithstanding, still harbored resentments about Landry, said of Thomas's intent to brand Landry in racist terms, "I don't think anyone on the team has had more differences with Tom Landry than me. But I respect him. I don't give a damn, black or white, that cat is a good coach and a good man."[13]

AFTER BEATING the Cardinals and Eagles—with Staubach starting both games when Morton's shoulder acted up again—the Cowboys had a 6–3 record when they went to Washington, DC, for the return grudge match against George Allen's 5–3–1 Redskins. It was a statement game, personally so for Landry, whose mild distaste for Allen had grown into full-blown detestation. Though he certainly respected Allen as a football man, he had also regarded him as someone with no limits on chutzpah. Indeed, Allen, whose kinship with Richard Nixon was a case of devious minds thinking alike, had no compunction wallowing in righteous indignation while having people skulk around his next opponent's practices, and he was the sorest of winners, piling on scores and postgame taunting.

Thus Landry—who would be kept from Coach of the Year validation when it went to Allen instead—must have certainly enjoyed it when the Cowboys vanquished and nearly humiliated Allen and the Redskins, winning 13–0 on November 21, Staubach coolly directing a balanced attack that gained 146 yards in rushing and 151 in passing, and scoring the only touchdown on a 29-yard scramble in the first quarter. Ironically, Allen himself was now going with a dual-quarterback scheme, which of course he made out to be his own brilliantly original idea, with the antediluvian Billy Kilmer and Sonny Jurgensen vying for time.

Primed and confident, the Cowboys pushed on no matter what. In

November, Ralph Neely broke his leg in a motorcycle accident—he lied to Landry at first that he had been thrown from a horse, believing it would be less offensive to the coach—and tackle Don Talbert broke a bone in his foot. After the loss to the Bears on Halloween, Don Meredith repeated his criticism of the shuttle on *Monday Night Football*. This time, however, Landry too had come to the conclusion that the shuttle had outlived its usefulness. It took until the season's eighth game, but Landry finally named Staubach the sole starter. Grateful, Staubach completed twenty of thirty-one passes for 199 yards and a touchdown in a 16–13 win in St. Louis. He then dismantled the Giants, throwing for 232 yards and three touchdowns, two to Hayes, winning 42–14.

The Cowboys ran out the schedule with seven straight wins, trampling the Cardinals in the finale, 31–12, running up their combined margin of victory over the last four games to 153–57. With Morton an afterthought, Staubach won all ten of his starts. His fifteen touchdown passes and only four interceptions, 59 percent completion rate, 8.9 yards per pass attempt, and a league-best 104.8 quarterback rating won him an invitation to the Pro Bowl. The team stats were no less gaudy. It ranked No. 1 in offense (and points, 406) and No. 2 in defense. The offense was a perfectly balanced machine, ranked second in passing and third in rushing. Thomas, in an abbreviated season, ran for eleven touchdowns, the most in the game.

The reward for all this was a road trip to Minneapolis to play the 11–3–0 Vikings in the opening playoff round, on Christmas Day, in another chamber of deep-frozen hell, Metropolitan Stadium, where the Nordic team almost never lost. The Cowboys had some added incentive going in. When the Pro Bowl selections were announced, only one of them, Bob Lilly, made the first team. Staubach did win the Bert Bell Award as the league's outstanding player, yet he was voted to the All-Pro second team behind Greg Landry. By contrast, five Vikings—including the core of the Purple People Eaters defensive line, Alan Page and Carl Eller—made it onto the first team, with cause. The Vikings led the league in defense, giving up an astounding 9.9 points a game and only *two* rushing touchdowns.

The temperature at game time was twenty-two degrees, balmy by Ice Bowl standards, and on this day it was the Cowboys' defense that stopped the Vikings on every critical play and bailed out an anemic offense. The Cowboys forced five turnovers, intercepting Bob Lee four times. A Thomas 13-yard touchdown run and a 9-yard scoring pass in the third quarter ran the score to 20–3, and the final was 20–12. Landry called it the best defensive effort of the season, and Vikings receiver Gene Washington said, "Dallas played a perfect game. The Cowboys just didn't make any mistakes."[14]

The ease with which they won made them a strong favorite in the NFC Championship Game, the first at the virginal Texas Stadium, held on January 2, 1972, in a redux with Dick Nolan's San Francisco 49ers, who had some incentive of their own. At 9–5, they seemed a long shot. The now gimpy, thirty-six-year-old John Brodie had a downer of a season, his eighteen touchdown passes offset by twenty-four interceptions. They also had some age on the defensive line and in the secondary. By the luck of the draw, though, they got to play the first-round game at home, against George Allen's Redskins, and managed to pull out the win, 24–20. When they came to Dallas, they were still smarting from the loss the year before at Kezar Stadium.

For Landry the 49ers were a tough old boot. No other coach knew the Cowboys' operating systems as well as Nolan, and his own version of the Flex defense brought Staubach back down to earth, literally. Harassed mercilessly by All-Pro defensive end Cedrick Hardman, Staubach was sacked six times and was constantly flushed from the pocket. Yet Staubach profited from his deep backfield, with Hill and Garrison keeping drives going, amassing 172 rushing yards on forty-six carries. Landry's defense was the difference. Brodie had little breathing room. Blitzed on nearly every play, he completed only fourteen of thirty passes, three of which found the Cowboys' defensive backs. Early on, in the second quarter, with the ball on his own 8-yard line, Brodie aimed a screen pass for fullback Ken Willard. Lilly came in high, blocking Brodie from seeing George Andrie spin off a block, and the ball floated right into Andrie's hands. Hill then plunged into the end zone for a 7–0 lead, which was all Landry needed. A late 2-yard touchdown run by Thomas iced the game, 14–3.

The most salient aspect of the victory was its joyless, mechanical inevitability. Though hardly a blowout, the game never seemed in doubt. When it was over, the Cowboys ambled into the locker room, not one of them in a celebratory mood. The only overt gesture of victory was Herb Adderley's forefinger haughtily stuck into the dewy air. These were the "new" Cowboys, after all, the team on a mission from God, about which Cliff Harris said, "We were never driven by emotion, but always by logic," and Cornell Green said, "We've had the Super Bowl on our minds since training camp."[15] Now it was upon them, the game to be played on January 16 in New Orleans's corroding Tulane Stadium. They drew as an opponent not a presumed AFC top cat like the Colts or the Chiefs but the Cinderella Miami Dolphins, who had beaten both en route to Tulane. Don Shula's precocious team, in only their fourth year, and their second under him, had risen into the league elite when the jut-jawed coach played to the strengths of his quarterback, Bob Griese, the former Purdue All-American who was the expansion Dolphins' first-round pick in 1967.

Griese's arm was not strong but it was surgically accurate, and when Shula took over the team in 1970, he put tight controls on him, centering the offense around a plundering rushing attack led by the tanklike fullback Larry Csonka, nimble Jim Kiick, and the aptly named Mercury Morris. They all ran behind some of the best young offensive linemen in the game, notably guards Larry Little and Bob Kuechenberg, and compiled the most rushing yards in the league. This softened up defenses, freeing Griese to launch precise throws to the Browns' expatriate Paul Warfield, who caught a league-best eleven touchdown passes. Griese's passer rating was second only to Staubach's, and he was both an All-Pro and the league MVP. But it was the quick, swarming Dolphins defense that was the story. The "No-Name Defense," as they were called, actually featured several stars, such as veteran middle linebacker Nick Buoniconti and safeties Dick Anderson and Jake Scott. The front four were light, but they rarely took themselves out of a play by falling for a play action or a trap block, with tackle Manny Fernandez an immutable boulder.

The contrast between the Dolphins and the Cowboys began at the top, in the personas of the two coaches—"SHULA'S FIRE VERSUS LANDRY'S PATIENCE" as the headline in the January 16 *Morning News* put it. On the surface, in many tangible ways, the contest shaped up much like the Jets-Colts affair three years before, with

Shula, the losing coach that day, now leading an upstart former AFL entry into war against the seemingly unbeatable establishment team, even if the Cowboys still saw themselves as the NFL's bête noir. Landry certainly seemed overdue. As one writer noted of him, "This man has more patience than any individual I've ever known," adding that the toll he had to pay—Meredith, Morton, Rentzel, Thomas, and so on—would have "been enough to kill a lesser man."[16]

THE COWBOYS' fans were eager to witness history being made. During the week following the win over San Francisco, seven thousand tickets to the Super Bowl were put up for sale at seven o'clock in the morning at the Cowboys' offices. They were all gone within an hour. By now these climactic games were a barometer of a changing culture. When Tex Schramm said he would not pay for the Cowboys' cheerleaders to make the trip to New Orleans, fans paid their way instead, the first time sexy window dressing became part of the NFL's annual circus, a small but significant cultural stamp of the ongoing sexual revolution.

Not that the culture beyond the gates was any easier to stomach. On the front page of the *Morning News* the day after the win against the 49ers, the game story went elbow to elbow with Richard Nixon's pronouncement that he would finally reveal his long "secret" plan to end the Vietnam War,[17] which entailed a fresh round of carpet bombing in North Vietnam. Nixon was still sitting atop the withering culture, his demagoguery of America's fearful "Silent Majority," which guaranteed his landslide victory over his antiwar challenger George McGovern in November, the last gasp of an antediluvian political culture. In fact, Nixon's career had mirrored the rise of the NFL, and as a fan, he appreciated the public's fancy with the pro game. Seeking some goodwill, he injected himself into the Super Bowl buildup, devising a play he graciously offered to Don Shula, a down-and-in pass to Warfield, appropriately a conservative play. That he did not make a play available to Landry may have been a tacit understanding that, good Republican that Landry was, not even a president could call plays for the Dallas Cowboys.

Landry would soon enough know how fortunate he was not being befriended by Nixon, who only a year later would be insisting "I'm not a crook" as he dragged the country through another convulsion, one that would batter quaint notions about the sanctity of men in high office. Even so, in Dallas, the fact that Nixon picked against Landry was taken as a personal snub, with *Morning News* editorial writer Mike Kingston, not knowing the future irony of it, venturing that it was "about as sound as visiting Red China."[18]

Landry, who was surely sanctified in *his* office, and culturally evolving in small increments, approached his second Super Bowl with far less rigidity than he had the first. Wisely, he eased off the sequestration of his players from their womenfolk during the team's stay in New Orleans and relaxed his curfew restrictions in a town where that would be dangerous. The Cowboys were a light, loose bunch, convincing Tex Maule that they were on the cusp of their promised land. Maule, returning to his old Cowboys boosterism, picked them to win in his preview, "by more than two touchdowns . . . by shutting off the Miami running game [and] dumping Griese for losses or forcing him to pass in a hurry as they did to John Brodie."[19] The bookmakers also signed off, making Landry's team a 6-point favorite.

At kickoff, back in Dallas the streets were nearly deserted and nearly every television was tuned to the broadcast on CBS. It was a day when nothing would be permitted to go wrong. And nothing did. Nixon's self-serving sideshow did get one thing right: defending Warfield was the microcosmic fulcrum of the game, though the down-and-in he urged on Shula was used only once, and it was broken up by Renfro, who manned the outside coverage lanes on Warfield. The inside lanes were assigned to Cornell Green, who mimicked the receiver's every move. When Warfield would go in motion before the snap, Green would migrate all the way across the field with him, then stick with him on the route. This sandwich effectively snuffed the lissome receiver, the task made easier by the Doomsday front line and linebackers locking down the Dolphins' runners and rendering their passes predictable. Warfield would grab only four passes for 39 yards, and flubbed several others, no doubt hearing footsteps closing in on him.

The young Dolphins played jittery. Larry Csonka, who hadn't fumbled all season, lost the ball the second time he ran, and Howley recovered it on Dallas's 48, setting up a field goal and a 3–0 lead. On the Dolphins' next series came the most memorable moment of the game, save for the halftime salute to the recently deceased Louis Armstrong featuring Ella Fitzgerald and Al Hirt. Griese dropped back to throw, saw Lilly and defensive end Larry Cole coming straight at him, pivoted, and began retreating. Hemmed off wherever he turned, Griese zigzagged like a rudderless speed boat, scrambling backward until Lilly wrapped him up at the 9-yard line—a Super Bowl record 29-yard sack that still holds. The Cowboys failed to score, but the tone was set. In the second quarter, Staubach capped off a long drive with a 7-yard touchdown pass to Alworth. The Dolphins countered, driving deep into the Cowboys' territory, but when Griese tried to get the ball to Warfield at the 2, Green broke up the pass, leaving the Dolphins to settle for a field goal.

It was only 10–3 at the half, but Landry's boys had severely outplayed Shula's. With many options to try, Landry, seeing how the Dolphins' defense bunched up to stop the run, had Thomas and Garrison go wide, then cutting back against the grain. The normally resolute front four of the Dolphins were confused. They allowed the Cowboys to gain 252 yards on forty-eight carries, a total that has been surpassed only three times in Super Bowl play. Staubach passed nineteen times, completing twelve for 119 yards. On the first drive of the third quarter, he passed only once on an eight-play sequence that saw a 37-yard burst by Thomas, a 16-yard reverse by Hayes, and a 3-yard sweep by Thomas for a 17–3 lead.

After yet another big-game interception by Howley, and an ensuing 7-yard touchdown pass to Ditka, the rout was on. It would end at 24–3, punctuated by a beaming Landry being ferried off the field on the broad shoulders of Renfro, Hayes, and Wright, at long last relieved of the yoke of monumental, inglorious defeat. It was Shula who now owned that animadversion, twice losing the big one. Accordingly, Shula's Teutonic facial features, bearing the same baffled exasperation Landry had had, admitted through gritted teeth afterward that his team had been "destroyed." Nick Buoniconti confirmed that he'd been "knocked senseless" by the Cowboys' line.[20]

Thomas, who gained 95 yards on nineteen carries, was the obvious choice as the game's MVP, but the editors of *Sport* magazine who chose the winner, apparently not wanting to chance being embarrassed, or even repudiated, by the querulous Thomas, instead gave the award, and the sports car that came with it, to Staubach,[21] who was not only a safer choice but a whiter one. Beyond that, there *was* no reason for the snub. A similar situation arose when Joe Namath was given the award after Super Bowl III, even though fullback Matt Snell gained 121 yards. But Namath's charisma, if not his conservative stats, dominated the event, something that could not be said of Staubach.

As it turned out, Thomas *did* dominate this event, but not in a way the league wanted. In the merry postgame locker room, with the players giddily pulling Clint Murchison Jr. into the shower, Thomas sat on his stool in his underwear, angrily shooing away reporters. The TV people first came looking for Landry, who, with Lilly towering over both of them, was handed the Lombardi Trophy by Pete Rozelle. Noting that the Cowboys franchise had been formed the year he had become commissioner, Rozelle jived that he had a "special interest watching you develop." When he mentioned the name of Lombardi, Landry flashed a thin smile, as if that bootheel had finally been lifted from his team's necks.

With the lights bathing his shiny pate, Landry looked cool and regal, his double-breasted blue suit unwrinkled. "I'm delighted we're still here after starting the franchise," he said, referring to his bumpy road. The ghost of Lombardi was still stalking him, however. When CBS announcer Tom Brookshier mentioned that, but for the two defeats to the Packers, he and not Lombardi would have had a 1960s' dynasty, he bowed to the ghost, saying he'd been "delighted just to be in it against them, even though we gave 'em a scare a couple of times." Then, "Hopefully, we've reached our point in history right now, and maybe we can go on from here."[22]

While the network was feverishly trying to get Thomas on camera, Brookshier interviewed Staubach and Hayes. Thomas finally relented after being urged by Jim Brown, and Brookshier was startled when he finished with Hayes and saw Thomas's eyes staring at him. Thoroughly unnerved, beads of sweat forming on his face, he stammered, "Duane, how are you? My name is Tom Brookshier." He then launched into a rambling prologue about Thomas being fast but never out of control, before finally asking, "Are you that fast? Are you that quick, would you say?" Still glaring, Thomas had a succinct answer. "Evidently," he said, in perfect deadpan.

Players and reporters who had gathered around them broke up, including the embarrassed Brookshier, who tried another question but in mid-sentence decided to have Brown answer it. Returning to Thomas, he said, meekly, "Duane, people don't know you," and as he began to frame a question, Brown twitted, "Are you nervous, Tom?" Brookshier, a good egg, admitted he was. Trying again, he managed to asked Thomas, "Do you like the game of football?" Quietly, came the reply: "Yes, I do. That's why I'm a football player."[23] Other questions seemed to drift away before they could be fully formed, and the bizarre colloquy ended, to gain as much attention as the game itself did—proving that even in glorious victory, Duane Thomas went his own way. And whether he knew it or not, it was the last time he would be seen in the employ of the Dallas Cowboys.

FOR LANDRY, the final gun sounded the end to his eleven-year wait for vindication. He wrote in his memoirs, "I couldn't seem to stop smiling for days."[24] To be sure, there was a little extra gusto in his lips when he met up with Alicia outside the locker room and bussed her on the cheek. Bob St. John, who believed he might never see a day like this, encountered him as the Cowboys waited at the airport for the flight back home. Landry was reading a paper. Seeing the tart-tongued scribe, he grinned and, for him, delivered a kidney punch: "Boy, you writers. I don't know what you're going to write about now. . . . You guys might just have to reevaluate," apparently meaning the writers' habitual plaints about Landry's failing to win the big ones. But St. John had a ready comeback. "What we'll do now," he said, "is ask the question, 'Can the Dallas Cowboys win two big ones in a row?'" Landry giggled at the line; in fact, the question was very much on his mind, too.[25]

The next day the papers laid on hands—"SUPER COWBOYS BOWL 'EM OVER," was the page-one headline in the *Morning News* ("Free at last," was St. John's lead sentence), with another confirming, almost as if with a pinch to make sure, "COWBOYS HAVE WON IT ALL." A sidebar asked, "A DYNASTY OR A DREAM?"[26] The players, unlike Landry, had no doubt about the last. "We really believed we had a dynasty," says Renfro. "We thought we'd win two, three more Super Bowls."[27] Tex Maule, taking his own bows for his not-so-daring prediction, quoted in his *Sports Illustrated* review of the game Tex Schramm's old axiom regarding the computers being only as good as the players they analyze—"You put garbage in, you get garbage out"—and added his affirmation. "There is no garbage on the Dallas Cowboys," he wrote. "Not anymore."[28]

Landry permitted himself none of that felicitation. The glow for him faded after the team received its mandatory welcome home from thousands of fans at Love Field that night. Recalls Renfro, "He told us, 'Enjoy it, now, boys, 'cause we've got a lot of work to do when you get to camp.' He was already thinking about next season. Tom knew how hard it would be to do it again, to keep our edge. It was like he filed away the Super Bowl two minutes after it happened. We, the players, had fun that off-season, we had guys who tended to overdo it anyway, win or lose. But Tom didn't rest on the win. He didn't want to talk about it. He'd lost too many big games to think winning again would be easy."

Alicia Landry saw little difference in her husband as the afterglow seemingly washed over everyone else in Dallas. "Oh, he was happy, in his way. He'd waited a *long* time for it, and you could just feel the weight that had been taken off his back. But he was uncomfortable when people would fawn over him. We took our vacation, a long driving trip out west, because he didn't want to be deluged by people. Then we came home and it was right back to the films, draft reports, meetings with the other coaches. I think I enjoyed all the success more than him. To me, it was the greatest thing in the world. To Tommy, it was what he always expected. I'll say it like this, he hated losing more than he loved winning. He didn't want that bitter taste again. But he knew he would."[29]

NOT EVEN winning a Super Bowl, and the $25,000 each player and coach pocketed for it, could make Landry and his men want to put up with Thomas for another year. Over the off-season, Thomas and his brother were pulled over by Texas highway cops—"for driving while black," wrote one wag[30]—and arrested for smoking marijuana. They escaped jail time when Tex Schramm got them legal representation and five years' probation instead.[31] As soon as camp convened in Thousand Oaks, Thomas missed the first meeting and practice. Landry and Schramm had held off on moving him, hoping he would change his ways, and the coach tried one last shot, going to Thomas's room and asking why he had missed the sessions. "I didn't feel like it," he said, adding that he wasn't paid to attend meetings, only to play on Sunday. Landry, bending no more, left the room and went to see Schramm.

"That's it," he said. "We have to trade Thomas."[32]

Landry was ready to admit that he had "made a mistake having one set of rules for the team and one for Duane."[33] Even so, he would later say he felt "sick" about having to cut Thomas adrift. "Duane was obviously a troubled young man. He needed help. And I hadn't been able to get through to him."[34] Mike Ditka, who had watched the coach twist himself into knots, and believed that "Duane is basically a good guy," called the Thomas saga the "worst anguish Tom ever went through," and said, "I've never seen a man suffer [like that] in trying to do what he thought was best for a football team . . . it was pure hell." Ditka's slant was that "Landry never really bent the rules for Thomas, but I think he bent himself a little bit."[35]

Maybe a lot. Schramm, no doubt relieved he wouldn't need to pay Thomas a superstar salary after his third year, sent the scowling enigma to the San Diego Chargers on August 1 for small change, two second-year players, running back Mike Montgomery and receiver Billy Parks, a southern California iconoclast in the Lance Rentzel mold. Pat Toomay believed the Cowboys would have taken just about anyone, calling the deal a "physical severance." Yet Toomay, now the last rebel on that squad, and soon to be dispatched himself, saw the moment in the long lens as a failure for Landry. Thomas, he said, had "cracked the arrogance that has encased the Cowboy front office for years [and forced] them to do something they did not want to do—to trade him. The Cowboys have never deliberately dumped a first-rate player unless that player was injured, or going over the hill."[36] What's more, Thomas had seemed to want nothing more than to please Landry.

If one can believe Pete Gent's take, it was Thomas who had been tormented and sent over the edge by *Landry*. Gent, who later befriended Thomas, once claimed that "Tom made Duane absolutely crazy . . . he was emotionally crippled . . . I don't think he ever recovered from it. None of us did."[37] Gent himself was so far gone that he swore the Cowboys were "behind the whole episode" of Thomas's drug bust, which in reality Schramm had helped defuse.[38]

Whatever the genesis of his mental state, Thomas made no friends in San Diego. Much as his weekend in New England, he ensured his fate by not showing up to work, landing him on the twenty-day suspension list. When he finally came in, he refused to stand for the national anthem before an exhibition game against the Cowboys, and drew a raft of boos. Unwilling to see what else he would do, the Chargers put him on the reserve list—the best runner in football would not play a single down that season.

THE 1972 campaign indeed proved Landry's assumptions about how difficult it is to stay on top in a league that Pete Rozelle liked to say was a model of "parity," the Lombardi-style domination out with the past. The 1971 run had blinded everyone to something Landry knew was the number-one problem to deal with: with or without Thomas, the Cowboys were getting old. Reeves and Gregg retired, the latter beginning his own coaching career with the offensive line in San Diego. Howley was thirty-six, Lilly thirty-three, both still ferocious but with a limited shelf-life. And Adderley grew seriously disaffected. If Adderley saw Lombardi as a strict but all too human Italian patriarch, Landry was a distant, autocratic prig. Despite Adderley's six championship rings, Landry continually called him out during film sessions, something fellow future Hall of Famer Mel Renfro had to live with his entire career.

"Adderley!" Landry screeched, his high-pitched voice cutting through the quiet room, "you're clueing," Landry-speak for freelancing. When he saved a touchdown by doing so in one game, Landry benched him anyway, telling him to do "what your keys tell you to do!"

"No, I don't play that way," Adderley said.

"Then you won't play at all. Stay or leave, I don't care."[39]

He would stay only that year, then retire. Concurrently, younger players were having their own difficult transitions to the Landry way. Tody Smith, the younger and nearly as massive baby brother of Bubba Smith, had an injury-prone college career, but the Cowboys gambled a first-round pick for him in 1971. He spent that year on the taxi squad, then tore up his knee playing basketball in the off-season and underwent surgery. Smith wasn't sure he was healed by training camp, but the team's doctors pronounced him fit, reflecting once more the long-held prevailing attitude in the Cowboys' locker room that the doctors served only their masters in the front office. The highly sensitive Smith left camp—a cardinal Landry sin—and when he came back, he felt the cold shoulder of the coach. "I feel like a stranger here," he said. "I don't feel I'm needed."

Still, Landry named him the starter at left defensive end, replacing Larry Cole, but Smith suffered a bout with mononucleosis late in the season. He insisted he couldn't get out of bed to play in the Thanksgiving game; the doctors said it was all in his head. After dragging himself through the end of the season, he found out all the physical stress had left him with an enlarged spleen, a dangerous condition that necessitated a month-long stay at the Mayo Clinic. That was when he resolved never to play for the Cowboys again.[40] He asked for a trade and in 1973 was sent to the Houston Oilers.

Beyond these new examples of Cowboys culture clash, Staubach during the preseason suffered a shoulder separation which raised Morton from the dead. Once again the starter, he excelled through most of the season, completing 56 percent of his passes, including 15 for touchdowns, though typically he forced matters, throwing twenty-one interceptions. The offense, minus the spontaneous combustibility of Staubach's legs, dropped from scoring an average of 29 to 22 points a game, but with Thomas gone, Cal Hill reemerged, rumbling for 1,036 yards, the first Cowboy to clear a thousand and sixth best in the league. Landry did add a new wrinkle, dusting off Red Hickey's old Shotgun formation, which he renamed the Spread, causing many younger fans to assume he had invented it. The defense held firm despite its creeping age, ushering the team to a 10–4 record, a game behind the surging Redskins, and earning them yet another date with their new whipping boys, the 49ers, in the first playoff round, at Candlestick Park.

It wasn't quite the same Niners. Dick Nolan in a general youth movement had begun phasing out John Brodie for his longtime backup Steve Spurrier, and they had to win their last two games to finish at 8–5–1. But Nolan always got his team pumped for Landry's. During the season they had come to Texas Stadium on Thanksgiving and, causing four turnovers, laid a 31–10 licking on the Cowboys. Now, on a hunch, Nolan started Brodie, who before he ever got the ball had a lead when Vic Washington ran back the opening kickoff 97 yards for a touchdown. Brodie would have a 21–3 lead late in the first half, 28–13 midway through the fourth quarter after Larry Schreiber ran in his third touchdown. On the other side, Morton was flailing—he would complete eight of twenty-one passes, including one touchdown pass, throw two interceptions, and fumble the ball inside his own 5, which gifted the 49ers another 7 points.

Early in the fourth quarter, Landry played his last card, Staubach, who had played only four games in a mop-up role. Morton, who was so reluctant to cede the job that he had played one game with pneumonia, now cast aside his own ego. "I have confidence in you," he said. "You can win it in some way."[41] The 49ers begged to differ. When Staubach came out of the huddle, linebacker Dave Wilcox called across the line, "How does it feel to lose?"[42] But the conditions were propitious for a comeback. Staubach had to run a hurry-up offense, meaning there was no time for Landry to send in plays. Staubach was on his own, improvising, and right away he took the Cowboys on a drive that ended in a 27-yard field goal by Fritsch.

As the clock ticked down, Nolan aided the Cowboys' cause by surrendering short yardage. Staubach flung twenty passes in the quarter, completing twelve for 174 yard, and ran three times for 23 yards. Hill was on his way to a 125-yard game, and the Cowboys would have a massive edge in the number of yards gained, 402 to 255. When Staubach hit Billy Parks with a 20-yard touchdown pass with less than two minutes left in the game, shrinking the 49ers' lead to 28–23, Nolan's defense was exhausted. Landry still needed a miracle, though—and he got it when Mel Renfro recovered the ensuing onside kick.

Now, as an incipient air of gloom swept through the grandstand,

Staubach again dragged the home team deep down the field. With fifty-two seconds left, Staubach, on the Niners' 10-yard line, called a pass to Parks, but when the Niners blitzed all three linebackers, Staubach, just before being buried, got a fleeting glance of an open Ron Sellers in the end zone and let the ball fly. Touchdown, for a 30–28 lead and, a few seconds later, the game. It ended with the Cowboys deliriously celebrating on the sideline, with Larry Cole in full pads turning somersaults. Landry called it "one of the most exciting and remarkable endings to a football game I'd ever seen,"[43] though it would be only the first of a litany of semi-habitual "miracles," a term the Cowboys players freely used to explain what had just occurred.

There was an even bigger miracle on a gridiron that day. Earlier, the Steelers had beaten the Raiders on an end-of-game pass that was deflected and then caught by Franco Harris on top of his shoe—the "Immaculate Reception." Staubach, off his own immaculate pass, was on top of the world that week, feeding off headlines like "ARTFUL DODGER RETURNS,"[44] living a kind of out-of-body experience, his confidence boundless. Before the title game, against the Redskins on New Year's Eve Day, he breezily told Bob St. John, "If things are going bad I'll come in and pull it out [again]."[45]

As it happened, he was in at the start, a move that George Allen before the game called "a little risky"[46] and that Lee Roy Jordan still calls a "mistake."[47] Landry spent the night preceding the game participating in a Bible marathon reading on a Christian radio program, but after the miracle in 'Frisco, his favors from above may have had limits. The next day, Staubach's bucolic week ended, painfully, when Allen brought his secondary close to the line of scrimmage, stopped the Cowboys' ground game, and made Staubach look "a little rusty," as defensive end Ron McDole would say later. "Once we took his first receiver away, he was lost."[48] This time the Doomsday boys went down too, pounded by Larry Brown, who ran thirty times for 88 yards, and Billy Kilmer's two touchdown passes to Charley Taylor, who ran right through the Cowboys' double coverages in the 26–3 blowout.

The most embarrassing thing about the loss for Landry was that, as Lilly said afterward, the 'Skins "just beat the hell out of us."[49]

Indeed, Paul Zimmerman conjectured that the game wrote in blood the feral nature of the rivalry, as a "trademark of Redskin-Cowboy games—bad guys against mad guys, aristocrats against working stiffs. There was an angle for everyone. The game became a perennial ratings-buster for CBS." He added that the 1972 title game was marked by "the viciously hard-hitting Redskins," and that the "lingering memory of the game [became] a constant stream of Cowboys being helped off or carried off the field."[50] Landry had to live with the same memory, carved deeper by the *Morning News* headline the next day: "NOTHING SUPER ABOUT COWBOYS." As people looked around for someone to blame, the whipping boy became Billy Parks, the Lance Rentzel clone who unlike Rentzel had limited passion for football and, as if sleepwalking, caught only one ball for 21 yards in the game. That was actually one more than Bob Hayes caught, but Parks's crime was that he seemed not particularly fazed by his performance, or the defeat, opining afterward, "We should be able to accept victory and defeat on the same level. . . . To me, losing isn't like dying. If everyone does his best, how can you be sad?"[51]

As lofty as Parks's words were, to Landry they were cause to cut loose yet another nonconformist. Parks would be bundled into the Tody Smith trade with Houston, which gave in return a first-round and a third-round pick in the 1974 draft—a throwaway deal that would end up anything but. For now, Landry could shrug and say, as if it was a blip, "The last two years we played great football in the stretch run and made it. We didn't today."[52] Allen meanwhile luxuriated, singing hymns to his Over the Hill Gang while his players rubbed the Cowboys' noses in the defeat, saying they had been glad to see Staubach as the starter. So too was Don Shula glad to see the 'Skins two weeks later in the Super Bowl. Grateful to draw a team older and more tenuous at more positions than the Cowboys were, his undefeated Dolphins won 14–7 in the LA Coliseum, though after beating Landry, Allen's team may have felt as if they had won their Super Bowl.

Allen would be the biggest challenge to a Cowboys renaissance the rest of the decade, one that Landry would be able to hold to a stand-off. But for Landry there would be other roadblocks ahead, which would reinforce the notion that patience was his greatest virtue.

Chapter 20

"A BIG TRANSMITTER TO GOD"

AS IF 1971 RESET THE CLOCK, the Cowboys' championship season seemed to wipe away the team's reputation of falling one or two steps short. Now, Tom Landry's Voltairian garden of optimism was free to flourish, without cynicism, his own lengthening tenure an organic staple, not only in the NFL but also within the wider, greener landscape of American sports and pop culture. Landry's ever-stern visage, hat propped on head, stone-carved profile silhouetted against a sun-drenched grandstand, exemplified the overarching profile of the league, which was now a sport/corporate giant, secure and even arrogant in its marketing power.

In its most widely followed market, Landry presided over a team of brilliant but flawed players and boiling discontents who had been kept submerged for the sake of the Cowboys family and the Landry way. He did so with a steady, unerring hand, as the last of the old guard relevant and capable of dominating pro football's modern incarnation. Once Richard Nixon fell, victim of the dystopian hole in his soul, Landry was left as a proxy of old-world sensibilities in a new world, a man of high respect and stability in a battered culture betrayed by its own leaders. Those who questioned his methods would be left stranded in the crowd of others bowing to him. What's more, *he* was enjoying being Tom Landry more. Following the defeat to the Redskins in the NFC Championship Game, Pat Toomay recalled, Landry had told his men that the season "had been one of his best, in fact, the most enjoyable he had experienced in a long time." Even a natural-born skeptic like Toomay felt the connectivity to him. "The players," he said, "shared his feelings."[1]

The era of Landry's vulnerability had long passed. His job security was close to that of a Banana Republic president, though Landry coached as if his very life depended on bringing home a championship-ready unit each year. Amazingly, he did. Through varying degrees of change in his lineups, the Cowboys would not suffer a throwaway season, a condition that had everything to do with Roger Staubach, whom Landry *still* hedged about starting. This, in retrospect, is one of the oddest anomalies about Landry's reign. It is tempting to make the simple case that Staubach—who soon would be given the tag "Captain America" and would wear it well—was the coach's ideal quarterback, and that their mutual devotion to the Lord Jesus Christ, public, blue-nosed humility, and unyielding fidelity to their wives and football so conjoined them. The truth was that Staubach irritated Landry far more than Don Meredith ever had, given Staubach's constant complaining and open confrontations with the coach. If anything, Craig Morton, the blithe flower child, was more perfect a tool in Landry's system because he followed the plan, stayed in the pocket, and didn't bitch and moan about starting or calling the plays. Staubach admitted later, "I was not a brilliant reader of defenses. Craig was much more in the mold of what Coach Landry wanted at quarterback."[2]

In fact, it was Landry's own intransigence that deepened his chasm with Staubach. For one thing, Landry's refusal to give his assistant coaches any real role—theirs seemingly being limited to holding the door open for him when he entered a room—directly affected Staubach's growth. There was no offensive coordinator, no one who worked personally with the players. Landry, Staubach recalled, "controlled everything, and he and I didn't have any dialogue until Saturday night when he'd call me up and go over the game plan." When asked to come to the blackboard and diagram a play, the quarterback wouldn't know where to begin. "I'd kid around and drive 'em crazy," he said. "I just knew [the plays] *instinctively*."[3]

This was why Landry, the quintessential control freak, kept waffling about his two quarterbacks. When the 1973 season began, however, Landry had promoted Jim Myers to offensive coordinator to placate Staubach, who would be under center. Still, Morton was apt to come in on a whim, a constant reminder of how fickle the coach could be. Elsewhere, Landry made room for new Cowboys generation, by necessity. Manders, Andrie, and Alworth retired, and Howley was in his last season. Needing fresh young legs, Landry allowed nine rookies onto the roster, most auspiciously Michigan State tight end Billy Joe DuPree; East Texas State's small-college All-American defensive end Harvey Martin, a native of Oak Cliff; and Rice's swift outside linebacker Rodrigo Barnes. Harvesting receivers for Staubach, he gambled on another Parks/Gent tintype, a blazing fast, blond-maned surfer-boy aptly named Golden Richards, who after flunking out at Brigham Young finished school at the University of Hawaii. In addition, Schramm pulled off a trade for Dolphins receiver Otto Stowe and signed Tulsa's Drew Pearson as an undrafted free agent for the minimum $14,500 and a $150 bonus.

Landry also needed assistant coaches, and when Dan Reeves retired as a player, he believed Landry would name him an offensive coach. But when Landry hired the great old passing guru Sid Gillman, Reeves, in a fit of pique, sat out of football for a year.[4] Ray Renfro also left the team, opening the door for the newly retired Mike Ditka, who would be of critical importance in transferring Landry's law into human, frothing terms. Ditka's function was more than that of a coach. He was an attack dog, trained to go off at a ref or a player, either his or the other team's, at a mere glance by the coach. When "Landry's eyes meet Ditka's," Dallas sportswriter Carlton Stowers once said, "it seemed like a 'sic 'em' signal because Ditka would immediately tear into a referee. The first time I saw it happen, Ditka's verbal tirade was certainly worthy of a pillar of salt. He even used a word I had never heard before. . . . The next time I saw that Landry-to-Ditka 'sic 'em' look, Ditka went nuts. He threw his clipboard at the feet of one official and stuck it in the turf like a hatchet. Tom Landry never blinked. His all-pro hit man was doing his job."[5]

As a classic Landry bobo, Ditka was almost comically obsequious, such as when at the coach's moment of glory, Ditka had used some of his best moves trying to cut the line and find a place under

Landry's behind when he was hoisted on his players' shoulders. But he would become an effective sideline and clubhouse force, his duties expanded to coaching special teams, which he could whip into a kamikaze frenzy. Indeed, the Cowboys on the field were far more overheated than the normally placid fans at Texas Stadium, which now seemed to reflect the ultra-corporate sheen of an organization that kept on growing fatter. By now the Cowboys' reach branched out across the border where the team was wildly popular, their games fed to a network of Mexican TV stations with a Spanish-speaking announcer at the mike.

On the field, meanwhile, the pieces of the corporate puzzle would shift markedly as the old-timers retired with little sentimentality, usually governed by whether Landry believed a player was no longer at peak effectiveness. Bob Lilly, long an underpaid superstar, would see his salary bumped up to $100,000 in his exit year, 1974, but only with the understanding that, because of his bad back, he wouldn't be welcomed back the next season. Lee Roy Jordan, at thirty-two, would do things in 1973 he'd never done before; in one game he had fourteen solo tackles against Philadelphia; in another he intercepted three passes in the *first quarter* against the Cincinnati Bengals. That year, he finally made All-Pro and used it as leverage to gain his own six-figure deal. But after his play deteriorated and he was done in 1976, he exited with barely a good-bye—and Schramm's lingering grudge that Jordan had held up the team.[6] Walt Garrison, the old cowboy's body beaten into pulp before he was thirty, didn't wait to be told he was through. Instead, he informed Landry that he was not coming back in 1975, with no argument.

For both Landry and Tex Schramm, there were no favors to be dispensed to the members of the "family"—just as, later, there would be none for them. Never looking back, the Cowboys rolled on, an ever-churning corporate dynasty, immune to emotion, always updating and upgrading, always generating gold ratings for the league and handsome fees from the sold-out houses they played to everywhere on the road, but not at home. Even on opening day in 1973, the year the home-team blackout was lifted by an order of the U.S. Congress as a condition for the league's signing a new eight-year, $214 million agreement with the three television networks, with no antitrust questions asked, the Cowboys drew 10,000 short of a sellout at the Irving Cheeseburger, where the artificial noise and flash seemed to temper real emotion.

Not that the well-dressed season-ticket crowds didn't demand complete satiation from the team. As Staubach once wryly cracked, "Cowboy fans love you, win or tie."[7] Or as Tom Brookshier said, "Dallas fans never feel the Cowboys have lost a game. It's always that the referees screwed 'em or the Good Lord or something. It's the toughest place to broadcast a game. Their fans don't know football, they just know something's wrong if the Cowboys aren't winning by two touchdowns."[8] Landry, a man who, like his team now, was taken much for granted in Dallas, nevertheless felt enormous pressure to win every game, and win big.

LANDRY'S COACHING style and methods did not vary while all the cosmetic changes in the NFL were taking place. Still a taskmaster, he only intensified the pain and suffering players had to endure in summer camp. While en route to Thousand Oaks to experience his first Cowboys camp, Harvey Martin read Jerry Kramer's book about his years with the Packers and wondered if anything Landry ordered could be as rough as Lombardi's old "grass drills," which had the players run in place and fall to the ground over and over again. After tasting the Cowboys' camp, Martin said, "Vince Lombardi could have passed for a sadist, but I found out Landry was worse than Lombardi."[9]

Landry knew his biggest task was countering another new strategic wave. By the early 1970s coaches had begun tinkering with an extra defensive back—something hardly new to Landry, who saw it in the Giants' Umbrella set—and four linebackers in prototypical 3–4 formations,[10] the early applications of which were to plug gaps and stop the run, though soon teams would be exploring endless permutations of blitzing. At the same time, the league's Competition Committee, a tight tribunal of ruling-class plutocrats that originally consisted of Lombardi, Paul Brown, Al Davis, and Tex Schramm, decided that the merged league needed big-play offenses. Consequently they banned cut and chop blocking of receivers off the line of scrimmage and allowed contact with them only once downfield. Landry saw the opening to dust off Red Hickey's old Shotgun formation for the offense, urged to do so not by Hickey, his top scout and ancilla for over twenty years, but by Mike Ditka. Landry renamed it the Spread and sprinkled it with additional options, not only for obvious passing downs but also for running out of it, forcing defenses to hold longer before committing.

This was typical for Landry, meshing old and new formulas for players who didn't fully comprehend but, even so, learned through repetition. He also had to navigate around the swamp of festering issues such as salary and racial unease—the latest apostate being Rodrigo Barnes, who swore his lack of advancement on the team was because he was black. Landry, he once said, "did not *want* me to make the team," a conclusion reinforced by his short stay in Dallas. There were, as well, ongoing problems with drugs and psychotic behavior.[11] In 1973, six-time Pro Bowler John Niland, who no one knew had been sexually abused as a child and carried excess emotional baggage, apparently hallucinated after taking acid and ran down the street yelling, "God, if you want me, if I'm going to die, take me."[12] It took seven cops to subdue him, yet after he came down from his high, he was on the offensive line as if nothing happened. Landry seemed to be placated by Niland's embrace of Christ, but only for another year before Niland was traded to Philadelphia. Niland, born-again or not, would often be in trouble after his career, and in 1993 he served a prison sentence for fraudulently obtaining a loan.

Landry clearly had as little sympathy for men who suffered mental breakdowns in their personal lives as he did for those who had intellectual breakdowns on the field. In 1974, ten-year veteran Dave Edwards suddenly had some frightening, deeply Freudian visions involving the coach, with whom he had never had any problems. He was so troubled that he went to Landry to unburden himself. "Coach," he said, "several nights ago I dreamed I killed you. I dreamed I pushed you off a cliff." Landry was shocked by the revelation but didn't think it was anything that required his linebacker to seek professional help. "Forget about dreaming," was Landry's curt suggestion. Instead, he told Mike Ditka to get drunk with Edwards, apparently to help him drown dreams like that out of his thoughts.[13]

✦ ✦ ✦ ✦

FOR ALL the internal madness that was a fixed Cowboys gene, by 1973 the team was likely at its most collaborative as a unit. As Pat Toomay recalled of his feelings during the 1973 season, "For the first time in years people are working together toward a common goal. Meetings are purposeful, practices are spirited, and at last I am enjoying myself."[14] Lilly noted that, as a Cowboy codger, he was still learning new pages in the playbook. "Tom's coaching isn't so hard to learn," he said. "What's hard is to believe it."[15] This was a covenant unchanged since Landry first demanded it with the Giants in 1952.

However, it rarely seemed as if Landry and Staubach were on the same page. In '73 the coach reluctantly allowed Staubach to call his own plays, then took back the responsibility late in the season, using the excuse that Staubach had too much else on his mind caring for his terminally ill mother and the injuries he'd battled during the season. He had also gotten Staubach, whose shoulder had separated in preseason, to protect himself on his mad scrambles by sliding on his knees to a stop when the defense converged on him. Staubach led the NFL with twenty-three touchdowns and a 94.6 passer rating that year. Hill ran for 1,142 yards. Hayes, Pearson, Stowe, and DuPree almost evenly divided ninety-six receptions and sixteen touchdowns. Again needing to beat the Redskins late in the season to tie them for the division lead, the Cowboys won 27–7 behind a thunderous ground game, pushing George Allen's team into the wild-card slot when each team finished with a record of 10–4.

Landry had the rare benefit of the two playoff games being at home. The Cowboys put away the Rams in the first round, 27–16, then met the Vikings in the NFC final. Staubach threw four interceptions, while the Vikings plundered for 203 rushing yards and walked off the winner, 27–10, only to be ravaged by the Dolphins in the Super Bowl. In Dallas, with the taste of a title still savory, Landry was given a mulligan for falling short, on condition that he would be able to update his aging roster for the next season. And in 1974 the replacement parts kept streaming in. The Cowboys cashed in on the delayed draft picks gleaned for Billy Parks and Tody Smith. With the first one, they took Tennessee State's menacing defensive end Ed "Too Tall"

Jones, a six-foot-nine, 270-pound mastodon who had led his college team to an undefeated season and the national black college championship in 1973. With the other pick, they landed Arizona State's All-American scrappy quarterback-punter Danny White.

Landry, too, had to deal with both another summertime players' strike, which gained the union little leverage, and the birth of a new claimant in the booming pro football market, the World Football League (WFL). In outposts stretching into Canada and Hawaii, millionaire owners looked to pilfer NFL players and landed a few novas, most to begin in 1975 when their contracts ran out, including the Dolphins' troika of Csonka, Kiick, and Warfield. But the primary targets for the WFL were the unhappily paid Cowboys, no less than seven of whom, more than from any other team, signed WFL contracts: led by Cal Hill, Rayfield Wright, Jethro Pugh, Otto Stowe, Pat Toomay, and linebacker D. D. Lewis.

Danny White was another, walking away from the Cowboys for the Memphis team after Landry said he would use the rookie merely as a punter, despite the fact that Craig Morton also signed a future contract with the outlaw league. Landry could have used White, who tore up the new league as one of its most productive quarterbacks just as, in Dallas, Morton became so irritated about being yanked in and out of the lineup that he asked for a trade. He was accommodated, sent after the sixth game of the season to the Giants for their first-round pick in 1975, though it wasn't until two years later that Morton would salvage his tattered reputation with the Denver Broncos.

All this didn't disturb Staubach, who had the starting job by default. However, his sole backup became a flaky kid with no pro experience, Abilene Christian Clint Longley, who was signed as a free agent after washing out with the Cincinnati Bengals. Longley was a self-proclaimed rattlesnake hunter and a descendent of an Old West outlaw who had been hanged for stealing a horse. He also made no bones about having little tolerance for just about everyone on the team, including Landry and Staubach. He would mostly be ignored, but his fate would be played out in one indelible moment.

Landry was still charmed. Only one of his men, Hill, would actually go to the WFL, which lasted for two seasons before folding, invalidating the future contracts inked by so many Cowboys. Yet, unlike Csonka, who commanded a huge contract with the Giants upon his return to the NFL, the would-be expatriates were hamstrung, precluded from moving to other teams by the "Rozelle Rule," which until 1993 required stiff compensation for any player who signed elsewhere as a free agent. Hill was boxed in too, having torn up his knee during his lone WFL season, reducing his market value. And so almost all came back. Schramm, licking his chops, resigned them at far below their fair market price, save for Toomay, who was shuffled off to Buffalo. Hill was granted his request to be traded to the Redskins. The rest, Wright in particular, stewed in their anger at being underpaid. One day, wrecked on several bottles of Boone's Farm Apple wine, he moaned to Mel Renfro, who knew exactly what he was going through, "Fro, they tell me I'm the best. Why won't they pay me like the best?"[16]

It was a question commonly asked among the Cowboys. And even if Landry left the dirty work of the contracts to Schramm, he considered it a personal betrayal when players chose to leave the team on their own, never mind that he would cashier those he soured on without as much as a good-bye. Thus, he had come to be thought of as a co-conspirator in the penury of the front office. Indeed, while few players cared much about what Schramm thought of them, the quiet wrath of Landry was really the price one had to pay for making the almighty dollar more important than playing for the Dallas Cowboys.

TOM LANDRY, no longer the dashing, wavy-haired campus hero, had aged with grace, though when he turned fifty on September 11, 1974, he looked every bit of it. He was also every bit a football monarch, subject to profound sycophancy and analysis. After a few more years of cogitation, Dandy Don Meredith, who had jumped in 1974 from the booth on *Monday Night Football* to an announcing/acting gig with NBC (only to return to his signature role in 1978), still spoke of Landry harshly, as "an unemotional man . . . so well organized that he really has no need to communicate. I think I've matured a lot over the past three years but it was impossible to mature in that regimented atmosphere. They told me I was a professional and then insulted my intelligence with ridiculous rules that implied I didn't know how to take care of myself."[17]

Others, from a distance, went deeper. Landry's image in the national discourse was fairly uncomplicated at an earlier time. Back in 1966, he had been aggrandized with a piffle profile in the *Saturday Evening Post* that was titled "The Thinking Man's Cowboy," wherein he was called "pro football's coaching genius" who had "built a contender out of castoffs, three basketball stars, a sprinter, and a hippy quarterback."[18] For those just discovering the Landry persona in the culture of the 1970s, and those who still revered it, he was the strongest link to the game's colloquial past. In 1974, the urbane *New Yorker* freely associated him with the mythical college coaches of yore and pro football giants like Halas and Brown. Landry, wrote the author, had a "brooding intensity [that] has always suggested a portrait Rembrandt might have done."[19] Another writer intending a compliment, would posit that Landry was a "coaching Bolshevik," in the visionary rather than the political sense.[20] When Landry read *that* one, he knew he had reached an entirely different level of public consciousness, one that he could in no way understand.

At the same time, a contra chorale was growing too. The first chord struck when *North Dallas Forty* came out blaring in the fall of 1973. Pete Gent's madcap allegory of a group of lovable rogues, based on thinly veiled Cowboys hieroglyphs, posed an immediate problem for an organization that had been carefully crafted as a hypoallergenic, All-American fable. Not for nothing did the Cowboys sell more team-related merchandise and earn more licensing fees than any other team in sports. Indeed, when Gent began to write his roman à clef, Dandy Don Meredith, his own neuroses and anti-heroic tendencies aside, wasn't eager to be traced to the quarterback character. "I don't want it to be me," he told Gent, who laughed and replied, "Well, it is you."[21]

The book's frenzied send-up of all things pious and politically correct was a full frontal attack on Landry's canonized, methodized structures and strictures that bred rebellion. Tex Schramm, his persona turned into a Praetorian buffoon in the movie by a superbly scaly Dabney Coleman, blasted the book as "a total lie" and explained, "What has happened is one person, who in my opinion has a sick approach to life, has indicted the whole NFL and the Dallas Cowboy organization. . . I consider the book offensive and malicious."[22] The Dallas sportswriters resented it for their own reasons. Having constructed and perpetuated the myths of Landry and the team, many chose to slime Gent, whom they had never understood anyway. Others—Frank Luksa, to his dying day—avoided it. "You're asking the wrong person about the book, 'cause I never did read it," he said decades after the book's release. "I thought Pete Gent was paranoid. He smoked so much weed he thought people were chasing him. There have been other books written about the Cowboys and I read them because I knew the intent wasn't to crap all over Landry."[23]

Landry, for his part, had nothing to say about it, as if unworthy of his attention. To be sure, the use of drugs, needles, or other forms of self-destruction as insulation from the pain and mandatory participation on game days was something Landry never recognized as being unique to the Cowboys, or even a sustainable fact. He could plausibly play dumb about or seem intentionally alienated from popular culture. He certainly would not have admitted to having the same interior vulnerabilities as the character modeled on him, coach B. A. Strother, whom Gent portrayed not so much as a bloodless ogre as a football man buried under the weight of a team grown beyond his ability to control. As the Gent character tells him in the story, "We're not the team—*they* are," meaning the suits upstairs. "We're just the equipment. They depreciate us, write us off."

Gent would admit that he was a most unsympathetic truth-teller. When he came back to Dallas to promote the book, "I got so fucked up . . . and so drunk and so doped up, that when I got to the stadium, I just hallucinated. I kept seeing Texas Stadium as a big transmitter to God." While in town, he was busted for public drunkenness and had to sweat out a court psychiatric hearing before he was let go. "I had turned out," Gent said, "to be exactly what Tom Landry said I would be: someone who should never be let out on his own."[24]

A YEAR after Gent broke the seal on Cowboys retro-literature and revision, Pat Toomay came out with a first-rate book of *non-*

fiction about the Landry Cowboys, an ingratiating tell-all called *The Crunch*, which he says he wrote to expose the "image reality contradiction" of pro football. Like Gent's work, it too became a best-seller and delineated two essentials of being a Cowboy. One, Landry's obsession to keep his players' heads free of long hair, and, two, this unspoken directive: "Pills: Take three yellow ones and four blue ones at all meals. *Duh*."[25] Toomay had left Dallas with the same ambivalence as Gent, cursing the environment of win-at-all-costs but craving Landry's blessing. As with Gent, it wasn't the coach who was evil; it was the town and the front office. Dallas, he said, is "the home of the anti-Christ. There's really no reason for this city to be here, so people end up living in their imagination. This was the perfect seed bed for what Schramm was trying to do."[26]

In this way, Schramm was always the ground wire for Landry, sucking up the static electricity around both. It was no doubt one reason why Landry was glad he had Tex around, even when they butted heads. Tex was the bad cop; Landry, on the other hand, was the fine, upstanding man who bred what Toomay called a "psychological dependence" that even the smartest players were helpless to resist. This could be seen, so the theory went, in the drafting done by Landry and Schramm, which often targeted young men from torn families who needed sanctuary and salvation. Linebacker D. D. Lewis, who soldiered under Landry for thirteen years and was the team's co-captain in 1977 and 1978, once said, "My personal theory was that the Cowboys gave you all those psychological tests before they drafted you because they wanted guys with a fear of abandonment. They wanted guys smart enough to play Tom's system but too scared to question it or ask for more money when the team won."[27]

Similarly, Cliff Harris, a ten-year man and six-time All-Pro, felt that Landry could be "a cold-blooded son of a gun" and that his system "worked on insecurity. I never knew whether I was going to be back, even in my All-Pro years."[28]

Says Mel Renfro, "You know, I never thought about it but a lot of our guys did have tough childhoods, had daddy problems, especially the black guys. Maybe they *were* looking for a father figure. That's really what Tom was for many of us. All of us saw in him something we wished we could be. Something we knew we'd never be. Some guys would never have admitted that, and that's why they needed to get over on him, to prove to themselves that they didn't need to be like Tom Landry. But you know what? Those were the guys who came to respect Tom the most later on down the road."[29]

Like many other undercurrents on his own team, Landry never quite made this connection himself—nor how much some players were scarred further when they didn't find in him what they needed. Calvin Hill, who was not one of those needy young men from broken homes reaching out for a paternal hand, and who believed that Gent had characterized Landry as "tougher than he was," said he once told Landry, "A lot of the players look at you as a father." However, Hill related, "Tom minimized it. . . . I don't think Tom ever understood how much they depended on him."[30] To that, Tom Landry Jr. says with a wry grin, "I think it's fair to say Dad loved his players but he had only one son, and one was enough."[31]

AS AMERICA moved further from the culture that bred him, Tom Landry cast an even more imposing shadow, such was the massive scale of his presence and already storied history. Unlike most coaches, he didn't *need* to win, which was helpful since he would have another wave of big-game flameouts. In a Cowboys universe in which the hole in their stadium roof beckoned to the stars, upholding the team's honed and polished image was Landry's closed roof against the intrusion of outside societal pollutants, though in reality they surely streamed in. The further seepage of drugs into locker rooms was fresh proof that the Cowboys were no more immune than anyone else to the burgeoning by-products of a more reckless and on-the-edge culture.

Things were surely getting rough out there. Watergate and the resignation of Richard Nixon in August 1974 had removed the last assumptions of a postwar America led by flesh-and-blood heroes and moral men—a gene pool that had been thinned to perhaps one man, the one in the hat. As the walls came tumbling down on society, creating a new social praxis codified by *Roe v. Wade* in 1973, the Dallas Cowboys' entrenched image, indivisible from Landry's, had already been basted in new-age juices, what with the computers, the theme-park stadium, and the half-nekked cheerleaders. And so Cowboys Inc. moved onward and upward. The 1974 season, as it turned out, would be the single rebuilding year Landry needed, and the only one for which he likely would have been pardoned. If any team seemed resistant to youthful turnover, it was the Cowboys. There was a reason why Landry rarely started rookies. As Harvey Martin recalled, "Like everyone else, I had trouble learning the very complicated Flex defense. It's been said that by the time you truly understand the Flex, you're too old to play."[32] Even so, freely running in green players, Landry managed an 8–6 record, finishing in the top ten in offense and defense.

The highlight of the season was the Thanksgiving Day match with the Redskins at Texas Stadium, which became the stuff of madcap myth. George Allen needed a win to clinch the division, and his team led 16–3 with ten minutes to go in the third quarter, with Duane Thomas settling a score with Landry by scoring a touchdown for Allen. Worse, Staubach was knocked out of the game. His backup, Clint Longley, hadn't played a down all season, stewing in his hatred of Landry for not playing him. Now, in the huddle, as Walt Garrison shouted out assignments, the kid told the veteran, "Shut the fuck up."[33] He then directed a smart drive, hitting DuPree with a 35-yard touchdown pass. Minutes later Garrison capped another drive, running the ball in from the 1 for a 17–16 Dallas lead. For once Texas Stadium was alive and crackling, a fire lit by the baby-faced rattlesnake hunter. The fire seemed to abate when Thomas scored his second touchdown in the fourth quarter, after a late Cowboys fumble. But Longley got the ball back again with 1:45 left.

Landry sent in a pass play for Drew Pearson deep down the middle, but Pearson said a better play was for him to fake inside and run a sideline pattern, and Longley went against the coach. He wound up and lofted the ball to Pearson, who grabbed it on the 4 and ran in to the end zone, a lightning bolt 50-yard touchdown play, sealing an inconceivable 24–23 win and setting off a postgame saturnalia that had never been seen before nor would be seen again in that stadium. Glaze-eyed, Landry could only say there was "no way" he thought that pass could have been successful. Blaine Nye found the wisest context. Longley's performance, he said, was "a triumph of the uncluttered mind."[34] The sheer un-Landry-ness of the victory turned Longley into a fictional caped crusader in Dallas, and no one believed the hype more than him.

THE COWBOYS, at 8–6, missed the playoffs by two games in '74, the first time in a decade Landry was frozen out. Yet the pluses were many, perhaps the biggest being the elusive, pipe cleaner–legged Drew Pearson. Catching sixty-two passes, with a 17.5-yard average, he was voted to the All-Pro first team. He had played every game with his gut in an uproar, so wound up that he developed a bleeding ulcer and constant nausea. Thomas Henderson, who played with him later, recalled a not-atypical moment: "I saw him talking to Landry one time during a game and the coach jumped back. Landry didn't move that fast. Here was this corn and pancakes coming through Drew's face mask."[35] Golden Richards had an even higher average per catch, rendering the aging Bob Hayes obsolete. Not thrown to very often, the once-elite Hayes caught only nine passes and would become another sacrifice to the altar of impersonal attrition.

Bullet Bob had been the good soldier for years despite many grievances, the biggest being, as he would say, that racism "ran through the whole organization." He remembered team executives' calling him "Supernigger" behind his back and white players' openly referring to the blacks' Afros as "Nigger hairdos."[36] But loyalty was often a one-way street for Landry, and when Hayes played out his option in '74, Landry kept him on the bench much of the season.[37] Then, just before training camp in 1975, Hayes was traded to the 49ers for a third-round draft pick, and he learned of it when, not Landry but Gil Brandt—"a glorified scout," as Hayes made him[38]—called to tell him. By then, Hayes had a long addiction to Quaaludes, which were readily available from the Cowboys team doctors[39] and had fringe benefits. As he noted, "Nothing would make a woman give it up quicker than a Lude." After his splendid career ended in 1978, he was arrested and charged with selling Quaaludes and cocaine to an undercover cop. He pleaded guilty but despite Cowboys notables, including Roger Staubach, Jethro Pugh, Pettis Norman, Drew Pearson, Tex Schramm, and Tom Landry, testifying as character witnesses, he was sentenced to five years in jail and seven years' probation.

Hayes would claim that during his stay in prison, "redneck" inmates told him, "We hate you, nigger" and that when Mike Ditka came to the prison to visit him, he had told them Hayes "didn't like whites."[40] When he got out, with no job, and his marriage over, he was hired briefly by Staubach to manage some of his real estate holdings, but by the mid-1980s Hayes was adrift and an alcoholic, in and out of rehab treatment paid for by Staubach, and avoided by old friends. "You have to believe me," he would say, "I am not a drug dealer."[41] During the off-seasons in Dallas, he frequently hung around the Cowboys' offices, hoping for just a few minutes with the coach from whom he needed benefaction. When he wrote his auto- biography, his last paragraph read, "Today Tom Landry and I have a great relationship" and "I still bleed Cowboy silver and blue. . . . I was a Dallas Cowboy yesterday, I'm one today, and I will be one tomorrow."[42]

Hayes vowed that if he was elected to the Hall of Fame, "I'll have to have someone stand with me and introduce me . . . and I will be proud if it's Tom Landry."[43] It didn't quite happen that way. Hayes was kept from his rightful place in the Hall of Fame for the rest of his life. In 2002, after battling prostate cancer and liver problems, he died of kidney failure at age fifty-nine. Two years later, he finally won induction. Landry had died four years before, and at the ceremony in Canton, a letter was read, purportedly written by Hayes before his death, in which he thanked "the Dallas Cowboys organization" he had once reviled. However, Hayes's family claimed the letter was a fake, fabricated to gauze over his hatred of the front office. It was a parable of Landry's Cowboys that fame could be so incomplete for even the most popular and brilliant of them. And that not even in death could Bob Hayes rest easy.[44]

THE SUBJECT of mortality, which had first entered Tom Landry's life when his brother perished over the North Atlantic, touched him again on May 12, 1975, when his mother died at the age of seventy- six. Ruth Coffman Landry, the woman who had influenced his own personality and temperament more than any other human, had lived and died peacefully in the uncomplicated, unadorned grotto of Mission, Texas. When Tom went back there to grieve with Ray Landry and his brother and sister, he could see that his father would not last long without her. Ray had suffered a stroke and was unable to rise from his bed or chair without help.

If Tom hadn't realized it yet, he knew then that life was cruelly tenuous, and that the alliterative order of priorities he so blithely preached—faith, family, and football—could not keep at bay the frailties of each. As for the last, the responsibilities of coaching men he understood little seemed to be more of a routine than an imperative from God. In some ways, it was even an escape from cold, hard reality. All he could hope to obtain from it now was the sanctity that came with the vindication of his genius. As he noted with wonder in his memoirs, "At thirty-five years of age, I'd been the youngest head coach in football. . . . When Paul Brown retired [in 1976] I became the dean of NFL coaches, starting my seventeenth season."[45]

It would behoove him, he reasoned, not to look too far into the future. Thus, when his eleven-year deal with Murchison ran out at the end of the 1974 season, he and the aging oilman struck an informal arrangement. Landry would continue on, his salary bumped up to around $400,000—still a bargain among the upper crust of NFL head coaches—but nothing was drawn up or signed; he would work on a handshake deal, year to year, with no more said. Now, too, Landry finally decided the time was right to exercise his ownership option, buying at the 1959 price 6 percent of Cowboys stock—the same as Schramm's interest. And when Murchison later asked Tex to sell his shares back, at a small profit, he did so. Not by surprise, Landry followed the same course.

"I was privy to the deal, I was handling it for Dad," says Tom Landry Jr. "Clint wanted him to sell the stock back because at the time Clint was beginning to have financial troubles and needed every cent he could get to pay his creditors. And Dad was okay with that. He didn't want to be a stockholder, he wanted job security and I'm sure there were assurances given. So he sold back his 6 percent at a very small profit. Today that 6 percent would be worth something like $20 million."

Both Landry and Schramm had the sort of relationship with Murchison that led them to believe, stock or not, they were set for life as Cowboys executives and thereafter as team elders. But that wasn't how pro football worked. As they would eventually learn, living as Cowboys would not necessarily mean they would die as Cowboys.

LANDRY TOOK his younger and higher-kicking team into the 1975 season, dropping into the engine more new parts—the most propitious and portentous being Thomas Henderson, a remarkably gifted outside linebacker with similarities to Duane Thomas. Henderson, too, was a native Texan, born in Austin to an indigent teenage mother and a father he didn't know. After he graduated from high school, he enlisted in the Air Force but changed his mind and played at the obscure, all-black Langston University in Oklahoma, where he was called "Wild Man" for the complete abandon of his game. He won small-college All-American honors twice and wowed the pro scouts, none more than Gil Brandt, who had never seen a better athlete than the six-foot-two, 220-pound Henderson. But, also like Thomas, NFL teams were chary of him for the old familiar "personality" reasons.

Always up for a good gamble, Schramm, who had two first-round picks, used one on Maryland's six-foot-four, 260-pound All-Pro defensive tackle/end Randy White, and the other on Henderson. But Landry took a very different approach with the two young studs. As Henderson recalled, "I woke up the next morning and splashed all over the sports section was a picture of Tom Landry shaking hands with . . . Randy White. I wasn't real pleased. He didn't have the time of day for me . . . but he was more than pleased to be making the papers with his big old hunk of a white boy." He took it up on himself to walk up to the coach and shake his hand. "You know," a chilly Landry told him, "we took a chance on you. . . . I hope it works out." Henderson, too, was miffed about his contract, a five-year deal with a remarkably paltry $25,000 first-year salary, embellished with a $60,000 bonus and incentives that could bump it up to $235,000. Years later he would note that White had gotten a six-figure bonus, and lower draftees, who happened to be white, pocketed higher salaries. While he felt like "a rich man" when he signed, in reality he concluded the Cowboys "ripped me off and made me like it."[46]

Henderson even as a rookie was unimpressed with the Cowboys' way, chafed by not only Landry but most everyone else. Mike Ditka, he said, was "a maniac . . . the Tasmanian Devil of NFL coaches" who subjected players to "fear and humiliation" for any mistake, calling ones who erred "cowardly shits." Sometimes he would lay in wait in the locker room and browbeat someone, "You're getting cut tomorrow. . . . Pack your shit, man," though it was merely a scare tactic. Said Henderson, "He couldn't humiliate you more, and he had your life in his hands. Walk out that door and your career was over."[47]

Yet Henderson said he had a far better relationship with Ditka, who at least *engaged* him and threw kind words his way, than with Landry. The latter's style, by contrast, was pure Big Brother. As Henderson put him in a historical perspective years later, "Landry was this dictator, this Castro, this Khrushchev, this Saddam Hussein, this Ayatollah. You know, you didn't talk back. It was religious. It was communism . . . people marched around like they were in the Red Army."[48] When the players were on the field carrying out his orders, "it wasn't as if real people were performing it . . . we could have been just big strong marionettes. There was nothing approachable about the man, you just didn't want to talk to him about anything. He seemed so emotionless, so untouchable, so far from the rest of us."

Henderson in college played what he called a "5-2, Sic 'em," a read-and-go system that was the antithesis of the Cowboys' hold-your-ground Flex. He, like every other Cowboy, was flummoxed by Landry's "Britannica playbook," as he called it.[49] He admitted, "I didn't have a clue"[50] what it all meant, and wondered what sort of obsessive-compulsive mind it took to create such a volume, writing in his 1987 autobiography,

> Did people really go to these lengths to win a football game? Tom Landry did. He went to that trouble and more: tendencies, which plays they had to run on first and ten, first and twenty, second and six, second and seven, second and eight . . . and what time was on the clock when these plays were run. . . . There were about a hundred pages of plays, then a hundred pages of tendencies. Like it would say, "On second and five, 40 percent of the time in a Brown formation on the right hash mark, they ran Slant 34." Well I'll be damned. Do they really?[51]

Sizing up Landry, a man Henderson recalled as "beyond thorough and into the world of the unconscious," he was more fascinated than fearful. While others cowered before Landry, he all but laughed at him. On his first day at camp he checked into the dorm stocked with a couple of hits of reefer and acid.[52] Stoned, he frequently ambled to practices late.[53] He incurred a profusion of $50 fines. Handsome, with an infectious toothy smile, he had already taken to calling himself "Hollywood" and sold that image to a press always eager for another mouthy apostate on the Cowboys. Nor did he worry about the consequences. "I knew they wouldn't cut me, because I was a No. 1 draft choice, so I didn't work," he said. "I didn't care. I couldn't count the number of times I fell asleep in meetings."[54]

Henderson had no indisposition to airily call Landry "Tom," a privilege normally allowed to the old-timers, and even then with trepidation. In his first practice, Henderson hauled off on Staubach, a no-no. Landry nearly fainted, yelling into his bullhorn, "You don't hit Roger Staubach! You don't hit the quarterback!"[55] Harvey Martin once said that Henderson "unquestionably ranks as the most talented linebacker ever to play the game, and also the most troubled."[56] And for the time being, a wary Landry treated him gingerly, playing him in spots, putting him in competition with Mike Hegman, another gifted and hungry linebacker who had played with Too Tall Jones at Tennessee State and then was drafted in the seventh round in 1975.

Landry also used Henderson on special teams, even calling a few reverses for him on kickoff returns. One of these produced a thrilling 97-yard touchdown, which Henderson punctuated with a flourish, leaping and slam-dunking the ball, basketball style, over the goal post, adding his own stamp to this seminal form of football as performance art. Nothing about Henderson was mundane, dull, or contrite. For all of Landry's primordial modes of control, Henderson said, "I was walking around going, 'What the fuck are you all doing around here? Lighten the fuck up. Fuck him. He's just a fucking coach.'"[57] And every minute Henderson wore the blue lone star, the coach would grimace and try to reconcile himself to the fact that he needed men like Thomas Henderson and Duane Thomas to win the big ones.

✦ ✦ ✦ ✦

STAUBACH, WHO took hellacious hits game in and game out, remained healthy most of the 1975 season, which became notable for the running game that came out of nowhere in the absence of Cal Hill. Three years earlier, Landry had plugged in his second-round draft choice from Houston, Robert Newhouse. At five foot nine, 200 pounds with thick, sawed-off legs, he was a smaller reincarnation of Tank Younger, a bowling ball of a fullback who could run hard into the line or swerve in a higher gear to run around the end. Landry and Schramm also struck gold by plucking from the waiver list Preston Pearson, a graceful zephyr of a halfback who'd been let go by Chuck Noll despite being the first backup to Franco Harris and Rocky Bleier on the Steelers' 1974 championship team. Though Pearson was thirty, Landry could not help but take into account that he had matriculated under Don Shula and Noll, his study skills being exemplary and his canniness a huge asset.

Pearson and Newhouse were an odd couple, but they combined for over 1,400 yards in rushing that season, and 500 more in receiving. Pearson was a killer on key third-down situations when he would float out into the shallow zones and be open for a pass when the receivers were bottled up. Other new arrivals in the draft found places in the starting lineup, including linebacker Bob Breunig, defensive back Randy Hughes, and offensive tackle Pat Donovan. From the start, the season breezed along. The Cowboys burst from the gate, winning their first four games before hitting a snag and falling to 5–3. They then went on another streak, winning five of the last seven to finish at 10–4 and claim a playoff spot as a wild card.

They were once again a remarkably balanced unit—ranked No. 4 in passing, No. 5 in rushing, No. 8 in points, No. 9 in defense, No. 3 against the run—though few believed they would go far under the burden of having to play each playoff game on the road. The first came in Minnesota on December 28, for another match with the Vikings on a field frozen over by a blustery twenty-five-degree temperature. The Vikings, having won their last ten games to go 12–2, were prohibitive favorites. The redoubtable Fran Tarkenton was a first-team All-Pro that season and the league's MVP, his mission being to get back to the Super Bowl after being embarrassed the previous year when the Steelers intercepted him thrice, ran for 249 yards, and held the Vikings' runners to a record-low *17* yards of rushing. Through three quarters of the first playoff game, Landry held a 10–7 lead. But Tarkenton took the ball with five minutes left and led a long drive that ended with a 1-yard touchdown run by Brent McClanahan. Now trailing 14–10 with less than two minutes to go, the Cowboys faced a fourth and sixteen on their own 25.

Steaming that it had come to this, Landry, who rarely intruded on Staubach when he was in a late-game comeback mode, again left him in charge. And Staubach, after mainly handing the ball off all game, had to switch to passing mode. He called a sideline pass to Drew Pearson, who had been lobbying Landry to call some long passes to him but had been thrown only one, which went incomplete. "I was upset—pissed off, really," Pearson recalled. "I spent the second half loud-talking on the sideline so Coach Landry would hear me. He heard but he wasn't listening."[58] Now freed, Pearson tore off the line of scrimmage, covered by cornerback Nate Wright. As the pass screamed toward him, Pearson leaped and caught it as Wright shoved him out of bounds at the 50. It was first down, with forty-four seconds left. As the Cowboys huddled, Pearson got Staubach's ear. "I can beat Wright deep, but give me a chance to catch my breath," he said.[59]

Staubach nodded. He threw one incomplete pass, then called out, "Streak Route." It was a no-frills play, just a foot race between Pearson and Wright down the same sideline. Working from the Shotgun, Staubach pump-faked to freeze safety Paul Krause, then came under heavy pressure and had to hurry his pass, which didn't have much juice. Pearson, slowing down to come back for it, ran into Wright, who fell to the ground. Pearson somehow clamped the ball to his hip, pinning it in place with his right forearm, and backed into the end zone as a small round object came rolling at his feet. It looked like it could have been a penalty flag, something most everyone expected for interference on Pearson or Wright, but it was actually an orange thrown from the stands.

Staubach, who was on his back from the rush, never saw any of it. Hearing the crowd, he thought, "Oh my God, maybe Drew caught the ball."[60]

Pearson gleefully heaved the ball into the stands then was mobbed by ecstatic teammates as the bundled crowd in Metropolitan Stadium sat in stunned silence. Viking players stomped around and argued with the officials—one of whom, back judge Armen Terzian, lay unconscious on the field, his forehead split open by a bottle of Seagram's also thrown from the stands. No one quite knew whether there should be a celebration, a show of outrage, or concern that an official might die on the field. Nothing happened until Terzian was revived and taken off the field, whereupon the Vikings resumed arguing, with a real flag thrown when Alan Page was hit with an unsportsmanlike conduct penalty. At the gun, the delirious Cowboys sprinted off the field, 17–14 winners, pelted with more garbage and shielding team executives from harm.

Staubach, who had put to bed another heavy-panting comeback, knew he'd had help. Before the fateful pass, said the good Catholic son, summoning up his youthful indoctrination at the St. John the Evangelist Catholic elementary school in Cincinnati, "I closed my eyes and said a Hail Mary"[61]—instantly coining new football patois for "miracle" passes that dragged victory from the well of defeat; in Cowboys lore, it would henceforth and forever known as "The Hail Mary Game." Pearson, a Baptist, had never heard of the term, but decades later he acquired trademark rights to use it on caps and shirts. Staubach wouldn't need to wear it on his sleeve to be constantly surrounded by the memory.

Tarkenton, on the other hand, walked in the darkness of the damned. In the locker room he learned his father had died of a heart attack while watching the game on TV. The day quantified the chasm between he and Staubach. Neither deserved beatification, but Staubach again found his way out of the darkness, even if by accident. To Landry, it was something on the order of providence.

THE COWBOYS' wild-card tour took them next to LA for the NFC Championship Game against the 12–2 Rams, who had the league's stiffest defense, allowing just under 10 points a game. There were five All-Pros on that side of the ball alone: Merlin Olsen, Jack Youngblood, and Fred Dryer, along with linebackers Jack Reynolds and Isiah Roberston. Three more were on offense, running back Lawrence McCutcheon, receiver Harold Jackson, and guard Tom Mack. The only Pro Bowlers on the Cowboys were Staubach and Cliff Harris. But the Rams almost always lost their edge in the playoffs, and it took only minutes after Landry led his men into the gaping basin of the Coliseum for it to happen again. Staubach hit Preston Pearson out of the backfield for an early 18-yard score, and just kept milking the same cow, hitting Pearson for *three* touchdowns, and Golden Richards for another, all in the first two quarters.

It was 21–0 at the half, 34–0 after three quarters, and 37–7 at the end, the Rams having been left for dead, trampled for 441 yards. Suddenly the rebuilding team that got into the dance as a wild card seemed a juggernaut, running on all cylinders. Next stop: Landry's third Super Bowl, on January 18 at the Orange Bowl—a field that had been bad luck for him before. Worse, he had the unenviable task of beating Noll's champion Steelers, at the peak of the Steelers' 1970s dynasty. They'd won eleven in a row during the season, finishing 12–2, and had survived a fumble-filled back-alley fight with the Oakland Raiders in the AFC final, winning 16–10. Over the season they had rushed for more yards than anyone except O. J. Simpson's Buffalo Bills. The defense had five All-Pros, and Mel Blount, the league's premier cornerback, intercepted eleven passes and was named Defensive Player of the Year.

The Steelers, as with many teams, had a hardy contempt for the Cowboys. Jack Lambert, the meanest cuss in football, the gap between two front teeth making him look like a deranged walrus, said of Landry's men before the game, "They mess up your head too much. If they beat you, you feel like you've been tricked instead of whipped. I hate teams like that." It didn't take much to make Lambert mad. When he learned that the Cowboys were being housed at a beachfront hotel while the Steelers stayed downtown, he said, "I hope the sharks eat Staubach."[62] Harvey Martin once called the Steel Curtain front four "a violent, semicrazed wrecking crew." As it happened, defensive end Dwight "Mad Dog" White had been Martin's roommate in college, and was a Dallas native, who, Martin said, "would spit in an opponent's face, slug him, knee him." Tackle Ernie Holmes, he said, was "a violent crazy man," a "monster" with "a passion to maim." Mean Joe Greene, the leader of the pack, "possessed nearly supernatural strength."[63]

The Steelers came in as a 7-point favorite, but Landry had his own weapons and momentum: he had beaten the Steelers the last seven times they met. His men were sky high for the encounter, not to mention contented, Landry having allowed the married men to spend the night before the game not at a sequestered location but with their wives at the hotel. Landry's playbook was no secret; he had to find a way to stop Franco Harris and Rocky Bleier from chewing up yardage and to disrupt Terry Bradshaw's pinpoint passing. If it was a tight, low-scoring game, Staubach might be the difference. The weather was crisp and cool, and so were the Cowboys that Sunday in Miami. They struck first, on the opening kickoff, when Landry didn't wait to get funky. Preston Pearson fielded the kick and, according to plan, handed the ball off to Thomas Henderson, who doubled back to meet him then carried it 48 yards. Staubach minutes later found Drew Pearson with a 29-yard touchdown lob. For most of the opening frame, wrote Dan Jenkins, "Dallas had done everything but cause the Orange Bowl floats to disapper."[64]

The Cowboys were ornery too. When the Steelers' kicker Roy Gerela hooked a field goal, Cliff Harris patted him on the helmet, prompting the scabrous middle linebacker Jack Lambert to pick up Harris and body-slam him to the ground. Harris also ragged Lynn Swann, who had been doubtful for the game after sustaining a mild concussion in the Oakland contest. After one pass to him went awry, Harris trash-talked, "You're lucky you didn't come back on that ball because I'm gonna take a shot at you. You better watch your head."[65] Swann clearly didn't pay heed. He played that day as if his feet hardly touched the ground. Bradshaw was able to put important points on the board late in the first quarter by finding him with a 32-yard pass, setting up the tying score. They also connected in the second quarter on a 53-yard pass Bradshaw launched from his own end zone, with Swann—"climbing into the air like the boy in the Indian rope trick," wrote Jenkins[66]—tapping the ball in the air, then nestling it in his fingertips as he tumbled to the turf, his legs tangled with Mark Washington's arms beneath him.

But while this play would be the most enduring memory of the game, making the cover of *Sports Illustrated*, it was the Cowboys who clung to a 10–7 lead entering the fourth quarter, even though the Steel Curtain had fairly savaged their line and Staubach. Now, however, things began to come apart. A Cowboys punt was blocked in the end zone for a safety. Staubach was intercepted deep in the Steelers' territory, killing a key drive. Two field goals later, Pittsburgh led, 15–10. Still, if the Cowboys' defense could hold the Steelers to four downs with just over three minutes left, Staubach would have another shot. It did hold on the first two plays. Then, on third and four at the Steelers' 36, Bradshaw dropped back in the face of a blizzard blitz, stepped up to escape D. D. Lewis, and fired a long missile down the middle for Swann—a split-second before Harris cracked Bradshaw across the face mask, nearly knocking him out cold. "I don't know how I got the ball off," Bradshaw said later. "I was hearing bells or something on the ground." As the pass traveled 70 yards in the air, Washington fell behind by a step and Swann didn't need to break stride to cuddle it in his hands. Washington, making a futile leap at him, clutched at Swann's shoulder pad and fell away, able only to watch the end of a 64-yard touchdown.

It was 21–10, but Staubach still wasn't through. It had been a bad day for him, with two interceptions and a fumble. He also was sacked seven times, a Super Bowl record. But this was his time of game, and here he came, capping a lightning-quick drive with a 34-yard touchdown strike to scrub receiver Percy Howard to make the score 21–17. Then, with 1:22 left, Staubach got the ball *again*, at midfield, with no time-outs, and one Hail Mary left. He gave it a go, lofting a long spiral roughly aimed for Howard in the end zone, but it was picked off by safety Glen Edwards to end a game that left everyone exhausted, and the Cowboys gracious losers. Swann, the game's MVP with a then-record 161 receiving yards, was given his due, Washington readily admitting that "Swann just beat me one time too many." Staubach looked for silver linings. "We had our chances," he said. "Overall, Pittsburgh is the best, but it was a good season."[67]

By now, most everything the Cowboys did was an echo of their checkered past. Just as after the two epic defeats to Vince Lombardi, players remonstrated about bum luck and being hosed by the referees, who were out to "get" the blackguards from Dallas, even if it was the Steelers who wore the black hats. In fact, Landry had ordered his men not to take the bait and lose their cool by paying the Steelers back for their dirty hits, and said that they couldn't win a purely physical battle. That was a command that not everyone could obey, and some would even blame it for the loss. An enduring postscript of the game was that the Steelers hadn't been flagged for a single penalty, not even Lambert's body slam of Harris and numerous other cheap shots. More than a few Cowboys ventured that the refs had been intimidated by the more psychopathic Steelers, though Harvey Martin merely left it that the refs "called a bad game"[68] and that with so much fierce hitting they "decided not to call *anything*." Indeed, the Cowboys were whistled for only two penalties.

Landry's measured, anodyne reactions, according to script, reassured everyone that any given season was a prelude to the next, when it would all end differently. Indeed, having brandished their bona fides as the vehicle of his genius, the Cowboys were more intriguing than ever, so enticing and encompassing an attraction that even Landry's biggest critic, and biggest mistake, wanted back in.

Chapter 21

THE LAST HAPPY ENDING

B Y 1976, DUANE THOMAS WAS hanging on by his finger-nails in the NFL. George Allen had given up a lot for Thomas in 1973, a number-one and number-two draft pick, and paid him well, around $65,000 a year for two years, plus incentives and a bonus. Allen's rationale was that because Thomas knew Landry's playbook, "Now we can beat Dallas."[1] Thomas, recalling later that "George was my type of guy," got along with Allen, and he worked hard.[2] He even spoke up, sometimes giving fiery pep talks. And yet, save for a few high points, he was stuck on the depth chart behind Larry Brown and Charley Harraway and never flourished. When his contract ran out, the team asked him to take a 15 percent pay cut. He refused, and before he could be released, he took a better deal, jumping to the WFL's Hawaii franchise, which paid him $25,000 plus $5,000 a game, to replace Calvin Hill, who had blown out his knee. However, he never got into playing in the Mickey Mouse league and soon had the team's owner complaining, "I thought I was getting a great player who wouldn't talk. Now he talks a lot but doesn't play."[3]

Whether he stuck or not became moot when the league folded before the season had finished, and now Thomas's new objective was to get back to the Cowboys, as if that could expunge his still-lingering demons—the demons he believed were caused by Landry. Pettis Norman, whose career had ended with a knee injury in 1973, befriended

Thomas and acted as his representative, Jim Brown apparently having tired of that role.

Duane said, "I want to finish my career in Dallas." I said, "Duane, it's not so easy." Once Landry cut you loose, you were dead to him. I told him, "You have to make up for all the stuff you messed up down there." He'd need to come in on a tryout, not expect a big salary, behave better. He said, "I'll do whatever Tom wants me to do. I know I messed up."

The first thing I did was, I called Tex and explained the whole thing. Tex always was thinking of the PR value. He liked the idea. He said, "It's okay with me, but it's Tom's call." So then I got on the phone with Tom, and he was not comfortable with it. He said, "Pettis, you know how much I like you, I appreciate the call, but I don't know whether we can go back like that." Well, the only thing I had left was that it was close to Christmas. "Tom," I said, "one of the things you taught us was to be forgiving of others. Isn't that what Christmas is all about?" It was shameless, yes—but it worked. He thought a minute and said, "Okay, Duane can come back."[4]

Signed to a free-agent contract in April 1976, Thomas kept his word. He came in to Thousand Oaks eager to please, easily bantering with teammates and sportswriters. But Landry knew the years had taken a toll, that Thomas's legs were gone. As Staubach recalled, "We were all pulling for him to make it. Tom, too. . . . The strangest thing is that Duane didn't look any different, except lighter. He was in good shape, he just wasn't the same Duane."[5] Actually, in some ways he was even weirder. In a truly inspired coupling, Schramm assigned Thomas's roommate to be Thomas Henderson, and though they seemed to have a lot in common in vanity and testing boundaries, Henderson would later say that "Duane was a strange guy. He ate mostly fruit and he used to bring big piles of it back to the room . . . he used to leave it on the top of the dresser but it would spoil, rot." When Thomas came to the room and found Henderson throwing out the rot, the two nearly came to blows.[6]

Landry knew early on that the clock could not be turned back, and his decision was made for him when after one preseason game, during which Thomas was cheered but was slow off the mark, he pulled a hamstring. Thomas made it to the last cut; then it was left to Gil Brandt to call him and tell him he was out. "Sorry it didn't work out," said Brandt, not sounding like he was. Says Norman, "Duane was disappointed but not bitter. He called me and said, 'Listen, I am completely satisfied. They gave me all the chance in the world. I just couldn't get myself in shape.'" The brief and oddly pleasant encounter at least allowed Landry and Thomas to part on better terms, though the latter had a long road of healing ahead of him, of learning how to resolve all the leftover baggage. It may have been a form of therapy that, in his 1988 autobiography, Thomas revealed his real-time impressions from a diary he had kept during his stormy days in Dallas, including some brutal capsule comments about the Cowboys' Big Three. Schramm, the diary said, was "a closet racist"; Brandt, a man with "the mentality of a street pimp," a "supplier of vices," and a "liar."

If anything, the scalding broadsides in the diary for Landry were worse. The coach, Thomas had written, was an "illusionist who used Christianity for his own vanity, greed, and power," had a "John Birchite mentality," and had used the computer "to create Landry's Humanoids." It went on: "[Landry] recruited predominantly southern players, both black and white, to keep separation active and maintain total control (because of the southern conditioning of his men). [He had a] large ego [and a] white supremacist mentality. His philosophy was intimidation, intimidation, intimidation, of the mind and body."[7] Even after making peace with Landry, Thomas would explain the team's failures to repeat as champion this way: "There was a level of talent that produced success, even though conditions were socially primitive. But once the talent slips on a team like that, there's no backlog of love to fall back on."[8]

Given what became a Cowboy's post-traumatic syndrome for Thomas, an affliction shared in varying degrees by others, no amount of therapy could have resolved his backwash of grievances and apparitions. Pete Gent, who had no problem with harsh judgments about Landry, nonetheless spoke of Thomas in later years as a man entombed by his resentments and quite nearly having lost his mind. As the years rolled on, it seemed the only thing that could make Thomas live easier with himself was to be forgiven by the man he had despised. Sadly, Gent recalled that Thomas came to believe "he had been wrong and Landry and Schramm had been right, that he had been a bad boy. And it was heartbreaking to see that."[9]

In 1984, five years after his football career ended, Thomas began to petition the courts to pardon him for his past drug conviction. Landry came to his aid by writing a letter to the presiding judge. "In my opinion," he wrote, "he had paid his debt to society and has proven his willingness to abide by the law. . . . I am confident that he has remorse over the offense and is now in a position to make a contribution to society."[10] Thomas got his pardon, which if it did not allow him to fully reclaim his lost soul, at least let him salvage enough of it to move on, and to let some old bitterness drain.

He bounced from job to job for years and spent some time in the legal department at the Twentieth Century Fox studio. He tried writing and painting. He recruited black businesses to establish marketing outlets in Nigeria. And, smartly, he began to burnish his Cowboys association, hanging out often in the team offices. In 1979, Tex Schramm asked if he wanted to be in a movie. Thomas said yes and wound up with a $20,000 paycheck for turning in some seriously bad acting in *Dallas Cowboys Cheerleaders II*, a grade-Z production designed to shake more profit from the cheerleaders' profit tree.[11] In the mid-2000s, Thomas agreed to be interviewed for a video about the 1971 title team, even putting on a Cowboys uniform for the occasion. "It's very interesting," he said of the corporate leviathan the team had become, calling it "a circus on wheels."[12]

He didn't seem to appreciate the irony that his own Cowboys teams had been called a circus, if not hell on wheels. Nor, as Gent saw, did he have any hesitation making peace with the man he once indicted as having a "white supremacist mentality." Landry, he now reasoned, had "dealt with things at the time in the best way he could. I accepted that so I could move on. There was no need in me staying angry at him," and "I couldn't have gone to two Super Bowls if it hadn't been for the personality of Tom Landry. And so this has all been worth it for me in terms of the experience. What you take with you is what you learn from experiences that help you grow mentally, psychologically and spiritually."[13] Thomas, who had pawned his Super Bowl ring two decades before, symbolically bought it back.[14]

Not that Landry would revise history for the sake of feel-good comity. He allowed in 1987 that "we get along very well."[15] However, when HBO ran a retro-documentary titled *The Strange, Silent World of Duane Thomas*, Landry didn't hold back. He said that Thomas "appeared to be on drugs" in his two seasons and that "he was just miserable to be around . . . a goldfish became a shark . . . he was a black sheep." As Paul Zimmerman noted of those remarks, "It was strange, indeed, to hear such a serious accusation leveled so casually. It was very uncharacteristic of Landry, who has never said that about another player" from the drug-riddled Cowboys teams of the early 1970s.[16]

Cliff Harris provided a knowing coda of the very complicated saga of Duane Thomas, saying that Thomas "represented rebellion, the rebellion of youth in the post-Vietnam period. They tolerated it for a while and then didn't tolerate it anymore. He arrived too soon. It's sad."[17]

Still, if being pitied after the fact by the old coach may not have been the perfect end to the story, it was the closest thing Duane Thomas would ever get to a pardon from Tom Landry.

LANDRY ALWAYS seemed to be burdened by someone who reminded him of Duane Thomas. Another in that mold, he believed, was Jean Fugett, who leaped from his status as a thirteenth-round draft pick to become a valuable property as Billy Joe DuPree's backup at tight end. A strong blocker and reliable third-down receiver, in 1975 he was the second-leading receiver on the team, grabbing thirty-eight passes. But Fugett sulked about not getting as many reps as DuPree, and Landry never felt comfortable with him. After the season Fugett was traded to the Redskins, a move approved of by some Cowboys who believed Fugett wasn't a team player—Harvey Martin, for one, said after the trade that "they could have him."[18] When Fugett made All-Pro a year later, he had some choice words for his old coach in a 1977 *People* magazine profile of Landry. "I knew him as a coach, but I never knew the man," he said. "I didn't agree with his philosophy.

Football is a cruel game, and it's more cruel when it becomes impersonal. After a loss he would say, 'I gave you a perfect game plan and you blew it.' He keeps bringing in new talent. You lived with the knowledge that you could always be replaced. George Allen believes that if the players are happy, they will win. Landry believes that if the players win, they can be happy."[19]

Fugett did all right for himself. After his career he got his law degree, founded his own law firm, and, with his lawyer brother, created management companies in America and Europe; in 1993 he took over TLC Beatrice Foods, the largest black-owned business in the United States then. He also became president of the Retired Players Steering Committee of the NFLPA, and legal counsel to several Wall Street investment firms.[20] The irony was that Fugett was the kind of man Landry liked to brag about, the kind who learned the meaning of life as a Dallas Cowboy. That a man like that, and not like, say, Pete Gent, could be rubbed wrong by Landry was probably more vexing than he let on. But more vexing still was that he realized he had not, in fact, gotten over the temptation to stick it out with talented but toxic players. In fact, on that front he hadn't seen nothin' yet.

LANDRY'S BIGGEST problem entering the 1976 season was his running game. Newhouse's and Preston Pearson's production had fallen off, opening the door for halfback Doug Dennison and second-year fullback Scott Laidlaw, the latter being increasingly used as the pass-catching threat out of the backfield. Looking to throw more, Staubach passed for over 2,700 yards for the first time. The Cowboys took their first five games, lost in St. Louis, then ripped out another four wins. Their 9–1 record at that point gave them enough of a cushion to prevent their final-game loss to the Redskins from denying them the division crown, at 11–3. But Landry knew there was something missing. Staubach had chipped a bone in his throwing hand in midseason, and while he soldiered on, the offense could sputter at times. The first playoff round had them at home, against the Rams, who always folded in the playoffs. Except this time they didn't. They came in with their rumbling ground game and plundering defense and snuffed Landry's offense, limiting the running game to 85 yards on twenty-eight carries and Staubach to a miserable fifteen completions out of thirty-seven passes, with three interceptions.

As the game crept on, Landry may have had a fleeting wish that he had kept Duane Thomas after all. The Rams stayed close for three quarters, then went on a killer drive ending in a 1-yard Lawrence McCutcheon touchdown run—which Thomas Henderson, inserted as an extra linebacker on the goal line defense, insisted was no touchdown at all. "Lee Roy and I stopped [the play] six inches short," he said. "But the referee gave it to him anyway. It was horrible."[21]

Bogus or not, in those quaint days predating instant replays, the touchdown stood. As did a number of other iffy calls, the most egregious coming after Staubach got the Cowboys down to the Rams' 17-yard line with under two minutes left, and then found backup receiver Butch Johnson for an apparent touchdown, only for the refs to rule that he had one foot out of bounds. Then, on fourth down, a pass to DuPree seemed to pick up the first down at the 5, but it was spotted a yard short, at the 6, to where DuPree had been pushed back after the catch. All of which allowed the Rams to walk out giddy, and sheepish, 14–12 winners, putting off by a week their inevitable fold, when they lost to the Vikings in the NFC title game.

Landry delicately cited the bad calls—"They just missed it," he said of the galling DuPree spot,[22] but let it go. By rote, he did what he had done with his earlier Cowboys teams that fell short, praising his men as "the best group I've had from the standpoint of character, morale, spirit, and teamwork. They're the type who give you your greatest reward from coaching, who really make it enjoyable."[23] He could get away with these bromides now, secure as he was, and an all too familiar figure of pity after such letdowns. He insisted he had learned to accept defeat. "There are coaches to whom winning or losing means something close to life or death," he said. "If they lose, then their life has somehow been diminished. I'm not that way, and it keeps me steady. I'm at peace with myself."[24]

If some might have wondered if he had become a bit too accustomed to losing these heartbreakers, it wasn't just that Landry was getting older and more sentimental. At the same time, the players were becoming less inured to losing in the clutch. Staubach, who was so depressed after the loss and, as he recalled, "in a highly emotional state," told Landry it might be better for everyone if he was traded. Landry put that to rest straightaway. "That's crazy," he said. "The team had problems with the running game and you were injured. You played well under the circumstances. We just didn't have much support in other areas."[25]

In Big D, where arrogance spouted like oil out of a big rig, there was an absence of the vitriol that had greeted similar losses in the late 1960s. It was almost as if the Cowboys, as with their coach, had become an endless, timeless set piece, more a run-on sentence than a finite one. Not only were games strung together, but the seasons were separated by commas, not periods. And Landry had the absolute authority to keep stretching it across the page, keeping it always within reason that he would deliver another happy ending.

THE COWBOYS ensured as much by entering the 1977 season after Tex Schramm pulled off another steal of the century. It happened as the result of the impetuous Clint Longley brawling himself out of town. The unlikely hero of the '74 Thanksgiving miracle had gone back to the bench in '75 save for one start when Roger Staubach sat out the last game of the season. In '76, he was demoted in summer camp to third-string quarterback with Danny White's return. Longley blamed Staubach for his woes and picked a fight with him, whereupon the goody two-shoes ex-middie beat the tar out of him. Two days later, Longley sneaked up on Staubach in the locker room and sucker punched him, splitting his lip.

Landry had no choice but to give Longley his walking papers, and Schramm was able to fleece from the Chargers their first- and second-round draft picks for him. Longley would play little in San Diego before disappearing into obscurity. On the eve of the 1977 draft, Schramm bundled those two picks into a package that pried from the Seattle Seahawks their first-round pick, which turned out to be the No. 2 selection in the draft. For weeks before, it was clear that this pick would be used to draft Tony Dorsett, Pitt's three-time All-American tailback. Dorsett was, by all the scouting reports, the best running back in the land, but he was left for the Cowboys to snag because of a very bold and very opaque bit of parochialism by John McKay, the wry, red-nosed coach of the second-year Tampa Bay Buccaneers.

The year before, McKay had left his highly successful run as coach of the USC Trojans to take the head job with the expansion Bucs, and had been humiliated when his new team went 0–14. That brought him the top draft pick, and with it he demanded to have Ricky Bell, the Trojans' splendid tailback whom he had coached for three seasons, during which the Trojans won a national title and Bell led the nation in rushing and set the school record in that category. As a senior, Bell had come in second in the Heisman Trophy voting, the winner being Dorsett, whose Panthers had won the national crown. But McKay had his way and Bell was given a bank-breaking, five-year, $1.2 million contract by the Bucs, the highest ever in the NFL. Dorsett, who had the same agent as Bell, Mike Trope, was not about to take any less, and his lawyers made it known to the lower-market Seattle team that he was "not desirous of playing professional football in Seattle, and request that your team does not draft Mr. Dorsett."[26] The Seahawks thus set about trading away the No. 2 pick, and all the alluring picks Schramm had in his pocket made it a deal.

Being able to pull in Dorsett—barely able to believe it, Ernie Accorsi, the Colts' general manager, reminded everyone that "the Cowboys got themselves a Hall of Famer for four draft choices"[27]— seemed another example of the Dallas team's haughtiness. "Dallas and Seattle must be sleeping together. I don't understand it at all," said Vikings coach Bud Grant. All Landry had to understand was that he had gotten himself a game-breaker. Though a tad undersized at a ropy five foot nine and 200 pounds, Dorsett was an amazing amalgam of speed, slickness, and uncanny balance, a natural from the get-go. Growing up in blue-collar, western Pennsylvania mining country, he was an instant star in high school then crashed right into the starting backfield at Pitt, finishing second in the nation in rushing as a freshman, the first plebe in three decades to be an All-American.

With a long and blinding first step and an instinctive sense of when and where a play might break open, he set the school's all-time rushing record as a sophomore, then as a junior ran for over 300 yards against Notre Dame. As a senior, as the top rusher in the land, he collected the Heisman, Maxwell, and Camp awards. His 6,082 career rushing yardage was a college record that stood until Ricky Williams broke it in 1998. Landry could thank John McKay for such a weapon. Schramm, giddy, pronounced "a brilliant new era" had begun for the Cowboys.[28] But it was also an expensive new era for them. Had Schramm been unable to swing the deal, he no doubt would have been the first league honcho to decry Bell's deal as outrageous, echoing Bears general manager Jim Finks, who called it "alarming" and added that "it makes for a whole new ball game."[29] Indeed, Lee Roy Selmon, the top pick the previous year, had pocketed only $315,000 for three years from the Bucs. And the last time Schramm had to pay up for a blue-chipper, Too Tall Jones, he needed to part with $450,000 over four years.

But Schramm, stripped of his usual imperious take-it-or-leave-it negotiating stance, had to more than double that for Dorsett. When Tex put his name on the five-year, $1.2 million contract, his hand was no doubt steadied by a double vodka.

DORSETT WAS just what Landry needed, given the fall-off of the Cowboys' running game in 1976. Robert Newhouse seemed an ideal complement, his head-rattling blocking able to pave holes for Dorsett to blow through. Still, million dollars or not, Landry didn't lift his normal precept with rookies, bringing Dorsett along slowly until he could adapt to the system and not be subject to immediate pressure. Not that Dorsett had any aversion to the high life and self-attention. Neither was he the most responsible guy. Back in college, he racked up $1,200 in unpaid parking tickets. When he made his grand entrance at Thousand Oaks, it was behind the wheel of a Porsche, wearing a full-length mink coat.[30] His first order of business was to instruct the reporters to pronounce his name as the more uptown Dor*sett*.

When the team returned to Dallas, he immediately became a fixture at the discos. At one North Dallas hot spot called Number 3 Lift, he got into an argument with a bartender who apparently taunted him about dancing with a white woman then ordered him to move to the other end of the bar. When Dorsett refused, the bartender came at him, spouting racist insults. Dorsett squared up as if he were a rushing linebacker and popped him on the jaw. Yet it was Dorsett who was charged with assault, and even though the case was later dropped, he had tasted what life could be like for a black man in Dallas, even a Cowboy.

He would need to adapt on many levels, his worldview having come from the urban Northeast. Dallas would pose for him a good deal of culture shock, and Tom Landry even more of it. Like many rookie Cowboys, Dorsett was not used to regimentation or a coach who was cold and aloof. When he realized he would not be automatically given star treatment, or play other than in a backup role, his confidence sank, negatively affecting his play and his study habits. He grew insular, as if in his own bubble. In another double standard, Landry went far easier on Henderson for such academic inattention, rationalizing that Henderson's game relied on instinctive, freestyle roaming. Dorsett, on the other hand, caught no slack. The coach was constantly on his tail.

Mel Renfro, playing his final season that year at age thirty-six, recalls, "It actually got to the point where we were embarrassed by it. I think Tom was making a point that nobody, not even the best runner in the world, was bigger than the system. I thought Tom was unfair to Tony, who was a nice kid, not a self-promoter like Thomas Henderson. But Tom was a master at getting peak performance out of every single player. He knew each one, which needed to be kissed, and which needed to be slapped. Players always disagreed with something Tom was doing, but in the end we were all wrong. Tom was almost never wrong in his judgment about a player."[31]

LANDRY INDEED knew exactly what he was doing. He had a powerhouse defense, arguably the best he'd ever had. And he was unwilling to mess with his inalienable philosophy, that the team was far bigger than the sum of the parts. Newhouse, Pearson, and the other runners had to feel they had a role to play, and Dorsett would be a better Cowboy only if he understood this dynamic. Besides, he had to. The 1977 season would begin with the holdover backfield alignment of Newhouse and Preston Pearson, with Dennison and

Laidlaw moved down the depth chart in anticipation of Dorsett's eventual elevation. Landry had also made key defensive changes for that year. Thomas Henderson, having served his apprenticeship as a backup, moved in at strong-side linebacker. Randy White, no longer needed at linebacker, was shifted to the defensive line, at right tackle, making the Flex defense quicker, rangier, and meaner, White's moniker—"Manster," as in half man, half monster—being well earned. D. D. Lewis was now set at weak-side linebacker, with Bob Breunig in the middle. This synergy freed up Harvey Martin to rush the passer hell-bent.

The opener posed the stiffest test Landry would have all season. It sent the Cowboys to Minnesota, this time on a sixty-eight-degree afternoon, not an icicle in sight. The defenses dominated, neither team clearing 300 total yards, and Staubach and Fran Tarkenton were stifled, the latter intercepted three times. Both teams ran well (Dorsett in his pro debut got four carries for 11 yards), but getting in the end zone was prohibitive. Then Staubach, on his way to another All-Pro season, caught fire right on schedule. In the fourth quarter, down 7–3, he led an economical drive and found Preston Pearson out of the backfield for a 7-yard touchdown pass to take the lead. A Vikings field goal tied it, but Staubach capped another drive by taking the ball into the end zone from the 4, yet one more routinely dramatic day at the office. From here, nothing stood in Landry's way. He won eight straight, none particularly close, among them a 34–16 victory over the hated Redskins.

By then, Landry had barely eased Dorsett into the meat of the attack, keeping his number of carries in the ten to fifteen range and getting remarkable dividends. The week before, in a 30–24 win over the Cardinals, Landry started him, then sat back and enjoyed the show as the kid piled up 144 yards on just fourteen attempts, with two touchdowns. Dorsett remained in a steady groove, getting more action than the other backs but his frustration level swelling. After one early-season game against Tampa, even though he had run for 72 yards in just ten carries—Ricky Bell, who was having even bigger problems, could only muster 7 yards on three carries—Dorsett questioned himself, saying, "Mentally, I just collapsed," and admitted that he had lined up wrong throughout the game.[32]

After the Cowboys lost their first game, to the Cardinals on November 14, in no small part because Staubach sprained his thumb during the game, Dorsett, who had not started but contributed 5 yards on sixteen attempts, told Landry that not starting and being put in and yanked out was affecting his concentration. Landry replied that he wanted to start him but that "the way you've been going, I have my doubts about all that." Dorsett allowed that if Landry had told him he would be starting at some point, "I would have busted my butt more."

"It's not too late," Landry said tersely.[33]

Dorsett turned up the intensity level during the next week and won a starting assignment against the Steelers at Texas Stadium, whereupon he promptly scored a first-quarter touchdown on a 13-yard burst. In a real oddity, only two men ran the ball that day, Dorsett (seventeen carries, 73 yards) and Newhouse (ten carries 63 yards). The Steelers, meanwhile, pounded out 228 yards on the ground, dished out a terrible beating to Staubach, and won 28–13, another uncomfortable reminder that Chuck Noll's team had the Cowboys' number. The two losses opened the door for the Redskins, who at 6–4 were now just two games behind Dallas and were next up on the schedule. On a bitterly cold late November day in Washington, Landry's team was trailing 7–0 in the third quarter, his defense holding but the offense somnolent, with Staubach on his way to completing just ten of twenty-four passes. But his zen was intact, and Staubach directed a tidy drive ending with a 4-yard scoring pass to Golden Richards. Then in the fourth quarter Staubach did it again, with Dorsett's 1-yard plunge gaining the lead and the win.

When December arrived, Dorsett *was* the meat of the attack. In a game against the Eagles, he ran twenty-four times, exploding into the open seemingly at will, his toll rising like the digits on a gas pump. At the gun he had rung up 206 yards—the first 200-plus-yard rushing game by a Cowboy and still the third best in the team's history, bettered only by Emmitt Smith in 1993 and DeMarco Murray in 2011. Dorsett would never have a better game. He scored twice, the last on a sensational 84-yard burst, the longest in the league that season, icing a 24–14 victory. "COWBOYS TD PHILLY, CLINCH NFC EAST: TONY STEPS 206 YARDS," was the headline of the game story in the

Morning News, which also placed on page one a stirring shot of Dorsett prancing over a would-be tackler. He was now indeed in full throttle, the no-doubt Rookie of the Year. The next game, he effortlessly gained 92 yards on twenty carries in a 42–35 victory against the 49ers in Candlestick Park, the kind of big-time performance that would become yawningly common. He was, wrote Bob St. John, "the New Dimension."[34]

THE COWBOYS, record now sat at 11–2, with the division in hand, their record being the best in the NFC. But Landry had another pin to knock down. The regular-season finale was against the 12–1 Denver Broncos, the "Orange Crush," as they called themselves for their voracious and quick defense. Playing the new-wave 3–4 defensive set, their linebackers ran highly coordinated and disguised blitzes through lanes cleared by the feral end Lyle Alzado. But the headliner for the Broncos turned out to be a prodigal Cowboy, none other than Craig Morton, who, at thirty-four, won Comeback Player of the Year award doing exactly what he never did in Dallas, running a safe, conservative, no-frills offense. That was the brainchild of Red Miller, a longtime league strategist who had landed the head coaching job before the season. Miller, who like Landry was his own offensive coordinator, used to be known as "Good Time Red Miller" during his years of heavy drinking, but he had now been clean and sober for a year and a half. When his team clinched the AFC West, he smuggled eight cases of champagne aboard the team plane for a surprise celebration, and may have been the only person on board who didn't touch a drop.[35]

Miller, who would keep Landry from his second Coach of the Year award, threw himself into the job, creating a near cult out of the color orange—in his office he had an orange telephone, an orange radio, an orange toilet seat, an orange shower curtain, and an orange Christmas tree. He also tapped into the ethereal. "Winning is in the mind of the player," he would tell his men. "We're a team of destiny."[36] Miller had a strict rule for Morton: Don't make a mistake. Even if it meant he wouldn't throw the ball much, if at all, on the Broncos' side of the 50-yard line. And Morton obeyed, throwing fourteen touchdowns and only eight interceptions. As a matter of personal pride and as a psychological lever should they meet in the Super Bowl, Landry wanted to win the game and did not rest his regulars. Miller said he would do the same, whetting the appetite of the Doomsday defenders who had the second-most sacks in the league and were dying to get their mitts on Morton. On second thought, Miller rested Morton after one pass attempt. And while the Crush still made it a tough game, the 14–6 Cowboys' win told Landry all he needed to know about the Broncos.

That closed out the season at 12–2, equaling the high-water mark of the 1968 Cowboys, though this was the best team Landry ever had. They had not a single flaw. Dorsett, his insecurity over, ended up with 1,007 yards in rushing—dwarfing the number for Ricky Bell, who missed three games with injuries and gained a mere 436 yards, with exactly one touchdown. The Cowboys attack amassed the most yardage in the league and the second-most points. The always dominating defense was rated No. 2 against the pass and No. 3 against the run. Three offensive players—Staubach, Drew Pearson, and DuPree—made All-Pro, as did three defensive players—Martin (the Defensive Player of the Year), Harris, and Waters—and the kicker Efren Herrera.

The Cowboys were so good and so deep that two extremely talented young receivers, second-year pro Butch Johnson and twenty-one-year-old rookie Tony Hill, were used sparingly, mainly as kick and punt returners. Having the luxury of home-field advantage in the NFC playoffs, the Cowboys barely broke a sweat, spanking the Chicago Bears 37–7 and the Minnesota Vikings 23–6, gaining a combined 793 yards. Against the Bears, the Cowboys blunted Walter Payton, who during the season had rushed for a league-high 1,852 yards and earned the Offensive Player of the Year award. Never seeing an inch of space, he managed only 60 yards on nineteen carries. They did the same the following week against Chuck Foreman, who had run for 1,112 yards during the season but came away with just 59 yards on twenty-one carries. Landry had never seen his defense as stifling.

The Super Bowl was his reward, indeed against the Broncos, who had conquered the defending-champion Raiders in the AFC playoffs, outlasting Al Davis's boys in a nasty bar brawl of a game, winning 20–17 as Morton racked up 224 yards on just ten completions, and two touchdowns. Thus the storyline was written for the Super Bowl: Morton's revenge on Landry with a small-scale team against the large-scale team that discarded him after he failed in the big ones. This inner drama overlooked the nuts-and-bolts approach of the two coaches. Red Miller's defensive coordinator, Joe Collier, had rigged perhaps the game's best application of the 3–4 defense, but Landry figured he had it smelled out. "Actually, we were a little disappointed to be playing Denver," says Mel Renfro. "We wanted to pay back the Steelers and avenge what happened two years before. We just hated the Steelers. We wanted to beat Craig, of course, but nobody hated Craig. He was a good guy. Plus, we'd beaten them in their place and we didn't think there was any way they could beat us."

The game would mark the first time a Super Bowl was played indoors, at New Orleans's massive Louisiana Superdome on January 15, 1978, and Landry cracked nuts to keep his team stoked and hungry, insisting that "our team is a couple years away."[37] He went back to the full-blown scrimmages he had gotten away from before big games. To keep the players away from the ample distractions of New Orleans, the team was put up in a hotel in West Kenner, Louisiana, near the airport, safely removed from Bourbon Street. Taking no chances, Landry also restored the curfews and celibacy rules the night before the kickoff. Not that a few industrious Cowboys weren't able to smuggle some willing women into their rooms. With pride, Harvey Martin recalled conning Jim Myers, Landry's curfew enforcer. When Myers found two room-service dinners in Martin's room, the big man insisted he had a big appetite that night. He wasn't lying either. The woman he had sneaked in was hiding in the john.[38]

Renfro's opinion that the game was a mismatch was shared by most observers. And as much as Landry hated for his players to mouth off before games, no one could keep Hollywood Henderson from trashing the Broncos while wearing a bright orange jump suit. "THE ORANGE IS DOOMED TO BE CRUSHED," was the headline of the *Sports Illustrated* preview story. Though the NFC hadn't won a Super Bowl in five years, the Cowboys would come in as a 6-point favorite, which seemed a bargain. Much attention, of course, was paid to Morton, who had evolved from "The Prince of Greenville Avenue"—a nickname he acquired from the strip of hot spots in Dallas he used to frequent—to a pious proselyte, having married, settled down in Denver, and, as he said, "accepted Christ into my life." But Morton had baggage. He was paying off an IRS lien for nearly $36,000 in unpaid taxes.[39] And he would need divine aid going up against the Cowboys' defense. The Broncos had gotten to the dance on a wellspring of emotion that made up for the cavities in their offense. Emotion, however, would not get them far while staring down the business end of a double-barrel Texas shotgun.

THE UPWARD progression of the league that Tom Landry had been a major part of for a quarter century reached a new peak with Super Bowl XII. In large part due to the almost mythic franchise he had constructed, the TV audience for the game was the largest ever to watch a sporting event at the time. CBS would pull a 67 percent share of national households and 78.9 million viewers.[40] Worldwide, the game would be beamed to an estimated 85 million people. These seem like puny numbers today, but in 1978, in a far more compact global universe, when the population of America was around 222 million—90 million less than it is today—they were profound, and a leap into the future of sports. The Superdome was a prime example of the coinciding of pro football and the culture it was influencing in myriad ways. Football stadiums rarely intended to hold over 60,000 people, but more than 74,452 fit comfortably, and loudly, in the world's largest living room. All seats were coveted, with $30 tickets sold by scalpers for ten times that on the street. Soon, nearly all new football stadiums were built to those excess specifications, and prices for tickets escalated wildly.

The TV-ready theme of the game was evident when the captains went to midfield for the coin toss, and Staubach and Morton shared a hug. It was the last time Morton felt any love. From the start, he and his teammates played as though they were there to be sacrificed to the altar of Landry, who came out looking decidedly at ease, wearing not his usual dark gray business suit but a sprightly, light blue blazer and matching hat, black slacks, and a loudly striped tie. The game posed a challenge only for as long as it took for the Cowboys to turn orange to black and blue. On the Cowboys' first punt, Henderson zeroed in on Rick Upchurch, who had led the league in punt returns, and wiped him out so viciously that he was called for roughing. Later, Henderson said that Mike Ditka had made him do it, telling him, "If you get a shot" at Upchurch, "take the penalty. Just take him out. Not hurt him, but get his attention." Landry, who never would have ordered up a dirty hit himself, was waiting for Henderson on the sideline and an explanation. "Well fuck, Ditka told me to do that,"[41] Henderson said. It was as good an explanation as the coach needed, and he said nothing more about it.

The Cowboys' defense pillaged the left side of the Denver line, Martin and White running roughshod over tackle Andy Maurer and guard Tom Glassic and boring in on a helpless, inert Morton. They were so accomplished at the art of the pass rush that they could even bend the rules without detection. "Randy and I reached deep into our bag of tricks," Martin would recall, including stunts called Limbo and Reverse Limbo, which entailed strategic, balletic pivoting by the two huge men, inducing the Bronco linemen to move the wrong way and leave gaping alleys for one or the other of the rushing Cowboys. They simply poured through all day, seeing, as Martin remembered, "nothing but green AstroTurf" between them and poor Morton.[42] A photo in the papers the next day showed Martin literally wrapped around Morton as if in an amorous embrace, helmet to helmet, his arms clamped around his old teammate's neck. As Dan Jenkins wrote, Martin "committed enough crimes against Morton to do a life term in Leavenworth."[43]

One of Morton's four first-half interceptions (a Super Bowl record), late in the first quarter, went straight to the Cowboys' nickel back Randy Hughes at the Broncos' 29. That set up Dorsett's 3-yard run off the right tackle for a 7–0 lead, just about all Landry would need. In the first half Dorsett gained 66 yards, 22 more than the entire Denver offense. Still, two fumbles by the Cowboys—two of a record ten fumbles in the game—kept the Broncos within 13–0 at intermission. That sent Landry into the locker room steaming under his fedora. "Oh yeah, he tore us a new one," Renfro says. "He hadn't coached his behind off all year for us to fumble it away. When Tom got mad it didn't matter who you were, your ass was on the line."[44]

Then came the deluge. At 13–3 midway through the third quarter, with the ball on Denvers' 45, Landry sent in a play he had named "Spread Orange Left, Ray 15," a down-and-in to Butch Johnson. But Staubach had seen free safety Bernard Jackson cheating to the strong side to help cover DuPree. "Don't run the in-pattern, run the post," Staubach instructed Johnson. That meant Johnson had to break deep and get behind Jackson. It also meant Staubach would have to brook Landry. Normally, he was permitted to call plays only in two-minute drills, when there was no time for huddles or messengers. He could change a play at the line, but in Landry's view, he did so "more times than I thought he should."[45] This issue always caused underlying tension between them. And, now, at a profound moment like this, Staubach recalled that rather than calling the play Johnson wanted in the huddle, and have everyone know he was brooking Landry, he whispered it to Johnson, one on one. If it worked, or didn't, he would own up to it later, either way.

As Johnson tore down the sideline, Staubach's pass was a little strong. Johnson laid his body out headlong, parallel to the ground, in the blink of an eye grabbing it in his long fingertips, doing a full revolution as he tumbled into the end zone. When he popped back up—without the ball, which had come loose—the back judge had his arms stuck in the air signaling a touchdown. Johnson instinctively scooped up the ball as cornerback Steve Foley halfheartedly pointed to the ground, claiming the pass was incomplete. But the call was made, and the TV replays confirmed that Johnson indeed had possession when he hit the turf, completing one of the most acrobatic and breathtaking touchdown hookups ever made. "It looked spectacular," someone would tell Johnson after the game. "It was," he said.

For once, Landry didn't confront Staubach for his modification. "He never said a word to me," said the quarterback. "He was curious, but he wasn't going to ask me."[46]

The rest of the game was candy. Not even a calf injury that kept backup tight end Jay Saldi out of the game, depriving Landry of the double-tight-end formation he liked to use, nor the exit of Dorsett after the third quarter with a sprained knee, stopped the Cowboys.

The Bronco defense was left with their heads spinning from Landry's endless nexus of formations, shifting, trap, and counteraction blocks that blew open huge fissures. The Cowboys outgained the Broncos 325 yards to 156—with the latter's passing stats an eyesore (eight of twenty-five for 61 yards)—and by the fourth quarter Miller took mercy on Morton, relieving him with backup Norris Weese. With seven minutes left, and the ball on Denver's 29, Landry was seemingly toying with Miller. He sent in a halfback option for Newhouse, whose pass perfectly floated into Golden Richards's soft hands on the goal line to close out the score at 27–10. As Jenkins put it, "Tom Landry nailed Denver's Red Miller to a blackboard and left him there."[47]

Martin and White would share the game's MVP award, a rare nod to the defense when it came to such honors—but not rare for a Landry team, what with Chuck Howley having won the award for Super Bowl V. They got the nod over Staubach, who had completed nineteen of twenty-eight passes for 182 yards in his second Super Bowl win, tying him with Bart Starr, Bob Griese, and Terry Bradshaw. Landry, his second title tying *him* with Lombardi, Don Shula, and Chuck Noll, was given another ride off the field for the second time in the same city, raising an arm into the air in triumph. In the press room, he admitted he "felt more satisfaction" in 1971, since "that team had gone through a lot of heartbreak, so it was a great feeling." But if that edition had more experience, this one, he said, "overall has more top athletes."[48] As the champagne flowed in the clubhouse, Clint Murchison Jr., handed the Lombardi Trophy by Pete Rozelle, paid tribute to his coach, leaving no doubt what he thought of Red Miller. "I'm going to give this to Tom Landry," he said, "who is not only Coach of the Year but Coach of the Century."[49]

Landry, hat still in place, smiled and tossed out some obligatory compliments to the Broncos, praised his men for their hard work and dedication, then changed clothes and, with Alicia, boarded the bus back to the hotel, where they waited patiently for the locker room rituals to conclude and the players to begin wobbling to their seats. Murchison had arranged a victory bash for that night, under a big tent erected in the parking lot of the hotel. It featured rack after rack of Texas barbecue meats, dance routines by the cheerleaders, and performances by Willie Nelson, Waylon Jennings, Jerry Jeff Walker, and Charley Pride. Some of the Cowboys got up and sang country songs. Staubach, one of the most un-country of players, turned up his collar, and tried to impersonate Elvis Presley. The party began at 2:30 and went on until the sun came up.

Those looking for Landry wouldn't find him. He chose to have a quiet dinner with Alicia. Preferring not to be tempted by all that flowing firewater, or to see his players as out of control as they had been in control on the field, he was fast asleep with Alicia by the time they toasted him at the party. The next day, when the Cowboys came home and were given a victory parade in a motorcade through a jammed downtown Dallas, the Landrys were about the only ones in the motorcade who were wide awake and hangover-free.

For Renfro, there was ambivalence in leaving what had consumed so much of his life. "I really felt great, going out on top. I could have played longer. I was only thirty-seven, but I knew Tom wanted to get younger guys in there and once he made his mind up about that, you were gone. I could look back and see how wrong I was about Tom in my early judgments. I'd come to appreciate him so much more, and I thought he really changed quite a bit. During the last years he wasn't nearly as hard on us. He would make an effort to care about your feelings more. You could come to him with ideas and he wouldn't just shut you down.

"I thought Tom was at the top of his game then, that no one could beat him on details and strategy. At the same time, I left with regret because we should have won a lot more championships. We were the best team in football for a decade and only won twice. That stuck in my craw, I can tell you that. But it stuck in Tom's a lot more. No matter how many times he'd win, it was the ones he lost that he thought about. Those were the ones he wanted to go back and fix. When I'd see him years later, he never talked about the games we won, only the ones we didn't. Because those games killed him inside."

In the glow of that day under the dome, however, victory needed to be savored, every inch of it. Tom Landry had, he likely believed, figured out this whole business of winning championships, once and for all.

Chapter 22

HOLLYWOOD
BABYLON

EVEN IN VICTORY, TOM LANDRY was now looking to get away from the demands and tedious routines in Dallas, a city that had grown by leaps and bounds around him, in no small part because of the seed he had planted at the Cotton Bowl. The off-season offered a respite that he enjoyed far more than the chronic, ossified mechanics of football. The family getaways were still a rule, but no more so than his participation in the Billy Graham Crusades and the Fellowship of Christian Athletes banquets, where he could pimp his faith without worry that he would be seen as a salesman trying to sell it to heathens. As the onetime Dallas sportswriter Skip Bayless noted, "A lot of people in the Bible Belt went to church on Sunday morning and then felt like they went to a second service presided over by Coach Landry." The line of demarcation never blurred for Landry. "There was the 'bid'ness' Tom and then there was the Christian Tom," Bayless believed. "It was quite a shocking dichotomy to me to watch Tom function through the football season and then change his entire nature."[1]

The case could be made that the only time Landry believed he was anything like "God's coach" was after the last whistle blew. Billy Graham ventured, jokingly but pointedly, given that Landry's first appearance in the new stadium had been for a crusade, not for football, that Landry was "gonna have his *second* team," the football-playing one, in the place on the day after. Landry wore an easy smile at that, and it widened when Graham went on to say that the crusade would "bring some sanctification to the stadium."[2] Landry's was the smile of a man who knew he could quit football and still carry an air of pristine grace. But football was a calling too, one he inevitably came to regard as necessary to carry on and renew his life as a Christian.

Said Alicia Landry, "He told me, 'This job I have gives me the best platform I could ever have. It's meant for me to stay in coaching, to be able to witness his Christian faith and influence people.'"[3]

To be sure, he was nothing like the football man in the hat during those public testimonials. First off, he left the hat home for the Graham rallies; he was beautifully and proudly bald, relaxed, eyes glinting, not reluctant to be seen or heard by thousands of people with a Bible in his hand. If his oratory didn't exactly soar, it was straight from the heart, not the manual of favorite coaching clichés. He could fixate you with that famous internal sense of commitment and character, even if you knew about the less than savory aspects of his team almost right from the beginning of his reign. Landry was able to make even those flaws in his kingdom seem like a test of *his* morality and character, for winning with men of wildly different inclinations.

To some, even on the team, the Landry tintype of the nagging Jesus freak was fodder for scorn, but he walked in his own shadow because of it, and minded not a bit wallowing in it. Nothing could have pleased him more than when the theme of any given interview with him turned to his faith. And almost all of them did. The *Saturday Evening Post*, for example, which had become less topical and more nostalgic as its circulation faded in the 1970s, grabbed at Landry as if he were a lifebuoy for the concurrently fading Americana the magazine had sold for years with its fabulous Norman Rockwell artwork on the cover. In a 1977 compilation of famous Christians who "openly profess their faith," Landry was front and center, declaring that "God and my family (for God's love is bound up in my relationship with my family) became the most important parts of my life."[4]

In 1980, Landry was given another profile in the magazine, entitled "Punt, Pass and Prayer," which came with a deliciously fanciful subtitle that said everything about Landry's power to control the media message: "Although he has never been called for interference in the lives of his Dallas Cowboys, coach Tom Landry's discreet Christian influence has contributed substantially to their wholesome image." In truth, little about Landry's influence was discreet, least of all the Christianity right there on his sleeve, and even less about the team could be called wholesome. Even within the article there were hints that Landry and his team were perhaps not quite as easily caricatured. Bob Lilly, queried about his old mentor, said that, notwithstanding the image of team and coach, "most people aren't aware [that] Tom Landry is an exceedingly complex man."[5]

Not that he wasn't completely sincere in his stated beliefs and ready to parry any nonbelieving niggles. In a puffy 1978 interview with *Reader's Digest*, hardly a forum for pickiness about God and country, Dave Anderson wrote, delicately, "To cynics who question if Christianity and football's physical violence aren't contradictory, [Landry] insists: 'It's a matter of intent. If you want to hurt people viciously, that's wrong. But if God gives you the talent to play football, he expects you to use it.'"[6] Out on the Billy Graham stump circuit, Landry was in a different, soothing sinecure in which he told the same story of his conversion from meandering young man to one giving his every fiber of being to the Lord, and how that kept him centered in "the crazy world of football." One of his favorite aphorisms—"The job of a football coach is to make men do what they want to do, in order to achieve what they've always wanted to be"—was based on a passage from the book of Corinthians. His diction would be perfect, his cadence quietly intense. Never did he enjoy himself more. Sometimes it seemed that he didn't want to go back home. Not to Dallas, anyway.

HIS TIME on Texas soil became divided between the home on Rock Cliff Place and new digs he purchased down in Austin, where he and Alicia could breathe and relive memories too soon faded of their school and courtship days, when the world was perilous and uncertain but held so much in store for him. The house, in the Hills of Lakeway, was initially sprawled across an acre of a golf course. A few years later, they would move farther up the hills, where they could look out at lakes and misty green forests from what seemed atop the world, vistas that comforted Tom Landry in his last years. He also made dutiful trips down to Mission, one on the sad day in 1975 when Ruth Landry was buried.

By then, Ray Landry had six grandchildren, but without Ruth he was virtually alone. His son Jack was living in Houston, his daughter Ruthie married and raising her own family in Tulsa, Oklahoma. Ray's brother Arthur was also in Oklahoma, in El Reno; only his two sisters, Lein and Pearl, had remained in Mission. But as long as he was alive, his oldest surviving son had resolved to maintain a chain between past and present, no matter how much fame he accrued. Tom had grown fairly distant from his brother and sister, yet for years he sent Bob Martin season tickets to Cowboys games, which the retired Mission High coach bragged about all over town. Between his vacations and commitments to Billy Graham, Tom would head south in his Lincoln Continental for the long trek back to his childhood, to sit with Ray, make small talk, and drive him to the Lions Club, where Ray in an earlier time warp had once performed in blackface. They prayed together at the old First United Methodist Church up on Doherty, where Ray had taught Sunday school for almost thirty years.

Ray, of course, had never considered moving out of Mission. There, where he had laid down his family's roots in the Texas soil that made men tough and self-respecting, he was venerated for the indelible mark of distinction he had left on the city, which was carved even deeper into these streets and parks than that of his world-famous son. For a time he taught what was called Fireman's School, a yearly symposium for firefighters at Texas A&M, and as he grew older, he was of such stature in town that when there were glowing stories about him in the local papers, it was almost never as the father of an illustrious Texan up in Dallas. When Tom was named Mission's Man of the Year after the Cowboys' first championship season, he was not the first Landry to receive the honor. Ray had gotten the award a few years earlier.

With his old spirit, Ray had fought his way out of his wheelchair and almost completely recovered, something his son would not have taken any credit for, though his wife did for him. "Tommy," she says, "really willed Ray back to health. I believe that. I saw it. It was like he was coaching Ray the way he coaches players."[7] Seeing that his father was well enough to travel, Tom had sent him a ticket to Super Bowl XII, where he had a good time playing the role of the rube with the media, ribbing his son the clothes horse, whom he barely recognized in his expensive tailored duds and matching Stetsons on the sideline. "I'll be darned if I know where he gets those hats," he said. "Some guy keeps him in hats. His wife helps on dressing him, too." Casting his memory back a ways, he told of the young boy in bare feet with big dreams and the iron-willed stoicism he got from his mother. "He was a guy you couldn't punish. You could beat his hide off but he wouldn't say a word. The only thing you could do was take away a privilege like not letting him go on a date or to the movies."[8]

The son believed it was that same single-mindedness that got Ray back on his feet and hardy again. Then, nine months later, on October 11, three days after the Cowboys beat the Giants at Texas Stadium, Ray was mowing his lawn at the old house when he was cut to his knees by a blinding pain inside his head and fell to the ground. He died shortly afterward, from a massive stroke, at age seventy-nine. Landry got word on the practice field and flew to Mission to bury another large slice of his past. In the town that had molded both father and son, he recalled, "It seemed most of Mission crowded into that little Methodist church for the service." A long line of cars led by the hearse bearing the casket made a slow procession through the town's winding, palm tree–lined streets, stopping for a short, silent tribute in front of the old firehouse and Ray Landry Park. All along the route, "people poured out of their homes and businesses to stand on sidewalks and line the curb in silent tribute to my father."

On that day, more than any other, the son would realize what the father had meant to the town, and to him. When he left Mission again, now for the last time, it was with a codification he didn't have the first time he left. "Dad never was very expressive about his feelings," he wrote in his memoirs. "Still I knew what so many friends and relatives told me after the funeral was true: 'Your dad was always so proud of you, Tom.'" He had waited fifty-four years to hear those words. He waited even longer before he could return the homage he had never paid directly to Ray.

"I wished," he added, "I had told him how proud I was of him."[9]

THE PASSAGE of time had not taken his own brood far afield. Tom Jr., now twenty-seven, earned his law degree and had a practice in Houston. His daughter Kitty, twenty-five, had gone into the advertising business and married Eddie Phillips, a man just like dear old dad, who had quarterbacked the Texas Longhorns from 1969 to 1971 and ran the Wishbone offense to its unbeaten, national championship season in 1970. Phillips, who led the team to a record thirty straight wins, was named captain in 1971 and had one of the most amazing games in history that year, passing for 199 yards and rushing for 164 in the Longhorns' Cotton Bowl loss to Notre Dame. Injuries killed his shot at a pro career, and he went into banking. In the mid-1990s, he founded a major private equity company and at the time of writing was an advisory director of Frost bank. He and Kitty continued to live in Austin, not far from the Landry's getaway home, as did Lisa Landry, who was attending school at the same campus her parents had lived on three decades before.

Tom Landry was every bit the patriarch his grandfather and father had been. Yet he continued to be fit and trim, with not an ounce of fat on him; his middle still measuring thirty-two inches. His face and forehead were etched by age, but his blue eyes remained fierce. Pacing the sideline, he was as familiar a figure as could be, his own constancy a factor in the seamless progression of the Cowboys. In 1978, in particular, he looked down from a metaphoric hilltop, as coach of the defending champions at a benchmark interim for the sport. In 1978, the NFL increased its revenue from both ticket sales and television proceeds by expanding the regular season from fourteen to sixteen games. Furthermore, the playoff format was expanded from eight to ten teams, enabling the league to give another postseason payoff perk to CBS and NBC. There were critical on-field changes too, the most important one setting Landry and Tex Schramm against each other.

That happened when the Competition Committee decided that the defenses had evolved to a higher degree than the offenses—

something Landry could take much credit for—resulting in lower-scoring, less exciting games. Seeking to juice up the passing offense, the committee adumbrated new rules creating a five-yard "bumper zone," which limited where defensive people could make contact with receivers coming off the line, sharply curtailing the hand-to-hand combat that used to be common all down the field until the ball was in the air. The "bump and run" had been a critical part of many cornerbacks' game, most notably that of the Raiders' Willie Brown, who by coincidence would retire after this season. Now, all such combat occurred within a few steps after the snap. A second alteration was the loosening of holding calls on offensive linemen, making some clutching and grabbing acceptable. While this would allow more time for Landry's multi-formation pass plays to develop, the timing of the Flex defense would be thrown off a bit.

As it was, both of his safeties, Charlie Waters and Cliff Harris, were among the slowest in the league, their skills predicated on being in the right place by instinct and mastering Landry's probabilities. Now, aging and getting no faster, they would need to cover receivers who blew past the cornerbacks, which became a problem after Mel Renfro retired and Mark Washington came up with career-ending leg injuries that same season. Their replacements would be Benny Barnes, a onetime linebacker at Stanford and not the fastest guy around, and Aaron Kyle, a first-round pick in 1976 whose knee and foot were brittle. Thus the rule changes could not have come at a worse time for Landry, whose strategies were affected in more ways than the obvious ones. As his longtime adjutant, defensive backfield coach Gene Stallings noted at the time, "The philosophy here has always been to stop the run. That means we have played our corner-backs and safeties in close to the line. In the past we could get away with this because we bumped the receivers as much as any team in the league."[10]

Regardless of how the new regulations shook out, Landry's dis-pleasure about them stoked speculation that, aside from the overall merits they might have for a league eager to cash in on the excitement of higher scoring rather than the purists' appreciation for tight, low-scoring games, Schramm wanted to establish his own arc of authority by not favoring Landry. For his part, Landry never said anything negative about Tex, but he didn't need to because others would, openly wondering if Schramm enjoyed overstepping his coach just a bit too much. As Paul Zimmerman wrote of the rule changes, Schramm and his committee confreres "had accomplished, with one swoop of their pen, something that should have been the job of the coaches; and Landry, who always enjoyed the challenges of the game plan and chart book, didn't think it was right. . . . He thought the basic problem of controlling defenses that were monopolizing the game should be handled through coaching ingenuity, not by lawmakers."[11]

Landry, however, was never enough of a politician to get himself on the committee, even if he wanted to, or to put up with the conflicting egos and hidden agendas of other members of note (read: Al Davis). It was Landry's job to adapt to whatever the league threw at him. Besides the new pass-defense rules, he would need to parry strategic evolutions that were also changing the game. Whether he could do this would determine how long the Landry way would remain inviolate—or even relevant. And he'd have to do it even as his championship team got old and his cast of characters changed.

With the Cowboys, musical chairs was a constant. Another loser in that game was Golden Richards, who had become progressively dependent on pain killers as part of the routine of dealing with terrible injuries to be ready for games. After the NFC title game win over the Vikings, Richards had sat in his car outside the stadium weeping uncontrollably. "I had to pull off to the side of the road," he recalled years later. "I had decided to get help after the season. I knew then it would be two more weeks of propagating my addiction. I cried my heart out." But he didn't get help, and Landry insisted later he had no idea how badly Richards had gotten hooked until that off-season, when he was taken by ambulance to Baylor University Medical Center for what was called a drug overdose. Physically unable to play for almost the entire 1978 season, Richards caught exactly one pass for 2 yards.

Landry and Schramm would deal with the problem all too typically. They would trade him after the first game of the 1979 season to the Chicago Bears, with whom he would play a season and a half, but he was never whole or able to kick the pills. He would hit bottom in 1993, when he was arrested in a Salt Lake City suburb and accused of forging his father's signature on checks to buy drugs. After three failed drug rehab confinements over the years, he finally got clean and sober in the late 1990s.[12] Cowboys who performed admirably then quickly fell out of Landry's favor. Yet another was Toni Fritsch, the kicker whom Landry had gone all the way to Austria to sign. He had made over 60 percent of his field goals from 1971 to 1975, but Landry, the old punter, was a stickler for technique. During one practice in 1975, he told him, "Toni, I want you to kick through the ball." Fritsch, who was neither starry-eyed about American football nor overly subservient to Landry, bristled. "Coach Landry," he said in his thick accent, "you don't tell me how to keeck the ball. . . . I keeck the ball. You don't know how to keeck the ball. I keeck the ball for one point. I keeck the ball for three points."[13]

He had logic on his side, but not the coach. After that season, he was traded to San Diego, then to Houston, and made the All-Pro team in 1979. Landry would quickly sign away from the Rams the Mexican-born Rafael Septien, who would be the Cowboys' kicker for the next nine seasons and an All-Pro in 1981. Septien had his own foibles, however. In 1987 he would be arrested for and cop a plea on a charge of indecency with a ten-year-old girl—the same age of the girl Lance Rentzel had exposed *himself* to in 1970. Septien received ten years' probation and a $2,000 fine.[14] The Cowboys, wasting no time, released him within twenty-four hours.

But most ominously of all there was Hollywood Henderson, who was going to be the ruination of either Landry or himself. Or perhaps both.

THE EASY breezes of 1977 were gone when the next season commenced. In the new sixteen-game format, they won three of their first four before losing a cage match, 9–5, to the Redskins but not to George Allen, who had ultimately failed to displace Landry from owning the division and retired from coaching after the '77 season. At 3–2, the Cowboys seemed suddenly old, and teams were indeed picking on Barnes and Kyle for big yardage. No one seemed ready to step up, and in Dallas the front-running fan base was beginning to get nervous. At that stage of the season, I was sent to Dallas on assignment from *Sport* magazine to spend a few days around the Cowboys' offices and practice grounds. The title of the piece I subsequently wrote was one that could move a lot of magazines—"Behind the Cowboy Struggle to Reach Super Bowl XIII"[15]—and in fact *Sports Illustrated* soon after had its own take, a Joe Marshall concern titled "It Could Be Doomsday for Dallas."[16]

The trip was a revelatory experience because it provided insight into Landry the man and the sangfroid of his leadership. He did indeed have a Big Brother–like presence, looming over the operation, his proverbs staring down from locker room and office walls, such as this one with an old theme: "The most important factor in building an excellent football strength and conditioning program is WILL POWER!!!!!"[17]

It was a Monday, an off-day, and over at the team's practice facility, a rather drab and makeshift-looking complex of fields and areas shaded by tents, all overseen by Landry's mobile cherry-picker tower, players straggled into the locker room. In spite of the hard times, they seemed to be an engaging bunch, cocky and very happy to be Cowboys. Cliff Harris, in his skivvies, sat at his locker strumming impromptu scatological tunes such as "Joe Theismann Is a Punk" on a guitar with two broken strings.

Some though were nursing pet peeves along with their bruises. Tony Dorsett bitched about the Cowboys' having sent a string of players and Dallas businessmen to remind him about the responsibilities of being a Cowboy—his lack of the proper "image" having apparently cost him both a commentary spot on NBC and a deal with Fabergé cologne after a woman friend was arrested on a drug charge. "I'm not a little kid," he told me. "I don't need people telling me how to act." He had recently moved from downtown Dallas to a quiet suburb but denied it was to stay away from trouble. "Nah, I don't need to go into town now to get what I want . . . they can come to me," leaving no mystery as to what he meant. I asked if we could meet up later at, say, the Playboy Club. He smiled the devil's smile. "Can't do that. I go with three bunnies, and they all think they're the only ones."

Roger Staubach griped about *his* image, of pristine Landry-approved godliness. "I'm not happy with the way the press treats me," he said. "They make me look like a joke: my religion, my feelings about family and country, my politics. . . . Those labels mean nothing to me; my philosophy is very basic and changes all the time. I'm not so blind as to deny that—while we stand for good things here—we don't provide equality for all. Even in the church there's incredible prejudice. And in the area of human rights, I'm as liberal as you can get."

There were other surprises in that room too. Randy White insisted it wasn't brutishness that made his game but rather new-age meditation. "I do something called psycho-cybernetics . . . 15 minutes a day visualizing positive things, like sacking quarterbacks. By Sunday, I'm in a shell. I don't know names and faces, just the guy I have to beat."[18]

With this diverse gene pool as prologue, back at Clint Murchison's own tower, I encountered the legendary figure who unified them all on Sunday afternoons. There Landry sat, under the fixed, staring eyes of his spiritual mentor Billy Graham, a giant oil painting of whom dominated the wall of his office, as if he were Landry's Big Brother. From behind a desk cluttered with papers, clad in a Cowboys polo shirt, he looked different *sans* fedora—Bob Hope once observed that seeing Landry without a chapeau was "like seeing Tammy Faye Bakker without makeup."[19] The face was taught and unlined, the blue eyes clear and bright, the bubble-gum-pink skin reaching up to the top of that beautifully bald head, an aging lion secure in his lair but restless. "The fire hasn't been there yet," he would say of the Cowboys. "Teams have a better idea of our tendencies. You never fool teams for long, but if you execute, it shouldn't stop you if you have good people playing a good system. But we're just not playing tough, determined football." In the end, though, as always, there were the comforting words of the Good Book. "The Apostle Paul," he went on, "says adversity can build character. We'll find out just how much character we have."

It was quintessential Landry. He was never a master of the lilting quote but always prepared to deliver one from his Bible to verbalize whatever greater cause or significance he needed to express, sometimes to the point of stupefaction. He could, however, still get grown men pumped up with such menial prose, and I could easily imagine Landry in the locker room before a game, uttering those same words, rousing emotions without raising his voice one octave. Landry was no mere windup toy, like George Allen. He had deep thoughts about the culture and the schisms of society that had carried over into the locker room. He didn't quite know what it all meant—the open sex, the drugs, the marching against war, the sexual revolution, feminism, gays coming out—but he tried to see things from a worldview not his own, and he could hold his generation accountable for the ills it caused.

"I respect the players more now than I used to," he went on. "Today's players are a product of the '60s, and an affluent society . . . the distractions hurt us, the endorsements, the appearances, the contract negotiations. You can't stop guys from getting all they can—but it's damn tough to try and run a football team with all of it. . . . The money thing is part of this era of freedom and individuality and a lot of it goes too far, but players are much more aware than we were. Something had to be done about race in the '60s and we didn't do it."

This was similar to what he had said five years before to Gary Cartwright: "People my age . . . we grew up with the Depression, the War . . . a time of ICBMs [intercontinental ballistic missiles] and pinstripe suits and rampant materialism. But times are changing. I see that and I make an effort to change, too."[20] Now, hearing him riff like that, as muted as he was, with a thin high-pitched trill of a voice and a trace of the childhood lisp that contributed to his introversion, the words rolling out as if plucked from a bluegrass guitar, with an intensity not easily heard but rather felt, a New York Jew was disarmed. Not all the suspicion was gone, nor was Landry without the flaws that would become clear decades later, but neither was he a cardboard cutout of a southern football daemon. He was an aging man being tested by tides he couldn't stop, though he was trying—more than many other coaches far less set in their ways than he was in his.

Landry's swiftly wielded ax, the one he had used in the early and mid 1970s to mete out Cowboys justice to heretics like Billy Parks, Tody Smith, Rodrigo Barnes, Toni Fritsch, and Jean Fugett, had been put back in the woodshed as he attempted somehow to tolerate Hollywood Henderson. In the locker room the day I was there, Henderson wore a bright yellow "HOLLYWOOD" T-shirt, his locker dressed up with baby pictures of himself, "because I like to remind myself of what a beautiful baby I was . . . and still am," he said. He had lines like that down pat, not that everyone in the room cared to hear them. Henderson, taking the tone down, related, "Last spring I got hepatitis and was in the hospital for eight days. And nobody sent me a card or called. . . . It's okay. I don't hold it against nobody. But it just told me you gotta care for yourself, that no one else will."

HENDERSON CAME to taunt Landry and turn him inside out. He was easily the hardest player Landry tried to understand. As such, Henderson was a different kind of rebel, posing for Landry much the same confusion that Muhammad Ali caused the white culture. Henderson, growing up in Austin—the side of it Landry had not seen when he was the campus hero there decades before—the youngest of fifteen children, and abandoned by his father, had seen his mother shoot and nearly kill his stepfather, a raging drunk who abused her. By age twelve, he was burglarizing homes, smoking dope, and snorting heroin. Though he was a natural on the field, no truer words were ever spoken than those of Harvey Martin, Henderson's closest friend on the Cowboys, at least for a while, who once said of him, "The Cowboy computers early on spotted this rare, once-in-a-lifetime talent. But the computers could only measure athletic statistics, not a man's character."[21]

Henderson's whole existence seemed to scream payback and vengeance on people he judged as causing him pain. "I know where I've been and I don't want to go back," he once said. "I had to create an identity. It's a miracle I found Hollywood."[22] He was in the Ali mold, but only on a surface level—after all, Cassius Clay became Muhammad Ali on religious principle, not "Hollywood Clay" on crass hype. Henderson neither understood nor could discourse about anything serious. Even his obligatory racial soundings were purely personal, based as they were on his skew of things and making for good copy. He drew a line between himself and Duane Thomas, whom he said "had racial contamination . . . he knew racism and he was angry . . . I was never angry. I was just proud. I was arrogant, free and uncontaminated." He was, also, he believed, "the new black man."[23]

In truth, there was little about him that bespoke of any goal larger than serving himself. He cut only himself slack for on-field mistakes, and off it he was a misanthrope and gratuitously cruel, using his smile and contrived one-liners to disarm the writers who helped make him a walking sideshow act. If Landry had to get used to Henderson slighting him, so did the other black Cowboys. "The other guys, particularly the older guys, were afraid of Landry," he once said. "Jethro Pugh, Rayfield Wright, Mel Renfro, some of the older black gentlemen on the Cowboys had experienced racism from a powerless point of view. And that doesn't mean that they weren't great men. But when they saw me being free and expressive, they would get all upset. I would even smoke cigarettes in my locker. Shit, some of those guys would go smoke in their car."[24]

Henderson created a persona that the Cowboys had never encountered before, his preening, solipsistic jive talking anathema to Landry's regimented uniformity. Indeed, when he began a frightful foray into the hell of cocaine addiction,[25] it portended something exponentially more ominous than, say, Don Meredith's escapades with the drug, because of Henderson's ever-expanding sense of dare and defiance. Thus, Henderson was profoundly significant on and off the field, changing the image of the Cowboys from under-the-radar reprobates playing the role of clean-nosed Landry analogs to a team led by the ultimate nonconformist. Schramm was said to believe that Henderson "dramatically changed sports history" by begetting the crude self-promotion that became the norm for ensuing football generations.[26]

If so, it was because of the high irony that it gestated on a Tom Landry team. In fairness, it is likely that any coach would have put up with Henderson, his talent being such a tipping point in any given game. But when it seemed that Landry's moral code became compromised, the entire football ecosystem broke down.

TO BE sure, Landry's legacy would be soured by the second, greater bargain he made with the devil. Skip Bayless once quoted an unnamed Cowboys source in the 1990s who said that in the late 1970s, when "the Cowboys were at their peak, the entire country had to put up with so much shit from them that the new regime is still paying for it."[27] Surely, Landry had to bite his lip when the Hollywood thing grew, turning as many people off to the Cowboys as it turned on. It was just one of many accommodations, concessions, and compromises he had to make with his own organization. As Frank Luksa described the Cowboys' evolution, by then the team "existed in a separate reality than any other team. It was like a fun house mirror, all distorted."[28] As for Hollywood, he grew more distorted as he got away with more and more. By the time he stepped into the starting lineup, he was hopelessly addicted to cocaine and not all that concerned with covering up his addiction. Yet in the decadent fast lanes of Dallas, Henderson seemed somewhat *understated* next to the more highly publicized Cowboys. He had also fallen in with two other black players who had achieved unbridled superstardom and free license around town: Too Tall Jones and Harvey Martin.

The latter had his own weekly radio program, *The Beautiful Harvey Martin Show*, one of several such forums hosted by Cowboys royalty, including Tex Schramm and Landry. Martin's hip, happening patter pulled the highest ratings of any radio show in Dallas and frequently irked the front office for not towing the bland company line. He also owned an "in" discotheque—named, of all things for a Landry player, Lucifer's—and lived in a sumptuous North Dallas house with a heated indoor swimming pool right off the master bedroom, a Jacuzzi, and a rock waterfall spilling into the pool. As Henderson, green with envy, liked to describe it, it was "a romantic-looking spot to take a white girl whose parents didn't like niggers."[29]

Jones had his own custom condominium in North Dallas, with mirrored walls and ceilings in every room and reputedly the biggest bed anyone ever saw. Henderson spent much time there, testing the dimensions and inner springs of the bed. "I mean, we could get eight women in that bed."[30] It didn't much matter to him that his wife had left him and that his current girlfriend, Wyetta, a former bunny at the Playboy Club, was pregnant with his child. Nor did it matter that in the off-season he would hang around Hollywood, the real one, and make the club scene on Sunset Boulevard with one of the singing Pointer sisters, Anita. He would then call Anita his girlfriend while the endlessly suffering Wyetta lived in his house awaiting childbirth, never knowing where he was and with whom.

His only priority was himself, and the coke, which one could get simply by reaching out a palm. As Martin said, "Drugs blanketed Dallas. . . . You could order them from waiters in the fanciest night-clubs, if you knew how to ask. You could pretend to be ordering from the menu and actually be buying cocaine."[31] Henderson knew how to play that game. He rented limos, borrowed sable and bea-ver coats, and looked for beds to spend the night in. He was a con man from the get-go, using his considerable charm and bluff to score the next hit of coke, and a huge stash of cash. The "Hollywood" brand got him a $100,000 payday for a 7UP television commercial.[32] Tex Schramm, unlike Landry, was a fan of crude commercialism and bumped Henderson's salary up to $120,000 before the 1976 season. The bigger bucks could buy Henderson his own showy crib in North Dallas, but not a sense of healthy values. "I just bought class," he bragged to Martin one day about the house. Martin, who knew how shallow Henderson was, had a pointed reply, aimed directly at him: "You can't buy class."

It was a lesson Henderson was loath to learn. "If people knew all the women I've gone to bed with, it would shock Dallas," he said during his career rise, as if it earned him class points. As Martin recalled, "I tried to talk sense to Thomas but he lived somewhere around the bend."[33] More and more so when he became captive to cocaine, which became inseparable from his game. In time, he needed a good shot of blow in his veins the morning of a game. He could barely get out of bed some mornings, and getting to practice was always a struggle, but at least he could crash and get some sleep—in the darkened room when Landry ran the films, his bloodshot eyes covered by dark glasses. So unfazed was he by Landry that he rel-ished telling the story of the time the coach, seeing him out cold in the back row, threw him out of the room. That was, Henderson would laugh, "the only time I ever heard Tom curse. . . . He said, 'If you can't stay awake, get your ass out of the meeting.'"[34]

Henderson was convinced he could get away with anything; some-times, it was too easy. When his daily cocaine snorting caused him a deviated septum, it provided him a useful con. As Martin said, "His nose always ran, and he'd blow huge gobs of snot and phlegm onto his T-shirt."³⁵ Henderson's explanation was that it was due to a sinus problem, for which he happened to carry an inhaler, which only he knew was filled not with medicinal nose drops but liquefied cocaine. To his delight, he could inhale the stuff right in front of Landry's own nose.

If Henderson could do a passable riff of Muhammad Ali—stealing the champ's lines about being "pretty in the face and narrow at the hip," delivered with the same twinkle of the eye and self-parody—he had an unremitting dark side. As if his treatment of his girlfriend wasn't grotesque enough, he would also physically abuse her during her pregnancy, later writing in his first memoir, *Out of Control*, published in 1987, that he knew at the time he had a pathological problem. During an argument about his infidelity, he wrote, "I slapped her on top of the head. I slapped her again and again. . . . I kept hitting her 'til my hand got sore. What went through my mind, right then, was, 'This is the way my stepdaddy hit my mother, this is heritage coming up here.'"

As any cad would, he downplayed the act of striking a woman pregnant with his child with the justification that "I always kept an open hand, I never hit her with my fist," though he also admitted, "I was hitting tight ends about the head with these same open hands." He later realized that all this was "the cocaine at work" and that "I never hit Wyetta when I wasn't loaded."³⁶ For her, however, the pain of his hands wasn't as humiliating as that of his words. Cowboys players would hear him rail about her in the locker room, calling her crazy, a gold digger, a whore, and worse. When she gave birth to a daughter, Thomesa Holly Henderson in March 1979, he would go right on philandering and ignoring them—just as his own father had done to his family. Wyetta had to file a paternity suit against him before he would agree to marry her, and then dropped the suit.

In his semi-contrite autobiography, his prose turned almost poetically sad when he wrote, "I used friendships and nobody ever called me on it. I smiled through gritted teeth, looking at people, looking at people as they were watching me work them. And they would let me work them. I always felt good about the conquest, and the fact that I could do it again and again. But there was something very empty about it. . . . The bottom line was that with no spiritual base, with no serious values, I was lost. I was out of control."[37]

The most grating aspect of Henderson's Cowboys days was that in his coke-crazed haze, he actually saw himself as the great upholder of the team's surface values. Once, he tried to haze a rookie in camp, demanding that he sing during meals at the dining hall. The rookie refused, prompting Henderson to go off on a rant in front of the team about how the rookie "disrespected all our traditions . . . he not only disrespected me, he disrespected all you assholes."[38] Of course, Henderson always convinced himself that he was the victim at all times. Even years later, with his life in ruins, this sense of self-pity was still evident, with Henderson clinging to the fiction that he, not those he hurt, had paid a great price in aggravation and indignity, and that was what caused him to run off the rails. "I was the first black linebacker to hold down that position . . . and I'm not sure that set right with them," he said, meaning just about everyone on the team. He said that an in-house team motto could have been "Keep America Clean; Keep the Linebackers White."[39]

Unknowingly, he wrote his own epitaph when he said, when all was going well, "Here I am, this dysfunctional black bastard in the biggest game in the world, and if they really knew me, they'd throw me out of here."[40]

HENDERSON WAS conning himself by believing he could walk all over Landry forever. Indeed, he had erected a wholly erroneous effigy of the coach, whom he once said wasn't a plastic man but rather "the Tin Man; if that sucker cried he'd rust." Landry did have his overly sentimental moments, which could arise in a heartbeat when he cut a player he truly liked. One of those was a linebacker, Ken Hutcherson, who had all the tools and was a deeply committed Christian. "This is the toughest part of the business," Landry said, nearly sobbing, after releasing Hutcherson. "I had to cut a fine young man, a good friend, a good Christian."[41] But Landry kept those moments fleeting, and Henderson himself had to duck for cover when the coach laid into him for missed assignments on the field. Even so, Henderson always assumed he could get away with doing as much cocaine as he wished, knowing how little Landry knew about such contemporary cultural deviations. On that ground, Hollywood may have been right. As Frank Luksa said of those times, "A lot of us were in the dark about coke. We were all naive about drugs."

What's more, Landry seemed not to mind having a couple of outlaws on the roster, mingled in with the straight arrows and rednecks. Henderson, giving cover to himself, relished telling tales of other Cowboys who came to meetings under duress. One veteran, he recalled, would "come in hung over on tequila and faint dead away on the locker-room floor. We'd revive him for the meeting and he'd go in and faint all over again."[42] He maintained that 40 percent of his Cowboys teammates were using drugs of some kind, and that "five whites and seven blacks I knew of, including myself . . . were using marijuana, pills, cocaine, and other mind-altering substances."[43] Some needn't have left the locker room to get high on something other than the challenge of the game. He recalled that "there was someone in the locker room passing out pills [who] said, 'This here is for pain, and this here is to get you up for the game.'. . . The black capsules we called Black Mollies or Niggers. We'd say, 'That boy's playing like a nigger today. Must have some nigger in him.'"[44]

That was another barometer of the racial divide on those Cowboys teams—Henderson and D. D. Lewis, an archetypical good ol' boy from Mississippi, once nearly had it out, with fists, in the showers—yet even among brothers, Henderson became increasingly isolated. He once noted that Too Tall Jones back then "was getting a little leery of my drug use. His agent was putting pressure on him, I'm sure, saying, 'You've got to get away from this guy,' and finally Ed gave in."[45]

Landry could be forgiven if he didn't want to know any of what Henderson or anyone else was doing. If the team kept on winning, perhaps such ways of blowing off steam were beneficial. Henderson, for his part, said in retrospect that the Cowboys' front office was more clued in than they let on. "See, I think Tex Schramm knew and Gil Brandt knew [and] I'm not sure they told Landry," he said. "And that's kind of the way the Cowboys were run in those days. They insulated and protected Landry from that sort of thing."[46] To be sure, the leeway given Henderson was extraordinary. But it was plausible to those who were there that, among grown men, one didn't ask or tell. Lee Roy Jordan, for example, says, "I truly didn't know what guys were doing. I didn't know if a guy had been drinking Gatorade or tequila. I didn't want to know. And neither did Tom."[47]

Henderson belittled Landry's obligatory attempts to put some old-time religion into him by often sending as his messenger line-backer Bob Breunig, a devout Christian who attended Fellowship of Christian Athletes banquets with Landry. To Henderson, the only compact he had with the coach was to help him win, and nothing more, given that, as he said in the 1980s, "I always felt that Landry looked down on me, I know that Landry is not a racist, but he acted like one . . . he acted holier-than-thou," and that "I never had a con-versation about anything normal with Tom Landry until *long* after my career was over."[48] In this, he was hardly alone. The difference was that Landry never stuck with any miscreant as long as he did Henderson, who got it into his head that he had Landry in the palm of his hand, for as long as he wanted him there, so he believed. That, perhaps, was the most deranged thought Henderson ever had.

IT WAS not Doomsday for the Cowboys. With a 6–4 record and Landry having taken a kick to the gut when Ray died in late Octo-ber, the Cowboys virtually replayed the 1971 season. They ripped off the last six games, a span that saw some ridiculous blowouts: 42–14 over the Packers, 37–10 in the return match with the Red-skins, 31–13 over the Eagles, 30–7 over the Jets in the finale. When the smoke cleared, the Cowboys' record was 12–4, kings of the NFC East by three games. Taking full advantage of the new rules, Landry's offense tallied a fat 384 points, by far the most in the league. Stau-bach, throwing forty-four more passes than he ever would in the longer schedule, compiled 3,000 yards and twenty-five touchdowns. Dorsett ran for 1,325 yards and became just the third back to clear a thousand yards in his first two years. They both made All-Pro, as did Tony Hill, who displaced the troubled Golden Richards and caught the most passes on the team. Another receiver also made a mark, even though he didn't catch a single pass: thirty-eight-year-old tight end Jackie Smith. A five-time All-Pro with the perennial loser Cardinals, Smith had wanted to finish his career with a winner. After Jay Saldi went down with a knee injury in midseason, the Cowboys signed Smith, mainly as a blocker in Landry's two-tight-end set.

The Cowboys also adapted to the rules defensively, surrendering the third-fewest points on the strength of the best rushing defense in the NFL, with a league-high fifty-eight sacks. Martin, Henderson, Waters, and Harris made All-Pro, and Too Tall Jones, who was snubbed, was arguably the most feared among them. With so much age and fragility to them, much of the team was admittedly held together by glue and spit, but Landry had wrung from them another remarkable season, and with the last Super Bowl to be played in the decade on the horizon, the old stone-face, if he could get there, would be playing for the laurel of best team of the 1970s.

At home for the first round of the playoffs, the Cowboys faced a surprisingly resilient Atlanta Falcons and had to come back from 20–13 at halftime—behind Danny White, who came off the bench when Staubach took a hard hit in the third quarter. White was superb, completing ten for twenty passes for 127 yards and a 2-yard touchdown flip to Jackie Smith—his first catch of the season—that tied the game. White then led the fourth-quarter drive that culminated with the nearly forgotten Scott Laidlaw, who would run seventeen times for 66 yards, taking the ball from the 1-yard line into the end zone to grab the game 27–20.

Staubach insisted he was okay when the NFC title contest took the Cowboys to the West Coast for yet another tangle with the Rams, the upset loss to them in Texas Stadium two years before still stinging Landry. The Rams had a new coach, the portly, red-nosed Ray Malavasi, who replaced Chuck Knox, and Merlin Olsen had retired, but Jack Youngblood and Fred Dryer were still on the defensive line, the linebackers were strong and mobile, and cornerbacks Pat Thomas and Rod Perry made the All-Pro team. After the game began, it surprised no one that neither offense could move much; at halftime, the game was scoreless.

In the third quarter came the big play. Deep in his own territory, the Rams' unremarkable quarterback, Pat Haden, tried a short pass. Waters, playing close to the line, read the play perfectly, stepped in front of the receiver, and intercepted the ball at the 10. Dorsett took it in from the 5 for a 7–0 lead. The Rams then went on a long drive, which stalled at Dallas's 13-yard line. Here Malavasi gambled, going for the first down on fourth down, but the Cowboys surged into the backfield and stuffed the runner. Minutes later Waters picked off another pass, setting up Staubach's 4-yard scoring pass to Laidlaw. After Staubach's pass to DuPree made the score 21–0 in the fourth quarter, Cowboys' schadenfreude surfaced. Henderson, who believed that Malavasi had assigned players to physically injure him during the game—just as he had gone after Rick Upchurch in the last Super Bowl—at one point got in Malavasi's face, called him a "fat drunk," and vowed, "I'm going to singlehandedly beat your fat ass today."[49] This was just a tad more uncivil than the way Landry had once mouthed off to Paul Brown, but then Malavasi was no Paul Brown. Now, after intercepting a pass and running 68 yards for a touchdown, Henderson rose font-like and slammed the ball over the goal post again, certifying the 28–0 rout.

For yet another week, Henderson's narcissism was no cause for concern for Landry. Not when the man could make plays like *that*.

FATE DELIVERED the Cowboys what it hadn't a year earlier, the return match at the summit with the "semicrazed" Steelers, who had rebounded strongly and gone 14–2 for the season. They would collide on January 21, 1979, in the Orange Bowl, which seemed ominous for Landry's men, though the game shaped up as a truly Olympian clash. Joe Marshall salivated, "At long last, the AFC and the NFC have *both* put their best teams forward."[50] *Newsweek* parroted the same theme in a January 22 cover story, "A Really Super Bowl," which carried a split image of Terry Bradshaw and Hollywood Henderson. Such exposure led Henderson to tell reporters, "I'm more famous than the Shah of Iran," albeit not much more popular than the recently deposed dictator who had taken exile in the United States. Henderson also wondered if pictures of him would show any powder under his nose.[51]

Even given the hype that had come to usher in each Super Bowl, this one was by any rational measure something special. Fourteen men who played that day would go to the Hall of Fame—Roger Staubach, Tony Dorsett, Randy White, Rayfield Wright, Jackie Smith, Terry Bradshaw, Franco Harris, Lynn Swann, Mean Joe Greene, Jack Lambert, Jack Ham, receiver John Stallworth, cornerback Mel Blount, and center Mike Webster—and no one could doubt that these were the two best teams of the decade. Yet everything seemed geared around Henderson, who popped up everywhere there was a camera or a pen in motion. He clearly was on—but *what*? To some, it was obvious. When Henderson uttered his immortal diss that Bradshaw "couldn't spell cat if you spotted him the c and the t," Bradshaw's lesser-reported unguarded rejoinder was far more lethal, and accurate: "We're going to beat the Cowboys, and Hollywood Henderson is going to lose and then get strung out on cocaine."[52] Henderson, in turn, had a promise. If the Steelers won, he said, "I'll bring my acetylene torch to the Orange Bowl and cut [the Steel Curtain] up."[53]

Landry, who had learned to grit his teeth and put up with Henderson's mouth even when he didn't know what he was blathering about, said of the crack about Bradshaw's IQ, "I cringed when I heard that."[54] He would have cringed more had he known that Henderson had made a deal in Miami that week, buying an ounce of cocaine in exchange for tickets, and that, on the morning of the game, he loaded his nose with liquid cocaine. Just before taking the field, he would tuck the inhaler into a pocket inside the waistband of his football pants for a quick snort during the game, in spite—or because—of how insanely depraved it was to do this.

With the Steelers favored by 4 points, Landry was working the referees in advance, bringing up the paucity of penalties in Super Bowl XI. The Steelers, he said, "got away with a good thing in 1976. Let's just hope it doesn't happen again."[55] Neither had the Steelers forgotten that win. Martin later said the Steel Town team believed the Cowboys were "sissies," and this stung more so now that the "Gucci" Cowboys were defending champions. Indeed, the sociological hues of the contest were evident in a *Dallas Morning News* pregame story that was headlined "COWBOYS, STEELERS IN CLASS STRUGGLE."[56]

The key to the game again lay in the trenches, where championship teams proved their working-class credentials. Beyond that, Landry could only hope that his secondary wouldn't crack. It was a tall task—too tall, one could say—but typical of Landry was that he and Ernie Stautner had developed a system with Harris and Waters to deal with the restrictions on the bump and run. The cerebral Waters had explained to me months before, "What we're doing is disguising inside coverage, then doubling up deep on the big receivers, kind of a safety zone . . . we're both coming up and jamming [our] receivers off the line, then breaking back with them in shadow coverage." This meant the Cowboys' safeties had to disrupt the receivers' timing and still adhere to them all the way down the field into a deep zone. It seemed almost Rube Goldberg–esque. But, Waters had promised, by December "no team will beat us on that rule."[57] He was right about that. But it was now late January, and the stakes couldn't be higher.

MIAMI WAS a humid seventy-one degrees at the opening kick, and the field hard and fast. Tony Dorsett seemed to find it a magic carpet ride. On the first drive, behind masterful blocking, he shredded the Steel Curtain, gaining 38 yards on three carries, moving the ball to the Steelers' 38. But here Landry got too cute. Eager to mess with Chuck Noll's head, he called for a reverse flea flicker, designed for Dorsett to hand off to Drew Pearson, who would then funnel it back to Staubach for a deep pass downfield. Landry had tried a variation of it, a *receiver* option, in the Rams game, with Butch Johnson coming back to take the hand-off, only to see Johnson fumble. Now, Pearson took the ball from Dorsett, and *he* fumbled it, with the Steelers recovering. "We practiced that play for three weeks," Pearson moaned later. "We practiced the play so much it was unbelievable we could fumble it."[58]

Bradshaw made the Cowboys pay, lofting a fluttery 28-yard touchdown pass to Stallworth behind the double coverage Waters boasted of. Despite the gift, though, Staubach soon after evened the score with a 39-yard strike to Hill. Then in the second quarter, Henderson and Mike Hegman chased Bradshaw out of the pocket. Both wrapped their arms around him, with Hegman prying the ball from him and running 37 yards for a touchdown. However, Bradshaw was nothing if not resilient. The Cowboys would sack him four times and batter him silly, but with his ground game shut off, he would find another way. He also profited from a chain of Cowboys errors. After falling behind, he threw a short pass to Stallworth, and Kyle missed the tackle, sending Stallworth on a 75-yard jaunt to tie the score.

The Cowboys got back up and moved to the Pittsburgh 25, but after Dorsett was hit late out of bounds, he stuck the ball in the offending Steeler's face mask, sustaining a 15-yard penalty. Staubach then sailed one for Drew Pearson on a crossing pattern but failed to see Blount hanging around the middle of the field. His interception killed the drive, and on the last play of the half Bradshaw found a leaping Bleier for a 7-yard touchdown and a 21–14 lead. It was an exhausting thirty minutes, full of bone-rattling hits and trash-mouthing—Henderson and Franco Harris were in each other's face all day. Yet the Cowboys seemed to have figured the Steelers out, holding them without a first down in the third quarter. However, after Staubach moved them to the Steeler's 11-yard line, Landry called for a three-tight-end passing formation, normally a play he used on the goal line to mask a short pass into the end zone. When Staubach received the play, he was confused and called a time-out. "Coach, that's a goal line play," he told Landry, who acknowledged his error—he mistakenly thought the ball was on the 1—but thought the call would work regardless.

"Run it anyway," he ordered.[59]

He looked like a genius when after the snap Staubach looked up and saw Smith in the end zone, completely uncovered, so open, Staubach said later, that "I could have punted it to him." So open that Staubach eased off just a bit on the pass. It was now dark, the lights glaring down from the top of the stadium, and the ball led Smith slightly to his right. All of these subtle factors mattered when Smith went for the ball. First his legs slid under him, causing him to lose sight of the ball for a split-second. The easiest pass he ever had to catch went right through his hands then glanced off his chest. The crowd, reflexively gearing up for the sure touchdown, suddenly emitted a collective gasp. Smith, with the ball spinning on the ground, collapsed in agony onto his back, punching together the hands that failed him.

Landry, in a beige sport jacket and brown hat, threw his arms into the air and jerked around as if a slug had entered his gut, not unlike the reaction he displayed when Don Meredith threw away the 1967 title game against the Packers. His eyes were jammed shut and his mouth contorted in an *oh no!* pantomime, which would be one of the images in the next day's *Morning News*. Beside him, Danny White angrily slammed his helmet to the turf. Other Cowboys stomped their feet and cursed. Once the initial shock faded, no matter who you were that day it was impossible not to feel sick for poor Smith, whose Hall of Fame career would forever be blackened by this one misplay, which he would explain without self-pity: "It was a beautiful play that Coach Landry conceived. When I slipped, I guess I was just trying to be overcautious, and that's why I dropped it."[60]

Having to settle for a field goal, the only score in the third quarter, the Cowboys trailed 21–17, and the game was still winnable. Even though Stallworth had gone out with a muscle cramp in his leg and would not return, Bradshaw would make Schramm pay for his rule changes. Shadow zones and all, Bradshaw's deadly passes, some key ones to unsung tight end Randy Grossman, led a desperate Waters to beg Henderson to detour from stalking Harris and give Grossman a bump at the line, to keep him from getting into the passing lanes. As it happened, Henderson had belittled Grossman all week as a nonentity, and had been getting by him with no trouble. Now, it was Henderson who was taken out of his game—as was Harvey Martin, literally, having left with a hamstring pull.

Bradshaw also got a huge break early in the fourth quarter when he heaved one long pass downfield. Jostling under it, Swann and Barnes became tangled and fell to the ground. No penalty was called until, from 20 yards away, referee Fred Swearingen threw a late flag, on Barnes, for interference. The Cowboys yowled, Barnes raging at Swearingen, who mercifully refrained from tacking on another 15 yards for unsportsmanlike conduct. Barnes, adamant later, insisted that Swann "shoved me, knocked me down and tripped over me. When I saw the flag, I was mad, damn right. It was the closest I'll ever come to punching an official."[61] From the Dallas 23, Bradshaw called a draw up the middle for Harris. Not only was Henderson late in plugging the gap, but Waters was accidentally knocked over by the umpire, who got in his way. Harris rumbled untouched for a 22-yard touchdown, gleefully taunting Henderson after he did.

Worse for Hollywood, he was coming down from his coke high

and was in severe pain from the shots he took. On the sideline late in the third quarter, he removed the inhaler and, as he would say, "took a couple of deep belts of my liquid cocaine."[62] No one in the Orange Bowl or across the country was any the wiser that an All-Pro whose face had represented the glory of the league on a national magazine cover—a man who played for *Tom Landry*—was committing a crime on national television before 75 million viewers, blasting himself with a controlled substance into the ionosphere right in the middle of America's biggest sports event. It was metaphoric of the dirty realities that lay beneath the flag-draped veil of pro football. And Henderson was especially pleased that "the coaches were out in the cold," one in particular.

Down 28–17, the Cowboys gifted the Steelers once more. The Steelers' kickoff went short and was fielded by, of all people, Randy White, who like Henderson played on special teams, as a blocker. White, wearing a cast for a broken thumb, was unable to grip the ball and fumbled on Pittsburghs' 18. Bradshaw threw a pass out to the buttery Swann, who smoothly elevated without losing his stride and grabbed the ball ahead of Barnes. It was Bradshaw's fourth touchdown pass, putting the Steelers safely ahead, 35–17, or so it seemed. But Staubach didn't surrender. He led two furious drives that had the prematurely roistering Steelers defenders running in circles. Wasting no time between snaps, calling his own plays, Staubach ended the first drive with a 7-yard touchdown lob to DuPree, then after a successful on-side kick, another of 4 yards to Johnson.

Just like that it was 35–31, but there was no time left for miracles. The clock ran out, not only on the game but also on the proposition that Tom Landry had coached the team of the 1970s. The decade he knew he should have owned, just like this microcosmic game, had gotten away.

Chapter 23

AMERICA'S TEAM—
OR THE ANTICHRIST?

THERE WAS NO LOMBARDI TROPHY for Landry, but instead plenty of recriminations and backbiting in the wake of the bitterly galling defeat to the Steelers. On the surface, Landry had nothing to apologize for, which was good since he had no intention of doing so. With both offenses scoring the most points in a Super Bowl to date, and ringing up 556 total yards, not to mention six turnovers and nine sacks, Dan Jenkins wrote that Super Bowl XIII "was everything professional football's championship game is supposed to be, but rarely is."[1] The Cowboys, however, seethed. Harvey Martin called the Steelers "very lucky"[2] for cashing in on the Cowboys' flubs, and pretty much everyone spoke of Fred Swearingen as the devil incarnate. A few days later, the NFL office felt compelled to clarify that the call was incorrect, not that this mea culpa changed a thing. It suddenly seemed relevant to some to recall that Swearingen had been good luck for the Steelers before, being the referee when Franco Harris made his controversial "Immaculate Reception," on a pass that might have been deflected by an offensive player, giving his team a last-second miracle victory over the Raiders in a 1972 playoff game.

Roger Staubach was so distraught that he had no use for Christian forgiveness, grumbling that the outcome was "a real crime"[3] and referring to "some idiot official throwing a flag when he'd been out of position to see the play right."[4] Even so, the Cowboys insisted they should have won, and would have had Staubach not simply run out of time—a hoary echo of Dandy Don and their first title loss to the Packers. Hollywood Henderson, who didn't burn down the Orange Bowl and with rare humility congratulated Bradshaw on the field, cried at his locker, nursing in his mind the excuse that Charlie Waters, not he, was to blame, both for taking him out of his game and for not making the tackle on Harris's key touchdown run.

Landry's postmortem was that "we tried hard" but "we didn't take advantage of what opportunities we had. . . . On a given day, Pittsburgh is no better team than we are," and allowed that the interference call was "a very expensive one. . . . It looked to me as if [Swann] jumped into Benny." Cornered a few days later by Sam Blair, after viewing the films, he went a bit further: "Unfortunately, he missed it," he said, meaning Swearingen, who, he charged, "had no idea what was happening." Blair's headline was "LANDRY FUMES OVER CALL."[5] These pretexts, which were repeated over and over at the morgue-like postgame party Murchison held at the hotel, were mostly hot air. Landry knew the Steelers had outplayed his boys again. Bradshaw, the game's MVP, enjoyed his most productive day as a pro, both his 318 yards and four touchdowns career highs for him at the time and Super Bowl records. He did it with his shoulder nearly dislocated by some ferocious hits. The Jackie Smith drop aside, there was some mild second-guessing of Landry's strategy, such as the trick play that blew up and whether he should have had Randy White out there on the bungled kickoff.

Drew Pearson was unusually pointed, noting that the team had practiced over-the-middle pass routes, but Landry hadn't called for them until the game was out of hand. "I don't know why," Pearson said. "If I did, I'd be head coach."[6] This was the first hint of a growing feeling on the team that Landry was becoming more uptight and proprietary about the plays, unwilling to bend to new winds and strategies. As it was, Bradshaw, the man who allegedly couldn't spell "cat" made the Cowboys' defense seem rudimentary, openly boasting, "Shoot, there was no big mystery about how to beat the Flex. You throw on first down [which Bradshaw did fifteen times, with nine completions and two touchdowns]. The corners were almost always man-to-man on first down because the Flex was geared to stop the run. I almost felt sorry for their cornerbacks. I had Lynn Swann and John Stallworth out there, and all I had to do was throw it and they'd go get it."[7]

What had happened in Miami was exactly what Landry feared when the pass defense rules were relaxed, and why he felt so betrayed by Tex Schramm, whom he would never forgive for the sin of putting the league ahead of his team. *Don't ever take sides against the family* was also the first rule of the Dallas Cowboys' godfather. Had he thought about it, Landry might have construed that, on some level, Tex was trying to tell him something: that the game had changed more than Landry thought, and if the team was to thrive, he would need to adapt, borrowing ideas from the new crop of sages rather than trying to find all the answers in his own mind. In this prism, Landry's continued use of trick plays, originally devised for their excitement quotient on a team needing to sell tickets, seemed to be like catnip, a shortcut to gratification. Landry's big attraction as a young coach was that he was a big thinker, especially for a conservative football man, had a sense of dare, and loved pyrotechnic, game-breaking plays. Now, he was mainly defending old habits. Yet, he was so far ahead of the crowd that he was still winning, with remarkable continuity. And still bowing to him, was the Dallas press corps, including younger writers hired to take a more abrasive, cynical approach. One, the *Morning News*' Skip Bayless, wrote after the Super Bowl,

> Tom Landry was dancing with the one who brung him—that usually faithful multiple offense. . . . Almost always, he plays by the printout, ignoring emotion or individual momentum, pressure or panic. Maybe he should have gone more to Dorsett or Drew Pearson. But, no, the game plan likely stipulated [otherwise]. And Landry, stubborn as he is honest, sticks by his game plan. Maybe Staubach, like Bradshaw, would have a better feel calling his own plays. But who can argue with Tom Landry's record? He perseveres. He endures.[8]

However, if Landry suspected paradise was lost in Miami, he was right. Even more than the two losses to Lombardi, this one hurt and took a toll of enormous historical consequences. It was Chuck Noll who would ride the whirlwind, winning his third championship and then his fourth the next year, drinking in the plaudits. The *Morning News'* page-one game-story headline on January 23—"STEELERS BRING CURTAIN DOWN ON DALLAS"—was more prescient than anyone could have thought, least of all the coach. What Tom Landry would be left with was the reigns of a commercial enterprise like no other in sports—a trade-off that, for him, would be nowhere near good enough.

THE COWBOYS lurched into 1979 with another big-game dunking to atone for, and a rising tide of problems. But they also received a fresh benediction that would forever be their brand. It began in the off-season when NFL Films needed an angle to play for the team's 1978 highlight reel, which like the highlight reels for all other teams was marketed for sale. In the football marketing crowd, the Cowboys were the "it" team, based on the empirical data that showed them as popular a TV attraction as a Dean Martin celebrity roast. After all, they had been seen in three of the four highest-rated sporting events in history, the highest-rated Super Bowl and division and conference championship games, as well as the most-watched Sunday game. In 1979, they would be in the highest-rated Thanksgiving and Monday night games. As Landry understated, "Those things have happened because we've won, and in those wins are a lot of memories to keep."[9]

Bob Ryan, the vice president of NFL Films recalled that his first choice for the title of the film was "Champions Die Hard," but that Tex Schramm and the Cowboys' PR department thought it sent the message that the team's winning days were over. Ryan thought about an alternative, about the lure of the brand. "Wherever the Cowboys played, you saw people in the stands with Cowboys jerseys and hats and pennants," he said. "Plus, they were always the national game on television." His new suggestion, "America's Team," was about as arrogant as could be, which is every reason why Schramm loved it and Landry detested it. As always on matters like these, Schramm waved it through. When the film was ready, the first line of Ryan's script went,

They appear on television so often that their faces are as familiar to the public as presidents and movie stars. They are the Dallas Cowboys, "America's Team."[10]

The insignia might have been a passing ray of hype, pleasing to the limited audience of the reel in school assemblies, rotary clubs, and team banquets around Dallas, had not Pat Summerall, Landry's old confrere, introduced it to a nationwide audience on the CBS broadcast of the Cowboys' season opener against the St. Louis Cardinals. Landry, who thought he might never again hear the phrase, had no such luck; rather, people began asking him about it all the time. Each time, he would cringe. "Tom found it unseemly; to stand on a stage and scream 'Look at me' was not who he was," said Brad Sham, the team's longtime radio broadcaster. Tom Jr. agreed: "He felt we had painted a target on our back."[11] As usual, Landry was right. When the name got around, appearing more and more in newspapers across the league, the backlash mounted. The Steelers especially took it as an insult. "We resented, and I think we still resent the fact that someone or anyone refers to the Cowboys as 'America's Team.' You know what America's football team is? The team that wins the Super Bowl. That's America's Team."[12] Similarly, Raiders safety Mike Davis asked, "If they're America's Team, what are we, Guatemalans?"[13]

Actually, such protests were a bit much. The Raiders could only have been America's Team if America was a prison farm. As for the Steelers, while they too represented an albeit fading American subset, as a sports and cultural symbol their blue-collar sensibility was reminiscent of Lombardi's Packers but with none of the overwhelming emotional mesmerism of Lombardi. The gruff and disheveled Chuck Noll was actually as inscrutable as Landry, and far more cultured, a longtime gourmand and wine connoisseur, yet he was swallowed by Landry's polished and buffed prudence and purity, which clashed wildly but seemingly compatibly with his team's images of burgeoning wealth, sexy accessories in hot pants, and ding-a-lings like Hollywood Henderson.

Lurking under the glitzy surface of the Cowboys was something dark and antiheroic, interconnected to Dallas itself, a booming but boorish place where Pat Toomay said the Antichrist was alive and well. The Cowboys' identity was controvertible, adaptable, and compatible with the eye of the beholder. That they would root themselves further into the culture was confirmed in a 1979 Gallup survey in which American teenagers chose the saintly Roger Staubach as their favorite sports personality, and sometimes sinner Tony Dorsett as their second favorite.[14] The Cowboys had the market cornered on archetypes. Landry, now a deeply embedded icon, smoothed rough edges into comforting continuity. Which was why, despite any dissidence about the Cowboys, all arguments stopped when it came down to the coach, who, without even trying, had put himself atop the most acclaimed and marketed team in sports, a dynasty of a different sort, one that existed mainly as a fable. America's team, indeed.

THE BOLD trademark did in fact become a target, which was apparent in times of trouble. When the Cowboys made one of their many appearances on *Monday Night Football* in late September 1979, and lost 26–7 to the Cleveland Browns, Howard Cosell called them, and not unfairly, "the most over-glamorized, most propagandized team in football," adding that had they been in the AFC, "they wouldn't have been to so many Super Bowls."[15] By that time, the Cowboys had won their first three games of the season, and after the loss to the Browns they went on to win their next four, including one over the AFC's Cincinnati Bengals, 38–13. Sticking it to the heretics was often their best riposte.

The 1979 season in fact played out as another tribute to the coach's wizardry. All signs pointed to a bumpy road before it got under way. In June, Dorsett's eighteen-year-old fiancé Gigi Clayton died of an undiagnosed illness that had, without warning, paralyzed her from head to toe. Dorsett seemed to have his own curse when it came to women. A year later another fiancé, Princes Collins, would also die of mysterious causes, and his 1981 marriage to Julie Simon ended in divorce four years later.[16] He wasn't so lucky with his own health, either. In July, he dropped a mirror on his right foot, breaking his big toe. In another bad sign in June, fifty-seven-year-old John Murchison, Clint's brother and minority owner of the team, complained of feeling faint and was being taken to the hospital when the ambulance ran a red light and struck another vehicle, the crash killing him.

The biggest blow to the team's alchemy came when Too Tall Jones, a big man with big dreams and a bigger ego, shocked Landry with a sudden career change. Steamed that he had never been voted to the All-Pro team and that his contract had run out, he told Landry and Schramm he was quitting the gridiron for the four-cornered ring. A Golden Gloves fighter in his younger days, with a condor-like eighty-eight-inch reach, he had his eye on an eventual fight with the aging champ Muhammad Ali that would leave him set for life. Boxing people took it as a joke reminiscent of the thankfully unfulfilled chimera by seven-foot NBA star Wilt Chamberlain to get in the ring with Ali in the mid-1960s. Around the Cowboys, more than a few believed it to be a ploy to squeeze more money out of the team, until Jones indeed walked away and quickly signed a deal with CBS to televise each of his fights.

The timing was awful for Landry. Jethro Pugh had also retired, meaning that the left side of the Doomsday line was gone. And the secondary was in chaos. Barnes, Kyle, and Waters had had surgery, Waters for a ripped-up knee in an exhibition game that forced him to miss the entire season. Cliff Harris, who, while only thirty, looked ready for Social Security from the crashes he had instigated on the field, sensed that Landry would bench him for Randy Hughes and wanted to beat him to the punch by retiring. When Hughes dislocated his shoulder in camp, Landry talked Harris into staying for one final year. On the other side of the ball, Danny White fractured his right thumb, Scott Laidlaw injured his hamstring, and Drew Pearson his knee. Hollywood Henderson suffered a hiatal hernia of the esophagus, the bright side of which was that he had to give his throat a rest for a while.

Gil Brandt, for once, was unable to pull a rabbit out of a hat in the draft—though two solid players did arrive: Santa Clara tight end Doug Cosbie, a third-round pick, would play ten seasons with the Cowboys, and Ohio State running back Ron Springs, a fifth rounder who would play six seasons. With the defense wafer thin, Landry had to run stopgap players in and out. Fortuitously, in October, when the Colts' three-time All-Pro defensive end John Dutton, who, in his prime at twenty-eight, was embroiled in a contract dispute with the team, Tex Schramm pounced, sending Baltimore the Cowboys' first- and second-round picks in the 1980 draft. At six foot seven and 266 pounds, Dutton had surprising speed, igniting the Colts' "Sack Pack" front four, notching seventeen sacks in 1975, a club record (though still unofficial). He fit right into the Flex, playing the next nine seasons in Dallas.

Landry's great hope for the line was Schramm's first-round pick the year before, Michigan State defensive end Larry Bethea, the first defensive player to win the Big Ten's MVP award since Dick Butkus, something not even Bubba Smith could do. Bethea was a physical monster, but for some reason he showed limited fire on the field. One reason soon became clear when Bethea began hanging with Hollywood Henderson, no doubt causing Landry to sigh to himself, *Oh no, not again,* with reason since Henderson later would relate that he and Bethea did cocaine together. Bethea had the same sort of big ego and stuck around for six seasons, always on the verge of a breakthrough that never came.

The defense struggled in 1979, finishing twelfth in the league, yet Harris, White, and Martin went to the Pro Bowl. Beyond stats and honors, however, Landry could still wring big plays from most everyone—not least Staubach, who kept the team on track, winning eight of the first ten games. Staubach, at thirty-seven, played through pain and had arguably his best season, with twenty-seven touchdowns and only eleven interceptions, his passer rating being 92.3 percent, making All-Pro for the fifth straight year. This was the Staubach Landry always wanted: staying longer in the pocket, only thirty-seven rushes, longer passes—his 7.9 yards per attempt his personal high and the most in the league. Staubach's big target, Hill, caught sixty balls and had a career-best ten touchdowns, and earned his second straight All-Pro year, and Drew Pearson caught fifty-five for eight touchdowns, both going over 1,000 yards, the first time it happened on the Cowboys.

Out of character for a Landry team, the pass now set up the run. Dorsett, who missed two games, rallied from his woes to gain 1,107 yards. The grittiest performer, however, had to be Robert Newhouse, who during the season fractured his leg and, because he never said a word about it, played *three weeks* before the injury was properly diagnosed—which Harvey Martin thought was typical on the team. "I myself would come to experience less-than-perfect medical treatment provided by the Cowboys," he said.[17] Still Newhouse missed only two games and started a full twelve, earning his stripes with Landry, who would keep him around through the 1983 season, increasingly as a backup for Springs. Newhouse would also be kept in the organization for decades as director of alumni affairs. For all the good vibes, however, the Cowboys suddenly faltered in November, which included a game in the nation's capital that would be Hollywood Henderson's Waterloo.

LANDRY'S SLOW boil about Henderson had continued, the coach wearily issuing regular warnings that were routinely ignored. While he was winning, he was reluctant to mess with a team playing over its head, but things were coming to a head. Before the October 28 grudge match with the Steelers in Pittsburgh, Henderson missed practice with the bug, thinking he had gotten permission to do so by the team's trainer, Don Cochran. Then after the team arrived at their hotel in Pittsburgh, Henderson was going over the game plan in the dining room when Landry walked over and sat down next to him. "You know what our deal is," Landry said, before telling him he was not going to start the game.

Henderson, who got off on the pomp and ego mania of being introduced with the starting lineup, burned as Landry walked away, Henderson later saying he was thinking. "I'm not scared of that baldheaded son of a bitch, fucking God on earth." As the coach was about to have his pregame breakfast with the assistant coaches, Henderson tapped him on the shoulder. "Coach," he said, "if I don't start tomorrow I ain't playing. Now you deal with that." He turned on his heel and stalked away to his room, unconcerned that he had crossed every line there was when dealing with Landry, the worst part of which was calling him out in front of his coaches. Half an hour later, Bob Breunig came to the door of Henderson's room and told him, "Thomas, I just had a talk with Coach. He said if you ever do that again he's going to get rid of you." "Bob," Henderson replied, "he can do whatever the fuck he wants."

Henderson didn't hear anything from Landry and on Sunday morning went to Three Rivers Stadium, where he sat in his underwear in limbo, not knowing Landry's decision. Then, ninety minutes before the kickoff, Landry, having apparently spoken with Cochran, ambled to Henderson's locker. "Thomas, you win this time," he drawled. "You can go ahead and start today."[18] It was a remarkable cave-in by Landry, a point Henderson giddily related to Harvey Martin, who told him, "You're crazy," half in envy that Henderson was nutty enough to have even tried to show up Landry, much less to do so and live to tell the tale. Henderson was more surprised than anyone, and totally pleased. He would later say, "My teammates saw something they had never seen before. . . . They would say things like, 'Do you believe that motherfucker would do that?'" Purely incidentally, he admitted, "It was probably the only time in my life I was right and he was wrong."[19]

The Cowboys took a frightful beating that day. The Steelers, killing any lingering doubts about their Super Bowl win and taunting the Cowboys about the "America's Team" insignia, thundered for 173 yards on the ground, held the Cowboys to one field goal, and won 14–3. L. C. Greenwood hit Staubach so hard that the latter came out of the game with a concussion and didn't begin to speak coherently until the plane ride back home. Typically, however, he started the next game against the Giants and tore it up, completing twenty of thirty passes for 266 yards in a furious 16–14 comeback win, the Cowboys scoring 10 points in the last minute, on a 32-yard touchdown pass to Drew Pearson and a 22-yard Septien field goal.

The following Sunday they lost at home to the Eagles, 31–21, another late rally snuffed when Wilbert Montgomery burst 37 yards for the icing touchdown. Next, in Washington against Jack Pardee's 7–4 Redskins, the Cowboys played their worst game of the season, going down 34–20, with Staubach throwing three interceptions and being sacked six times. It was during this downer that Hollywood Henderson met his Waterloo. He had missed the Giants game with a hamstring injury and had wanted to stay home in Dallas, but Landry ordered him to travel to New York with the team and to dress for the game even though he was inactive. Instead, he stood on the sideline in a full-length mink coat. Against the Redskins, he played like he was still inactive, not making a single tackle in the game.

Late in the first half, he was playing with so little fire that defensive coach Jerry Tubbs, upstairs in the press box, ordered him to the bench for the rest of the quarter and warned him during halftime about his lack of hustle. Then, in the third quarter, with Dallas down 24–6, Henderson, on the sideline, pulled out a bandanna with the team logo and "Cowboys' Number One!" on it and began mugging and pointing at it for a TV camera. The back story was that Preston Pearson had designed the bandanna as an answer to the "Terrible Towel" ritualistically waved around by the Steelers' fans, and hoped to place them in stores for sale. He had asked Henderson to get some publicity for it, though when he did the timing could not have been worse, with the Cowboys looking nothing like number one. Martin, standing next to him, recalled, "I felt like throttling him right on the spot." It seemed to Martin that Henderson had given up on the game.

"We can still win this," he told him.

"I don't care," Henderson said.[20]

The hard-boiled Tubbs, seeing him jerking around on the TV monitor, flipped out. After the final gun, he again visited Henderson's locker and tore into him, saying, "If I was the coach I'd cut you today." Henderson, who had snorted his liquid cocaine and popped a few bennies during the game, thought he had done nothing wrong. "I thought I was doing something for a friend," he would recall of the brouhaha. "But I get crucified like Jesus and Preston Pearson never says a word."[21] Still smarting from Tubbs's halftime dress-down, Henderson snapped at him, "Get out of my motherfucking face, punk!" He was so wired he probably would have done the same with anyone, even Ditka, and entered very dangerous territory when he went on, "Get your ass back over where all them other punks are. Fuck you! I can do whatever the fuck I want."[22]

It was life imitating art—a scene eerily similar to Pete Gent's fictional locker-room run-in between an overwrought player and an unsympathetic assistant coach, and as in the literature, everything stopped in the room in anticipation of a brawl before Tubbs backed down, possibly saving his life. Henderson then went around the room yammering, "I'm Hollywood! Trade me! Every team in the world wants me!" Martin sat there, as he said, "mouth agape, knowing I was watching a madman." He turned to Drew Pearson and told him, "He's not home no more. The boy's here, but the mind isn't."[23]

Henderson continued his tirade in the shower, sputtering at teammates who were suddenly imaginary enemies: "Fuck all of you punks! All of you hen-pecked, kiss-ass motherfuckers around this fucking franchise. Ain't none of you got no fucking balls. Those fuckers say 'Jump,' your ass comes a mile high. They say, 'Go to church,' you all pile in there. All of you doing drugs before the god-damn games. All you married assholes out trying to fuck cheerlead-ers and every little bitch you can catch on the road and you look at me and judge me, you punks."[24] It went on like this, uninterrupted, for several minutes, the screams reverberating off the tile walls and through the steam. Reporters who had heard the tantrum in the locker room kept a distance. Amazingly, those who did kept it out of their game stories, even though nothing like this had ever hap-pened before. It seems inconceivable today, but no one asked Landry about it, and the whole Henderson bandanna incident was not given major play in the news.

Tubbs told Landry about the psychotic kabuki, but the coach chose not to do anything until he could discuss it with Schramm. The plane ride home became a continuation of the melodrama as Henderson, who took a Quaalude and snorted more coke in the lavatory, then drank straight gin from the miniature bottles passed out by the stew-ardesses. No one came near him, and he began shouting to no one specifically, "Trade me, I don't give a fuck." He walked past Landry and shot him a dirty look. He hissed at Jim Myers. "Don't you say nothing, I'll bust you in your nose. I've got nothing to lose here," a clear indication that he knew he had buried himself with Landry. He also told reporters on board, "I want to get traded from this fran-chise, all these sorry-ass motherfuckers. Nobody on this plane's got nuts."[25] As Martin said, "I could only wonder what terrible thing possessed him."[26]

When the plane landed, Henderson hopped into a Volkswagen with two girls in it and took off into the night. He later spoke of scoring cocaine before going home in the wee hours and crashing on his couch. At around eight in the morning he was awakened by a call from Landry's secretary asking him to come to the office right away, hours before the team was to practice that day. He got up, laid out a line of coke, snorted it, and hit the freeway.

LANDRY HAD been up much of the night too, hashing out the situation with Tex Schramm. They agreed they could not possibly let Henderson get away with his latest ugly scene. It all had a familiar ring, a rerun of the end of the Duane Thomas fiasco, and if Schramm had been keeping Landry ignorant of the full extent of the Henderson madness, he probably told him of it now. Though both liked Henderson personally, they faced the reality that his skills were declining, and that if and when the cocaine business became public, it would be hell on the "America's Team" image. They would also need to deal with his problem medically, another complicated issue before the era of *de rigueur* trips to celebrity drug clinics.

To avoid all that, Schramm, who knew the clauses of the standard player contract top to bottom, formulated a way out for the Cowboys that would neither cost them a dime nor come back to bite them if they traded Henderson and the team he went to claimed he was damaged goods. If he put Henderson on waivers, it would serve two purposes. One, it would seem more punitive than a trade. More important, however, it would be a clear blow to his pride, with any team that claimed him needing to kick in only a hundred bucks for arguably the best linebacker around. And—this was either genius or evil—*because* Henderson's pride would be singed, he would almost surely refuse the waiver route, which would be the only way he could go on being paid his salary and benefits. Rather, in pique and pride, he would no doubt quit outright, landing him on the retired-reserve list, meaning the Cowboys would not need to pay him a dime while still owning his rights. If he changed his mind and made a comeback, any team that wanted to sign him would have to kick back compensation to the Cowboys, and Schramm would insist on a first- or second-round draft pick. It was perfect in its simplicity and cunning.

Henderson, full of himself as he was, had neither a lawyer nor an

agent working for him who might be familiar with this legal minutiae. What's more, as he sped down the freeway, he had forgotten
all about his trade demands and was content to be a Cowboy. He
assumed the craziness in Washington would blow over, with Landry
meting out another slap on the wrist. When he got to the Cowboys
offices, Landry was the only one there. And it was obvious this time
was different. "I don't know what's wrong with you," Landry began,
then went on to upbraid him for his "disrespect" and for being a "disruptive influence." Ladling in some sociology, Landry said, "I know
you didn't have a daddy, that you didn't have any discipline growing
up," but that didn't excuse his atrocious behavior. He said nothing
about drugs.

Henderson sat, stony and stoned, knowing the ax was about to
fall. It happened when Landry said he could bench him, but that he
"would be disruptive," and the only alternative was for him to "play
football for somebody else." The old softie in Landry once again surfaced, with tears coming to his eyes when he reiterated that "this is
the damn toughest thing" about his job but that "I just can't handle
you anymore. I'm putting you on waivers." Henderson would recall,
dubiously, that he actually was *relieved* to be taken to the curb like
yesterday's trash, and that he had no pity as "this sorry motherfucker
shed these tears for me." Also dubiously, he believed that if he apologized to Landry, "I might have won him over." Instead, he said his
piece. "Well, you do what you've got to do," he wheezed. "I ain't
making enough money here to go through any more of this bullshit."

Addressing the stuffy coach with intentional discourtesy, he said,
"Landry, you know you never told me I could play football. You never
told me I was good but once. Once . . . But I'll tell you what. You
are going to miss me." Landry let him vent about being so unappreciated, then said that the 49ers would likely claim him off waivers. He then turned to his paperwork; for the case was closed in his
mind. Henderson wasn't done, however. Falling into the trap set by
Schramm, he sputtered, "No, no, no. You ain't going to put me on
shit. You can't fire me 'cause you know what I'm going to do? I quit.
I'm retiring as of this moment. I quit! You can't do no more to me,
Landry . . . and you know what else? You ain't going to the Super
Bowl this year, and no other year."[27]

✦ ✦ ✦ ✦

WITH THAT, the short, lunatic, manic-depressive career of Hollywood Henderson as a Cowboy was over. Having railed at being a tool for five years, he left by being the perfect tool—unwittingly approving of the last three years of his contract being flushed down the tubes. He walked out the door, down the empty hallway, and went to God-knows-where to score a quarter ounce of coke, relieving him of the need to think about how he screwed up. He called Schramm and told him to arrange a farewell press conference later that day. When he got back home, he slid off his finger the glowing championship ring he would soon pawn, yanked all his phones out of the wall, dressed to the nines, snorted more coke, and drove back to the Cowboy's offices for his valediction[28]—another echo of Duane Thomas, except that Henderson chose to go out on a high note, saving his diatribes for private company.

Living up to his sobriquet, Henderson at the press conference put on an Oscar-level acting job. With a chance to stick it to Landry right on his own turf, he instead went limp and played for pity. "It hurts a lot," he began. "This is the most hollow feeling I've ever had in my life." While he owned up to his "poor performance" in Washington, he steered clear of any admission of drug usage. His release, he said, was mainly because of "my air, my personality. I guess Dallas just isn't big enough for both of us." He was quitting the game, he insisted, not out of pique but because "I don't want to be passed around the league. I know I'm still the greatest linebacker in football and I would like to be remembered as a Dallas Cowboy." His only dart was a throwaway, noting that he wasn't a "traditional" Cowboy, and was in good company. "Just ask Duane Thomas, Bob Hayes, and Jean Fugett." But he ended, "I'm not holding a grudge. There's nothing bad I can say about the situation." He had big plans too— "Maybe now it's time for me to go to Hollywood."

Landry, explaining the move, spooned up more sweet cream. He said that Henderson "went to extremes . . . from brilliant to whatever [word] you want to use," and that "it hurts me a great deal to have to do what I've done. If you care about someone, it's no fun." In the end, he explained, "It was my personal decision that it is best for him not to be a contributing member of our team." Schramm, if he had hatched the perfect plan, was understandably smug and generous. Henderson, he said, would not be placed on waivers after all, unless he requested it, though in any case there would still be compensation. "This," he said, looking serious, is "a very sad day for me."[29]

Had Henderson been able to step back and think clearly, or discuss the situation with a lawyer or an agent—or if he had had working phones to answer calls from the NFLPA when its lawyers wanted to tell him he had given away his rights and that the union would back him in an illegal termination lawsuit—he would have known what he later acknowledged: announcing his retirement was "a big mistake."[30] When Henderson realized this, he knew Schramm had conned *him* when he wondered to Tex if it would be better if he kept playing, and was told it would be "better if you retired," though Schramm didn't clarify it would be better for management.

The elephant in the room of the Henderson matter—cocaine—went unnoticed and unspoken, if never unused by Henderson. The stories in the papers avoided it like the plague it was, the writers either willfully blind or helpfully protective of Landry and the team image. The *Morning News* on November 20 headlined the termination "A TECHNICOLOR TRAGEDY" and "THE DIVINE TRAGEDY" but in the end a simple case of insubordination gone too far. In these dispatches, no Cowboys spoke up for Henderson or expressed any worry that the team would suffer without him, a point made adamantly by Landry.

Thus Henderson, like Lance Rentzel and Duane Thomas, quickly faded from sight and mind. Henderson had given *Playboy* a saucy interview months before that was due to run in the January 1980 issue. When he was canned, the magazine leaked some quotes, which of course included jabs at Landry, including one that went, "He'll be smiling at you one minute, screaming at you the next . . . everybody is so paranoid about his job, and everyone knows who's on the way out."[31] It was a particularly ironic end note, but that sort of thing seemed as old as some of Landry's fedoras. Suddenly, it was easy to ignore Hollywood Henderson.

✦ ✦ ✦ ✦

IN THE months that followed, Henderson went from bad to worse. He floated back and forth between Dallas and Hollywood, with no salary and no league benefits. The 7UP people pulled his commercial, and he was whittling away what resources he had left on more and more coke.[32] At one point he did call the NFLPA back, and papers were drawn up for a lawsuit, but then he disappeared again and the union dropped the case before it could begin. He was even too wavy for Pete Gent, who was assigned to write a story on Henderson for *Esquire*. Gent, of course, took Henderson's side. "Why all the fuss over this nappy-headed boy waving at the television camera," he wrote, "when football is, after all, show-biz, based on illusion rather than reality?"[33] Yet after being stood up for a promised interview, Gent judged Henderson not as heroic but as a deranged and self-serving train wreck, though nothing about cocaine was mentioned. "Hollywood's alligator mouth," Gent concluded, "finally overloaded his hummingbird ass."[34]

I was luckier than Gent. A few months before, Henderson had given me an interview for *Inside Sports*. He had kept me waiting for two days, during which his beleaguered girlfriend Wyetta obligatorily apologized for his absence, then he straggled in, utterly charming, and began to lacerate Landry and the Cowboys players who had done him dirt, though his best lines came when it was noted that his night crawling had hurt him with the front office. "Is that right? So why did *they* fool around so much?" he roared, making his case by dispensing details about Murchison marrying Brandt's ex-wife and adding, "There's so much going on you wouldn't believe it."[35]

As Gent noted, that was perhaps not the smartest thing to say for a man who wanted back in with the Cowboys. And Henderson did. Earlier in the spring of 1980, he had gone to see the coach, as he put it, "on bended knees," telling him he would "clean cleats and mow the lawn" if need be. Landry said no thanks.[36] Still, Henderson insisted *Landry* would soon be on bended knee, begging *him* to come back. And if not, he swore some other team would meet his asking price—a million dollars.

Eventually Landry did change his mind when Bill Walsh called Schramm and proposed a trade. Henderson, impressed when Walsh invited him to his home—"Coach Landry," he said, "hadn't invited me to Kentucky Fried Chicken"[37]—signed, not for a million dollars but for $125,000 plus incentives. Schramm got his number-one draft choice and Walsh, his 49ers coming off a 2–14 record in his rookie season as coach, got a badly needed defensive player. Henderson, meanwhile, had taken an even more perilous turn, smoking far more potent rock cocaine from a pipe—freebasing.[38] Unlike Landry, Walsh apparently figured out what Henderson was doing; rather than trying to get him help, he put him on waivers before the season began.

He then signed with Houston, as an add-on for a team that would go all the way to the AFC title game, but Henderson pulled a hamstring and played in only seven games, later relating that he had brought his coke pipe to one game and freebased in the toilet stall beforehand.[39] Late in the season, Wyetta left with their daughter and filed a restraining order against him; soon after, they divorced. He was also having blackouts, which scared him enough to call the head of NFL security and tell him, "I'm fucked up. I'm freebasing . . . I'm sick. I need some help. This cocaine is killing me!"[40] This was the first time a player had ever voluntarily admitted to cocaine addiction, and the first to be sent to rehab and to a prototypical celebrity sanctuary for it. He spent two months at the Camelback treatment facility in Phoenix, but that was not long enough to keep him from straying. After sneaking out and getting drunk, he was put in a psychiatric lockup.[44]

The Oilers didn't want him back, but he got one more shot when he called Don Shula and said he had been in treatment and "was better." Although it was a lie—he went right back to coke—Shula bought it, giving him a contract for $125,000. In the spring Landry allowed Henderson to work out at the Cowboys grounds, whereupon he promptly got into a fight with Randy White, who pinned him to the floor and had to be pulled off him. Henderson joined the Dolphins, carrying on a charade by having Shula accompany him to AA meetings, then when they parted he would head to downtown Miami for some more coke. However, a serious neck injury in the last preseason game ended his career for good, though he would pocket all of his salary.

With no need for pretense left, he came clean publicly for the first time about cocaine, writing an article for the December 1981 *Playboy* titled "Confessions of a Cocaine Cowboy." Flat broke now, Henderson bummed money from old teammates, including Roger Staubach, Tony Dorsett, and Drew Pearson, even from Tex Schramm, but his old amigo Too Tall refused, knowing exactly what Henderson would do with it.[42] For a time he lived in a hotel room at the DoubleTree, which was raided by federal drug enforcement agents. Luckily for him, they found nothing.[43] Unable to afford the room, he lived for a year with country singer B. J. Thomas and his wife, who supported him until they tired of his erratic behavior and kicked him out. The next anyone heard of Henderson was in 1983 when he was busted for sexual assault on two teenage girls, one of whom was confined to a wheelchair. One of the girls went to the police, and he tried to bribe her with $10,000 to drop the charges.[44] When he was busted, Henderson's defense was that the sex was consensual, which hardly helped. After he accepted a plea bargain, he was sentenced to four years and eight months.

Henderson had been off cocaine for three months at the time of his sentencing, and if he needed any more reason to stay off it, he learned the day before he went to jail that his brother Allen, a hopeless freebaser, had committed suicide. Henderson resisted readily available supplies of the drug in prison, which may have been the hardest part of the twenty-eight months he served. When he was released in November 1984, he was still clean. And lucky. A lot more so than, say, Larry Bethea, who would be released by Landry following the 1983 season and, addicted to cocaine, went from coke to crime. He was arrested for setting fires in Mount Rainier National Park, then for stealing his mother's life's savings. On April 24, 1987, he robbed two convenience stores at gunpoint in his home state of Washington. When cops tracked him down, they found him dead with a bullet wound in his head. The death was ruled a suicide.[45]

By contrast, Henderson moved into a clean and sober phase, showing contrition for all those whose lives he had darkened. Of one of his foils, he said, "Terry Bradshaw is obviously smarter than I am. He made much smarter life decisions than I did."[46] But it was his old coach from whom he needed to court forgiveness the most. He was never completely contrite, however. Henderson would blame Landry for letting the drug situation get out of hand, maintaining that if Landry had really cared for him as a person he would have sent him to rehab[47]—again conflicting with his theory that Schramm had kept the coach in the dark about it. Indeed, even Martin didn't know the full extent of Henderson's drug use until he revealed it, but Martin believed Landry *had* tried to help Henderson, in his way.

"I know Coach Landry would do almost anything, even swallow his considerable pride, if he felt the slightest chance existed of helping [Henderson]," he said. "Landry not only went the extra mile with Thomas, he went many more miles."[48] Martin would need the same forbearance from Landry soon enough. In Roger Staubach's opinion, Landry's handling of Henderson showed both compassion and a finality that would become a dying concept in big-time sports, in which shoving drug-addled players off to designed rehab clinics spared coaches from decisive action. "It's not dealt with now," Staubach said. "You have to deal with it. Thomas was dealt with when he went too far."[49]

It became almost compulsory for Landry's critics to attach a racial motive to Henderson's release, and reflexively trace it through other black men dealt with similarly, such as Thomas and Hayes. As Martin pointed out, many black players around the league assumed that a black man who stood up for himself didn't stand a chance in Dallas. To be sure, a man like Tom Landry could not have conceivably understood black men like that, men who didn't understand their own impulses. But Henderson always pulled back from the edge of that cliff, making his distinction that Landry wasn't a racist, it only *seemed* that way, knowing it would be something like a misdemeanor to call him the worst thing a black man can say about a white man he also called "the smartest man in football."[50] "That's one thing I can't lay on Tom," he had told me. "I think if I'd been white and did the same things, he'd have gotten rid of me the first year, as a flake, a Joe Don Looney." Landry, he said, "tried to understand me."[51] And in the end, "I don't think he understood the new black man [but] his name would not appear on my list of racists."[52]

After all the smoke and powder had subsided, Henderson knew that Landry really wasn't the archfiend. Henderson managed to snort away what should have been a Hall of Fame career, and he had done all that to himself. The years of cocaine dissipation left him a physical shell, leading to a mild stroke in the late 1990s. Eventually he did find salvation, through the dumbest of luck when in 2000 he won $28 million in the Texas state lottery. When the news got out, a good many clean-living, hard-working people lamented, *My Lord, where's the justice?* He did have the good timing by then of being clean and sober since 1983, and was indeed a changed man. No longer an *enfant terrible*, he remarried in 1985, and over the next decade he began to lecture about the crutch of drug use. He formed a drug rehabilitation foundation, raised funds among the well-heeled and even shook hands with President Bill Clinton. In 1997 he did public penance, writing a letter to the editor of the *Morning News*, apologizing for his ill deeds with the team.[53] With the lottery winnings he built a stadium for children's sports events in East Austin.

His opinion of Landry became more respectful. He said Landry had "given me plenty of warning. I was a disruptive influence, disrespectful of the coaches, caught up in my own agenda," though he couldn't help but add, "Landry did the right thing, but he paid a huge price. He never took a team to the Super Bowl again."[54]

For Landry, the Henderson scars didn't heal as easily as the Duane Thomas welts. Landry felt he was duty-bound to come to the aid of former players who made an effort to reform, not to mention venerate him. As he had with Thomas, he spoke warmly of Henderson at an event to mark the ten-year anniversary of his sobriety in 1993. But although Landry put a good deal of ink into the Duane Thomas episode in his memoirs, there was not a word in those pages about Henderson's dismissal from the Cowboys, or even his later contrition. *Pravda* could not have disappeared that phase of the team's history any more obviously than Landry's selective amnesia.

When Henderson came to the Landry home late in the coach's life for a pleasant visit, it was perhaps worth more to him than all the lottery money. For Landry, however, it was a fleeting reminder that he had seen far too many Hollywood Hendersons in his time. Indeed, in 1979, the unresolved dysfunction that had escalated with Henderson would carry into another decade that Tom Landry would not be able to make sense of, a decade his reign would not survive.

✦ ✦ ✦ ✦

THE 1979 season proceeded apace, but on a rocky road. Mike Hegman, with only a few practices under his belt before the Thanksgiving Day game against the Oilers, was plugged in as strong-side linebacker but was virtually invisible against Earl Campbell. The league's leading rusher and MVP, Campbell carried the ball thirty-three times, storming through the lanes formerly patrolled by Henderson to gain 195 yards, and the Oilers would pull out a see-saw contest, 30–24, on a late touchdown pass from Dan Pastorini to Ken Burrough. Few called for Hollywood to come back. In fact, the bigger loss was thought to be Too Tall Jones. Paul Zimmerman would write that without Jones the team was "in a state of flux, not flex, and, for the first time since the early expansion years, was pushed around. . . . The opposition loaded up on the strong side and the Cowboys were overrun."[55]

On a less empirical level, many around town were concerned that the America's Team brand was taking a toll on the field. Skip Bayless, for example, stewed after the loss in Washington, DC, that "the label may have sold a few zillion more calendars, but it hadn't done much for the Cowboys' competitive edge. Before, maybe, the Cowboy aura actually frightened opponents into clammy-handed fumbles. The Cowboys would crush you with class and character. But now it's America's Team. . . . The fear has turned to loathing. . . . It's almost like an unspoken conspiracy. This season, opponent after opponent vows to keep America's Team out of the playoffs."[56]

That seemed a distinct possibility with the Cowboys at 8–5, tied with the Redskins' record. Three weeks later they were still tied, at 10–5, when Pardee brought his team into Texas Stadium on a freezing day, the winner of the game to take the division. With Dorsett out nursing a bruised shoulder, little-used Ron Springs ran for 79 yards and a touchdown, Staubach threw for two more, and Dallas led 21–17 going into the fourth quarter. But 'Skins fullback John Riggins, who ran twenty-two times for 151 yards, scored twice, for a 34–21 lead with four minutes to go, leaving the 62,867 fans in a sour mood. However, Staubach was in his element. After a key fumble recovery by Randy White, Staubach, who would throw forty-two times in the game, completing twenty-four for 226 yards, the second most of his career, had the freedom to call his own plays and drove the offense 59 yards on three passes, hitting Springs with a 26-yard touchdown pass with 2:20 left. One Redskins' first down would have killed the clock, but the defense held on a three and out and the ball was Staubach's, on his own 14, with 1:48 left. He faded back and hit Tony Hill with a 20-yard pass, Preston Pearson twice for 22 and 25 yards, dodging a heavy rush both times. From the Redskin's 33, he moved the ball to the 8-yard line with 42 seconds left.

Staubach now called "Hot Left 17," a pass play for DuPree similar to the one in the Super Bowl that wound up slipping through Jackie Smith's hands, but Staubach told Hill, "Be ready." When an all-out blitz made the pass to DuPree undoable, Staubach blindly lofted one for Hill, who instinctively broke outside instead of inside. Beating cornerback Lemar Parrish, Hill saw the ball floating down and coddled it in his arms, tying the game. Rafael Septien's extra point won it, 35–34, sending the fickle fans into delirium. Landry, who had switched to wearing an overcoat at halftime, stuck his arms up in a touchdown signal when Hill made the catch. He was ecstatic after the game, calling it Staubach's finest, though it had lots of company since this was his twenty-first fourth-quarter win and the fourteenth he had stolen in the final two minutes.

Carlton Stowers went overboard in his game story, writing, "Move aside. If you will please, Santa. Out of the way, Tooth Fairy. Take a backseat, Mr. Easter Bunny and all you other charitable creatures of fantasy and folklore. And kindly make way for flesh-and-blood Roger Staubach, as remarkable a benefactor as any storybook ever has designed." Staubach called it "the most thrilling 60 minutes" he'd ever played. For Pardee it was hell. "There we were, divisional champions with 40 seconds to play, then nothing," he said.[57] After the game Harvey Martin, who had been sent a funeral wreath by Redskins fans during the week, went to the Washington locker room and flung the wreath in. Landry later made him publicly apologize, calling what he did "gauche."[58]

The Cowboys finished with the fifth-most potent offense in the league, the passing game producing the second-highest number of touchdowns. Dorsett stumbled but still cleared 1,000 yards. Hill caught sixty balls and made ten touchdowns; Drew Pearson, fifty-five and eight. Hill and Staubach (twenty-seven touchdowns, eleven interceptions, NFL-best 92.3 passer rating) went to the Pro Bowl, as did Martin, White, and Pat Donovan. Still, Landry knew this was a dissipated edition of the 1977 and '78 teams, and when the Rams came in for another playoff go-around, he wasn't nearly as confident as the prevailing attitude that the 9–7 Rams were a warm-up. While they seemed mediocre, with only Jim Youngblood making All-Pro, they always thirsted for revenge against the Cowboys. Ray Malavasi could also be relieved that Hollywood Henderson wasn't around to make his day miserable.

Dorsett, his shoulder healed, rushed for 87 yards, but he was nearly matched by Wendell Tyler. And after White sacked Vince Ferragamo in the end zone for a quick safety, Ferragamo, who had battled Pat Haden all season for the starting job, began dissecting the Cowboys' secondary and went in at halftime leading 14–5. Ferragamo would complete only nine passes but rack up 210 yards and three touchdowns, while Staubach was harried and completed twelve of twenty-eight for just 124 yards, his longest pass only 29 yards. Still, the Cowboys came out for the second half aroused. Springs scored on a 1-yard run in the third quarter, cutting the deficit to 14–12. Then, early in the final stanza Staubach took his offense down the field and found Jay Saldi from 2 yards out.

But the Rams didn't fold. Down 19–14, they allowed the Cowboys nothing more, and with two minutes left Ferragamo, imitating Staubach, led his team on a dramatic march. And now came the back-breaker. From the 50-yard line, with the Cowboys in zone coverage, he laid one out for Billy Waddy over the middle—consciously attacking Mike Hegman, who had the responsibility Henderson had had, to cover any receiver who came through the shallow zone. As the pass zipped over him, Hegman leaped, his arm outstretched, and tipped the ball slightly, but Waddy was able to grab it and run it all the way into the end zone for the lead. As Henderson, who watched the game on TV, noted with glee, "I could always outjump Mike Hegman. As far as I was concerned, Tom Landry lost that game when he fired me . . . I sat there with a bag of coke and loved it."[59]

At 21–19, Staubach still had a minute or so to pull off another miracle, but he was semi-dazed after taking a whack earlier from Jack Reynolds, and the Rams now pressured him heavily as he dropped back. He tried to throw the ball away short, but guard Herb Scott happened to be there and instinctively caught it—illegally, as Scott was an illegal receiver, costing a 15-yard penalty, which put Staubach in a deeper hole he couldn't dig out of. It was the strangest completion Staubach ever had, and as Landry and the Cowboys walked off afterward, few believed he would let it stand as his final pass.

But Staubach, who had had to leave five games in 1979 with concussions, was seriously contemplating quitting. Coming off another terrific year, he was about to turn thirty-eight and was concerned for his future health. In older days, team doctors kept smelling salts for the purpose of getting players with concussions back up on their feet and into the game. Now, players were starting to realize the cumulative toll of head injuries, though it would take a couple more decades of survivors' being left brain-damaged from head injuries—and lawsuits filed by their families and the players' union against the league—before teams and the league began to keep concussed players out of games. Smart as he was, Staubach was ahead of that curve. His wife, Marianne, wanted him to quit, and on his own he went to see a neurologist in New York who said he had had slight neurological changes in the left side of his brain that could lead to scar tissue syndrome. His advice was to retire. Staubach saw another doctor in Dallas who was less pessimistic but told him, "If you retired, it wouldn't be a decision you would regret."[60]

Undecided, Staubach, as had Dandy Don Meredith a decade before, went to see Landry and told him he was hanging up his jock, but he was prepared to stick it out another year if the coach would ask him to. He never did. Staubach recalled the meeting as "brief and businesslike," and there was not even a parting handshake. When he walked toward the door, Staubach in jest asked if he did return, would Landry let him call his own plays.

"Sure," Landry said, smiling thinly. "You can call some from the press box."

"Seriously," Staubach persisted, "what if I came back? If I played again, could I call plays?"

Landry, though, wasn't in a jocular mood. As with Meredith,

Landry wanted to move Staubach out, and as with Craig Morton, Landry believed Danny White was ready for his close-up and might otherwise grow stale on the bench. Not getting with the joke, Landry all but put the best quarterback he would ever have in mothballs, as if he were an old warship.

"No," he said, cold as ice, "we have a system."[61]

In truth, Staubach, like Dandy Don, wanted to hear Landry tell him he was needed, wanted. Naïve as Staubach was, he came in that day thinking he owed it to Landry to go on. It wouldn't have hurt for Landry to say he owed Staubach too. But this was a coach looking ahead, to very uncertain times, and as always with little room for sentimentality. The rub was that the end of the Staubach era took more from Tom Landry than he would ever be able to recover.

Chapter 24

STARING INTO
THE DARK

A S THE LAST DECADE OF LANDRY'S reign began, spilling off a decade when he had won seven NFC championships
and two Super Bowls—and had saved the pride of the old NFL guard
by being the only NFC team to win it all in the 1970s—he was no
longer necessarily the savviest coach in the game. Indeed, his station
was shared by younger and just as seasoned and intellectually acute
men with names like Noll, Walsh, and Gibbs. No longer, too, was he
quite the grump he once was. Nearing sixty, he was more a doyen,
still stoic and intransigent as ever, but a little less hardboiled in spots,
and the edge he gave his team game was baked into any given Sunday
or Monday.

"Playing against the Cowboys and coach Landry, he was just such
an icon on the sideline," said Ron Jaworski, the ESPN broadcaster
who quarterbacked the Philadelphia Eagles to the Super Bowl in 1981
and whose career covered the second half of Landry's tenure. "It was
almost like the Cowboys had seven points on the board before kickoff because of the way everyone respected coach Landry as a coach,
as a leader and the way he handled his football team. There was a
certain intimidation factor that was involved in playing the Cowboys
just because the man with the hat was on the sideline."[1]

But the old "family" feel of the team was gone, replaced by a
business-like mindset. As long as Murchison was around—not to

mention Tony Dorsett, Too Tall Jones, and Randy White—Landry could swim against any current, hat securely cocked, his set-in-stone Flex and multi-formations ready to withstand another round of football evolution. Yet the magic of those 1970s drafts had to end, and the damage left by Staubach's and Henderson's exits created cavities that could not be filled. Neither could the one left by Cliff Harris, though Landry himself came to his home to tell him he should retire, something Harris could sense coming. As a result, he and Charlie Waters had started a gas marketing company that grew into a major enterprise. "I never knew whether I was going to be back," Harris said, "even in my All-Pro years."[2]

Waters wouldn't allow himself to quit without one more go after his knee injury. When he returned in 1980, he had some new concepts for Landry to consider. As he recalled, "I was firmly convinced we should go to the 3–4 defense. . . . I'd prepared what I thought was a good presentation. I thought Coach Landry would welcome the idea of an older veteran coming in to offer ideas to help the team. Well, I got all wrapped up in my little speech, and then I took a look at Coach Landry. His eyes were cold and steely, his jaw muscles were tight. He was staring off into space, waiting for me to finish. Right then I knew I'd done the wrong thing. I'd tampered with something that was his, that was special to him. Our relationship was never the same after that."[3] Waters has gotten a lot of mileage out of that story, with different punch lines; once, he said Landry reacted to his suggestion "as if I'd accosted his daughter,"[4] another time that "he looked at me like I was a traitor."[5] This wasn't merely glib hyperbole; Landry no doubt felt all those ways when his pride and joy, his signature defensive set, was questioned.

Rather than change strategy in midstream, Landry's province was to change horses. Staubach's retirement was something close to a traumatic event, especially among those he had made into stars. Drew Pearson was so distraught that he couldn't bring himself to attend Staubach's retirement press conference, "because I didn't want the whole world to see me crying."[6] Staubach himself said later he wished he had stuck around because he thought the Cowboys had more Super Bowls in them. And, given the near-grief mode that greeted Staubach's retirement—over three hundred media credentials were issued for his announcement—White, at twenty-eight, was on the griddle, ready in Landry's opinion, but he was about to enter a snake's nest and did so with a question mark: Did he have the right stuff deep inside him?

White had all the tools. Smart as a man could be—the entire time they were teammates Harvey Martin believed that Danny White was the son of the Supreme Court justice and former football legend Byron "Whizzer" White—he was able to process and effectuate Landry's playbook. His arm wasn't a howitzer, but he rarely missed his target by much. He could scramble a bit, but unlike Staubach, that was always a last option. He had come from Frank Kush's Arizona State passing machine, setting seven NCAA passing records, and Landry salivated at the thought of what White could do on a pro gridiron. Some would say that if Landry ever regarded any player as a son, White came closest. After he had jumped the Cowboys as a rookie to sign with the WFL, he had sat quietly for four seasons, paying his dues, sucking up the Landry method, never expressing his impatience as Staubach had done, to Landry's pique. He dutifully did his job as a punter, something Landry in particular could value. He was also handsome in that generic, country-club-brochure way the Cowboys' brass liked. He was humble, appropriately religious, and said all the right things.

"Dad really believed in Danny," said Tom Landry Jr. "It was almost as if he were looking at himself in a time tunnel. A really intense guy who didn't lose control of himself. A smart guy, almost professorial. A punter. Good family guy. Sound familiar? I don't think Dad wanted to push Roger out. I'm sure if not for all the concussions Dad would have loved to have Roger around, I mean, the guy was only what, twenty-nine, thirty? But Danny just seemed to be the ideal guy to keep the roll going. Hell, Dad thought Danny was going to be the last quarterback he would need, that they'd both retire together."[7]

White, smart as he was, knew what kind of load he was carrying. Not that he wouldn't have to endure what Meredith, Morton, and Staubach had to, Landry's cold, admonishing stare and barbed remarks, when he didn't follow plays to the letter and dared to change a play call at the line, even if the play he called worked. Cowed by that, White, who was naturally judgmental and volatile, refrained from doing anything that might annoy Landry. In 1979, when he had come in for an injured Staubach in a game against the Steelers, he decided on his own to fake a punt and failed to make the first down. When he got to the sideline, Landry grumbled to him, "Danny, you just can't do that. You just can't do that." White felt like digging a hole for himself. Then, he recalled, "I was worried the next week and got a little paranoid when I felt he wasn't talking to me."[8]

Sometimes he seemed like an automation with none of Staubach's mercurial habits and behind-the-scenes cheekiness, and that was fine with Landry, who swore by White, adamantly—though if White believed that meant Landry would stick with him in perpetuity, he would learn a hard lesson. For now, however, White was the man. Knowing how sensitive he was, Landry did not keep any immediately viable alternative quarterbacks in reserve. White's backups—Glenn Carano, a former second-round pick from the University of Nevada, Las Vegas, who seemed to be renting space on the bench for two years, and rookie Gary Hogeboom, a sixth-round pick out of Central Michigan—were strictly mop-up men.

White wasn't the only one on the spot. The secondary was an ongoing problem. Cliff Harris's worries that Randy Hughes would take his job proved unfounded. Hughes never bloomed enough in Landry's eyes to become a starter, and Harris's place at free safety was filled by third-year-man Dennis Thurman, an eleventh-round draft pick out of USC in 1978. There would also be new starting cornerbacks. Aaron Kyle and Benny Barnes were displaced by two more young, unproven talents, Aaron Mitchell and Steve Wilson. Suddenly, the aging Cowboys were sprinkled with youth, but not necessarily blue-chip players. As Zimmerman noted, "The past two seasons the draft has yielded virtually nothing for the Cowboys, and thus it is that dynasties become history."[9] Indeed, Schramm's top pick that season was at No. 78, in the third round, and Colorado linebacker Bill Roe would wash out after one season.

From out in never-never land, Thomas Henderson piped in, chortling that "the Cowboys used to be America's Team. This year they're going to be Iran's Team. . . . Now, they need me more than they ever will. That's just a rebuilding team without me. They'll be lucky to finish at .500."[10] Still, Landry got Too Tall Jones back, his fight career over after six fights against tomato cans in less than two months, all wins, five by knockouts, none anything but a novelty freak show. After the last fight, a one-round KO in Jackson, Mississippi, over one Rocky Gonzalez in January 1980, CBS, which had paid him $300,000 to broadcast these stinkers, terminated the contract. With no one clamoring for another fight, and sickened by the sleazy fight game, Too Tall remembered he was a football player.

Landry had resolved to fix his wobbly defense, and after two decades he went back to his roots, running the defense himself—at least for the duration of summer camp—and leaving the offensive play-calling to Dan Reeves, which was a tectonic shift for Landry. By the end of preseason, Landry was satisfied with his work, opining, "I'm not worried about our pass rush," which was so bold a statement for Landry that Zimmerman wrote, "That pronouncement from Mr. Conservative should send up distress flags around the league. No one can remember Landry ever being satisfied with a pass rush, even in the Bob Lilly days."[11] Then when the calendar turned to September, Landry fooled 'em all again, which was more striking given that his re-rigged defense was only marginally improved—it would finish the season ranked thirteenth. Conversely, the offense White ran was unstoppable, Landry's best ever.

Tony Dorsett for once had no disasters, little or big, and ran for 1,185 yards, though one of the oddest circumstances in football was the reluctance of Dallas to cotton to him. While they liked to call him "Touchdown Tony"—to his teammates he was "Hawkeye" for his buglike eyeballs—the sedate Texas Stadium crowds and the sportswriters found something not genuine about him, as if he didn't know who he was himself. He had supposedly settled down with a wife and an eight-year-old stepdaughter, but there were still regular sightings of him at the clubs and the lingering memories of smug irruptions like "No one's gonna badmouth me in Pittsburgh, Dallas, or Timbuktu" and the pretentious faux-French pronunciation of his name.[12]

In fact, Dorsett *had* been booed, and the press *did* bad-mouth him, causing him to return the favor. He had been the recent beneficiary of one of the numerous dubious honors that dilettantes automatically bestowed on Cowboys players, deserving or not, this being

Best-Dressed Man in Professional Sport by the Custom Tailors Guild in New York. Dorsett belittled the papers for reporting on something as inane as that. Trying to set a narrative, the Cowboys' PR department had been pumping the theme that Dorsett had finally grown up now that Landry had named him a co-captain.

This being the Cowboys, there were others who appeared headed in the opposite direction. Given the team's darker moments, Mike Hegman's brush with the law was almost quaint. He was charged in the off-season with forging a friend's name on $10,534 worth of checks, causing Henderson to gloat that Hegman "may be playing only for the prison team."[13] However, being a Cowboy had its rewards, provided Landry thought a player was worth keeping. He did with Hegman. After Dorsett, Harris, Staubach, and Bob Breunig chipped in $2,000 each to help pay back what Hegman had forged, he was given two years' probation—with some claiming he had received special treatment—and Landry had no compunction keeping Hegman around for eight more years.[14]

LANDRY WAS always able to normalize problems, or at least hide them behind the furniture. Playing it coy, he predicted his team would go 8–8. When the gate opened, however, they won five of the first six, and seven of nine. And this time, they didn't hit a wall. They ended the season with a 12–4 record, tied with the newly resurgent Philadelphia Eagles, who because of tie-breaking criteria won the division. Moving into the Danny White era without pause, the offense was ranked No. 1, having scored 454 points, the most by a Cowboys team save for the 2007 unit, which would score 455. That worked out to 28.4 points a game. White, while not throwing as often as Staubach did in 1979, threw twenty-eight touchdown passes, beating Staubach's club record by one, and had a 60 percent completion rate—but he also threw twenty-five interceptions, which was a recurring problem. Dorsett, Newhouse, and Springs were a potent backfield. Hill, Drew Pearson, and DuPree were now highly experienced and highly reliable catchers.

Landry, with the previous year's first-round exit from the playoffs on his mind, had his boys primed—and their first opponents, the

Rams, paid for it. This time they had to come to Irving, and they left in tatters, 34–13 losers, the game blown open in the second half by White's touchdown passes to Dorsett, Butch Johnson, and Drew Pearson. White had his first career 300-yard passing game, but he was aided by a pulverizing ground game that softened up the defense the way Ulysses S. Grant softened up Richmond. The Cowboys ran forty-six times for 338 yards—at the time, the second most ever in a playoff game.

That prefaced White's football baptism. The next playoff round took the Cowboys to Atlanta to play Leeman Bennett's Falcons, a team on a one-year high, with four All-Pros on offense led by quarterback Steve Bartkowski, and another on defense, tackle Mike Kenn. The game soon developed into an air war, both teams racking up 642 passing yards and five touchdowns. After three quarters, Bartkowski had the clear edge, his team up 24–10 when he found fullback William Andrews from 12 yards away.

Now White had to be Staubach, snatching victory from defeat. Cool as the man he replaced, he directed a drive capped by a 1-yard touchdown run by Newhouse to get the scores a little closer. Then, after the Falcons made a field goal, with 3:40 left and down by 10, White went back to work, ultimately finding Drew Pearson with a 14-yard touchdown pass to make it 27–24. Less than two minutes remained when White got the ball back on his own 29-yard line. He methodically moved it to Atlanta's 42, with 1:48 left and no time-outs. Bennett unwittingly lent him some help by having the Falcons play a prevent defense even though the Cowboys needed to move the ball only 40 yards to get into field-goal range. Taking what he was given, White would throw to Butch Johnson at midfield, then Preston Pearson to the 36, with twenty-nine seconds left. He called a screen pass for Dorsett, who rambled to the 24. With the Falcons in a daze, White took the next snap and, not playing it safe, threaded the needle with a dart between two defensive backs to find Drew Pearson in the end zone with the game-winning pass.

The drive was smart, slick, surgical, deadly. And one game too soon. Back in the NFC title game, the Cowboys had a January 11 date with a new rival for conference preeminence, the Eagles, coached back to the big time by Landry's exact negative image. Dick

Vermeil, a bantam cock of a man who, like George Allen, led sing-alongs with his players and often broke into tears when he spoke, no matter what the topic was. Like Allen too, Vermeil measured his own team by how it did against Landry's. Having infrequently beaten the Cowboys, veteran Eagles needed no additional motivation. Kicker Tony Franklin, a Fort Worth native who had come of age basted by the Cowboys' mythology of arrogance, now was a sworn enemy of it, the blue-collar, unglamorous environs of Philadelphia motivation in itself, even if it smacked of Cowboys envy.

Franklin would say, "You cannot believe how much this team and this city hate the Dallas Cowboys"[15]—a commonly heard statement around the league, "this team" being just about any. By contrast, while Cowboys players had no love and plenty of scorn for any team in their way, and by habit breathed hard through their nostrils when facing the Giants, they really hated only one team to the marrow, the Redskins. Still, the Cowboys simply didn't believe the Eagles could take them in a title match. Landry had beaten Vermeil in eight of ten games, and while they would split the last four, the Cowboys had taken the most recent one, the season finale in Dallas, 35–27.

But the overconfidence was misplaced. The Eagles were the stingiest team in the NFL, yielding only 13.9 points a game, its 3–4 alignment fast and savvy. All-Pro nose tackle Charlie Johnson could read the play off the snap so well that he had been in position to make *three interceptions* that season. With advantageous field position, the unspectacular but cerebral Jaworski threw twenty-seven touchdowns and just twelve interceptions, had a 91 passer rating, and went to the Pro Bowl, as did his six-foot-eight receiver Harold Carmichael. The Eagles had pounded the Vikings in Minnesota in the first round, 31–16, and were salivating about playing the Cowboys in an igloo-like Veterans Stadium. At game time the temperature was twelve degrees, the wind chill factor was minus three, with gusts putting it in the minus thirty range. Landry hadn't felt as goose-fleshed since that most gelid afternoon in Green Bay. Danny White, the Arizonan, had never seen conditions as primitive, and with his unusually small hands for a quarterback, he had trouble gripping the frosted ball.

It would be a dreadful day for him, completing just twelve of thirty-one labored throws for 127 yards, his passes cut from the sky by the howling winds. Luckily, Jaworski was no better, the so-called Polish Rifle misfiring often, going nine of twenty-nine for 17 yards with two interceptions. The game was tied, 7–7, at halftime, but Jaworski had what White didn't that day: a running game. On the game's second play, the Eagles' fullback Wilbert Montgomery slashed his way to a 42-yard touchdown, the main guts of a killer rushing attack that devoured 263 yards. On the other hand, the Cowboys could manage only 90 running yards, Dorsett just 41 on thirteen attempts.

Still the game hung in the balance until White and Dorsett coughed up third-quarter fumbles. White's occurred as he was being sacked by Carl Hairston, and it set up a field goal by Franklin that gave the Eagles a 10–7 lead. On the very next drive, Jerry Robinson picked up the ball after Dorsett's fumble and carried it to the Dallas 38, and early in the fourth quarter Leroy Harris ran it in from 9 yards out, to give the Eagles a 17–7 lead. It was still possible for White to pull off another rally, but Montgomery kept the ball from him, in all gaining 194 yards on twenty-six carries, at the time just 2 yards shy of Steve Van Buren's 1947 playoff record. White could do nothing when he did get the ball, and Franklin's very satisfying field goal in the last quarter put a win out of reach.

For Vermeil, it was a fleeting taste of nectar. In the Super Bowl, the Oakland Raiders would turn it to vinegar with a 27–10 thrashing in New Orleans, the venue that was always so kind to the Cowboys. The spin that made the rounds in Dallas that off-season was that Landry, and not Al Davis, had deserved such an easy game. Landry, though, had to face up to an even colder reality than the one he had endured in Philadelphia: that chances like this were going to be harder to come by.

THAT OFF-SEASON, as well, Landry lost a son, in the football sense, when Dan Reeves became the second Landry lieutenant to ascend to his own head coaching job, having accepted a lucrative offer from the Denver Broncos following the 1980 season. Reeves had previously been given due consideration by several teams, and Landry never stood in his way. But reminiscent of the sly manner in which Wellington Mara juggled Landry's and Lombardi's ambitions back during their Giants days, Landry would leave the impression that Reeves might well someday be his hand-picked successor as the Cowboys' head coach. However, Reeves began to feel much the way Landry and Lombardi had, unappreciated, his loyalty to Landry self-defeating and even stunting. According to one report, Reeves "often complained privately, bitterly, about Landry's inflexibility"[16] when it came to updating his age-old strategies. It didn't help that during the 1980 season Landry took back the responsibilities for play-calling, making Reeves feel like he was being downgraded. After the season, the Broncos made him an offer and Reeves leaped at it, becoming head coach and vice president of the organization. When the 1981 season began, Red Miller was out, and Landry's scion was on the sideline in a suit, surrounded by men in orange uniforms, the youngest head coach in the league. Stiffening up Miller's relaxed ways, and keeping Joe Collier's 3–4 defense intact, Reeves took the Broncos to a 10–6 record in his first year. In 1984 the Broncos would be division champs, on course to winning five titles and making it to the Super Bowl in 1986, 1987, and 1989. Still, his Landry pedigree also came with heartbreak and big-game failure: he lost all three of those Super Bowls (and another, in 1998, as head coach of the Atlanta Falcons).

Landry, knowing how unhappy Reeves had become in Dallas, wished him well. He then went outside the organization to replace Reeves, hiring Wake Forest coach John Mackovic as the quarterbacks coach, though, as always; Landry was intent now on controlling every aspect of the product the Cowboys put on the field, and no longer did he consider youthful slipups to be acceptable to the greater good. Tony Dorsett might not have completely matured, but on a surface level he was playing the role of captain convincingly, though a leadership role was obviously suited to him. Earning a cover story in *Sports Illustrated*, he told Rick Telander, "You hope in this life that you grow and you don't always repeat your mistakes," adding, "I don't want to waste anything now. I've made adjustments," even if he seemed not altogether convinced, adding with a shrug, "I mean, I guess I've matured."

He certainly needed to convince no one of his talents. But it was off the field where he was said to have made his biggest strides, his defensiveness explained by Telander as a product of childhood, when Dorsett saw his alcoholic older brother die of a heart attack. He was so scarred by that, he couldn't sleep in his own house and moved in with his older sister. Wrote Telander, "Dorsett doesn't like to reveal any of these things about his past; in fact, he'd be happy now if reporters sort of left him alone." Dorsett added, "I'd say that things did come at me too fast, and that I was a little naive. But everything was so easy. Going from nothing at Pitt to the national championship and the Heisman. Then the Super Bowl. Then Rookie of the Year. . . . It still freaks me out."[17]

Behind the fluffy narratives, though, Dorsett was getting himself into trouble financially, failing to pay his taxes[18] and associating with shady types. There were also rumors afoot about cocaine.[19] Whatever was known or unknown about him, there was a vague sense of angst about Touchdown Tony, a sense that would persist among the fans and the local reporters. Indeed, Telander's last sentence, deviating from the script, was portentous, almost sinister: "He sits there now, a young man staring into the dark with his immense, relentlessly searching eyes, ready to play the game."[20]

FOR NOW, Dorsett could run through the dark into daylight. He was at the top of his game. Having missed the All-Pro team in 1980, he charged back onto the first team with a 1,646-yard trophy season in 1981, his career best. Retrenching to a more conservative attack generally conducive to championship teams, the ground game rolled like a diesel. Danny White, knowing where his Texas toast was buttered, was effusive in his praise of the coach for that. When the Cowboys and the Eagles met again at Veterans Stadium in early November, Dallas, at 6–2, was a game behind in the division, and the team was down 14–3 after three quarters, having been stunned by an 85-yard touchdown bolt from Jaworski to Carmichael. Then came the fourth quarter and two lovely drives by the Cowboys, one capped by a 17-yard touchdown pass from White to Cosbie, the other a 9-yard run by Dorsett to seal the comeback, 17–14. Afterward, wrote Paul Zimmerman,

White stood by his locker and launched into a speech heard so often in Dallas locker rooms through the years. It's known as the Tom Landry Soliloquy.

"Today he was the best I've ever seen him," White said. ". . . We could've scored 38 points today. Coach Landry's play-calling was brilliant; he was constantly one step ahead of them. They'd overload against Tony Hill, and he'd come back with the counter play. Then they'd just about defense that, and he'd go back to the way we started, play-action stuff and the passing game."

Now the houselights were dimming; there was soft organ music in the background. "He's the hub of the wheel behind everything here," White was saying. "It's just like he has his hand in your back, pushing you along." . . . Segue to Landry, who's sitting on a chair in the coaching room, studying the Coke he's sipping; his bald head reflects the overhead light. A messenger has just relayed the news to him that White said he was one step ahead of the Eagles. The hub-of-the-wheel and the hand-in-the-back parts were not mentioned. "Well," Landry said, looking up. "We won."[21]

He could say that twelve times in 1981, a year in which the core of the Cowboy's another year older, was reinforced on defense by two amazing rookies Schramm had gotten on the cheap, Everson Walls from Grambling State University and Michael Downs from Rice. Both Dallas natives, they were unbelievable ball hawks but judged too slow by the scouts. Signed for the bare minimum as undrafted free agents, they came to Thousand Oaks and stuck like glue to receivers. Landry was so impressed that when the season began, Walls was the starting left cornerback, and after Randy Hughes hurt his shoulder, Downs started at free safety. Together, they were the second and third rookies to ever start a season for Landry.

These were chancy moves, but Walls picked off a league-high eleven passes and made the Pro Bowl, while Downs stole seven. When teams threw the ball away from the area they covered, the other defensive backs prospered. Right corner Dennis Thurman had nine interceptions, and Charlie Waters marked his last year with three of his own. Suddenly, the Cowboys' secondary, formerly the team's Achilles' heel, had become the cream of the league—intercepting a remarkable *thirty-seven* passes. Walls would become a fixture for nine years and a four-time All-Pro, leading the league in interceptions three times, a feat shared since only by the Baltimore Ravens' Ed Reed. By 1987, Walls would own a $5.05 million, three-year contract and be the second-highest-paid cornerback in the league.

Landry also found valuable backups in linebackers Anthony Dickerson and Guy Brown and defensive backs Ron Fellows and Steve Wilson. With the old team balance back, the offense finished the season ranked sixth, the defense seventh, and the rushing game second, fueled by Dorsett and Springs. White threw for over 3,000 yards, with twenty-two touchdown passes and just thirteen interceptions. Hill averaged over 20 yards a catch. White, Jones, Scott, and Donovan went back to the Pro Bowl. When Landry's team beat the Eagles in early November, he gained a share of first place in the division, and stayed there as Vermeil's team faded and the Cowboys won four of their last five games. Another win over the Eagles, 21–10, secured, by two games, Landry's twelfth division crown.

His immediate reward for that was a cookie, a first-round playoff game against the 9–7 Tampa Bay Buccaneers at Texas Stadium. By now Ricky Bell was gone, and the man John McKay had passed up for him ran for 86 efficient yards on sixteen carries, though Dorsett took a back seat to the defense, which stuffed quarterback Doug Williams into a trash can. All four of the Cowboys' running backs notched a touchdown in a 38–0 ego boost as the team returned yet again to the NFC Championship Game, a January 10,1982, date with the newest flavor in the league, the San Francisco 49ers.

LANDRY HAD never lost to the 49ers in the playoffs. Now, however, he would need to do it against Bill Walsh, who in 1980 was in his third season as the team's head coach. It was the kind of position he had to wait far too long for. The white-haired, avuncular-looking Walsh had served as an assistant coach under Al Davis in Oakland and Paul Brown in Cincinnati, helping to develop two distinct passing systems. One was the long, go-for-broke "vertical" game that Davis had learned from Sid Gillman, and the other a controlled scheme designed for the weak-armed Virgil Carter to complete short, safe passes from one sideline to the other. These tosses were tantamount to a running game, though with careful blocking the player catching them could break for long yardage.

Walsh put in eight years in Cincinnati but not as a silent partner. He was an opinionated taciturn fellow who clashed with the similar Brown. Still, he assumed that when Brown quit coaching, he would get the job. However, when Brown decided he would run the Bengals from upstairs, he stiffed Walsh for the job, leaving him shattered.[22] Walsh then jumped to the Chargers as an assistant, then to Stanford University as head coach. Then in 1979 Ed DeBartolo Jr., the young owner of the 49ers, signed him to coach his team, whereupon they went 2–14 in his first year. But the next season Walsh made the move that turned it all around: he elevated his third-round pick from the year before, the dashing Notre Dame All-American Joe Montana, to be his starting quarterback.

The 49ers' record improved to 6–10 in 1980, and Walsh had, in his new quarterback, the ideal vehicle to transplant his deceptively cautious offense to the West Coast—in short order, to be christened the "West Coast offense." Montana, another product of western Pennsylvania mining country, seemed to have steel in his blood and the Roger Staubach late-game gene. In Montana's last game at Notre Dame, played in the Cotton Bowl against Houston, he was so sick that he had to have intravenous fluid injections at halftime and sipped chicken soup on the sideline, but he came in with two seconds left to throw the winning touchdown. He brought that sort of magic into the pros, where his quick release, convincing play fakes, and sprint-outs in a moving pocket made the Walsh method flourish like never before.

Montana was only one of Walsh's prize picks. He also drafted receiver Jerry Rice, defensive back Ronnie Lott, and linebacker Charles Haley—who with Montana were the core of four championship teams in the new decade. Every bit the control freak that Landry was, Walsh at age fifty was a demanding taskmaster who called all the plays. He also laid out an ironclad game plan in which the first fifteen plays were scripted in advance and had to be followed to the letter. He and Montana had a kind of sixth sense between them. Often by the time Walsh sent in the play via a hand signal, Montana had already called it and the team was up at the line for the snap.

Montana in 1981 completed a league-high 63.7 percent of his passes, threw for 3,565 yards, and had nineteen touchdowns and twelve interceptions. He also had a target that made the Walsh passing schematic leap from the blackboard to points on the scoreboard. That was Dwight Clark, a tenth-round pick from Clemson in 1979 who had sat on the bench his first year until Montana gave him a function. At six foot four and 200 pounds, Clark had inordinately long arms, which allowed Montana to keep the ball up high where only Clark could catch it. Both went to the Pro Bowl, for Montana the first of eight times, after a lethal season when Clark reeled in eighty-five passes, though he was used more as a third-down, possession receiver, only catching four touchdown passes.

Montana threw to virtually everyone, backs, receivers, tight ends, popcorn vendors, whomever, giving Landry an enormous challenge planning for the game, one made greater by the fact that Walsh had also built the NFL's second-toughest defense. Giving up just 15.6 points a game, Walsh and his defensive coordinator Chuck Studley cemented their version of the 3–4 alignment when Jack Reynolds came over from the Rams to play the inside lanes with Dan Bunz. What's more, Walsh did Landry one better by starting *three* rookies in the secondary, including cornerback Ronnie Lott, the team's first-round pick who made All-Pro and would go on to a Hall of Fame career. The 49ers surged to a 13–3 record and in the first round of playoffs trampled the Giants, 38–24. Then came Landry's boys.

IT WAS misting and gray, a crisp forty-three degrees, at Candlestick Park on game day, and the sloppy turf would contribute to a dizzying affair, the lead changing hands seven times and the unsteady footing and moist ball helping to cause nine turnovers, six by the home team. Taking advantage, the offenses ruled, bringing touchdown catches by Freddie Solomon, Hill, and Clark, along with touchdown runs by Dorsett and Johnny Davis, the last giving the 49ers a 21–17 lead entering the fourth quarter. Montana would complete twenty-two of thirty-five passes for 286 yards, dwarfing White's sixteen of twenty-four for 173 yards, but Landry's cleverly cloaked zone defense led to three Cowboy interceptions. And as time began getting short, the

Cowboys took control. A Septien field goal cut the deficit to one, 21–20. Then Danny White led a deliberate, time-eating drive, ultimately finding Cosbie with a 21-yard scoring pass that put the Cowboys ahead 27–21 with 4:54 to go.

That gave Montana time to pull out a win, though he would need to do it on this drive, which began from his own 11-yard line. As the drive went on, Walsh ordered running plays to take advantage of the hard-charging defensive linemen, and as a result the clock ran down fast. After passes to Clark and Solomon put the 49ers at the Dallas 13—Landry believed the latter one, with Solomon sliding off a "pick" by the tight end, was illegal—there was just 1:15 left. Two plays later, it was third down with 3 yards to go at the 6, and 58 seconds left. Stomach-bubbling time. On the sideline during a 49ers time-out, Landry paced like a puma in a black suit and hat. Unlike Walsh across the field, he had no headset on and said not a word to anyone as he clutched a sheet of paper in his right hand. As the camera found him, Vin Scully, announcer of the game on CBS, said, "Tom Landry is six yards away from his sixth Super Bowl . . . and for the upstart 49ers, six yards from Pontiac," the site of the Super Bowl.[23] For the next play, Walsh had stationed two running backs behind Montana and had Clark and Solomon lined up to the right. At the snap, Montana rolled right in a moving pocket. As he neared the sideline, Martin, Jones, and Lewis all had him in their sights. Deftly, Montana pump-faked once, then as Jones bore in on him, he did it again, causing Jones to stop and leap so he could get in the way of a pass.

With just that little crack of daylight, Montana caught sight of Clark moving from left to right along the back of the end zone, having broken his route when he saw Montana in trouble. Montana, falling backward, flung a high pass, too high seemingly to be caught. Though Montana would deny it, many assumed he was trying to throw the ball away and bank everything on fourth down, such was the tilt of the ball out of his hands. But this was exactly the kind of pass Montana loved to funnel to Clark, who looked like he was climbing up a stepladder to reach it, stretching out to his full height in a perpendicular line over Benny Barnes, who could only look up and see Clark tickle the ball with his long fingertips, steady it, and come down to earth, in bounds. It was so sudden that, as if a lightning bolt had hit the end zone, there was a moment of quiet, then the sound of rumbling thunder when it became clear the game was now tied. Clark spiked the ball and was mobbed by teammates. The crowd erupted in waves of celebration, as if in rapture.

Landry clenched his jaw tighter but never changed his expression. There were fifty-one seconds left, and when the extra point was made, to give the Niners a 1 point lead, he motioned to summon his kick-return team and studied the paper in his hand. Tom Landry Jr., who was in the stands a few rows behind the Cowboys' sideline, recalls, "That was the classic example of how Dad went about his business. We were all deflated, angry, crushed. But that whole drive he was thinking about what he would do if they scored. He had his plan of attack all ready to come back and win." White indeed had enough time and time-outs to move the scale back one last time. The kickoff return gave him the ball at his own 25. "What a magnificent, wild game," Scully teased, awaiting the first snap.

White, given his first call by Landry on the sideline, dropped back, unencumbered by any rush. He squared up and sent a beautiful spiral for Drew Pearson on a down-and-in pattern. The perfectly timed pass hit him in the numbers at the 50-yard line between three defensive backs. Pearson took it in full stride and for a fraction of a second had an open field in front of him, but then cornerback Eric Wright reached out with his left arm, desperately grabbing for *anything*. Wright's fingers found Pearson by the scruff of the neck, tugging him down from behind by the shirt. But for that, Scully said, "Pearson would have busted it," for a 75-yard touchdown. With thirty-eight seconds to go, the ball on the 49ers' 44, and one time-out, White was near field goal territory. A television shot of a nervous DeBartolo came up—"the young owner growing very old," said Scully. Then one of Landry, head down, lost in thought—"but Landry," Scully segued, "has been through it all many times." White, though, hadn't. He took another deep drop, this time under heavy pressure. He put his arm up to throw, pulled it back down as he waited for Hill to make his break, then was engulfed by tackle Lawrence Pillers. The ball squirted loose, to be recovered by end Jim Stuckey, finally putting the Cowboys to sleep. White argued that his arm was moving forward, thus it was an incomplete pass, but he was ignored.

It was a particularly cruel way to lose, even for Landry, who had lost cruelly enough for ten men. As CBS cross-cut glimpses of a grim, silent Landry and a relieved, animated Walsh, Scully's narrative became a eulogy, contrasting "Bill Walsh in his ascendancy as one of the great young coaches" with the forlorn, graven images of "one of the greatest coaches in history standing on the [other] side, Tom Landry.[24] Indeed, even though Walsh was only seven years younger than Landry, it felt like there had been a great generational change that day. Almost immediately, Clark's touchdown was the stuff of legend—"The Catch" was all that was needed to replay it in the mind—and sent the 49ers tripping lightly to the first of their four Super Bowl wins in the Walsh/Montana era. For the Cowboys there was the consolation again of what might have been—*if only*.

Landry was, as ever, gracious, giving Montana his due props. Asked what the key to the game was, he said, "Montana has to be the key. There really is nothing else there except the quarterback."[25] But he was covering up, according to his son. "It was just so crushing to me, and to Dad. If Wright doesn't get a piece of Drew's shirt, it's our best comeback ever, we go to the Super Bowl, maybe it's a new dynasty. Danny White's career would have been made. And then . . . not."

A laugh. "You know, people who hated the Cowboys said God hated us, too, that's why we lost that game. Well, the Catholics believe in fate but not the Methodists. We believe pain is a trial, you endure it, learn from it, and it leads to redemption. You're responsible for your own fate. It was all on him, not God. And when he looked at games like that from the long view, he was proud that he'd been in so many of those. He went to his grave believing deep in his heart that the Cowboys were the best team of his era."

But were the Cowboys themselves getting a little too resigned to inevitable defeat? Drew Pearson, for one, was spitting mad, carrying on in the locker room that "I got my number called just twice. People tell me this is supposed to be my time of year. I'm supposed to be the clutch player in the playoffs. But it's tough when you don't get the ball. I just don't understand it." Otherwise the room was fairly free of sulking. Bob Breunig said, "It's a sickening kind of feeling, but you got to remember it's just a game," recalling the untroubled postgame attitude that got Golden Richards cashiered.[26] In the paper the next day, Skip Bayless, believing God had indeed turned the page, pronounced that time had run out on more than a game.

"Cowboy mystique died a little Sunday," he wrote. "Metallic-blue tradition was tarnished some in the mud and the blood that was Candlestick. All of Schramm's computers and all of Landry's men couldn't put the Cowboys back together again. . . . In the very end zone in which Ron Sellers caught Roger Staubach's 30–28 miracle in '72, SF's Dwight Clark rose into 49er heaven and caught six points of Destiny. . . . The Dallas Cowboys had done it so many times to so many people. Sunday, the Good Lord looked the other way."[27]

BUT THE world went on for Landry, if anything with more affinity and respect for being so graceful in the face of living death. As always, win or lose, he turned his attention to the next task, the next season—but not before there was some scuttlebutt that the defeat might drive him into retirement, which, in the aftermath of the game, he did not entirely dispel. "Right now, I'm disappointed," he said, "and when I'm disappointed, I don't make decisions. No, I'm not ready to make a decision right now."[28]

His son knew better. "He couldn't even begin to think of retiring until he won it all again. He just couldn't quit with a bitter taste like that in his mouth." Landry of course returned, but with another shakeup of assistants precipitated by Mike Ditka's exit. Ditka had passed on a number of head coaching jobs, not only out of loyalty to Landry but also because he wanted only one job, from the Bears, his old team, and he was willing to wait for it. A few years earlier, he had sent a letter to Papa Bear Halas saying he would be available when Halas "was ready" to hire him.[29] When the Bears went 6–10 in 1981, Halas was, and in a flash the gum-chewing, profanity-spewing pile of rusty nails was gone, with Landry's blessing but with a certain regret. Behind the cartoonish tough-guy act, Ditka knew football inside and out. It was he, after all, who had realized the modern-day application of the Shotgun, and his sharp eye for little nuances during games led Landry to alter his game plans. Perhaps most important in Landry's purview, Ditka had maintained order in the locker room, not counting that day in Washington, DC, when Hollywood Henderson threw his temper tantrum. No other assistant had anywhere near the same slack or respect from the players.

It was of some pride to Landry that his lieutenants were fanning out across the league, spreading his gospel, or so he had a right to believe, even if none of them would run their own ship like he did. On the other hand, Landry had to contemplate Ditka's exit as another omen that the old communal unity was breaking up. Still, Landry felt very paternal about men like Ditka and Reeves, and for years after they left his bosom, they dutifully had regular phone conversations with him. Little of these discussions had anything to do with football. They were more calls of duty, and perhaps a bit of guilt-easing that they had left him before he won another championship.

The upshot of this spread of Landry protégés throughout the league was that the coaches who didn't get the call became stewed about it. Gene Stallings, for example, had been a fixture on the staff since 1972, and he believed that a man who had served both Bear Bryant and Tom Landry, the two most eminent football coaches of modern times, deserved a chance to run a team. But he would have to keep waiting. Back in Big D, it was less about confederation and loyalty than raw ambition—with some daring to think about who would get the most coveted job of all, Landry's. That this was even a subject for speculation indicated that, despite his continued despotic methods, Landry may not be as inviolate as it seemed.

As always, he gave the impression that such idle hearsay was beneath his ken. Yet it seems more than coincidence that with Reeves and Ditka gone, and no one on his staff worthy in his eyes of succeeding him, Landry brought home Dick Nolan as an assistant two years after his original prodigal son had hit bottom, fired by the New Orleans Saints after a 0–12 start. Nolan was given Ditka's title as receivers coach, though he would also coach the defensive backs. But if Nolan thought he was quietly being groomed to follow in Landry's infinite footsteps, there was too much on the horizon that would get in the way of that.

REMARKABLE, INDEED, was the magnetic pull and commanding presence of a team that *wasn't* reaching the pinnacle, but whose allure kept growing. Seasons were interstitial, slavishly followed, endlessly pimped on Monday nights and Thanksgiving. Ratings for their games were still going through the ceiling. Bayless was wrong, or at least premature. Nothing about the Cowboys' mystique expired in Candlestick Park. Not yet. If the America's Team title was a self-fulfilling prophesy, they had made it so, if not by winning it all then by being in so many climactic games and losing them so damn entertainingly. They surely were fat and firmly entrenched in an era when Ronald Reagan and Gordon Gecko represented the same national values—greed was good, as Gecko said. It was for the Cowboys and the NFL, and beyond. The Cowboys' appeal in Mexico was reflected in their network of two hundred radio stations in fourteen states, including sixteen Spanish-language stations. Even the team's self-promotional newsletter, begun in 1975, had reached a circulation of over a hundred thousand.

It was around this time that Butch Johnson, one of the more flamboyant of the Cowboys, sensed a superficiality beginning to set in on the club. As he recalled, "We really were no longer a football team. We had become rock stars with people lining up at hotels to see us. It was insane." Each player, he said, "had developed his own image, down to his attire. . . . If you didn't have a mink or an Armani or something really sharp, other players would really talk bad about you." Much more improbably, *Landry* seemed to be preening a bit. "Tom had his image, too," Johnson noticed; which in cold weather entailed bringing out "his full-length cashmere coat and fur-lined hat."

Not that Landry ever gave in to some of the team's pop culture standards. He intentionally kept his eyes from wandering to the Cowboys' cheerleaders for fear of some photographer snapping that money shot. Some players told of wearing their helmets backward on the bench so they could sneak a peak through the ear holes at the formations going on behind them. This soft-porn Cowboys subfranchise was unstoppable within the culture. A Cowgirls' cheesecake poster had surpassed sales of the iconic kittenish Farrah Fawcett poster from the late 1970s, and a made-for-TV movie called *The Dallas Cowboys Cheerleaders* racked up the second-highest ratings of any TV movie ever made. The cheerleaders even toured around the world, and would add only more and more media credits, an industry with a life of its own that continues to thrive to this very day despite almost every other team having its own squad of professionally trained, sequined, pole-dancers bounding out of pushup bras on the sideline. Schramm was provident: it wasn't the steak, it was the sizzle that sold; not the flesh but the brand it was wrapped in.

Hollywood Henderson may not have been right about much, but he never was righter than when he told me, "The Cowboys were the best vehicle to push myself. They're on national TV all season long. America's Team. I always exploited them for personal gain."[30] Landry, then, shouldn't have felt so bad about Henderson. It was never personal, only business. Dallas itself, as heavily invested as it was in boosting the Cowboys, had become an overpriced, inflated metropolis, its ozone layer of inane, idle rich obsessions very profitably caricatured by an absurdly overplayed TV series about the rapacious fables of an oil family much like the Murchisons and an immoral patriarch named J. R. Ewing. Week after week, the greed and family betrayals on *Dallas* weren't deviations but *requirements*, the surreality of capitalist chauvinism etched by the pastiche of glamorous exterior shots in the opening, including an aerial view of the "God's portal" roof of Texas Stadium, the house that Murchison built on Tom Landry's shoulders.

Indeed, the oversized nature of the Cowboys made oversized capitalism seem cool, even God blessed. It had God's coach, after all. One could argue that the enormous profit turned by the league, and shared with the Cowboys, was the sole doing of the onetime joke team in Dallas. All of it painted a picture of overflowing mercantilism and arrogance that needed a strong, compatible coach who dominated but was not a slave to the operation. A hip coach in white shoes and dark shades would have made it all a farce. Landry, on the other hand, kept injecting his hip-to-be-squareness into the middle of every new generation. In the early 1980s Paul Zimmerman wrote,

> History will evaluate Landry as the captain of the smoothest ship in the game for many, many years. Ask him what his trademarks are and he'll say, "Consistency, proper organization, proper preparation." A lot of people get a lot of credit within the organization,

but, as former Bear GM Jim Finks said, "It's that bald-headed guy who runs the show."[31]

He was a bargain too, making not a lot of money, accepting less than he could have when he sold his stock back to Murchison. Still, as much as Landry had hated the America's Team label, consciously or not he began to play his part with more pomp, looking either more regal or more arrogant, depending on one's allegiance. And beating him became the same sort of obsession it had once been for George Allen, who had perished trying, never slaying the team he had called "a goddamn bunch of front-runners."[32] Indeed, outlasting rivals and kibitzers gave Landry an immunity from the miasma of Cowboys hatred all around him. When, in 1982, John Wilbur ventured that his old team was "a monolithic computer; there was a real antihuman spirit there, [a] corporate mentality, total conformity,"[33] after two decades and the many rebels Landry had put up with, such talk seemed tired and dated.

LIKE THE aging actor in the White House, Landry's Teflon coating shielded him from the alleged crimes and misdemeanors going on in his midst, and the natural backlash to the America's Team hype that Landry, after all, had predicted. More and more, Dallas sportswriters like Bayless and Randy Galloway were getting openly cynical about the label, Bayless to the point that Schramm called him "that little cocksucker."[34] There was a niche for literature such as the *Cowboy Haters Handbook*. And when *Sports Illustrated*'s 1982 football preview issue focused on the Cowboys, it came with both a pro and a con article about them. The pro was William Oscar Johnson's article "There Are No Holes at the Top," an elegiac bronzing of Landry, Schramm, and Brandt as the three horsemen of the sports kingdom who collectively, wrote Johnson, had an "aura of myth—or miracle . . . as if it were a cathedral or a shrine where one can go to be cured of everything from lumbago to losing poker hands."[35]

The counterpoint was "Dallas Can Have 'em," in which Paul Zimmerman catalogued Cowboys put-downs from numerous football people, such as Jack Lambert, who said, "Talk to anyone around the league and they'll tell you, 'We don't care who wins, as long as it isn't the Cowboys,'" and John Brodie, who added, "Nobody ever beats the Cowboys. They always do something to beat themselves. They never give anyone credit. Whenever someone beats them, all you hear is 'Well, those weren't the real Dallas Cowboys they beat.'" The paranoid Al Davis insisted, "The Cowboys are wired to the league office, everyone knows that. And you can bet every game official knows that, too. If there's one team that's going to get a break, it's Dallas—on the calls, on the scheduling, on the Competition Committee, on everything else relating to league matters"—a plaint that would have amused a few Cowboys who still saw Fred Swearingen lurking in their own conspiracy theories. Zimmerman's piece also related a memorable one-liner by CBS publicist Beano Cook, who was quoted as telling Schramm, "You're one of the two most efficient organizations in the 20th century."

"What's the other?" asked Schramm.

"The Third Reich."[36]

As the article trenchantly pointed out, though, being envied to the point of hatred was the ultimate form of flattery to the Cowboys. Decades later, it still is. "Oh, we *loved* wearing that America's Team thing," says Tom Rafferty, who was draped in it for almost all of his fourteen years as the Cowboys' center. "The way we looked at it, a lot of people had worked a lot of years to develop that, and every guy who came through felt that tradition. We felt we had a completely unique image, and we meant a lot to people halfway around the world. Tom didn't build that image, but he sure sold it."[37]

And no one begrudged him. No backlash ever really dirtied up his pretty face. Some things never changed. Landry was one of them. He wasn't just Landry; he was *Landry*. And if it seemed the Cowboys could never lose without psychodrama, it was just as reasonable to expect any lull in winning to be temporary simply because of that granite effigy, who would never let them slide. If winning Super Bowls wasn't absolutely required, being close to it was. As Schramm said, "The season is always a failure for us when we don't make the Super Bowl. We don't have the luxury of being a contender or just a playoff team."[38] Having held up his end, Landry was content enough in his station that he could joke about his longevity. Asked to comment on the fact that he was the only coach in his team's history, he said, "That's one way to look at it. The other is that I haven't had a promotion in 21 years."[39]

Good-humored as he was about it, there was a certain bite to those words. Landry had to know he was taken very much for granted, such as by being given Coach of the Year honors only once. If like Vince Lombardi, who also took home that honor just once, those kind of ego balms meant little to him, some form of symbolic reward clearly seemed in order to commemorate that Landry was coaching a declining team to some of its best seasons.

THE PROBLEM for Landry was that the game was changing faster than he could figure it out. Mostly, this had to do with non-football matters. In 1982, the NFL's entrenched narratives were shaken up like pickup sticks when the players' union shockingly called a strike early in the season. Landry had enough problems as it was. Waters and Lewis had retired, their places filled by Barnes—who shifted to strong safety—and Guy Brown at weak-side linebacker. Otherwise, the roster was unchanged. Their toughest game came first, hosting the Steelers in a Monday night game. Again Chuck Noll prevailed, 36–28, behind three Terry Bradshaw touchdown passes—and despite four scoring tosses by White, who threw for 347 yards but also two interceptions. The following Sunday, the Cowboys rebounded, beating the Cardinals in St. Louis, 24–7, White producing two more touchdowns and interceptions.

White had emerged as a real gunslinger, for better or worse, as Landry was prepared to let him chuck his way through the season. But then, before the third game, the season went on hold, the union finally getting tough with the owners, demanding that 55 percent of league revenue be set aside for players' salaries. The negotiator for the owners, predictably, called such a thing "socialism" and the league held firm, expecting the union to fold. Talks, getting nowhere, went on for seven weeks, and before long the players became divided. Some, badly in need of a paycheck, began lobbying for an end to the strike, but no one was more harmful to the union than Danny White, who took management's side, calling the walkout a "farce," and met with Schramm to ask what he could do to end it on management's terms.

In truth, there was not a thing he could do. And when word of his sellout became public, White became a pariah. Some Cowboys said they would never play on the same team with him. When the owners agreed to pay players severance when they retired early, the union gave up the fight, which had done great damage to both the players and the league, and returned in November to finish what would be a nine-game season. Landry, who had been agnostic about the strike, could feel the bad vibes. As a former player who never had to take a union stand or pay a dollar in union fees, Landry viewed labor issues with ambivalence. He wanted players to be better paid but not necessarily be given greater power, and he detested the chain of disruptions every summer by the union. But White's heresy was strictly a matter of causing unnecessary disruption on the team.

White, Landry recalled in his memoirs, bluntly for him, "had upset some of his lower-paid teammates [and] some people questioned whether he had the ability or the confidence of the team to rally the Cowboys to a championship."[40] He worried about it enough to pump up Gary Hogeboom when the scrimmages began in preparation to resume the season, which was a shock to White, who, if he thought he was further inveigling Landry by his pro-management stance, learned he had read him wrong. Landry had no overriding loyalty to White, and indeed liked what he kept seeing in Hogeboom, a bigger, stronger, purer prototype for the position and an outgoing, well-liked bloke.

When the players returned, Landry boldly announced that Hogeboom was his starter for now, though his intention was to force White to win back his teammates' trust by having to win his job all over again. When the schedule resumed on November 21, White had in fact done that. He was at the helm against Tampa Bay, leading the Cowboys to a close, 14–9 win and leaving poor Hogeboom to brood that he had been played, used as a prop. To be sure, building Hogeboom up just to let him down wasn't the most graceful thing Landry had ever done, but it did pave over the mess White had made for himself, and in the larger lens it helped to rekindle team esprit, something that would be pivotal in the abbreviated schedule, when a stumble might prove fatal to making the playoffs.

The Cowboys didn't do that until after they went over a month without losing, storming through five games before they lost to the Eagles, then on the road in the finale at Minnesota. With a record of 6–3, they were seeded second to the Redskins and began a three-stage playoff series by trouncing the Buccaneers 30–17 behind Dorsett's 110 yards and White's two touchdown passes. They then brushed the Packers out of the way, 37–26, with Dennis Thurman having an otherworldly game, intercepting three Lynn Dickey passes and running one back 39 yards for a touchdown. Just like that, barely breaking a sweat, the Cowboys were playing for the NFC championship again, a long-running TV series the public never seemed to tire of. By then, fan discontent over the strike had evaporated, the usual excitement and full houses were back, and there would be nothing to apologize about for a Super Bowl win.

Similar to what had happened the year before in San Francisco, a victory over Landry would go a long way for another coach of distinction on the cusp of aristocracy, Joe Gibbs, in his second season in command in Washington. Like Bill Walsh, Gibbs had to wait a long time to get his chance as head coach. He spent seventeen years as an assistant, three times under Don Coryell, at San Diego State, then in the pros with the St. Louis Cardinals and later the San Diego Chargers. Like Walsh, the short, professorial-looking Gibbs made his bones as an offensive savant, creating the ultra-sophisticated, long-passing scheme dubbed the "Air Coryell" attack. It had *averaged* 400 yards a game in 1980 and finally earned Gibbs a top job in 1981. That year, he improved the sagging Redskins' record to 8–8, and in the truncated 1987 season, to 8–1—in no small part because of a mobile, All-Pro, if not exactly young, quarterback in Joe Theismann, and a stifling defense, run by Richie Petitbon, the most unyielding in the league.

The NFC Championship Game, played on January 22, 1983, on a cold, crisp day in RFK Stadium, made Landry's illusory season disappear. The Cowboys were ranked fifth in offense, third in defense, and White went to the Pro Bowl with Dorsett, though he was the most-sacked quarterback in the league. In the big one, though, White did little. On the plus side, he probably didn't remember any of it. Sacked hard by end Dexter Manley late in the first half, he had to leave the game with a concussion and was replaced by Hogeboom, who was itching to show what he could do. The Cowboys were down 14–3, and John Riggins was running wild on them behind the blocking by the "Hogs" on the front line. The flaky Riggins would carry the ball thirty-six times, gaining 140 yards and scoring two touchdowns.

Throwing out the game plan, Landry gave Hogeboom free reign to throw, and he let fly a blizzard of passes, twenty-nine times in just one half, completing fourteen for 162 yards. Down 14–3, he hit Pearson with a 6-yard touchdown pass, then after a critical Cowboys special teams breakdown—allowing a 76-yard punt return, which set up a Riggins touchdown—he found Butch Johnson with a 23-yard shot, cutting the lead to 21–17 entering the last quarter. But Hogeboom's adrenaline rush ended here. He threw two interceptions, the last one with a minute to go, the ball being tipped by Manley then caught and run in for the clincher by tackle Darryl Grant, which sealed the victory, 31–17.

For some Cowboys who had been through these walks of shame, there was no self-delusion. Harvey Martin, who had made All-Pro again, was ready to pronounce judgment. "When a team consistently comes close . . . and falls short each time, it is not by accident," he would later say. "Great teams do not consistently lose the close game." The Cowboys, he said, "had a serious flaw, maybe several of them."[41] He didn't mean on the field, but within the soul. If so, Landry once more escaped any real heat for it. For some, in fact, delusion was a comforting ally, in this case that the season itself was somehow bogus in its brevity. Joe Gibbs would beg to differ; his team went on to beat the Miami Dolphins in the Super Bowl in Pasadena, the first of his three title runs over the next decade. For Landry, the hardest part of losing might have been seeing the ascension of the team he disliked the most, and thought he lad left in the dust.

RATHER THAN good-cop Landry, when people got on the Cowboys' case the whipping boys were almost always the two front-office bad cops, Tex Schramm and Gil Brandt. Schramm had ridden the Cowboys boom to become the most powerful broker in the league, Pete Rozelle's point man for every pressing matter. The biggest one was the NFL's war against Al Davis after he sought to move the Raiders, against the league's wishes, to Los Angeles subsequent to the Rams' move to Anaheim in 1980. Davis was an old friend, but when he sued the league on antitrust grounds, making it a personal war against his old foil Rozelle, Tex had no option but to go to war against Davis. Schramm was a constant presence in the courtroom during the trial, passing notes to the league's lawyers, but Davis eventually won, opening the door for a hopscotch of franchise jumping—one that would include the mercurial *Davis*, who would shift the Raiders *back* to Oakland in 1995.

Brandt, meanwhile, had transformed *his* role into a demesne not unlike that of J. Edgar Hoover, sitting atop stacks of files with the darkest of secrets to use as leverage. One writer said that when it came to contracts, "Players always felt that the hand of Tex Schramm was somehow behind the numbers . . . which generally followed a team scale and were very low, compared to the league average. . . . But when they thought they had been lied to or somehow cheated, there was the feeling they'd been worked over by a Schramm-Brandt combination."[42] As Pete Gent said, "In my next book, I'm gonna create the most evil person I can think of and call him Schrandt!"[43]

Landry could have cared less about what the other two honchos were doing. As long as they did their jobs in service to the Cowboys, their business was not his business. There was nothing he could have ever done about them, anyway. But if they ever believed they were more important to the Cowboys than Landry, Clint Murchison Jr. would shoot that right down. The problem for all three legs of the Cowboys' triangle was that the game was changing too fast for them, and worse for Landry, Murchison was nearing his own abyss. But what Landry had to fear most had to do with something Hollywood Henderson once said, that "the main reason Tom fired me was to try to show the team he had control. The truth was, he never really had control. He was just a guy who made everybody think he had control."[44] If that was wishful thinking by Henderson, Landry had to wonder now if his players were starting to believe it.

Chapter 25

LIVING ON
A PRAYER

FIFTY-NINE-YEAR-OLD TOM LANDRY looked around in 1983 and realized he was at another of many crossroads, standing over a dissipating team with an enormous brand value and multiple problems. The decline was a product of the usual factors, such as age and instability at the quarterback position, but more egregiously for Landry was the one of runaway egos. If opponents painted a target on their backs, the Cowboys gave them a clear one to shoot for by acting as if they were entitled to win based on rating numbers, sales figures, and outside earning potential.

Confirming Butch Johnson's analysis, the Cowboys acted more like rock stars all the time, In fact, observers at the Dallas hotel where the Cowboys would hunker down on the eve of games might have wondered if the Rolling Stones were staying there. Just before a Monday night game finale against the Vikings, Johnson, according to Skip Bayless, whispered to him; "These guys don't understand anymore, man. Girls were all over the floor last night. You watch: We'll lose tonight and we'll live to regret it."[1] He was right. They did lose, and went into the playoffs on a sour note that became more sour against the Redskins.

The Cowboys had never had to pretend they were emotionally wrapped in any game, and the America's Team backlash had at first fed into their emotional ovens. Yet as much as the players still loved to be tarred with the label, it was more to buff their personal media stars. There could be no doubt the grandeur had gone to their heads, and for some up their noses.

Harvey Martin, for example, as the latest casualty of living way too large and too reckless, had become part of the problem rather than the solution. Like Clint Murchison Jr., Martin fell on hard times, done in by his own lack of restraint. Undeterred by the economic downturn of the late 1970s, when America endured long gas lines and interest rates climbing to over 20 percent, Martin sank money into any investment that was pitched to him. Besides Lucifer's, he went in on a restaurant called Smokey's, as well as land investments, all of which went under in the early 1980s and left him a mountain of debt and a $300,000 tab from the IRS. In 1982 he declared bankruptcy, which, when it went public, gave more ammunition to the Cowboys' haters. During the NFC title game in Washington, Redskins fans threw coins at him.

Martin, who kept secret his regular cocaine use since 1980,[2] had clearly lost much. He didn't make the All-Pro team in 1982, and his number of sacks fallen to eight in the truncated season, his concentration drained by his financial collapse and negative publicity during the trial of the two major Dallas drug dealers who tried to divert attention by dropping his name as a client. Martin had to go into denial mode. He claimed he knew only one of the men, not as a dealer but as a hairdresser whose barbershop he frequented—as did a number of other Cowboys including, it was pointed out, Tom Landry, Tex Schramm, and Gil Brandt.[3] The situation would get only worse for Martin. Soon it became public knowledge that he was also being investigated in connection with a mob of Brazilian cocaine dealers in Dallas. Martin's story was that the only one of those guys he knew was a soccer player for the Brazilian national team who had been charged with selling drugs, but that he had never gotten cocaine from him.[4]

Both trials ended in convictions, leaving Martin tarnished for no reason other than guilt by association—a sting also felt by seven other Cowboys, including Dorsett, Tony Hill, Ron Springs, and Larry Bethea, who had been implicated by the Brazilians as clients in a plea bargain for a lighter sentence, a story so volcanic that it was broken by the *New York Times*. It turned out that none of the players were called to testify at the trial or charged with any crime, a much less hysterical and overlooked story, but months of blaring headlines, gossip, and the Damoclean sword hanging over their heads about imminent indictment took a serious toll on each of them.

None more so than Martin. After the coin-littered loss to the Redskins, he had told Landry, "I'm tired of fighting" and that he was quitting. Landry talked him down, but if he was any the wiser about Martin's drug use than he was about Henderson's, he handled this version of cocaine madness almost as badly. To be sure, Landry had a far greater affection for Martin, who had never given him a minute of trouble or missed a meeting. Rather than come out and ask Martin if he had a drug problem, and with Martin unwilling to admit to one, Landry was more intent on defusing numerous government investigations into drug use by the Cowboys, something that could rip the mask right off the team's image. As it was, new rumors had it that some of the players were preparing to turn on each other, and one Cowboy who was not implicated, Drew Pearson, seemed to be turning against those who had been, promising to "stay as far away [from them] as possible."[5]

When Landry met with Martin after the 1982 season, he seemed to be less concerned with Martin's mental and physical health than he was with the health of the Cowboys' public image, which had already been sullied by slurs such as "South America's Team." "I feel if we show that we as an organization are trying to curtail these wild activities, the government will ease up," Landry told him.[6] It had been decided that the best course of action was to send Martin to the Hazelden rehab facility in Minneapolis, where Landry had recently attended a seminar about players and drugs. But rather than doing this to get Martin straight, Landry said he wanted him to "go to Hazelden and come back and report to the team. Bring back as much literature as you can. Talk to the players about what you learn." Martin couldn't understand how the trip would help him, or anybody, and resisted until Landry said, "You're a leader, Harvey" and then dropped the only compelling reason necessary for a Cowboy to do almost literally anything.

"You're doing this for the team," he said.[7]

Unless Landry was as clueless as he had been during the Henderson years, it's possible he was trying some reverse psychology. It's possible he figured Martin might take a hint and check into the place on his own. Martin, however, construed the odd marching order as Landry's being more concerned about *other* players, many of whom Martin later would say "had become obvious embarrassments to the Cowboys, with obnoxious, blatant displays of public drunkenness." Even more strangely, the trip was intended to be a top-secret mission, though it didn't take long for word to leak out, perhaps by Cowboys sources for the benefit of the Feds. By the time Martin ended his one-day "fact-finding" visit to Hazelden and boarded the flight back to Dallas, several reporters were waiting for him on the plane.

With Martin's cover blown, Landry's phone rang off the hook as reporters sought answers from him about the mysterious mission. Getting himself into trouble, he insisted he hadn't sent Martin to a drug clinic because he suspected he was on drugs but rather because he wanted him to "evaluate the program for us, not to dry out. I don't feel he's involved with drugs right now,"[8] which if true meant he *was* clueless. His spin didn't stop the press from running with the more obvious assumption. The *Dallas Morning News* ran a story headlined "COWBOYS' MARTIN IN REHAB CENTER," and quoted an anonymous Cowboys player ridiculing Landry's tale and saying Martin never would have made the trip to Minnesota "unless he needs the help."[9]

Seeing the story getting out of hand, the Cowboys called a press conference to clear the air, or so they hoped. Before it began, Landry had a few instructions for Martin. "They're going to ask some tough questions," he said. "I want you to tell the truth. Tell them why you went to Hazelden. Then I'll talk to you and back you up."[10] This was reasonable enough, but the truth here was actually meant to further protect reputations, the team's and Martin's. What Landry would back up in the larger scope was Martin's continued denials about using cocaine. In fact, by way of self-defense Martin said that during his brief stay at Hazelden he had taken a urine test that was negative for cocaine. But Landry had created a storm and cast him in the worst light he had ever been.

Randy Galloway, incredulous at what sounded like Landry playing the media for suckers, lamented, "Tom Landry has been around long enough to know better, but he says it was a story he never expected the newspapers to cover. . . . Unfortunately, Tom fumbled that one. . . . [W]hen it comes down to a game of who-do-you-believe, Tom Landry can score at will against anyone [but] the explanation seemed perfectly ridiculous. Even to other Cowboy players." As if hesitant to even use the word in relation to God's coach, Galloway asked, "But would Tom Landry lie to us?"[11] If so, Galloway insisted with great sorrow, it would be the first time in twenty-three years that Landry had told a lie, or at least not the full truth. Added a sympathetic Martin later, "I couldn't remember Dallas ever doubting Coach Landry's word before, but this time it did."[12]

Actually, Landry hadn't really lied. The more one looks into the episode, it becomes clear that he had gone to lengths to keep from finding out that Martin had a drug habit. Learning so would have demanded that Landry hold to the example he had set when he fired Henderson, and he still wanted Martin around. Landry wasn't deceitful, he was duplicitous, and dishonest with himself, and in the long lens of a man who lived beyond reproach, that may have been worse than a little fib. Fleeting as the manic events of that off-season would be, they marked a turning point for Landry, when his bullet-proof Teflon began to fray.

Remarkably, he had to all but admit he had made matters worse for Martin, saying, "I'm sorry his visit became public. I can see where there would be confusion on this, but it's just not what people are going to think." Martin agreed, concluding that going was "a mistake," and when he returned for another season he was more embroiled in drug rumors than before. Landry took pity on him, saying he had chosen Martin for the ill-fated excursion only because "he's been through so much lately, because he's suffered,"[13] without any mention of cocaine, which Martin went right on using. Just what Landry had hoped to accomplish other than getting the government off his team's back was unclear. In the end, beyond that, he accomplished nothing.

DISSIPATED AS Martin was, Landry needed every available body he had going into the 1983 season, which, for the hundredth time, seemed to signal a steep fall for the team. The *Sports Illustrated* pre-season issue ran with the cover line "DALLAS DIGS IN" and included a story by Bruce Newman alluding to the fact that a bad season was not an option in Dallas. The Dallas Cowboys, it said, "are something different—a kind of majestic nation-state. Just as there are Kremlin-ologists, there are Cowboyologists, who watch the team closely."[14] Anyone who did could see a team in a manic meltdown, the drug rumors forcing Dorsett to hold a press conference in Thousand Oaks to deny it. "The whole thing would never have been more than a city case if it hadn't been the Dallas Cowboys," he recognized. "When you're America's Team, you gotta stay clean."

Those were famous last words if ever there were any, considering how few could stay clean, and for Touchdown Tony the PR campaign to sell him as a responsible leader was over. Like Martin, he too had seen business investments fail and had an IRS bill for back taxes of $414,000,[15] which would be more difficult to pay off when several of his endorsement deals were terminated.[16] His value to the Cowboys was still great, but he had only one more All-Pro season left in him, and as for being loved by the fans, that dream was also over.

The investigations prompted Tex Schramm to hire a grim-faced ex-FBI agent, Larry Wansley, as director of counseling services, his job, as Newman wrote, being "to keep America's Team off America's front pages by ferreting out trouble before it happens. His duties this season will include keeping 'undesirables' away from the play-ers' rooms when the Cowboys are traveling on the road. Presumably this means that if any Brazilian soccer-playing hairdressers carrying cameras and tiny spoons show up in the vicinity, Wansley will get suspicious."[17] One of the players sure to occupy Wansley's attention, Harvey Martin, called Thousand Oaks "Fort Landry," with check-points, barricades, and round-the-clock security patrols.[18] For all the revelations over the years about the Cowboys and drugs, there had never been any great urgency to know what the players were up to, or to do much even if the front office did know. Now, there was. Tex Schramm had no compunction admitting that if he went back and read *North Dallas Forty*, he would settle for things being "that way versus the problems we have today."[19] As Landry saw it, with typical understatement, "This is not a routine camp."

Indeed, Landry, who was ticked off that the new Players Association agreement with the league limited fines to $100 per offense, had had his stormy camps in the past, but there had never been a sheriff on the payroll and roaming the grounds, and the players weren't happy about it. "There's a tendency to feel like I'm a grown man, and I don't need that," Dorsett complained. "I don't think that's what we need to bring unity to this team. If we can't do it without a security man, we're in trouble."[20] Beyond drugs, curfew busting, and an unsettled quarterback situation—Lord, did *anything* ever change on this team?—the "serious flaws" Martin had sensed during the failure of the previous season presented a bigger problem, though for Landry it went no deeper than his players "not doing the things you need to do to get to the Super Bowl."

That may have been a subtle slap at Danny White, whose performance in the NFC title game left Landry cold and revived his doubts that White had the right stuff of leadership. Landry resumed his flirtation with Gary Hogeboom, but as the season neared, neither man excelled in the exhibition games, leading *Sports Illustrated* to wonder, allegorically, headlining its preseason Cowboy's story, "WHERE HAVE YOU GONE, ROGER STAUBACH?"

AS PREDICTABLE as Landry was in gumming up such pronouncements of his team's demise, the answer to that question came within mere weeks: *never mind*. When the curtain went up on the 1983 campaign, the "majestic nation-state" lived. Rock stars or not, Landry could still get through to his men, and the old spit and fire rose up from game one, which had them in Washington playing against the hated Redskins, now champions of the world, in the first Monday night game of the year. Both Landry and Gibbs prepared as if it were a Super Bowl, and on a sweltering eighty-four-degree evening, it seemed Gibbs had done it better, his team taking a 23–3 lead at the half. Then came a Cowboys avalanche. White, who was back under center again, completed only nine passes all game, but he left the Redskins' secondary shell-shocked with third-quarter touchdown bombs of 75 and 51 yards to Hill, then White ran across the goal line from a yard out in the fourth quarter for a 24–21 lead.

Minutes later, again at the 1-yard line, he found Doug Cosbie in the end zone. They couldn't stop Theismann from coming back on a touchdown drive but held on to win a 31–30 thriller, sending a tingle up millions of legs in Cowboys Nation.

That indeed set the course. Landry's team won the next six games, one a 37–7 blowout of the Eagles, preceded by an overtime win over Tampa Bay. It was the first time the Cowboys had been undefeated after seven games. They then had another memorable adventure when the LA Raiders—en route to Al Davis's third and last championship season—came to Texas Stadium. Landry's welcome gift was a trick play on the first drive that had White give the ball to Springs, who then passed to *White* for a 15-yard touchdown. But while the Cowboys hung in, forcing six turnovers, the Raiders would put up 519 yards and hold on for a 40–38 win. Landry might have had his team at 12–2 late in the season, but it dropped the last two games, 31–10 to the Redskins at home and 42–17 in San Francisco. At 12–4, the Cowboys stumbled into the playoffs as a wild card.

Dorsett in particular faltered, going from first in the league in rushing during the strike-shortened season to sixth, with 1,321 yards. He was still always one quick burst away from an unforgettable play, the memory of his 99-yard run the year before in Minnesota—the longest run in NFL history—still fresh. But he was a step slower. Fortunately, Danny White was on fire. Even if some of his teammates gritted their teeth while on the same field with him, he fired twenty-nine touchdown passes, the club record until Tony Romo's thirty-six in 2007. He also completed 62.7 percent of his passes and racked up 334 completions and 3,980 yards, all also records at the time, though he was never far from an interception, throwing twenty-three.

The Cowboys' offense was ranked No. 2 in the league, but the game against the Raiders exposed their fatal flaw, an aging defense vulnerable to the pass, finishing twenty-seventh in that category. As well, the offensive line was problematic. The Cowboys had the home field in the first playoff round, against the 9–7 Rams, but they could not produce a rushing attack. White, forced to throw fifty-three times, gained 330 yards and two touchdowns, but his three interceptions sealed another postseason failure, LA leaving as winners, 24–17. It was White who took the most heat for it. His playoff performances were cause for great derision, with Skip Bayless pinning on him the label of "Master of Disaster."[21] And to be sure, there was something missing in those games, his cool smarts replaced by stuttering indecision—the same something missing in a future Cowboys quarterback with the same puzzling qualities. Indeed, in Cowboys history four quarterbacks are yoked according to the big-game gene: the ones who had it—Staubach and Troy Aikman—and the ones who didn't—White and Tony Romo.

Not even showy emotional displays of confidence could mask the Cowboys' decline. Before the game, they seemed to be in a lather. As Paul Zimmerman wrote, "They came out for introductions in a full sprint, fists thrust high. They pounded each other's shoulders. In the TV booth, Pat Summerall and [John] Madden were remarking how unusual this was, how unlike the Cowboys. They really want it today,'" said Summerall. "Then the Rams took the opening kickoff and drove 85 yards for a touchdown." When it was over, Tony Dorsett admitted, "Emotion is something that's got to be genuine. It's got to be real. You can't force it or turn it on or off. By game time it was too late. We'd already become the team we were going to be."[22]

THE SADDEST postscript of the 1983 season was Harvey Martin. His season and his life in tatters, he quit for good. At thirty-three, he was old before his time, his skills gone. With his sack total for the season falling to an embarrassing two, Landry had taken to lifting him from games for rookie Jim Jeffcoat. Only after Larry Wansley had seen Martin in a club that had been ruled off-limits to players did Landry ask him to take a drug test. Martin, feeling he was being picked on, broke down and cried, telling Landry he had him competing against players who, unlike him, "never bought a breakfast for the Cowboys."[23] Martin refused the test, but after the season as he was working out, Wansley approached him, urine bottle in hand. "We need you to take a sample," he said.

Exploding, Martin barked, "Fuck you!"

"We need it," Wansley persisted.

"I retire!"

It was a reply given in haste, much as Hollywood Henderson had done, and perhaps was the same reaction the Cowboys wanted to provoke. The sportswriters speculated about this. Indeed, a common assumption was that Landry, seeing Martin decline, pushed him out the door. In truth, Landry, making an exception to his dispassionate judgments about who was no longer useful, tried to talk him into staying, even with Martin's refusal to take a drug test. In the end, there would never be one. Martin held his own farewell press conference on May 3 and, like Henderson, took the high road, with dignity and all due reverence for Tom Landry and a team to which he would later say, "I gave much more loyalty than I received."[24]

Landry, who stood beside him, dewy-eyed, extolled Martin effusively and guilelessly, saying he was "very instrumental in the great teams we had." Tex Schramm and Gil Brandt, who almost always attended these mawkish, self-serving Cowboys rituals, stayed away, "probably thankful to be rid of Harvey's headlines," jabbed Bayless the wiseacre.[25] To them, Martin may have been yesterday's news, but to Landry it was another reason to raise a final toast to one of the men who had gotten him to the dance, and to sadly gaze backward and hold onto, for a last moment, what he had lost.

For Martin, the struggle was only beginning. Stubbornly avoiding drug treatment, he had some success in local business and did some acting and pro wrestling gigs. He was next heard from in 1996, when he went through a second bankruptcy and was arrested for domestic violence and cocaine possession, getting off lightly with an eight-month probation and court-ordered drug rehabilitation. He was given a job selling chemical products by his old teammate John Niland and apparently stayed clean and sober, but as Drew Pearson looked back a few years later, "It's almost like you could see him heading for a dead end, and you just hope that dead end—and this is real hard for me to say, but it's true—is not death."[26] Alas, it was. Soon afterward, Martin contracted pancreatic cancer. On Christmas Eve 2001, he died at age fifty-one. He had lived in Dallas his entire life, had been a Super Bowl MVP for America's Team, and was on the NFL's 1970s All-Defensive team. But when the end came, he was virtually alone.

✦ ✦ ✦ ✦

TOO MANY forlorn press conferences had now been held for the Cowboys' greats bowing out too soon. The next one to go was Pearson, only months after Martin, following a horrifying tragedy. On March 23, 1984, he fell asleep at the wheel of his Dodge Daytona and crashed into a parked tractor-trailer on Interstate 635. His twenty-seven-year-old brother, Carey Mark Pearson, died in the accident. Pulled out of the wreck, Drew Pearson underwent emergency surgery to stop the bleeding in his liver. Just weeks before the accident, Pearson had aired out the tension he'd had with Landry, calling the coach "callous" and "uncaring." Landry, seeing the remarks, told him he was hurt by them. But when Pearson was wheeled out of the operating room and opened his eyes, he saw Roger Staubach, which didn't surprise him. Then he saw Tom Landry, which did. "We were starting minicamp that Monday after the accident. He addressed the team and then left to be with me at the hospital."[27]

Pearson had heretofore questioned Landry's sanctimony about his faith. "I'd watch him jump on a player and think, 'How can he do a player that way?'" Now, seeing Landry almost every day at his bedside during his recovery, he had a whole new perspective. "That's when I knew he was a genuine Christian."[28] Pearson wanted to try to play again, but Landry convinced him to quit, at age thirty-three; the announcement was made on July 15. He retired owning the record for the most yardage gained by any Cowboys receiver, yet feeling unappreciated—what Cowboys player *didn't*? He did continue a loose relationship with the team. In 1985, Schramm gave him a job as scout and special assistant, but Pearson found his ideas ignored and left one game into the season. He became a feature reporter for the growing cable network HBO and later entered the sporting goods business, with some seed money from Schramm. He also, for a time, hosted the Cowboys radio pregame show. Despite the trying times with Landry, he was able to resolve his differences as others had, by separating Landry the humanist—in the way Landry had not meant it—and Landry the absolutist. Indeed, that was really the only way to do it.

✦ ✦ ✦ ✦

FOR LANDRY the truest test of his leadership was having to make do with a caliber of athlete he'd rarely had to settle for in the past. It was a prodigious task, one that required him to give more of himself to teaching and technique than ever before. It wasn't just that Brandt was losing his touch out on the scouting trails, or that the crop of football players in the 1980s was thinner. As always, the Cowboys' handicap was that winning kept them from the highest draft picks, and now the hidden prizes that only Brandt used to ferret out were already well scouted and snapped up. Brandt still knew more than most and could have made a steal of a trade here and there—if other teams wanted to do business with the Cowboys, which none did, not wishing to play the fools anymore.

Brandt had seen it coming, way back when the scouting combines were formed using his sort of computerized databases. By 1982, he felt as if he were on an island. "You know," he said, "it's extremely hard for us to make a trade anymore. We used to pick up draft choices from lots of teams, but now they're all trying to do the same thing." One of the Cowboys' scouts, John Wooten, said that "there was just too much animosity" for the team to get anything done.[29] Landry grew frustrated with what Brandt was giving him, but had to resign himself to working with what he had. He did amazingly well, even if he was clearly on less stable ground. And for the first time, he would have to face pitfalls down the road without his safety blanket, Clint Murchison Jr., the first of the great Cowboys pillars to fall.

ALMOST RIGHT up until word came, shockingly, in 1983 that he was tapped out, Clint Murchison Jr. was, for those who had a passing interest in him, still the apotheosis of baronial privilege and envy. Men like Murchison—the entrepreneurs, the cream of the crop in profit-taking—were not supposed to fall victim to the feckless investments they made, or be at the mercy of recessions and bursting real estate bubbles. Murchison, in no small part due to his standing as the hidden power bankrolling the Dallas Cowboys and Tom Landry's boss, lived as high and ostentatiously as seemed possible, and he reveled in it.

Most people knew that Murchison owned property, high-tech companies, and the most famous sports team in the world, not to mention a few Caribbean islands. But few knew that he had managed to lose every acre and every penny he had. In 1984, *Forbes* still ranked Murchison as one of the nation's richest men, worth over $250 million. That number may have been true on paper, but it had been eaten away by debt. Even so, this was $100 million less than what had been estimated only the year before. In truth, the "Texas Croesus," as he had been called in better days, had actually lost $1.2 *billion*—within a year.[30]

Murchison had been in severe trouble since the early 1970s, when he began investing in jeopardous real estate and other ventures pitched to him by any grafter with a good line. Clint always believed money was not stagnant, that it was there to be gambled with, and that he had a Midas touch. But he hit a losing streak that continued without end, and one of his failures symbolized all of them: a cockamamie scheme to convert cow manure into gas. The company's acronym was CRAP, and the $10 million he sunk into it indeed went down the crapper. Another big idea, a ski resort in *Iran*, had predictable results.[31] It meant nothing to the insouciant Murchison that he had to borrow heavily to stoke his investments, and when interest rates went through the roof, it would make it impossible to pay back debts that, by the 1980s, were greater than his assets.

Complicating matters, the late John Murchison's son, John Dabney Murchison, learned that his uncle had secretly raided his $30 million trust fund and cleaned it out, leading him to sue Clint for the amount. In turn, Clint persuaded Dabney's mother, Lucille "Lupe" Murchison, one of Dallas's most esteemed art collectors, that Dabney was the one who squandered her family money, and Clint got her to sue her own son to remove him as co-executor of John's fortune. Dabney agreed to take a $3 million payout and cranked up his legal battle with Uncle Clint. This highly entertaining intra-dynasty wrangle, with dollar signs floating all around it, made the fictitious scripts on *Dallas* seem like something from *Xanadu*. There was even a terrifying break-in at Lupe's home, during which masked gunmen tied her up, though no one was hurt or apprehended, and some speculated it was a feeble attempt by Clint to make Lupe think Dabney was behind the clumsy incident.[32] Whether he was or not, Murchison was desperate for any angle that might work. His oil and gas holdings had tanked when the Arab oil cartel overproduced supplies, sending prices crashing. At the same time, the real estate bubble burst. Suddenly, Murchison was saddled with an estimated $75.7 million in debt, a number that would continue to grow exponentially. Every bit and piece of his erstwhile empire was held as collateral by the banks, and they were all after him to make payments on his debt.

The Cowboys organization was one of those pieces, even if Murchison reinvested every cent of its earnings back into it. His biggest nightmare was a judge ordering him to sell the crown jewel of his empire to satisfy a judgment. As it was, he had taken the Cowboys' financial profile down a few notches, and the possibility loomed that the team that had rewritten all the profiteering rules in pro sports franchise ownership could become insolvent. Murchison, though, ever the cockeyed optimist, expected a turnaround in his fortunes any day. But now even his own children were nipping at his heels, forcing him to give up control of their trust funds before he could raid them. And so just after the new year of 1983 arrived, he knew he had no viable option but to sell his precious football duchy. As if things could get any worse for Murchison, his physical health was declining as fast as his economic health. In the late 1970s he had been diagnosed with a rare degenerative nerve disorder with no known cure called olivopontocerebellar atrophy, and began losing motor functions, including equilibrium and speech. Landry was taken aback when, during a team plane ride, Murchison rose from his seat and nearly collapsed to the floor.[33]

It seemed that Clint also had a cocaine problem. As the veteran Dallas investigative reporter Mark Lane wrote in 2013, "In his early fifties, when most people are burned out and their lives ruined from cocaine, Clint had just begun. He found the drug helped aid him in his concupiscent escapades. While some Jerry [Jones] detractors claim he's on drugs, Clint Murchison actually was."[34]

Actually, Murchison was able to wiggle a tiny bit off the hook when the easing of bankruptcy laws during the Reagan era cushioned men of great wealth and not incidentally Republican leanings. Under a revamped Chapter 11 law, Murchison was allowed to avoid many of his debts and sell off his assets and insurance policies to raise cash to satisfy certain other liabilities that could not be written off. After making the gut-wrenching decision to sell the Cowboys, he called Tex Schramm to his home and told him the game was over for him. Tex was understandably the first person to know. He was Clint's first hire for the organization, the man who ran the team and made more millions for him, and a man he trusted so much he had agreed to finance a golf resort in Key West that Tex and two partners had conceived—and that went bust, costing Clint $130 million.[35] That venture was a rare swing and miss for Schramm, whose next big project was to find a buyer for America's Team.

Word broke on January 9, 1983, with the *Dallas Morning News* reporting, "MURCHISON MAY BE TRYING TO SELL COWBOYS," the reason given being his health. Schramm, pledged to secrecy, denied the team was up for sale, and the paper a month later noted that such a sale made no sense because Murchison would have had to pay more in capital gains taxes than his estate would have had to pay after he died.[36] It was relevant, as well, that at the time the NFL was facing the newest challenge by a renegade league, the United States Football League (USFL), a well-financed twelve-team venture whose owners would include one Donald Trump. Avoiding direct competition, the USFL would begin as a spring/summer league starting in March 1983, with a raft of free agents and college stars, some as underclassmen (then verboten in the NFL), including the last three Heisman Trophy winners, Herschel Walker, Mike Rozier, and Doug Flutie, as well as future NFL Hall of Famers Reggie White, Jim Kelly, and Steve Young. George Allen was lured out of retirement to coach the Chicago team, and Red Miller the Denver one, though he would be replaced by Craig Morton.

The USFL, with a former NBC Sports president as commissioner, scored a shocking $70 million, four-year contract from ABC *and* the nascent all-sports network ESPN. The USFL posed far too grave a threat to the NFL for the Dallas Cowboys to be in limbo, and for Pete Rozelle not to have Schramm on his usual perch of power. Early in 1983, there was talk that a team might be put in Dallas, to play in the

Cotton Bowl. It didn't happen, but only because the Cowboys' arrogant might could quash a potential lease at their former stadium. Rozelle did some praying that the Cowboys sale would be taken care of as soon as possible. Yet no matter who that owner might be, it was clear that the Cowboys would never be the same.

Dallas itself was a metaphor of changing times. For decades it was a playpen for millionaires, a crudely cut emerald that had acquired a reputation as the only place in Texas where the idle rich could go to party, blow endless supplies of money, and consider it worth every lost penny. Now, falling oil prices and property values had people on pins and needles, not to mention finding solace in white powder. The cocaine trials that rocked the Cowboys and the town seemed a perfect collocation of everything that was going wrong. Like Harvey Martin, other Cowboys lost money impetuously by investing in Dallas night clubs and restaurants without doing much research or getting good advice—many of them black players, who came to the self-absolving conclusion that men of color faced impossible odds in Dallas.

Tom Landry, a level-headed man who rarely saw the world through starry eyes, was dumbstruck by Murchison's troubles. He had always regarded Clint as bulletproof, a titan of industry too smart and too rich to lose it all so precipitously. "I think that more than anything else altered Dad's world view," says Tom Landry Jr., who had noticed how much trouble Murchison was getting into. "He believed if you worked hard, the amount of effort one put into something would bring rewards. He loved Clint because Clint was the essence of a good man who always made good business decisions. It was an idealistic take, sure, but Dad was no bumpkin, he knew that in high-stakes business you take risks and you can lose. He just never thought Clint wouldn't survive. I told him I had serious doubts about that, and I was anything but happy that I was right."

The induction was powerfully obvious to Tom Landry: both he and Murchison had built the eighth wonder of the capitalist sports world. And if that great profit machine could rise higher and higher while its owner fell through the floor, no mere mortal was on safe ground. "I don't know if he became cynical," Tom Jr. says, "because that wasn't him. It was more like the old rules he grew up with and practiced were changing. He knew men like him had less of a place in that world, but he knew he still had a place in football. He worked harder in the eighties than he ever did. And for the first time he had to think more in terms of being more rewarded for it. I always handled his contracts with the Cowboys, and no matter who the new owner would be, we were going to make sure he was well taken care of. The days of the handshake agreements were over."[37]

DESPITE HOW badly he felt for Murchison, Landry had to wonder about his own future as a result of the team's changing hands. This was an issue that had obviously become more important to him as he aged, and it prompted him to do something he had, for decades, resisted. The year before, he had filmed an amusing, gently self-mocking TV commercial for American Express—no used-car lot spots for him, he began at the top. In it, Landry, a tenderfoot in an Old West scene, dismounts from a horse in a long-rider coat and ten-gallon hat. "Do you know me? I'm the most famous cowboy in Texas," he drawls as he enters a noisy saloon, explaining how helpful the credit card is, then, hemmed in by large men in familiar red helmets and shoulder pads, he goes on, "'Cause you never know when you're gonna be surrounded . . . by Redskins." As they glare at him, he looks up and chirps one word: "Howdy."[38] Alicia Landry had to convince him to fly to Hollywood and do the gig but, once there, he worked tirelessly to get the nuance of the dialogue right and was delighted with the result.

"What people didn't realize," she says, "is that Tommy loved to make fun of himself. And I think at that stage of his career and his life, he was a lot less self-conscious about how he would look to people. He didn't think it reflected badly on the Cowboys to have a little fun with the image he'd lived with for so long. When it came to football, he wasn't any less serious but he also wanted people to see that he wasn't all stiff and everything. He had a wonderful personality, and he didn't mind if the world saw that."[39]

It seems a fair number of the fair sex of a certain age caught on to that. Paul Zimmerman wrote in the mid-1980s that "Landry, incidentally, is my mother's favorite coach. She loves watching him on

the sidelines. 'Such dignity,' she says. 'The way he carries himself
. . . he's a real man.'"[40] Alicia Landry muffles a laugh at this revelation. "Maybe that's why that commercial was so good. It showed he
wasn't a cardboard character. He was a regular guy. He even had to
learn to ride a horse! And when he finished it was like he'd ridden all
his life. [Laugh] If he was going to do something, he was going to do
it right."

The commercial, one of the best with a sports theme ever made,
no doubt because of the revelation that Tom Landry was actually
lovable, was up and running in the 1983 off-season. Yet even with
greater fame for Landry, everything about the Cowboys was up in the
air. His contract had to be renewed—but by whom? As the *Morning
News* headlined on March 19, "LANDRY WAITS ON OWNER CHANGE
BEFORE TALKS ON FUTURE." Some, in fact, were already openly venturing that a new top dog might want to bring in a new coach. In
reality, that could not have happened unless Landry chose to walk
away. That was one condition Murchison placed on the sale, and
Schramm, even though he had experienced growing personal friction
with Landry, was also loyal to him, or at least joined too solidly at
the hip to separate. The last thing Tex wanted was to be seen as plot-
ting the removal of the soul of the Cowboys, though it might well
have given him a rush to know he held Landry's future in his hands.

Landry himself was not uneasy. As he coyly put it in his autobiography, "I didn't worry about any threat to my job because I
understood Clint wanted to protect everyone in the organization and
preserve the Cowboys' tradition."[41]

Schramm indeed made that a condition of any new ownership,
which might have helped queer his first couple of potential sales.
That and the flat economy that made the asking price of $100 mil-
lion a harder sell. Harder still was that Schramm was after a deal
that would reap for Murchison a nice pile of cash but not send
the team into future debt. As well, the deal had to include buying
Texas Stadium, which cost a fortune to operate. Some high-rollers
were very interested, then fell away, one being radio network entre-
preneur Gordon McLendon and the owners of Mary Kay Cosmet-
ics, raising the prospect that Texas Stadium might be painted pink.
Others, such as Florida land developer George Barbar and Dallas

oilmen W. O. Bankston and Vance Miller—the latter a former business partner of Murchison—were more serious but cautious, asking to finance the purchase by borrowing, using the team as collateral, which was a definite no-no for Schramm. What's more, men like that were, as Schramm said, "very high profile,"[42] precisely what he *didn't* want, fearing an owner who might meddle with him and Landry. Schramm put these prospects on hold and moved toward another sugar daddy who had put in an initial bid, one who also had partnered with Murchison in the now-faded past: Harvey Roberts "Bum" Bright.

Small world that Texas's coincidental arc of football and money is, this was the same Bum Bright who had interviewed Landry in 1959 when the Texas A&M head coaching job opened up, and who had found him so unimpressive. Both men had moved down the road a long way since then, the Oklahoma-born Bright making a Murchison-like fortune in oil, real estate, transportation, and now primarily banks, savings and loan institutions, the prime movers of perverted 1980s neo-capitalism. Bright, who was now chairman of the Board of Regents at A&M, had corporate assets valued at $500 million, personal assets at $125 million. As importantly as having wealth equivalent to the budget of a small country, Bright had a low profile, or at least *lower* than your typical Texas oil bigwig, and was known to delegate authority, which he would need to do with the Cowboys.

Bright's offer was $85 million, $60 million for the team and $25 million to assume the remaining sixty-five years on the lease for Texas Stadium. Bright, who was nowhere near as reckless as Murchison, had some doubts, so to share the wealth, and the risk, he formed a syndicate of eleven limited partners; as managing partner, he would own no more than 17 percent of the team's stock. The snag here, or so Schramm led Bright to believe, was an NFL policy that a single investor in a team should own at least 51 percent. The truth was that the Cowboys had bent that policy for decades since the two Murchison brothers had owned 50 percent each. Cunningly, Schramm assured Bright he could get Rozelle to approve of the deal, but only if Bum made him managing partner, a title usually reserved for the majority stockholder, such as the most famous managing partner in sports, Al Davis. The title would put Tex, not Bum, in charge of all matters pertaining to the team, and as such, Tex would be almost impossible to fire. He played it right too, because Bum agreed and in short order Rozelle was "persuaded" to accept the sale, reinforcing the notion that the commissioner really worked for Tex Schramm.

On March 20, 1984, the deal was announced at the first press conference called by Murchison since 1964, when he made a struggling coach into a potentate with a ten-year contract and a security blanket seemingly for as long as Landry wanted it to be. In the end, a side note was that Schramm's loyalty to Landry, and the need to find a hands-off owner, cost Murchison and himself a good chunk of money. Barbar, who thought he'd had the inside track, complained for years about being screwed, but everyone involved was sold on the idea that Bum Bright was the right man to carry on the Murchison legacy.

Clint said he was leaving a happy man, but he did not want to go feeling guilty that he had besmirched the status and vanity of the Dallas Cowboys. Even though his personal fortune had evaporated, and nearly every dollar of the sale money had been earmarked for all the lawyers, his last official act was to find $5 million to say "thank you" to his Big Three. Schramm was given a $2.5 million bonus, and his salary was bumped up to $400,000. Landry got $2 million; Brandt, $500,000. This would not help Bright as he tried to get a grip on the team's runaway budgets. And Schramm rewarded himself by reclaiming the 3 percent in Cowboys stock he had sold back to Murchison, though he had to pay $1.8 million out of his pocket for it. Once Bright settled in, he did what Murchison was going to do and signed Landry to a three-year contract extension, at $350,000 a year.

Landry was pleased with the outcome, but he was also fatalistic. Regardless of the covenant Bright had made to keep the old order in place, Landry was under no illusion that Bum was another Murchison. "You can't be sure how tough these new owners will be," he said. "Clint was a different type of person. In bad times Clint always believed we'd come out all right, which we did. Bum Bright didn't get where he is by taking care of everybody along the way. He's a tough cookie, and I don't know what pressures might be asserted on somebody like Tex if, say, we continued a string of losing seasons. . . . Everything is fine when you produce. If you don't you never know what will happen."[43]

Landry was right. Bright was a ruthless man with little senti-mentality or sense of entitlement for anyone but himself, a streak that carried over from his far-right conservative beliefs that ranged near Clint Murchison Sr. territory and made Landry seem like Wal-ter Mondale by comparison. Bright didn't go on record often, but when he did, he was not so bright. When John Kennedy was gunned down in the streets of Dallas, he co-sponsored a blatantly political advertisement criticizing Kennedy's policies that ran in the *next day's* paper.[44] Decrying government alms for those not nearly as fortunate as him, he once said, "Our unrestrained welfare programs encourage people to be non-productive and, therefore, hungry and helpless."[45] Bright kicked off his tenure as a Cowboys owner paying his head coach proper obeisance and compensation, but Landry couldn't help but be wary that the old Aggie who had such a negative first impres-sion of him would not be so enamored after all of the old Longhorn.

Indeed, there seemed to be a lingering, mutual wariness, even mis-trust, between the two. If Landry was a man of the Texas soil, Bright still had the soil of Muskogee on his boots. Making a fortune from Texas oil did not necessarily make a man a Texan. "I'm sure that kind of thing was part of it to Dad," says Tom Landry Jr. "Some-times there's a natural barrier between two men who have to work together. Listen, they tried hard to make Bum Bright into another Clint Murchison because everybody wanted that. But that was never gonna happen. When Clint left, he took with him the way the Cow-boys *were*, and now they were gonna be something else, something that might not be so good."

After Murchison gave him his bonus, which Landry said "stunned" him, Tom and Alicia went to Clint's home to express gratitude. They didn't know how badly withered Murchison was until Anne Mur-chison let them in and had to prop up her husband in a chair in the living room. As Landry remembered, "His speech sounded slurred, but he seemed happy and surprised to see us. And when we thanked him for his overwhelming generosity, Clint acted almost embarrassed by out gratitude."[46]

If there was an upside for Landry, other than the one Murchison had gilded, it was that Murchison, a meek-looking man who had lived his life doing what preachers like Landry sermonize about *not* doing, became a born-again Christian as his health began to slip away. The days of him basking in the Cowboys' sunshine were gone, but after hearing him attest to God's love and strength as a way toward salvation, Landry reckoned the long journey, for both him and Clint, had not been in vain.

LANDRY HAD enough security with his new contract and the characteristically safe investments he had made in real estate around Dallas and Austin to stop worrying about his future, and anything else but football. After the tumultuous off-season in 1984, all he had to do was take an aging team with a porous defense back into the penthouse. Tex Schramm, *his* security seemingly inviolate, regarded going out-and-out in the playoffs as a crime against nature and had vowed, "We are not going to play with the same deck again,"[47] not necessarily meaning the players. Over the off-season, he met with Landry and suggested there be a shakeup of the assistant coaches, a crew that had the look of a group in Bermuda shorts playing poker around the pool at a Miami Beach hotel. Jim Myers was sixty-four; Ernie Stautner, fifty-nine; Dick Nolan, fifty-four; Jerry Tubbs, fifty-one; Gene Stallings, fifty; and Jim Shofner, the latest offensive coordinator not allowed to call plays, fifty. Tex wanted to bring in a younger assistant to help run the offense, someone wired into the newer football metrics, but Landry told him, candidly, that he didn't have the time to groom someone who would master the Cowboys' system, and preferred playing with the hand he had.

"Maybe after two years," he said, sounding not unlike Jim Lee Howell, "I'll quit and everything will resolve itself," meaning that one of the king's men would take over.[48]

Schramm backed off, for now, but it was the last time such non-committal future planning would suffice. In retrospect, 1984 would be the last season Tom Landry was allowed to be Tom Landry, czar. The problem for him wasn't his assistants but the holes on either side of the ball. Landry came into the season without Martin, Pearson, DuPree, Donovan, and Newhouse. He had precious little to plug the gaps, certainly not with draft picks. His first-round pick was Texas A&M linebacker Billy Cannon Jr. Given a big dose of hype, the son of the original AFL star running back and receiver suffered a season-ending spinal injury while making a tackle in the eighth game. He tried to come back the next year, but the team doctors said he had a congenital spine defect and refused to clear him, ending his career. He then became the latest player to sue the Cowboys, bringing a $9.6 million negligence suit, which would be settled in 1992.[49]

By now, only fourteen players from the previous eight drafts were on the roster, and just one was a starter, Jeffcoat. On the offensive line would be the No. 164 pick from 1977, right tackle Jim Cooper, and the No. 105 pick from 1980, right guard Kurt Peterson. The right cornerback was Ron Fellows, a seventh-rounder chosen at No. 173 in 1981. But two picks by Schramm in 1984 would be notable, in time. One was a gamble, fifth-round pick Herschel Walker, who was playing in the USFL and was eligible for the NFL since his class at the University of Georgia had graduated. Less notable was another fifth-rounder, Washington quarterback Steve Pelluer, who was earmarked as no more than a third-stringer. Pelluer, however, would almost by accident have his day, though a short one—and the distinction of being Tom Landry's last starting quarterback.

The privilege of being Landry's quarterback of the moment was a continuing mystery that kept the two leading men unsure from day to day who would lead. Danny White might have believed he could end a player strike by himself, but he couldn't—ever, it seemed—permanently clinch the starting job in Dallas. The lingering echoes of his endorsing the owners in the fight with the players never faded, and after the 1983 season, a group of players openly called for Landry to go with Hogeboom as the No. 1 quarterback.[50] Landry seemed to bend to their will, saying he had a "feel" that Hogeboom was the right man for the job.

Hogeboom, again convinced his time had come, seemed to justify the switch when in the opener against the Rams in LA, he led a gusher of an attack, the Cowboys gaining 436 yards, 343 of them from his arm, as he completed thirty-three of forty-seven passes, with one touchdown. The Cowboys won 20–13, shutting the Rams out in the fourth quarter and suddenly quieting the usual preseason worries stoked by all the retirements. Landry always kept his team in contention with fast starts, and he did it again, the Cowboys winning four of their first five games. Hogeboom was a bit uneven, but Landry had him throw long and throw a lot, to good effect. It wasn't until the sixth game, at home against the Cardinals, that he blew up, going thirteen of twenty-eight for 143 yards and throwing two interceptions. By contrast, the Cardinals' quarterback, Neil Lomax, threw three touchdown passes. When the Cowboys fell behind 31–13 in the fourth quarter, Landry benched Hogeboom for White, who threw a late touchdown pass, but too late to change the result, a 31–20 loss, but again altering the equation.

In the next game, the Redskins mauled the Cowboys in Washington, 34–14, and Landry yanked Hogeboom early after he threw two interceptions. They nearly lost the next one too, at home against the Saints, who ran 235 yards on the ground, but this time White saved the game by putting up 21 fourth-quarter points to take it into overtime, when a Septien field goal won it, 30–27. Hogeboom could read the tea leaves. On the following Sunday, in a home game against the Colts—the *Indianapolis* Colts now—White was the starter, throwing for 262 yards and two touchdowns in a 22–3 breeze, and Hogeboom was history, for a second time.

However, White could not keep the fire lit. In what was becoming a disturbing trend, the Cowboys showed their age toward the end of the season. At 9–5 with two games to go and a playoff spot at stake, they had a rematch with the Redskins at home and were up at the half 21–6, White having thrown three touchdown passes. Gibbs's team, however, took the lead in the third quarter with 17 unanswered points. White hit Hill with a 43-yard touchdown pass to take the lead back, but with Landry needing his defense to hold, they bent and broke, the 'Skins pounding out a drive that ended with a John Riggins touchdown run for an excruciating 30–28 win.

The Cowboys still could have made the playoffs with a win in Miami in the last Monday night game, and after falling behind 14–0, they battled back to a 21–21 tie in the fourth quarter when White heaved an electrifying 66-yard touchdown strike to Hill. Once more, though, the defense broke. Dan Marino sent the ball deep to Mark Clayton, who caught it for a 63-yard touchdown, and the winning score in a 28–21 victory. Tom Landry walked off the field to end the season without making the playoffs. It was the first time this had happened since 1974, his winning record leaving him with no illusions that he could get back to postseason play without younger Cowboys. However, the question now was: *Could* Landry think younger?

LANDRY SURELY was no more inured to the postmodern football culture chic, as two intrepid Cowboys learned, to their regret. One, Butch Johnson, had constantly chafed about being used sparingly as a receiver, allowing him few chances to re-create his indelible tumbling touchdown catch in the second Super Bowl victory. Feeling a need to accentuate any touchdown he could score—he was always a big-play guy, having led the team with five in 1981—the unveiled a shimmying dance/spike he called "The Quake," working with a choreographer to develop the routine. While fans debated which Johnson had a better boogie, Butch or the oilers' theatrical Billy "White Shoes" Johnson with his "Chicken Dance," Landry did another slow boil and finally told Butch during the 1983 season to spike the dance.

Johnson, who was having his best season in Dallas, catching forty-one balls that year, took the order personally, another grievance by a black Cowboy about Landry just not understanding or caring about the sociology of black players' displays of individualism on or off the field. More than once, Johnson was so upset about his playing time, he called Landry a liar for misleading him. He even pleaded to the coach to "get me out here," though like nearly all disaffected Cowboys who made that demand, he wanted desperately to stay. However, late in the season he announced he was through and skipped out to Cancun, but then returned for the next game. For Landry, Johnson seemed to be following Hollywood Henderson in open sedition. The real problem with the team, the receiver said, "if they wanted to acknowledge it, is that we're living on mystique instead of all-out playing football." Moreover, whenever the Cowboys were recently on *Monday Night Football*, Howard Cosell had dinner with him, gleaning comments like that which he could milk on the air.[51]

Landry put up with a lot, but after the season he shipped Johnson to Houston, not even the loss of Drew Pearson making Landry want to keep him around. Retribution or not, it worked out nicely, the trade bringing to the Cowboys Mike Renfro, a smallish but leather-tough Texas Christian receiver who had had six productive seasons in Houston, and a fifth-round draft pick in the next year's draft—the one Schramm cashed in for Herschel Walker.

A year later, Landry did the same with Ron Springs after Springs had been arrested for a fracas at a Dallas topless bar. He had been charged with punching a female cop, which Springs said was an accident, and was given probation.[52] Springs, who in 1983 had set a club record for running backs, making seventy-three catches for 589 yards and rushing for 541 yards with eight touchdowns, was perhaps the Cowboys' only rah-rah type of guy left, and one who was voluble about racial injustice. He believed the Cowboys' front office was just waiting for him to take a misstep to get rid of him, and when he was released in camp before the 1985 season he said, "There isn't a plane fast enough to get me out of Dallas," a sentiment shared no doubt by Landry and Schramm. Springs, who played two more years in Tampa, had a sad denouement. He was a diabetic, and as his health deteriorated, he had a foot amputated, underwent a kidney transplant, slipped into a three-year coma, and then in 2008 died at age fifty-four, another classic Cowboy known to too few.[53]

Johnson and Springs left with memories cherished and tarnished, two more black Cowboys some would claim were done dirt by Landry. As further proof, Danny White had also been involved in an off-field encounter, with a seventeen-year-old driver whose car nearly collided with White's. At a stoplight, White got out and slapped the kid, who filed assault charges. Along with Roger Staubach, Landry testified for White helping him win an acquittal, saying under oath that under the same circumstances, "I might do the same"—a stunning admission.[54] Landry also went to Chicago as a character witness for Mike Ditka when his old factotum was arrested for driving drunk during the 1985 season, after which Ditka's license was suspended for six months.[55] By contrast, he didn't stand up for Springs in court, and Schramm reprimanded several black players for doing so. Was it a double standard based on race? When black men were involved, were the Cowboys America's Most Wanted, and when whites were, America's Most Misunderstood?

A better question might be, Did only those who earned their lone star in Landry's eyes, regardless of color, receive the full force of the

Cowboys' indemnification? Backup defensive lineman Don Smerek in the early 1980s got into a scrape in a parking lot and was shot in the chest, amazingly, without serious injury. Although a vial of white powder was found on him, as if by magic no charges were filed against either man, and the incident never made it into the papers.

The best escape artist was Too Tall Jones. He was once arrested for DWI after leading cops on a wild chase. Another time a woman accused him of rape for trying to have intercourse with her while she was asleep. Yet another, he and a woman friend were busted for threatening cops outside a disco. Jones insisted he was innocent but during his trial he pleaded no contest and was given three years' probation and fined $750.[56] Too Tall was a Cowboy for as long as Landry stayed the coach, and if ever there was a man the team would try to pull some strings for, it was Jones, a man no one ever took for white.

Landry had no time or the inclination to defend himself to those who might have drawn racial conclusions from any outside events. He simply did what he always did, smooth out any roughness he could, get everyone more or less on the same page, and then turn it. But more and more, what was on the next page was something he didn't wanted to see.

IN THE 1985 season, the Cowboys once more broke out fast, humbling the Redskins in the opener in the ninety-degree Irving heat. It was again the kind of Monday night affair that stimulated ratings and titillated the legion of Cowboys followers, and the final score, 44–14, seemed to presage that if there was a Super Bowl season left in Landry, this was it. The biggest obstacle was his defense, which aside from Jones and Randy White was pretty much a patchwork of low-draft choices and undrafted free agents. By necessity, he had two starters who were only twenty-four, Jeffcoat and middle linebacker Eugene Lockhart, the latter a wily Texan and a sixth-round draft pick in 1984 who would hold down the position until 1992. But the secondary was still remarkably opportunistic. Against the 'Skins they suffocated receivers and intercepted the baffled Joe Theismann *five* times.

That year the Cowboys would rack up thirty-three interceptions, one less than the Bears, who were on their way to a 14–2 season, two playoff shutouts, and a 46–10 execution of the Patriots in the Super Bowl. The Bears also gave Landry a rare reason to borrow from another team's blueprint, in this case some elements of the "46" defense unleashed by Mike Ditka's prickly defensive coordinator, Buddy Ryan. The alignment, named for the number worn by Bears safety Doug Plank, who often played as an extra linebacker, had the front seven lining up in spots that made it hard for offenses to pick them up. The result was open holes for deadly blitzing by everyone— eight Bears defenders had at least one sack, and *six* of them went to the Pro Bowl, four on the first team. For that year, while the 46 was new, nobody could figure it out.

Landry had sometimes lined a backer up on the line, as a lineman, and now he did more of that, as well as flipping linebackers from the weak to the strong side and blitzing more than he ever had. Many of the defense's interceptions were the result of that, though Everson Walls seemed not to need much help; his league-high nine picks made him the first man to lead the NFL in interceptions three times. The free-wheeling blitz attack was infectious; figuring it out on their own, the back seven didn't wait for a defensive call, they just came in if they saw an opening. There were also sixty-two sacks, tops in the league. And Landry could still preen that he never had to go to a 3–w4 set.

In the literature intended to deconstruct Landry, retroactive claims have been made that Landry's in-game instructions and calls were being ignored by now, and that the fear of bucking him was undercut by the fact that there were no talented backups who might replace straying starters. The use of the 46 defense, it was said, was more the doing of Gene Stallings, who coached the defensive backs. One of his charges, Dextor Clinkscale, quoted Stallings as saying, "Now Tom doesn't agree with this, but this is the way we're going to do this."[57] It was dubious at best that Stallings ever made the statement, and Clinkscale made the claim in the bitter aftermath of his own trade. Indeed, the thought that Randy White, who was Landry's on-field captain, would have tolerated such freelancing is preposterous.

"There was never a time," White says, "that Tom wasn't in charge of what we did. Gene Stallings never would have done anything without running it by Tom. It might have seemed to some of those guys back there that they were on their own and brilliant as all hell and didn't need Tom or anyone else, but that was the weakest defensive secondary we ever had. Without Tom, those years would've been a disaster. We were very controlled. We weren't much like the Bears, and neither were the Bears after that year. The league learned how to exploit the 46 and then it was gone. The Flex was around for 29 years."[58]

Definitely not controlled, however, was the collective ego of the secondary, the members of which were by far the biggest "rock stars" on the team, by their own design. After the six-interception game in Washington, DC, Danny White mused that "they were like thieves—Thurman's Thieves."[59] He was referring to Dennis Thurman, the senior defensive back who, while he was mainly a backup now, was regarded as the leader of that pack. He and Dextor Clinkscale arranged for a poster to be shot of the six-man secondary, clad in "gangsta" attire, in black overcoats, shades, and snap-brim hats. Before a game against the Giants, Clinkscale ominously warned, "The Thieves are coming. Lock up your jewels."[60]

This was a pernicious sign of the times, when rap records were romanticizing gang violence. Many veteran Cowboys, including some of the black players, such as Jim Jeffcoat, detested it, leading to clashes on the field before sixty thousand pairs of eyes. In one game, Randy White and Thurman began blaming each other for a blown play. Thurman pushed White, who was held back by teammates before he could go for Thurman's throat. As well as the Thieves played, and with as little patience as he had for such tawdry spectacles, Landry simply could not have this sort of internecine strife and told the renegades they were no longer to wear the hats or act out the gangsta motif. "Hell, no," Everson Walls said at first, "I paid $50 for this hat."[61]

Reluctantly, the Thieves did put the act to bed, but Landry still broke them up, giving Thurman's right cornerback job to Ron Fellows after five games. By the start of the 1986 season, Thurman—a man Landry had been considering as a defensive back coach—and Clinkscale would be gone, Thurman already released and signed by the Cardinals, Clinkscale also released after a holdout and signed by the Indianapolis Colts. Landry had it right; neither would play beyond another season, though Thurman did in fact become an assistant coach, at USC, then with the Baltimore Ravens, and then the Jets as defensive coordinator.

On the other side of the ball, Danny White in '85 passed for 3,157 yards and twenty-one touchdowns. In the second game, in Detroit, when White went down and the Lions fell behind, Hogeboom went crazy, heaving twenty-four passes, completing seventeen for 255 yards and two touchdowns. He also ran one in, closing Detroit's lead though losing in the end, 26–21. For the next game, against the Browns, he was back on the pine. When White couldn't start against the Eagles in midseason, Hogeboom did and had the Cowboys up 14–6 before the Eagles won it late, 16–14.

The next time White saw action came on a day when the Cowboys didn't show up. This was when the petrifying Bears, undefeated after ten games, came to Texas Stadium in mid-November. It seemed a real test for Ditka, on the road, against his mentor, whose Cowboys were 7–3. But this was a game that tore the mask off Landry's overachieving team, with the real 46 burying the Cowboys' offense, savaging both Dallas quarterbacks, who were sacked six times and intercepted four times. Early on, end Richard Dent picked off White at the 1-yard line and ran the ball in for a touchdown. In the second quarter cornerback Mike Richardson ran another in from the 36. Walter Payton ran for 132 yards. The Cowboys rushed for 52 yards, passed for 167. Final score: 44–0.

Leave it to Landry, though, to rebound from a cuffing like that, and arguably a worse one three weeks later, when the Cowboys lost in Cincinnati, 50–24, his worst defeat ever. The following Sunday, the Giants, with the same record, 9–5, came into town. They were a team on the rise, led by quarterback Phil Simms and outside linebacker extraordinaire Lawrence Taylor. A win would clinch the division, and with White banged up, Landry elected to start Hogeboom. In the first quarter, he delivered a 58-yard touchdown bolt to Mike Renfro, who bloomed that season, catching sixty passes. However, Simms threw two scoring passes to take the lead. Hogeboom then had to leave the game with an injury.

This was do-or-die time for Landry, and he got the play of the year from Jeffcoat, who intercepted a batted Simms pass and ran the ball back 65 yards for the tieing touchdown. On the ensuing drive, the Giants' punter fumbled the snap, and the Cowboys recovered the ball on the Giant's 12. In came White, who found Renfro from 12 yards out for the lead, 21–14, but he couldn't go any longer. That meant Steve Pelluer had to protect the lead, which he did. Running a smooth show in the last quarter, he directed a time-consuming 72-yard drive—keeping it alive on a third-and-fifteen play by hitting scrub receiver Karl Powe for a 28-yard pickup, leading to an insurance touchdown in the 28–21 win. Landry had his thirteenth division title, twentieth consecutive winning season, and eighteenth playoff season, something never accomplished before or after by any coach.

The Cowboys ended with a season record of 10–6. Tony Dorsett had passed the milestone of 10,000 yards of rushing, the sixth to do so, and did it in a most satisfying way, in the win over the Steelers in October. But there were some red flags. While the Cowboys were ranked third against the pass, there were no thieves up front on the aging line, which kept the team rated twenty-third against the rush. And Landry had a hobbled quarterback for the opening-round playoff game against the Rams in Anaheim on January 4, 1986—his record thirty-sixth postseason game, and his last.

On that day, Landry had to squirm for sixty minutes of abject despair, watching helplessly as the Cowboys fell 20–0, the Rams getting the kind of effort from All-Pro running back Eric Dickerson—248 yards on thirty-four carries—that had now become a fantasy for Tony Dorsett, who managed all of 8 yards on seventeen carries. White hoisted up forty-three passes, completed twenty-four for 217 superficial yards, and had three interceptions. It was an utter humiliation for Landry, the upshot of which was that getting back to the Super Bowl wasn't the goal now as much as keeping himself around to rebuild a team he could be proud of.

Chapter 26

"ASSAULT ON MOUNT LANDRY"

AT SIXTY-ONE, AND WITH OVER a quarter century in pro football under his belt, Thomas Wade Landry was still one very impressive-looking man, as the mums who watched football could attest. He was a grandfather—Kitty had given birth to his second grandchild, a girl named Jennifer, in 1983. He also walked his youngest daughter, Lisa, down the aisle when she got married at Highland Park United Methodist Church. Family was more important than it ever had been back when it was just part of the equation that sounded so good in interviews—faith, family, football. Tom Jr. had strayed a bit, making a go of it in business in Las Vegas, but had moved back to Dallas and began spending the time with his father he never had before.

Handsome a figure as Tom Landry cut, he had begun to show and feel his age. He had a bad knee that prevented him from his daily jog around the track, and he needed spectacles, as fashionable as the hats and suits, though they didn't look quite so on him. He had begun to broach the subject of retirement with the family, leaving them with the impression that one more championship would provide the ideal last chapter of his football days, even if pursuit of it changed his own equations. "The end of that '85 season," he reflected in his memoirs, "would have been a logical time to retire,"[1] the improbable division title his valediction. But Landry didn't fool himself. The team was, he said, on "a downward slide," and if he left, it would seem as if he did so before the deluge came. Better to right the ship, or go down with it. No one who knew him had the slightest doubt of that.

Besides, why should he go? As it was, he was sharp and just as fastidious a teacher of technique and theory, and at his age, he wanted to show he was a hip kind of grandpa. Every now and then he sprinkled his vocabulary with the sort of neologisms that Hollywood Henderson said Landry would start using five years after they had become jejune, one being to remark that players liked to "do their thing," usually things he hated. Still, he was squarely Landry, usually the last to know the nicknames of his own players. When he heard someone say "'Fro," meaning Mike Renfro, he thought it referred to *Mel* Renfro. He also had a habit of calling his on-again, off-again quarterback *Hogenbloom*, and when he had announced his starting quarterback for the 1984 season, it somehow came out *Pozderac*, transposing the name of offensive tackle Phil Pozderac.[2]

Landry would have denied to the moon that he was out of touch with his own team—veteran Landry observers could point out that he never was good with names—and he could laugh about such *faux pas*, a sign that he was becoming less self-conscious about his squareness, something his new mercenary side accommodated. That side was important to him now. His outside commercial work didn't stop with the American Express gig. He also recorded promos for Dallas radio stations—*rock 'n' roll* stations, no less—teasers that would go something like, "Hi I'm Tom Landry and even I listen to K-Rock." One time he agreed to perpetuate an April Fool's joke by "revealing" the Cowboys had traded for the draft rights to John Elway. When a news reporter dropped by and gave him a hair dryer, he didn't miss a beat. "And I wanted a curling iron," he said.[3]

Some who thought they could read him saw the unveiling of the Landry charisma as conscious vainglory. Skip Bayless believed he knew Landry well enough to say he was "as skilled an image-maker as Schramm" and concerned to a fault with what was written about him in the press, even taking assistants to task if he believed something they said reflected badly on him.[4] As secure as he was financially now, he surely didn't do the commercials for the money. It may simply have been, as Alicia noticed, that he was less uptight and self-serious as he passed sixty. She tells the story of what might have been a gaffe by her after Roger and Marianne Staubach arrived late to Lisa's wedding, when she jokingly told a reporter, "Roger got lost? No wonder Tommy had to call the plays for him." When it made the papers she was mortified what her husband would think. Instead, both men found it hysterical. "Serves Roger right," said Landry, milking an old issue turned gag, "for changing so many of my plays."[5]

Looking back surely seemed a lot more amusing now than looking ahead. Indeed, the failure of the Cowboys to get younger may have been due to not just the draft busts and the league's catching up to Gil Brandt's file of sleepers. As distant as he was from most players, Landry had a real soft spot for his still productive veterans and wanted to keep them around. Paul Zimmerman wrote that "maybe as he gets older Landry is mellowing and he feels closer to his older people."[6] If so, it may have finally dawned on Tom Landry that youth was wasted on the young.

As for himself, he admitted that being the "man in the hat" when hats had gone out of style made him "an endangered species."[7] Only he didn't know how endangered.

AMONG THE projects Bum Bright was bound to continue was the expansion of Texas Stadium, adding 118 new luxury boxes and building a spanking new and wholly unnecessary office building and practice facility over two hundred acres in a suburban North Dallas hamlet called Valley Ranch. Named Cowboys Center, the brainchild of Tex Schramm was another adventure into gross excess. Schramm liked to call the facility Cowboy Town, making it sound like a summer camp where Tom Landry would be playing Spencer Tracy for adorable pugs who looked like Mickey Rooney. But this camp had a movie theater, a dance studio for the cheerleaders, a travel agency, and an endless maze of hallways to nowhere—a fun house in a horror movie that cost $70 million at a time when the middle class was drowning.

Landry worked almost under cover in a glorified coat closet–sized space at the rear of one of the buildings. He also had no objection to clearing out of the place for training camp, heading still to Thousand Oaks, away from the decadent comforts of Cowboy Town, which most of the players found creepy. Thousand Oaks was the preferred choice as well for the Cowboys' philanderers who spent summers away from their wives. But that had always been one of those commandment violations Landry overlooked when it came to the men he led. Some traditions were so sacred that they overrode commandments.

WITH HIS contract set to expire again after the 1986 season, Landry could no longer talk Schramm out of infusing some youth into the coaching staff. The shutout loss to the Rams in the playoffs rankled Schramm, who had ranted and raved, swilling booze and shouting profanity, in the press box all during the game. His new pet expression was that the team needed "young blood," and he believed he had found it, in Paul Hackett, the offensive coordinator of Bill Walsh's 49ers. At thirty-nine, Hackett was still thought of as a whiz kid after eleven years of coaching on the college and pro levels. His resume included stints at Cal, USC, and the Cleveland Browns, running the same kind of upbeat, keep-'em-guessing attack Walsh had brought to the game. Though Walsh swore by Hackett, he also had to deal with his brazenness, Hackett freely telling Walsh when he thought he was full of it.

Hackett was clearly not someone suited to work for Tom Landry, but Schramm needed more than another yes man. He wanted someone he could call his own, someone he could move into the head coach's office in time. This was not something Hackett was averse to. He knew he would be perceived and judged in that light, and he relished the chance. To be sure, nothing about him suggested a yes man. A high-strung, ingratiating man averse to neither attention nor ambition, he presented himself as a generational lodestar, hoping that Landry would accept him but intending to make his mark regardless.

Landry, who was determined to cling to the authority Schramm had chipped away at, gave ground but only up to a point. Even though Hackett was Tex's man, not his, he played the good soldier, traveling to a college all-star game in New Orleans to interview him for the coordinator's job—albeit so perfunctorily that Hackett thought he had no chance. For the media he agreed with Schramm's decision to bring a "fresh look" to the team and insisted that Tex wasn't encroaching on his turf, that the decision to hire Hackett or anyone else was strictly his. However, in his autobiography, he told of serious reservations that he didn't bring up at the time, about the "conflict of philosophy" between Hackett's one-size-fits-all, prefabricated offense and the Cowboys' chain link of reads and adaptations after the snap. The two systems, he said, were "fundamentally different."[8]

He kept such thoughts sublimated after Hackett was hired, and at the announcement they stood shoulder to shoulder singing hosannas to each other. Hackett said he was eager to be able to "learn from one of the masters."[9] The last three words titillated the press, writing its own story line. As soon as training camp began, he was being called "the next Landry" in the papers. When asked about it he would say coyly, "We'll see what happens." For Landry, such speculation was exactly the kind of diversion he didn't need, and he never played along with it. Rather, his attitude was a thinly veiled contempt for the outsider he had consented to hire. As Bayless reported after the introductory press conference, "While Hackett [was] earnestly explaining his offensive philosophy, Landry [was] craning his neck sideways, turtlelike, with a squint that appear[ed] to say, 'Who is this whippersnapper?'"[10]

Hackett clearly didn't know what he was in for, though he could guess. It didn't help that he replaced Shofner, who knew his place and whom the players loved. Shofner, offended by the shuffle, was offered a job in the Cowboys' front office, but he quit and went to St. Louis as an assistant to the Cardinals' new head coach—Gene Stallings, who had finally received an offer to become a head coach and left Landry's bosom. Even before he arrived, Hackett wore a black hat around the team, and the players seemed to take their cues from Landry in their tepid responses about the new guy. To the reporters, Hackett was a cause célèbre, even a savior. "Welcome to Dallas, 39-year-old Paul Hackett," wrote Randy Galloway. "Dallas, home of the Dull-as Cowboys. Can you cure the boredom, Paul? Can you juice up this jalopy?"[11]

Not that Hackett could explain what his juice would be. Com-

pared with Landry's way of simplifying the complexities of his system into simple language for the masses, Hackett was professorial
and abstruse. Blackie Sherrod, who had taken his drollery to the
Morning News, wrote, "We heard that Dr. Paul Hackett was being
imported from the San Francisco Institute of Technology to install a
new passing offense for the Cowboys. We just didn't understand he
was going to teach it in Russian."[12] Landry, not ceding control of the
offense to Hackett, began for the first time to wear a headset under
his fedora. He was linked to Hackett up in the press box, and often
overruled the plays Hackett sent down. "Let's be real," says Sam
Blair, "Hackett was window dressing for Tom. It was Tom's team,
his offense. You don't think Tom would have let some guy he didn't
even want come in and make him look bad by changing the basics
around, do you? The worst thing that could have happened was what
happened: trying to make Tom into Bill Walsh. He would have to be
kicked and dragged into that system or any other system. Tom barely
mentioned Paul; it was like he wasn't even there."[13]

In fairness to Hackett, Landry likely would have done the same
with anyone brought in to take his job, something he wanted to handle himself, his way, with *his* guy. Indeed, when Tex Schramm was
asked if Hackett would be the next in line, his stock answer was,
"It's tough to replace God."[14] Especially when God was going to
make it so tough. Schramm may have had his way in bringing in the
new blood, but it stopped there. "The way it played out," said Frank
Luksa, "it wasn't Tom versus Hackett, it was Tom versus Tex. Tom
and Tex had a very complex relationship. Though they never spent
an hour together off the field, they had a real bond when it came
to defending each other. But when Tom thought Tex was stepping
into his domain, he got his back up. Hackett was just caught in the
middle."[15]

Hackett saw the writing on the wall early: if he was to succeed
Landry someday, it wouldn't be with the coach's blessing. Landry
made Hackett as irrelevant as possible. He certainly didn't think
he needed to overhaul the offense to accommodate him. The year
before, Landry himself modified the passing attack, using more
shorter-range patterns over the middle to Mike Renfro, who caught
sixty balls and scored eight touchdowns. Now, trying to drop some

of Hackett's ideas in disrupted the team's flow, and Renfro's numbers fell to only twenty-two catches. Some of this had to do with the arrival of UCLA's All-American receiver Mike Sherrard, for whom Schramm traded up to be able to pick in the first round the year before, the first receiver taken by the team in that round since 1968. Sherrard was the fastest receiver the Cowboys had since Bob Hayes, and he caught forty-one passes and made five touchdowns in 1985, opening up the passing game quite enough. The biggest influence on the Cowboys' offense in 1986, however, would not be a new passing charter. It would be a running back who made Tony Dorsett obsolete.

LANDRY'S LAST big break in his charmed life came when the USFL, its ranks shrinking and losses increasing despite all that TV money, had a change of tactics. After the 1985 season its owners decided the only way to save itself was to go head to head with the NFL in the fall, while suing the elder league to force a merger by filing a $567 million antitrust suit. After a six-week trial, a jury decided in the spring that the NFL was indeed a monopoly. It was a pyrrhic victory, though, since the jury also ruled that the USFL was responsible for its own failures. The USFL was then awarded exactly one dollar in damages, tripled under antitrust law to three dollars. Unable to continue, the league folded, to formally dissolve in 1988 after an appeal failed, and players began streaming to the NFL.

Tex Schramm, who had as usual been on the front lines of another legal and guerilla war against a concocted league, had kept a sharp eye on the USFL's operation and appropriated for the NFL a number of useful elements, including instant replay, which began immediately with the 1986 season, and the two-point conversion, which would be adopted in 1994. For his own team, he took a human asset, a two-legged ball of rolling thunder named Herschel Walker. His contract with the USFL had expired, and he had been set free by the New Jersey Generals' owner, Donald Trump, to make a deal for himself. The Cowboys, who had drafted him, had no legal right to him after three years, but Walker was thrilled to be able to play for Landry. To sweeten the pot, Schramm gave Walker a five-year,

$5 million contract—making him the highest-paid Cowboy—and a $500,000 bonus.

At six feet one and 225 pounds, Walker was built and blocked like a fullback, wiping out linemen and linebackers as if he were a Jeep, but he also had the speed and shiftiness of a tailback and the instincts of a great pass receiver. Not resting on talent alone, he sat through Landry's chalk talks, scribbling notes furiously on a pad. Even if he was a bit of a brownnoser, his easy smile and gratitude to be playing in Dallas was a welcome breath of humility in a hornet's nest of rock stars, thieves, and malcontents. He had it all—including the bonus, which made Tony Dorsett flip out. Along with Too Tall Jones, Dorsett was the most seriously underpaid Cowboys superstar ever, his own insecurity and poor representation allowing Schramm to take advantage of him. Even now, his salary of $550,000 was around half that of Walker's and Walter Payton's.

When the news about Walker broke, Dorsett could not feign glee at being in a "dream backfield." Instead, he seethed, "I'm not playing second fiddle to anybody," and threatened that he could be "a very disruptive force on this team"[16] unless the Cowboys paid him the same. Quite simply, this could not be done because Schramm *had* paid him more, having renegotiated Dorsett's seven-year contract the year before, pumping it up to $6.4 million and leaving the three years left on it as non-negotiable. He had also saved Dorsett from ruination when his IRS tab had swelled to $414,000 and the revenuers placed liens on his paychecks, both of his homes, and his cars. Doing something radical for him, Schramm arranged for the Cowboys to lend Dorsett $500,000, restructured his contract to free up some back-end money, and saved $3 million, almost half, as an annuity to be carried over thirty years. Regardless, Dorsett now threatened to hold out, prompting Schramm to bat not an eyelash. With his usual smugness, he said, "I feel . . ." He also had no problem discussing Dorsett's heretofore private financial problems.[17]

Insecure as he was, Dorsett could never win a dogfight like that with a pit bull like Schramm. After a few days of being AWOL, he came in to camp properly chastened, apologizing for his "disruptive force" remark and another that Schramm had "double-crossed" him. He promised to give his all. He praised Walker. Sympathetically to

Dorsett, Landry went slow with Walker, bringing him in on selected downs for the first few games then started him in the fourth game. In a late September 31–7 rout of St. Louis, Dorsett was out with a bum ankle, and Walker exploded for 120 yards of rushing and four catches for 37 yards, the latter a skill that was a gift. But Landry still held him back a bit, despite pleas from the fans and the press to go big with Walker. When Dorsett was healthy, Landry used the archaic full-house backfield, with Walker and Dorsett as tailbacks and the 235-pound battering ram fullback Timmy Newsome to lead them through the line.

Landry, though, was still loath to make Walker the focus of the attack, lest he lose Dorsett. Both men, however, wanted more carries, which was nothing new for Dorsett, who had long bitched about Landry's limiting his runs due to concern for his size and brittleness. The mutual demand for more touches underlined why two Heisman winners had never been paired in the same backfield—and why Landry's try at it was doomed.

DANNY WHITE seemed to have conquered his own challenges. During the 1984 off-season, the *Morning News'* Gary Myers conducted a poll that had readers voting for whom they wanted to be the starting quarterback. He also did a survey of Cowboys players to weigh in, anonymously, on the same question. Both polls agreed, though the latter was the more significant: "COWBOYS WANT HOGEBOOM, BUT THINK THEY'LL GET WHITE," read the headline.[18] This was hardly surprising, and it proved that the resentments from the 1982 strike were cooked into the team's psyche, but the depth of animosity toward White shook even Landry, who normally would have laughed off reader polls. After one more season waiting for him to bloom, he traded "Hogenbloom" to Indianapolis for a second-round draft pick, a move that would not haunt the Cowboys—Hogeboom would be out of football in two years. As the 1986 season shaped up, White had the job as usual, with Steve Pelluer and sixth-round-pick Reggie Collier the new suitors.

The going was never easy for White, who would now hear chants for *Pelluer*, but he again proved he knew how to win—in the regular season, when he was healthy. In the Monday night opener, a 31–28 thriller against the Giants, he threw for 279 yards and two touchdowns, leading a late drive that beat the same defense that would lead the Giants back to their first championship since Landry played for them. Notably, Dorsett scored the first touchdown, Walker the clincher. After eight games the Cowboys had parlayed that success to a 6–2 record. Then came a killer bad break. Early in the rematch against the Giants in the Meadowlands, Carl Banks came in on a blitz and slammed White to the ground, fracturing his throwing wrist and ending his season, his injuries having become an all too familiar story.

Enter Pelluer, throwing. He filled the air with thirty-eight passes, completing twenty-eight for 339 yards and a touchdown pass to Renfro that put the Cowboys ahead in the second quarter. But he was also sacked five times, and the Giants prevailed 17–14. Worse, Walker hurt his ankle in the game, and it would not be fully healed for the rest of the season. Pelluer, who had an old-world gentility about him, proved he had an arm and mettle, as Paul Zimmerman wrote, a "hidden fire beneath his 'yes, sir' and 'no, sir.'"[19] Still, Pelluer was not overly mobile, the offensive line was a patchwork, and without Walker in every play the backs weren't picking up blitzes. Pelluer was buried each week, sacked an incredible forty-seven times—eleven times by the Chargers in one game, one shy of the NFL record, a game the Cowboys *won*. In the end, the offense allowed sixty sacks, second most in their history, turning Pelluer into "a basket case."[20]

The Cowboys were still 7–4 after the San Diego game, but the last five games were a blur of misery. Pelluer wound up with eight touchdown passes and seventeen interceptions, and heard the fans calling for Reggie Collier. For Landry, it was like trying to hold back a cracking dam. He had failed in recent years to prevent late-season collapses, and even with his backfield horses, things seemed disjointed, partly because both horses battled nagging injuries. In the next to last game, at home against Philadelphia, Walker, finally recovered, ran for 122 yards on only six carries. He ran 84 yards in one play for a score in the first quarter, then snared a pass for *another* 84-yard touchdown in the fourth to give the Cowboys a 21–16 lead, before a late touchdown gave the game to the Eagles.

Walker's number of rushing touchdowns, twelve, was amazing given that, after his ankle injury, he played basically as a receiver, even technically a man-in-motion flanker and *tight end*. In the game before the Cowboys lost to the Giants, he had carried the ball twenty-six times against St. Louis, but thereafter he never did more than eight times. Of his twelve rushing touchdowns, just three came in the final seven games. Still, Walker ran for 727 yards, only 11 behind Dorsett, who had thirty-three more carries. He caught seventy-six balls, the most on the team and the most by a back in the Cowboys' history. His average rush was 4.9 yards, second in the NFL. As titillating as his rookie NFL season was, however, the 1986 season, with its 7–9 record, is remembered for only one thing: being Landry's first sub-.500 season since 1964.

Landry had a lot to work on to prove it was an aberration. The defense was as unsettled as the offense. He had done much to shore it up against the run, but plugging one leak opened another. The defense was ranked No. 27 against the pass, the secondary never recovering from Landry's dispatch of Dennis Thurman, the head "Thief," to St. Louis before the season. Many of the team's problems were traced back to Landry as a common source, and it was either alarming or flattering to Landry that during one of the late-season losses, against the Rams in Anaheim, Larry Wansley had clamored down from the press box and told him, "Coach Landry, there's been a threat on your life . . . there might be a sniper up there somewhere."[21] Wansley took him off the field for his own protection, causing a stir in the stadium when he handed his clipboard to Danny White and was led to the locker room. Wansley borrowed a bulletproof vest from an LA cop, and Landry wore it under his jacket when he went back out, against Wansley's wishes. On the sideline, White eased the mood by saying the way his season had gone, the sniper would probably miss Landry and hit him instead.

Football had surely changed from the days when few paid it much attention to now, when it served as an incubator for deranged fans threatening to kill Tom Landry. Landry, shrugging the incident off, had much bigger problems than deranged fans. He would spend the off-season vowing his toughest summer camp ever, and put his softening veterans on notice that next season they might be out, that nearly every position was up for grabs. Indeed, if the feeling was getting around in the football orbit that the old coach was not on top of things anymore, Landry was sanguine that he was needed more than ever to resurrect the Dallas Cowboys.

MAYBE THE biggest reason why, other than pride and vanity, was that he felt he owed it to Clint Murchison not to leave his proud franchise in ruins. Landry thought the saddest thing he ever lived through, next to his family trying to deal with his brother's death in the skies over the North Atlantic, were the last weeks of Clint's life. By the new year of 1987, Murchison was dying. He was wheelchair-bound, unable to speak or move, withering away. Tom and Alicia would drop by once in a while so that he would know he wasn't forgotten, and were pleased that Clint's born-again Christianity gave them an added bond. Like Clint's wife, Annie, they hoped it would purge Clint of his life of debauchery and adultery. Landry considered that a victory of good over evil and maybe even a reward for having to put up with Murchison's sinful ways in the glory years—though when Landry wrote his memoirs, he danced around that subject. Of the "wild and profligate life he supposedly lived," he said, "I don't know much, if any, of that is true. I never saw that side of Clint."[22]

The last time he saw Murchison was when Clint was taken to a hospital with pneumonia in late March. He and Tex Schramm went there and knew Clint would not last long. They said their last good-byes. On March 30, the man who facilitated the Landry legend died at age sixty-three. Landry spoke at the funeral, weaving old stories into the peace he said Clint had found by devoting himself to God. After Murchison was set down in his grave, Alicia said on their way home how sad it was that Clint died just after becoming a Christian. For Tom Landry, though, it seemed a relief. Clint, he told her, had found God just in time.

ALTHOUGH NO one knew it, the machinery leading to the biggest Cowboys shakeup of all was in place. Landry simply assumed that he was safe because Tex Schramm was in command, which wasn't naive as much as logical. However, Schramm, whose power far out-weighed his 3 percent stock—Bum Bright gushed that Tex was "my CEO"[23]—wasn't making Bright happy. There was, above all, his untethered spending. The biggest money pit was Cowboy Town, but Bright was fortunate that the weak real estate market halted Schramm's planned projects, like a Cowboys hotel, a Cowboys golf course, a Cowboys ice-rink, and a promenade with Cowboys restaurants. Soon, wrote one critic, the place was "a sandstone elephant stalked by tusk-hunting creditors."[24] Those creditors came right to Bright's office. Overdue bills had to be paid. To make matters worse, the politicians, even the great messiah of the privileged in the White House, were causing him headaches. For one thing, they passed into law the Tax Reform Act of 1986, severely limiting depreciation of property, property like the Dallas Cowboys Inc., which was losing money, a lot of money. Bright also began to do what he had pledged not to: question the coach, whose contract was up. However, if the previous season had seemed to Landry the logical time to quit, he would do Bright no favors a year later.

As Tom Landry Jr. says, "Dad would have liked to retire, he didn't need all the aggravation. If it was Clint he might have, but he wasn't going to roll over for Bum Bright, who seemed to have his own agenda and wasn't really supportive of Dad. Then you had Tex taking shots at him. He felt it was him against the world. He'd been there twenty-six years, Bright three. He felt he was the only one who had a handle on the future. And so if he was made to walk the plank, he wasn't gonna jump."[25]

Indeed, Bright later claimed that he wanted Landry out when his contract was up, but that Schramm wouldn't move on it, with the alibi that he didn't have a successor in place yet.[26] Bright's opinion was that, as he recalled later, "Something needed to be done. A new direction was needed on the coaching staff from Tom on down. But despite the fact he appears gruff at times, Tex is a sentimentalist. He didn't have the stomach to do what needed to be done." Months went by, and what Bright didn't know was that Schramm not only disobeyed his order but had unilaterally decided to resign Landry for a good deal more of Bright's tightening money supply. A year later, Schramm, clearly talking about Bright, reflected that "the popular game . . . was to point out things that Landry should have done and things that proved he had done a poor job. These opinions came from people who had no idea what was going on internally with our football team," people who he said "had no fucking idea what should be done."[27]

Neither was Landry cowering in a corner waiting for the sky to fall on him. Sub-.500 season or not, reduced leverage or not, he didn't want anyone thinking he was ready to chuck it all. Perhaps it mattered to him that Paul Hackett had turned down an offer to become head coach at USC and was itching to take over Landry's job. Whatever the case, feeling frisky after having arthroscopic surgery to remove bone spurs from his left knee, he decided he had to come back, with the security of the kingly presence he was. For him, the issue was not in doubt. "Tex," he recalled, "had always assured me I could coach as long as I wanted. When one of my contracts ran out Tex would come and tell me what he could do on the next one. He was always more than fair; we never quibbled about any of the terms."[28] Schramm, moreover, did not believe Landry needed to walk that plank. Indeed, both he and Landry agreed that had White not gone down, the Cowboys were playoff-bound. And so there was nothing standing in the way when the two men met on unrelated business and Landry suddenly digressed.

"I need a three-year contract, Tex," he said.

"Okay, Tom," came the near-automated response.[29]

"And that," Landry later remembered, "was that."

He wanted the years more than the top-shelf money, but he certainly believed he should keep pace with the highest-paid coaches, who made around $1 million a year, those being Bill Walsh, Joe Gibbs, Don Shula, and Chuck Noll, all of whom he predated. Schramm could not quibble, nor could Bum Bright when Tex came to him to approve the deal. Bright, however, had one condition: he wanted Landry to sign three, unconnected one-year contracts. That would reserve the right to terminate him after either of the first two years and not owe him a dime more. The next he heard, Schramm had signed Landry for three years, at $800,000 for the first year, $900,000 for the second, $1 million for the last—all in one contract, all of it guaranteed. Bright only learned of it on July 17, when Tim

Cowlishaw broke the story in the *Morning News*, writing, "Tom Landry was looking for a commitment this off-season. From players. From coaches. From everyone. Landry did not exclude himself from the search. As a result, he has reached an oral agreement with Tex Schramm to remain as head coach for three more seasons."

Said Landry, "That figure was pretty much my idea. I wanted to try to bring us back to the level we once were at and I knew that was going to take more than a year."[30]

It was as if Bright didn't exist and had no say. Suddenly his favorite CEO seemed less than the most honest man in the world—the opinion of, well, everyone else in the world. Schramm, he said later, had misled him, that Tex had hemmed and hawed about the contract going through lawyers and went off on vacation, leaving the status quo.

Reading about the signing in the newspapers, Hackett was floored too, betraying his motives for staying. Rather than congratulate Landry, he went to Schramm, who had led him to believe he would succeed Landry when the old man's contract expired. He asked him what gives. "It was out of my hands," Tex told him,[31] a preposterous fable that proved Bum Bright correct; Schramm *couldn't* be trusted, and the chain of command was essentially a mystery. "This place is unbelievable," Bright told Skip Bayless. "No one ever tells anyone anything. . . . We just have to read about it in the papers. You never really know who's responsible for anything." Hackett had become so paranoid that he wondered if his own stock would fall among the league's general managers because of Landry's coolness to him.[32] He also thought the Cowboys' people had put the word out that he was disloyal and hard to get along with, and that it was true that he had walked a very fine line between open hostility to Landry and placating him, not very gracefully. Indeed, his own injudicious comments to the press were jarring. By example, late in the 1986 season he had concluded, "We cannot win in this league with the tackles we have," and "It is staggering how poorly this team has drafted for the last eight years. You compare this team to the 49ers, man for man, two deep, and it's a joke."[33]

Bum Bright, who had his own litany of things to kvetch about, for now could do nothing except pretend to be excited about Landry pulling the Cowboys out of the doldrums. Landry, with brass in pocket, allowed that he had only this chance left, being that "I've reached the point . . . that I'm not going to coach a lot longer."[34] It sounded like the right and humble thing to say, but he may not have believed it. If he could get back into the winner's circle, God only knew when he'd consent to go.

BOTH LANDRY and Schramm fully expected the 1987 season to be a revival. Going back to the early Landry, he promised a back-breaking training camp with two-a-day scrimmages daily. Showing he meant business, before camp opened he waived Tony Hill, who had led the team for the last nine seasons in the number of receiving yards and even now ranks second in team history, as well as third in the number of touchdowns and fourth in the total number of yards. But Landry—passing the buck by saying he was relying on Hackett's evaluation—believed Hill, at thirty-one and last an All-Pro in 1985, had slipped in his ability to play and, in Landry-speak, "didn't fire up" during the previous season. As Paul Zimmerman noted, "It was practically unheard of for Landry to demote a starter in the off-season, let alone cut him."[35] But he was right about Hill, who signed with the 49ers and was cut before the season, ending his career. The move also signaled that change was in the air. Another sign was that the annual Cowboys' highlight film that year was titled *Make Way for Tomorrow*.

The exception, of course, was the head coach, who entrenched himself even more while the man chosen as his putative heir apparent, Paul Hackett, accepted blame for the second-half collapse of the previous season. His West Coast offense, he admitted, was too much for Pelluer, who couldn't handle the split-second decision-making demands to pick out first-, second-, and third-option receivers.[36] Landry, having phased that system in, would now phase it out. By the time the team opened camp, Schramm had rammed through another new assistant coach, offensive line pit boss Jim Erkenbeck, who came from the New Orleans Saints, though hardly as young blood. Erkenbeck, a fifty-one-year-old ex-Marine who had once been on the same staff as Hackett at Cal, replaced longtime Landry fixture Jim Myers and was expected to re-create his history of developing dominating offensive lines.

The Cowboys had drafted with that, and perhaps Hackett's diatribe, in mind. They reeled in 316-pound guard Jeff Zimmerman and 310-pound tackle Kevin Gogan. Already there was 335-pound USFL expatriate guard Nate Newton, who would play the next thirteen years on that line (and later serve thirty months in federal prison for drug trafficking).[37] Gogan would also play for thirteen more seasons, seven in Dallas. Center Tom Rafferty was the only veteran left now. At left tackle was 320-pound converted defensive lineman Mark Tuinei, one of Brandt's last finds, a 1983 rookie free agent (whose sad postscript was that he would be found dead in 1999 of a heroin and ecstasy overdose).[38] Clearly, Landry wanted bones to rattle.

The way coaches were dropping, Gene Stallings may have gotten out just in time. His stay in St. Louis was brief, but it led to a bigger job, as head coach of the Alabama Crimson Tide in 1990, and a checkered path, the Tide being sanctioned for rules violations but making Stallings the Southeast Conference's Coach of the Year twice. Coaches aside, Gil Brandt was also on thin ice, his rotten drafts now as notorious as his long-ago gems. It didn't help Brandt that the tough old nail Ernie Stautner, who was seemingly joined at the hip with Landry, remarked that Brandt "should have been let go ten years ago."[39] If Landry wouldn't openly say that, Schramm's actions spoke loudly enough. He had limited Brandt's purview, restricting him from signing players and hiring new scouts not affiliated with Gil to run the entire scouting department. Brandt spent most of his time during summer camp on the Thousand Oaks golf course, killing time. That, and the fact that few in the team's office missed him being there did not bode well for Gil, even if Tex was not going to cut him out of the picture entirely.

In microcosm, this was the conundrum Schramm faced with Landry. He could cut into his authority, but if he felt Landry had lost it as a coach, he was beholden to the old holy trinity. Of course, Tex had no doubt about himself. He hadn't lost a thing off his own fastball, he reckoned. All three of them had survived too much and made too much history to be sent to pasture. With the Cowboys, it was, as always, complicated.

✦ ✦ ✦ ✦

PRODUCING A revival in 1987 would be complicated too. Dorsett had both of his knees operated on in the off-season and would need to be pampered. Danny White's wrist wasn't completely healed either, meaning that Steve Pelluer would be on standby. Rafael Septien was arrested early in camp on the underage sex charge, and by the end of camp he was the kicker no more.[40] Early in August, Mike Sherrard broke his leg, one of the most grotesque injuries anyone had ever seen. As he was taken off the field in agony, with the bone in his leg protruding through his shin, players couldn't bear to watch. Sherrard would not play for three seasons, which was a devastating loss for Landry.

There were strike clouds again gathering over camp, with the players' union turning the screws on the owners, threatening to walk out—during the season this time—on the long-delayed issue of free agency, something the league's management council, chaired by Tex Schramm, would not budge on. With this as a backdrop, the first two regular-season games went on, with the Cowboys on the road for both. They lost the opener in St. Louis, 24–13, when the defense rolled over and surrendered 21 points in the fourth quarter—it was Landry's only second opening-day loss in the last twenty-three years—then beat the champion Giants in a snarling, warlike defensive battle, 16–14, the Cowboys having to hold their breaths as the Giants missed a last-second field goal. And then the union called its strike, which Schramm had prepared for wisely and cunningly. As the owners' battle strategy formed, they weren't going to sit idly by as they had during the 1982 strike. This time, the games would go on with replacement players culled from among their own low draft picks, unsigned free agents, semipros, and opportunistic truck drivers, bartenders, gym teachers, and gravediggers.

After the third game of the season went dark, all the teams had scab teams ready for the next week, and Schramm had marshaled his fellow plutocrats. His reply to the union's proposals was to vow that "there will never be free agency" even if the players struck for thirty years.[41] Another time, he said, "Free agency won't work. We found that in baseball,"[42] a statement long ago proved inoperative.

Schramm went on the TV news shows regurgitating this position, gladly making himself the face of the enemy. And players regarded him as that, calling him "the architect of scab ball," "a smart man but a moral-less person," and "Mikhail Schramm." One cynic claimed Schramm wanted the strike because he knew how bad the Cowboys were. In turn, Schramm, who seemed stuck in an earlier era, labeled the union leadership "revolutionaries who want to destroy the structure of the NFL," "radical," and "militant."[43]

Schramm meanwhile dealt with his own labor force just as severely. As the striking Cowboys were deciding to stay or go, he went right for the jugular, playing divide and conquer by putting their future money on the table. He sneaked into every players' contract a clause that any annuities would be revoked if a player missed a game or practice for non-injury reasons. No one knew if this was legal, but it was threatening to a good half-dozen stars who, like Dorsett, had an annuity for their own protection. These included Danny White, Randy White, Too Tall Jones, Doug Cosbie, and Everson Walls, all of whom stood to lose a lot of deferred cash.

Jones and Randy White were the first to cross the line, galling Cowboys players who had supported White in his holdout a few years before. "Hey, if it was just my salary, I'd sit out as long as the next player," said Jones, sadly and with cause, since thirty-three other defensive linemen made more than he did in salary. "But this is my retirement thing, this is what I've worked for."[44] Cosbie, the Cowboys' union representative, and Walls stuck to their principles, as did Dorsett, who blasted White as "selfish" and for "letting the team down," calling him "Captain Scab."[45] Danny White, with 1982 in mind, wavered but was an easy mark for Schramm. At the time, a truck parts company he owned was being investigated for mail fraud, and he owed $230,000 to creditors.[46] Helping him out, Schramm had advanced him $300,000, which would need to be repaid if he walked the line.[47] White had no choice but to buckle, lamely clarifying that he was "supporting my teammates," not management. Then, days later, a shamefaced Dorsett caved too, "forced" into it, he insisted, by Schramm.

Actually, the Cowboys had only the third-highest defection rate, with twenty-one players crossing the picket line. No other team,

however, took more heat from so many, owing to Schramm's methods, which led the NFLPA to make noise about suing the Cowboys
for illegal coercion. Even some management types felt Schramm had
gone too far. Most owners were content to stick with the replacements rather than diluting their real teams, and spoke of respecting
the dignity of striking players, inferring that Schramm had not. Some
tried to convince Schramm not to play the regulars, given that players
all over the league were breaking ranks and it was becoming obvious
the strike wouldn't last long. Tex, though, never looked for halfway
victory, and in a right-to-work state like Texas he had no problem
bludgeoning workers with impunity.

Dorsett particularly was in a real bind. He was only 598 yards
short of breaking Jim Brown's all-time rushing record and was mortified by the idea of doing it in tainted games. Thus he said he would
"go out on the 50-yard-line at Texas Stadium and beg them not to
play me . . . don't make me do it this way."[48] It was a pathetic plea,
leading one writer to opine that "a proud athlete had been reduced
to almost cartoon-figure dimensions."[49] Landry, who had tired of
Dorsett's blaming everyone else for his own decline, such as the
offensive line, was loath to comply, but he did hold all the regulars
out of the first scab game, against the Jets in New Jersey, playing
only the replacements Schramm had put together with great care.
While striking players from both teams picketed outside the stadium,
and signed autographs for fans, most of the attention inside was on
quarterback Kevin Sweeney, a seventh-round pick out of Fresno State
whom Schramm had wanted Landry to find a spot for but was cut
because of his smallish size, barely six feet.

In the sparsely populated Meadowlands, Landry gave his team
of strangers a no-frills game plan, mainly running Alvin Blount, a
ninth-rounder, who carried the ball twenty-eight times for 72 yards.
Sweeney completed just six of fourteen passes, but three went for
touchdowns, and he came up a winner, 38–24. Landry would play
his regulars in the next game, the home opener against the Eagles,
though for only a few plays—no doubt influenced by the way the
crowd, a surprisingly robust 40,622, turned on the regulars, booing
whenever they were on the field. The sort-of Cowboys ran the sort-
of Eagles out of Texas Stadium, 41–22, and when Sweeney threw

another touchdown pass, the stadium erupted; when Dorsett ran for a touchdown from 10 yards out, it was as if the enemy had scored. In right-to-work Texas, the fans had little sympathy for the liberal trade unions or their striking millionaires, even the ones who defected, but they swooned over nonunion workers making $3,125 a game, waving banners that said things like "Scab Boys We Love You" and "Honor Thy Mother and Thy Father and Thy Contract."

In most NFL cities the games were largely ignored, but in Dallas the ratings were as high as for most regular Cowboys games. Local support for the scab boys was described as "hysterical." And Schramm, of course, took credit for all of it, having put them together. After being derided by fans on his own weekly radio show for gumming up the new team with old stars, Tex now shamelessly advised Landry to keep the regulars *out*. This surreal, inverted football wonderland ended quickly. The strike was over before the next weekend, and the union, or what was left of it, sent its members back to their teams, though not soon enough for the fill-in teams to bask in one last moment of glory. Fans in Dallas had already made the Cowboys' Monday night game against the Redskins a sellout, and Landry's announcement that he was starting Danny White brought out more banners, one reading, "White's a Weenie, We Want Sweeney."

That night, more than sixty thousand people booed Dorsett and White, both of whom had poor games as the 'Skins came on at the end to win, 13–7. When it was over, the replacements left the field to an ovation, soon to be forgotten, and few in a mood to thank Schramm, who withheld $1,000 from their last paycheck, to make up for the $1,000 bonus he had given them at the start. (He insisted it had been an advance.)[50] As was predicted, the Cowboys did become even more reviled. At the end of the Eagles game, with the win in the bag, Landry had brought in his regulars and even ran a reverse for a touchdown, leaving Buddy Ryan sputtering that Landry ran up the score and calling God's favorite coach a "hypocrite" and a "phony."[51] Landry had never been accused of this breach of coaching etiquette. Granted, this was Buddy Ryan, who created enemies by the peck, but when it came to Landry, it was easier now to do what would once have been unthinkable, or at least unspeakable.

In fact, Schramm, who was just as furious that Sweeney wasn't used, stomped like a child during the Redskins game, cursing as always but now at Landry, calling him a "son of a bitch"[52] and not caring who overheard. Bum Bright, also enamored of the kid, apparently felt Tex was in the right state of mind to take action. He called him during the following week and fulminated, "Call Landry and let's fire him," but Schramm had to quickly retrench. "No," he said, "we can't do that just yet." Bright said he would fire Landry himself. "No," Tex assured him, "let me handle it my way."[53] His way, though, was to do nothing. As the weeks went by, Bright would see him fiddling, and burned with anger.

AS THE union took its case for free agency to court, the same way baseball players had won theirs, the replacements were sent home with the notable exception of Sweeney, who was kept as the third-string quarterback. Landry had a 3–2 team with ten games left, but also a team with lingering divisions. Some returning Cowboys had nothing but contempt for the defectors and for Dallas fans, whom one player called "stupid" for being "led by the nose" by Schramm to accept an inferior product.[54] Schramm's end around with the annuity clauses would carry over too, it becoming part of the union's lawsuit against the NFL, and while Cosbie and Walls—who were treated as heroes by players around the league for standing up to Schramm—would have their annuities restored, they could not look Schramm in the eye. The Cowboys' holy trinity seemed anything but. Schramm and Brandt were loathed by the players, and Landry was losing the unconditional loyalty, and affinity, his players always had for him. Indeed, Butch Johnson said Landry once "made everyone live in fear of losing their job," but now the "fear slowly became hatred."[55]

That might have applied most viscerally to Tony Dorsett. He never recovered from the tremors Schramm had caused him, and Landry didn't make him feel any better. Despite his iffy knees, Dorsett wanted to carry the load, but it seemed that Landry's summer camp proclamation—that "this is Herschel Walker's team now"—still stood, not that Landry was having *Walker* carry the load. His reluctance to commit to either man was just plain odd. The Cowboys' first post-strike game brought them helmet to helmet again with the Eagles, with Buddy Ryan thirsting for payback.

The game was tight for a half, Walker's 1-yard touchdown run bringing the Cowboys to within 3 points, 13–10. The defense limited Randall Cunningham to only 127 yards of passing while White was going twenty-two of thirty-six for 257 yards. Dorsett carried the ball only eleven times for 32 yards and Walker, twelve for 54. The monster line was in tatters, with Nate Newton injured and requiring knee surgery and tackle Phil Pozderac mysteriously quitting three days before the game. The Cowboys turned the ball over three times and had a field goal blocked. Eagles halfback Keith Byars ran for 94 yards. By late in the fourth quarter, Ryan's team was ahead, 30–20, and had the ball with time running out. *Perfect!* he must have thought. Sticking it to Landry, he called for a long pass, which brought an interference penalty in the end zone. Then from the 1, Byars scored what Ryan would call "a very gratifying" touchdown.

Landry, his anger melting his frozen veneer, seemed to have amnesia about the game two weeks before. Clearly indignant, he said of Ryan's rub-it-in score, "I wouldn't justify it with a comment," and "I wouldn't run up the score on anybody. A lot of people will be upset. I wasn't really happy with it." Someone asked if he would forget it. "No, I'll probably remember," he said, seething with a bravado that would prove empty.[56] Actually, Landry was just as upset with White, who had strayed from the pocket too often and was yanked in the fourth quarter for Pelluer, who then tried to run for a first down, was slammed hard, and sustained a mild concussion, requiring Landry to put White back in. Other observers returned to an old critique of the team: not enough emotion. And both Dorsett and Walker were griping that Landry needed to choose one tailback and demote the other.

With static noise surrounding him, all a weary Landry could do was say it didn't do the team any good to "have comments like that."[57] He stood pat in a critical Monday night home date against the Giants, when Dorsett ran fourteen times and gained 3 yards—a mortifying career low—and Walker ran nine times for 28. In all, the Cowboys gained 36 yards on twenty-four carries, a club record for futility. The game turned into a shootout between White and Simms, who threw for nearly 500 yards combined, and when Simms was injured, his backup, Jeff Rutledge, added 50 more. Walker lined up as flanker at times and caught six passes, though in the end five Giants turnovers and a career game by Too Tall Jones—who had four sacks and forced two interceptions and a fumble—gave Landry the game, 33–24, sweeping the Giants for the season and outcoaching the newest genius in the fraternity, Bill Parcells.

The Cowboys were 4–3 and carrying some old swagger, until they walked in front of a bus in Detroit, losing to a terrible Lions team 27–17, a dreadful White throwing four interceptions. Schramm, knowing how costly the defeat was, blurted out on his radio show, "Some of the things we're doing are frankly mystifying," adding, "I'm not sure it's all on the players. . . . There's an old saying, 'If the teacher doesn't teach, the students don't learn.'"[58] Oblique as it was, there was no doubt he was talking about Landry, whose old-world sensibilities mandated that such intra-team criticism remain out of the public eye, and who would later say nothing he ever read or heard hurt him more.

In the following game against the Patriots in Foxborough, Landry all but gave up on Dorsett. Walker, carrying the ball twenty-eight times and gaining 173 yards, was the entire running game save for one carry by Dorsett and one by Newsome, in another feral, tense contest that went into overtime. Then, Walker bolted for a thrilling 60-yard touchdown for the win, 23–17. Schramm, no longer mystified, wore a smug look that must have said to Bum Bright, "Now what was that you were saying about firing Tom Landry?" The Cowboys came home for a match against the Dolphins, and Landry, acting on one of his hunches, started Pelluer, who mainly handed the ball off to Walker and watched him scamper for 156 total yards. Dorsett rode the bench. In the end, the Cowboys went under, 20–14, a killer of a loss that made the following contest *big*.

They played the mediocre Vikings at home, and Landry seemed to have settled on Pelluer as the starting quarterback. Then, inexplicably, he went with White, who went wild, throwing for 341 yards and four touchdowns—and three interceptions. Walker ran for a total of 167 yards. Once more a game went into stomach-roiling overtime, and this time, with the defense exhausted from being dragged up and down the field all day, the Vikings took the ball in, game over, 44–38.

Dorsett, who entered that game for seven carries, gaining 19 yards, was now a spot player, a spare part, telling people with a sad laugh that they should "come and see me get my three runs."[59] Rumors were swirling that the Cowboys would move him to Denver, to play for Dan Reeves, at the trading deadline, rumors that Dorsett was wishing and hoping were accurate. But the deadline passed, chaining him to the Cowboys for at least the rest of the season. By now the team as a whole was starting to capsize, with everyone but Walker pretty much disintegrating. And then it *really* got bad.

Their record was 5–6, with the season hanging by a thread, but a gift was up next: a home game against the Atlanta Falcons, who were 3–8 and approaching a rare achievement, finishing dead last in scoring, offense, defense, rushing, and kicking. They scored 13 points a game and gave up nearly 30, they had yielded 34 points or more five times, 48 in their first game, and were coming off a 34–21 beat-down by the Cardinals. In Dallas, few felt it was worth buying a ticket to see the game. Only 40,103 fans showed up, a pittance compared with the last scab game and the smallest crowd ever for a regular-season game at Texas Stadium. Before the Cowboys knew what hit them, the Falcons scored twice, on a 28-yard pass and a 20-yard fumble return. Dallas clawed back to a score of 14–10, but then . . . nothing. A useless White was pulled for Pelluer, who put up a lot of passing yards but no points. Walker, who had taken a lot of accumulated punishment, ran fifteen times for 35 yards.

The Falcons rammed in another touchdown to win, 21–10. It was a walkover, alright, by the worst team in the world, whose players celebrated by chanting expletives about Tex Schramm. Schramm, no longer smug, called this the "lowest point in my career," and had to save Landry his job that day. As the mess deepened, Bum Bright, with the booing ringing in his ears, kept burning hotter and at one point instructed Tex to fire the coach right there.

"What? *Now?*" Schramm replied, incredulously, "in the middle of a game?"[60]

Naturally, Tex talked him down again, but Bright didn't cool off. That night, he was cornered by *Morning News* sportswriter Steve Pate and let his temper fly again. Bright, the renowned football expert, said he was "horrified" at the play-calling, that "it doesn't seem like we've got anybody in charge that knows what they're doing other than Tex," and "the aura of the Cowboys is dying." Bright concluded, "I'm not satisfied with the results we get. We can't go along like we are." All this, of course, reflected directly and indirectly on Landry, who when Pate read him the quotes cracked wise. "At least he didn't give me a vote of confidence," he said. "so I've still got hopes—I guess."[61]

LANDRY WAS not as flippant about the game, his analysis being that "we just weren't quick enough up front. Why, I don't know. I just know we weren't moving as fast as they were."[62] A day later, on December 6, when Bright's rant hit the papers, and the *Morning News* was filled with headlines like "HITTING BOTTOM WITH A THUD," "BRIGHT CRITICIZES COACHING," "IT DOESN'T GET ANY WORSE THAN THIS LOSS," and "LOW LOWER LOWEST," Landry couldn't find a positive, nor could he deny the obvious. Then, even worse news came along: Eugene Lockhart had broken his leg in the game and was gone for the year. "I just thought things were bad until I heard that," Landry said. "That makes things hit bottom for us."[63] The middle linebacker now was Ron Burton, a free-agent rookie. Actually, the worst of it was that the loss to the Falcons struck few as overly surprising. Sherrod mused that the game had "the underwhelming significance of neighborhood hopscotch [and] caused nary a tremor in the NFL scheme of things. At the most, there may have been a fleeting wonder about the Great Cowboy Collapse. The Cowboys have dangled so long off the yardarm, they are easily omitted from any playoff conversation. Oh, America's Team lost another? Pass the dip. So what."[64]

It had taken some time and doing but the Cowboys were past tense. In a crafty parable, Randy Galloway, ostensibly writing about Texas Stadium but aiming at its tenants, eulogized, "That does it. That peels the paint off the franchise walls. That rots the woodwork, cracks the foundation, caves in the ceiling and brings down the rafters. This property is hereby condemned. Level it."[65] In case the point was missed, he added, "The Cowboys are homeless, helpless, and prideless. Worst of show, as in dog show." Frank Luksa, now with the

Times Herald, wrote that they had "no heart. . . . No leadership. No character. No pride," and applied the worst slur one can use against a team—the Cowboys, he said, had "quit."[66]

Landry could only try to steer past the squall, and having said their pieces, Schramm and Bright were backing down. Tex had apologized for his radio comments, saying he made them under "stressful circumstances. I wish I hadn't said them, because they created a misimpression. Obviously, I don't have any criticism of Tom's coaching today any more than I've had in past years."[67] In truth, the odd semiotic—*misimpression*—seemed just a bit too fine. After all, he didn't say he was *wrong* about the teacher not teaching. As for Bright, he amended his remarks this way: "I'm not going to get into any of those kinds of discussions. I'm not even going to recognize those questions," but he too didn't exactly take his imprecations back. And the more he spoke, the less repentant he sounded. "Goodness knows," he said a few days later, "Tom Landry has a reputation for being a good coach," emphasizing *reputation*, "I don't say his coaching is good. I don't say it's bad. . . . I just know we're not winning. We might not have the right leadership on the field or off the field."[68]

Landry found he couldn't hold his tongue, either, about Bright, a man he considered an interloper whose football knowledge could be printed on the head of a pin. Sprinkling a little dirt on his words about Bright, he said, "Do the remarks bother me? Yes, of course they do. I'm human . . . maybe it's a reaction to all the other bad things that have happened to him—the economy around here, for instance. It's just been devastating." It was harder he said, on Alicia than him. "Sure my wife was upset by those quotes. That's what a wife is for, support, and I've got a good wife."[69] He would recall Bright's criticisms as "spouting off."[70] Now it was getting personal.

Even with all the screaming ink, the Dallas sportswriters still couldn't bring themselves to lobby for what Bright wanted; in a popularity contest with Tom Landry, Bum Bright had no chance. To be sure, no one wrote that *Landry* had quit, only his players. Thus, guessing games about who might replace Landry were treated as a joking matter. When rumors flew that Dan Reeves was being considered, Galloway teased, "This is not a demand, or a suggestion, or even a hint, but Tom Landry needs to retire. One of these years, anyway. . . . When he's good and ready, Tom will simply excuse himself, walk right out through the hole in the roof, and he won't be back."[71]

Still, Landry was clearly under fire, and digging in. *Sports Illustrated* in December ran an article entitled "Assault on Mount Landry," with Zimmerman writing, "They have brought out the chisels, and in the still Dallas air you can hear the clink, clink as they take pieces out of the monument that most people thought would stand for all time."[72] Perhaps hardest to take for Landry was that voices from the glorious past were joining in. Roger Staubach, for example, said, "It's a team of whiners, of guys who play to their weaknesses instead of forgetting about them and playing to their strengths. . . . Instead of leadership, they had a bunch of people making excuses, and that's still the mood around there. And when you have that, you don't have a team."

Landry still had his defenders, basically everybody in the game, on every level, past and present, outside of Dallas. Otto Graham, for one, couldn't believe the carping, saying, "There's no way he deserves the abuse he's getting."[73] Sentiment among Cowboys from better years was divided, with some feeling the game had passed him by, while others cast the blame on Schramm for sniping at him. "Tom used to be in charge. Now I believe it's Tex," said the old tough guy Lee Roy Jordan, who theorized that "over the last year and a half management has worked on promoting the image that Tom can't coach anymore. It's not us. It's Tom's fault."[74] Jordan, as with most Cowboys from the glory days, hadn't grown any closer to Landry. Believing the Flex was obsolete, he once spoke to Landry about it. "It wasn't just, hey you gotta go to the 4–3. I had thought it out. I had some ideas about some positioning within the Flex, moving people around so people couldn't recognize what would happen." Pause. "Let's just say Tom wasn't very receptive."[75]

But he didn't despise Landry the way he did Schramm. Few did. And when the pressure eased on the coach, Schramm changed the focus of his criticism to outsiders who had dared quote him. To Tex, the rule was that if Landry was a problem, he was *our* problem, and ours to criticize. Outsiders, on the other hand, were just out to destroy us. "The higher you get, the farther you fall," he said. "The media around the country are just as anxious to see us come down as to do well. But there's one thing the media don't want of the Dallas Cowboys, and that's to see us go away." Bright tried to pull back, too, saying of Landry, "I don't watch him coach, and I don't try to evaluate his coaching versus anyone else's." Asked if he would ever fire Landry, Bright weaseled, "That's an awfully harsh word to use," he hawed. "I don't think that would ever come about. Tom Landry would not be fired. The relationship with Tom and Tex is such . . . well, it just wouldn't happen that way."[76]

But another way was out there on the horizon.

Chapter 27

"YOU'VE TAKEN MY TEAM AWAY FROM ME"

THE LAST THREE GAMES of the 1987 season were, for the first time in memory, a closing stretch of a Dallas Cowboys schedule with no real significance. As it happened, the Cowboys won two of those games, Herschel Walker running for 100 yards in the final two. But as soon as the Cowboys were eliminated from playoff competition, they were a tarnished hallmark. In Paul Zimmerman's view, "America's Team had become America's Cream Puff,"[1] and "an average team with average to less-than-average talent, magnified in the public eye because of what they once were."[2]

The same thing could be said about its hoary head coach, an iconic totem immune to the evolving notion of what a coach should look like. By now, Tom Landry was the only one in his fraternity who clad himself in a carefully tailored suit and matching hat. The others wore a motley swatch of sweater vests, rumpled sweat suits, baseball caps, and muddy spiked shoes. Indeed, if judged on cosmetic appeal alone, Landry was an anachronism, hanging out in God's waiting room. There is no doubt he never would have accepted being just another coat rack for NFL sponsors to hang their sportswear collections on as part of multimillion-dollar deals with the league. By the 2000s, it was actually *illegal* for a coach to wear a suit instead of league-approved Reebok garb. When the 49ers' Mike Nolan, whose father Dick had been the first Landry protégé to coach a team, asked for permission to don a suit in tribute to his old man, who died in 2007, even he was denied. Lord knows the hassle Roger Goodell would have getting Landry into a jumpsuit.

Landry's visage may have attenuated, but under the circumstances, getting out of the 1987 season with a 7–8 record and his team giving up just 8 points more than they scored, didn't seem so horrific, and it eased the siege mentality around Landry, if temporarily. Nothing, though, could ameliorate the siege Tony Dorsett felt he was under. Withering away on the bench, he finished with 456 yards of rushing, a career low and still short of Brown's record, and a distant second to Walker's 891. Dorsett had no desire to set the all-time rushing record in Dallas, and over the off-season he asked to be traded. Landry, who was dreading another year of Dorsett's sad descent, was only too happy to accommodate him, dealing him to the Broncos for a fifth-round draft pick. Touchdown Tony fled to Denver, his star faded.

Dorsett finally broke the record in his last gem, running thirty-two times for 119 yards and two touchdowns in a Broncos game against the Raiders in September 1988. He finished the season with 703 yards and five touchdowns. He intended to play again in 1989 but tore up his knee in practice. His career was over, ending with a total of 12,739 yards, still the eighth highest in league history, but with bitter recriminations and the growing feeling that his years as a Cowboy had negatively affected his life and health. As with many players of his generation, the head shots he took lingered. By the 2000s, he was suffering from memory loss and possibly Alzheimer's. Landry, he said, had once told him he could play despite a broken bone in his back, and the Cowboys' trainers "would see me and just point to the training room [and say] 'Get some ice and heat and come on back out here.'"[3]

If Landry had hung Dorsett out to dry, it was because, as always, he had other plans, for other players. Indeed, he pledged to be more like the first-year coach he was in 1960, working late in the night, concerned only with turning things around. This Landry, the one in his twilight, may have been most conscious of the image he had created by accident for himself, and even his critics saw him in these desperate times as a man seriously after redemption. "As Schramm's monster grew out of control," recalled a florid Bayless of the Landry on his last legs, "Landry hung on for dear life. That's the Landry I liked: the guy behind the curtain frantically yanking the levers that worked the great and powerful Mount Landry."[4] But soon the assault on Mount Landry would regather, led by Bayless yanking some greasy levers of his own.

BY 1988, when he really did deserve a life of leisure, Landry was still making football history, even if at a price to his legacy. He had thrived during America's many transitions, from a postwar to post–Cold War state of mind, from a middle-class boom to a suburban boom. His place seemed to be that of a last gasp of conventionalism, a breath of Ronald Reagan's "morning in America" as it turned to a less romantic afternoon. Men like Landry, giants of a day now done, were facing extinction, only he didn't know it. He could pretend he still mattered as much, but he could not pretend to understand a culture with pastel-colored *Miami Vice* macho, gay chic, and the epidemic of AIDS. Landry had dutifully participated in an AIDS awareness event, feigning sympathy as best he could for those caught in a plague he might well have believed was the price paid for the ultimate biblical sin. As for the game he loved, if he ever did believe football was immune to cultural trends, players like Thomas Henderson had taught him a hard lesson. His losing teams also carried a lesson, that he had fewer answers.

Landry wanted to believe that he was not a relic, and maintained that pose with a grim tenacity. He had a contract he could offer as proof, and still wielded his power swiftly, as shown by his kissing-off of Dorsett. Schramm had seemingly given up trying to foist assistants on him which led Landry to reclaim his old imperial authority. No longer would he give any ground to Paul Hackett, announcing over the off-season that the Cowboys had been retarded by the forced integration of two conflicting offensive systems. Now he would go with a simplified attack built around Walker, making things easier for the quarterback—whoever that would be. Landry had five of them in camp, and went into the season with four, the first time he had ever done that, which would make the continuity anything but simple given that he *still* couldn't choose and stick with just one.

Hackett had little to do now and would ride out the season, trying to stay relevant by tossing in his two cents to the quarterbacks and saying unkind things about Landry's coaching to reporters on the sly. Although he feared Landry had slimed him to owners and general managers, it seemed that on merit he never would get an offer to coach an NFL team. After Landry was deposed, Hackett, offered a front-office paper job, took his Wham and Madonna records back to the college game to become offensive coordinator for Mike Gottfried at Pitt. Hackett ascended to the top spot there when Gottfried quit before the last game of that season, and held it for another three years, without success, before in 1998 he took the job he had once declined, head coach at USC. Only two years later he would be replaced by Pete Carroll. Hired as offensive coordinator for the Jets, he was eventually run out of town by fans and the media for his now conservative offense, before becoming quarterbacks coach for the Bucs and Raiders. In the end, Landry's resistance to him as his successor may have been the best proof that Hackett never was the head coaching material Schramm had rashly judged him to be.

Landry began the 1988 season with Pelluer under center, and Danny White as backup. White would get into two games, and in the second one he suffered a season-ending knee injury, unable to enjoy a new target for his passes. That year's first-round draft pick out of the University of Miami was Michael Irvin, the speed-burning, hot-dogging All-America receiver who had set every school receiving record. He also left the lingering memory of a 73-yard touchdown against Florida State that put the Hurricanes into the Orange Bowl against Oklahoma, where they won the national championship. Irvin was full of bluff, bluster, and self-promotional hype, meaning he was perfect for the Cowboys. Schramm predicted Irvin would fuel the Cowboys' "return to the living."[5] Landry had no hesitation rushing him into the lineup, the first Cowboy rookie receiver to start in twenty years.

Pelluer's first touchdown pass of the season wound up in Irvin's hands, in the opener in Pittsburgh, a 35-yard strike in the third quarter that cut the Steelers' lead to 17–14. Pelluer performed well in the game, completing twenty-four of thirty-seven passes for 289 yards and two touchdowns, but he also threw two interceptions, the second one costing the game. The Cowboys, deep in the Steelers territory, were trailing 24–21 with 3:21 left. They had a third and two on the 4-yard line, a free play in effect to go for the win, with a chip-shot field goal in reserve to tie. Landry called a safe pass—"37" in play-book terminology—to Tim Newsome floating left out of the back-field. But Pelluer, perhaps groggy from a big hit he had taken on the previous play, thought he heard the messenger say "36" in the huddle, and so while everyone else went left, he rolled right—into a swarm of Steelers. Rather than throw the ball out of bounds, he attempted a pass back over the middle for Cosbie, and it was easily picked off by linebacker David Little. Landry, who looked like he had heartburn after the game, covered for Pelluer by saying, "We called the wrong play."[6] And he stuck with him.

To some observers, Pelluer was way in over his head, and it didn't help that there were too many cooks on the Cowboys' sideline, with both Landry and Hackett constantly barking instructions at him, and players getting in his face about being open downfield. Unlike Staubach, who shut out everyone, including Landry at times, Pelluer always seemed unsure of what to do. He also began to feel the heat in the newspapers, which nicknamed him "Wrong Way Pelluer." But he hung in and found other helpful hands in Ray Alexander, a refu-gee from the Canadian Football League (CFL) who signed as a free agent. Alexander caught Pelluer's second touchdown pass in Pitts-burgh and would go on to be the Cowboys' best receiver that season, with fifty-four catches and six touchdowns. Irvin would have thirty-two receptions, averaging over 20 yards a catch, and five touchdowns. Walker rumbled for 79 yards in the opener and was a monster all season, running for 1,514 yards, second to Eric Dickerson, and grab-bing fifty-three passes for 505 yards, just the tenth player in history to break 2,000 total yards of offense.

The Cowboys' problem was that they moved the ball well but couldn't get it into the end zone, scoring only 16.6 points a game. Worse, Landry's defense was held together by baling wire, still rely-ing on thirty-seven-year-old Too Tall Jones for the big stops. Randy White, thirty-five and battered, was benched for rookie Danny Noonan at left tackle and finished his Hall of Fame career nearly invisible. One linebacker, Ron Burton, was an undrafted free agent; another, Gary Cobb, a ninth-round draft pick. Everson Walls and

Michael Downs were slowing down in the secondary. With the dam often broken, the Cowboys gave up 381 points, the twenty-fifth worst in the league, and forced the least number of turnovers, nineteen.

It was all Landry could do to compete each week, and after four weeks he had. The second game was a Monday night visit to the new NFL outpost in Phoenix, Arizona, against the Cardinals, relocated from St. Louis. In the arid desert air at Sun Devil Stadium, he kept the ball on the ground, Walker rushing for 149 yards and a touchdown. Pelluer's 1-yard touchdown run put the game out of reach, and the Cowboys won 17–14. They then had the home opener against the Giants, which became a tight defensive wrangle. In a near replay of opening day, Pelluer blew up at the end. The Giants were up 12–10, but the Cowboys were at New York's 9-yard line on third down, with the game on the line. This time, Pelluer got the play right but threw a blind pass into the end zone, and it was picked off by linebacker Harry Carson.

These were the kind of losses that tried Landry's soul, and they were coming too frequently now. The Falcons came in next, and Landry got even for last year's fitful defeat, but just barely. The Cowboys led 14–0 early but then trailed 20–19 late, setting up a dramatic Pelluer-led comeback that climaxed with a 29-yard touchdown pass to Alexander. The 26–20 victory put their record at 2–2. And then the roof, what there was of it, fell in.

OVER THE next ten weeks, Landry came up snake eyes. Some games were close, some not, and a few were horrendous—35–17 against the Redskins, 43–3 against the Vikings, 38–24 against the Bengals, the latter two in successive games, by which time any dream of a revival was gone. By then, Landry had made some embarrassing slips. Against the Eagles in Philadelphia, sitting on a 23–17 lead with 2:25 left, he misread the yard line. On third and three with the ball on the Eagles 23, a reasonable 40-yard field goal would have put the game away. But Landry thought the ball was on the 30-yard line and called a pass play. Under pressure, Pelluer was called for grounding, resulting in the ball being moved out of field-goal range. The Cowboys had to punt, and Randall Cunningham led an 85-yard drive to win the game at the final gun, 24–23. In his postgame encounter with the writers, Landry explained that he called the ill-fated pass because he wasn't comfortable about a field goal from the 30, though a 47-yarder certainly was makable. When corrected, he insisted he was right. Only later did he realize he was wrong, and he took the blame for that but not the pass. "As far as I was concerned," he said, "the line of scrimmage never mattered because I still hadn't wanted to risk a field goal."[7]

It was as brutal a loss as Landry had ever suffered, and it became exhibit A for those who questioned whether he still belonged on the sideline. Landry called the resulting furor "a public roasting."[8] But if a few writers and TV commentators had broken from the Landry-worshipping commentariat in Dallas, none did so with the venom of Bayless, who now went where no one else would. In his column he disowned the man pulling those clever levers. He called him "senile"[9] and asked, "Will anyone ever save this poor man from himself?"[10] The slur didn't sting Landry as much as it did Alicia, who in a rare interview made a stirring public defense of her husband. "Everyone who knows anything about the game still thinks he's doing a great job," she said. "I know Tommy can coach. He's proved that, hasn't he?" She even challenged him not to waver, saying rhetorically that "if you can't stand the critics you need to get out."[11]

Looking back now, she says, "Actually, I didn't need to challenge him. Tommy knew what it was like to be under fire. It only made him stronger. Besides it was just so silly. That could have happened to any coach, at any age. He coached in hundreds of games and was still a great coach. To call him senile was completely unfair. It was someone trying to get attention. Anyone who would have said a thing like that knew nothing about football, and nothing about Tom Landry."[12] It was surely not what a real man would do, in Tom and Alicia's estimation—and by the cut of Sam Houston's jib, not what a *Texan* would do (Bayless was coincidentally an Oklahoman). In his memoirs Landry's pride and anger flared when he turned the mistake around, upbraiding Bayless, not by name but as "my most vocal critic," for an attack that "reeked of age discrimination"[13]—perhaps the first and only time Landry ever posed as a liberal, taking up the cudgels to protest one of those new-age social causes like ageism.

Bayless, admitting that his salvos about Landry made him a pariah around town, even within the brethren of sportswriters, said, "In Dallas it was difficult for me to criticize Landry's lapses without fans criticizing me for taking a cheap shot at the lovable old nutty professor." He said that while other writers called out Landry, in much milder terms, for his slipup in Philadelphia, "You could have shown some Cowboy fans a tape of the play, and they still wouldn't have believed the ball was on the 23. If Tom Landry said it was on the 30, it was there, sure as God is in heaven."[14] Two years later, hacking away at the Landry legend in his book *God's Coach*, Bayless belittled him by comparing him to Slim Pickens's boneheaded cowboy in *Blazing Saddles*. With much treacle, he wrote, "I often was embarrassed by Landry. How could anyone who knew even a little about football watch this slapstick offense and think Landry was adding to his legend?"[15]

Perhaps one reason for this wild swing at Landry may have been that the coach, not surprisingly, had stopped talking to Bayless directly and responded to his questions with vacant platitudes. But then Landry took a few of the scribes seriously, maintaining close ties only with guys who had come through time with him, such as Sam Blair, Frank Luksa, and Bob St. John, none of whom ever would have turned on the coach. In truth, Landry took flak from writers far less seriously than he did criticism from a minority owner, Ed Smith, a seventy-five-year-old Texas millionaire who owned 25 percent of the team's stock. Though few around the Cowboys knew who he was, Smith traveled with the team on the road, lived conspicuously high on the hog, and assumed he would one day own the majority of stock. In treating Landry like dirty laundry, Smith felt it was his place to step in where Bum Bright had left off the year before. Days after the first loss to the Giants, Smith, infuriated about the last-minute interception that cost the game, phoned Landry in his office and complained about the play called.

Not getting proper deference from the coach, Smith then shot off his mouth in public, repeating his criticism on a radio talk show. And Landry did hear from him again, after the sorry loss in Philadelphia, and again deflected him like a Texas blister beetle. Smith would later get downright nasty about Landry, saying, "Tom had a huge ego.

His attitude was 'I'm a legend' because he read it every day in the paper." And that "Bum should've said, 'bang, 'Landry, you're gone.' But Bum didn't have the courage." Landry, he said, "should have gotten out two or three years ago. He shouldn't have had to tell him to get out. But what are you going to do when you have only 38,000 people showing up at the stadium and you are losing hard cash?"[16]

Landry was almost smugly confident that no writer, not even Bum Bright or Ed Smith, would run him out of Texas Stadium. And he was right. With the added hubris of coming as far as he had intact, he believed he held the keys to the Cowboys' surging into another new era. He was even apparently willing to accept some less than savory aspects of the modern sports culture. One was the rising use of steroids in football. Performance-enhancing drugs were surfacing in baseball and football in the late 1980s, under cover even though they were neither illegal nor expressly banned. Football in particular seemed to demand a shortcut for those not genetically gifted to keep pace with those who were. Players looked to be twice as big as they were in the 1950s and 1960s, and Landry issued no orders banning needles full of juice to anyone who wanted to get bigger and stronger.

According to one source, that would have included around 25 percent of the team then. And Landry equivocated that while he was opposed to steroid use because of health concerns, players needing to keep up with the crowd was "the American way." This was a clear instance of the Cowboys hardly being alone in the football crowd, which didn't legislate against steroids for years. But Pat Toomay cut typically to the bone in saying that Tex Schramm, more so than any others in the game, "envisioned the day all players would be bionic,"[17] at least all on the Dallas Cowboys.

But there was no one bionic on the Cowboys. Only dinosaurs facing extinction.

EVEN AT the start of the 1988 season, the speculation about the *next* head coach of the Cowboys became a running story. "POSSIBLE LANDRY SUCCESSORS" read a *Morning News* headline on September 2, with Gary Myers throwing out Don Shula as a possibility, as Shula, the second-longest tenured coach in the NFL, was "best friends" with Tex Schramm. Various reader polls were taken about whether Landry should stay, with one saying he should, one saying he shouldn't. These were easy games to play, but no one in the press, or Landry, knew what was happening in secret. Over the summer, Bum Bright had quietly begun the same process that Clint Murchison Jr. had under the same shroud of secrecy. This was to be, he knew, his final autumn of putting up with the madness that was the decline and fall of America's Team. The reason was that his own financial burden was as dire as Murchison's had been.

Bright had avoided the same fate until the October 1987 stock market crash, which caused a chain reaction that crippled his extensive savings and loan holdings. Over the next year *Forbes* magazine would chart his net worth plunging from $600 million in 1984 to $300 million in 1988. Then in February 1988, the biggest asset he owned, Bright Banc Savings Association, based in Dallas, was declared insolvent and taken over by federal regulators.[18] The Cowboys organization, which was supposed to be the cherry on his sundae, was more like a sour grape. It lost around $9 million in 1988 alone. Bright's big plans for raising capital by selling penthouse sky boxes at Texas Stadium, called Crown Suites, had fallen flat. Rather than a stampede for them, a good ninety were put up for sale by the lessees.

If 1988 was bad for Bright on the field, it was far worse in his real arena. The crude oil and real estate markets collapsed into free fall, creating an apocalypse for bankers who had stoked all manner of oil-related projects that were now abandoned, leaving the bankers holding the bag. Hundreds of savings and loans closed shop nationwide, and down in the heart of Texas, Bright took another kick to the gut when his two glittering gilt-lined baubles, First Republic Bank Corporation and Bright Banc, collapsed. Early in 1989, newly inaugurated President George H. W. Bush, a semi-Texan to whom Bright had donated hundreds of thousands of dollars to help elect, signed off on government regulation to keep the savings and loan scandal from tanking the entire economy. Bright's banks alone had rung up $4.1 *billion* of debt, which the taxpayers would pay for as they did with the other savings and loans in the form of bailouts— and Bright was removed from the boards of his banks. He also had to begin spending millions to fight government lawsuits against him

and his son-in-law—his business partner, James "Boots" Reader,—
that charged them with fraud, negligence, and lying to regulators. In
1972, when the Resolution Trust Corporation would ask for damages
of $160 million,[19] Bright could only bluster that he was the victim of
an "unprincipled witchhunt . . . against honest men and women to
extort money from them."[20] But he had needed no help in losing half
his fortune, which was a still hefty $300 million.[21]

It was metaphoric that the two owners of the Dallas Cowboys
turned out to be counterfeit wheeler-dealers whose self-indulgent
greed caused America's Team to become just so much terra-cotta
crockery in a rummage sale. In the end, while their facades of wealth
and privilege couldn't keep the creditors away, their stockpiled con-
nections to power did spare them any kind of penalty, or, in Bright's
case, continued millionaire and noblesse oblige status. Still, like
Murchison, there was no way out for Bum. The ego rub of owning
America's Team had turned to leveraging it. Bright set out to get as
much as $180 million for the team, including the stadium leases and
the outstanding debt. He wouldn't even come close to that, but he
had no dearth of offers. This time, however, the difference would
be that Tex Schramm was cut out of the loop. Having been bitten
once too many times by his favorite CEO, whom he rightly knew
would never betray Landry, Bright chose an outsider, a broker from
the Salomon Brothers investment banking giant named Jack Veatch,
to conduct the search for someone whom he knew *would* fire Landry.

It didn't take long for rumors to seep out, though Schramm did
not believe for a second that another sale of the franchise could
happen without his invaluable presence. Asked if there really was
another sale of the Cowboys impending, he said, Of course not. Yet
the pieces of a new Dallas Cowboys regime were already in place
months before the dotted line was signed. Back in August 1988, at
the training ground of the freshly minted national champion Miami
Hurricanes, Jimmy Johnson, he of the mercurial moods and plas-
ter of Paris–perfect hair, casually mentioned to his assistant coaches
that he had a friend who was trying to buy a pro football franchise.
What he also knew was that if his friend succeeded, Johnson would
have a new job. Months later, early in 1989, while jogging with one of
the coaches, he dropped word that a new coach would be needed at

Miami. "You better be ready to push spring practice back," he said. "Looks like the guy's going to buy the team."[22]

THE "GUY," of course, was Jerral Wayne "Jerry" Jones, the most determined rich guy who wanted the Cowboys in his portfolio. Like Bright, Jones was not a Texan but an Arkansan, raised in Little Rock. Always an overachiever, he was a six-foot, 180-pound guard and co-captain on Frank Broyles's 1964 Razorback national championship team. Broyles's staff included Hayden Fry, Johnny Majors, and Barry Switzer, and Jones's roommate was Jimmy Johnson. Unlike the others, Jones didn't have football in his future—not yet. He went into his father's insurance business then struck gold with oil and gas, his Jones Oil and Land Lease company raking in at least $50 million and a subsequent company, Arkoma, another $40 million. He then sold Arkoma for $174 million. Bucking the economic crises of the decade, unlike Murchison and Bright, he would run up a fortune of $300 million.[23]

Nearly all of Jones's drilling explorations were in Arkansas and Oklahoma, and he had no particular fondness for the Cowboys. In fact, in past years he had tried to buy the San Diego Chargers. Now forty-seven, dashing, and ruddy-faced with a tight-jawed smile, he had money, a former Arkansas beauty pageant winner as a wife, and craved a trophy team of his own. He was belatedly seduced by the Cowboys' mystique and bottom line—the realities of which Bright was not eager for him to know. Jones had one condition: he would buy the team only if Jimmy Johnson, an old friend who had coached at Oklahoma State before going to Miami, would be the head coach. Pointedly, he called Johnson "the best coach in football." Soon, Jones had another condition. He had decided he didn't need to pay a general manager because he knew enough about the game and the business of football to annex that role as well. This, he trusted, would force Schramm to voluntarily quit and require him to sell his 3 percent stock to Jones. With the departure of the downgraded Gil Brandt a given, that would mean the entire Dallas Cowboys' power structure would fall before Jerry Jones's feet.

Bright had no problem with Jones's stipulations. Though he

wouldn't say it, he was out not just for money but for blood. According to the sports anchor at channel 8, Dale Hansen, "Bright wanted Schramm and Landry to be stuck just like they were. He reveled in it. He called me bragging about it—'Schramm spent more of my money buying goddamn houses for his girlfriends, and that sonofabitch Landry treated me like shit. To hell with both of them.'"[24]

Jones's impulsiveness, which set him apart from many of the bidders who were terrified by the prospect of having to fire Landry, gave him the inside track. That Schramm was kept out of the loop was evident by the fact that he too had his eye on Jimmy Johnson, envisioning him joining the Cowboys' staff in 1989 and being tutored by Landry, who would make a farewell tour of the league and then, when his contract was up, exit gracefully. Tex figured Johnson would leap at the chance, more so because Brandt had known him since the mid-1960s, when Johnson began his coaching career as an assistant at Louisiana Tech and claimed the then-unknown Johnson had gotten the Miami job in 1984 on his recommendation.

Meanwhile the season dragged on, miserably, in a hail of dropped balls, penalties (the most ever by a Cowboys team), blown assignments, and general confusion on the sideline—all accompanied by shriveling crowds, booing, and tart headlines, but no real assumption that Landry was coaching his last games. Landry's what-me-worry stance about his future was reflected in a story that noted, "It's easy for critics to point to Tom Landry's age, but those who know him best insist he's still able."[25] Another told of Landry's evaluations "with an eye toward '89" and reported that Landry had "moves under his hat, and being able to look ahead is one of the rare benefits of being 2–8."[26] Still, Landry's definitive plans to continue on, with yet another contract extension, created a sticky wicket. As the headline of a Blackie Sherrod column read, "CHANCE FOR A GRACEFUL RETIREMENT PASSES LANDRY BY."[27]

Sherrod, in another column late in the season, dropped into the mix an early clue that the Cowboys would soon be under new ownership again, construing it as good news for Landry: "This week, the hunch hints that Cowboys sale is right on the brink, to [Dallas Mavericks] owner Don Carter. And if indeed Carter becomes the new Cowboy owner, it would probably mean Tom Landry could coach as long as he dang well wants to."[28] By then, the season had become a disaster. In November, Landry had given Schramm's beau ideal, Kevin Sweeney, a shot at starting quarterback, but after two mediocre games he went back to Pelluer, putting Tex in a foul mood. In mid-December, Schramm got into a scuffle with a local TV reporter in the hallway outside the Cowboys' locker room at Texas Stadium.

If it was to be Landry's last season, however, the team had to have a moment when they would win one for the old man. It happened in the penultimate game, in Washington, eliminating the Redskins from the playoff chase with a throwback effort, Landry's defense holding them to 24 yards of rushing and intercepting three Doug Williams passes, and Pelluer throwing three touchdowns passes to Irvin, the last in the fourth quarter to win, 24–17. In the locker room the Cowboys celebrated like fresh-faced boys, and Tom Rafferty called Landry over and gave him the game ball, tears streaming down both of their faces. "This is for the guy who stuck by us when we were 2–12," the grizzled center said. "He's taken a lot of shit. And he's going to be the guy who gets us back on top."[29] Yet he couldn't finish the season with a win, losing ignominiously to Buddy Ryan, who again ran up the score, 23–7. In the end the Cowboys finished at 3–13, territory Landry had not tread since his first two seasons in Dallas. As he left the field that day there was a palpable sense that he might be walking off for the last time, as a loser, a parenthetical figure in the NFL galaxy, leaving not on a trail of huzzahs and flower pedals but barely noticed, small and irrelevant.

No one really knew what to say to make anyone feel better. The Cowboys were ranked No. 21 in offense and No. 25 in defense, but for the first time since they landed Too Tall Jones in 1973, Dallas would have the No. 1 pick in the draft. Landry was confident he had the essentials in Walker and Irvin and was itching to spend that pick on a quarterback he lusted for, UCLA's All-American Troy Aikman, the classic big, strong pocket-passer. He got to see Aikman up close when the Bruins came to Dallas for the Cotton Bowl against the Arkansas Razorbacks on January 2. Landry watched him during practices at Texas Stadium and then attended the game, sitting in the VIP lounges not far from Jerry Jones, who was there to root for his old alma mater. Landry came away pumping up Aikman, who threw a touchdown pass in the 17–3 Bruins win and was the game's co-MVP, as the next great quarterback. "He said, 'This guy is something else. Whoever has him within three years is gonna be the Super Bowl champions,'" recalls Alicia Landry. The feeling was mutual. Aikman said it would be like a dream to play for Landry. "And his mother told me the same thing: that her son was ecstatic he'd be playing for Tommy."

THE JERRY JONES business was being kept hush-hush. Indeed, with the Super Bowl being in Miami, Schramm invited Jimmy Johnson to sit in the Cowboys' box so he could work him, given that the Eagles' owner, Norman Braman, was also interested in him. Johnson, playing it coy, was delighted to sit alongside the Cowboys' legendary brain trust, but he knew more than he was free to say. Moreover, Landry, none too pleased at having to put up with another young coach who wanted his job, said almost nothing to Johnson, making it clear that even if Johnson would have accepted the offer, the plan would never have worked. As a championship head coach, Johnson was far more important than Hackett, and if it hadn't worked with Hackett, it would have been disaster with Johnson.

Jerry Jones was first mentioned in the Dallas papers two days before Christmas. In a *Morning News* story headlined "ARKAN-SAS MAN SHOWS INTEREST IN COWBOYS" came word that "Arkansas businessman Jerry Jones confirmed making a bid [and said] 'I have shown an interest, and I have been doing my homework.' . . . The size of the thing is that it is in Dallas, Texas. If it were in any other city in the United States, I wouldn't be interested."[30] At the time, Jones was still one of many suitors. The one getting the most attention was Ed Smith, who planned to expand his stock to majority status. Others were heavy hitters with a higher profile than Jones, such as Don Carter, LA Lakers owner Jerry Buss, oilman and movie mogul Marvin Davis, Donald Trump, hotelier Bob Tisch, and a consortium of Japanese businessmen, though the symbolic impact of America's Team being owned by Japan made Bum Bright reel.

By February, Jones was just about home. Almost none of the bidders would pay for the lease at Texas Stadium. Jones, who would, had been given a tour of Valley Ranch by Jack Veatch, and word of an impending deal began to seep into the papers. Only now did Schramm know he had been, as Landry would later say, "totally shut out,"[31] but he still knew nothing about Jones and Bright's merged plan to depose Landry and himself. On Thursday, February 23, Landry conducted meetings at Valley Ranch with his coaching staff. One of them was the new quarterbacks coach, who, unlike Hackett, was someone from the "family": Jerry Rhome, Dandy Don Meredith's old backup. Landry had also finally relented about the 3–4 defensive set. He was counting on a busy off-season. That night, however, he and Alicia were in the den in front of the TV, his nose buried in paperwork, when at 9:30 a teaser ran on channel 5 about the sale of the Cowboys and the new head coach. Alicia bolted upright on the couch. "Did you hear that?!" she said.

Not only did he hear, it seemed all of Dallas did. In the next half hour the phone kept ringing, some of the calls from reporters asking what was happening. Landry accurately said he knew nothing about the sale or a new coach. Neither did Schramm, who was adamant that there was nothing to it. When a reporter from another station called him, Schramm was in a snit, raging that the reporter who broke the story "just fucked up his entire career. That stupid fucker is dead," adding, "Do you really think they'd sell the Cowboys and I wouldn't fuckin' know about it?" When the report was amplified on the ten o'clock news, Alicia said, "It can't be true." Landry said he thought the story was "farfetched" and assured her, "If Tex doesn't know about it, there may be nothing to it."[32] They went to bed expecting better news in the morning.

Actually, Schramm's ire may have been a reaction to his slow realization that he was being played. That day he had gotten a call from Don Shula, who told him that Jimmy Johnson had contacted his son David, an assistant coach with the Dolphins, about joining his Cowboys staff.[33] So there was plenty to the rumor, which was fed to channel 5 by Jack Veatch a day before, but with the proviso that the station sit on the news until Landry could be informed he was out. Both the outgoing and the incoming owner wanted no part of such a chore, neither wanting to be the villain. They could have easily marched into Landry's office at Valley Ranch and done it themselves, but instead they sat waiting for Tex to deliver Landry's head to them. Neither did Landry feel he needed to call Bright for answers.

And so nothing happened. The deal wasn't even finalized yet, but Veatch's leak had exploded. Jones was becoming freaked out by the fevered coverage. "I had no idea of the impact the media was about to have," he said. "I'd just never dealt with that quantity or quality of reporting."[34] Scores of reporters descended on Valley Ranch, others outside Bright's downtown office. Landry still went about his work, every passing minute shaking his head that a rumor could create such a circus. On Friday, he again spoke with Schramm, who seemed to Landry in "obvious distress. Beneath his obvious agitation, I sensed a frustrated helplessness I'd never known in Tex Schramm before."[35] Tex was still shrewd though. If Jones was setting him up to be the fall guy for Landry's impending dismissal, the game plan for Schramm was to turn the table on Jones. If the new guy wanted Landry out, he would be the one who would catch hell for it.

JONES, ANOTHER shrewd man, had come to realize the very same thing. He told Bright he would not sign the deal until he could meet with Landry personally, that he owed the old coach that much. He wanted to do it that afternoon at Valley Ranch, but by the time he summoned up enough nerve to do it, Landry had left. Then, seeking to avoid the media crush that weekend, Tom and Alicia decided to head down to Austin Friday night to spend the weekend and to be with their daughter Lisa, whose birthday was in a few days. Landry called Schramm and asked him if he should. "Go ahead," Tex told him.

That night, Jones and Johnson and their wives chose to have dinner at Mia's, a Tex-Mex restaurant in downtown Dallas that happened to be one of Landry's favorite eateries, with signed photos of the coach festooning the walls. That choice was either a colossal mistake or a colossal affront to Landry, and when they were spotted, gasps went up, calls were made, and reporters were sent running there. A smug Jones told them not to assume anything, and he seemed to greatly enjoy the attention as they munched on their burritos. A few hours later, at three o'clock in the morning, Jones signed the deal with Bright—on a napkin, he said—at the latter's Bright Banc office.

The deal was for a good chunk less than Bright shot for, $90 million for the team, $50 million for the stadium leases. Jones also assumed the $10 million mortgage on the Valley Ranch grounds. And he had to earmark $1 million for the man he was about to cut loose after twenty-nine years from the team he built, and another $3 million to buy back Schramm's stock. As it was, to be able to afford the deal, Jones needed to keep the self-important Ed Smith around as a minority stockholder, to kick in $18 million toward the sale—though Jones could be relieved that neither Landry nor Schramm had kept their original stock at 1959 prices, and might have appreciated the roundabout irony that Clint Murchison, by buying back that stock, had paved the way for the second sale of his team to a man who would seek to extirpate the history Murchison had built.

On Saturday morning, Johnson returned to Miami, knowing he was the de facto coach of the Cowboys. A sign painter at the private airport where Jones had parked his Learjet had painted the image of a silver-and-blue Dallas Cowboys helmet on the plane's tail. The sale would be announced that day, but there was still one piece of business left, the most vexing one, and Jones would have to chase Landry hundreds of miles to do it. Landry, who had returned to the cockpit and earned his pilot's license a few years before, would fly his single-engine Cessna 210 to Austin. He arose early and called the airport for the weather and a flight plan. He then grabbed his *Morning News* to read over breakfast. On page one, he nearly had to rub his eyes when he saw a photo of Jones and Johnson laughing it up at Mia's, in a booth he had probably sat in a hundred times. When Alicia saw it, she had no doubt what the intention was—"They were sticking it to us."

Yet Landry still hoped for the best. In fact, he left for the airport after taking a call from a businessman friend who said he was trying to put together a late bid that would beat Jones's. As the Cessna rose above the hazy skyline, the last thing Landry would believe was that he was peering down, for the last time as coach, at the tempestuous geography he had ruled. But he still had no idea what had been decided down there. Indeed, at that very hour Schramm was at Bright Banc. Tex had promised he would call him in Austin with any news.

There would be news, big news. Once the papers were signed and vetted, Jones still wanted Schramm to fire Landry for him, but Tex had made that a moot point. A few hours later, Jones had his Learjet gassed up, and he and Schramm prepared for a trip to Austin. When they arrived in the early afternoon, Landry, Alicia, and Lisa, along with her husband, Gary Childress, were on a newly built golf course in Hidden Hills near Lake Travis, a few miles from Lakeway. Tom Jr. had flown in as well and joined them there for a leisurely eighteen holes. They had just completed the first hole when an attendant found the coach and said there was a phone call for him at the clubhouse, from Mr. Tex Schramm. When Landry picked up, Tex had to say only three words for him to know it was over: "It isn't good."[36]

Schramm said he and Jones were going to fly down to Austin to see him. Landry's first instinct was to say, "Don't bother. Save your gas." A face-to-face firing may have been something Jones felt he owed Landry, but Landry didn't feel he owed Jones the honorable way out of the mess he had made for himself. But this was *Landry*, the man who practiced the honor that he preached, at least to his own satisfaction. And so he would play his execution like a nobleman. He even gave Schramm directions to Hidden Hills for the execution. He then returned to the course and told his family what was about to happen.

"He was hurt, I could see it in his eyes," recalled Alicia, "but he was trying to be as upbeat as he could. He said, 'Well, I guess this is it.' He told Lisa and me to go back to our house and he'd meet us there. We were all very upset that Jerry Jones never gave him a chance to leave gracefully. Mr. Jones didn't even know Tommy, never had spoken with him. My God, this was no ordinary coach. I just felt so bad for him. Before I left I gave him a big hug, something we usually refrained from doing in public, and we just sort of stood that way for a minute, not saying a word. We'd always wondered what it would be like when it was over. Now we knew."

Landry finished the round with his son and Childress while waiting for Jones and Schramm. They arrived two hours later and climbed out of a golf cart in their business suits, looking very out of place. Jones nervously stuck out his hand. Landry shook it, said,

"We can talk over here," and led them to an office inside the club. Inside the small room, Jones found it hard to look the old man in his eyes. Landry and Schramm sat in easy chairs, Jones on a plump couch across from them, with Tom Jr. standing behind him, making him more nervous.

As Jones stammered on for a bit trying to find the right way to say what he had to, Schramm, the man who allegedly ran the NFL, the man who had shared a thousand intimate conversations in small rooms with Tom Landry and always dominated the conversation, sat limp and silent, letting Jones fend for himself. Later, he would be described as "emotionally wounded" by the entire sequence of events,[37] in particular by Landry's response when Jones confirmed he had bought the Cowboys and was bringing in Jimmy Johnson as coach, a response typically simple and declarative, framing the disbelief deep within his Texas soul that it could have come to this.

"You've taken my team away from me," said Tom Landry.[38]

LANDRY LATER would call the meeting "a blur" and say that "a jumble of feelings crowded my mind. Anger. Sadness. Frustration. Disappointment. Resignation."[39] When Jones said, "I wish I could make this easier for you," Landry, thinking of how Jones let him twist in the wind, held him accountable for "not handling the situation the way it should have been." Jones, who was itching to get out of there, apologized without really accepting blame and got up to leave with Schramm, the necktie party for God's Coach having taken perhaps ten minutes. The deed done, he looked to Landry "visibly pale." Schramm got up and clutched Landry's hand, looking to his old confrere like "a disaster survivor—wounded and in shock. Tears filled his eyes." Almost in a whisper, he mouthed the words, "I'm sorry."[40] Recalled Landry, "My own eyes misted over and I mumbled something. . . . There weren't any adequate words for that moment. Just raw emotion." Both men could tell that something had died inside each of them that day.

Jones strode to the parking lot, so disoriented that he got into the wrong car and tried to start it. Tom Jr., shaken by what he had just witnessed, could only say, "I'm sorry, Dad."[41] They went to change clothes in the dressing room, and Landry called Alicia with the news she already knew, then she and Lisa drove back to Hidden Hills for Lisa's birthday dinner at the country club. "It wasn't a wildly happy occasion," Landry noted, but it was the last time for a while he had some degree of solitude before the reporters would descend on him wherever he went. That afternoon, when word broke about his firing, TV crews began to camp out in front of the Landrys' house at Lakeway. Incredibly, a helicopter from a local station landed in front of the clubhouse there before being ordered to take off again by the club manager. Up north, Dallas reporters headed for Valley Ranch for the press conference introducing Jones and Johnson that night, which would be carried on stations all across the state. At Hidden Hills, meanwhile, Landry tried to ignore the whirlwind.

"Tommy was never one to get emotional or show anger," Alicia says, "but I was angry and showed it. It was mishandled so badly. At that point Tommy just wanted to fulfill his contract and rebuild the team. One more year and that would have been it. That's how they should have handled it. I just couldn't believe they had done that to him. It took a long time to get over it. For both of us."

Tom Jr.: "It could have been done with dignity. Tex got it right: Let Dad finish his contract and walk away with his head high and hand the reigns to Jimmy. But it was a done deal, without any discussion. Everyone was kept in the dark, then all of a sudden there was the restaurant thing and guys are coming onto the golf course to fire you. There wasn't anything dignified about it. Dad could take it, but when you're made to feel like a pile of trash, how are you supposed to feel? That wasn't a firing, it was a degrading spectacle. You don't treat a Tom Landry like that."

Naturally, Jones had a much different recollection about those ten minutes of infamy. He would tell of a testy Landry who told him his vigil to Austin was self-serving "grandstanding," throwing Jones back on his heels. Landry, he said, was unfair to *him*, given that "I really thought I was going out of my way to do the right thing. . . . I honestly don't know what else I could have done under the circumstances."[42] He also insisted that Schramm had backed him up. The one thing he could not claim, however, was that he ever gave Landry a chance to plead his case. Nor that Landry wasn't entitled to every ounce of his pride.

AT VALLEY RANCH, the announcement would be described by the *New York Times* as "an emotional, Texas-sized news conference . . . one more unbelievable act in the drama that has grabbed not only North Central Texas, but has created an entire state of mind as well."[43] That state was obvious from the start when reporters began peppering Jones, Schramm, Bright, and Johnson about the manner in which Tom Landry had been fired. All said nothing but wonderful things about him, Schramm with watery eyes that gleamed in the bright lights. In the *Morning News* Gary Myers wrote that as Schramm went on, "his voice cracked and he cried. It was almost too much to comprehend." Of the fateful golf course termination, Schramm managed to say, "It was a very difficult meeting. It's very, very sad. It's tough when you break a relationship you've had for 29 years. That's an awful long time. For Tom, he was emotional."[44]

Jones had no tears to shed, but he breathlessly paid homage to Landry in words he could not muster when face to face with him. "This man is like Bear Bryant to me, like Vince Lombardi to me. If you love competitors, Tom Landry's an angel! . . . He was magnificent to me for what he had been through. He's special. Tom Landry is the Cowboys." Waving his arms and pounding the table in front of him, he went on, "Jimmy Johnson would be the first to tell you that he couldn't carry Tom Landry's water bucket!" But then, pivoting, he stressed "I wouldn't have bought the Dallas Cowboys if Jimmy Johnson couldn't be my coach!"[45]

Clearly, Jones wanted to have it both ways, something he never would be able to pull off. Mostly, he tried to butter up his new town. "I will sell my house in Little Rock and move to Dallas," he said, only underlining his carpetbagger status. "My entire office and my entire business will be at [the Cowboys'] complex. This will be a hands-on operation. I want to know everything there is to know, from player contracts to socks and jocks and television contracts. This is my company, and I will be making all the decisions. The Cowboys will be my life!" Football fans would learn for the first time that night that a good way to listen to Jerry Jones was with their hands over their ears. And Jimmy Johnson learned how immense his problem was replacing a legend. Thankfully, he didn't try any of Jones's bluster. A native of Port Arthur, he leaned on his roots, "I'm extremely proud to be back in Texas," he said, conceding, "I wish there could have been better circumstances about me coming into this situation. . . . It hurts me when someone says I did something out of disrespect. If I did, I'm sorry. But I've always wanted to be head coach of the Dallas Cowboys."

That Jones wanted to be the general manager of the Dallas Cowboys was also clear. If anything, Jones had less use for Tex than Tom, and far less reason to be respectful of him. During the press conference, he had a good laugh noting that Schramm, who usually positioned himself closer to the cameras than anyone else, hung in the background, leaning against a wall. "Tex is used to standing out front, but he's a little behind me here tonight," giggled Jones, who then lied, "He's still going to be an important part of the Cowboys, but it's my vote. I'm the owner."[46] Schramm blanched at that. Afterward, Tex invited some of his favored reporters into his office for a round of scotch and sodas and told them in confidence, "I have a lot of work to do with this sonofabitch." Then, after a long belt, "Goddammit, I can't believe he'd say those things."[47]

ON THAT Sunday morning, Landry flew home and went right to Valley Ranch to clean out his office. By then, the early editions were out, and they were not kind to Jones. In the *Morning News* Frank Luksa tarred him for the "undignified, thoughtless manner" in which Landry was let go, and columnist David Casstevens minced no words; Jones, he wrote, was "dumber than a box of rocks, public-relations wise."[48] Wrote Gary Myers, "Jones' sudden firing of coach Landry . . . before bothering to discuss the matter with him should stun and infuriate people who don't even follow professional sports. In a society where there still is a sometimes naive belief that great performance and loyal service will be rewarded, the callous dismissal of the Dallas Cowboys coach stings like the snap of a wet towel . . . [and] indicates he still has a lot to learn about the relationship between the Cowboys and their fans." Myers suggested that a "fitting tribute" would be to rename the Irving Cheeseburger as Tom Landry Stadium.[49]

Landry for his part did not wallow in self-pity. He didn't arrange his own press conference. After the crush of the night before, the Cowboys' playland was yawningly empty except for a solitary cameraman and reporter from a Dallas TV station, whom he allowed to follow him on his sad rounds as he moved among drafty corridors, lingering in private thought as he passed one or another photograph on the wall. When the footage ran that night, the hyper-cynical Bayless, Jones's lone ally in the media, was sure Landry had plotted all this as a play for sympathy, acting out "his every sigh and shake of the head." Landry, he wrote, had even "dressed perfectly for the part: open-collared flannel shirt, work-in-the-garden pants, bifocals, no hat. . . . He moved slowly, as if what Jones had done to him had suddenly aged him twenty years."[50]

However, if Landry thought he had earned sympathy, he hardly had to choreograph it. He was moving in a cloud of cumulus condolence. On Monday morning, he would be back at Valley Ranch to say good-bye to his staff and whatever players would be there for an off-season workout. Earlier he said a tearful good-bye to Tex Schramm, whom *he* pitied, having figured out what Tex refused to see: that his days of power were soon over.

Landry had to hold himself together as he told his troops, "This will be our last meeting together." He aggrandized them, saying they would never quit, then broke down, his shoulders heaving as he sobbed, unable to go on. The dozen or so players looked down at the floor, crying along with him. Landry, dabbing at his eyes, went on, "The thing I'm going to miss most is my relationship with the coaches and you, you the players, I'll be with you in spirit, always. I love you guys. God bless you and your families."[51] It had taken him twenty-nine years to give in to the softness of the heart, enough to tell grown men he loved them, an affection he had always reserved exclusively for his family and his God, not even for his team as an abstraction. When he began to walk away, the players started to applaud, one by one, then in unison. He went to his office, had pictures taken with the secretaries, said farewell to the coaches, and drove away from Valley

Ranch. Only then, without looking back, did he accept the reality. It was over.

The departure suggested that of an abdicating king, though predictably to Bayless it was a sham. Some of the players who cried with Landry and gave him an ovation, he claimed, told him they had in private celebrated, with one unnamed player allegedly saying, "Guys kept raising a glass and saying 'Here's to the baldheaded motherfucker. He got it just the way he treated so many of us.'" Then Bayless reached beyond chutzpah and unctuously wrote that he was "relieved" for Landry, and worse, that "Jerry Jones was the best thing that could have happened to Tom Landry. . . . I believe God used Jones to free God's Coach from himself."[52] Such audacity, he later admitted upon reflection, came off as "incomprehensible blasphemy" to his readers. Not to mention to the troops Landry had commanded, like Bob Lilly, who said that day, "A lot of old Cowboys are crying tonight."[53]

ON THAT Sunday, February 26, the new regime was almost an afterthought. The media coverage fixated on the deposing of Mount Landry." "SHOCK. DISBELIEF. ANGER," "GOODBYE TOM. HELLO JIMMY," "TO THE END, LANDRY TRUE TO HIMSELF," "FANS SORRY LANDRY NOT PART OF FUTURE," and, simply, "GOODBYE," were some of the headlines. Editorials drew all sorts of allegorical lessons from his legacy. Sam Blair, who had grown old with him, penned Landry's Cowboys obituary in a column titled "End of an Era," writing, "When I was a rookie in 1961, Tom Landry was just like he is now—a coach with strong beliefs. [He] ran the Cowboys the way he ran his life—with faith."

The story had gone nationwide, the topic of sullen veneration from the establishment elites, led by Pete Rozelle, who said he hadn't felt this way since Vince Lombardi's death and that Landry was "a tremendous role model for kids and our fans."[54] Rozelle, with only one season left before retiring, had cause to be melancholic. Papa Bear Halas and Steelers patriarch Art Rooney had died during the decade. Paul Brown was in ill health and would go in 1991. And now the last of the old-guard coaches was out.

To some, the victimization of Landry owed its genesis to the descent of Dallas itself, and in a larger lens, Texas itself, an argument that had merit given the factors that led to the changes of ownership, factors that had buckled the state's economy. It was still a fresh story in May when Randy Galloway wrote, "In this town, the biggest sports story of the year, of the decade—the biggest ever—actually was 'Tom Landry Fired.' Call it The Impossible Scheme." And Jerry Jones would never escape from what became in Dallas, inevitably, the "Saturday Night Massacre."[55]

"In a way, Jerry got a bum rap," reflected Frank Luksa. "It was Bum Bright who brought Tom down. Jerry isn't a bad guy. He just got caught in a trap. He had to play his card—Jimmy Johnson—to get the team, and that left no way to change coaches slowly. And let's face it, Jerry never figured out how to make it look like he cared about Tom Landry."[56]

Jones would try, painfully and insincerely at times, to do that, always watching what he said about Landry, who reciprocally had to be careful with his words about Jones, which were few and far between. Jones, he would say as sincerely as he could, had a right to bring in his own coach and wished him well. But what else did he need to say? After all, Bright and Jones had managed to do what Landry never could do for himself: make him a figure of deep sympathy. Besides, he would talk all day about his old teams and players with not a hint of circumspection, knowing that to the masses he was talking about the *real* Cowboys.

With the media crawling over them, Landry and his wife took a month-long vacation in Palm Springs. When they returned in early April, the mayor and business and civic leaders, with Roger Staubach as point man, had raised $90,000 for a Tom Landry Day celebration. It would include a Civic Center Plaza tribute and a "Hats Off to Tom Landry" parade—or, as a sour Bayless clucked, "charade"[57]—with marching bands and floats. When Staubach had told him of the plans in February, Landry was duly flattered but wondered if anyone would actually show up two months hence. His answer came as they drove downtown for the event on April 11. There were around a hundred thousand people along the parade route, some seven deep, and nearly a hundred of his former players had turned out for the proceedings, including Staubach, Tony Dorsett, Herschel Walker, Drew Pearson, Walt Garrison, Bob Lilly, and Lee Roy Jordan. Tex Schramm wasn't there, having gone to Europe on league business. Jerry Jones wisely stayed in his office. There were no Cowboys officeholders there, no cheerleaders. Miss Fort Worth rode on a float.

The players rode in classic cars behind the 1954 Buick Skylark carrying the Landry family, who waved to the throngs, Tom looking overwhelmed. People yelled things like, "We love you Tom!" and carried banners. There were marching bands, a choir singing "The Battle Hymn of the Republic." At the ceremony, telegrams were read from President George Bush and Billy Graham. Bob Hope called in a tepid comedy bit—"You've had winning teams for so long that a lot of people thought that Tom Landry was the capital of Texas." Governor Bill Clements made the old Army Air Corps veteran an honorary admiral in the Texas Navy. After the bash, Landry was taken by helicopter to Texas Stadium to coach a flag-football game between the old-goat Cowboys and a team of old-goat Redskins. He then was driven to a TV station for a thirty-minute interview.

Not even when the Cowboys won the Super Bowl was there a hoedown like this. Some sharklike Republican Party operatives began trying on that day to talk him into running for governor, senator, whatever he preferred. He likely would have won too, but Tom Landry, a man smarter than most, wanted no part of it. The politics of football had been vulgar, soul-robbing, and corrupting enough.

BACK AT Valley Ranch, Jones had taken over Schramm's luxurious office suite for himself and, poring over the books, became as shocked by Schramm's profligate spending as Bum Bright had been. The Cowboys had 109 nonplaying employees, three times the number on the normal NFL team. For such reasons, the Cowboys organization, for all its scent of wealth, had never turned much of a profit. Unlike Bright, Jones was prepared to take a pickax to that budget and payroll. He would run the Cowboys, he vowed, as a bottom-line business, not a vanity project—famous last words, to be sure.

Jimmy Johnson, much more of a martinet than Landry, with none of the gooey nougat beneath Landry's hard shell, had no qualm telling reporters how shocked he was at the shambles Landry had left him. He immediately fired most of the coaches, ending Jerry Rhome's tenure before it began, and brought in several of his Hurricane assistants, but he kept, for now, five Landry holdovers, foremost being Dick Nolan. Dave Shula indeed became his offensive coordinator. Johnson also released players he prejudged would not make the cut, big and small names alike. When Randy White came up to him after one of the first bone-rattling practices and said he might not be able to always complete all the drills, Johnson sent him walking, as he did with Too Tall Jones. The Cowboys, he groused, had gotten too soft and too used to a "country club" environment.

Landry must have been faintly amused that, in this revisionist light, he had morphed from the archetypical "strong" coach to that of a weak sister. The plain truth, not the revision, was that Landry for all his flaws had never been a weak coach, and his controlled temperament was the perfect preachment of his longevity, in loud contrast to Johnson, who blew hot and cold and would clash with the equally mercurial Jones even in victory, sending Johnson to a broadcasting career within a few years. Seen in the prism of Jones's stormy reign, a silent owner and a near-silent coach wasn't such a bad deal.

In a farewell missive to the inscrutable yet somehow endearing man under the hat, Paul Zimmerman wrote, "In over 20 years, I got to know Landry as a writer gets to know a coach, never anything more. But I never asked him a question that was not answered honestly. I've written plenty of negative stories about the Cowboys, but not once has he mentioned any of them or shown any resentment."[58] That was how he came in, and how he left. Within a year of his expatriation, he was still *Landry*, a man of sublime grace and rectitude, but no longer was football part of that old correlation with faith and family. By the end of the 1989 season, a season he largely ignored, he said, "I felt strangely detached from the Dallas Cowboys. Because the old Cowboys were gone forever."[59]

He didn't need to say it, but he had closed the door on that extended era. He was, he knew, the last Cowboy.

THE
APOSTLE

ALL THE POSTDATED ADULATION aside, being fired from what had seemed not like a job as much as a permanent state of mind had left Tom Landry feeling lifeless. The Saturday night after Jerry Jones violated his golf game with the most awkward termination of employment ever carried out, the ex-coach of the Dallas Cowboys had a fitful sleep and awoke, for the first time in his life, not wanting to get out of his bed. Indeed, it was the lowest he ever had been. "Worse," he would say, "than any playoff loss marking the sudden end of a season. After this, there were no more seasons."[1]

Yet the most trenchant irony about Tom Landry was that this rugged individualist from the plains of South Texas was never really a fan of the Dallas Cowboys, not in the sense humans who follow a team arc. He had never stepped back far enough to know the vicarious joy and agony of rooting. Thus when Jerry Jones took his cost-cutting to the mortally insulting level of taking away the tickets of Cowboys players and coaches, including Tom and Alicia Landry's, the practical effect was far less than the symbolic one. As Alicia makes clear, neither of them would have used those tickets anyway. Neither would have felt that Texas Stadium required their presence after church on Sundays, and their Monday nights didn't need after-midnight drives home. Landry now knew less about the league than most fans; he had prepared for each game, one at a time, without following the trends, streaks, and achievements. He needed to check the standings in the papers to know who was winning and losing.

Loyalist that Landry was, he and Alicia had a strong attachment to only one team—the Giants. Their memories of those rollicking, nascent days on a team that introduced them to the big town, and a new world of culture and social diversity, only became more golden as the madness in Dallas intensified. The Landrys were nearly as happy when the Giants won the Super Bowl in 1987 as they were when the Cowboys left New Orleans twice as champions; and they would be again when the Giants won it in 1991. Landry took his enforced exile as an opportunity to do what he hadn't before. Pointedly, just as the first Cowboys season without him neared, he and Alicia traveled to Europe on a five-week sojourn, taking advantage of the free tickets for life given to them by Southwest Airlines. They toured Switzerland, Austria, France, Germany, and Italy—being recognized in varying degrees at each stop. That same year he also wrote his autobiography. He was named to serve on President George Bush's Drug Strategy Council—drugs being a subject he knew all too well about—and as chairman of the Dallas International Sports Commission. He made endless rounds for the Billy Graham Crusade and the Fellowship of Christian Athletes, which might not have sustained if not for his association with and appearances for it. Graham, who hailed him as "one of the finest Christian gentlemen I've ever known" and "like a John the Baptist to me,"[2] was the recipient of around $100,000 that Landry donated to the Crusade.

Graham told him the best years of his life were ahead of him, and these became the words Landry echoed in his memoirs when he envisioned a future of even greater rewards. Toward that end, he resolved immediately that the Cowboys were part of a past now ended. As was football itself. While it was possible he could have gotten another job, he considered his body of work a closed book, and any return to walking along an alien sideline a mercenary act of desperation. He was coaching for God now, traveling far and wide for appearance fees of no more than $500. Not much else mattered as much.

If there was something to be glad about his dismissal, besides the overwhelming feeling of relief, it was that he knew Schramm hadn't done him in. They had ended their era together after Schramm's head went rolling a few weeks after his, following Landry and Gil Brandt into a post-Cowboys existence. Brandt, unable to find work in the league, could only hop the fence, taking a gig in the new century as a columnist for a football website. Jones did to Tex what he had done to Landry, giving him no chance to justify his continuation. Jones had fired most of Schramm's staff, including his righthand man, Joe Bailey, whom Tex had been grooming to one day take over the presidency of the team. Feeling sorry for his old confrere, Landry mused, "I got out easy. I got out when it happened. Tex didn't. He had to live with them."[3] As Jones had anticipated, Schramm could take only so much humiliation. After a blowout in Jones's office, Tex was either canned or quit. It was never really known, nor did it matter.

Schramm though had a lot more leverage than Landry did, with unequaled clout in the league's high council, and could demand a severance package that included a lifetime suite at the Cowboys' home games and a $1.2 million annuity. Jones, in fact, was told that the league's approval of the Cowboys' sale would be, ahem, held up until he satisfied Tex. Jones satisfied Tex. The sale went through. Schramm saved face by pretending he left because he was a big cheese in the World League of American Football, an NFL-subsidized spring "developmental league" in North America and Europe that Tex saw as a potential worldwide NFL. And who better to oversee the NFL's megalomania than Tex Schramm? But even with Schramm as commissioner of the league, it fell short of world domination, losing steam quickly and becoming a strictly European circuit by 1995. At that point, Schramm retired from the game, to live out his life idly rich and decreasingly famous until his death in July 2003, at eighty-three, no more powerful and significant man ever having lived within the borders of pro football.

WHEN JONES took away the tickets of the old Cowboys, it was a small part of a massive expansion of the team's revenue. With the money he cut from the operations of the club, he built thirty new luxury boxes at Texas Stadium, where he also sold corporate advertising space on the scoreboards and walls. He did something else Murchison and Bright refused to do—he prevailed on the Irving city council to lift the ban on sales of beer and wine on Sunday. As a result, for the first time, Cowboys fans could imbibe at games without smuggling hooch in. He sold space under big tents in the parking lot for swank parties.[4] And of course he and Johnson dismantled the Landry-Schramm regime from top to bottom.

Jones would in fact pay more than lip service to Landry's legacy, commissioning a bronze statue of him that would be located outside Gate 1 at Texas Stadium and then later uprooted and placed on the curb outside Cowboys Stadium. However, before the 1989 season began, Landry stalwarts were gone or on the way out. Danny White was released from his contract and retired as the Cowboys' all-time passing leader, with 21,959 yards, 155 touchdowns (and 132 interceptions), and the fifth-best completion percentage in NFL history—but also with the rap that he was a big-game flop, though Landry's gracious coda for him was that White was "a solid winner." Steve Pelluer was also gone, and Kevin Sweeney, for whom Schramm had waited so patiently to rise, all three sacrificed to the altar of Jones and *his* new bauble, Troy Aikman, who had to get over his disappointment that he would never get to play for Landry.

As good as Herschel Walker was, he too was a Landry guy, and on borrowed time. Five games into the season, Jerry Jones made his first blockbuster trade, moving Walker to the Vikings for five key players and *six* draft picks, from which would come no less than Emmitt Smith and safety Darren Woodson, who would play thirteen seasons and be the all-time Cowboys leader in tackles. Jones would be able to preen about that trade for a long time, more so since Walker would go downhill quickly and make stops in Philadelphia and New York before finishing his career in 1995—in Dallas. Too Tall Jones and Tom Rafferty would slog through one final season, leaving Everson Walls, at thirty-one, the senior Cowboy a year later. Even Thousand Oaks would be junked, starting in 1990 when summer camp was moved to Austin, a money-saving decision that left a lot of leeches and kept women high and dry. Jones, said Tex Schramm, "didn't give a damn about history . . . no feeling for the past. You almost expected him to take the stars off the helmets."[5] The biggest rub, said Bob Ward, who had been retained as conditioning coach, was that "Jones completely destroyed our myth."[6]

The reward for picking the Cowboys' bones clean was a 1–15 season in 1989. Jones decreed that Johnson had to start Aikman at quarterback, knowing that was something Landry never would have done with a rookie, and he was plagued by interceptions and benched for five games for his backup Steve Walsh, Johnson's quarterback at Miami. With each loss, signs could be seen at the Irving Cheeseburger reading, "Bring Landry Back," and booing of Jones became mandatory when he made himself public—most egregiously when he trolled the sideline during games. Jones began having stress and an irregular heartbeat. He couldn't sleep.[7] It was hard to sell that Landry couldn't have done better. Indeed, while keeping any overt schadenfreude to himself, Landry had no problem telling his old press favorites that he wouldn't have made moves that Johnson did that he thought cost the Cowboys games.

Johnson's nightmare rookie season, however, was a prelude to a climb not unlike Landry's own in the early years, only Johnson's was faster. With Smith and Woodson in tow, the team went 7–9 in 1990 and 11–5 with a playoff berth in 1991 and Aikman an All-Pro for the first of six straight years. In 1992, the Cowboys soared, going 13–3 and marching to a 52–17 ravaging of the Bills in the Super Bowl. "LANDRY LOYALISTS AREN'T ATTACKING JONES NOW," a headline read.[8] Jones even did something Landry never could, repeat, blasting the Bills again, 30–13, in the next Super Bowl. In the newest age of pro football, an erratic but profit-making blowhard could earn a valuable place in the sports' infrastructure. In 1992, he was appointed to the Competition Committee, the first owner since Paul Brown to be on it. Jones showed that he was not above firing a coach who had won two straight titles, and he could claim vindication when Barry Switzer replaced Johnson. Only two years later, Switzer did something Landry hadn't, beating the Steelers in a Super Bowl. Yet Jones's ability to endure as a winner faded a good deal faster than it had for Landry. In 1997, when Switzer missed the playoffs, he too was axed by Jones, and the Cowboys' now epic reign of gnawing failure began.

Still, none of it had any effect on the team's glittery facade and its fat bottom line. Any edition of America's Team, it seems, is immune from much PR damage, and for this they owe Landry, who gave the team a figurative waiver of immunity when it came to wild excesses.

And Landry of course has looked better and better with each new failure. He had to wait only one year to receive his Hall of Fame plaque, elected in 1990 along with Bob Griese, Franco Harris, Jack Lambert, Ted Hendricks, Buck Buchanan, and Bob St. Clair. Introduced by Roger Staubach, and wearing the iconic hat, he rose to the lectern and insisted in his speech that if he didn't look emotional, "the emotion is all within." It had been quite a time in his life, he noted, "being fired and being elected to the Hall of Fame in the same year." He was all grace and class, dedicating most of the speech to praising Clint Murchison Jr.[9]

Such rituals, by alleviating the football withdrawal pains, were easy for Landry, who was also wise enough to know he need not say anything untoward about Jones to come off looking like the better man. Indeed, Frank Gifford recalled that, shortly after the firing—which Gifford called "brutal"—Landry had told him, "They have every right to do what they want with their football team. It's time to move on."[10]

Another old confrere, Pat Summerall, now a Dallas resident, regularly joined him on the golf course, seeing a far different man than the humorless drill instructor he once knew. Landry, he said, had learned to laugh at himself, as he did when Summerall would remind him of the time Landry had once proudly spoken of going to "the Lood"—meaning of course the Louvre—on a trip to Paris.[11] Landry was also a lot easier to please. After Summerall told him that he had been recently baptized, Landry grew misty. "This is one of the happiest days of my life because of what you've told me," he said.[12] In the early 1990s, he went into business with Tom Jr., who had made him a grandfather again, three times, the last a son named Thomas Landry III. They opened an office downtown under the name Landry Investment Group, brokering oil and real estate deals. Mostly, it served as a booking agency for appearances and endorsements by the old coach. Among the latter was a reprise of his mid-1980s American Express TV commercial, in which he now unpacked a guitar in a hotel room and warbled a very off-key, "Mamas, don't let your babies grow up to be . . . Redskins."

He had succeeded in retaining every drop of his majesty, turning old critics into pillars of stone. When Bayless's book of Landry nullification was published at the same time as Landry's autobiography, a year after Landry was fired, Ron Fimrite wrote in a dual review, "*Landry* is neither as interesting nor as sanctimonious as his literary assailant [and] explains a fact of athletic life that Bayless should have understood: A good coach never gets too emotionally attached to his players. Landry also seems to think that his associates, the infamous Murchison, Schramm and Brandt, were pretty damn good at their jobs, just as he himself was. The evidence . . . would seem to substantiate this uncritical view."[13] Although Bayless by then claimed to be a born-again Christian himself, Gene Lyons, the sage-like Arkansas newspaper columnist, slammed Bayless's "religious prating" as an "attempt to use God to sanctify an old-fashioned rip job."[14]

Walking hallowed ground, Landry was still marketable long into his retirement. He posed for print ads for Abercrombie & Fitch and Quality International motels. Of the former, Alexander Wolff and Kostya Kennedy noted that at seventy, Landry "looks surprisingly at ease in the black-and-white portraits currently running in *The New Yorker* and *Vanity Fair*. The A&F connection isn't the most incongruous thing about the ads: Landry is posing at a Montauk, N.Y., home once owned by someone from an even more remote world, the late Andy Warhol."[15] As much fun as he was having fusing into these new markets, though, he never fully adapted to a world beyond the game. "I wouldn't say he missed football as much as making a difference in people's lives," says Tom Jr. "Dad never could be alone very long. He'd get restless. He preferred working with guys, molding them into a winning unit and now he couldn't do that. He still had that spark in him, but he didn't know what to do with it."[16]

He had plenty of life left, and he found it easier now to break his self-imposed exile from Texas Stadium. In 1993, four years after he fired Landry, Jones faced a second-most awkward matter as it related to him, when Landry would be inducted into the Cowboys' in-house hall of fame, the Ring of Honor. Jones had wanted badly to get that out of the way, but Landry wouldn't hear of accepting the honor as long as some major Cowboys he had coached were being ignored. It was also an implicit nod to Tex Schramm, since the Ring had been Schramm's personal domain, the honorees exclusively his choice, sometimes based on his grudges—Lee Roy Jordan, for instance, wasn't given his rightful place in the Ring until 1989, after Tex was gone, apparently a victim of his having bested Tex in a contract holdout. Now that the Ring had become a vessel for Jones's grudges, *Schramm* would be denied his place until 2003, when his induction was posthumous.

Jones in truth could not have cared less about the Ring, at least until *his* Cowboys became eligible. He had inducted no one since Jordan, pushing the Cowboys' heritage further into the dust bin of history. But the longer Landry went without being honored, the more heat Jones took. And so, when Jones gave in, first agreeing to honor Tony Dorsett and Randy White, Landry was there at Texas Stadium to lay on hands. A year later, on November 7, 1993, the old coach would have the spotlight to himself, for his induction during halftime of a game with the Giants. He donned the Ring of Honor jacket, flanked by previous honorees Staubach, Jordan, Lilly, Renfro, Howley, Meredith, and Don Perkins. He looked fit and trim, his only concession to time being the oversized, rose-tinted aviator-style eyeglasses, but the distance between he and Jones on the platform was a measure of their mutual contempt.

Jones made a stiff introduction, dutifully saying Landry "represents what we all in sports would like to represent, a higher cause and a bigger meaning" and "this would not be the Ring of Honor, Coach Landry, without you in it." Landry, speaking with no prepared remarks, said that this was a "really outstanding day for me," effusively praised Murchison and Schramm, and saluted "my old team the New York Giants" and Wellington and Ann Mara as "great friends of mine through the years." Only when he finished did he get around to thanking "Jerry for all he's done to make this a special day."[17] Landry did what Jones cringed at: turning back the clock, even if only for a few minutes. But the owner needn't have worried that Landry would want to come back more often. He had better things to do. Things that had to do with life and death.

LISA LANDRY CHILDRESS, who was working as a teacher in Austin, had been diagnosed in 1991 after she became pregnant and an ultrasound revealed three tumors in her liver. Doctors urged her to have an abortion and begin chemotherapy, but she toughed out the pregnancy, giving birth to her daughter, Christina, in August. Without treatment, the cancer had worsened, and doctors said she had two months to live unless she had a liver transplantation. Ten days later, a donor was located and she had her new liver, but the drugs she was given could not fight off her body's rejecting the organ. Landry, burying his nose in medical books and getting counsel from numerous other authorities, read of a doctor in Pittsburgh who was using a new antirejection drug and contacted him. After Lisa was put on the drug, her condition improved, and she began giving lectures about organ transplantation.

A year later, however, new tumors were found in her lungs. She underwent surgery but the cancer kept spreading and she was diagnosed as terminal. As Sam Blair recalls, "When Lisa got sick, I'd gotten the story just by chance and called Tom. He said, 'Sam, I know it's a story but hold off a while, we're gonna try and get some treatment for her so wait a while.' And I did. That was the only time I never went ahead on a story. I wouldn't have for anyone else."[18] Lisa hung on until May 1995, when she died at age thirty-seven. It was as if, says Tom Landry Jr., the wind had been knocked out of his father. "He just hurt so much, we all did. It was so sad, a brilliant, vibrant young woman taken from us all like that, with a young daughter. She was so brave. All she wanted was to live to see her baby born and she lived four years after that. But then she passed on and it seemed so unfair."

He goes on, "By then Dad had established in his head a predicate for crises of faith. He had gone through a lot of personal pain. He'd lost a family member as a young man and he'd had so many bitter disappointments in football. He had come to deal with the worst pain in life and move forward. His feeling was that nobody lived without pain, that out of pain comes a fuller life."

"It was a terrible thing and it changed our lives," says Alicia Landry, the glint in her eyes never being the same since. "Tommy was broken up. Those things can shake your faith but he stayed strong. He looked at the good things, that Christina had gotten to know her mother before she passed away. He was so proud of her."[19]

Landry began a foundation in his daughter's name and held periodic charity golf tournaments for it. He indeed moved forward, sometimes at high altitudes. In early March 1995, he was flying his Cessna, Alicia and their granddaughter in the cabin, on a flight to Austin. He had been in the air only a few minutes, on a path over Ennis just southwest of Dallas, when the engine began to sputter. Although it had been exactly fifty years since the last time he'd had to deal with engine trouble while high in the sky, he may as well have been back over flak-filled skies in Europe. His instincts took over.

"The plane had a new rod and it punched a hole in the oil container, which began to drip," recalls Alicia. "We knew we were going down but we weren't afraid because Tommy had landed a lot of planes, and I always thought he could take care of anything. He was calm, he told us what was happening and looked for a place to land, and found a big open spot."

Almost beyond belief, but on second thought the most perfect sanctuary for him, it was a *football field*, behind a high school. "It was kind of muddy and when we hit it just kind of nestled us, and he gently turned the plane sideways because we were headed for a highway. We stopped in the mud, he turned off the engine, and that was it." Remarkably, no one sustained as much as a scratch, and the plane sat undamaged. The FAA did a routine investigation and found nothing amiss. After a brief flash on the nightly news, which is when his son learned of the incident, Landry was soon back in the air, neither man nor machine having grounded him yet.

IN HIS twilight, he remained *Landry*, consciously rigorous in refusing to allow himself to be used by huckster politicians who craved his public endorsements. The one time he loosened that standard, and mildly at that, by inviting President Gerald Ford to the Cowboys' practice facility during the 1976 campaign, he took some criticism. Now, he cared a great deal about his pristine legend, and keeping it that way required him to walk above any hint of crassness or crudity.

That rule applied in his final years, when few people knew he was fighting for his life. In early May 1999, feeling run down, he went for a checkup and was given a grim diagnosis: he had leukemia, specifically acute myelogenous leukemia, which despite the name is not necessarily a death sentence. If he received chemotherapy and treatment right away, the prognostic variables were his age and whether the disease was caught early enough. Landry's reaction was typical. He told no one except his family, and resolved to live his life without giving in to fear or depression. Indeed, he went right from the doctor's office to watch his grandson play in a Little League baseball game. He also committed to several charity golf functions.

Frank Luksa once again got the story first, when Tom Landry Jr. revealed it to him. On May 8, Luksa wrote in the *Morning News* that Landry "is undergoing treatment for leukemia in a local hospital. . . . He is expected to remain under the care of physicians for the next 30 days. 'Fortunately, this was diagnosed at an early stage and treatment was begun immediately,' said Mr. Landry Jr. The family and doctors are optimistic.'"[20] Letters and cards began to pour into Landry's office and the Cowboys. A month later, feeling good, even cocky, he checked out of Baylor University Medical Center after the first stage of his treatment. Wrote Luksa, "The voice sounded the same as the one I have heard for almost 40 years of news conferences, interviews and in post-game locker rooms. The only difference I detected was an extra degree of vibrancy. Almost a trill."

"They've turned me loose, and I'm on my way to Austin," Landry said brightly,[21] seemingly on the way to beating another opponent. In late August, Luksa reported that "Tom Landry's reaction to treatment of leukemia continues to improve with two exceptions. His golf game is on the blink, and he has gotten, well, borderline chubby. Otherwise, all is well with the former Cowboys coach relative to his condition. The results of a blood test taken Tuesday morning at Baylor University Medical Center indicated the disease at least had been brought to a stage of temporary remission. He's to repeat the procedure next month."[22] In November, after he went back in for more treatment, *USA Today* ran a story that Landry was not responding to it, prompting Alicia to deny it, saying she was "optimistic." A month later, he was out again. He made another appearance at Texas Stadium, performing a ceremonial coin toss but no more fond of the game. "It's a new era, the hotdogging and all that, the big salaries, people like Deion [Sanders]," he said. "It's just not football as we knew it."[23] But he was facing fourth and long, very long.

"Dad started taking a turn for the worse," his son says. "He went back into the hospital shortly after that and they couldn't do anything. He had given it a good fight but it took a lot out of him. He began drifting in and out of consciousness and the doctors said it was just a matter of time. We tried everything but he didn't respond, he was basically comatose that last month and had pretty much withered away to nothing, which was heartbreaking. We were there every day with him. Mom spent every night there, sleeping in the room. And I'm grateful that I was able to have a few long talks with him when he was awake and lucid because those are the last memories I have of him. Even then, his mind was sharp."

Luksa also caught him on one of the good days. "He was very ill but stoic to the end. He battled it, he really believed he could beat it, but he was honest with himself. Near the end he said, 'It's my time. I'm ready to go.' Those may have been the last words he ever said, and they were so typical of him. He was satisfied with what he accomplished and that he had lived a good life. He faced his death the way he had his life, with class and dignity. He didn't fear dying."[24]

Tom Jr. sensed that, as well. "He knew he'd given life all he had, and now he had his family around him, could feel how much we loved him, and that God loved him. To a man like Dad, that was all you could ask for out of life. As sad as it was to be on death vigil, we were happy that he was at peace with himself. And then on the morning of the twelfth, at around 6 a.m., we were all around his bed. Dad opened his eyes but you could tell he couldn't see anything. Then he just quit breathing. We all held each others' hands and silently prayed. Mom was very strong, she was like him in that respect. She held us all together. She said, 'He's gone but he'll always be with us.' Each of us said good-bye, kissed him on the forehead, and filed out. And Mom was right, he's been with all of us ever since. I feel him there every day."

The news broke almost immediately, across the time zones. The *New York Times*' obituary began, "He was known as Ol' Stone Face, and on the sideline it was easy to see why. However well or poorly the Dallas Cowboys were playing, Coach Tom Landry's expression under his snap-brim fedora never changed. But that's the way he wanted it."[25] The *Wall Street Journal*'s obit was titled, admiringly,

"Organization Man." Luksa, chosen to write the *Morning News'*
front-page obituary, "Farewell, Coach," began,

> Those who tagged along with the Cowboys for any length of time
> eventually reached an identical conclusion about Tom Landry. There
> was no man behind the mask. Discovery didn't mean he lacked sub-
> stance or depth. Nor did it reveal the man in the funny hat as a con
> hiding his essence behind the ice-blue gaze of a glacier. On the con-
> trary, my dear Watson. Landry inspired mystery because everyone
> assumed there was more to him than met the eye.[26]

The tributes streamed in, from the president to the governor to
dozens of his former players. Tex Schramm called him "a great individual." Roger Staubach said, "If Coach Landry isn't in heaven,
we're all in trouble."[27] Billy Graham said he was "one of the greatest Christian gentlemen I ever knew."[28] Flags were ordered flown at
half-mast throughout the state. Fans began leaving flowers on the
sidewalk outside Texas Stadium. Jones issued a statement saying
Landry's "legacy and influence" reached far beyond the Cowboys,
that he "captured the essence of this sport, the spirit of this state,
and all of the virtues that athletic competition provides our society."[29] There were three memorials for Landry, two open to the public, at his Highland Park church and downtown at the Morton H.
Meyerson Symphony Center. The private funeral service on February
17 took place at the Sparkman Hillcrest Funeral Home in North Dallas across the street from the SMU campus.

That morning, Tom Landry lay in repose in a prim navy-blue jacket,
gray slacks, and his Hall of Fame tie. A blue fedora was propped next
to the casket, which Tom Landry Jr. placed inside it when his father
was lowered into his grave; an image of the famous hat would be
carved into his headstone. The chapel overflowed with guests who had
requested that Alicia invite them, including ex-players and assistants
who as a group grew to around four hundred. On the stage beside
the casket, Schramm sat next to Commissioner Paul Tagliabue, sobbing uncontrollably. Also there were surviving copilot veterans he
had served with in World War II. Jerry Jones was present with Troy
Aikman and Jones's latest coach, Dave Campo. And even though

Jones had offered the use of Texas Stadium for a mass public tribute, on this mournful day he would be reminded, stingingly, of that now long-ago Saturday night in Austin. During the service, Dr. Howard Hendricks of the Dallas Theological Seminary, Landry's Cowboys' chaplain from 1974 to 1982, said at one point that Landry's "convictions were forged in the furnace of real life with the loss of Lisa and the graceless firing as a coach."[30]

A long line of speakers rose to lionize the old coach, though only Don Perkins touched on his complex nature, calling him "an enigma." Tom Landry Jr. said his father "was everything he seemed to be." The reformed Thomas Henderson called Landry "the greatest man I've ever known." Staubach delivered the eulogy, breaking down several times, saying, "This is one of the most difficult things I've ever had to do. . . . A chunk has been taken out of me by the death of Coach Landry. . . . He was our rock, our hope, our inspiration. He was our coach." Staubach then read a poem that had been written by Lisa Childress Landry, the last line of which was: "Our bodies will become glorious and perfectly made. For Christ made sure our ransom was paid." Concluded Staubach, "Coach, give our love to Lisa. We miss you both."[31]

Handkerchiefs dabbed at red, watery eyes and wails of grief were heard as the congregation sang "Amazing Grace." Then the men chosen as pallbearers—Tony Dorsett, Randy White, Bob Lilly, Mel Renfro, Charlie Waters, Drew Pearson, Pettis Norman, and Dan Reeves—slowly carried the casket outside for burial in Sparkman Hillcrest Memorial Park. Barely noticed, standing alone in the back of the hall, loudly crying, was Thomas Henderson, the thorniest of the 506 players Landry had coached.

All of Dallas cried that day. And as the years fanned out without him, it almost seemed as if all the statuary dedicated to Tom Landry was more than tribute; it was a yearning for resurrection.

TODAY, HIS image endures, as the icon carved into his headstone: the stern man peering from under a hat, holding a clipboard tucked under his folded arms. And nearly a quarter century after Landry was sacked, the Cowboys still have a cachet, not as America's Team but America's most riveting, entertaining, and profitable train wreck. Polls have found them to be the least popular team in sports, and Jones the least popular sports personality in Texas.[32] Ironies abound, one occurring when Jimmy Johnson ragged the Cowboys of Jason Garrett as "a country club"—the exact insult used by Jerry Jones about the Tom Landry regime.[33] For Jones, what went around seems bound to come around.

The metropolis of Dallas is a different animal too, not nearly as dependent on the fortunes of the Cowboys but just as surely a better place now than when Landry found it in 1960. While only those with long memories and broad, keen perspectives would have traced the connection, when the city, in 2006, elected its first black county district attorney in Texas, in Dallas County, a brash man named Craig Watkins, he owed his job to men like Mel Renfro and Pettis Norman. Indeed, these men were brought to a city of racial exclusion by Tom Landry, who was likely the most important conduit the game ever had between past and future. Still, Dallas is Dallas; Watkins in his reelection campaign was accused by an opponent of stealing his tires,[34] the kind of charge against black men not entirely unexpected in the South, even against sitting district attorneys.

Landry existed when football and its gentry came of age, and the growing pains that tested him actually foreordained much greater rewards and ills for his successors. Landry couldn't prevent the game's progression into psychosis any more than he could prevent his own team's. But more than most, he created continuity and collegiality out of chaos, in times when that seemed impossible in an America tearing itself apart. One can define Landry in empirical ways, such as Bill Walsh's coda that Landry was a coach who invented his own offense and defense, something no other coach has done. But it's in a wider window that most who knew Landry remember him, usually in simple terms.

Frank Luksa, who died in 2012, said, "He appealed to people for the unbending way he lived. His priorities were family, faith and football and it would have seemed disingenuous from anyone else. He was that kind of man. He was a real guy who lived a helluva life. I felt privileged to have been there for so much of it." Sam Blair, who was there for the entire run, and had a near symbiotic relationship with

Landry, still delights in saying, "He'd tell people, 'Sam Blair is the only writer I can talk to about anything.' He'd always take my call, direct, even at his height. That was like a direct line to God."

Roger Staubach remembers him as "a great football coach. You can pick on his weaknesses, but you have to look at history. Over a long period, what he did was pretty darn special."[35] Danny White says, "He cared about the players far more than the wins and losses."[36] With Landry, it boiled down to simple human values, the things he loved and had such a hard time expressing but fortunately never really needed to. Landry in this way left a certain nostalgic, American Gothic permanence to a game that has no place for men like him now. He belonged to his era, tooth, nail, and fedora. But for his fellow travelers he endures. Lee Roy Jordan gets the same feeling whenever he's inside AT&T Stadium, a structure Tom Landry didn't live to see. "I think of Coach Landry," he says. "He built every inch of this place."[37] In that way, AT&T Stadium *is* Tom Landry Stadium, whether Jerry Jones knows it or not.

DOWN IN Austin, where a great Texas love story began, the forgotten matriarch of the Cowboys sits in her living room beneath the old photos, telling stories of the Landry she knew. That Landry was a man who indeed wasn't perfect and may never have found the answer to everything by looking heavenward, but he came close enough without compromising himself.

"He was really a good man, a kind man, and more fun than anyone ever knew," she is saying now. "You would have liked him." Pause. "The Cowboy fans now, they don't know what he meant, how much of himself he gave to make this team's success. What I loved the most about him was his fairness and gentlemanliness. Those were outstanding assets. You noticed it. You felt it."

You had to. It was something involuntary, something undefinable but tangible. From beginning to end, it was the only thing it could have been. It was a Texas thing.

ACKNOWLEDGMENTS

Many voices helped to tell and shape the story of Tom Landry that emerged in these pages, and many were needed. In its essence, this is a story that could not have been accurate or complete without the detail and nuance needed to bring truth and texture to a visionary man like Landry. Unlike perhaps any major figure in the pantheon of sports demigods, Landry was far more nuanced than he ever let on—or perhaps, even realized. But if by his nature such delicate contouring was not particularly important to Landry himself, lagging well behind the overriding, and heartburn-inducing, task of winning football games and surviving the treacherous tidal waves of life in the NFL over nearly three decades, it is an absolute requirement for anyone who dares take on the daunting challenge of producing the definitive biography of an inscrutable man so often subject to caricature in previous literature. Thus, even the smallest details are subject to verification, corroboration, and substantiation. Judgment comes only with the safety and sanctity of truth.

Luckily, my efforts to relate the full and accurate story, one of the greatest stories ever told in the American sporting culture, were blessed by the patience and forbearance of the only person left from the glory of the Landry years who shared them with him. Alicia Wiggs Landry not only was bonded to Tom Landry by marriage but by the interlocking of their Texas souls. Different as they were in outward temperament and personality, no one ever understood what made the great old coach tick like she did, and though she had no stake in this project other than as a source, she seemed to sense that it might well be the last chance for history to get the story right about the man she loved, and always saw as deeply misunderstood.

Indeed, I was stunned by how remarkably cooperative she was. During the seminal phase of the researching, I had left one message for her, hopeful but not anywhere near certain that she would return the call. Only days later, as I walked through an airport on the way to Lord knows where, my phone rang. It was Alicia, not someone tapped to decline an interview for her, and when I explained my vision for the book she scheduled a visit right then and there, pledging to give me all the time I would need. As I learned, it wasn't her intention to sugarcoat or paint him in the celestial hues of perfection; like him, she never pretended that Tom Landry was a saint, nor that he was fault-free.

Through the ensuing months, she was always prepared to discourse about the good times and the bad when the Landrys were the first couple of Texas, filling in crucial perspective about what made this inscrutable man tick, and hurt. Quite simply, this book could not have flourished without her. Adding his own trenchant reflections of the dad with whom he had a sometimes distant relationship was Tom Landry Jr., a man both blessed and cursed by sharing his father's name and many of the same facial features.

No Landry biography would be complete without the observations of the players he molded in his image and his theories. Though some believed he was a despot, no Cowboy ever came away from playing for Landry without unending respect born originally from fear, even resentment. There are tricky issues in the Landry story, including to what extent he knew of the drug use going on in his own locker room, but none more so than race. As with Landry's football theories, these issues cannot be dispensed with on a superficial level, as normally they have been in the past, and I am indebted to some all-time great Cowboys for thoughtfully and candidly discussing them. These include two of the most eloquent, strong-willed, and influential African American players to play for Landry, Mel Renfro and Pettis Norman, as well as Landry-era icons Lee Roy Jordan and Hall of

Famer Bob Lilly and original Cowboys Mike Connelly and Bob Fry. I am also grateful to have been enlightened and entertained by the man Landry turned into the game's first superstar middle linebacker while coaching the New York Giants' defense: the redoubtable Sam Huff, who with little prompting revealed some of the most intensely personal and revelatory thoughts ever uttered about Landry.

As a journalist, it was a pet kick for me to consult two of Dallas's legendary sporstwriters who soldiered with Landry and crafted the narratives that framed the Cowboys on the journey from peonage to perfection: Sam Blair and Frank Luksa, the latter of whom sadly died shortly after the manuscript was completed. Because that journey began a good deal before Landry arrived in Dallas, investigating his extraordinary life required dogged research, and I was aided in that highly rewarding but sometimes tedious task by archivists Cassandra Karl and Cindee Pelfrey at the Mission (Texas) Historical Museum. As well, digging up long-ago pictorial images of Landry as a dashing Texas Longhorn hero was the chore of Susan Allen Sigmon and Joy Lawrence at the University of Texas Athletic Department and Aryn Glazer and Margaret Schlankey at the Dolph Briscoe Center for American History in Austin, Texas. Thanks to one and all for their time, and for putting up with me. The same can be said of my agent, Jim Fitzgerald, and my editor at Liveright, Phil Marino, both of whom recognized that the Landry story was far more transcendent and entwined with mid- and late-twentieth-century sports and culture than most historians have realized. The result was a team effort, one I suspect Tom Landry himself would have approved of.

NOTES

Introduction

1. Marianne Bickle, "According to Tom Landry, A Winner Never Stops Trying," *Forbes*, June 13, 2011.

2. BrainyQuote, http://brainyquote.com/quotes/quotes/t/tomlandry388204.html.

3. Peter Golenbock, "The Organization Man," *Wall Street Journal*, February 16, 2000.

4. Herbert Warren Wind, "Coach," *New Yorker*, December 16, 1974, p. 122.

5. Gary Cartwright, "The Lonely Blues of Duane Thomas," *Texas Monthly*, February 1973.

6. Bob Hayes with Robert Pack, *Run, Bullet, Run: The Rise, Fall, and Recovery of Bob Hayes* (New York: Harper and Row, 1992); Lance Rentzel, *When All the Laughter Died in Sorrow* (New York: Bantam Books, 1973); Thomas "Hollywood" Henderson and Peter Knobler, *Out of Control: Confessions of an NFL Casualty* (New York: Putnam, 1987); Harvey Martin, *Texas Thunder: My Eleven Years with the Dallas Cowboys* (New York: Rawson, 1986); "Sports People: Septien Pleads Guilty," *New York Times*, April 9, 1987; "Bethea Apparent Suicide," *New York Times*, April 24, 1987.

7. Skip Bayless, " 'boys Will Be 'boys," *Sports Illustrated*, January 13, 1997.

8. Robert Wilonsky, "The Comeback of Harvey Martin," *Dallas Observer News*, January 8, 1998.

9. Martha Frankel, "Boys Will Be Boys: The 1990 Cowboys Were Menaces on and off the Field," *New York Post*, August 31, 2008.

10. Gary Cartwright, "Melting the Plastic Man," *Texas Monthly*, November 1973.

11. Jeff Merron, "Reel Life: 'North Dallas Forty,' " ESPN Page Two, http://espn.go.com/page2/s/closer/021101.html.

12. Cartwright, "Melting the Plastic Man."

13. Stan Grossfeld, "A (Silent) Voice of Experience," *Boston Globe*, September 10, 2003.

14. "Reversing His Field: Duane Thomas Has Returned to the Cowboys—As an Author," *Los Angeles Times*, July 23, 1987.

15. Charean Williams and Tim Price, "Remembering Tom Landry," *Fort Worth Star-Telegram*, February 14, 2000.

16. Mark Ribowsky, "Behind the Cowboy Struggle to Reach Super Bowl XIII," *Sport*, November 1978, p. 32.

17. Dwight White quoted in Martin, *Texas Thunder*, p. 214.
18. Henderson and Knobler, *Out of Control*, p. 66.
19. Peter Golenbock, *Cowboys Have Always Been My Heroes* (New York: Warner Books, 1997), p. 653.
20. "Tom Landry," *Up Close Classics*, ESPN, May 17, 2001; *Landry: The NFL's Man in the Hat*, NFL Films, 2010.
21. "Reversing His Field."
22. "Oklahoma's Landry Jones Combines Faith and Football," *Black Christian News*, August 27, 2011, http://blackchristiannews.com/news/2011/08/oklahomas-landry-jones-combines-faith-and-football.html.
23. Jennifer Briggs Kaski, *The Book of Landry* (Nashville: Towle House, 2000), p. 12.
24. Gary Cartwright, "Turn Out the Lights," *Texas Monthly*, August 1997.
25. "Tom Landry," *Up Close Classics*.
26. Skip Bayless, *God's Coach: The Hymns, Hype, and Hypocrisy of Tom Landry's Cowboys* (New York: Fireside, 1990), pp. 112–113.
27. Brian D. Sweany, "Styles and Styles of Texas," *Texas Monthly*, March 2009.
28. Tom Landry with Gregg Lewis, *Tom Landry: An Autobiography* (New York: Harper-Collins, 1990), p. 33.

Prologue: "IT'S A TEXAS THING"

1. Sara Anderson, "Tom Landry's Head Cheerleader," *Athletes in Action*, Fall 1989, p. 5.
2. Alicia Landry interview. All Alicia Landry quotes in this chapter from author interview.
3. Paul Zimmerman, *The New Thinking Man's Guide to Pro Football* (New York: Simon and Schuster, 1984), p. 246.
4. Walt Garrison with John Tullius, *Once a Cowboy* (New York: Random House, 1988), p. 55.
5. John Steinbeck, *Travels with Charley in Search of America* (New York: Viking Press, 1962).
6. "Notable Quotes of Sam Houston," Sam Houston Memorial Museum website, http://shsu.edu/~smm_www/History/quotes.shtml.
7. "Top 10 Best Texas Quotes," http://www.top10-best.com/t/top_10_best_texas_quotes.html.

Chapter 1: MISSIONARY MAN

1. Tom Landry Jr. interview.
2. Cindee Pelfrey interview.
3. Tom Landry with Gregg Lewis, *Tom Landry: An Autobiography* (New York: Harper-Collins, 1990), p. 40.
4. *The Handbook of Texas Online*, Texas State Historical Association, http://www.tshaonline.org/handbook/online/articlesqdw01.
5. Landry with Lewis, *Tom Landry*, p. 41.
6. Ibid.
7. *Upper Valley Progress*, October 12, 1977.
8. Landry with Lewis, *Tom Landry*, pp. 44–45.
9. Ibid.
10. *The Eagle* (Mission, Texas), November 6, 1928.
11. "The New Game of Football: Radical Changes in This Year's Rules Revolutionizing the Sport," *New York Times*, September 30, 1906.
12. Gary Cartwright, "Tom Landry: God, Family, and Football," *Sport*, October 1969; Landry with Lewis, *Tom Landry*, p. 49.
13. Landry with Lewis, *Tom Landry*, p. 51.

14. Ibid.
15. Bob St. John, *Landry: The Legend and the Legacy* (Nashville: W Publishing Group, 2000), p. 128.
16. Ibid., p. 129.
17. Ibid., p. 127.
18. Landry with Lewis, *Tom Landry*, p. 51.
19. Ibid., p. 47.
20. *Mission Times*, undated.
21. St. John, *Landry*, p. 130.
22. Ibid., p. 131.
23. Ibid., p. 132.
24. Landry with Lewis, *Tom Landry*, p. 60.

Chapter 2: A GRIM REAPER

1. "Boeing B-7 Flying Fortress," *Wikipedia*, en.wikipedia.org/wiki/B-17_Flying_Fortress.
2. Tom Landry with Gregg Lewis, *Tom Landry: An Autobiography* (New York: Harper-Collins, 1990), pp. 62–65.
3. Ibid.
4. Ibid.
5. Ibid.
6. "Austin, Texas," *Wikipedia*, en.wikipedia.org/wiki/Austin,_Texas.
7. "Charles Whitman," *Wikipedia*, en.wikipedia.org/wiki/Charles_Whitman.
8. Jim Nicar, "Bevo," Mackbrown-Texas Football.com, http://www.mackbrown-texas-football.com/sports/m-footbl/spec-rel/bevo.html.
9. Bob St. John, *Landry: The Legend and the Legacy* (Nashville: W Publishing Group, 2000), pp. 137–138.
10. Ibid., p. 137.
11. Landry with Lewis, *Tom Landry*, p. 67.
12. Skip Bayless, *God's Coach: The Hymns, Hype, and Hypocrisy of Tom Landry's Cowboys* (New York: Fireside, 1990), p. 53.
13. Alicia Landry interview.
14. Landry with Lewis, *Tom Landry*, p. 69.
15. Ibid., p. 71.
16. Ibid., p. 73.

Chapter 3: BIG MAN ON CAMPUS

1. "Sweatt v. Painter," *Wikipedia*, en.wikipedia.org/wiki/Sweatt_v._Painter.
2. Tom Landry with Gregg Lewis, *Tom Landry: An Autobiography* (New York: Harper-Collins, 1990), pp. 74–75.
3. Ibid.
4. Bob St. John, *Landry: The Legend and the Legacy* (Nashville: W Publishing Group, 2000), p. 147.
5. Alicia Landry interview. All Alicia Landry quotes in this chapter from author interview.
6. *Dallas Morning News*, October 8, 1947.
7. "Mustangs Defeat Steers in Nerve-Tingler, 14–13," *Dallas Morning News*, November 2, 1947.
8. Landry with Lewis, *Tom Landry*, p. 75.
9. Ibid.
10. "Mustangs Defeat Steers."
11. St. John, *Landry*, p. 156.
12. "Steers Smash Louisiana, 33–0," *Dallas Morning News*, September 19, 1948.

13. "Tars Smash Texas, 34–7," *Dallas Morning News*, September 26, 1948.
14. Landry with Lewis, *Tom Landry*, p. 79.
15. Ibid., p. 80.
16. Ibid.

Chapter 4: A TEXAS YANKEE

1. Tom Landry with Gregg Lewis, *Tom Landry: An Autobiography* (New York: Harper-Collins, 1990), p. 80.
2. Alicia Landry interview. All Alicia Landry quotes in this chapter from author interview.
3. Landry with Lewis, *Tom Landry*, p. 84.
4. Herbert Warren Wind, "Coach," *New Yorker*, December 16, 1974, p. 128.
5. Landry with Lewis, *Tom Landry*, p. 85.
6. Ibid.
7. Ibid., pp. 87–88.
8. Ibid., p. 87.
9. Barry Gottehrer, *The Giants of New York: The History of Professional Football's Most Fabulous Dynasty* (New York: G. P. Putnam's Sons, 1963), pp. 42–43.
10. Arthur Daley, "Expensive Rubbernecking," *New York Times*, November 7, 1957.
11. Ibid.

Chapter 5: "OKAY, TOM, YOU EXPLAIN IT"

1. *New York Post*, October 20, 1950, p. 94; *New York Post*, October 23, 1950, p. 52.
2. Tom Landry with Gregg Lewis, *Tom Landry: An Autobiography* (New York: Harper-Collins, 1990), p. 92.
3. *New York Post*, October 23, 1950, p. 52.
4. "Television," *Wikipedia*, en.wikipedia.org/wiki/Television.
5. "Tunnell in Action with Giant Eleven; Rowe, Landry Also Ready for Eagles," *New York Times*, October 17, 1951.
6. Paul Zimmerman, *The New Thinking Man's Guide to Pro Football* (New York: Simon and Schuster, 1984), p. 128.
7. *New York Times*, October 2, 1950.
8. Zimmerman, *New Thinking Man's Guide to Pro Football*, p. 127.
9. *New York Post*, October 23, 1950.
10. *New York Post*, October 16, 1950, p. 95.
11. Bob St. John, *Landry: The Legend and the Legacy* (Nashville: W Publishing Group, 2000), p. 168.
12. Ernie Palladino, *Lombardo and Landry* (New York: Skyhorse Publishing, 2011), p. xxiii.
13. *New York Daily News*, December 18, 1950.
14. Alicia Landry interview.
15. Landry with Lewis, *Tom Landry*, p. 95.
16. *New York Times*, November 15, 1951.
17. Landry with Lewis, *Tom Landry*, p. 91.
18. St. John, *Landry*, p. 171.
19. David Maraniss, *When Pride Still Mattered: A Life of Vince Lombardi* (New York: Simon and Schuster, 1999), p. 61.
20. Carlo DeVito and Sam Huff, *Wellington: The Maras, the Giants, and the City of New York* (Chicago: Triumph Books, 2006), pp. 127–128.
21. Landry with Lewis, *Tom Landry*, p. 98.
22. Peter Golenbock, *Cowboys Have Always Been My Heroes* (New York: Warner Books, 1997), p. 51.

23. Palladino, *Lombardi and Landry*, p. 12.
24. Zimmerman, *New Thinking Man's Guide to Pro Football*, p. 171.
25. *Denver Post*, September 14, 1986.
26. Golenbock, *Cowboys Have Always Been My Heroes*, p. 45.
27. Landry with Lewis, *Tom Landry*, p. 104.
28. Ibid.
29. Jack Cavanaugh, *Giants among Men* (New York: Random House, 2008), pp. 25–26.

Chapter 6: "SAM'S MY MAN"

1. "Giants Dispute Graham Hint of 'Dirty Football,'" *New York Times*, November 9, 1955.
2. Gary Cartwright, "Tom Landry: God, Family, and Football," *Sport*, October 1969.
3. David Maraniss, *When Pride Still Mattered: A Life of Vince Lombardi* (New York: Simon and Schuster, 1999), p. 161.
4. Official Website of the Chicago Bears, http://www.chicagobears.com/tradition/bears-in-the-hall/bill-george.html.
5. Jack Cavanaugh, *Giants among Men* (New York: Random House, 2008), p. 176.
6. Peter Golenbock, *Cowboys Have Always Been My Heroes* (New York: Warner Books, 1997), p. 51.
7. Tom Landry with Gregg Lewis, *Tom Landry: An Autobiography* (New York: Harper-Collins, 1990), pp. 104–105.
8. Sam Huff interview. All Huff quotes in the chapter from author interview.
9. Cavanaugh, *Giants among Men*, p. 18.
10. Frank Gifford, *The Whole Ten Yards* (New York: Random House, 1993), pp. 99–100.
11. *New York Times*, October 16, 1956.
12. Landry with Lewis, *Tom Landry*, p. 106.
13. Robert Riger and Tex Maule, *The Pros: A Documentary of Professional Football in America* (New York: Simon and Schuster, 1960).
14. Cavanaugh, *Giants among Men*, p. 37.
15. Ibid.
16. Gifford, *Whole Ten Yards*, pp. 96–97.
17. Sam Blair, *Dallas Cowboys, Pro or Con? A Complete History* (Garden City, NY: Doubleday, 1970), p. 17.
18. Ibid., p. 18.

Chapter 7: "AS DIFFERENT AS DAYLIGHT AND DARK"

1. Pat Summerall, *Giants: What I Learned about Life from Vince Lombardi and Tom Landry* (Hoboken: John Wiley, 2010), p. 90.
2. Frank Gifford with Peter Richmond, *The Glory Game* (New York: HarperCollins, 2003), pp. 20–21.
3. Sam Huff interview. All Huff quotes in this chapter from author interview.
4. David Maraniss, *When Pride Still Mattered: A Life of Vince Lombardi* (New York: Simon and Schuster, 1999), p. 161.
5. Tom Landry with Gregg Lewis, *Tom Landry: An Autobiography* (New York: Harper-Collins, 1990), p. 112.
6. Gifford with Richmond, *Glory Game*, pp. 82–83.
7. Landry with Lewis, *Tom Landry*, p. 111.
8. Maraniss, *When Pride Still Mattered*, p. 161.
9. Landry with Lewis, *Tom Landry*, p. 112.
10. Maraniss, *When Pride Still Mattered*, p. 172.
11. Carlo DeVito and Sam Huff, *Wellington: The Maras, the Giants, and the City of New York* (Chicago: Triumph Books, 2006), p. 136.

12. Maraniss, *When Pride Still Mattered*, p. 161.
13. Ibid., p. 76.
14. Ernie Palladino, *Lombardi and Landry* (New York: Skyhorse Publishing, 2011), p. 3.
15. "Giant among Giants," *New York Times*, December 31, 1956.
16. DeVito and Huff, *Wellington*, p. 129.
17. Jack Cavanaugh, *Giants among Men* (New York: Random House, 2008), p. 26.
18. DeVito and Huff, *Wellington*, p. 129.
19. Ibid.
20. Gary Cartwright, "Tom Landry: God, Family, and Football," *Sport*, October 1969; "Why Worry When Your Assistants Are Lombardi, Landry," *Los Angeles Times*, January 27, 1987.
21. http://www.profootballhallof.com/history/release.aspx?release_id=1894.
22. Louis Effrat, "Giants Have Patterns for Work in Addition to Patterns for Play," *New York Times*, October 25, 1958.
23. Landry with Lewis, *Tom Landry*, p. 112.
24. Alicia Landry interview. All Alicia Landry quotes in this chapter from author interview.
25. Landry with Lewis, *Tom Landry*, p. 112.
26. Arthur Daley, "The Big, Bad Bears," *New York Times*, December 18, 1956.
27. "Giants Memorize Key Bear Threats," *New York Times*, December 20, 1956.
28. Tex Maule, "Notes on a Gelid Afternoon," *Sports Illustrated*, January 7, 1957, p. 50.
29. Landry with Lewis, *Tom Landry*, p. 108.
30. *New York Post*, December 29, 1956.
31. *New York Daily News*, December 29, 1956.
32. *New York Post*, December 29, 1956.
33. Tom Landry Jr. interview.
34. Landry with Lewis, *Tom Landry*, p. 108.
35. *New York Times*, August 19, 1956.
36. Gay Talese, "Nolan Is Giants' Top Choice for All-Anonymous," *New York Times*, October 20, 1957.
37. Gifford with Richmond, *Glory Game*, p. 15.
38. Landry with Lewis, *Tom Landry*, p. 113.

Chapter 8: "LORD, I NEED YOUR HELP TODAY"

1. Tom Landry with Gregg Lewis, *Tom Landry: An Autobiography* (New York: HarperCollins, 1990), p. 113.
2. Sam Huff interview. All Huff quotes in this chapter from author interview.
3. Arthur Daley, "The Boy from Syracuse," *New York Times*, November 2, 1958.
4. Ernie Palladino, *Lombardi and Landry* (New York: Skyhorse Publishing, 2011), p. 164.
5. Pat Summerall, *Giants: What I Learned about Life from Vince Lombardi and Tom Landry* (Hoboken: John Wiley, 2010), p. 59.
6. Sam Blair, *Dallas Cowboys, Pro or Con? A Complete History* (Garden City, NY: Doubleday, 1970), p. 17.
7. Arthur Daley, "One for the Book," *New York Times*, December 30, 1958.
8. Frank Gifford with Peter Richmond, *The Glory Game* (New York: HarperCollins, 2003), p. 23.
9. Ibid.
10. Daley, "One for the Book."
11. Landry with Lewis, *Tom Landry*, p. 118.
12. David Maraniss, *When Pride Still Mattered*: A Life of Vince Lombardi (New York: Simon and Schuster, 1999), p. 198.
13. Ibid.
14. Anthony Summers, *Official and Confidential: The Secret Life of J. Edgar Hoover* (New York: Putnam, 1993).

15. Joe David Brown, "Big Man Even in Big D," *Sports Illustrated*, January 21, 1963; Jane Wolfe, *The Murchisons* (New York: St. Martin's, 1991); Peter Golenbock, *Cowboys Have Always Been My Heroes* (New York: Warner Books, 1997), pp. 10–14; Skip Bayless, *God's Coach: The Hymns, Hype, and Hypocrisy of Tom Landry's Cowboys* (New York: Fireside, 1990), p. 72.

16. Horace Sutton, "Country Club in Hawaii," *Sports Illustrated*, November 12, 1956, p. 62.

17. Bayless, *God's Coach*, p. 72.

18. Golenbock, *Cowboys Have Always Been My Heroes*, p. 18.

19. Tom Landry Jr. interview.

20. Landry with Lewis, *Tom Landry*, pp. 116–117.

21. Blair, *Dallas Cowboys, Pro or Con?* p. 17.

22. Landry with Lewis, *Tom Landry*, p. 118.

23. Ibid., pp. 119–120.

24. Alicia Landry interview.

25. Landry with Lewis, *Tom Landry*, p. 293.

26. Peter Gent, "North Hollywood Forty and Other Morality Plays from the NFL," *Esquire*, September 1980, p. 40.

27. Summerall, *Giants*, p. 60.

28. Jack Cavanaugh, *Giants among Men* (New York: Random House, 2008), p. 189.

29. Summerall, *Giants*, p. 81.

30. Bayless, *God's Coach*, p. 57.

31. Tex Maule, "Tom Thumb's Adventures with the Giants," *Sports Illustrated*, October 26, 1959.

32. Arthur Daley, "Counsel for the Defense," *New York Times*, December 23, 1959.

Chapter 9: BIG DOG

1. Gary Cartwright, "Turn Out the Lights," *Texas Monthly*, August 1997.

2. Skip Bayless, *God's Coach: The Hymns, Hype, and Hypocrisy of Tom Landry's Cowboys* (New York: Fireside, 1990), pp. 73.

3. Ibid., p. 60.

4. Bob St. John, *Tex! The Man Who Built the Dallas Cowboys* (Englewood Cliffs, NJ: Prentice Hall, 1988), p. 168.

5. Peter Golenbock, *Cowboys Have Always Been My Heroes* (New York: Warner Books, 1997), p. 30.

6. "Texas Schramm," *Encyclopedia.com*, http://www.encyclopedia.com/topic/Tex_ Schramm.aspx.

7. Golenbock, *Cowboys Have Always Been My Heroes*, p. 32.

8. Bayless, *God's Coach*, p. 62.

9. Ernie Palladino, *Lombardi and Landry* (New York: Skyhorse Publishing, 2011), p. 213.

10. Charles Burton, "Landry Delaying Decision on Job," *Dallas Morning News*, December 20, 1959.

11. Tom Landry with Gregg Lewis, *Tom Landry: An Autobiography* (New York: Harper-Collins, 1990), p. 127.

12. *New York Times*, December 28, 1959.

13. Alicia Landry interview. All Alicia Landry quotes in this chapter from author interview.

14. Golenbock, *Cowboys Have Always Been My Heroes*, p. 31.

15. Landry with Lewis, *Tom Landry*, p. 127.

16. *Time*, November 30, 1959, pp. 56–58.

17. Sam Huff interview.

18. *Dallas Morning News*, December 23, 1958.

19. *Dallas Morning News*, July 25, 1959.

20. Sam Blair interview.

21. *Dallas Morning News*, December 9, 12, 20, and 28, 1959.
22. Charles Burton, "Rangers Hire Tom Landry," *Dallas Morning News*, December 29, 1959.
23. Bayless, *God's Coach*, p. 78.
24. Sam Blair, *Dallas Cowboys, Pro or Con? A Complete History* (Garden City, NY: Doubleday, 1970), p. 19.
25. Mike Connelly interview.
26. Golenbock, *Cowboys Have Always Been My Heroes*, pp. 35, 38.
27. Ibid., p. 38.
28. Ibid., p. 24.
29. Tex Maule, "Born in an NFL Storm," *Sports Illustrated*, February 8, 1960.
30. "The Playboy Interview," *Playboy*, June 1978.
31. Golenbock, *Cowboys Have Always Been My Heroes*, p. 24.
32. Maule, "Born in an NFL Storm."
33. "Rangers Will Get Help from Rivals," *New York Times*, January 29, 1960.

Chapter 10: "IS THERE A TEAM IN DALLAS?"

1. Charles Burton, "Rangers Hire Tom Landry," *Dallas Morning News*, December 29, 1959.
2. Tex Maule, "The Cowboys Can Ride High on Better Defense," *Sports Illustrated*, September 9, 1963.
3. Skip Bayless, *God's Coach: The Hymns, Hype, and Hypocrisy of Tom Landry's Cowboys* (New York: Fireside, 1990), p. 74.
4. "Lynching Statistics," Classroom: The Charles Chestnutt Digital Archive, www.chesnutt archive.org/classroom/lynchingstat.html.
5. Peter Golenbock, *Cowboys Have Always Been My Heroes* (New York: Warner Books, 1997), p. 72.
6. Ibid., pp. 76–77.
7. Ibid., p. 109.
8. Mike Connelly interview. All Connelly quotes in this chapter from author interview.
9. Golenbock, *Cowboys Have Always Been My Heroes*, p. 192.
10. Bayless, *God's Coach*, pp. 33, 35.
11. Golenbock, *Cowboys Have Always Been My Heroes*, p. 37.
12. Sam Blair interview.
13. Frank Luksa interview.
14. Sam Blair, *Dallas Cowboys, Pro or Con? A Complete History* (Garden City, NY: Doubleday, 1970), p. 42.
15. *Dallas Morning News*, July 12, 1960.
16. "The Six-Minute Mile," *Sports Illustrated*, July 27, 1960.
17. Bob St. John, *Landry: The Legend and the Legacy* (Nashville: W Publishing Group, 2000), p. 215.
18. Gary Cartwright, "Melting the Plastic Man," *Texas Monthly*, November 1973.
19. Bob Fry interview.
20. Curt Sampson, "Don Meredith: The First Dallas Cowboy," *D Magazine*, September 22, 2010.
21. *Dallas Morning News*, August 22, 1960.
22. "Cowboys Confident Victory's in Store," *Dallas Morning News*, August 7, 1960.
23. *Dallas Morning News*, August 18, 20, and 21, 1960.
24. Blair, *Dallas Cowboys, Pro or Con?* p. 36.
25. *Sports Illustrated*, September 26, 1960.
26. *Dallas Morning News*, September 26, 1960.
27. Blair, *Dallas Cowboys, Pro or Con?* p. 54.
28. *Dallas Morning News*, September 27, 1960.

29. Blair, *Dallas Cowboys, Pro or Con?* p. 54.
30. Tom Landry with Gregg Lewis, *Tom Landry: An Autobiography* (New York: Harper-Collins, 1990), p. 135.
31. *Dallas Morning News*, December 1, 1960.
32. Arthur Daley, "In the Home Corral," *New York Times*, December 4, 1960.
33. Golenbock, *Cowboys Have Always Been My Heroes*, p. 130.
34. Sam Huff interview.
35. St. John, *Landry*, p. 219.
36. Landry with Lewis, *Tom Landry*, p. 136.
37. Golenbock, *Cowboys Have Always Been My Heroes*, p. 132.
38. Landry with Lewis, *Tom Landry*, p. 136.

Chapter 11: A VIRTUE OUT OF WEAKNESS

1. Sam Blair, *Dallas Cowboys, Pro or Con? A Complete History* (Garden City, NY: Doubleday, 1970), p. 63.
2. *Dallas Morning News*, August 25, 1961.
3. *Landry: The NFL's Man in the Hat*, NFL Films, 1982.
4. Edwin Shrake, "Why Is This Man Laughing," *Sports Illustrated*, September 18, 1972.
5. Bob Fry interview.
6. Mike Connelly interview. All Connelly quotes in this chapter from author interview.
7. Bob St. John, *Landry: The Legend and the Legacy* (Nashville: W Publishing Group, 2000), p. 214.
8. Bob Lilly with Kristine Setting Clark, *A Cowboy's Life* (Chicago: Triumph Books, 2008), p. 50.
9. *Dallas Morning News*, August 1, 1961.
10. *Dallas Morning News*, November 15, 1960.
11. St. John, *Landry*, p. 215.
12. Blair, *Dallas Cowboys, Pro or Con?* p. 74.
13. *Dallas Morning News*, September 18, 1961.
14. Ibid.
15. *Dallas Morning News*, September 21, 1961.
16. *Dallas Morning News*, October 10, 1961.
17. Tex Maule, "A Shuttle Shakes Up the Pros," *Sports Illustrated*, November 5, 1962.
18. *Dallas Morning News*, October 10, 1961.
19. St. John, *Landry*, p. 220.
20. Peter Golenbock, *Cowboys Have Always Been My Heroes* (New York: Warner Books, 1997), p. 144.
21. Ibid.
22. Skip Bayless, *God's Coach: The Hymns, Hype, and Hypocrisy of Tom Landry's Cowboys* (New York: Fireside, 1990), p. 71.
23. Blair, *Dallas Cowboys, Pro or Con?* p. 88.
24. Ibid.
25. "Cornell Green (defensive back)," *Wikipedia*, en.wikipedia.org/wiki/Cornell_Green_ (defensive back).
26. H. W. Wind, "The Sporting Scene," *New Yorker*, December 16, 1974, p. 144.
27. *Dallas Morning News*, December 17, 1962.
28. Blair, *Dallas Cowboys, Pro or Con?* p. 118.
29. *Dallas Morning News*, September 18, 1962.
30. *Dallas Morning News*, September 24, 1962.
31. Tom Landry with Gregg Lewis, *Tom Landry: An Autobiography* (New York: Harper-Collins, 1990), p. 141.
32. Gary Cartwright, "Tom Landry: God, Family, and Football," *Sport*, October 1969.
33. Landry with Lewis, *Tom Landry*, p. 146.

34. Ibid.
35. Joe David Brown, "A Big Man Even in Big D," *Sports Illustrated*, January 21, 1963.
36. Bayless, *God's Coach*, p. 74.
37. Brown, "Big Man Even in Big D."
38. Blair, *Dallas Cowboys, Pro or Con?* p. 109.
39. Curt Sampson, "Don Meredith: The First Dallas Cowboy," *D Magazine*, October 2010.
40. Gary Cartwright, "The Shadows of the Image," *Dallas Morning News*, January 17, 1963.
41. Sam Blair interview.
42. Landry with Lewis, *Tom Landry*, pp. 144–145.
43. *Dallas Morning News*, December 17, 1962.

Chapter 12: "IT WASN'T DALLAS. IT WAS DANTE'S INFERNO"

1. Sam Blair interview. All Blair quotes in this chapter from author interview.
2. Mike Connelly interview. All Connelly quotes in this chapter from author interview.
3. *Dallas Morning News*, September 1, 1963.
4. Tex Maule, "The Cowboys Can Ride High on Better Defense," *Sports Illustrated*, September 9, 1963.
5. Gary Cartwright, "Meredith: Dallas' All-Time Man on the Spot," *Dallas Morning News*, November 16, 1963.
6. Sam Blair, *Dallas Cowboys, Pro or Con? A Complete History* (Garden City, NY: Doubleday, 1970), p. 146.
7. Pettis Norman interview. All Norman quotes in this chapter from author interview.
8. Skip Bayless, *God's Coach: The Hymns, Hype, and Hypocrisy of Tom Landry's Cowboys* (New York: Fireside, 1990), p. 76.
9. Tom Landry with Gregg Lewis, *Tom Landry: An Autobiography* (New York: HarperCollins, 1990), p. 147.
10. *Dallas Morning News*, November 23, 1963.
11. Ibid.
12. *Dallas Morning News*, November 25, 1963.
13. Bud Shrake, "No Day for Games," *Dallas Morning News*, November 24, 1963.
14. Landry with Lewis, Tom Landry, p. 148.
15. Bud Shrake, "Growing Old with the Cowboys," *Dallas Morning News*, February 6, 1964.
16. Ibid.
17. Landry with Lewis, *Tom Landry*, p. 149.
18. Bob St. John, *Tex! The Man Who Built the Dallas Cowboys* (Englewood Cliffs, NJ: Prentice Hall, 1988), p. 266.
19. Bob Lilly with Kristine Setting Clark, *A Cowboy's Life* (Chicago: Triumph Books, 2008), pp. 66–67.
20. Lee Roy Jordan interview. All Jordan quotes in this chapter from author interview.
21. Paul Zimmerman, *The New Thinking Man's Guide to Pro Football* (New York: Simon and Schuster, 1984), p. 244.
22. Ibid.
23. Michael MacCambridge, *America's Game* (New York: Anchor, 2005), p. 214.
24. Duane Thomas and Paul Zimmerman, *Duane Thomas and the Fall of America's Team* (New York: Warner Books, 1988), p. 47.
25. Sam Blair, "Changing Costumes," *Dallas Morning News*, January 22, 1964.
26. Ibid.
27. Gary Cartwright, "New-Look Cowboys Tackle Cards," *Dallas Morning News*, September 12, 1964.
28. Blair, *Dallas Cowboys, Pro or Con?* p. 158.
29. Ibid., p. 61.

30. "Tex Schramm," Answers, http://www.answers.com/topic/tex-schramm#ixzz1oLI0tRHF.

31. Jeff Merron, "Reel Life: 'North Dallas Forty,' " ESPN Page 2, http://espn.go.com/page2/s/closer/021101.html.

32. "Bear Bryant," *Wikipedia*, en.wikipedia.org/wiki/Bear_Bryant.

33. Mel Renfro interview. All Renfro quotes in this chapter from author interview.

34. Peter Golenbock, *Cowboys Have Always Been My Heroes* (New York: Warner Books, 1997), p. 347.

35. Frank Luksa interview.

36. Golenbock, *Cowboys Have Always Been My Heroes*, pp. 284, 353.

37. Alicia Landry interview.

38. Jimmy Brown with Myron Cope, *Off My Chest* (New York: Doubleday, 1964).

39. "Malcolm X," *Wikipedia*, en.wikipedia.org/wiki/Malcolm_X.

40. Gary Cartwright, "Of Black and White," *Dallas Morning News*, October 1, 1964.

Chapter 13: "WE'RE READY TO CONTEND"

1. Curt Sampson, "Don Meredith: The First Dallas Cowboy," *D Magazine*, September 22, 2010.

2. Tom Landry with Gregg Lewis, *Tom Landry: An Autobiography* (New York: Harper-Collins, 1990), p. 142.

3. Pettis Norman interview. All Norman quotes in this chapter from author interview.

4. Mel Renfro interview.

5. Frank Luksa interview. All Luksa quotes in this chapter from author interview.

6. Lee Roy Jordan interview.

7. Mike Connelly interview. All Connelly quotes in this chapter from author interview.

8. Skip Bayless, *God's Coach: The Hymns, Hype, and Hypocrisy of Tom Landry's Cowboys* (New York: Fireside, 1990), p. 81.

9. Ibid.

10. Sam Blair, *Dallas Cowboys, Pro or Con? A Complete History* (Garden City, NY: Doubleday, 1970), pp. 175.

11. Ibid., p. 182.

12. Ibid., p. 184.

13. Peter Golenbock, *Cowboys Have Always Been My Heroes* (New York: Warner Books, 1997), p. 259.

14. Blair, *Dallas Cowboys, Pro or Con?* p. 187.

15. Golenbock, *Cowboys Have Always Been My Heroes*, p. 260.

16. Landry with Lewis, *Tom Landry*, p. 158.

17. Sam Blair interview. All Blair quotes in this chapter from author interview.

18. Landry with Lewis, *Tom Landry*, p. 158.

19. Tom Landry Jr. interview. All Tom Landry Jr. quotes in this chapter from author interview.

20. Landry with Lewis, *Tom Landry*, p. 159.

21. *Dallas Morning News*, November 2, 1965.

22. *Dallas Morning News*, November 22, 1965.

23. Golenbock, *Cowboys Have Always Been My Heroes*, p. 270.

24. Richard Sandomir, "Little Consolation in Third-Place Game," *New York Times*, February 6, 2011.

25. Bob St. John, *Tex! The Man Who Built the Dallas Cowboys* (Englewood Cliffs, NJ: Prentice Hall, 1988), p. 4.

26. Bayless, *God's Coach*, p. 42.

27. "Excerpt: Chapter One: The Next Voice You Hear," *AWOC Books*, http://www.awocbooks.com/Book.cfm?b=41&f=e.

28. Joe David Brown, "A Big Man Even in Big D," *Sports Illustrated*, January 21, 1963.

29. Bayless, *God's Coach*, pp. 73, 79.

30. Brown, "Big Man Even in Big D."

31. Gary Cartwright, "Turn Out the Lights," *Texas Monthly*, August 1997.

32. Golenbock, *Cowboys Have Always Been My Heroes*, p. 317.

33. Steve Elliott, "American Heroes: Willie Nelson Smoked Pot with Don Meredith," *Toke of the Town*, December 7, 2010, http://www.tokeofthetown.com/2010/12/american_ heroes_willie_nelson_smoked_pot_with_don.php.

34. Golenbock, *Cowboys Have Always Been My Heroes*, p. 283.

35. Bayless, *God's Coach*, p. 91.

36. Golenbock, *Cowboys Have Always Been My Heroes*, p. 243.

37. Bob Lilly with Kristine Setting Clark, *A Cowboy's Life* (Chicago: Triumph Books, 2008), p. 65.

38. Bob St. John, *Tex! The Man Who Built the Dallas Cowboys* (Englewood Cliffs, NJ: Prentice Hall, 1988), p. 263.

39. Landry with Lewis, *Tom Landry*, p. 153.

40. Jeff Merron, "Reel Life: 'North Dallas Forty,' " ESPN Page 2, http://espn.go.com/ page2/s/closer/021101.html.

41. Landry with Lewis, *Tom Landry*, p. 146.

42. Lilly with Clark, *Cowboy's Life*, p. 26.

43. Sampson, "Don Meredith."

44. Landry with Lewis, *Tom Landry*, pp. 143–144.

45. Gary Cartwright, "Tom Landry: Melting the Plastic Man," *Texas Monthly*, November 1973.

46. Sampson, "Don Meredith."

Chapter 14: "THE BASER INSTINCTS OF MEN"

1. Dave Goldberg, "Football War Ended with Merger 25 Years Ago," *Los Angeles Times*, June 9, 1991; "AFL-NFL Merger," *Wikipedia*, en.wikipedia.org/wiki/AFL%E2%80%93NFL_ merger.

2. *Dallas Morning News*, November 5, 1966.

3. "Walt Garrison," *Wikipedia*, en.wikipedia.org/wiki/Walt_Garrison.

4. Tex Maule, "A Shuttle Shakes Up the Pros," *Sports Illustrated*, November 5, 1962.

5. Bob Lilly interview.

6. Michael MacCambridge, *America's Game* (New York: Anchor, 2005), pp. 232–233.

7. Mike Connelly interview. All Connelly quotes in this chapter from author interview.

8. *Orange County Register*, October 10, 2011.

9. Peter Golenbock, *Cowboys Have Always Been My Heroes* (New York: Warner Books, 1997), p. 327.

10. Tom Landry Jr. interview. All Tom Landry Jr. quotes in this chapter from author interview.

11. David Maraniss, *When Pride Still Mattered: A Life of Vince Lombardi* (New York: Simon and Schuster, 1999), p. 415.

12. Herbert Warren Wind, "Coach," *New Yorker*, December 16, 1974, p. 147.

13. *Dallas Morning News*, September 8, 1966.

14. *Dallas Morning News*, October 4, 1966.

15. *Dallas Morning News*, October 10, 1966.

16. Sam Blair, *Dallas Cowboys, Pro or Con? A Complete History* (Garden City, NY: Doubleday, 1970), p. 224.

17. *Dallas Morning News*, October 22, 1966.

18. *Dallas Morning News*, December 19, 1966.

19. *Dallas Morning News*, December 29, 1966.

20. *Dallas Morning News*, December 31, 1966.

21. Tex Maule, "Green Bay Rolls High," *Sports Illustrated*, January 9, 1967.

22. Ibid.

23. *Dallas Morning News*, December 31, 1966.

24. "Turn Out the Lights: Dandy Don Meredith Dies," *San Mateo Daily Journal*, December 7, 2010.

25. *Dallas Morning News*, January 2, 1967.

26. Pettis Norman interview. All Norman quotes in this chapter from author interview.

27. Frank Luksa interview. All Luksa quotes in this chapter from author interview.

28. Bob Hayes, *Run, Bullet, Run: The Rise, Fall, and Recovery of Bob Hayes* (New York: Harper and Row, 1992), p. 180.

29. Sam Blair interview.

30. *Dallas Morning News*, January 2, 1967.

31. "Best NFC Championship Games," *SI.com*, http://sportsillustrated.cnn.com/multimedia/photo_gallery/1001/nfl.playoffs.best.nfc.championship.games/content.1.html #ixzz1w76xL5nM.

32. Blair, *Dallas Cowboys, Pro or Con?* p. 231.

33. Tom Landry with Gregg Lewis, *Tom Landry: An Autobiography* (New York: HarperCollins, 1990), p. 164.

34. Maule, "Green Bay Rolls High," p. 13.

35. Golenbock, *Cowboys Have Always Been My Heroes*, p. 265.

36. *Dallas Morning News*, January 2, 1967.

37. Golenbock, *Cowboys Have Always Been My Heroes*, p. 355.

38. Jeff Merron, "Reel Life: 'North Dallas Forty,' " ESPN Page 2, http://espn.go.com/page2/s/closer/021101.html.

39. Ibid.

40. Ibid.

41. Ibid.

42. Walt Garrison with John Tullius, *Once a Cowboy* (New York: Random House, 1988), p. 64.

43. Ibid.

44. Ashley Withers, "SMU's Playboy Past: Off Campus Office Building Has a Unique Story of Its Own," *Daily Campus* (SMU), September 13, 2011.

45. Landry with Lewis, *Tom Landry*, p. 219.

46. Alicia Landry interview.

47. Withers, "SMU's Playboy Past."

48. Duane Thomas and Paul Zimmerman, *Duane Thomas and the Fall of America's Team* (New York: Warner Books, 1988), p. 46.

49. Peter Gent, "North Hollywood Forty and Other Morality Plays from the NFL," *Esquire*, September 1980, p. 40.

50. Edwin Shrake, "A Rich Man Is Odd Man Out," *Sports Illustrated*, December 9, 1968.

51. Lance Rentzel, *When All the Laughter Died in Sorrow* (New York: Bantam Books, 1973), p. 120.

52. Golenbock, *Cowboys Have Always Been My Heroes*, p. 315.

53. Ibid., p. 317.

54. Blair, *Dallas Cowboys, Pro or Con?* p. 238.

Chapter 15: LESS THAN ZERO

1. Sam Blair, *Cowboys, Pro or Con? A Complete History* (Garden City, NY: Doubleday, 1970), p 252.

2. *Dallas Morning News*, September 30, 1967.

3. Blair, *Dallas Cowboys, Pro or Con?* p. 254.

4. Edwin Shrake, "A Cowboy Named Dandy Don," *Sports Illustrated*, September 16, 1968.

5. Tom Landry with Gregg Lewis, *Tom Landry: An Autobiography* (New York: HarperCollins, 1990), p. 166.

6. Blair, *Dallas Cowboys, Pro or Con?* p. 265.

7. *Dallas Morning News*, December 25, 1967.

8. Pettis Norman interview.

9. David Maraniss, *When Pride Still Mattered: A Life of Vince Lombardi* (New York: Simon and Schuster, 1999), p. 389.

10. *Dallas Morning News*, December 24, 1966.

11. Blair, *Dallas Cowboys, Pro or Con?* p. 263.

12. *Dallas Morning News*, December 30, 1967.

13. Alicia Landry interview. All Alicia Landry quotes in this chapter from author interview.

14. Landry with Lewis, *Tom Landry*, p. 167.

15. Mike Connelly interview.

16. Peter Golenbock, *Cowboys Have Always Been My Heroes* (New York: Warner Books, 1997), p. 330.

17. Landry with Lewis, *Tom Landry*, p. 167.

18. Lee Roy Jordan interview. All Jordan quotes in this chapter from author interview.

19. Mel Renfro interview. All Renfro quotes in this chapter from author interview.

20. Shrake, "Cowboy Named Dandy Don."

21. Tex Maule, "The Old Pro Goes in for Six," *Sports Illustrated*, January 8, 1968.

22. Curt Sampson, "Don Meredith: The First Dallas Cowboy," *D Magazine*, September 22, 2010.

23. *Dallas Morning News*, January 1, 1968.

24. Ibid.

25. Blair, *Dallas Cowboys, Pro or Con?* p. 275.

26. Maule, "Old Pro Goes in for Six."

27. *Landry: The NFL's Man in the Hat*, NFL Films, 2010.

28. Bill Plaschke, "Ice Bowl: It's Still Considered among Best NFL Games, but Plenty of Myths Surround Packers' Defeat of Cowboys in 1967 Championship Game," *Los Angeles Times*, January 9, 1996.

29. Maule, "Old Pro Goes in for Six."

30. *Landry: The NFL's Man in the Hat*.

31. Maule, "Old Pro Goes in for Six."

32. Lance Rentzel, *When All the Laughter Died in Sorrow* (New York: Bantam Books, 1973), p. 152.

33. *Dallas Morning News*, January 1, 1968.

34. Blair, *Dallas Cowboys, Pro or Con?* p. 282.

35. Landry with Lewis, *Tom Landry*, p. 170.

36. Blair, *Dallas Cowboys, Pro or Con?* pp. 278–279.

37. Shrake, "Cowboy Named Dandy Don."

38. *Dallas Morning News*, January 1, 1968.

39. Tom Landry Jr. interview.

40. Duane Thomas and Paul Zimmerman, *Duane Thomas and the Fall of America's Team* (New York: Warner Books, 1988), p. 44.

41. *Dallas Morning News*, January 1, 1968.

42. Larry Harris, "Woodson Was First with 'Frozen Tundra,'" *Press Box*, http://www.pressboxonline.com/story.cfm?id=6428.

43. Golenbock, *Cowboys Have Always Been My Heroes*, pp. 332, 339.

44. *Dallas Morning News*, January 4, 1968.

45. Ibid.

Chapter 16: "WE NEED TO REVERSE THIS TREND"

1. Bob St. John, *Landry: The Legend and the Legacy* (Nashville: W Publishing Group, 2000), pp. 255–258.

2. David Maraniss, *When Pride Still Mattered: A Life of Vince Lombardi* (New York: Simon and Schuster, 1999), pp. 452, 118, 446; Jud Lounsbury, "Starr's Claim That Lom-

bardi Would Endorse Romney Is Absurd: Lombardi Was a Strong Democrat," *Daily Kos*, November 4, 2012, http://www.dailykos.com/story/2012/11/04/1155332/-Starr-s-Claim-That-Lombardi-Would-Endorse-Romney-is-Absurd-Lombardi-was-a-Strong-Democrat.
3. Lounsbury, "Starr's Claim."
4. *Dallas Morning News*, April 5, 1968.
5. "Cronkite, Who Defined the Role of Anchor, Dies at 92," Associated Press, July 18, 2009.
6. Sam Blair, *Dallas Cowboys, Pro or Con? A Complete History* (Garden City, NY: Doubleday, 1970), p. 290.
7. Peter Golenbock, *Cowboys Have Always Been My Heroes* (New York: Warner Books, 1997), p. 348.
8. Ibid., pp. 349–350.
9. Edwin Shrake, "A Cowboy Named Dandy Don," *Sports Illustrated*, September 16, 1968.
10. Ibid.
11. Ibid.
12. *Dallas Morning News*, September 18, 1968.
13. *Dallas Morning News*, December 4, 1968.
14. Ibid.
15. Blair, *Dallas Cowboys, Pro or Con?* pp. 318, 320.
16. Tom Landry with Gregg Lewis, *Tom Landry: An Autobiography* (New York: HarperCollins, 1990), p. 172.
17. Blair, *Dallas Cowboys, Pro or Con?* p. 320.
18. Pettis Norman interview.
19. Bob Hayes with Robert Pack, *Run, Bullet, Run: The Rise, Fall, and Recovery of Bob Hayes* (New York: Harper and Row, 1992), p. 112.
20. Blair, *Dallas Cowboys, Pro or Con?* p. 322.
21. *Dallas Morning News*, December 22, 1968.
22. Golenbock, *Cowboys Have Always Been My Heroes*, p. 366.
23. Ibid.
24. Landry with Lewis, *Tom Landry*, p. 172.
25. *Dallas Morning News*, December 22, 1968.
26. Jeff Merron, "Reel Life: 'North Dallas Forty,' " ESPN Page 2, http://espn.go.com/page2/s/closer/021101.html.
27. Walt Garrison with John Tullius, *Once a Cowboy* (New York: Random House, 1988), pp. 76–77.
28. Ibid., p. 77.
29. *Dallas Morning News*, December 22, 1968.
30. Landry with Lewis, *Tom Landry*, p. 177.
31. Shrake, "Cowboy Named Dandy Don."
32. *Dallas Morning News*, June 29, 1969.
33. Golenbock, *Cowboys Have Always Been My Heroes*, p. 370.
34. Landry with Lewis, *Tom Landry*, p. 177.
35. Matt Mosley, "Saying Goodbye to 'Dandy Don' Meredith," NFL Nation: Gary Cartwright, *NFL Nation Blog*, December 6, 2010, http://espn.go.com/blog/nflnation/tag/_/name/gary-cartwright.
36. Landry with Lewis, *Tom Landry*, p. 177.
37. Blair, *Dallas Cowboys, Pro or Con?* p. 333.
38. *Dallas Morning News*, July 6, 1969.
39. *Dallas Morning News*, July 7, 1969.
40. Golenbock, *Cowboys Have Always Been My Heroes*, p. 370.
41. Frank Gifford, *The Whole Ten Yards* (New York: Random House, 1993), p. 149.
42. Merron, "Reel Life: 'North Dallas Forty.' "
43. Ibid.
44. Mike Connelly interview.
45. *Sports Illustrated*, September 22, 1969.
46. Blair, *Dallas Cowboys, Pro or Con?* p. 352.

47. Golenbock, *Cowboys Have Always Been My Heroes*, p. 385.
48. Blair, *Dallas Cowboys, Pro or Con?* p. 361.
49. Ibid.

Chapter 17: THE LORD TAKETH . . .

1. Sam Blair, *Dallas Cowboys, Pro or Con? A Complete History* (Garden City, NY: Doubleday, 1970), p. 373.
2. Bob Hayes with Robert Pack, *Run, Bullet, Run: The Rise, Fall, and Recovery of Bob Hayes* (New York: Harper and Row, 1992), p. 229.
3. Blair, *Dallas Cowboys, Pro or Con?* pp. 377–378.
4. Peter Golenbock, *Cowboys Have Always Been My Heroes* (New York: Warner Books, 1997), p. 411.
5. Blair, *Dallas Cowboys, Pro or Con?* p. 379.
6. Golenbock, *Cowboys Have Always Been My Heroes*, p. 413.
7. Blair, *Dallas Cowboys, Pro or Con?* p. 381.
8. Golenbock, *Cowboys Have Always Been My Heroes*, p. 413.
9. Blair, *Dallas Cowboys, Pro or Con?* p. 381.
10. *Dallas Morning News*, December 30, 1969.
11. Blair, *Dallas Cowboys, Pro or Con?* p. 370.
12. Tom Landry with Gregg Lewis, *Tom Landry: An Autobiography* (New York: HarperCollins, 1990), p. 180.
13. *Dallas Morning News*, December 30, 1969.
14. Blair, *Dallas Cowboys, Pro or Con?* p. 420.
15. Jeff Merron, "Reel Life: 'North Dallas Forty,' " ESPN Page 2, http://espn.go.com/page2/s/closer/021101.html.
16. *Dallas Morning News*, December 30, 1969.
17. Skip Bayless, *God's Coach: The Hymns, Hype, and Hypocrisy of Tom Landry's Cowboys* (New York: Fireside, 1990), p. 74.
18. Paul Zimmerman, *The New Thinking Man's Guide to Pro Football* (New York: Simon and Schuster, 1984), p. 292.
19. Peter Gent, "North Hollywood Forty and Other Morality Plays from the NFL," *Esquire*, September 1980, p. 39.
20. Bob St. John, *Texas Sports Writers: The Wild and Wacky Years* (Plano, TX: Republic of Texas Books, 2002), p. 2.
21. William Oscar Johnson, "There Are No Holes at the Top," *Sports Illustrated*, September 1, 1982.
22. Hayes with Pack, *Run, Bullet, Run*, p. 109.
23. Mike Connelly interview.
24. David S. Neft and Richard M. Cohen, *The Sports Encyclopedia: Pro Football, the Modern Era, 1960–1988* (New York: St. Martin's Press, 1988), p. 188.
25. Duane Thomas and Paul Zimmerman, *Duane Thomas and the Fall of America's Team* (New York: Warner Books, 1988), p. 41.
26. Ibid., p. 52.
27. Golenbock, *Cowboys Have Always Been My Heroes*, p. 428.
28. Hayes with Pack, *Run, Bullet, Run*, p. 112.
29. Walt Garrison with John Tullius, *Once a Cowboy* (New York: Random House, 1988), pp. 62–63.
30. "Pat Toomay Talks about His Career: Commodore History Corner by Bill Traughber," *Vanderbilt Commodores*, October 29, 2008, http://www.vucommodores.com/sports/m-footbl/spec-rel/102908aaa.html.
31. Bob Lilly with Kristine Setting Clark, *A Cowboy's Life* (Chicago: Triumph Books, 2008), p. 90.
32. Mel Renfro interview. All Renfro quotes in this chapter from author interview.

33. Tex Maule, "Big Ifs in Big D: The Cowboys, Who Haven't Won a Big Game, Are Plagued by Quarterback Doubts, Complacent Vets, Angry Blacks and No Confidence," *Sports Illustrated*, August 31, 1970.

34. St. John, *Texas Sports Writers*, p. 66.

35. Ibid., p. 67.

36. Golenbock, *Cowboys Have Always Been My Heroes*, p. 432.

37. Hayes with Pack, *Run, Bullet, Run*, p. 218.

38. Ibid.

39. Ibid., p. 111.

40. Ibid., pp. 231, 113.

41. Thomas and Zimmerman, *Duane Thomas*, pp. 57–58.

42. Hayes with Pack, *Run, Bullet, Run*, p. 133.

43. Mark Ribowsky, *Howard Cosell: The Man, the Myth, and the Transformation of American Sports* (New York: W. W. Norton, 2011), pp. 231, 324.

44. Golenbock, *Cowboys Have Always Been My Heroes*, p. 436.

45. Landry with Lewis, *Tom Landry*, pp. 186–187.

46. Golenbock, *Cowboys Have Always Been My Heroes*, p. 437.

47. Ibid.

48. Landry with Lewis, *Tom Landry*, p. 187.

49. Pettis Norman interview.

50. "Pokes Rentzel Charged with Indecent Exposure,"*Dallas Morning News*, December 1, 1970.

51. Golenbock, *Cowboys Have Always Been My Heroes*, p. 442.

52. Lance Rentzel, *When All the Laughter Died in Sorrow* (New York: Bantam Books, 1973), p. 214.

53. Ibid., p. 208.

Chapter 18: "A VEHICLE FOR CORPORATE EGO"

1. *Dallas Morning News*, December 31, 1970.

2. *Dallas Morning News*, January 4, 1971.

3. Ibid.

4. Morton Sharnik, "For an Opening, He Might Come Out and Growl," *Sports Illustrated*, January 18, 1971.

5. Joe Nick Patoski, *The Dallas Cowboys: The Outrageous History of the Biggest, Loudest, Most Hated, Best Loved Football Team in America* (New York: Little, Brown, 2012), p. 242.

6. Lee Roy Jordan interview. All Jordan quotes in this chapter from author interview.

7. Tex Maule, "Eleven Big Mistakes," *Sports Illustrated*, January 25, 1971.

8. *Super Bowl III Highlights*, NFL Films, 1969.

9. "Super Bowl V," *Wikipedia*, en.wikipedia.org/wiki/Super_Bowl_V.

10. Maule, "Eleven Big Mistakes."

11. Eric Neel, "The Super Bowl Barely Makes the Grade," ESPN Page 2, http://espn.go.com/page2/s/neel/030122.html.

12. *Dallas Morning News*, January 18, 1971.

13. Peter Golenbock, *Cowboys Have Always Been My Heroes* (New York: Warner Books, 1997), p. 462.

14. *Dallas Morning News*, January 18, 1971.

15. Bill McGrane, "A Mad, Mad, Mad Super Bowl," in Pete Rozelle, *The Super Bowl: Celebrating a Quarter-Century of America's Greatest Game* (New York: Simon and Schuster, 1990).

16. Tom Landry with Gregg Lewis, *Tom Landry: An Autobiography* (New York: Harper-Collins, 1990), p. 188.

17. Mel Renfro interview.

18. Pat Toomay, *The Crunch* (New York: W. W. Norton, 1975), p. 60.

19. *St. Petersburg Times*, February 27, 1971; "Kiner Hearing Moved to 31st," *Dallas Morning News*, June 23, 1972.

20. "Drug Charges Dropped," *New York Times*, February 1, 1972.

21. Toomay, *Crunch*, p. 60.

22. "Duane Thomas," *Wikipedia*, en.wikipedia.org/wiki/Duane_Thomas.

23. Duane Thomas and Paul Zimmerman, *Duane Thomas and the Fall of America's Team* (New York: Warner Books, 1988), p. 72.

24. Golenbock, *Cowboys Have Always Been My Heroes*, p. 473.

25. Thomas and Zimmerman, *Duane Thomas*, p. 73.

26. Ibid., p. 75.

27. *Dallas Morning News*, July 22, 1971.

28. Golenbock, *Cowboys Have Always Been My Heroes*, p. 450.

29. Landry with Lewis, *Tom Landry*, p. 191.

30. Golenbock, *Cowboys Have Always Been My Heroes*, p. 458.

31. Thomas and Zimmerman, *Duane Thomas*, pp. 64–65.

32. *Dallas Morning News*, July 22, 1971.

33. Thomas and Zimmerman, *Duane Thomas*, p. 78.

34. *Dallas Morning News*, July 22, 1971.

35. Ibid.

36. *Dallas Morning News*, July 29, 1971.

37. Thomas and Zimmerman, *Duane Thomas*, p. 80.

38. Ibid., p. 81.

39. Ibid.

40. "Duane Thomas," Everything Dallas Cowboys, August 25, 2012 everything-dallascowboys.com/cowboys-history/players-and-coaches/running-backs/duane-thomas.

41. Pettis Norman interview. All Norman quotes in this chapter from author interview.

42. Thomas and Zimmerman, *Duane Thomas*, p. 192.

43. *Dallas Morning News*, May 16, 1971.

44. Thomas and Zimmerman, *Duane Thomas*, p. 59.

45. Tex Maule, "Big Ifs in Big D: The Cowboys, Who Haven't Won a Big Game, Are Plagued by Quarterback Doubts, Complacent Vets, Angry Blacks and No Confidence," *Sports Illustrated*, August 31, 1970.

46. Toomay, *Crunch*, p. 196.

47. "Lance Alworth Trade," Professional Football Researchers Association, pfraforum.org/index.php?showtopic=1064.

48. Jaimie Aron, *Breakthrough 'Boys: The Story of the 1971 Super Bowl Champion Dallas Cowboys* (Minneapolis: MVP Books, 2011), p. 46.

49. "Lance Rentzel," *Wikipedia*, en.wikipedia.org/wiki/Lance_Rentzel.

50. Ibid., p. 45.

51. *Dallas Morning News*, September 6, 1971.

52. Ibid.

53. Golenbock, *Cowboys Have Always Been My Heroes*, p. 476.

54. Maule, "Big Ifs in Big D."

55. Thomas and Zimmerman, *Duane Thomas*, p. 118.

56. Ibid.

57. Patoski, *Dallas Cowboys*, p. 260.

58. Landry with Lewis, *Tom Landry*, p. 191.

59. Ibid.

Chapter 19: . . . AND THE LORD FINALLY GIVETH

1. Pat Toomay, *The Crunch* (New York: W. W. Norton, 1975), p. 86.

2. "Texas Stadium," Ballparks.com, http://football.ballparks.com/NFL/DallasCowboys/index.htm.

3. Gary Cartwright, "Turn Out the Lights," *Texas Monthly*, August 1997.

4. "Why Does Texas Stadium Have a Hole in Its Roof? So God Can Watch His Team Play," Associated Press, December 12, 2008.

5. Sam Blair, *Dallas Cowboys, Pro or Con? A Complete History* (Garden City, NY: Doubleday, 1970), p. 383.

6. Jane Wolfe, *The Murchisons* (New York: St. Martin's Press, 1991), p. 307.

7. Joe Nick Patoski, *The Dallas Cowboys: The Outrageous History of the Biggest, Loudest, Most Hated, Best Loved Football Team in America* (New York: Little, Brown, 2012), p. 239.

8. Peter Golenbock, *Cowboys Have Always Been My Heroes* (New York: Warner Books, 1997), p. 283.

9. Duane Thomas and Paul Zimmerman, *Duane Thomas and the Fall of America's Team* (New York: Warner Books, 1988), p. 79.

10. Tom Landry with Gregg Lewis, *Tom Landry: An Autobiography* (New York: HarperCollins, 1990), p. 190.

11. Patoski, *Dallas Cowboys*, p. 256.

12. Golenbock, *Cowboys Have Always Been My Heroes*, p. 482.

13. Ibid.

14. *Dallas Morning News*, December 26. 1971.

15. *Dallas Morning News*, January 4, 1972.

16. Will Grimsley, "Coaching Contrast," Associated Press, January 16, 1972.

17. *Dallas Morning News*, January 4, 1972.

18. Mike Kingston, "Nixon's Football, Political Strategy Bad," *Dallas Morning News*, January 7, 1972.

19. Tex Maule, "Cowboys, in a Walk," *Sports Illustrated*, January 17, 1971.

20. John Underwood, "The Blood and Thunder Boys," *Sports Illustrated*, August 7, 1972.

21. Alan Schmadke, "Super Bowl Skinny," *Orlando Sentinel*, January 2008.

22. CBS telecast, January 16, 1972.

23. Ibid.

24. Landry with Lewis, *Tom Landry*, p. 193.

25. *Dallas Morning News*, January 17, 1972.

26. Ibid.

27. Mel Renfro interview. All Renfro quotes in this chapter from author interview.

28. Tex Maule, "A Cowboy Stampede," *Sports Illustrated*, January 24, 1972.

29. Alicia Landry interview.

30. Patoski, *Dallas Cowboys*, pp. 279–280.

31. Ibid.

32. Landry with Lewis, *Tom Landry*, p. 196.

33. Skip Bayless, *God's Coach: The Hymns, Hype, and Hypocrisy of Tom Landry's Cowboys* (New York: Fireside, 1990), p. 109.

34. Toomay, *Crunch*, p. 196.

35. Golenbock, *Cowboys Have Always Been My Heroes*, p. 483.

36. Toomay, *Crunch*, p. 85.

37. Golenbock, *Cowboys Have Always Been My Heroes*, p. 473.

38. Ibid., p. 499.

39. Patoski, *Dallas Cowboys*, p. 301.

40. Golenbock, *Cowboys Have Always Been My Heroes*, p. 522.

41. Patoski, *Dallas Cowboys*, p. 302.

42. Bayless, *God's Coach*, p. 121.

43. Landry with Lewis, *Tom Landry*, p. 198.

44. *Dallas Morning News*, December 24, 1972.

45. *Dallas Morning News*, December 31, 1972.

46. Ibid.

47. Golenbock, *Cowboys Have Always Been My Heroes*, p. 515.

48. *Dallas Morning News*, December 21, 1972.

49. *Dallas Morning News*, January 1, 1973.
50. Thomas and Zimmerman, *Duane Thomas*, p. 118.
51. Golenbock, *Cowboys Have Always Been My Heroes*, p. 523.
52. *Dallas Morning News*, January 1, 1973.

Chapter 20: "A BIG TRANSMITTER TO GOD"

1. Pat Toomay, *The Crunch* (New York: W. W. Norton, 1975), p. 179.
2. Skip Bayless, *God's Coach: The Hymns, Hype, and Hypocrisy of Tom Landry's Cowboys* (New York: Fireside, 1990), p. 122.
3. Ibid.
4. Peter Golenbock, *Cowboys Have Always Been My Heroes* (New York: Warner Books, 1997), p. 518.
5. Nick Gholson, "Gholson: For Dallas, Ditka Was Landry's Hit Man," *TimesRecord News*, October 31, 2009, http://www.timesrecordnews.com/news/2009/oct/31/for-dallas-ditka-was-landrys-hit-man.
6. Golenbock, *Cowboys Have Always Been My Heroes*, p. 629.
7. George Will, "America's Shifting Reality," *Jewish World Review*, November 4, 2004.
8. Duane Thomas and Paul Zimmerman, *Duane Thomas and the Fall of America's Team* (New York: Warner Books, 1988), p. 125.
9. Harvey Martin, *Texas Thunder: My Eleven Years with the Dallas Cowboys* (New York: Rawson, 1986), p. 18.
10. Carlton Stowers, *Staubach: Portrait of the Brightest Star* (Chicago: Triumph Book, 2010), p. 136.
11. Golenbock, *Cowboys Have Always Been My Heroes*, p. 524.
12. "Out of Bounds: Domestic Violence Scarred This Ex-Cowboy's Life Until He Learned to Fill a Void within Himself," *Fort Worth Star-Telegram*, July 31, 1994.
13. Peter Gent, "North Hollywood Forty and Other Morality Plays from the NFL," *Esquire*, September 1980, p. 41.
14. Toomay, *Crunch*, p. 179.
15. Ibid., p. 200.
16. Ibid., p. 196.
17. Joe Nick Patoski, *The Dallas Cowboys: The Outrageous History of the Biggest, Loudest, Most Hated, Best Loved Football Team in America* (New York: Little, Brown, 2012), p. 283.
18. Edward Linn, "The Thinking Man's Cowboy," *Saturday Evening Post*, December 17, 1966.
19. Herbert Warren Wind, "Coach," *New Yorker*, December 16, 1974, p. 122.
20. Curt Smith, "Punt, Pass and Prayer," *Saturday Evening Post*, October 1980, p. 63.
21. Golenbock, *Cowboys Have Always Been My Heroes*, p. 367.
22. Matt Schudel, "Peter Gent, Football Player-Turned-Author, Dies at 69," *Washington Post*, October 1, 2011, http://www.washingtonpost.com/local/obituaries/peter-gent-football-player-turned-author-dies-at-69/2011/10/01/gIQAQhedDL_story.html.
23. Frank Luksa interview.
24. Golenbock, *Cowboys Have Always Been My Heroes*, pp. 376–377.
25. Toomay, *Crunch*, p. 8.
26. Bayless, *God's Coach*, p. 115.
27. Ibid., p. 18.
28. Ibid., p. 146.
29. Mel Renfro interview.
30. Thomas and Zimmerman, *Duane Thomas*, p. 95.
31. Tom Landry Jr. interview. All Tom Landry Jr. quotes in this chapter from author interview.

32. Martin, *Texas Thunder*, pp. 46–47.

33. rabblerousr, "Top Ten Cowboys Regular Season Games: #3: The Mad Bomber Saves the Day," *Blogging the Boys* (blog), July 13, 2012, http://www.bloggingtheboys.com/2012/7/13/3157372/top-ten-dallas-cowboys-regular-season-games-3-enter-the-mad-bomber.

34. Stowers, *Staubach*, p. 133.

35. Thomas "Hollywood" Henderson and Peter Knobler, *Out of Control: Confessions of an NFL Casualty* (New York: Putnam, 1987), p. 209.

36. Bob Hayes with Robert Pack, *Run, Bullet, Run: The Rise, Fall, and Recovery of Bob Hayes* (New York: Harper and Row, 1992), pp. 232–233.

37. Golenbock, *Cowboys Have Always Been My Heroes*, p. 569.

38. Hayes with Pack, *Run, Bullet, Run*, p. 113.

39. Ibid., pp. 273–274.

40. Golenbock, *Cowboys Have Always Been My Heroes*, p. 573.

41. Hayes with Pack, *Run, Bullet, Run*, p. 305.

42. Ibid., p. 11.

43. Mike Fisher, "Conning the Cowboys?" *TheRanchReport.com*, February 2, 2009, http://dal.scout.com/2/835595.html.

44. Ibid.

45. Tom Landry with Gregg Lewis, *Tom Landry: An Autobiography* (New York: Harper-Collins, 1990), p. 205.

46. Henderson and Knobler, *Out of Control*, pp. 64, 82.

47. Golenbock, *Cowboys Have Always Been My Heroes*, p. 582.

48. Joe Marshall, "My, How You Do Run On and On," *Sports Illustrated*, January 29, 1979.

49. "They Said It," *Sports Illustrated*, December 19, 1977.

50. Henderson and Knobler, *Out of Control*, pp. 84–85.

51. Ibid.

52. Martin, *Texas Thunder*, p. 61.

53. Henderson and Knobler, *Out of Control*, p. 81.

54. Ibid.

55. Martin, *Texas Thunder*, p. 61.

56. Golenbock, *Cowboys Have Always Been My Heroes*, p. 582.

57. Barry Horn, "Staubach, Pearson Discuss Genesis of 'Hail Mary' Pass," *Dallas Morning News*, January 17, 2010.

58. Dan Jenkins, "On a Wing and a Prayer," *Sports Illustrated*, January 5, 1976.

59. Horn, "Staubach, Pearson Discuss."

60. Ibid.

61. Dan Jenkins, "Dallas Feels the Steeler Crunch," *Sports Illustrated*, January 26, 1976.

62. Martin, *Texas Thunder*, pp. 75–76.

63. Ibid.

64. Jenkins, "On a Wing and a Prayer."

65. Martin, *Texas Thunder*, p. 80.

66. Jenkins, "On a Wing and a Prayer."

67. Ibid.

68. Martin, *Texas Thunder*, p. 80.

Chapter 21: THE LAST HAPPY ENDING

1. Duane Thomas and Paul Zimmerman, *Duane Thomas and the Fall of America's Team* (New York: Warner Books, 1988), p. 206.

2. Ibid.

3. Ibid.

4. Pettis Norman interview. All Norman quotes in this chapter from author interview.

5. Thomas and Zimmerman, *Duane Thomas*, p. 212.

6. Thomas "Hollywood" Henderson and Peter Knobler, *Out of Control: Confessions of an NFL Casualty* (New York: Putnam, 1987), p. 47.

7. Thomas and Zimmerman, *Duane Thomas*, p. 9.

8. Skip Bayless, *God's Coach: The Hymns, Hype, and Hypocrisy of Tom Landry's Cowboys* (New York: Fireside, 1990), p. 117.

9. Peter Golenbock, *Cowboys Have Always Been My Heroes* (New York: Warner Books, 1997), p. 502.

10. Thomas and Zimmerman, *Duane Thomas*, p. 114.

11. Ibid., p. 216.

12. http://dallascowboys.com/news/news.cfm?id=62343770-B8AD-DCB4-4CECE6E34DF F4C98.

13. David Barron, "Ex-Cowboy Duane Thomas 'Found Peace in the Game,'" *Houston Chronicle*, February 1, 2004.

14. Thomas and Zimmerman, *Duane Thomas*, p. 215.

15. "Reversing His Field: Duane Thomas Has Returned to the Cowboys—As an Author," Associated Press, July 23, 1987.

16. Thomas and Zimmerman, *Duane Thomas*, pp. 86–87.

17. Ibid., p. 245.

18. Harvey Martin, *Texas Thunder: My Eleven Years with the Dallas Cowboys* (New York: Rawson, 1986), p. 90.

19. Kent Demaret, "Tom Landry Is a Believer: In Himself, His Printouts, His Cowboys and His Lord," *People*, December 19, 1977.

20. "Jean Fugett," *Wikipedia*, en.wikipedia.org/wiki/Jean_Fugett.

21. Golenbock, *Cowboys Have Always Been My Heroes*, p. 615.

22. Joe Nick Patoski, *The Dallas Cowboys: The Outrageous History of the Biggest, Loudest, Most Hated, Best Loved Football Team in America* (New York: Little, Brown, 2012), p. 369.

23. Golenbock, *Cowboys Have Always Been My Heroes*, p. 608.

24. Demaret, "Tom Landry Is a Believer."

25. Golenbock, *Cowboys Have Always Been My Heroes*, p. 615.

26. Joe Marshall, "This Agent's No Secret," *Sports Illustrated*, May 16, 1977.

27. Golenbock, *Cowboys Have Always Been My Heroes*, p. 617.

28. Greg Hansen, "Bucs Get Ricky Bell . . . Dallas Gets Tony Dorsett," *Evening Independent* (Tampa), May 3, 1977.

29. Demaret, "Tom Landry Is a Believer."

30. Golenbock, *Cowboys Have Always Been My Heroes*, p. 618.

31. Mel Renfro interview. All Renfro quotes in this chapter from author interview.

32. Golenbock, *Cowboys Have Always Been My Heroes*, p. 621.

33. Ibid.

34. *Dallas Morning News*, December 5, 1978.

35. Joe Marshall, "The Orange Is Doomed To Be Crushed," *Sports Illustrated*, January 16, 1978.

36. Dan Jenkins, "Doomsday in the Dome," *Sports Illustrated*, January 23, 1978.

37. Patoski, *Dallas Cowboys*, p. 381.

38. Martin, *Texas Thunder*, p. 106.

39. Marshall, "Orange Is Doomed To Be Crushed."

40. Bill Gorman, "Super Bowl TV Ratings," TV by the Numbers, January 18, 2009, http://tvbythenumbers.zap2it.com/2009/01/18/historical-super-bowl-tv-ratings/11044.

41. Golenbock, *Cowboys Have Always Been My Heroes*, p. 633.

42. Martin, *Texas Thunder*, p. 111.

43. Jenkins, "Doomsday in the Dome."

44. Bayless, *God's Coach*, p. 134.

45. Tom Landry with Gregg Lewis, *Tom Landry: An Autobiography* (New York: Harper-Collins, 1990), p. 211.
46. Jenkins, "Doomsday in the Dome."
47. Ibid.
48. *Dallas Morning News*, January 16, 1978.
49. Patoski, *Dallas Cowboys*, p. 385.

Chapter 22: HOLLYWOOD BABYLON

1. *Tom Landry: A Football Life*, NFL Films, 2011, part 4 available at http://www.youtube.com/watch?v=2ZTnts952X8&feature=related.
2. Ibid.
3. Ibid.
4. "Call the Next Witness," *Saturday Evening Post*, April 1977, p. 44.
5. Curt Smith, "Punt, Pass and Prayer," *Saturday Evening Post*, October 1980, p. 63.
6. Dave Anderson, "Tom Landry: Spur of the Dallas Cowboys," *Reader's Digest*, November 1978, p. 227.
7. Alicia Landry interview.
8. Joe Nick Patoski, *The Dallas Cowboys: The Outrageous History of the Biggest, Loudest, Most Hated, Best Loved Football Team in America* (New York: Little, Brown, 2012), p. 384.
9. Tom Landry with Gregg Lewis, *Tom Landry: An Autobiography* (New York: Harper-Collins, 1990), p. 206.
10. Joe Marshall, "It Could Be Doomsday for Dallas," *Sports Illustrated*, January 22, 1979.
11. Paul Zimmerman, *The New Thinking Man's Guide to Pro Football* (New York: Simon and Schuster, 1984), p. 244; Duane Thomas and Paul Zimmerman, *Duane Thomas and the Fall of America's Team* (New York: Warner Books, 1988), p. 47.
12. Barry Horn, "Going Deep—Into a Hell: Former Cowboy Richards Has Seen Life Become Anything but Golden Because of Drugs," *Dallas Morning News*, January 25, 1993.
13. Thomas "Hollywood" Henderson and Peter Knobler, *Out of Control: Confessions of an NFL Casualty* (New York: Putnam, 1987), p. 88.
14. "Septien Pleads Guilty," *New York Times*, April 9, 1987.
15. Mark Ribowsky, "Behind the Cowboy Struggle to Reach Super Bowl XIII," *Sport*, November 1978, pp. 27–28.
16. Marshall, "It Could Be Doomsday for Dallas."
17. Ribowsky, "Behind the Cowboy Struggle," pp. 27–28.
18. Ibid., pp. 32–33.
19. Alexander Wolff and Kostya Kennedy, "Look What's in Landry's Laundry," *Sports Illustrated*, September 4, 1995.
20. Gary Cartwright, "Tom Landry: Melting the Plastic Man," *Texas Monthly*, November 1973.
21. Harvey Martin, *Texas Thunder: My Eleven Years with the Dallas Cowboys* (New York: Rawson, 1986), p. 60.
22. Mark Ribowsky, "The Inside Track: Thomas Henderson," *Inside Sports*, June 30, 1980, p. 90.
23. Thomas Henderson with Frank Luksa, *In Control* (Champaign, IL: Sports Publishing, 2004), pp. 313, 315.
24. Peter Golenbock, *Cowboys Have Always Been My Heroes* (New York: Warner Books, 1997), p. 582.
25. Thomas "Hollywood" Henderson with Walter Lowe Jr., "Confessions of a Cocaine Cowboy," *Playboy*, December 1981.
26. Skip Bayless, *God's Coach: The Hymns, Hype, and Hypocrisy of Tom Landry's Cowboys* (New York: Fireside, 1990), p. 141.
27. Ibid.

28. Frank Luksa interview. All Luksa quotes in this chapter from author interview.
29. Martin, *Texas Thunder*, p. 182.
30. Ibid., p. 168.
31. Ibid., p. 118.
32. Ibid., p. 142.
33. Ibid.
34. Ribowsky, "Inside Track," p. 89.
35. Martin, *Texas Thunder*, p. 144.
36. Henderson and Knobler, *Out of Control*, p. 144.
37. Ibid., p. 183.
38. Ibid., p. 218.
39. Ibid., p. 224.
40. Gary Cartwright, "Comeback: Thomas 'Hollywood' Henderson," *Texas Monthly*, September 2000.
41. Henderson and Knobler, *Out of Control*, p. 89.
42. Ribowsky, "Inside Track," p. 89.
43. Golenbock, *Cowboys Have Always Been My Heroes*, p. 635.
44. Henderson and Knobler, *Out of Control*, p. 147.
45. Ibid., p. 168.
46. Golenbock, *Cowboys Have Always Been My Heroes*, p. 635.
47. Lee Roy Jordan interview.
48. Golenbock, *Cowboys Have Always Been My Heroes*, p. 638.
49. Ibid.
50. Joe Marshall, "Super Bowl XIII Should Be Super Lucky," *Sports Illustrated*, January 22, 1979.
51. Golenbock, *Cowboys Have Always Been My Heroes*, p. 638.
52. "What Did Terry Bradshaw Say about Thomas 'Hollywood' Henderson during Super Bowl Week?" *Sports Comet*, www.sportscomet.com/Football-American/78921.htm.
53. Henderson and Knobler, *Out of Control*, p. 204.
54. Tom Landry with Gregg Lewis, *Tom Landry: An Autobiography* (New York: Harper-Collins, 1990), p. 207.
55. Martin, *Texas Thunder*, p. 129.
56. *Dallas Morning News*, January 21, 1979.
57. Ribowsky, "Behind the Cowboy Struggle," p. 32.
58. "Super Bowl XIII," *Wikipedia*, en.wikipedia.org/wiki/Super_Bowl_XIII.
59. Golenbock, *Cowboys Have Always Been My Heroes*, p. 641.
60. Dan Jenkins, "What a Passing Parade!" *Sports Illustrated*, January 29, 1979.
61. Ibid.
62. Henderson and Knobler, *Out of Control*, p. 212.

Chapter 23: AMERICA'S TEAM—OR THE ANTICHRIST?

1. Dan Jenkins, "What a Passing Parade!" *Sports Illustrated*, January 29, 1979.
2. Harvey Martin, *Texas Thunder: My Eleven Years with the Dallas Cowboys* (New York: Rawson, 1986), p. 133.
3. Peter Golenbock, *Cowboys Have Always Been My Heroes* (New York: Warner Books, 1997), p. 641.
4. Martin, *Texas Thunder*, p. 133.
5. Sam Blair, "Landry Fumes Over Call," *Dallas Morning News*, January 23, 1979.
6. Skip Bayless, "Ungodly Godly Terry," *Dallas Morning News*, January 22, 1979.
7. Skip Bayless, *God's Coach: The Hymns, Hype, and Hypocrisy of Tom Landry's Cowboys* (New York: Fireside, 1990), p. 140.
8. Skip Bayless, "XIII Replay: A Final Angle," *Dallas Morning News*, January 23, 1979.

9. Curt Smith, "Punt, Pass and Prayer," *Saturday Evening Post*, October 1980, p. 128.

10. "America's Team," *Wikipedia*, en.wikipedia.org/wiki/America%27s_Team.

11. *Landry: The NFL's Man in the Hat*, NFL Films, 2010.

12. "Lynn Swann on America's Team," YouTube, http://www.youtube.com/watch?v=x BLUotbreas.

13. Duane Thomas and Paul Zimmerman, *Duane Thomas and the Fall of America's Team* (New York: Warner Books, 1988), p. 122.

14. Rick Telander, "How to Be a Real Cowboy," *Sports Illustrated*, December 7, 1981.

15. Joe Nick Patoski, *The Dallas Cowboys: The Outrageous History of the Biggest, Loudest, Most Hated, Best Loved Football Team in America* (New York: Little, Brown, 2012), p. 424.

16. "Tony Dorsett and his DEAD Fiance's??" Lipstick Alley, http://www.lipstickalley.com/f154/tony-dorsett-his-dead-fiances-147789.

17. Martin, *Texas Thunder*, p. 148.

18. Thomas "Hollywood" Henderson and Peter Knobler, *Out of Control: Confessions of an NFL Casualty* (New York: Putnam, 1987), p. 231.

19. Golenbock, *Cowboys Have Always Been My Heroes*, p. 652.

20. Martin, *Texas Thunder*, p. 145.

21. Mark Ribowsky, "The Inside Track: Thomas Henderson," *Inside Sports*, June 30, 1980, p. 88.

22. Henderson and Knobler, *Out of Control*, p. 232.

23. Martin, *Texas Thunder*, p. 145.

24. Henderson and Knobler, *Out of Control*, pp. 232–233.

25. Ibid.

26. Martin, *Texas Thunder*, p. 145.

27. Henderson and Knobler, *Out of Control*, pp. 234–235.

28. Ibid., p. 236.

29. *Dallas Morning News*, November 20, 1979.

30. Henderson and Knobler, *Out of Control*, p. 236.

31. *Dallas Morning News*, November 20, 1979.

32. Peter Gent, "North Hollywood Forty and Other Morality Plays from the NFL," *Esquire*, September 1980, p. 33.

33. Ibid.

34. Ibid., p. 39.

35. Ribowsky, "Inside Track," p. 90.

36. Ibid., p. 32.

37. Henderson and Knobler, *Out of Control*, p. 239.

38. Ibid., p. 246.

39. Ibid., p. 259.

40. Ibid., p. 266.

41. Ibid., p. 285; Mike Downey, "Hollywood Henderson Went through Hell and Lived to Tell about It," *Los Angeles Times*, September 7, 1987.

42. Henderson and Knobler, *Out of Control*, p. 285.

43. Ibid., p. 244.

44. Ibid., p. 294.

45. "Bethea Apparent Suicide," *New York Times*, April 24, 1982.

46. "Henderson Apologizes for Calling Bradshaw Dumb," *SunSentinel*, January 22, 1996, http://articles.sun-sentinel.com/1996-01-22/sports/9601220020_1_henderson-s-career-thomas-hollywood-henderson-terry-bradshaw.

47. Golenbock, *Cowboys Have Always Been My Heroes*, p. 643.

48. Martin, *Texas Thunder*, p. 146.

49. Michael Graczyk, "NFL and Players Need to Address Drug Problem, Staubach Says," Associated Press, September 14, 1996.

50. Ribowsky, "Inside Track," p. 89.

51. Ibid.

52. Thomas Henderson with Frank Luksa, *In Control* (Champaign, IL: Sports Publishing, 2004), pp. 314–315.

53. Thomas Henderson, "Dear Dallas . . . : An Open Letter of Confession and Apology from Former Cowboys Linebacker Thomas 'Hollywood' Henderson," *Dallas Morning News*, January 5, 1997, available at hollywoodhenderson.com/news/news8.asp.

54. Gary Cartwright, "Comeback: Thomas 'Hollywood' Henderson," *Texas Monthly*, September 2000.

55. Paul Zimmerman, "NFC," *Sports Illustrated*, September 8, 1980.

56. Skip Bayless, "Put Flag at Half-Mast for America's Team?" *Dallas Morning News*, November 19, 1979.

57. Carlton Stowers, "Staubach Rallies Cowboys in Comeback over Redskins," *Dallas Morning News*, December 18, 1979.

58. Martin, *Texas Thunder*, p. 149.

59. Henderson and Knobler, *Out of Control*, p. 237.

60. Carlton Stowers, *Staubach: Portrait of the Brightest Star* (Chicago: Triumph Books, 2010), p. 210.

61. Ibid.

Chapter 24: STARING INTO THE DARK

1. Charean Williams and Tim Price, "Remembering Tom Landry," *Fort Worth Star-Telegram*, February 14, 2000.

2. Duane Thomas and Paul Zimmerman, *Duane Thomas and the Fall of America's Team* (New York: Warner Books, 1988), p. 82.

3. Ibid.

4. *Landry: The NFL's Man in the Hat*, NFL Films, 2010.

5. Thomas and Zimmerman, *Duane Thomas*, p. 82.

6. Peter Golenbock, *Cowboys Have Always Been My Heroes* (New York: Warner Books, 1997), p. 667.

7. Tom Landry Jr. interview. All Tom Landry Jr. quotes in this chapter are from author interview.

8. Bob St. John, *Landry: The Legend and the Legacy* (Nashville: W Publishing Group, 2000), p. 371.

9. Paul Zimmerman, "NFC," *Sports Illustrated*, September 8, 1980.

10. Mark Ribowsky, "The Inside Track: Thomas Henderson," *Inside Sports*, June 30, 1980, p. 88.

11. Zimmerman, "NFC."

12. Rick Telander, "Hell on Wheels," *Sports Illustrated*, December 7, 1981.

13. Ribowsky, "Inside Track."

14. "Cowboys' Hegman Bargains for Plea," Associated Press, February 26, 1981; "Hegman's Treatment Not Special," United Press International, February 28, 1981.

15. Skip Bayless, *God's Coach: The Hymns, Hype, and Hypocrisy of Tom Landry's Cowboys* (New York: Fireside, 1990), p. 173.

16. Ibid., p. 204.

17. Telander, "Hell on Wheels."

18. Denne H. Freeman, "Money Woes Keep Tony Dorsett Down," Associated Press, August 11, 1985.

19. Martin, *Texas Thunder*, p. 181.

20. Telander, "Hell on Wheels."

21. Paul Zimmerman, "The Eagles Have Landed—CRASH," *Sports Illustrated*, November 9, 1981.

22. "Coaching Legend Bill Walsh Dies at 75," *San Jose Mercury News*, July 31, 2007.

23. CBS telecast, Cowboys-49ers, January 10, 1982.

24. Ibid.

25. Paul Zimmerman, "Off on the Wrong Foot," *Sports Illustrated*, January 18, 1982.

26. *Dallas Morning News*, January 11, 1982.

27. Skip Bayless, "Mystique Strikes Out," *Dallas Morning News*, January 11, 1982.

28. *Dallas Morning News*, January 11, 1982.

29. *America's Game: The Super Bowl Champions, #2. 1985 Chicago Bears*, NFL Films, February 3, 2007.

30. Ribowsky, "Inside Track," p. 88.

31. Paul Zimmerman, *The New Thinking Man's Guide to Pro Football* (New York: Simon and Schuster, 1984), pp. 244–245.

32. *Tom Landry: A Football Life*, NFL Films, 2011, www.youtube.com/watch?v=coKnEfVxiQ8.

33. Zimmerman, "Off on the Wrong Foot."

34. Joe Nick Patoski, *The Dallas Cowboys: The Outrageous History of the Biggest, Loudest, Most Hated, Best Loved Football Team in America* (New York: Little, Brown, 2012), p. 435.

35. William Oscar Johnson, "There Are No Holes at the Top," *Sports Illustrated*, September 1, 1982.

36. Paul Zimmerman, "Dallas Can Have 'Em," *Sports Illustrated*, September 1, 1982.

37. Tom Rafferty interview.

38. *Dallas Morning News*, January 11, 1982.

39. "They Said It," *Sports Illustrated*, February 16, 1981.

40. Tom Landry with Gregg Lewis, *Tom Landry: An Autobiography* (New York: Harper-Collins, 1990), p. 230.

41. Martin, *Texas Thunder*, p. 189.

42. Thomas and Zimmerman, *Duane Thomas*, p. 48.

43. Ibid.

44. Bayless, *God's Coach*, p. 150.

Chapter 25: LIVING ON A PRAYER

1. Skip Bayless, *God's Coach: The Hymns, Hype, and Hypocrisy of Tom Landry's Cowboys* (New York: Fireside, 1990), p. 196.

2. Harvey Martin, *Texas Thunder: My Eleven Years with the Dallas Cowboys* (New York: Rawson, 1986), p. 81.

3. Bruce Newman, "Where Have You Gone, Roger Staubach?" *Sports Illustrated*, August 29, 1983.

4. Martin, *Texas Thunder*, p. 198.

5. Ibid., p. 188.

6. Ibid., p. 199.

7. Ibid., pp. 199–200.

8. Ibid., p. 200.

9. *Dallas Morning News*, May 28, 1983.

10. Martin, *Texas Thunder*, p. 205.

11. *Dallas Morning News*, May 28, 1983.

12. Martin, *Texas Thunder*, p. 205.

13. *Dallas Morning News*, May 28, 1983.

14. Newman, "Where Have You Gone, Roger Staubach?"

15. Bayless, *God's Coach*, p. 233.

16. Martin, *Texas Thunder*, p. 206.

17. Newman, "Where Have You Gone, Roger Staubach?"

18. Martin, *Texas Thunder*, p. 211.

19. Bayless, *God's Coach*, p. 208.

20. Newman, "Where Have You Gone, Roger Staubach?"

21. Bayless, *God's Coach*, p. 170.
22. Duane Thomas and Paul Zimmerman, *Duane Thomas and the Fall of America's Team* (New York: Warner Books, 1988), p. 126.
23. Thomas "Hollywood" Henderson and Peter Knobler, *Out of Control: Confessions of an NFL Casualty* (New York: Putnam, 1987), p. 239.
24. Martin, *Texas Thunder*, p. 217.
25. Ibid., p. 216.
26. Robert Wilonsky, "The Comeback of Harvey Martin," *Dallas Observer News*, January 8, 1998.
27. robertdknight, "Managing Emotions: Drew Pearson Sees a Lot of Tom Landry in Jason Garrett," *The Boys Are Back* (blog), December 20, 2012, http://theboysareback.wordpress.com/2012/12/20/managing-emotions-drew-pearson-sees-a-lot-of-tom-landry-in-jason-garrett.
28. Bayless, *God's Coach*, p. 203.
29. Ibid., p. 177.
30. William Oscar Johnson, "A Chapter Closed," *Sports Illustrated*, March 6, 1989.
31. "Clint Murchison Jr.," Everything Dallas Cowboys, September 22, 2012, http://www.everything-dallascowboys.com/dallas-cowboys-history/owners-and-execs/clint-murchison-jr/clint-murchison-jr.
32. "Murchison Widow Robbed by 2 Bandits," *Dallas Morning News*, April 4, 1981; "Murchison Withdraws as Executor of Estate," *Dallas Morning News*, April 10, 1981.
33. Tom Landry with Gregg Lewis, *Tom Landry: An Autobiography* (New York: Harper-Collins, 1990), p. 231.
34. Mark Lane, "Clint Murchison: Craziest Dallas Cowboys Owner Ever," *TLH: The Landry Hat*, April 11, 2013, the landryhat.com/2013/04/11/clint-murchison-craziest-dallas-cowboys-owner-ever/.
35. Golenbock, *Cowboys Have Always Been My Heroes*, p. 688.
36. "Sale Would Make No Estate-Tax Sense," *Dallas Morning News*, February 15, 1983.
37. Tom Landry Jr. interview. All Tom Landry Jr. quotes in this chapter are from author interview.
38. "American Express Commercial Featuring Tom Landry (1986)," YouTube, http://www.youtube.com/watch?v=8do9Y1rwQeA.
39. Alicia Landry interview. All Alicia Landry quotes in this chapter are from author interview.
40. Paul Zimmerman, *The New Thinking Man's Guide to Pro Football* (New York: Simon and Schuster, 1984), p. 246.
41. Landry with Lewis, *Tom Landry*, p. 231.
42. Bob St. John, *Tex! The Man Who Built the Dallas Cowboys* (Englewood Cliffs, NJ: Prentice Hall, 1988), p. 323.
43. Ibid., p. 313.
44. "Businessman, Philanthropist Bright Dies," *Battalion Online*, January 18, 2005, http://www.thebatt.com/2.8485/businessman-philanthropist-bright-dies-1.1202429.
45. John Anderson and Christine Carroll, "Texas 100: The 100 Richest People in Texas," *Texas Monthly*, September 1990.
46. Landry with Lewis, *Tom Landry*, p. 232.
47. St. John, *Tex!* p. 302.
48. Ibid.
49. *Sports Illustrated: Dallas Cowboys, 50 Years of Football* (New York: Sports Illustrated Books, 2010), p. 110.
50. Ibid., p. 111.
51. Bayless, *God's Coach*, p. 172.
52. "Springs Found Guilty, Will Ask Probation," Associated Press, September 1, 1985.
53. "Former Cowboy RB Ron Springs, 54, Dies after Four-Year-Coma," *Dallas Morning News*, May 12, 2011.

54. "Staubach Testifies in White's Assault Trial," Associated Press, June 21, 1984.
55. "Ditka Loses Driver's License 6 Months for Drunken Driving," United Press International, February 15, 1986.
56. "Cowboy Gets Fine on Driving Charges," Associated Press, October 18, 1985.
57. Bayless, *God's Coach*, p. 222.
58. Randy White interview.
59. *Dallas Morning News*, September 10, 1985.
60. Rick Telander, "Dallas Does It," *Sports Illustrated*, December 23, 1985.
61. Ibid.

Chapter 26: "ASSAULT ON MOUNT LANDRY"

1. Tom Landry with Gregg Lewis, *Tom Landry: An Autobiography* (New York: HarperCollins, 1990), p. 234.
2. Skip Bayless, *God's Coach: The Hymns, Hype, and Hypocrisy of Tom Landry's Cowboys* (New York: Fireside, 1990), p. 214.
3. Ibid., p. 160.
4. Ibid., p. 161.
5. Landry with Lewis, *Tom Landry*, pp. 230–231.
6. Paul Zimmerman, *The New Thinking Man's Guide to Pro Football* (New York: Simon and Schuster, 1984), p. 246.
7. Landry with Lewis, *Tom Landry*, p. 219.
8. Ibid., p. 236.
9. Bayless, *God's Coach*, p. 243.
10. Ibid., p. 241.
11. Randy Galloway, "Cowboys Put Lot of Stock in Hackett," *Dallas Morning News*, February 13, 1986.
12. Blackie Sherrod, "Cowboys: No Loss of Optimism on Offense," *Dallas Morning News*, September 1, 1986.
13. Sam Blair interview.
14. Bayless, *God's Coach*, p. 164.
15. Frank Luksa interview.
16. Bob St. John, *Landry: The Legend and the Legacy* (Nashville: W Publishing Group, 2000), p. 382.
17. "Schramm Doesn't Intend to Trade Dorsett," Associated Press, August 15, 1986.
18. *Dallas Morning News*, May 20, 1984.
19. Zimmerman, *New Thinking Man's Guide*, p. 133.
20. Ibid., p. 178.
21. St. John, *Landry*, p. 368.
22. Landry with Lewis, *Tom Landry*, p. 237.
23. Zimmerman, *New Thinking Man's Guide*, p. 228.
24. Bayless, *God's Coach*, p. 23.
25. Tom Landry Jr. interview.
26. "Ex-Cowboys Owner Bright Almost Fired Landry in '87," Associated Press, February 26, 1990.
27. Bob St. John, *Tex! The Man Who Built the Dallas Cowboys* (Englewood Cliffs, NJ: Prentice Hall, 1988), pp. 308–309.
28. Landry with Lewis, *Tom Landry*, p. 239.
29. Ibid.
30. Tim Cowlishaw, "Hill Waived; Landry 'Commits,' " *Dallas Morning News*, July 17, 1987.
31. Bayless, *God's Coach*, p. 253.
32. Ibid., p. 254.

33. Peter Golenbock, *Cowboys Have Always Been My Heroes* (New York: Warner Books, 1997), p. 695.

34. St. John, *Tex!* p. 306.

35. Duane Thomas and Paul Zimmerman, *Duane Thomas and the Fall of America's Team* (New York: Warner Books, 1988), p. 154.

36. St. John, *Tex!* p. 310.

37. "Cowboys' Newton Sentenced in Drug Case," Law Center, *CNN.com*, August 20, 2002, http://articles.cnn.com/2002-08-20/justice/ctv.penalty.box_1_flight-attendants-drug-charges-kidnapping-charges?_s=PM:LAW.

38. "Autopsy Finds Tuinei Died of Drug Overdose," *New York Times*, May 12, 1999.

39. Golenbock, *Cowboys Have Always Been My Heroes*, p. 692.

40. "Sports People: Septien Pleads Guilty," *New York Times*, April 9, 1987.

41. Golenbock, *Cowboys Have Always Been My Heroes*, p. 697.

42. St. John, *Tex!* p. 152.

43. Ibid., p. 145.

44. Ibid., pp. 154, 167.

45. Thomas and Zimmerman, *Duane Thomas*, p. 163.

46. "Investors Say Danny White Firm Diverted Funds," *Dallas Morning News*, June 19, 1988,

47. Golenbock, *Cowboys Have Always Been My Heroes*, p. 698.

48. Thomas and Zimmerman, *Duane Thomas*, p. 166.

49. Ibid., p. 167.

50. St. John, *Tex!* p. 147.

51. Peter Golenbock, *Landry's Boys: An Oral History of a Team and an Era* (Chicago: Triumph Books, 2005), p. 427.

52. Bayless, *God's Coach*, p. 259.

53. Ibid.

54. Thomas and Zimmerman, *Duane Thomas*, p. 172.

55. Bayless, *God's Coach*, p. 197.

56. Thomas and Zimmerman, *Duane Thomas*, p. 175.

57. Ibid.

58. Landry with Lewis, *Tom Landry*, p. 243.

59. Thomas and Zimmerman, *Duane Thomas*, p. 236.

60. Joe Nick Patoski, *The Dallas Cowboys: The Outrageous History of the Biggest, Loudest, Most Hated, Best Loved Football Team in America* (New York: Little, Brown, 2012), p. 479.

61. *Dallas Morning News*, December 7, 1987.

62. Ibid.

63. Ibid.

64. Blackie Sherrod, "Hitting Bottom with a Thud," *Dallas Morning News*, December 7, 1987.

65. Randy Galloway, "It Doesn't Get Any Worse Than This Loss," *Dallas Morning News*, December 7, 1987.

66. *Dallas Times Herald*, December 7, 1987.

67. Landry with Lewis, *Tom Landry*, p. 244.

68. Thomas and Zimmerman, *Duane Thomas*, p. 230.

69. Ibid., pp. 236–237.

70. Landry with Lewis, *Tom Landry*, p. 243.

71. Randy Galloway, "Successor to Landry? Put the Accent on Reeves," *Dallas Morning News*, October 5, 1986.

72. Paul Zimmerman, "Assault on Mount Landry," *Sports Illustrated*, December 21, 1987.

73. Thomas and Zimmerman, *Duane Thomas*, p. 231.

74. Ibid., p. 232.

75. Lee Roy Jordan interview.

76. Zimmerman, "Assault on Mount Landry."

Chapter 27: "YOU'VE TAKEN MY TEAM AWAY FROM ME"

1. Duane Thomas and Paul Zimmerman, *Duane Thomas and the Fall of America's Team* (New York: Warner Books, 1988), p. 126.
2. Ibid., p. 239.
3. S. L. Price, "The Heart of Football Beats in Aliquippa," *Sports Illustrated*, January 31, 2011.
4. Skip Bayless, *God's Coach: The Hymns, Hype, and Hypocrisy of Tom Landry's Cowboys* (New York: Fireside, 1990), p. 314.
5. "Michael Irvin," *Wikipedia*, en.wikipedia.org/wiki/Michael_Irvin.
6. *Dallas Morning News*, September 5, 1988.
7. Tom Landry with Gregg Lewis, *Tom Landry: An Autobiography* (New York: Harper-Collins, 1990), p. 245.
8. Ibid.
9. Ibid., p. 246.
10. Bayless, *God's Coach*, p. 266.
11. Landry with Lewis, *Tom Landry*, p. 246.
12. Alicia Landry interview. All Alicia Landry quotes in this chapter not otherwise documented are from author interview.
13. Landry with Lewis, *Tom Landry*, p. 246.
14. Bayless, *God's Coach*, p. 270.
15. Ibid., p. 269.
16. "Cowboys Are Sold; Landry Out as Coach," Associated Press, February 26, 1989.
17. Thomas and Zimmerman, *Duane Thomas*, p. 114.
18. William Oscar Johnson, "A Chapter Closed," *Sports Illustrated*, March 6, 1989.
19. "RTC Sues Former Texas Bankers; Seeks $160 Milllion from Bum Bright and Associate," *American Banker*, May 18, 1992.
20. "U.S. Sues Bright in S&L Fall; Ex-Cowboys Owner Alleges 'Witch Hunt,'" *Dallas Morning News*, May 15, 1992.
21. Bob St. John, *Landry: The Legend and the Legacy* (Nashville: W Publishing Group, 2000), p. 55.
22. Johnson, "Chapter Closed."
23. Joe Nick Patoski, *The Dallas Cowboys: The Outrageous History of the Biggest, Loudest, Most Hated, Best Loved Football Team in America* (New York: Little, Brown, 2012), pp. 497–498.
24. Ibid., p. 500.
25. *Dallas Morning News*, October 30, 1988.
26. *Dallas Morning News*, November 12, 1988.
27. *Dallas Morning News*, December 7, 1988.
28. Blackie Sherrod, "Some Hither, Others Yon," *Dallas Morning News*, December 18, 1988.
29. Golenbock, *Cowboys Have Always Been My Heroes*, p. 708.
30. *Dallas Morning News*, December 23, 1988.
31. Landry with Lewis, *Tom Landry*, p. 26.
32. Ibid, pp. 23–24.
33. Ibid., p. 27.
34. Golenbock, *Cowboys Have Always Been My Heroes*, p. 287.
35. Landry with Lewis, *Tom Landry*, p. 23.
36. Ibid., p. 31.
37. *Dallas Morning News*, February 27, 1989.
38. Johnson, "Chapter Closed."
39. Landry with Lewis, *Tom Landry*, p. 32.
40. Ibid., p. 33.
41. Tom Landry Jr. interview. All Tom Landry Jr. quotes in this chapter are from author interview.

42. Joe Nick Patoski, "Turnover!" *Texas Monthly*, October 2012.

43. *New York Times*, March 1, 1989.

44. Gary Myers, "Jones Buys Cowboys, Fires Landry," *Dallas Morning News*, February 26, 1989.

45. Johnson, "Chapter Closed."

46. Myers, "Jones Buys Cowboys, Fires Landry."

47. Patoski, *Dallas Cowboys*, p. 505.

48. Ibid., p. 506.

49. *Dallas Morning News*, February 27, 1989.

50. Bayless, *God's Coach*, p. 21.

51. Landry with Lewis, *Tom Landry*, p. 292.

52. Bayless, *God's Coach*, pp. 285–286.

53. Patoski, *Dallas Cowboys*, p. 506.

54. Ibid.

55. Randy Galloway, "Jones Faces Long Climb to Win Fans," *Dallas Morning News*, May 3, 1989.

56. Frank Luksa interview.

57. Bayless, *God's Coach*, p. 295.

58. Paul Zimmerman, "The Other Tom Landry," *Sports Illustrated*, March 6, 1989.

59. Landry with Lewis, *Tom Landry*, p. 265.

Epilogue: THE APOSTLE

1. Tom Landry with Gregg Lewis, *Tom Landry: An Autobiography* (New York: Harper-Collins, 1990), p. 36.

2. Skip Bayless, *God's Coach: The Hymns, Hype, and Hypocrisy of Tom Landry's Cowboys* (New York: Fireside, 1990), p. 157.

3. Ed Werder, "Way Schramm Was Fired Still Makes Landry Angry," *Dallas Morning News*, August 30, 1992.

4. Joe Nick Patoski, *The Dallas Cowboys: The Outrageous History of the Biggest, Loudest, Most Hated, Best Loved Football Team in America* (New York: Little, Brown, 2012), p. 512.

5. Ibid.

6. Bayless, *God's Coach*, p. 306.

7. Ibid.

8. Ken Murray, "Landry Loyalists Aren't Attacking Jones Now," *Baltimore Sun*, December 17, 1991.

9. "Tom Landry," YouTube, youtube.com/watch?v=InZKoR+qxQE.

10. Frank Gifford, *The Whole Ten Yards* (New York: Random House, 1993), p. 150.

11. Pat Summerall, *Giants: What I Learned about Life from Vince Lombardi and Tom Landry* (Hoboken: John Wiley, 2010), p. 208.

12. Ibid., p. 109.

13. Ron Fimrite, "Two Views of a Famed Dallas Coach," *Sports Illustrated*, September 3, 1990.

14. Gene Lyons, "God's Coach (Review)," *Entertainment Weekly*, August 10, 1990.

15. Alexander Wolff and Kostya Kennedy, "Look What's in Landry's Laundry," *Sports Illustrated*, September 4, 1995.

16. Tom Landry Jr. interview. All Tom Landry Jr. quotes in this chapter are from author interview.

17. "Tom Landry," YouTube.

18. Sam Blair interview. All Blair quotes in this chapter are from author interview.

19. Alicia Landry interview. All Alicia Landry quotes in this chapter are from author interview.

20. Frank Luksa, "Landry Hospitalized for Leukemia Treatment; Ex-Coach's Cancer Diagnosed Early, Son Says," *Dallas Morning News*, May 8, 1999.

21. Frank Luksa, "Landry Says 'I Feel Good' and Thanks All That Knew He Would," *Dallas Morning News*, June 14, 1999.

22. Frank Luksa, "Landry Battling; Now It's the Bulge," *Dallas Morning News*, August 25, 1999.

23. Peter Golenbock, *Cowboys Have Always Been My Heroes* (New York: Warner Books, 1997), p. 722.

24. Frank Luksa interview. All Luksa quotes in this chapter are from author interview.

25. "Sports of the Times; Landry Was in Control as Cowboys' Coach," *New York Times*, February 13, 2000, http://www.nytimes.com/2000/02/13/sports/sports-of-the-times-landry-was-in-control-as-cowboys-coach.html.

26. Frank Luksa, "Farewell, Coach," *Dallas Morning News*, February 13, 2000.

27. Bob St. John, *Landry: The Legend and the Legacy* (Nashville: W Publishing Group, 2000), p. 5.

28. Ibid.

29. Ibid.

30. "Relatives, Friends Bid Landry Farewell; Coach Laid to Rest with Trademark Hat," *Dallas Morning News*, February 17, 2000.

31. St. John, *Landry*, p. 25.

32. December 21, 2011, Public Policy Polling, as reported at http://sportsillustrated.cnn.com/magazine/features/si50/news/2003/10/09/press.

33. Gregg Rosenthal, "Jimmy Johnson: Dallas Cowboys Now a 'Country Club,'" Around the League, NFL.com, November 8, 2012, http://www.nfl.com/news/story/0ap1000000091657/article/jimmy-johnson-says-jerry-jones-runs-a-country-club.

34. Jennifer Emily, "Attorneys Who Oppose Craig Watkins' Re-election as Dallas County District Attorney Fault Actions of His Conviction Integrity Unit," *Dallas Morning News*, October 26, 2010, http://www.dallasnews.com/news/politics/local-politics/20101025-Attorneys-who-oppose-Craig-Watkins-688.ece.

35. Bayless, *God's Coach*, p. 132.

36. "The Man in the Hat," *People*, February 28, 2000.

37. Lee Roy Jordan interview.

INDEX

ABOUT THE AUTHOR

Mark Ribowsky has written twelve highly acclaimed books encompassing a wide range of pop culture topics, including the definitive biographies of the legendary sportscaster Howard Cosell (*Howard Cosell*) and Negro League legends Satchel Paige (*Don't Look Back*) and Josh Gibson (*The Power and the Darkness*), maverick Oakland Raiders owner Al Davis (*Slick*), controversial music producer Phil Spector (*He's a Rebel*), and a trilogy of Motown biographies about the Supremes (*The Supremes: A Saga of Motown Dreams, Success, and Betrayal*), Stevie Wonder (*Signed, Sealed, and Delivered*), and the Temptations (*Ain't Too Proud to Beg*). He has also written the exhaustive *A Complete History of the Negro Leagues, A Complete History of the Home Run*, and the autobiography of eccentric real estate baron Abe Hirschfeld (*Crazy and in Charge*), as well as hundreds of articles for national magazines including *Playboy, Penthouse, Sport, Inside Sports*, and *TV Guide*, his subjects including Eddie Murphy, David Letterman, Kareem Abdul-Jabbar, Larry Bird, Magic Johnson, Peyton Manning, Charles Barkley, Alex Rodriguez, and O. J. Simpson. He lives in Florida.